HARVARD ECONOMIC STUDIES
Volume 159

The studies in this series are published under
the direction of the Department of Economics
of Harvard University. The department does not
assume responsibility for the views expressed.

Productivity and U.S. Economic Growth

Dale W. Jorgenson, Frank M. Gollop, and
Barbara M. Fraumeni

HARVARD UNIVERSITY PRESS

Cambridge, Massachusetts   1987

Copyright © 1987 by the President and Fellows
    of Harvard College
All rights reserved
Printed in the United States of America
10 9 8 7 6 5 4 3 2 1

This book is printed on acid-free paper, and its binding
materials have been chosen for strength and durability.

Library of Congress Cataloging-in-Publication Data

Jorgenson, Dale Weldeau, 1933–
    Productivity and U.S. economic growth.

    (Harvard economic studies; v. 159)
    Bibliography: p.
    Includes index.
    1. Industrial productivity—United States.
    2. Capital investments—United States.
    3. United States—Economic conditions—1945–
    I. Gollop, Frank M.   II. Fraumeni, Barbara M., 1949–
    III. Title.   IV. Series.
HC110.I52J67   1987   338'.06'0973   87–12098
ISBN 0–674–71175–0 (alk. paper)

Acknowledgments

The development of the data base described in this book has left us with a series of obligations that we can acknowledge but never adequately repay. Our colleagues William Barger, Peter Chinloy, and Charles Hulten contributed to the development of both methods and data. The results of their own work are reported in their doctoral dissertations, included in our list of references. However, we would like to express our appreciation to them for their contributions to our work. We have also much appreciated the valuable advice and assistance by Martin Sullivan in the construction of our capital data and by Peter Derksen and Mieko Nishimizu in the generation of our labor input data. Without their help the development of these data would have been impossible. Finally, we wish to acknowledge the able research assistance of Brian Alves, David Carvalho, Blake Evernden, Gary Ferrier, Denise Gaudet, Nelda Hoxie, Stephen Karlson, Betsy O'Boyle, Mark Roberts, and David Robinson.

Our capital and output data owe much to the efforts of Jack Faucett, president of Jack Faucett Associates, and his staff. We are very grateful to them and to Ron Kutscher and John Tschetter of the Bureau of Labor Statistics and Ken Rogers of the Bureau of Industrial Economics for assisting us in the effective use of the results. Thomas Vasquez of the Office of Tax Analysis kindly made available his unpublished study of depreciation practices. Finally, the staff of the Bureau of Economic Analysis has been extremely helpful in all phases of our work. We wish to mention, especially, the assistance of Robert Clucas, Tony Eckman, Don Eldridge, Jack Gottsegan, William Gullickson, John Hinrichs, Mimi Hook, Shirley Loftus, James Milton, John Musgrave, Robert Parker, the late Phil Ritz, Eugene Roberts, Colleen Scanlon, Arlene Shapiro, Al Walderhaug, and Paula Young.

Financial support of our work was provided by the Program on Technology and Economic Policy, Kennedy School of Government, Harvard University. Additional support by the Federal Emergency Management Agency, the Department of Labor, the U.S. Postal Service, and the National Science Foundation is gratefully acknowledged. None of the individuals or institutions listed above shares our responsibility for any deficiencies remaining in this book.

Contents

1 Overview

This book analyzes economic growth in the United States during the years from 1948 to 1979. These three remarkable decades were dominated by a powerful upward thrust in the level of U.S. economic activity. In 1979 the output of the civilian economy stood at 1.516 trillion constant 1972 dollars; by contrast, output in 1948 was only 524 billion. The increase in the level of economic activity from 1948 to 1979 was almost twice the rise over all preceding American history.

The growth record of the U.S. economy over the period 1948–1979 is all the more striking in view of the experience of the preceding two decades. The years from 1929 to 1948 were dominated by the Great Depression of the 1930s and the Second World War. For this period Christensen and Jorgenson (1970) estimated the rate of growth of the U.S. private domestic economy at 2.1 percent per year. For the period 1948–1966 the U.S. growth rate rose to 3.7 percent per year. From 1966 to 1979 the growth rate averaged 3.0 percent.

In this book we put forward a new perspective on postwar U.S. economic growth. We show that the driving force behind the massive expansion of the U.S. economy between 1948 and 1979 was a vast mobilization of capital and labor resources. The single most important contribution to U.S. economic growth during this period was made by capital input. The contribution of capital input averaged 1.6 percent per year for the period 1948–1979. The contribution of labor input was another important source of U.S. economic growth, averaging 1.1 percent per year from 1948 to 1979.

Capital and labor inputs combined contributed 2.6 percent per year to the growth rate of 3.4 percent for the output of the U.S. civilian economy from 1948 to 1979. These two inputs accounted for more than three-fourths of the growth of output in that period. By contrast, advances in the level of productivity contributed only 0.8 percent per year to the growth of output, less than one-fourth the combined contributions of capital and labor inputs. Accordingly, we have emphasized capital and labor resources rather than advances in productivity in our analysis of postwar U.S. economic growth.

Our perspective on U.S. economic growth has important intellectual antecedents, beginning with the seminal contribution of Denison (1962) to the measurement of labor input. Increases in hours worked through gains in employment contribute to the growth of labor input in the approach pioneered by Denison. In addition, labor input grows through increases in the proportion of hours worked by more productive members of the work force. We identify this component of growth in labor input with growth in labor quality. In our approach the growth of labor input is the sum of growth in hours worked and growth in labor quality.

The second stage in the development of our viewpoint on U.S. economic growth was the contribution to the measurement of capital input by Christensen and Jorgenson (1969; 1970). Growth in capital input results from increases in capital stock through capital formation in this approach. Capital input also grows as a result of increases in the proportion of more productive capital goods in the capital stock. We identify the second component of growth in capital input with growth in capital quality. In our approach the growth of capital input is the sum of growth in capital stock and growth in capital quality.

The third stage in the development of our perspective on U.S. economic growth was the extension of principles underlying the work of Christensen, Denison, and Jorgenson to the sectoral level. This phase was completed by Gollop and Jorgenson (1980), incorporating intermediate input with capital and labor inputs. Extension of our approach to the sectoral level had important antecedents in the measurement of intermediate and labor inputs by Leontief (1953) and the measurement of capital and labor inputs by Kendrick (1961a).

In this book we complete the integration of intermediate, capital, and labor inputs at the sectoral level into an analysis of sources of growth for the U.S. economy as a whole. This integration makes it possible for us to attribute U.S. economic growth to its sources at the level of individual industries. We allocate sources of U.S. economic growth among contributions of growth in capital and labor inputs, changes in the level of productivity at the sectoral level, and intersectoral shifts of outputs and inputs.

Our new perspective on U.S. economic growth emphasizes the contribution of the mobilization of resources within individual industries. The explanatory force of this perspective is overwhelming at the sectoral level. For forty-six of the fifty-one industrial sectors included in our study, the contributions of intermediate, capital, and labor inputs were the predominant source of growth of output. Changes in the level of productivity account for the major portion of growth in output for only five industries.

To implement our approach to the analysis of U.S. economic growth we have developed a methodology based on explicit models of production. At the sectoral level this methodology is based on production functions, giving outputs as functions of intermediate, capital, and labor inputs and time. At the aggregate level the methodology is based on an aggregate production function, giving output as a function of capital and labor inputs and time.

We have constructed a complete set of U.S. national accounts for inputs as well as outputs at sectoral and aggregate levels. This system of accounts complements the existing U.S. national accounts for outputs presented by the Bureau of Economic Analysis (1977b). Our accounts can be integrated with the Bureau of Economic Analysis interindustry transactions accounts and with the national accounts for income and expenditure, capital formation, and wealth constructed by Jorgenson (1980).

To analyze the sources of U.S. economic growth we allocate the growth of output at both sectoral and aggregate levels between the contributions of inputs and changes in productivity. We also separate the contribution of each input into growth in an unweighted sum of its components and growth in input quality. Input quality is defined as the ratio between the input index and the unweighted sum of its components.

We complete our analysis of economic growth by determining changes in productivity and the distribution of the value of output among the productive inputs. For this purpose we generate econometric models of production at both sectoral and aggregate levels. We employ the same forms of the sectoral and aggregate production functions as we use to generate our accounting data.

The major innovations in our study are in the development and implementation of a common methodology for data generation, analysis of economic growth, and modeling of production. We will conclude this chapter by listing the major innovations in our methodology and describing its most important limitations.

Methodology

Our methodology is based on models of producer behavior. By using explicit production models we are able to unify the treatment of a large and diverse range of problems—data generation, analysis of the sources of economic growth, and determination of productivity growth and the distribution of the value of output among productive inputs. In this section we outline the main features of our methodology at sectoral and aggregate levels and describe the integration of sectoral and aggregate models of production. In the following section we discuss the application of our methodology to data generation. A detailed presentation of our methodology is given in Chapter 2.

An important innovation in our methodology at the sectoral level is that intermediate, capital, and labor inputs are treated symmetrically.[1] Output is represented as a function of all three inputs and time; substitution possibilities among intermediate inputs and primary-factor inputs are modeled explicitly. This approach can be contrasted with a more restrictive approach based on the existence of a value-added aggregate within each sector.[2] In this alternative approach output is represented as a function of intermediate input and the quantity of value-added. Value-added is represented in turn as a function of capital and labor inputs and time.

A second important innovation in our methodology at the sectoral level is that we distinguish among components of intermediate, capital, and labor inputs that differ in marginal productivity. For each sector, intermediate input is represented as a function of deliveries from all other sectors.[3] Capital input is represented as a function of types of capital input, broken down by class of asset and legal form of organization within each sector.[4] Sectoral labor input is represented as a function of types of labor input, broken down by characteristics of individual workers such as sex, age, education, employment status, and occupation.[5]

Symmetric treatment of intermediate, capital, and labor inputs makes it possible to integrate productivity measurement, the analysis of sources of growth of output, and econometric modeling of substitution and productivity growth with interindustry analysis. We can determine the coefficients of the interindustry model endogenously, taking into account changes in the prices of primary-factor inputs and changes in productivity.[6] Given the coefficients and final demand for the output of each sector, we can determine levels of industry output, interindustry transactions, and employment of primary-factors of production. This approach to interindustry analysis does not require the existence of a value-added aggregate within each sector.[7]

A third important innovation in our methodology at the sectoral level is that we treat prices and quantities symmetrically.[8] In our models of production we combine the production function and intermediate, capital, and labor inputs as functions of their components with necessary conditions for producer equilibrium. In equilibrium the share of each input in the value of output is equal to the elasticity of output with respect to that input. Similarly, for intermediate, capital, and labor inputs the share of each component is equal to the elasticity of the corresponding input with respect to that component.

To disaggregate intermediate, capital, and labor inputs into components that differ in marginal productivity, we measure the prices of individual inputs along with input quantities. For each sector we measure prices and quantities of deliveries of intermediate inputs from all other sectors. We measure rental prices as well as quantities of capital inputs, broken down by class of asset and legal form of organization. Finally, we measure wage rates as well as hours worked, for labor inputs, broken down by characteristics of individual workers. Our methodology generates price and quantity index numbers for output, intermediate input, capital input, labor input, and the rate of productivity growth.[9]

To implement our methodology we consider specific forms for sectoral production functions. We take these functions to be translog in form, so that output is an exponential function of linear and quadratic terms in the logarithms of inputs and in time.[10] Given the translog production functions for all sectors, we can generate translog quantity index numbers of the rates of productivity growth. The average rate of productivity growth between any two periods is the difference between the growth rate of output and a weighted average of growth rates of intermediate, capital, and labor inputs. Weights are given by the average share of each input in the value of output for the two periods.[11]

Similarly, we consider specific forms for the functions giving sectoral intermediate, capital, and labor inputs in terms of their components. Again we take these functions to be translog in form. Given translog intermediate, capital, and labor inputs for all sectors, we can generate the corresponding translog quantity index numbers for the inputs. The growth rate of each input between any two periods is a weighted average of growth rates of its components. Weights are given by the average share of each component in the value of the input for the two periods. The corresponding price indices are defined as ratios of the values of the inputs to the translog quantity indices.[12]

A novel feature of our methodology at the sectoral level is that we employ the same models of production in analyzing sources of growth and in modeling productivity growth and the distribution of the value of output. Translog index numbers for intermediate, capital, and labor inputs and rates of productivity growth are employed in our analysis of the sources of growth. Translog production functions are used to specify econometric models for determining the distribution of the value of output among the productive inputs and the rate of productivity growth. In estimating the parameters of these models we employ as data translog quantity indices of inputs, the corresponding price indices, and translog indices of the rate of productivity growth.[13]

We employ a much more restrictive framework at the aggregate level than at the sectoral level.[14] This framework requires a value-added aggregate in each sector. We formulate an aggregate model of production by combining sectoral value-added functions with market equilibrium conditions for each factor of production. We construct a production possibility frontier for the economy as a whole by maximizing aggregate output, defined in terms of quantities of value-added in all sectors. We distinguish among inputs that differ in marginal productivity at the aggregate level as well as the sectoral level. Aggregate output is a function of quantities of sectoral value-added and sums of each type of capital and labor input over all sectors. Deliveries to intermediate demand by all sectors are precisely offset by receipts of inter- mediate input, so that transactions in intermediate goods do not appear at the aggregate level.

We obtain an even more restrictive form of our aggregate model by requir- ing that an aggregate production function exists.[15] In this model, value- added is defined as a function of quantities of value-added in all sectors, and capital and labor inputs are defined as functions of all types of capital and labor inputs. Value-added is represented as a function of capital and labor inputs and time. The existence of an aggregate production function imposes very stringent restrictions on the sectoral models of production. All sectoral value-added functions must be identical to the aggregate production function. In addition, the functions giving capital and labor inputs for each sector in terms of their components must be identical to the corresponding functions at the aggregate level. It is important to emphasize that we do not employ these restrictions in modeling production at the sectoral level.

We implement our methodology for the economy as a whole by consider- ing specific forms for the production function and for capital and labor inputs as functions of their components. We take these functions to be translog in form, to generate a translog quantity index number for the rate of produc- tivity growth. The average rate of productivity growth is the difference between the growth rate of value-added and a weighted average of growth rates of capital and labor inputs. Similarly, we can generate translog index numbers of capital and labor inputs, giving the growth rate of each input as a weighted average of growth rates of its components.

The translog index numbers for capital and labor inputs and the rate of productivity growth for the economy as a whole are employed in our analysis of the sources of economic growth. The translog production function is used to specify an econometric model for determining the rate of productivity growth and the distribution of value-added between the primary-factor inputs. We employ the translog quantity indices of inputs, the corresponding price indices, and the translog index of the rate of productivity growth as data to estimate the parameters of this econometric model.

The final innovation in our methodology is that we combine sectoral and aggregate models of production to analyze economic growth. Using the aggregate model we can allocate the growth of output among contributions of primary-factor inputs and the rate of productivity growth. Using the sectoral models we can express the rate of aggregate productivity growth in terms of the rates of sectoral productivity growth and reallocations of value-added, capital input, and labor input among sectors.[16] The rate of productivity growth in each sector is weighted by the ratio of the value of output in that sector to value-added in all sectors. These weights reflect the direct contribution of sectoral productivity change to economic growth through deliveries to final demand and the indirect contribution through deliveries to intermediate demand.

The existence of an aggregate production function implies that all sectoral value-added functions are identical. If all sectors pay the same prices for primary-factor inputs, the reallocations of value-added, capital input, and labor input among sectors have no effect on aggregate output. The contributions of these reallocations can be regarded as measures of departure from the assumptions that underlie the aggregate model of production. Our methodology makes it possible to assess the significance of these departures.

The benefits of such a model must be weighed against the costs of departures from the stringent assumptions that underly the existence of an aggregate production function. Where these assumptions are inappropriate we can employ the approach to interindustry analysis outlined above to analyze patterns of production for the economy as a whole. This approach is based on sectoral models of production rather than an aggregate production model.

Data Generation

Implementation of our sectoral and aggregate models of production requires data on output and on intermediate, capital, and labor inputs for each industrial sector. In this section we will outline the generation of data for the U.S. economy for the period 1948–1979. In the following section we will discuss the application of these data to the analysis of sources of U.S. economic growth. The generation of labor and capital input data is described in detail in Chapters 3 and 4, respectively. A description of data on intermediate input and output is presented in Chapter 5. The generation of data for our aggregate model of production is described in Chapters 8 and 9.

A novel feature of our data on sectoral labor input, as described in Chapter 3, is that we utilize data from both establishment and household surveys. We have controlled estimates of employment, hours worked, and labor compensation for each industrial sector to totals based on establishment surveys that underlie the U.S. national income accounts. On the basis of household surveys we have allocated these totals among categories of the work force, cross-classified by the characteristics of individual workers. The resulting estimates of hours worked and average compensation per hour for each sector provide the basis for our price and quantity indices of labor input.

In Chapter 3 we describe sectoral data on prices and quantities of labor input, cross-classified by the two sexes, eight age groups, five educational groups, two employment classes, and ten occupational groups. For each of fifty-one industrial sectors, we will provide annual data from 1948 to 1979 on hours worked and average labor compensation per hour for components of the work force cross-classified by all of these characteristics. For this purpose we allocate employment, hours, weeks, and labor compensation within each sector on the basis of less detailed cross-classifications, using a new methodology that enables us to exploit the available detail on each component of labor input, from the *Census of Population* and the *Current Population Survey*. This methodology is based on the method of iterative proportional fitting which will be described in Chapter 3.[17]

Our first step in developing sectoral measures of labor input is to construct employment matrices cross-classified by sex, age, education, employment status, and occupation for each year, on the basis of household surveys from the U.S. census and the *Current Population Survey*. The resulting employment matrices are controlled to employment totals for each sector on the basis of establishment surveys from the U.S. national income and product accounts.

Establishment surveys provide an enumeration of jobs rather than persons at work, while household surveys count only persons actually at work during the survey week. By using establishment-based estimates of the number of jobs in each sector and assigning to absent workers the average annual hours worked by individuals with comparable characteristics, we are able to estimate hours worked for each type of worker on an annual basis.

We estimate hours worked by workers, cross-classified by demographic characteristics on the basis of household surveys. We adjust the resulting estimates to control totals for each industrial sector from the U.S. national income accounts. We define hours worked for each category of labor input as the product of employment, hours worked per week, and the number of weeks in the calendar year, fifty-two. The concepts employed in our estimates of labor input reflect the conventions used in the most recent *Census of Population* and in the *Current Population Survey*.

Our third step in developing sectoral measures of labor input is to construct labor compensation matrices for each year on the basis of the U.S. census. These data provide estimates of average compensation per person rather than average compensation per job. To combine these data with estimates of the number of jobs from establishment surveys, we first convert average compensation per person to average compensation per job. For this purpose we generate matrices of weeks paid per year for each category of workers.

Labor compensation is the product of average compensation per person, the number of jobs per person, and the number of jobs. Estimates of average compensation per person and the number of weeks paid per year are based on household surveys; estimates of the number of jobs are based on establishment surveys. Control totals for annual labor compensation are taken directly from the U.S. national income accounts.

To estimate average hourly compensation per person for employees we begin with data on wage and salary income from the *Census of Population* for 1950, 1960, and 1970. Differences in outlay on labor input per person reflect differences in marginal products among workers, but, the cost of labor input from the point of view of the producer also includes supplements. Differences in wage and salary income must be adjusted to incorporate employers' contributions to social security and unemployment compensation and other supplements to wages and salaries.

Earnings reported by the census for self-employed workers and the income of unincorporated enterprises from the U.S. national income accounts include both labor and property income. We have divided income from unincorporated enterprises between labor and property components, assuming that after-tax rates of return are the same for corporate and noncorporate business. Labor compensation is distributed among the self-employed on the basis of wage differentials among employees in the corresponding industrial sector. To derive labor compensation per hour worked for each category of labor input, we divide total labor compensation by annual hours worked for each category.

Our final step in constructing data on labor input for each of the fifty-one industrial sectors is to combine price and quantity data, cross-classified by sex, age, education, employment class, and occupation, into price and quantity indices of labor input. A novel feature of our approach is that we employ a translog quantity index of labor input for each sector. The growth rate of labor input from period to period is a weighted average of growth rates of hours worked for the components of labor input. Weights are given by the average shares of each component in labor compensation for the two periods. We also derive a measure of total hours worked for each sector by adding hours worked across all categories of labor input within that sector.

We define the quality of hours worked as the ratio of labor input to hours worked, for each sector. Changes in the quality of hours worked represent the differences between changes in an index of labor input with hours worked weighted by average labor compensation, and changes in an unweighted index. Indices of the price and quantity of labor input, labor input quality, employment, weekly hours per person, hourly compensation, hours worked, and labor compensation are presented for each industrial sector in Appendix B.

In Chapter 8 we will describe aggregate data on prices and quantities of labor input, cross-classified by sex, age, education, employment class, and occupation, but not by industry. For the economy as a whole we add hours worked and labor compensation for each category over all industries. To derive labor compensation per hour worked for each category we divide total labor compensation by annual hours worked. Finally, we combine price and quantity data into price and quantity indices of aggregate labor input, using a translog quantity index. We derive a measure of total hours worked for the economy as a whole by adding hours worked across all categories of labor input. We define the quality of aggregate hours worked as the ratio of labor input to hours worked.

An important innovation in the construction of our data on capital input, which will be described in Chapter 4, is that our approach is strictly analogous to the approach we have outlined for data on labor input. Capital services represent the quantity of capital input, just as labor services represent the quantity of labor input. Measures of capital services for depreciable assets are derived by representing capital stock at each point of time as a weighted sum of past investments. The weights correspond to the relative efficiencies of capital goods of different ages, so that all weighted components of capital stock have the same efficiency.

Rental rates for capital services provide the basis for property compensation, just as wage rates provide the basis for labor compensation. Information on rental transactions would be required to employ data sources for capital input that are analogous to those we have used for labor input. These data are not available in a readily accessible form, even for the substantial proportion of assets with active rental markets. We have imputed rental values on the basis of estimates of capital stocks and property compensation.

Data on rental rates for depreciable assets are generated by allocating property compensation among return to capital, depreciation, and taxes. Depreciation is the decline in value of a capital good with age at a given point in time, so that estimates of depreciation depend on the relative efficiencies of capital goods of different ages. A novel feature of our estimates of capital input is that we incorporate the same data on relative efficiencies of capital goods into estimates of both capital stocks and rental rates.[18]

In Chapter 4 we describe sectoral data on prices and quantities of capital input, cross-classified by six asset classes—producers' and consumers' durable equipment, residential and nonresidential structures, inventories, and land—and three legal forms of organization—corporate business, noncorporate business, and households and institutions. For each of forty-six industrial sectors we provide annual data from 1948 to 1979 on capital stock and its rental rate for all categories of capital input. Data on capital input are unavailable for the five government sectors included in our analysis of labor input.

Our first step in developing sectoral measures of capital input is to construct estimates of capital stock by industry for each year from 1948 to 1979. For producers' durable equipment and nonresidential structures we employ investment data distributed among industries on an establishment basis. We have controlled estimates of investment for all sectors to totals from the U.S. national product accounts.

The time series for investment in producers' durable equipment starts in 1920, and the time series for investment in nonresidential structures starts in 1890. Given investment for each industrial sector, we have compiled estimates of capital stock by expressing the stock for each year as a weighted sum of past investments, using geometrically declining patterns of relative efficiency of capital goods with age. Since the weights assigned to investments before 1920 for equipment and before 1890 for structures are negligible, we have set investments for these early years to zero.

For residential structures we employ investment data from the U.S. national product accounts. Tenant-occupied housing is assigned to the finance, insurance, and real estate sector, and owner-occupied housing to the private household sector. To obtain estimates of investment in equipment and structures in constant prices, we employ deflators based on investment goods prices from the U.S. national product accounts.

Our estimates of stocks of land by industry begin with estimates of the stocks of land for the economy as a whole. We employ balance sheet data to allocate land among industrial sectors and between corporate and noncorporate business within each sector, again with the exception of private households and nonprofit institutions. The Bureau of Economic Analysis has constructed estimates of inventory stocks in current and constant prices by sector. These estimates are consistent with data on inventory investment for the U.S. economy as a whole from the national product accounts. These data are broken down by legal form of organization within each industry.

The second step in developing sectoral measures of capital input is to construct estimates of prices of capital services on the basis of data on property compensation. For each asset the price of investment goods is a weighted sum of future rental prices, discounted by a factor that incorporates future rates of return. Weights are given by the relative efficiencies of capital goods of different ages. The same weights are used to construct estimates of rental prices and capital stocks. For depreciable assets the weights decline with age; for nondepreciable assets the weights are constant.

Differences in the tax treatment of property compensation among legal forms of organization result in differences in rental prices of capital services. A novel feature of our estimates of the rental prices of capital services in the corporate sector is that we include data on the corporate income tax. We also include data on property taxes for corporate business. We allocate property compensation for corporate business within each industrial sector among equipment, structures, land, and inventories. Corporate property compensation is the sum of rental payments for capital services for all four classes of assets.

Similarly, for the noncorporate sector we include data on property taxes for noncorporate business in our estimates of the rental prices of capital services in the noncorporate sector. We assume that the noncorporate rate of return is equal to the corporate rate of return after corporate taxes. This enables us to allocate noncorporate income between labor and property compensation. Noncorporate property compensation is the sum of rental payments for capital services for all four classes of assets.

To derive prices of capital services for private households and nonprofit institutions, we first estimate the rate of return on owner-occupied housing. We assume that the rate of return for private households and nonprofit institutions is the same as the rate of return on owner-occupied housing. We incorporate data on property taxes for private households into our estimates of the rental prices of capital services used in this sector. Property compensation for households and institutions is the sum of rental payments for all classes of assets.

The final step in constructing data on capital input for each of our forty-six private industrial sectors is to combine price and quantity data, cross-classified by class of asset and legal form of organization, into price and quantity indices of capital input. A novel feature of our approach is that we employ a translog quantity index of capital input for each sector. The growth rate of capital input from period to period is a weighted average of growth rates of capital stocks for the components of capital input. Weights are given by the average shares of each component in the property compensation for the two periods.

We derive a measure of capital stock for each sector by adding capital stocks across all categories of capital input within that sector. We define the quality of capital stock as the ratio of capital input to capital stock. Changes in the quality of capital stock represent differences between changes in an index of capital input, with capital stocks weighted by rental rates, and changes in an unweighted index. Indices of the price and quantity of capital input, capital input quality, the price and quantity of capital stock, and property compensation are presented for each industrial sector in Appendix C.

In Chapter 8 we describe aggregate data on prices and quantities of capital input, cross-classified by asset class and legal form of organization, but not by industry. For the economy as a whole we add capital stock and property compensation for each category over all industries. To derive property compensation per unit of capital stock for each category we divide total property compensation by capital stock. Finally, we combine price and quantity data into price and quantity indices of aggregate capital input, using a translog quantity index. We derive a measure of capital stock for the economy as a whole by adding capital stock across all categories of capital input. We define the quality of aggregate capital stock as the ratio of capital input to capital stock.

In Chapter 5 we describe sectoral data on prices and quantities of output and intermediate input, where intermediate input is classified by sector of origin. For fifty-one industrial sectors we provide annual data from 1948 to 1979 on output and its price. Data on intermediate input are unavailable for the five government sectors and for private households. We provide annual data from 1948 to 1979 on intermediate input and its price for forty-five industrial sectors. Output is equal to input in both current and constant prices for private households and the five government sectors. Our analysis of productivity is limited to the forty-five industrial sectors for which we have data on all three inputs.

Data on output in current and constant prices are available from the Interindustry Economics Division of the Bureau of Economic Analysis (1974b) for the manufacturing sectors and from a study by Jack Faucett Associates (1975) for the Bureau of Labor Statistics for nonmanufacturing sectors. To evaluate output from the point of view of the producing sector we subtract excise and sales taxes and add subsidies to the value of output. The resulting deflator of output from the producer's point of view is equal to the ratio of the value of output in current prices to the value of output in constant prices.

An important innovation of our approach to productivity measurement at the sectoral level is that intermediate, capital, and labor inputs are treated symmetrically. We employ all three inputs to analyze the sources of growth in sectoral output and to model the distribution of the value of sectoral output among inputs. The value of output at the sectoral level includes the value of intermediate input, as well as the values of capital and labor inputs. In measuring output we use the industry definitions employed in the U.S. national income accounts. These definitions are based on establishments within each industry.

To disaggregate intermediate input by the sector of origin of intermediate goods, we employ data on interindustry transactions, published by the Bureau of Economic Analysis.[19] These data are based on industry definitions employed in the interindustry accounts. To bring our measures of intermediate input into conformity with industry definitions from the U.S. national income accounts, we reallocate data on interindustry transactions among sectors, taking into account reclassifications, redefinitions, and transfers used in the interindustry accounts.[20]

To construct prices and quantities of intermediate input by sector of origin, we deflate the value of intermediate input originating in each sector by an index of purchasers' prices for the output of that sector. We have described the construction of an index of producers' prices for the output of each sector. These indices are transformed to purchasers' prices by adding sales and excise taxes and subtracting subsidies. The final step in constructing data on intermediate input for each of our forty-five industrial sectors is to combine price and quantity data, classified by sector of origin, into price and quantity indices of intermediate input.

A novel feature of our approach to measuring intermediate input is that we employ a translog quantity index of intermediate input for each sector. The growth rate of intermediate input from period to period is a weighted average of growth rates of intermediate inputs classified by sector of origin. Weights are given by the average shares of each component in the value of intermediate input into the sector for the two periods.

We derive an unweighted index of intermediate input for each sector by summing the intermediate inputs from all originating sectors. We define the quality of intermediate input as the ratio of our translog quantity index of intermediate input to an unweighted index of intermediate input for each sector. Indexes of the price and quantity of output and intermediate input, intermediate input quality, the unweighted quantity index of intermediate input and the corresponding price, and the value of intermediate input are presented for each industrial sector in Appendix D.

In Chapter 9 we describe aggregate data on the price and quantity of value-added. Value-added for the economy as a whole is the sum of value-added in all industries. The quantity of value-added for each sector is derived by combining price and quantity data on output and intermediate input into price and quantity indices of value-added, using a translog quantity index. The quantity of aggregate value-added is the sum of quantities of value-added in all industries. Finally, the price of aggregate value-added is the ratio of value-added to the quantity of value-added for the economy as a whole.

A very important limitation of our approach is that we have based our estimates of the value of output and the value of intermediate, capital, and labor inputs on accounting conventions employed in the U.S. national income accounts. The utilization of our data for interindustry analysis would require the generation of data on output and all categories of input on the basis of accounting conventions used in the U.S. interindustry accounts. Complete implementation of the United Nations' System of National Accounts (1968) for the United States would make it possible to provide data by industry on the basis of both sets of accounting conventions.

Sources of Economic Growth

We allocate U.S. economic growth of output over the period 1948–1979 among the contributions of productive inputs and changes in productivity. We present an analysis of the sources of growth of output at the sectoral level in Chapter 6, and an analysis of the sources of growth for the U.S. economy as a whole in Chapters 8 and 9.

To allocate the growth of sectoral output among the contributions of intermediate, capital, and labor inputs and changes in productivity, we first construct data on the rate of productivity growth for each sector. As shown in Chapter 6, we combine price and quantity data for outputs and inputs into an index of the rate of productivity growth. We employ a translog quantity index of productivity growth for each sector. This index is the difference between the growth rate of output from period to period and a weighted average of growth rates of intermediate, capital, and labor inputs. Weights are given by average shares of each input in the value of output in the two periods.

The starting point for the construction of data on sectoral productivity growth is a sectoral production account in current prices. The fundamental accounting identity is that the value of output is equal to the value of input. The value of output excludes all sales and excise taxes and includes subsidies paid to producers; the value of input includes all taxes and supplementary payments made by producers, as well as the compensation received by the suppliers of each input. Valuation from the producers' point of view is essential for the integration of our data on output and input into models of production at the sectoral level.

Our concept of valuation from the point of view of the producer is intermediate between the national accounting concepts of valuation at market prices and valuation at factor cost. The value of output at market prices includes taxes paid by producers and excludes subsidies received by producers. The value of output at factor cost excludes these taxes and includes subsidies. Control totals for the value of output and the value of intermediate, capital, and labor inputs in our sectoral production accounts are based on the U.S. national income accounts.

For the five government sectors included in our study, output is equal to labor input; for private households output is equal to an index of capital and labor input. For these six sectors the rate of productivity growth is zero by definition. We construct measures of productivity growth for the remaining forty-five sectors for the period 1948–1979. Translog indices of rates of productivity growth are presented on an annual basis for all forty-five industrial sectors in Appendix D.

The rate of growth of sectoral output is the sum of the contributions of intermediate, capital, and labor inputs and the rate of productivity growth. The contribution of each input is the product of the average value share of the input and its growth rate. Table 1.1 compares the average annual growth rate of output in each industry with the average annual contributions of each input and the rate of productivity growth for the period 1948–1979. The sum of the contributions of intermediate, capital, and labor inputs is the predominant source of growth of output for forty-six of the fifty-one industrial sectors included in our study. The rate of productivity growth is a more important source of sectoral growth for only five industries.

Comparing the contribution of intermediate input with other sources of growth in output, the contribution of this input is by far the most significant source of growth. If we focus attention on the contributions of capital and labor inputs and, exclude intermediate input, the sum of the contributions of these two inputs is a more important source of growth than changes in productivity. Our overall conclusion is that the contributions of intermediate, capital, and labor inputs predominate over productivity growth in accounting for sectoral growth.

We present a detailed analysis of the sources of growth in sectoral output in Chapter 6 where we decompose the growth rate of intermediate input into the sum of growth rates of an unweighted index of intermediate input and an index of the quality of intermediate input. Similarly, we decompose the growth rate of capital input into the sum of the growth rates of capital stock and the quality of capital stock. Finally, we decompose the growth rate of labor input into the sum of the growth rates of hours worked and an index of the quality of hours worked.

Table 1.1. Growth in sectoral output and its sources, 1949–1979 (average annual rates)

| Industry | Contributions to growth in output | | | | |
	Rate of output growth	Intermediate input	Capital input	Labor input	Rate of productivity growth
Agricultural production	0.0216	0.0128	0.0040	-0.0097	0.0146
Agricultural services	0.0297	0.0173	0.0068	0.0111	-0.0055
Metal mining	0.0142	0.0075	0.0127	-0.0004	-0.0056
Coal mining	0.0038	0.0112	0.0069	-0.0116	-0.0027
Crude petroleum and natural gas	0.0213	0.0291	0.0104	0.0031	-0.0214
Nonmetallic mining and quarrying	0.0409	0.0153	0.0178	0.0039	0.0038
Contract construction	0.0271	0.0169	0.0022	0.0074	0.0006
Food and kindred products	0.0281	0.0134	0.0018	-0.0002	0.0131
Tobacco manufacturers	0.0072	0.0116	0.0039	-0.0015	-0.0068
Textile mill products	0.0345	0.0157	0.0026	-0.0030	0.0192
Apparel and other fabricated textile products	0.0264	0.0130	0.0016	0.0009	0.0109
Paper and allied products	0.0401	0.0322	0.0054	0.0041	-0.0016
Printing and publishing	0.0323	0.0176	0.0023	0.0066	0.0058
Chemicals and allied products	0.0591	0.0329	0.0091	0.0050	0.0121
Petroleum and coal products	0.0271	0.0422	0.0024	0.0005	-0.0179
Rubber and misc. plastic products	0.0477	0.0259	0.0062	0.0113	0.0043
Leather and leather products	-0.0047	-0.0023	0.0005	-0.0054	0.0025
Lumber and wood products except furniture	0.0288	0.0245	0.0045	-0.0011	0.0009
Furniture and fixtures	0.0373	0.0281	0.0029	0.0038	0.0026

Table 1.1 continued

	Contributions to growth in output				
Industry	Rate of output growth	Intermediate input	Capital input	Labor input	Rate of productivity growth
Stone, clay and glass products	0.0382	0.0281	0.0057	0.0038	0.0007
Primary metal industries	0.0128	0.0154	0.0023	0.0011	-0.0059
Fabricated metal industries	0.0350	0.0200	0.0037	0.0062	0.0050
Machinery, except electrical	0.0417	0.0240	0.0062	0.0080	0.0036
Elec. machinery, equipment, and supplies	0.0580	0.0262	0.0058	0.0102	0.0158
Trans. equipment and ordnance, except motor vehicles	0.0559	0.0408	0.0013	0.0100	0.0039
Motor vehicles and equipment	0.0451	0.0285	0.0053	0.0022	0.0091
Professional photographic equipment and watches	0.0569	0.0217	0.0102	0.0170	0.0081
Misc. manufacturing industries	0.0340	0.0243	0.0037	0.0015	0.0046
Railroads and rail express services	0.0053	-0.0046	0.0019	-0.0108	0.0187
Street rail., bus lines, and taxicabs	-0.0217	-0.0063	0.0036	-0.0044	-0.0147
Trucking services and warehousing	0.0488	0.0222	0.0072	0.0078	0.0116
Water transportation	0.0040	0.0058	0.0011	-0.0019	-0.0009
Air transportation	0.0957	0.0421	0.0103	0.0153	0.0281
Pipelines, except natural gas	0.0493	0.0133	0.0282	-0.0014	0.0093
Transportation services	0.0268	0.0488	0.0034	0.0049	-0.0304
Telephone, telegraph, and misc. communication services	0.0688	0.0077	0.0234	0.0087	0.0290
Radio and television broadcasting	0.0132	-0.0064	0.0185	0.0216	-0.0205
Electric utilities	0.0628	0.0227	0.0275	0.0034	0.0092

Table 1.1 continued

| Industry | Contributions to growth in output | | | | |
	Rate of output growth	Intermediate input	Capital input	Labor input	Rate of productivity growth
Gas utilities	0.0531	0.0403	0.0106	0.0024	-0.0001
Water supply and sanitary services	0.0328	-0.0031	-0.0001	0.0048	0.0312
Wholesale trade	0.0425	0.0064	0.0090	0.0127	0.0145
Retail trade	0.0293	0.0091	0.0043	0.0056	0.0103
Finance, insurance, and real estate	0.0493	0.0341	0.0031	0.0076	0.0044
Services, exc. private households and institutions	0.0377	0.0286	0.0064	0.0078	-0.0052
Private households	0.0491	0.0000	0.0499	-0.0008	0.0000
Institutions	0.0373	0.0146	0.0105	0.0182	-0.0059
Federal public administration	0.0173	0.0000	0.0000	0.0173	0.0000
Federal government enterprises	0.0141	0.0000	0.0000	0.0141	0.0000
State and local educational services	0.0457	0.0000	0.0000	0.0457	0.0000
State and local public admin.	0.0362	0.0000	0.0000	0.0362	0.0000
State and local enterprises	0.0363	0.0000	0.0000	0.0363	0.0000

Growth in input quality is not an important source of growth in intermediate input. Our inferences about the predominant role of growth in intermediate input would be unaffected by omission of changes in input quality. Excluding intermediate input from consideration, however, the relative importance of the rate of productivity growth and the contributions of capital and labor inputs would be reversed.

As shown in Chapter 9, we allocate the growth in aggregate output between growth in capital and labor inputs and changes in productivity. We construct data on the rate of productivity growth by combining price and quantity data for value-added, capital input, and labor input. We employ a translog quantity index of the rate of productivity growth, equal to the difference between the growth rate of value-added and a weighted average of the growth rates of capital and labor inputs. The weights are given by average shares of each input in value-added for the two periods.

The starting point for our measure of the rate of aggregate productivity growth is a production account for the U.S. economy as a whole, in current prices. The fundamental accounting identity for the economy as a whole is that the value of output is equal to the value of input from the producer's point of view. The value of output excludes sales and excise taxes and includes subsidies received by producers. The value of input includes the value of primary-factors of production, incorporating supplementary payments and payroll taxes included in labor compensation and property taxes and other taxes in property compensation. Our concept of valuation is essential for integration of our data on aggregate output and input into a model of production for the economy as a whole.

We present the translog index of the rate of productivity growth for the U.S. economy as a whole on an annual basis for the period 1948–1979 in Chapter 9. The growth rate of the quantity of value-added is the sum of the contributions of capital and labor inputs and the rate of productivity growth. The contribution of each input is the product of its average share in value-added and its growth rate. Table 1.2 compares the average annual growth rate of value-added with the contributions of the two primary-factor inputs and the average annual rate of productivity growth for the period 1948–1979 and for seven subperiods: 1948–1953, 1953–1957, 1957–1960, 1960–1966, 1966–1969, 1969–1973, and 1973–1979.

The seven subperiods are not chosen arbitrarily. The endpoints of each period are years in which a cyclical peak occurred. The growth rate presented for each period is therefore the average annual growth rate between cyclical peaks. Since we report average annual growth rates, the unequal lengths of the periods do not affect comparisons among these periods. The sum of the contributions of capital and labor inputs is the predominant source of growth in value-added for the period as a whole and for all seven subperiods. Productivity growth is a much less important source of U.S. economic growth.

The contribution of capital input is the most significant source of growth for the period 1948–1979 as a whole. Capital input is the most important source of growth for six of the seven subperiods, and productivity growth is the most important source for only one, 1960–1966. The contribution of capital input exceeds the contribution of labor input for all seven subperiods, while the contribution of labor input exceeds productivity growth in four of the seven subperiods. Our overall conclusion is that growth in capital input is the most important source of growth in value-added, growth in labor input

Table 1.2.   Growth in aggregate output and its sources, 1948–1979

Variable	1948–1979	1948–1953	1953–1957	1957–1960	1960–1966	1966–1969	1969–1973	1973–1979
Value added	0.0342	0.0404	0.0302	0.0274	0.0444	0.0326	0.0308	0.0283
Contribution of capital input	0.0156	0.0195	0.0153	0.0105	0.0145	0.0190	0.0156	0.0144
Contribution of labor input	0.0105	0.0124	0.0035	0.0084	0.0141	0.0134	0.0095	0.0105
Rate of productivity growth	0.0081	0.0085	0.0113	0.0084	0.0159	0.0002	0.0058	0.0034

the next most important source, and productivity growth is the least important.

We present a detailed analysis of the sources of growth of value-added for the U.S. economy as a whole in Chapter 9. We decompose the growth rate of capital input into the sum of the growth rates of capital stock and the quality of capital stock. Similarly, we decompose the growth rate of labor input into the sum of the growth rates of hours worked and an index of the quality of hours worked. Finally, we decompose the rate of aggregate productivity growth into a weighted sum of the rates of sectoral productivity growth and reallocations of value-added, capital input, and labor input among sectors.

Growth in the quality of capital stock accounts for over one-fourth of the growth of capital input during the period 1948–1979. This quantitative relationship also characterizes the seven subperiods. For the period as a whole, the growth of hours worked exceeded the growth of labor quality. For the period 1948–1966 the growth in hours worked actually fell below the growth in the quality of hours worked. For the period 1966–1979 the contribution of hours worked accounted for almost two-thirds of the contribution of labor input. For the period 1948–1979 sectoral productivity growth is the predominant component of the rate of aggregate productivity growth. Contributions of reallocations of value-added, capital input, and labor input among sectors are small but not negligible.

In Chapter 8 we present a more detailed decomposition of the sources of quality change in aggregate capital and labor inputs.[21] For this purpose we first introduce partial indices of labor input, adding hours worked and shares of labor compensation over some characteristics of the labor force and constructing a translog index over the remaining characteristics. Labor input is cross-classified by sex, age, education, employment class, and occupation.

We analyze the impact of changes in the composition of the work force, among components classified by all six of these characteristics, on the growth of labor quality.

Similarly, we introduce partial indices of capital input by adding capital stock and the share of property compensation over some characteristics of the capital stock and constructing a translog index over the remaining characteristics. Capital input is cross-classified by asset class and legal form of organization. We analyze the impact of changes in the composition of the capital stock among components classified by both characteristics on the growth of capital quality.

The existence of an aggregate production function implies that all sectoral value-added functions are identical. Under this very stringent assumption and the additional assumption that all sectors pay the same prices for primary-factor inputs, the reallocations of value-added and the primary-factor inputs among sectors have no effect on the growth of aggregate output. The contributions of these reallocations to aggregate productivity growth can be regarded as measures of departure from the assumptions that underlie the aggregate model of production. In Chapter 9 we show that these contributions are far outweighed by the contribution of rates of sectoral productivity growth.

Substitution and Productivity Growth

Our sectoral models of production are based on sectoral production functions, giving output as a function of intermediate, capital, and labor inputs, and time. We describe the distribution of the value of output in terms of value shares, defined as ratios of the value of each input to the value of output. Necessary conditions for producer equilibrium at the sectoral level are that the value shares are equal to the elasticities of output with respect to the corresponding inputs. We assume that the production functions are characterized by constant returns to scale, so that the elasticities and the value shares sum to unity for each sector.

Substitution among inputs and productivity growth are treated symmetrically in our model of production. We describe productivity growth in terms of rates of productivity growth, defined as growth rates of output, holding intermediate, capital, and labor inputs constant. Under constant returns to scale the rate of productivity growth can be expressed as the growth rate of output less a weighted average of the growth rates of the three inputs. Weights are given by the corresponding value shares. If the production function is increasing in all three inputs, the value shares must be nonnegative.

To characterize the implications of patterns of production for productivity growth and the distribution of the value of output, we began with models of production that abstract from specific forms for the production functions. To characterize the implications of patterns of substitution at the sectoral level, we introduce share elasticities, defined as changes in value shares with respect to proportional changes in the quantities of intermediate, capital, and labor inputs.[22]

To characterize patterns of productivity growth we introduce biases of productivity growth, defined as changes in the value shares with respect to time.[23] These biases can be employed to characterize the implications of patterns of substitution for the rate of productivity growth. Under constant returns to scale the sum of biases with respect to all three inputs is equal to zero. Patterns of productivity growth can be characterized by introducing the acceleration of productivity growth.

We consider the restrictions on sectoral patterns of substitution and productivity growth implied by Hicks neutrality of productivity growth and by the existence of a value-added function.[24] Hicks neutrality implies that substitution among inputs is independent of time. The existence of a value-added function implies that sectoral productivity growth does not involve intermediate input.

In determining the rate of productivity growth and the distribution of the value of output among the three inputs, we consider specific forms for the sectoral production functions. For this purpose we take the share elasticities with respect to intermediate, capital, and labor inputs; the biases of productivity growth with respect to all three inputs; and the acceleration of productivity growth as fixed parameters.

To indicate the interpretation of the fixed parameters we can characterize the form of the production function as the *constant share elasticity production function*.[25] For this production function output is an exponential function of linear and quadratic terms in the logarithms of all three inputs and in time. To indicate the role of the variables we have referred to this form of the production function as the *translog production function*.

An important innovation in our modeling of production is that we employ the same form for sectoral production functions in modeling producer behavior and in constructing index numbers. Using the interpretation of the parameters of the translog production function as constant share elasticities, we express the conditions for concavity of the production function in terms of these elasticities. Similarly, we can express the conditions for Hicks neutrality of productivity growth and the existence of a sectoral value-added function in terms of restrictions on the share elasticities and biases of productivity growth.

Our sectoral models of production consist of four equations for each sector, giving the rate of productivity growth and the value shares of all three inputs as linear functions of the logarithms of the inputs and time. To formulate econometric models of production we add stochastic components to each of these equations. To estimate the unknown parameters of the translog production function for each sector, we combine equations for two of the value shares with the equation for the rate of productivity growth, to obtain a complete model.

We obtain estimates of the parameters of our econometric models of production and test statistics for Hicks neutrality of productivity growth and the existence of a value-added aggregate for forty-five of the fifty-one industries listed in Table 1.1. These estimates and test statistics are based on time series data for the period 1948–1979 on prices and quantities of intermediate, capital, and labor inputs and output described in Chapters 3–5.

Under Hicks neutrality, biases of productivity growth with respect to all three inputs are equal to zero; the results show that biases of productivity growth are significantly different from zero for thirty-nine of the forty-five industries. We conclude that the measures of the rate of sectoral productivity growth presented in Chapter 6 should be regarded as functions depending on quantities of intermediate, capital, and labor inputs, as well as on time. Similarly, conditions that are jointly necessary and sufficient for the existence of sectoral value-added functions are rejected for forty of the forty-five industries. We conclude that intermediate input should be treated symmetrically with capital and labor inputs in modeling sectoral patterns of substitution and productivity growth.

In estimating the parameters of our sectoral models of production we do not impose restrictions on these parameters that are implied by Hicks neutrality of productivity growth or the existence of a value-added function. We do impose the restrictions on these parameters implied by concavity of the production functions. Necessary conditions, that the production function is increasing in intermediate, capital, and labor inputs, are satisfied for all forty-five sectors included in our study. Necessary conditions that the sectoral production functions are increasing in time are satisfied for only thirty of the forty-five sectors.

Under the conditions for concavity, the estimated elasticities of the share of each input with respect to its own quantity must be nonpositive. This condition, together with the condition that the sum of all the elasticities of the value share of a given input with respect to all three inputs must be equal to zero, implies that only one of the two share elasticities with respect to quantities of the other two inputs can be negative. All three of these share elasticities can be nonnegative; this condition holds for forty-one of the forty-five industries.

The estimated elasticity of the share of labor with respect to the quantity of capital is negative for only one of the forty-five industries. For the remaining forty-four industries the value shares of input do not decrease with increases in the quantities of capital input, holding the quantities of intermediate and labor inputs and time constant. The estimated elasticities of the share of intermediate input with respect to the quantities of capital are negative for only three industries; for the remaining forty-two industries the value shares of intermediate input do not decrease with respect to the quantities of capital input, holding intermediate and labor inputs and time constant. Finally, the estimated elasticities of the value shares of intermediate input do not decrease with respect to the quantities of labor input for all forty-five industries.

If the bias of productivity growth with respect to an input is positive, productivity growth is *input using* for that input; if the bias is negative, productivity growth is *input saving* for that input. The sum of the three biases is equal to zero under constant returns to scale, so that we can rule out the possibility that all three biases are either all negative or all positive. Each of the remaining six logical possibilities—any two biases negative or any two biases positive—occurs for at least one of the forty-five industries included in our study.

The pattern of productivity growth that occurs most frequently among the forty-five industries is labor-saving in combination with capital-using and intermediate-input-using productivity growth. This pattern characterizes seventeen of the forty-five industries. For this pattern the rate of productivity growth is increasing in intermediate and capital inputs and decreasing in labor input. Labor-saving, capital-saving, and intermediate-input-using productivity growth occurs for ten industries, while productivity growth is labor-using, capital-using, and intermediate-input-saving for eight industries. Labor-saving, capital-using, and intermediate-input-saving and labor-using, capital-saving, and intermediate-input-saving patterns of productivity growth occur for four industries each. Productivity growth is labor-using, capital-saving, and intermediate-input-using for only two industrial sectors.

Our final objective is to determine the rate of aggregate productivity growth and the distribution of value-added between capital and labor inputs for the U.S. economy as a whole. Necessary conditions for producer equilibrium at the aggregate level are that the value shares are equal to the elasticities of the quantity of value-added with respect to the corresponding inputs. Similarly, we describe productivity growth in terms of the rate of productivity growth, defined as the growth rate of the quantity of value-added, holding capital and labor inputs constant.

We have already pointed out that the existence of an aggregate production function has very stringent implications for sectoral models of production. A value-added function must exist for all sectors, and all sectoral value-added functions must be identical to the aggregate production function. At the sectoral level we reject the existence of a value-added function for forty of the forty-five industries included in our study. We have concluded that it would be inappropriate to employ value-added functions in analyzing patterns of production at the sectoral level.

The measures of departure from the assumptions underlying our aggregate model of production are sizable but far from predominant in the decomposition of the rate of productivity growth for the U.S. economy as a whole. We conclude that an aggregate production function may provide a useful simplification in analyzing patterns of production at the aggregate level.

We characterize the implications of substitutability among inputs for the distribution of aggregate value-added, in terms of share elasticities. As before, share elasticities are defined as changes in value shares of capital and labor inputs with respect to proportional changes in the quantities of both inputs. Similarly, we characterize the implications of patterns of productivity growth for the distribution of value-added in terms of biases of productivity growth, defined as changes in value shares with respect to time. Finally, we employ the acceleration of productivity growth to characterize the implications of patterns of productivity growth.

We consider restrictions on aggregate patterns of substitution and productivity growth implied by Hicks neutrality, Harrod neutrality, and Solow neutrality of technical change.[26] Hicks neutrality implies that substitution between capital and labor inputs is independent of productivity growth. A necessary and sufficient condition for Hicks neutrality is that both biases of productivity growth with respect to quantity are equal to zero. Harrod neutrality implies that aggregate productivity growth does not involve capital input, while Solow neutrality implies that aggregate productivity growth does not involve labor input.

A necessary condition for Harrod neutrality is that the elasticity of the value share of labor input with respect to capital input and the bias of productivity growth with respect to capital input are proportional to the value share of capital input and the rate of productivity growth. For Solow neutrality the roles of capital and labor inputs are reversed. Any two of the three types of neutrality of productivity growth imply the third; under these restrictions the production function is linear logarithmic in value-added, capital input, labor input, and an arbitrary function of time.

In developing a model of production for determining the rate of productivity growth and the distribution of value-added between capital and labor inputs for the economy as a whole, we consider a specific form for the production function. For this purpose we take as fixed parameters the share elasticities with respect to capital and labor inputs, the biases of productivity growth with respect to both inputs, and the acceleration of productivity growth. As before, we can refer to the resulting form of the production function as the constant share elasticity production function, emphasizing the interpretation of the parameters. Alternatively, we can refer to this form as the translog production function, emphasizing the role of the variables.

Our aggregate model of production consists of three equations giving the rate of productivity growth and the value shares of both inputs as linear functions of the logarithms of the inputs and time. To formulate an econometric model of production we add a stochastic component to these equations. To estimate the unknown parameters of the translog production function we combine the equation for one of the value shares with the equation for the rate of productivity growth.

We obtain estimates of the unknown parameters on the basis of time series data for the period 1948–1979 on prices and quantities of capital and labor inputs, described in Chapter 8, and value-added, described in Chapter 9. We also obtain test statistics for Hicks neutrality, Harrod neutrality, and Solow neutrality of productivity growth. None of the three forms of neutrality is rejected, so we conclude that the production function can be taken to be linear logarithmic.

In estimating the parameters of our econometric model of production, we impose the restrictions implied by concavity of the production function, but we do not impose restrictions implied by Hicks neutrality, Harrod neutrality, or Solow neutrality of productivity growth. Necessary conditions for the aggregate production function to be increasing in capital and labor inputs and time are satisfied. All share elasticities are equal to zero under the concavity restrictions, so that the production function can be represented in Cobb–Douglas form.

The estimated value of the bias of productivity growth with respect to labor input is negative, so that aggregate productivity growth is labor-saving and capital-using. Alternatively, we can say that the rate of productivity growth is increasing with respect to the quantity of capital input and decreasing with respect to the quantity of labor input. The estimated value of the acceleration of productivity growth is negative, so that the rate of productivity growth decreases with time, holding capital and labor inputs constant.

Conclusion

In this chapter we have outlined a methodology for analyzing postwar economic growth in the United States. We have also outlined the application of this methodology to the generation of data and the analysis of sources of U.S. economic growth. Finally, we have outlined an extension of this methodology to encompass determination of the rate of technical change and the distribution of the value of output among inputs.

Our methodology is based on explicit models of production. The principal innovations in this methodology are the following:

1. At the sectoral level, intermediate, capital, and labor inputs are treated symmetrically to model substitution among inputs and productivity growth. At the aggregate level, capital and labor inputs are treated symmetrically.

2. At the sectoral level we distinguish components of intermediate, capital, and labor inputs that differ in marginal productivity within each industrial sector. At the aggregate level we distinguish components of capital and labor inputs that differ in marginal productivity.

3. At both sectoral and aggregate levels we treat prices and quantities of inputs and outputs symmetrically. We construct index numbers of prices and quantities on the basis of models of the underlying production process.

4. We employ the same models of production to generate data, analyze sources of growth, and model the distribution of the value of output and the rate of productivity growth.

5. We combine sectoral and aggregate models of production to analyze economic growth at the aggregate level.

We first apply our methodology to the generation of data on outputs and inputs. Our principal innovations in the generation of data are the following:

1. At the sectoral level we take the intermediate, capital, and labor inputs to be translog functions of their components. Similarly, at the aggregate level we take capital and labor inputs to be translog functions of their components.

2. We have utilized data from both establishment and household surveys to measure labor input. Control totals for employment, hours worked, and labor compensation for each sector are based on establishment surveys; these totals are allocated among categories of the work force on the basis of household surveys.

3. Our approach for measuring capital input is strictly analogous to our approach for measuring labor input. Capital services represent the quantity of capital input, just as labor services represent the quantity of labor input. Rental rates for capital services provide the basis for property compensation, just as wage rates provide the basis for labor compensation.

4. We generate estimates of prices and quantities of output and intermediate input on the basis of the same classification of economic activities as the classification employed in our estimates of capital and labor input.

5. For each sector we construct price and quantity indices of value-added by combining price and quantity data on output and intermediate input. We construct data on prices and quantities of value-added, capital input, and labor input for the U.S. economy as a whole, by summing data for all sectors.

The second application of the methodology is to analyze the growth of output at both sectoral and aggregate levels. Our principal innovations in analyzing sources of economic growth are the following:

1. To allocate the growth of outputs among contributions of the productive inputs and changes in productivity, we employ indices of the rates of productivity growth based on translog production functions.

2. The starting point for the construction of data on rates of productivity growth is a system of production accounts in current prices. For each account the value of output is equal to the value of input. Outputs and inputs are evaluated from the point of view of the producer.

3. We present a detailed analysis of growth at the sector level, among the contributions of intermediate, capital, and labor inputs and the rate of productivity growth. We allocate the contributions of each of the three inputs between the contribution of an unweighted index of the components of that input and the contribution of input quality, where input quality is defined as the ratio of an index of input quantity to an unweighted sum of its components.

4. We present an analysis of growth at the aggregate level among the contributions of capital and labor inputs and the rate of productivity growth. We decompose the sources of quality change in labor input among all components of the labor force. Similarly, we decompose the sources of quality change in capital input among all components of the capital stock.

5. We decompose the rate of aggregate productivity growth among the contributions of rates of sectoral productivity growth and the contributions of reallocations of value-added, capital input, and labor input among sectors.

The final application of our methodology is to model patterns of substitution and productivity growth and their implications for the rate of productivity growth and the distribution of the value of output among productive inputs. Our principal innovations in modeling substitution and productivity growth are the following:

1. We employ the same form of the production function to determine the rate of productivity growth and the distribution of the value of output among the productive inputs as to construct index numbers of productivity.

2. We treat substitution among inputs and productivity growth symmetrically. We describe patterns of substitution in terms of share elasticities, defined as changes in the shares of inputs in the value of output with respect to proportional changes in all inputs.

3. We describe patterns of productivity growth in terms of biases of productivity growth, defined as changes in the rate of productivity growth with respect to proportional changes in all inputs, and the acceleration of productivity growth.

4. At the sectoral level we do not impose the existence of a value-added function for each sector; we test the restrictions on the parameters of our sectoral models of production implied by the existence of a value-added function.

5. We do not impose restrictions on the form of productivity growth. At the sectoral level we test restrictions on the parameters implied by Hicks neutrality of productivity growth. At the aggregate level we test restrictions on the parameters implied by Hicks neutrality, Harrod neutrality, and Solow neutrality of productivity growth.

While our methodology makes it possible to unify data generation, analysis of the sources of economic growth, and determination of the rate of productivity growth and the distribution of the value of outputs among productive inputs, it is important to keep in mind the following limitations of this methodology:

1. We assume that sectoral production functions are characterized by constant returns to scale. This assumption implies that the aggregate production function is characterized by constant returns to scale. Constant returns are essential to the allocation of the value of output among productive inputs on the basis of accounting data at both sectoral and aggregate levels.

2. We assume that the prices of inputs and outputs can be taken as fixed at the sectoral level. This assumption implies that prices of inputs and outputs can be taken as fixed at the aggregate level. Fixed prices are required for the identification of marginal products with prices of productive inputs at both sectoral and aggregate levels.

3. The most important limitations of our methodology at the aggregate level arise from the use of an aggregate production function. The existence of an aggregate production function imposes severe restrictions on the representation of sectoral production patterns, and it is important to emphasize that we have not employed these restrictions to analyze production patterns at the sectoral level. Accordingly, our aggregate model of production must be regarded as a useful simplification for representing production patterns for the U.S. economy as a whole, rather than the result of aggregation over the models we utilize at the sectoral level.

2 Methodology

This chapter describes our methodology for analyzing postwar patterns of economic growth in the U.S. economy. The theory of production provides the framework that identifies the variables to be included at both sectoral and aggregate levels, determines how each variable should be measured, and establishes the link between sectoral and aggregate measures of productivity. The theory also provides an explicit characterization of sectoral and aggregate models, based on value-added.

We describe a model of producer behavior that permits an analysis of sources of growth in output for individual industrial sectors. The model includes a production function for each sector—giving output as a function of time and capital, labor, and intermediate inputs. Time and all inputs are treated symmetrically. The production function and necessary conditions for producer equilibrium are combined to generate index numbers for productivity and for capital, labor, and intermediate inputs.

We present a model of capital as a factor of production. The distinguishing feature of capital as a factor of production is that durable goods contribute capital services to production at different points of time. The services provided by a given durable good are proportional to the initial investment. In addition, the services provided by different durable goods at the same point of time are perfect substitutes.

A more restrictive version of our methodology is based on a model with output as a function of value-added and intermediate input. Value-added is in turn represented as a function of capital input, labor input, and time. In this alternative approach, time and capital and labor inputs are separable from intermediate input, so that productivity growth can occur only through value-added.

We will also derive a model of production that permits an analysis of sources of growth in aggregate output. This model is based on a production possibility frontier expressing aggregate output as a function of time, value-added in each sector, and the primary-factors of production. A more restrictive version of our aggregate model is based on a production function giving output as a function of time and capital and labor inputs. Combining this production function with conditions for producer equilibrium, we generate index numbers for productivity for output, and for capital and labor inputs.

A link between aggregate and sectoral productivity is also established. Our multisectoral model of production includes production functions for all sectors and conditions for producer equilibrium. It also includes market equilibrium conditions to balance demand and supply for the primary-factors of production. Growth in aggregate productivity depends on sectoral productivity growth and on changes in the distribution of value-added and the primary-factors of production among sectors of the economy.

Sectoral Productivity Growth

Our methodology for productivity measurement is based on a model of producer behavior. The point of departure for this model is a production function for each industrial sector, giving output as a function of intermediate input, capital input, labor input, and time. To analyze substitution among inputs, we combine the production function with necessary conditions for producer equilibrium. To analyze changes in substitution possibilities over time, we employ the rate of productivity growth. The conditions for producer equilibrium can be combined with growth rates of intermediate input, capital input, labor input, and output to produce an index number for the rate of productivity growth.

Our models of production are based on production functions $\{F^i\}$ for each of the n sectors, characterized by constant returns to scale:

$$Z_i = F^i(X_i, K_i, L_i, T), \qquad\qquad (i = 1, 2,..., n),$$

where T is time, $\{Z_i\}$ is the set of outputs, $\{X_i\}$, $\{K_i\}$, and $\{L_i\}$ are the intermediate, capital, and labor inputs. We can define the shares of intermediate input, capital input, and labor input, say $\{v_X^i\}$, $\{v_K^i\}$, and $\{v_L^i\}$, in the value of output by

$$v_X^i = \frac{p_X^i X_i}{q_i Z_i},$$

$$v_K^i = \frac{p_K^i K_i}{q_i Z_i} \, ,$$

$$v_L^i = \frac{p_L^i L_i}{q_i Z_i} \, , \qquad (i = 1, 2,..., n),$$

where $\{q_i\}$, $\{p_X^i\}$, $\{p_K^i\}$, and $\{p_L^i\}$ denote the prices of outputs and intermediate, capital, and labor inputs, respectively. Outputs are valued in producers' prices, while inputs are valued in purchasers' prices.

Necessary conditions for producer equilibrium are given by equalities between the shares of each input in the value of output and the elasticities of output with respect to that input:

$$v_X^i = \frac{\partial \ln Z_i}{\partial \ln X_i} \, (X_i, K_i, L_i, T),$$

$$v_K^i = \frac{\partial \ln Z_i}{\partial \ln K_i} \, (X_i, K_i, L_i, T),$$

$$v_L^i = \frac{\partial \ln Z_i}{\partial \ln L_i} \, (X_i, K_i, L_i, T), \qquad (i = 1, 2,..., n).$$

Under constant returns to scale the elasticities and the value shares for all three inputs sum to unity. Conditions for producer equilibrium imply that the value of output is equal to the sum of the values of intermediate, capital, and labor inputs:

$$q_i Z_i = p_X^i X_i + p_K^i K_i + p_L^i L_i, \qquad (i = 1, 2,..., n).$$

Our data on output, intermediate input, capital input, and labor input in current prices satisfy this equality as an accounting identity.

The production function is defined in terms of output, intermediate input, capital input, and labor input. Each of the inputs is an aggregate that depends on the quantities of individual intermediate inputs, capital inputs, and labor inputs:

$$X_i = X_i (X_{1i}, X_{2i},..., X_{ni}),$$

$$K_i = K_i (K_{1i}, K_{2i},..., K_{pi}),$$

$$L_i = L_i (L_{1i}, L_{2i},..., L_{qi}), \qquad (i = 1, 2,..., n),$$

where $\{X_{ji}\}$ is the set of n intermediate inputs from the jth sector ($j=$ 1,2,..., n), $\{K_{ki}\}$ is the set of p capital inputs, and $\{L_{li}\}$ is the set of q labor inputs, all into the ith sector ($i = 1, 2,..., n$). We say that the production function is *separable* in the n intermediate inputs, the p capital inputs, and the q labor inputs.[1] If each of the aggregates is homogeneous of degree one in its components, we say that the production function is *homothetically separable*.[2] Homogeneity implies that proportional changes in all inputs that comprise each aggregate result in proportional changes in the aggregate. The aggregates for each sector are characterized by constant returns to scale. If the production function is homogeneous of degree one in the n intermediate inputs, the p capital inputs, and the q labor inputs, separability of the production function implies homothetic separability.[3]

We can define the shares of the individual intermediate, capital, and labor inputs, say $\{v_{Xj}^i\}$, $\{v_{Kk}^i\}$, and $\{v_{Ll}^i\}$, in the value of the corresponding aggregate in the ith sector ($i=1, 2,..., n$) by

$$v_{Xj}^i = \frac{p_{Xj}^i X_{ji}}{p_X^i X_i}, \qquad (i, j = 1, 2,..., n),$$

$$v_{Kk}^i = \frac{p_{Kk}^i K_{ki}}{p_K^i K_i}, \qquad (i = 1, 2,..., n; k = 1, 2,..., p),$$

$$v_{Ll}^i = \frac{p_{Ll}^i L_{li}}{p_L^i L_i}, \qquad (i = 1, 2,..., n; l = 1, 2,..., q),$$

where $\{p_{Xj}^i\}$, $\{p_{Kk}^i\}$, and $\{p_{Ll}^i\}$ are the prices of individual intermediate, capital, and labor inputs.

Necessary conditions for producer equilibrium are given by equalities between the shares of the individual inputs in the value of the corresponding aggregate and the elasticities of the aggregate with respect to the individual inputs:

$$v_{Xj}^i = \frac{\partial \ln X_i}{\partial \ln X_{ji}} (X_{1i}, X_{2i},..., X_{ni}),$$

$$v_{Kk}^i = \frac{\partial \ln K_i}{\partial \ln K_{ki}} (K_{1i}, K_{2i},..., K_{pi}),$$

$$v_{Ll}^i = \frac{\partial \ln L_i}{\partial \ln L_{1i}} (L_{1i}, L_{2i},..., L_{qi}), \qquad (i = 1, 2,..., n).$$

Under constant returns to scale, the elasticities and the value shares sum to unity for each of the three aggregates. Conditions for producer equilibrium imply that the values of intermediate, capital, and labor inputs are equal to the sums of the values of their components:

$$p_X^i X_i = \sum p_{Xj}^i X_{ji},$$

$$p_K^i K_i = \sum p_{Kk}^i K_{ki},$$

$$p_L^i L_i = \sum p_{Ll}^i L_{li}, \qquad\qquad (i = 1, 2,..., n).$$

Our data on the components of intermediate, capital, and labor inputs for each sector satisfy these equalities as accounting identities.

Finally, we can define the rate of productivity growth, say $\{v_T^i\}$, for each sector as the rate of growth of output with respect to time, holding intermediate input, capital input, and labor input constant:

$$v_T^i = \frac{\partial \ln Z_i}{\partial T} (X_i, K_i, L_i, T), \qquad\qquad (i = 1, 2,..., n).$$

It is important to note that our definition of the rate of productivity growth does not impose any restriction on substitution patterns among intermediate, capital, and labor inputs.

We say that the production function is *separable* in intermediate input X_i, capital input K_i, and labor input L_i if and only if output Z_i can be represented as a function of aggregate input, say W_i:

$$Z_i = F^i[W_i(X_i, K_i, L_i), T], \qquad\qquad (i = 1, 2,..., n),$$

where aggregate input is independent of the level of technology T. We say that the production function F^i is *homothetically separable* in these inputs if aggregate input W_i is homogeneous of degree one. Under constant returns to scale, the production function is homogeneous of degree one in input W_i, so that productivity growth is *Hicks neutral*[4] and we can rewrite the function in the form

$$Z_i = A_i(T) \cdot W_i(X_i, K_i, L_i), \qquad\qquad (i = 1, 2,..., n).$$

If productivity growth is Hicks neutral, the rate of productivity growth is independent of intermediate, capital, and labor inputs and depends only on time:

$$v_T^i = \frac{d \ln A_i(T)}{dT}, \qquad\qquad (i = 1, 2,..., n).$$

Similarly, input W_i is independent of time and depends only on intermediate, capital, and labor inputs. Under constant returns to scale the existence of aggregate input is equivalent to Hicks neutrality. Our models of production do not require the existence of such an input aggregate in constructing an index of productivity growth; equivalently, we do not require that productivity growth is Hicks neutral.

Up to this point we have discussed indices of productivity growth and intermediate, capital, and labor inputs. We also require corresponding price indices. For this purpose we introduce the dual to our model of production, based on a function that gives the price of output as a function of the prices of intermediate input, capital input, labor input, and time.

Given the necessary conditions for producer equilibrium, we can express the price of output as a function, say $\{P^i\}$, of the prices of intermediate input, capital input, labor input, and time:

$$q_i = P^i(p_X^i, p_K^i, p_L^i, T), \qquad\qquad (i = 1, 2,..., n).$$

We refer to these functions as *sectoral price functions*.[5] The price functions $\{P^i\}$ are homogeneous of degree one in the input prices. Homogeneity implies that a proportional increase in all input prices results in a proportional change in the price of output.

Under constant returns to scale the production function is homothetically separable in the n intermediate inputs, the p capital inputs, and the q labor inputs, if and only if the price function is homothetically separable in the corresponding input prices.[6] The prices of intermediate, capital, and labor inputs are homogeneous of degree one in the prices of their components:

$$p_X^i = p_X^i(p_{X1}^i, p_{X2}^i,..., p_{Xn}^i),$$

$$p_K^i = p_K^i(p_{K1}^i, p_{K2}^i,..., p_{Kp}^i),$$

$$p_L^i = p_L^i(p_{L1}^i, p_{L2}^i,..., p_{Lq}^i), \qquad\qquad (i = 1, 2,..., n).$$

Homogeneity of the sectoral price functions implies that proportional changes in the prices of all inputs that comprise each aggregate input result in proportional changes in the price of the aggregate.

We can define the rate of productivity growth for each sector, say $\{v_T^i\}$, as the negative of the rate of growth of the price of output with respect to time, holding the prices of intermediate input, capital input, and labor input constant:

$$v_T^i = -\frac{\partial \ln P^i}{\partial T} (p_X^i, p_K^i, p_L^i, T), \qquad (i = 1, 2,..., n).$$

If output is a function of an aggregate input, the price of output can be expressed as a function of the price of input, say p_W^i:

$$q_i = \frac{p_W^i (p_X^i, p_K^i, p_L^i)}{A_i(T)}, \qquad (i = 1, 2,..., n).$$

The rate of productivity growth depends only on time; the price of input depends only on the prices of intermediate, capital, and labor inputs. The existence of a quantity aggregate for input is equivalent to the existence of a price aggregate for input and either is equivalent to Hicks neutrality of technical change. It is important to emphasize that we do not employ the assumption of Hicks neutrality to construct our indices of productivity.

In defining output, intermediate, capital, and labor inputs, and productivity in terms of data on quantities and prices, we consider a specific form of the production function for each sector $\{F^i\}$:

$$Z_i = \exp[\alpha_0^i + \alpha_X^i \ln X_i + \alpha_K^i \ln K_i + \alpha_L^i \ln L_i + \alpha_T^i \cdot T$$

$$+ \frac{1}{2} \beta_{XX}^i (\ln X_i)^2 + \beta_{XK}^i \ln X_i \ln K_i + \beta_{XL}^i \ln X_i \ln L_i$$

$$+ \beta_{XT}^i \ln X_i \cdot T + \frac{1}{2} \beta_{KK}^i (\ln K_i)^2 + \beta_{KL}^i \ln K_i \ln L_i$$

$$+ \beta_{KT}^i \ln K_i \cdot T + \frac{1}{2} \beta_{LL}^i (\ln L_i)^2 + \beta_{LT}^i \ln L_i \cdot T + \frac{1}{2} \beta_{TT}^i \cdot T^2],$$

$$(i = 1, 2,..., n).$$

For this production function, output is a transcendental or, more specifically, exponential function of the logarithms of inputs. We refer to these forms as *transcendental logarithmic production functions* or more simply, *translog production functions.*[7]

As before, necessary conditions for producer equilibrium imply that the value shares of intermediate, capital, and labor inputs are equal to the elasticities of output with respect to these inputs:

$$v_X^i = \alpha_X^i + \beta_{XX}^i \ln X_i + \beta_{XK}^i \ln K_i + \beta_{XL}^i \ln L_i + \beta_{XT}^i \cdot T,$$

$$v_K^i = \alpha_K^i + \beta_{XK}^i \ln X_i + \beta_{KK}^i \ln K_i + \beta_{KL}^i \ln L_i + \beta_{KT}^i \cdot T,$$

$$v_L^i = \alpha_L^i + \beta_{XL}^i \ln X_i + \beta_{KL}^i \ln K_i + \beta_{LL}^i \ln L_i + \beta_{LT}^i \cdot T, \qquad (i = 1, 2,..., n).$$

Similarly, rates of productivity growth are equal to rates of growth of output, holding all inputs constant:

$$v_T^i = \alpha_T^i + \beta_{XT}^i \ln X_i + \beta_{KT}^i \ln K_i + \beta_{LT}^i \ln L_i + \beta_{TT}^i \cdot T, \qquad (i = 1, 2,..., n).$$

The translog production function is characterized by constant returns to scale if and only if the parameters satisfy the conditions

$$\alpha_X^i + \alpha_K^i + \alpha_L^i = 1,$$

$$\beta_{XX}^i + \beta_{XK}^i + \beta_{XL}^i = 0,$$

$$\beta_{XK}^i + \beta_{KK}^i + \beta_{KL}^i = 0,$$

$$\beta_{XL}^i + \beta_{KL}^i + \beta_{LL}^i = 0,$$

$$\beta_{XT}^i + \beta_{KT}^i + \beta_{LT}^i = 0, \qquad (i = 1, 2,..., n).$$

If we consider data at any two discrete points of time, say T and $T-1$, the growth rate of output can be expressed as a weighted average of the growth rates of intermediate, capital, and labor inputs plus the average rate of productivity growth:

$$\ln Z_i(T) - \ln Z_i(T-1) = \bar{v}_X^i [\ln X_i(T) - \ln X_i(T-1)] + \bar{v}_K^i [\ln K_i(T) - \ln K_i(T-1)]$$

$$+ \bar{v}_L^i [\ln L_i(T) - \ln L_i(T-1)] + \bar{v}_T^i, \qquad (i = 1, 2,..., n),$$

where the weights are given by the average value shares:

$$\bar{v}_X^i = \frac{1}{2} [v_X^i(T) + v_X^i(T-1)],$$

$$\bar{v}_K^i = \frac{1}{2} [v_K^i(T) + v_K^i(T-1)],$$

$$\bar{v}_L^i = \frac{1}{2} [v_L^i(T) + v_L^i(T-1)], \qquad (i = 1, 2,..., n),$$

and

$$\bar{v}_T^i = \frac{1}{2} [v_T^i(T) + v_T^i(T-1)], \qquad (i = 1, 2,..., n).$$

We refer to the average rates of productivity growth $\{\bar{v}_T^i\}$ as *translog rates of productivity growth*.

Similarly, we can consider specific forms for intermediate, capital, and labor inputs. For example, intermediate input can be expressed as a translog function of individual intermediate inputs:

$$X_i = \exp[\alpha_1^i \ln X_{1i} + \alpha_2^i \ln X_{2i} + ... + \alpha_n^i \ln X_{ni}$$

$$+ \frac{1}{2} \beta_{11}^i (\ln X_{1i})^2 + \beta_{12}^i \ln X_{1i} \ln X_{2i} + ...$$

$$+ \frac{1}{2} \beta_{nn}^i (\ln X_{ni})^2], \qquad (i = 1, 2,..., n).$$

As before, necessary conditions for producer equilibrium imply that the value shares of individual intermediate inputs $\{X_{ji}\}$ are equal to the elasticities of intermediate input with respect to its components:

$$v_{Xj}^i = \alpha_j^i + \beta_{1j}^i \ln X_{1i} + ... + \beta_{jn}^i \ln X_{ni}, \qquad (i = 1, 2,..., n).$$

Intermediate input is characterized by constant returns to scale if and only if the parameters satisfy the conditions

$$\alpha_1^i + \alpha_2^i + ... + \alpha_n^i = 1,$$

$$\beta_{11}^i + \beta_{12}^i + ... + \beta_{1n}^i = 0,$$

$$\beta_{1n}^i + \beta_{2n}^i + ... + \beta_{nn}^i = 0, \qquad (i = 1, 2,..., n).$$

Considering data on intermediate inputs into an industrial sector at any two discrete points of time, we can express the growth rate of intermediate input as a weighted average of growth rates of individual intermediate inputs, with weights given by average value shares:

$$\ln X_i(T) - \ln X_i(T-1) = \sum \bar{v}_{Xj}^i [\ln X_{ji}(T) - \ln X_{ji}(T-1)], \qquad (i = 1, 2,..., n),$$

where

$$\bar{v}_{Xj}^{i} = \frac{1}{2} \ [v_{Xj}^{i}(T) + v_{Xj}^{i}(T-1)], \qquad\qquad (i = 1, 2,..., n).$$

Similarly, if capital and labor inputs are translog functions of their components, we can express the growth rates in the form

$$\ln K_i(T) - \ln K_i(T-1) = \sum \bar{v}_{Kk}^{i} \ [\ln K_{ki}(T) - \ln K_{ki}(T-1)],$$

$$\ln L_i(T) - \ln L_i(T-1) = \sum \bar{v}_{Ll}^{i} \ [\ln L_{li}(T) - \ln L_{li}(T-1)], \qquad (i = 1, 2,..., n),$$

where

$$\bar{v}_{Kk}^{i} = \frac{1}{2} [v_{Kk}^{i}(T) + v_{Kk}^{i}(T-1)], \qquad\qquad (i = 1, 2,..., n; k = 1, 2,..., p),$$

$$\bar{v}_{Ll}^{i} = \frac{1}{2} [v_{Ll}^{i}(T) + v_{Ll}^{i}(T-1)], \qquad\qquad (i = 1, 2,..., n; l = 1, 2,..., q).$$

We refer to the expressions for intermediate, capital, and labor inputs $\{X_i, K_i, L_i\}$ as *translog indices of intermediate, capital, and labor inputs.*[8]

The product of price and quantity indices of intermediate, capital, and labor inputs must be equal to the values of the individual intermediate, capital, and labor inputs. Accordingly, we can define the price index of intermediate input as the ratio of the value of intermediate input to the translog quantity index. Price indices for capital and labor inputs can be defined in the same way. The resulting price indices of intermediate, capital, and labor inputs do not have the form of translog price indices, but they can be determined from data on prices and quantities at any two discrete points of time.[9]

Capital as a Factor of Production

We can refer to durable goods acquired at different points in time as different *vintages* of capital. The flow of capital services is a quantity index of capital inputs from durable goods of different vintages. Under perfect substitutability among the services of goods of different vintages, the flow of capital services is a weighted sum of past investments. The weights correspond to the relative efficiencies of the different vintages of capital.[10]

In the durable goods model of production the relative efficiency of a capital good depends on the age of the good and not on the time it is acquired. Replacement requirements are determined by losses in efficiency of existing capital goods, as well as actual physical disappearance or retirement of capital goods. When a capital good is retired, its relative efficiency drops to zero.

We first characterize each capital good by means of the relative efficiency of capital goods of different ages. For each type of asset the efficiency of a capital good of age τ relative to the efficiency of a new capital good is denoted $d(\tau)$. The sequence of nonnegative numbers $\{d(\tau)\}$ describes the *relative efficiencies* of capital goods of different ages; by definition, the relative efficiency of a new capital good is equal to unity: $d(0) = 1$.

We assume that relative efficiency is nonincreasing with age, so that:

$$d(\tau) - d(\tau - 1) \leq 0, \qquad\qquad (\tau = 1, 2,....,).$$

Finally, we assume that every capital good is eventually retired or scrapped, so that relative efficiency declines to zero:

$$\lim_{\tau \to \infty} d(\tau) = 0.$$

Investment represents the acquisition of capital goods at a given point in time. The quantity of investment is measured in the same way as the durable goods themselves. For example, investment in equipment is the number of machines of a given specification; and investment in structures is the number of buildings of a particular description. The price of acquisition of a durable good is the unit cost of acquiring a piece of equipment or a structure.

By contrast with investment, capital services are measured in terms of the use of a durable good for a stipulated period of time. For example, a building can be leased for a period of years, an automobile can be rented for a number of days or weeks, and computer time can be purchased in seconds or minutes. The price of the service of a durable good is the unit cost of using the good for a specified period.

In the durable goods model of production, capital input plays a role that is analogous to that of any other input. To present the durable goods model of production, we first assume that the production function is homothetically separable in the services of different vintages of capital. The quantity index of capital input is homogeneous of degree one in the services from capital goods of different ages.

We assume that the quantity index of capital input is characterized by perfect substitutability among the services of different vintages of capital, and that the services provided by a durable good are proportional to initial investment in this good. Under these assumptions the quantity of capital input is proportional to capital stock, where capital stock is a weighted sum of past investments.

The sequence of relative efficiencies of capital goods of different ages $\{d(\tau)\}$ allows characterization of capital stock at the end of each period, say

$A(T)$, as a weighted sum of past investments,

$$A(T) = \sum_{\tau=0}^{\infty} d(\tau)\, I(T-\tau)\,,$$

where $I(T-\tau)$ is investment in period $T-\tau$ and the weights are given by the sequence of relative efficiencies.

Capital goods decline in efficiency at each point in time, generating needs for replacement of productive capacity. The proportion of an investment to be replaced at age τ, say $m(\tau)$, is equal to the decline in efficiency from age $\tau-1$ to age τ:

$$m(\tau) = -\,[d(\tau) - d(\tau-l)]\,, \qquad\qquad (\tau = l,\ 2,...,T)\,.$$

We refer to these proportions as *mortality rates* for capital goods of different ages.

Since the relative efficiency of a capital good is nonincreasing, the mortality rates are nonnegative:

$$m(\tau) \geqq 0, \qquad\qquad (\tau = 1,\ 2,...\ )\,.$$

Further, the sum of mortality rates over all ages is equal to unity:

$$\sum_{\tau=1}^{\infty} m(\tau) = \sum_{\tau=1}^{\infty} [d(\tau) - d(\tau-1)] = d(0) = 1\,.$$

We refer to the sequence of mortality rates $\{m(\tau)\}$ as the *mortality distribution* of a capital good.

We can define *replacement* as the level of investment required to keep capital stock unchanged. First taking differences of the expression for capital stock in terms of past investments, we can express replacement requirements, say $R(T)$, in terms of past investments and the mortality distribution:

$$A(T) - A(T-1) = I(T) + \sum_{\tau=1}^{\infty} [d(\tau) - d(\tau-1)]\, I(T-\tau)$$

$$= I(T) - \sum_{\tau=1}^{\infty} m(\tau)\, I(T-\tau)$$

$$= I(T) - R(T)\,,$$

where

$$R(T) = \sum_{\tau=1}^{\infty} m(\tau) I(T-\tau) .$$

Replacement requirements can also be expressed by means of the proportion of an initial investment replaced τ periods after the time of acquisition. This proportion includes replacement requirements generated by the decline in efficiency of the initial capital stock, together with all subsequent replacements of each succeeding replacement. We refer to these proportions, say $\delta(\tau)$, as *replacement rates* for capital goods of different ages.

The sequence of replacement rates can be computed recursively from the sequence of mortality rates, by means of the *renewal equation* (Feller, 1968, 311–313, 329–331). The proportion of an initial investment replaced at time v and again at time $\tau > v$ is $m(v)\delta(\tau-v)$, where $m(v)$ is the mortality rate for an asset of age v and $\delta(\tau-v)$ is the replacement rate for an asset of age $\tau-v$. The proportion of an initial investment replaced at age τ is the sum of the proportions replaced first in periods 1, 2,..., and later at period τ:

$$\delta(\tau) = m(1)\delta(\tau-1) + m(2)\delta(\tau-2) + ... + m(\tau)\delta(0) , \qquad (\tau = 0, 1,...).$$

We refer to the sequence of replacement rates $\{\delta(\tau)\}$ as the *replacement distribution*. Using the replacement distribution we can express replacement requirements in terms of past changes in capital stock:

$$R(T) = \sum_{\tau=1}^{\infty} \delta(\tau) [A(T-\tau) - A(T-\tau-1)].$$

The durable goods model of production is characterized by price–quantity duality. The rental price of capital input is a price index that corresponds to the quantity index given by the flow of capital services. The rental prices for all vintages of capital are proportional to the price index for capital input. The constants of proportionality are given by the relative efficiencies of the different vintages of capital.[11]

To present the dual to the durable goods model of production, consider the price function that corresponds to the production function under constant returns to scale. The price function is homothetically separable in the rental prices of different vintages of capital if and only if the production function is homothetically separable in the corresponding capital services. The price index of capital input is homogeneous of degree one in the rental prices of capital goods of different ages.

PRODUCTIVITY AND U.S. ECONOMIC GROWTH

Under perfect substitutability among the services of different vintages of capital the price index of capital input is the price of the services of a new capital good. Under the additional assumption that the prices provided by a durable good are proportional to the initial investment, the rental prices of capital goods of different ages are proportional to the rental price of a new capital good. The constants of proportionality are given by the relative efficiencies of capital goods of different ages.[12]

For each asset the relative efficiency of capital goods of different ages enables us to characterize the price of investment goods in each period, say $p_I(T)$, as a weighted sum of future rental prices:

$$p_I(T) = \sum_{\tau=0}^{\infty} d(\tau) \prod_{S=1}^{\tau+1} \frac{1}{1+r(T+S)} p_K(T+\tau+1) ,$$

where $p_K(T+\tau+1)$ is the rental price in period $T+\tau+1$ and the weights are given by the sequence of relative efficiencies $\{d(\tau)\}$. In this expression $r(T)$ is the rate of return on capital in period T and $\prod_{S=1}^{\tau+1} \frac{1}{1+r(T+S)}$ is the discount factor in period T for future prices in period $T+\tau+1$.

We can define depreciation as the value that must be recovered in every period to keep wealth intact. Taking first differences of the expression for the price of investment goods in terms of future rental prices, we can express depreciation on a capital good in period T, say $p_D(T)$, in terms of future rental prices and the mortality distribution $\{m(\tau)\}$:

$$p_I(T) - [1 + r(T)] p_I(T-1)$$

$$= -p_K(T) - \sum_{\tau=1}^{\infty} [d(\tau) - d(\tau-1)] \prod_{S=1}^{\tau} \frac{1}{1+r(T+S)} p_K(T+\tau),$$

$$= -p_K(T) + \sum_{\tau=1}^{\infty} m(\tau) \prod_{S=1}^{\tau} \frac{1}{1+r(T+S)} p_K(T+\tau),$$

$$= -p_K(T) + p_D(T),$$

where

$$p_D(T) = \sum_{\tau=1}^{\infty} m(\tau) \prod_{S=1}^{\tau} \frac{1}{1+r(T+S)} p_K(T+\tau).$$

Alternatively, we can express depreciation in terms of present and future changes in the price of investment goods, using the replacement distribution $\{\delta(\tau)\}$:

$$p_D(T) = -\sum_{\tau=1}^{\infty} \delta(\tau) \left[\prod_{S=1}^{\tau} \frac{1}{1+r(T+S)} \, p_I(T+\tau) - \prod_{S=1}^{\tau-1} \frac{1}{1+r(T+S)} \, p_I(T+\tau-1) \right]$$

In the absence of taxation the rental price of capital services in period T can be expressed in terms of the price of investment goods, the rate of return, and depreciation:

$$p_K(T) = p_I(T-1)r(T) + p_D(T) - [p_I(T) - p_I(T-1)].$$

The rental price is the sum of the nominal return to capital $p_I(T-1)r(T)$ and depreciation $p_D(T)$, less revaluation $p_I(T) - p_I(T-1)$. We can also express the rental price of capital services in terms of the price of investment goods, the own rate of return on capital in period $T, r(T) - \dfrac{[p_I(T) - p_I(T-1)]}{p_I(T-1)}$, and depreciation:

$$p_K(T) = p_I(T-1) \left[r(T) - \frac{p_I(T) - p_I(T-1)}{p_I(T-1)} \right] + p_D(T).$$

To illustrate the application of the perpetual inventory method, consider three examples of sequences of relative efficiencies. First, suppose that efficiency is constant for a lifetime of L periods and zero thereafter:

$$d(\tau) = \begin{cases} 1, & (\tau = 0, \ 1,..., L-1), \\ 0, & (\tau = L, \ L+1,...). \end{cases}$$

The mortality distribution is equal to zero for ages through $L-1$, unity for age L, and zero thereafter:

$$m(\tau) = \begin{cases} 0, & (\tau = 1, \ 2,..., L-1), \\ 1, & (\tau = L), \\ 0, & (\tau = L+1, \ L+2,...). \end{cases}$$

Finally, the replacement distribution is periodic, with period equal to the lifetime L:

$$\delta(\tau) = \begin{cases} 0, & (\tau = 1,\, 2,\dots,\, L-1,\, L+1,\dots), \\ \\ 1, & (\tau = L,\, 2L,\dots). \end{cases}$$

Second, suppose that efficiency declines linearly for a lifetime of L periods and is zero thereafter:

$$d(\tau) = \begin{cases} 1 - \dfrac{\tau}{L}, & (\tau = 0,\, 1,\dots,\, L-1), \\ \\ 0, & (\tau = L,\, L+1,\dots). \end{cases}$$

The mortality distribution is constant for ages through $L-1$ and zero thereafter:

$$m(\tau) = \begin{cases} \dfrac{1}{L}, & (\tau = 1,\, 2,\dots,\, L), \\ \\ 0, & (\tau = L+1,\, L+2,\dots). \end{cases}$$

Finally, the replacement distribution takes the form

$$\delta(1) = \frac{1}{L},$$

$$\delta(2) = \frac{1}{L}\left(1 + \frac{1}{L}\right),$$

. . .

Third, suppose that efficiency declines geometrically at the rate δ:

$$m(\tau) = \delta(1-\delta)^{\tau}, \qquad\qquad\qquad\qquad (\tau = 0,\, 1,\dots).$$

The mortality distribution also declines geometrically at the same rate:

$$m(\tau) = \delta(1-\delta)^{\tau-1} \qquad\qquad (\tau = 1, 2,....,).$$

Finally, the replacement distribution is constant:

$$\delta(\tau) = \delta, \qquad\qquad (\tau = 1, 2,...).$$

If efficiency is constant over a lifetime of L periods and zero thereafter, replacement requirements follow a "one-hoss-shay" pattern,

$$R(T) = I(T-L),$$

or, in terms of past changes in capital stock,

$$R(T) = [A(T-L) - A(T-L-1)] + [A(T-2L) - A(T-2L-1)] + ...$$

If efficiency declines linearly, replacement requirements follow a "straight-line" pattern:

$$R(T) = \frac{1}{L} \sum_{\tau=1}^{L} I(T-\tau)$$

or

$$R(T) = \frac{1}{L} [A(T-1) - A(T-2)] + \frac{1}{L} (1 + \frac{1}{L}) [A(T-2) - A(T-3)] + ...$$

Finally, if efficiency declines geometrically, replacement requirements follow a "declining balance" pattern:

$$R(T) = \sum_{\tau=1}^{\infty} \delta(1-\delta)^{\tau-1} I(T-\tau)$$

or

$$R(T) = \delta A(T-1).$$

To illustrate the application of the dual to the perpetual inventory method, we first suppose that efficiency is constant for a lifetime of L periods and zero thereafter. Depreciation can be expressed in terms of future rental prices,

$$p_D(T) = \prod_{S=1}^{L} \frac{1}{1 + r(T+S)} \, p_K(T+L),$$

or in terms of future changes in prices of investment goods,

$$p_D(T) = \sum_{\sigma=1}^{\infty} \left[\prod_{S=1}^{\sigma L} \frac{1}{1+r(T+S)} \, p_I(T+\sigma L) - \prod_{S=1}^{\sigma L-1} \frac{1}{1+r(T+S)} \, p_I(T+\sigma L-1) \right].$$

Second, if efficiency declines linearly for a lifetime of L periods and is zero thereafter, we obtain the following expression for depreciation:

$$p_D(T) = \frac{1}{L} \sum_{\tau=1}^{L} \prod_{S=1}^{\tau} \frac{1}{1+r(T+S)} \, p_K(T+\tau),$$

or, in terms of future changes in prices of investment goods:

$$p_D(T) = -\frac{1}{L} \left[\frac{1}{1+r(T+1)} \, p_I(T+1) - p_I(T) \right]$$

$$-\frac{1}{L} \left[1 + \frac{1}{L} \right] \left[\prod_{S=1}^{2} \frac{1}{1+r(T+S)} \, p_I(T+2) - \frac{1}{1+r(T+1)} \, p_I(T+1) \right]$$

$$- \ldots$$

Third, if relative efficiency declines geometrically at the rate δ, depreciation is proportional to the price of investment goods:

$$p_D(T) = \sum_{\tau=1}^{\infty} \delta(1-\delta)^{\tau-1} \prod_{S=1}^{\tau} \frac{1}{1+r(T+S)} \, p_K(T+\tau),$$

$$= \delta p_I(T).$$

Since we have assumed that replacement requirements follow a declining balance pattern for each asset, depreciation is a constant proportion of the price of investment goods. The constant of proportionality δ is the rate of depreciation, which is equal to the rate of replacement.

In the perpetual inventory method, data on the quantity of investment goods of every vintage are used to estimate capital formation, replacement requirements, and capital stock. Data on the acquisition prices of investment goods of every vintage are required in the price counterpart of the perpetual inventory method. The price of acquisition of an investment good of a given age is a weighted sum of future rental prices of capital services. The weights are relative efficiencies of the capital good in every future period.

An array of acquisition prices for capital goods of each vintage at each point of time provides sufficient information to enable us to calculate the service prices of capital goods of each vintage. These data—together with current investment, capital stock, replacement, and investments of all vintages at each point of time, constitute the basic data on quantities and prices required for a complete vintage accounting system. Price and quantity data that we have described for a single durable good are required for each durable good in the system. These data are used to derive price and quantity indices for each durable good, and these indices play the role of prices and quantities of individual inputs in the theory of production.[13]

For each durable good with a full set of data for each time period, price and quantity indices for capital input can be constructed at each point in time. For durable goods with a less complete set of data, a simplified set of price and quantity indices can be constructed on the basis of the assumption that the decline in efficiency is geometric.[14] Under this assumption the rate of replacement is constant and equal to the rate of decline in efficiency. Vintage accounts are unnecessary, since replacement is proportional to capital stock and depreciation is proportional to the current acquisition price of investment goods.

Sectoral Value Added

A more restrictive version of our methodology for sectoral productivity measurement is based on the concept of value-added. Output is represented as a function of intermediate input and value-added; value-added is represented in turn as a function of capital input, labor input, and time. The existence of the value-added aggregate requires that time and capital and labor inputs are separable from intermediate input. Given the quantities of intermediate input and value-added, output is independent of time. In the value-added approach, intermediate input is not treated symmetrically with capital and labor inputs.

The unrestricted version of our methodology, as described in the previous section, treats all inputs and time symmetrically. Our sectoral models of production do not require the existence of a value-added aggregate to construct an index of productivity growth. Both the restricted and unrestricted versions of our methodology require the same data for full implementation—prices and quantities of output and of intermediate, capital, and labor inputs. The value-added approach is based on more restrictive assumptions but requires precisely the same data.

We have employed a model of production based on a production function $\{F^i\}$ for each of the n sectors. The production function gives output $\{Z_i\}$ as a function of intermediate input $\{X_i\}$, capital input $\{K_i\}$, labor input $\{L_i\}$, and time T. We can specialize this model by introducing a value-added function $\{G^i\}$ for each sector, giving the quantity of value-added, say $\{V_i\}$, as a function of capital input, labor input, and time:[15]

$$V_i = G^i(K_i, L_i, T), \qquad\qquad (i = 1, 2,..., n),$$

where

$$Z_i = F^i(X_i, V_i),$$

$$= F^i[X_i, G^i(K_i, L_i, T)], \qquad\qquad (i = 1, 2,..., n).$$

We say that the production function is *neutral* with respect to intermediate input. If the value-added function is homogeneous of degree one in capital and labor inputs, we say that the production function is *homothetically neutral* with respect to intermediate input. Homogeneity implies that proportional changes in capital and labor inputs result in proportional changes in value-added. The value-added function is characterized by constant returns to scale. If the production function is homogeneous of degree one in intermediate, capital, and labor inputs, neutrality of the production function implies homothetic neutrality.

Denoting the price of value-added by $\{p_V^i\}$, we can define the share of value-added, say $\{v_V^i\}$, in the value of output by

$$v_V^i = \frac{p_V^i \, V_i}{q_i \, Z_i}, \qquad\qquad (i = 1, 2,..., n).$$

Necessary conditions for producer equilibrium include equalities between the share of value-added and the elasticity of output with respect to value-added:

$$v_V^i = \frac{\partial \ln Z_i}{\partial \ln V_i} (X_i, V_i), \qquad\qquad (i = 1, 2,..., n).$$

Under constant returns to scale, the elasticities and the value shares for intermediate input and value-added sum to unity. Conditions for producer equilibrium imply that the value of output is equal to the sum of the values of intermediate input and value-added:

$$q_i Z_i = p_X^i X_i + p_V^i V_i, \qquad\qquad (i = 1, 2,..., n).$$

Necessary conditions for producer equilibrium also include equality between the shares of capital and labor inputs in value-added and the elasticities of the quantity of value-added with respect to those inputs. Conditions for producer equilibrium imply that value-added is equal to the sum of the values of capital and labor inputs:

$$p_V^i \, V_i = p_K^i \, K_i + p_L^i \, L_i, \qquad\qquad (i = 1, 2,..., n).$$

Up to this point we have discussed quantity indices of value-added; we also require the corresponding price indices. Given the necessary conditions for producer equilibrium, we can express the price of output as a function of the prices of intermediate input and value-added:

$$q_i = P^i(p_X^i, p_V^i), \qquad\qquad (i = 1, 2,..., n).$$

As before, we refer to these functions as *sectoral price functions.*[16] The price functions $\{P^i\}$ are homogeneous of degree one in the prices of intermediate input and value-added. Similarly, we can express the price of value-added as a function of the prices of capital input, labor input, and time:

$$p_V^i = p_V^i(p_K^i, p_L^i, T), \qquad\qquad (i = 1, 2,..., n).$$

We refer to these functions as the *sectoral price of value-added functions.* These functions are homogeneous of degree one in the prices of capital and labor inputs.

In defining value-added in terms of data on quantities and prices, we consider a specific form of the production function for each sector $\{F^i\}$:

$$Z_i = \exp\left[\alpha_0^i + \alpha_X^i \ln X_i + \alpha_V^i \ln V_i + \frac{1}{2}\, \beta_{XX}^i (\ln X_i)^2 \right.$$

$$\left. + \beta_{XV}^i \ln X_i \ln V_i + \frac{1}{2}\, \beta_{VV}^i (\ln V_i)^2 \right] \qquad (i = 1, 2,..., n).$$

Output is a translog function of intermediate input and value-added.

Necessary conditions for producer equilibrium imply that the shares of intermediate input and value-added are equal to the elasticities of output with respect to intermediate input and value-added:

$$v_X^i = \alpha_X^i + \beta_{XX}^i \ln X_i + \beta_{XV}^i \ln V_i,$$

PRODUCTIVITY AND U.S. ECONOMIC GROWTH

$$v_V^i = \alpha_V^i + \beta_{XV}^i \ln X_i + \beta_{VV}^i \ln V_i, \qquad\qquad (i = 1, 2,..., n).$$

The translog production function is characterized by constant returns to scale if and only if the parameters satisfy the conditions

$$\alpha_X^i + \alpha_V^i = 1,$$

$$\beta_{XX}^i + \beta_{XV}^i = 0,$$

$$\beta_{XV}^i + \beta_{VV}^i = 0, \qquad\qquad (i = 1, 2,..., n).$$

If we consider data at any two discrete points of time, say T and $T-1$, we can express the growth rate of output as a weighted average of growth rates of intermediate input and value-added:

$$\ln Z_i(T) - \ln Z_i(T-1) = \bar{v}_X^i[\ln X_i(T) - \ln X_i(T-1)]$$

$$+ \bar{v}_V^i[\ln V_i(T) - \ln V_i(T-1)], \qquad\qquad (i = 1, 2,..., n),$$

where the weights are given by the average value shares:

$$\bar{v}_X^i = \frac{1}{2}\,[v_X^i(T) + v_X^i(T-1)],$$

$$\bar{v}_V^i = \frac{1}{2}\,[v_V^i(T) + v_V^i(T-1)], \qquad\qquad (i = 1, 2,..., n).$$

The growth rate of value-added can be expressed in terms of growth rates of intermediate input and output and the average value shares:

$$\ln V_i(T) - \ln V_i(T-1) = \frac{1}{\bar{v}_V^i}[\ln Z_i(T) - \ln Z_i(T-1)]$$

$$-\frac{\bar{v}_X^i}{\bar{v}_V^i}[\ln X_i(T) - \ln X_i(T-1)], \qquad\qquad (i = 1, 2,..., n).$$

We refer to these expressions for value-added $\{V_i\}$ as *translog indices of value-added*.[17]

The product of price and quantity indices of value-added must be equal to value-added. Accordingly, we can define the price index of value-added as the ratio of value-added to the translog quantity index. The resulting price index does not have the form of a translog price index, but it can be determined from data on prices and quantities of output and intermediate input at any two discrete points of time.

Aggregate Productivity Growth

Our next objective is to develop the methodology for productivity measurement at the aggregate level. Our point of departure is a multisectoral model that includes value-added functions for all sectors. The model also includes market equilibrium conditions between the supply of each primary-factor of production and the sum of demands for that factor by all sectors:

$$K_k = \sum K_{ki}, \qquad\qquad (k = 1, 2,..., p),$$

$$L_l = \sum L_{li}, \qquad\qquad (l = 1, 2,..., q),$$

where $\{K_k\}$ is the supply of capital input and $\{L_l\}$ is the supply of labor input.

To derive an aggregate model of production we choose a set of quantities of value-added for all sectors. We then maximize aggregate output—defined as a proportion of all quantities of value-added—subject to the value-added functions for all sectors, the market equilibrium conditions, and the supplies of primary-factors of production.[18] We can express the maximum value of aggregate output, say λ, as a function of all quantities of value-added, all supplies of primary-factors of production, and time:

$$\lambda = H(V_1, V_2,..., V_n; K_1, K_2,..., K_p; L_1, L_2,..., L_q; T).$$

The constraints of our maximization problem—sectoral value-added functions and market equilibrium conditions—are linear homogeneous functions in the supplies of primary-factors of production, sectoral quantities of value-added, and demands for factors of production. The function H is homogeneous of degree minus one in the quantities of value-added $\{V_i\}$, homogeneous of degree one in the factor supplies $\{K_k, L_l\}$, and homogeneous of degree zero in quantities of value-added and factor supplies together. We conclude that our model of aggregate output is characterized by constant returns to scale.

To define a model of production for the economy as a whole, we first fix the level of aggregate output at unity:

$$1 = H(V_1, V_2,..., V_n; K_1, K_2,..., K_p; L_1, L_2,..., L_q; T).$$

PRODUCTIVITY AND U.S. ECONOMIC GROWTH

This expression defines the *production possibility frontier*. We can define the shares of value-added for all sectors, capital inputs, and labor inputs—say $\{w_i\}$, $\{w_{Kk}\}$, and $\{w_{Ll}\}$—in aggregate value-added by

$$w_i = \frac{p_V^i V_i}{\sum p_V^i V_i} \qquad (i = 1, 2,..., n),$$

$$w_{Kk} = \frac{p_{Kk} K_k}{\sum p_V^i V_i} \qquad (k = 1, 2,..., p),$$

$$w_{Ll} = \frac{p_{Ll} L_l}{\sum p_V^i V_i} \qquad (l = 1, 2,..., q),$$

denoting the prices of value-added, capital inputs, and labor inputs by $\{p_V^i\}$, $\{p_{Kk}\}$, $\{p_{Ll}\}$, respectively.

Necessary conditions for producer equilibrium involve the shares of value-added in each sector and shares of each capital and labor input in value-added for the economy as a whole. These value shares are equal to elasticities of aggregate output with respect to the quantities of value-added in each sector and the quantities of capital and labor inputs:

$$w_i = \frac{\partial \ln H}{\partial \ln V_i} \ (V_l, V_2, 1,..., V_n; K_1, K_2,..., K_p; L_1, L_2,..., L_q; T),$$

$$(i = 1, 2,..., n),$$

$$w_{Kk} = \frac{\partial \ln H}{\partial \ln K_k} \ (V_1, V_2,..., V_n; K_1, K_2,..., K_p; L_1, L_2,..., L_q; T),$$

$$(k = 1, 2,..., p),$$

$$w_{Ll} = \frac{\partial \ln H}{\partial \ln L_l} \ (V_1, V_2,..., V_n; K_1, K_2,..., K_p; L_1, L_2,..., L_q; T),$$

$$(l = 1, 2,..., q),$$

Under constant returns to scale for the economy as a whole, both the elasticities and the shares of value-added for all sectors sum to unity. Similarly, the elasticities and value shares of all capital and labor inputs sum to unity.

We can define the rate of productivity growth for the economy as a whole, say v_T, as the growth rate of aggregate output with respect to time, holding all quantities of value-added, capital input, and labor input constant:[19]

$$v_T = \frac{\partial \ln H}{\partial T}(V_1, V_2,..., V_n; K_1, K_2,..., K_p; L_1, L_2,..., L_q; T).$$

A more restrictive form of our methodology for productivity measurement is based on a production function. If the production possibility frontier can be expressed in terms of value-added—capital input, and labor input—say V, K, and L—we can write this frontier in the form

$$l = H[V(V_1, V_2,..., V_n), K(K_1, K_2,..., K_p), L(L_1, L_2,..., L_q), T],$$

where the aggregates $\{V, K, L\}$ are characterized by constant returns to scale. We say that the production possibility frontier is homothetically separable in value-added, capital input, and labor input.

Value-added can be expressed as a function, say F, of capital and labor inputs and time:

$$V = F(K, L, T).$$

This expression defines the *aggregate production function*; this production function is characterized by constant returns to scale. The quantities of capital and labor inputs are functions of the quantities of their components:

$$K = K(K_1, K_2,..., K_p),$$

$$L = L(L_1, L_2,..., L_q).$$

The existence of an aggregate production function implies that the value-added functions of all sectors are identical up to a scalar multiple.[20] Under this condition we can write the value-added functions in the form

$$V_i = G^i(K_i, L_i, T),$$

$$= a_i F(K_i, L_i, T), \qquad\qquad (i = 1, 2,..., n),$$

where F is the aggregate production function and the constants of proportionality $\{a_i\}$ are fixed. We can choose dimensions for measuring value-added in each sector so that these constants are equal to unity for all sectors; for this choice of dimensions all value-added functions are identical to the aggregate production function. In addition, sectoral capital and labor inputs $\{K_i\}$ and $\{L_i\}$ are identical functions of their components.

Given the existence of an aggregate production function, we can define the shares of capital and labor inputs, say v_k and v_L, in value-added by

$$v_K = \frac{p_K K}{p_V V},$$

$$v_L = \frac{p_L L}{p_V V},$$

where p_V, p_K, and p_L denote the prices of value-added, capital input, and labor input, respectively. Necessary conditions for producer equilibrium are given by equalities between the value shares of each input and the elasticity of output with respect to that input:

$$v_K = \frac{\partial \ln V}{\partial \ln K} (K, L, T),$$

$$v_L = \frac{\partial \ln V}{\partial \ln L} (K, L, T).$$

Since the value-added functions of all sectors are identical to the aggregate production function, the elasticities and the value shares are identical for all sectors. Under constant returns to scale the elasticities and the value shares for each input sum to unity.

We can define the shares of components of capital and labor inputs, say $\{v_{Kk}\}$ and $\{v_{Ll}\}$, in the value of the corresponding aggregate by

$$v_{Kk} = \frac{p_{Kk} K_k}{\sum p_{Kk} K_k}, \qquad\qquad (k = 1, 2,..., p),$$

$$V_{Ll} = \frac{p_{Ll} L_l}{\sum p_{Ll} L_l}, \qquad\qquad (l = 1, 2,..., q).$$

Necessary conditions for producer equilibrium are given by equalities between the value share of each component and the elasticity of the aggregate with respect to that component:

$$v_{Kk} = \frac{\partial \ln K}{\partial \ln K_k} (K_1, K_2,...,K_p), \qquad\qquad (k = 1, 2,..., p),$$

$$v_{Ll} = \frac{\partial \ln L}{\partial \ln L_l} (L_1, L_2,...,L_q), \qquad\qquad (l = 1, 2,..., q).$$

As before, the elasticities and value shares are identical for all sectors. Under constant returns to scale, the elasticities and the value shares sum to unity for each aggregate.

If, in addition, value-added V can be expressed as a function of aggregate input, say W, we can write this function in the form

$$V = F[W(K, L), T],$$

where input is homogeneous of degree one in the inputs, K and L. The production function F is homogeneous of degree one in input W, so that productivity growth is Hicks neutral, and we can write the function in the form

$$V = A(T) \cdot W(K, L).$$

Identical restrictions hold for the sectoral value-added functions.

If productivity growth is Hicks neutral, the rate of productivity growth is independent of capital and labor inputs and depends only on time:

$$v_T = \frac{d \ln A(T)}{dT} .$$

Similarly, input W is independent of time and depends only on capital and labor inputs. We do not require Hicks neutrality to construct an index of productivity growth.

Up to this point we have discussed quantity indices of the rate of productivity growth and capital and labor inputs. As before, we require the corresponding price indices. For this purpose we introduce a dual to our aggregate model of production. The dual is based on the price possibility frontier, giving the price of output as a function of the prices of value-added in all sectors, the prices of primary-factors of production, and time.

Under constant returns to scale the necessary conditions for producer equilibrium imply that the sum of value-added in all sectors is equal to the sum of the values of capital and labor inputs in all sectors:

$$\sum p_V^i V_i = \sum p_{Kk} K_k + \sum p_{Ll} L_l.$$

Our data on value-added, capital input, and labor input satisfy this equality as an accounting identity. Given this identity and the necessary conditions for producer equilibrium, we can define the price of output, say μ, as a proportion of the prices of value-added in all sectors. We can express the price of output as a function of the prices of value-added in all sectors, the prices of primary-factors of production, and time:

$$\mu = R(p_V^1, p_V^2, ..., p_V^n; p_{K1}, p_{K2}, ..., p_{Kp}; p_{L1}, p_{L2}, ..., p_{Lq}; T).$$

The function R is homogeneous of degree minus one in the prices of value-added $\{p_V^i\}$, homogeneous of degree one in the prices of the primary-factors of production $\{p_{Kk}, p_{Ll}\}$, and homogeneous of degree zero in the prices of value-added and factors of production together.

To define the rate of productivity growth, we first fixed the price of output at unity:

$$l = R(p_V^1, p_V^2, ..., p_V^n; p_{K1}, p_{K2}, ..., p_{Kp}; p_{L1}, p_{L2}, ..., p_{Lq}; T).$$

The expression defines the *price possibility frontier* for the economy as a whole.[21] We can define the rate of productivity growth as the negative of the rate of change of the price of output with respect to time, holding constant the prices of value-added in all sectors and primary-factors of production:

$$v_T = -\frac{\partial \ln R}{\partial T} (p_V^1, p_V^2, ..., p_V^n; p_{Kl}, p_{K2}, ..., p_{Kp}; p_{L1}, p_{L2}, ..., p_{Lq}; T).$$

If the production possibility frontier can be expressed in terms of value-added, capital input, and labor input, we can write the price possibility frontier in terms of prices of these aggregates:

$$l = R[p_V(p_V^1, p_V^2, ..., p_V^n), p_K(p_{K1}, p_{K2}, ..., p_{Kp}), p_L(p_{Ll}, p_{L2}, ..., p_{Lq}), T].$$

The price of value-added can be expressed as a function, say P, of the prices of capital and labor inputs and time:

$$p_V = P(p_K, p_L, T).$$

This expression defines the *aggregate price function.* The price function is homogeneous of degree one in the prices of capital and labor inputs. The prices of capital and labor inputs are functions of the prices of their components:

$$p_K = p_K(p_{K1}, p_{K2}, ..., p_{Kp}),$$

$$p_L = p_L(p_{L1}, p_{L2}, ..., p_{Lq});$$

These functions are also homogeneous of degree one.

The existence of an aggregate price function implies that the price of value-added functions for all sectors are identical up to a scalar multiple.

Under this condition we can write the price of value-added functions in the form

$$p_V^i = p_V^i \, (p_K^i, p_L^i, T),$$

$$= b_i \, P(p_K, p_L, T), \qquad\qquad (i = 1, 2,..., n),$$

where P is the price function, p_k and p_L are the prices of capital and labor inputs, and the constants of proportionality $\{b_i\}$ are fixed. As before, we can choose dimensions for measuring value-added in each sector so that these constants are equal to unity in all sectors. For this choice of dimensions all sectoral price-of-value-added functions are identical to the aggregate price function. In addition, all prices of capital and labor inputs are identical functions of the prices of their components. If the prices paid for primary inputs are the same for all sectors, the sectoral prices of value-added $\{p_V^i\}$ are identical to the aggregate price of value-added p_V.

Constant returns to scale for the economy as a whole implies that aggregate value-added is equal to the sum of value-added in all sectors:

$$p_V V = \sum p_V^i \, V_{i.}$$

Our data on value-added satisfy this equality as an accounting identity. If all sectoral prices of value-added are identical to the aggregate price of value-added, this identity implies that the quantity of value-added for the economy as a whole can be expressed as the sum of the quantities of value-added in all sectors:[22]

$$V = \sum V_{i.}$$

Similarly, constant returns implies that the values of capital and labor inputs are equal to the sums of the values of their components:

$$p_K K = \sum p_{Kk} \, K_k,$$

$$p_L L = \sum p_{Ll} \, L_{l.}$$

Again, our data on capital and labor inputs satisfy these equalities as accounting identities.

If value-added can be expressed as a function of input, the price of output can be expressed as a function of the price of input, say P_W:

$$p_V = \frac{p_W(p_K, p_L)}{A(T)} \ .$$

The rate of productivity growth depends only on time, and the price of input depends only on the prices of capital and labor inputs. The existence of a quantity aggregate for input is equivalent to the existence of a price aggregate for input, and either is equivalent to Hicks neutrality of technical change. Corresponding restrictions hold for the sectoral price-of-value-added functions.

As before, we consider a specific form for the production function in defining value-added in terms of data on quantities and prices:

$$V = \exp\left[\alpha_0 + \alpha_K \ln K + \alpha_L \ln L + \alpha_T \cdot T + \frac{1}{2} \beta_{KK}(\ln K)^2 \right.$$

$$+ \beta_{KL} \ln K \ln L + \beta_{KT} \ln K \cdot T + \frac{1}{2} \beta_{LL}(\ln L)^2$$

$$\left. + \beta_{LT} \ln L \cdot T + \frac{1}{2} \beta_{TT} \cdot T^2 \right] .$$

Value-added is a translog function of capital and labor inputs. The sectoral value-added functions are identical to the aggregate production function.

Necessary conditions for producer equilibrium are given by equalities between the value share of each input and the elasticity of output with respect to that input:

$$v_K = \alpha_K + \alpha_{KK} \ln K + \alpha_{KL} \ln L + \alpha_{KT} \cdot T ,$$

$$v_L = \alpha_L + \alpha_{KL} \ln K + \alpha_{LL} \ln L + \alpha_{LT} \cdot T .$$

Similarly, the rate of productivity growth is equal to the rate of growth of output, holding both inputs constant:

$$v_T = \alpha_T + \beta_{KT} \ln K + \beta_{LT} \ln L + \beta_{TT} \cdot T .$$

The sectoral value shares and rate of productivity growth are identical to the corresponding aggregate value shares and rate of productivity growth.

The translog production function is characterized by constant returns to scale if and only if the parameters satisfy the conditions

$$\alpha_K + \alpha_L = 1 ,$$

$\beta_{KK} + \beta_{KL} = 0$,

$\beta_{KL} + \beta_{LL} = 0$,

$\beta_{KT} + \beta_{LT} = 0$.

If we consider data for the economy as a whole at any two discrete points of time, say T and $T-1$, the growth rate of output can be expressed as a weighted average of the growth rates of capital and labor inputs plus the average rate of productivity growth:

$$\ln V(T) - \ln V(T-1) = \bar{v}_K [\ln K(T) - \ln K(T-1)] + \bar{v}_L [\ln L(T)$$

$$- \ln L(T-1)] + \bar{v}_T \,,$$

where weights are given by average value shares:

$$\bar{v}_K = \frac{1}{2} [v_K(T) + v_K(T-1)],$$

$$\bar{v}_L = \frac{1}{2} [v_L(T) + v_L(T-1)],$$

$$\bar{v}_T = \frac{1}{2} [v_T(T) + v_T(T-1)].$$

We refer to the expression for the average rate of productivity growth $\bar{v}_T$ as the *translog index of the rate of productivity growth*.

Similarly, we can consider specific forms for capital and labor inputs as functions of their components. For example, the quantity of capital input can be expressed as a translog function of its components:

$$K = \exp[\alpha_1 \ln K_1 + \alpha_2 \ln K_2 + ... + \alpha_p \ln K_p$$

$$+ \frac{1}{2} \beta_{11} (\ln K_1)^2 + \beta_{12} \ln K_1 \ln K_2 + ...$$

$$+ \frac{1}{2} \beta_{pn} (\ln K_p)^2] \,.$$

As before, the corresponding sectoral functions are identical to the aggregate function. Necessary conditions for producer equilibrium imply that the share of each component of capital input in the value of capital input is equal to the elasticity of capital input with respect to that component:

$$w_{Kk} = \alpha_k + \beta_{1k} \ln K_1 + \beta_{2k} \ln K_2 + ... + \beta_{pk} \ln K_p, \qquad (k = 1, 2,..., p).$$

The quantity of capital input is characterized by constant returns to scale if and only if the parameters satisfy the conditions

$$\alpha_1 + \alpha_2 + ... + \alpha_p = 1,$$

$$\beta_{11} + \beta_{12} + ... + \beta_{1p} = 0,$$

$$\beta_{12} + \beta_{22} + ... + \beta_{2p} = 0,$$

. . .

$$\beta_{1p} + \beta_{2p} + ... + \beta_{pp} = 0.$$

Considering data on capital input at any two discrete points of time, we can express the growth rate of capital input as a weighted average of growth rates:

$$\ln K(T) - \ln K(T-1) = \sum \bar{v}_{Kk} [\ln K_k(T) - \ln K_k(T-1)],$$

where weights are given by average value shares:

$$\bar{v}_{Kk} = \frac{1}{2} [v_{Kk}(T) + v_{Kk}(T-1)], \qquad (k = 1, 2, ... p).$$

Similarly, if labor input is a translog function of its components, we can express the growth rate of labor input in the form

$$\ln L(T) - \ln L(T-1) = \sum \bar{v}_{Ll} [\ln L_l(T) - \ln L_l(T-1)],$$

where

$$\bar{v}_{Ll} = \frac{1}{2} [v_{Ll}(T) + v_{Ll}(T-1)], \qquad (l = 1, 2,..., q).$$

We refer to the expressions for capital input K and labor input L as *translog indices of capital and labor input*.

Using the translog indices, we can write the rate of productivity growth in the form

$$\bar{v}_T = \ln V(T) - \ln V\ (T-1)$$

$$- \bar{v}_K \cdot \sum \bar{v}_{Kk}[\ln K_k(T) - \ln K_k(T-1)]$$

$$- \bar{v}_L \cdot \sum \bar{v}_{Ll}[\ln L_l(T) - \ln L_l(T-1)].$$

Again, the sectoral rates of productivity growth are identical to the aggregate rate of productivity growth.

The product of price and quantity indices must be equal to the corresponding value. For example, we can define the price index of capital input as the ratio of the value of capital input to the translog quantity index. The price index of labor input can be defined in the same way. The resulting price indices of capital and labor inputs do not have the form of translog price indices, but can be determined from data on prices and quantities at any two discrete points of time.

Aggregation over Sectors

Our final objective is to compare methodologies for productivity measurement at the aggregate and sectoral levels. Our sectoral models of production are based on a production function for each sector, giving output as a function of intermediate input, capital input, labor input, and time. The production function is combined with necessary conditions for producer equilibrium. A more restrictive model is based on a value-added function for each sector, giving the quantity of value-added as a function of capital input, labor input, and time.

Our aggregate model of production is derived from a multisectoral model of production that includes value-added functions for all sectors. The multisectoral model also includes market equilibrium conditions for each primary-factor of production. Our aggregate model is based on a production possibility frontier and conditions for producer equilibrium. A much more restrictive model is based on an aggregate production function. The existence of an aggregate production function implies that all sectoral value-added functions are identical and that capital and labor inputs within each sector are identical functions of their components.

Conditions for producer equilibrium at the sectoral level are defined in terms of prices for the output of each sector and prices paid for intermediate goods and for the primary-factors of production by each sector. Conditions for producer equilibrium at the aggregate level are defined in terms of prices for value-added and the primary-factors of production for the economy as a whole. Conditions for producer equilibrium at the sectoral and aggregate levels are equivalent only under the restrictive conditions that there exist for all sectors value-added functions that are identical to the aggregate production function, that capital and labor inputs within each sector are identical functions of their components, and that the prices paid for primary-factor inputs are the same for all sectors.

If conditions for producer equilibrium at sectoral and aggregate levels are equivalent, we can express the rate of productivity growth for the economy as a whole in terms of sectoral rates of productivity growth.[23] If prices of value-added differ among sectors, due to differences among sectoral value-added functions or to differences in prices paid for the primary-factors of production, we can express the aggregate rate of productivity growth in terms of sectoral rates of productivity growth and changes in the distribution of value-added and the primary-factors of production among sectors.[24]

We can define the price of value-added for the economy as a whole, p_V, in terms of prices of value-added in all sectors $\{p_V^i\}$:

$$p_V V = p_V \sum V_i,$$

$$= \sum p_V^i V_i.$$

Value-added for the economy as a whole is equal to the sum of value-added over all sectors. Our data on value-added satisfy this equality as an accounting identity.

Similarly, we can define the prices of capital inputs for the economy as a whole $\{p_{Kk}\}$ in terms of prices paid for each type of capital input in all sectors $\{p_{Kk}^i\}$:

$$p_{Kk} K_k = p_{Kk} \sum K_{ki},$$

$$= \sum p_{Kk}^i K_{ki}, \qquad\qquad (k = 1, 2, ..., p).$$

The value of each of the capital inputs for the economy as a whole is equal to the sum of values over all sectors. Our data on capital input satisfy these equalities as accounting identities.

Finally, we can define the prices of labor inputs for the economy as a whole $\{p_{Ll}\}$ in terms of prices paid in all sectors $\{p_{Ll}^i\}$:

$$p_{Ll} L_l = p_{Ll} \sum L_{li},$$

$$= \sum p_{Ll}^i L_{li}, \qquad\qquad (l = 1, 2,..., q).$$

The value of each of the labor inputs is equal to the sum of values over all sectors. Our data on labor input satisfy these equalities as accounting identities.

We can express the rate of productivity growth for the economy as a whole in terms of sectoral productivity growth rates and changes in the distribution among sectors of value-added and the primary-factors of production. First, write the rate of productivity growth for the economy as a whole in the form

$$\bar{v}_T = \ln V(T) - \ln V(T-1) - \bar{v}_K[\ln K(T) - \ln K(T-1)]$$

$$- \bar{v}_L[\ln L(T) - \ln L(T-1)].$$

Using the translog indices of capital and labor inputs, the rate of productivity growth can be written

$$\bar{v}_T = \ln V(T) - \ln V(T-1) - \bar{v}_K \sum \bar{v}_{Kk}[\ln K_k(T) - \ln K_k(T-1)]$$

$$- \bar{v}_L \sum \bar{v}_{Ll}[\ln L_l(T) - \ln L_l(T-1)].$$

Second, we can express the rate of productivity growth for each of the n sectors in the form

$$\bar{v}_T^i = \ln Z_i(T) - \ln Z_i(T-1) - \bar{v}_X^i[\ln X_i(T) - \ln X_i(T-1)]$$

$$- \bar{v}_K^i[\ln K_i(T) - \ln K_i(T-1)] - \bar{v}_L^i[\ln L_i(T) - \ln L_i(T-1)],$$

$$(i = 1, 2,..., n).$$

Using the translog indices of value-added, the sectoral rate of productivity growth can be written

$$\bar{v}_T^i = \bar{v}_V^i[\ln V_i(T) - \ln V_i(T-1) - \bar{v}_K^i[\ln K_i(T) - \ln K_i(T-1)],$$

$$- \bar{v}_L^i[\ln L_i(T) - \ln L_i(T-1)],$$

$$(i = 1, 2,..., n).$$

Finally, using the translog indices of capital and labor inputs for each of the n sectors, rewrite the sectoral rate of productivity growth in the form

$$\bar{v}_T^i = \bar{v}_V^i[\ln V_i(T) - \ln V_i(T-1)] - \bar{v}_K^i \sum \bar{v}_{Kk}^i \ [\ln K_{ki}(T) - \ln K_{ki}(T-1)]$$

$$- \bar{v}_L^i \sum \bar{v}_{Ll}^i[\ln L_{li}(T) - \ln L_{li}(T-1)] \ ,$$

$$(i = 1, 2,..., n).$$

Multiplying the sectoral rates of productivity growth by the ratio of value-added in the corresponding sector to value-added in all sectors, summing over all sectors, and subtracting the results from the rate of productivity growth for the economy as a whole, we obtain

$$\bar{v}_T = \sum \frac{\bar{w}_i}{\bar{v}_V^i} \cdot \bar{v}_T^i + [\ln V(T) - \ln V(T-1)] - \sum \bar{w}_i[\ln V_i(T) - \ln V_i(T-1)]$$

$$+ \sum \bar{w}_i \cdot \frac{\bar{v}_K^i}{\bar{v}_V^i} \sum \bar{v}_{Kk}^i[\ln K_{ki}(T) - \ln K_{ki}(T-1)] - \bar{v}_K \cdot \sum \bar{v}_{Kk}[\ln K_k(T) - \ln K_k(T-1)]$$

$$+ \sum \bar{w}_i \cdot \frac{\bar{v}_L^i}{\bar{v}_V^i} \sum \bar{v}_{Ll}^i[\ln L_{li}(T) - \ln L_{li}(T-1)] - \bar{v}_L \cdot \sum \bar{v}_{Ll}[\ln L_l(T) - \ln L_l(T-1)],$$

where

$$\bar{w}_i = \frac{1}{2}[w_i(T) + w_i(T-1)], \qquad\qquad (i = 1, 2,..., n),$$

$$w_i = \frac{p_V^i V_i}{\sum p_V^i V_i}, \qquad\qquad (i = 1, 2,..., n).$$

The first term in this expression for the rate of productivity growth is a weighted sum of sectoral productivity growth rates. The weights reflect the ratios of output to value-added by all sectors; the sum of these weights exceeds unity.[25] The remaining terms reflect the contributions of changes in the sectoral distribution of value-added, all types of capital input, and all types of labor input to the rate of aggregate productivity growth.[26]

Conclusion

The sectoral models of production presented in this chapter imply a methodology for analyzing sources of growth in output for each sector. We have used this methodology to generate index numbers for intermediate, capital, and labor inputs and rates of productivity growth. These index numbers are employed in constructing data on labor input in Chapter 3, capital input in

Chapter 4, intermediate input in Chapter 5, and rates of productivity growth in Chapter 6.

A distinctive feature of our methodology is that intermediate input and the primary-factor inputs are treated symmetrically at the sectoral level. Second, components of intermediate, capital, and labor inputs that differ in marginal productivity are treated separately in measuring sectoral input aggregates. Finally, output and all three inputs are valued from the point of view of the producer. Input prices must include all taxes paid by the producer and all supplements to wages. Output prices must exclude taxes paid and must include subsidies received by producers.

We employ the sectoral models of production presented in this chapter to analyze patterns of substitution among inputs and changes in these patterns over time, as will be shown in Chapter 7. For this purpose we develop and implement econometric models of production that incorporate the features we have employed to analyze the growth of output. These models determine the rate of productivity growth and the distribution of the value of output among intermediate, capital, and labor inputs.

To develop an aggregate model of production we have introduced value-added functions for each sector, giving quantities of value-added as functions of capital input, labor input, and time. We have used this more restrictive methodology to generate index numbers of the quantity of value-added for each sector. It is important to emphasize that we do not employ these restrictions in our analysis of the growth of sectoral output, reported in Chapter 6, or the analysis of sectoral patterns of substitution and technical change, reported in Chapter 7.

Second, we have combined value-added functions for all sectors with market equilibrium conditions for the primary factors of production to derive a production possibility frontier for the economy as a whole. We further specialize this methodology by requiring the existence of an aggregate production function. We generate index numbers for aggregate capital and labor inputs as reported in Chapter 8, and aggregate productivity growth, as reported in Chapter 9.

By contrast with our methodology at the sectoral level, transactions in intermediate goods do not appear at the aggregate level. Deliveries to intermediate demand by all sectors are precisely offset by receipts of intermediate input. Components of capital and labor inputs that differ in marginal productivity are treated separately at both sectoral and aggregate levels. Finally, aggregate output, capital input, and labor input are valued from the point of view of the producer. Input prices include taxes paid and supplements to wages; output prices exclude taxes and include subsidies.

The existence of an aggregate production function implies that value-added functions are identical for all sectors and that capital and labor inputs within each sector are identical functions of their components. While this highly restrictive framework is not employed in our analysis of sectoral production patterns, reported in Chapters 6 and 7, we utilize an aggregate production function to analyze the growth of aggregate output in Chapter 9. Using this framework, we represent the growth rate of output as the sum of a weighted average of growth rates of capital and labor inputs and the rate of productivity growth.

We combine sectoral and aggregate models of production, as shown in Chapter 9, to decompose the aggregate rate of productivity growth into a weighted sum of sectoral rates of productivity growth and components that reflect changes in the sectoral distribution among sectors of value-added, all types of capital input, and all types of labor input. The contributions of these distributional changes can be regarded as a reflection of departures from the assumptions that underlie the existence of an aggregate production function.

Finally, in Chapter 9 we extend the aggregate model of production to analyze patterns of substitution between capital and labor inputs and changes in these patterns over time. We develop and implement an econometric model of production that determines the rate of productivity growth and the distribution of the value of output between capital and labor inputs.

3 Sectoral Labor Input

Our initial objective in analyzing postwar patterns of productivity growth is to construct measures of labor input for each industrial sector.[1] These are index numbers constructed from data on hours worked and compensation per hour. The data on hours worked and labor compensation for each industry are cross-classified by sex, age, education, employment status, and occupation of workers.

We construct measures of labor input that are consistent with the U.S. national income and product accounts. For this purpose we have introduced control totals for each industry, based on establishment surveys. To disaggregate labor input by demographic characteristics we have exploited the detail on employment, hours worked, weeks paid, and compensation that is available from household surveys. To achieve consistency between establishment and household survey data, we have used the household survey results to distribute industry totals based on establishment surveys.

We have disaggregated the labor input of all employed persons into cells, cross-classified by the two sexes, eight age groups, five educational groups, two employment classes, ten occupational groups, and fifty-one industries, as listed in Table 3.1. This breakdown of labor input is based on the groupings employed by the Bureau of Census in reporting data from household surveys. The census data provide the primary source for consistent time series, cross-classified by industrial, occupational, and demographic characteristics.

Data on labor input for the fifty-one industry groups listed in Table 3.1 are available from establishment surveys employed in construction of the U.S. national income and product accounts. No existing household or establishment survey, including the recently expanded *Current Population Survey* data set, is designed to provide annual data from 1948 to 1979 on the complete distribution of laborers among the 81,600 cells of a matrix cross-

69

Table 3.1.   Characteristics of labor input

Sex

(1) Male
(2) Female

Age

(1) 14–15 years
(2) 16–17 years
(3) 18–24 years
(4) 25–34 years
(5) 35–44 years
(6) 45–54 years
(7) 55–64 years
(8) 65 years and over

Employment class

(1) Wage or salary worker
(2) Self-employed or unpaid family worker

Occupation

(1) Profession, technical, and kindred workers
(2) Farmers and farm managers
(3) Managers and administrators, except farm
(4) Clerical workers
(5) Sales workers
(6) Craftsmen and kindred workers
(7) Operatives
(8) Service workers, including private household
(9) Farm laborers
(10) Laborers, except farm

Education

(1) 1–8 years grade school
(2) 1–3 years high school
(3) 4 years high school
(4) 1–3 years college
(5) 4 or more years college

Industry

(1) Agricultural production
(2) Agricultural services, horticultural services, forestry, and fisheries
(3) Metal mining
(4) Coal mining
(5) Crude petroleum and natural gas extractions
(6) Nonmetallic mining and quarrying, except fuel
(7) Construction
(8) Food and kindred products
(9) Tobacco manufactures
(10) Textile mill products
(11) Apparel and other fabricated textile products
(12) Paper and allied products
(13) Printing, publishing, and allied industries
(14) Chemicals and allied products
(15) Petroleum (refining) and coal products
(16) Rubber and miscellaneous plastic products
(17) Leather and leather products

Table 3.1 continued

---

(18) Lumber and wood products, except furniture
(19) Furniture and fixtures
(20) Stone, clay, and glass products
(21) Primary metal industries
(22) Fabridcated metal industries
(23) Machinery except electrical
(24) Electrical machinery, equipment, and supplies
(25) Transportation equipment, except motor vehicles, ordnance
(26) Motor vehicles and motor vehicle equipment
(27) Professional photographic equipment, watches
(28) Miscellaneous manufacturing industries
(29) Railroads and railway express service
(30) Street railway and bus lines and taxicab services
(31) Trucking services, warehousing, and storage
(32) Water transportation
(33) Air transportation
(34) Pipelines, except natural gas
(35) Services incidental to transportation
(36) Telephone, telegraph, and miscellaneous communication services
(37) Radio and television broadcasting
(38) Electric utilities
(39) Gas utilities
(40) Water supply, sanitary services, and other utilities
(41) Wholesale trade
(42) Retail trade
(43) Finance, insurance, and real estate
(44) Services
(45) Private households
(46) Nonprofit institutions
(47) Federal public administration
(48) Federal government enterprises
(49) Educational services, government (state and local)
(50) State and local public administration
(51) State and local government enterprises

---

classified by the characteristics given in Table 3.1.[2] What the existing surveys do provide are marginal totals cross-classified by two, three, and sometimes four characteristics of labor input. These marginal distributions, available for each year from 1948 to 1979, become the basis for our model of labor input and compensation.

Our first task is to construct annual matrices for labor input for each year from 1948 to 1979, cross-classified by the industrial, occupational, and demographic characteristics listed in Table 3.1. To accomplish this goal we utilize the method of iterative proportional fitting, generalizing the RAS method introduced by Stone (1962). The statistical principles underlying this method are a straightforward extension of those that underlie the application of the RAS method to the biproportional matrix model of Bacharach (1965). We discuss the method of iterative proportional fitting in the next section.

We have employed all the published marginal totals for each component of labor input, from the *Census of Population* and the *Current Population Survey*. In the following sections we outline the sources for data on employment, hours, weeks, and labor compensation, and the procedures we have adopted in constructing the matrices that underlie our index numbers for labor input. A complete listing of the data sources appears in Appendix A.

The desirability of disaggregating labor input by industrial, occupational, and demographic characteristics of the work force has been widely recognized, for example by Denison (1962), Griliches (1960), Jorgenson and Griliches (1967), Kendrick (1961a), and others. Kendrick has developed measures of labor input disaggregated by industry for much of the postwar period, but his measures do not incorporate cross-classification of labor input by age, sex, education, or other demographic characteristics of the work force. Denison has developed measures of labor input for the U.S. economy as a whole, based on data disaggregated by sex, age, education, and employment status, but not by occupation or industry.[3]

In the absence of data disaggregated by industrial, occupational, and demographic characteristics, measures of labor input and compensation that fail to reflect differences among workers remain in common use. Our data base can be used to generate indices of labor input cross-classified by each of the characteristics we have employed in compiling data on hours worked and compensation per hour. In a later section we present indices of labor input for each of the fifty-one industries listed in Table 3.1.

Iterative Proportional Fitting

For each year from 1948 to 1979 we construct matrices of data on hours worked and labor compensation per hour, cross-classified by the demographic, occupational, and industrial characteristics of labor input listed in Table 3.1. This cross-classification involves a total of 81,600 entries for each matrix for each year. Data on the components of labor input—employment, hours per week, weeks per year, and labor compensation—are not available in published form for such a detailed cross-classification, but considerable detail is available for individual years on the basis of two-way, three-way, and even four-way cross-classifications. Data from the decennial *Census of Population* are more detailed than data from the annual *Current Population Survey*. Our objective is to exhaust the detail available from both sources in constructing matrices for each component of labor input for each year.

The task is to generate annual estimates of each component of labor input for all 81,600 cells of the cross-classification presented in Table 3.1. For this purpose we have utilized the method of iterative proportional fitting, generalizing the RAS method introduced by Stone (1962) and formalized by Bacharach (1965).

To illustrate the method of iterative proportional fitting, we find it useful to consider the biproportional matrix model as an example. Consider two non-negative matrices, **A** and **B**. The elements $\{a_{ij}\}$ of the first matrix are known. The problem is to estimate the unknown elements $\{b_{ij}\}$ of the second matrix, where only the row and column sums $\{u_i\}$ and $\{v_j\}$, respectively, are known:

$$\sum_{j=1}^{n} b_{ij} = u_i, \qquad\qquad\qquad (i = 1, 2,..., m),$$

$$\sum_{i=1}^{m} b_{ij} = v_j, \qquad\qquad\qquad (j = 1, 2,..., n).$$

To specify the problem of estimating the unknown elements $\{b_{ij}\}$ more precisely, we introduce the assumption that the matrix **B** is *biproportional* to the matrix **A**, that is:

$$b_{ij} = r_i s_j a_{ij}, \qquad\qquad (i = 1, 2,..., m; j = 1, 2,..., n),$$

where r_i is a factor associated with the ith row of **A** and s_j is a factor associated with the jth column of **A**.

The problem of estimating the unknown elements of the matrix **B** reduces to the problem of choosing row and column factors $\{r_i, s_j\}$ so that the row and column sums are equal to the known row and column sums $\{u_i, v_j\}$ and the elements of **B** are nonnegative. To state the problem more formally we can introduce the diagonal matrix $\hat{r}$ with diagonal elements $\{r_i\}$ and the diagonal matrix $\hat{s}$ with diagonal elements $\{s_j\}$. We can represent sequences of such matrices by $\{\hat{r}^t, \hat{s}^t\}$. The set **B** of matrices that are biproportional to the matrix **A** is defined by the conditions

$$B = \lim_{t \to \infty} \hat{r}^t A \, \hat{s}^t,$$

$Bi = u$,

$i'B = v$,

where i is a vector of ones, u is a vector with elements $\{u_i\}$, and v is a vector with elements $\{v_j\}$.

The matrices $\mathbf{B}$ that are biproportional to a given matrix $\mathbf{A}$ can be written in the "RAS" form:

$B = \hat{r} A \hat{s}$,

or as the limit of such matrices. Bacharach shows that for any matrix $\mathbf{A}$ such that every row and every column has at least one positive element, and for any vectors u and v with all elements positive and $\sum u_i = \sum v_j$, there exists a unique nonnegative matrix $\mathbf{B}$ that is biproportional to the nonnegative matrix $\mathbf{A}$ (Bacharach, 1965, pp. 302–308).

The method for constructing the matrix $\mathbf{B}$ proposed by Stone (1962) and others involves an iterative process. The first iteration requires two steps:

1. Multiply the ith row by a scalar, say r_i^1, such that the row sum is equal to the given total u_i.

2. Multiply the jth column by a scalar, say s_j^1, such that the column sum is equal to the given total v_j.

The result of this process is a new nonnegative matrix $\mathbf{A}^1$ that serves as the starting point for the next iteration. Successive iterations of the process define a sequence of matrices $\{\mathbf{A}^t\}$ defined by

$$A^t = \hat{r}^t A^{t-1} \hat{s}^t , \qquad\qquad (t = 1, 2,..., T),$$

where $\mathbf{A}^0 = A$ Bacharach shows that the process converges to the unique biproportional matrix $\mathbf{B}$.

We next consider the method of iterative proportional fitting. In presenting this method we find it useful to rewrite the nonnegative matrix $\mathbf{A}$, where

$$\mathbf{A} = [a_1, a_2,...,a_n]$$

and $\mathbf{a}_j$ is the jth column of $\mathbf{A}$:

$$\mathbf{a}_j = \begin{bmatrix} a_{1j} \\ a_{2j} \\ \\ a_{mj} \end{bmatrix}$$

Next we consider any partition of the elements of $\mathbf{a}_j$, that is, any set of subsets of the elements of $\mathbf{a}_j$ such that each element is assigned to one and only one subset. We restrict consideration to partitions of the elements of $\mathbf{a}_j$ such that each subset contains at least one positive element. As before, the elements of the matrix $\mathbf{A}$ or the column vector $\mathbf{a}_j$ are known. The problem is to estimate the unknown elements of a matrix $\mathbf{B}$, where

$$\mathbf{B} = [b_1, b_2,...,b_n],$$

and $\mathbf{b}_j$ is the jth column of $\mathbf{B}$:

$$\mathbf{b}_j = \begin{bmatrix} b_{1j} \\ b_{2j} \\ \\ b_{mj} \end{bmatrix}.$$

We consider a partition of the vector $\mathbf{b}_j$ corresponding to any given partition of the vector $\mathbf{a}_j$, denoting the sum of all elements in the ith subset of the jth partition of $\mathbf{b}_j$ by u_i^j, where all such sums are positive and the sum over all subsets is the same for all partitions. We say that the vector $\mathbf{b}_j$ is *multiproportional* to the vector $\mathbf{a}_j$ if the following conditions are satisfied:

1. There are factors $\{\mathbf{r}_i^j\}$, one for each partition, such that each element of $\mathbf{b}_j$ can be represented either as the product of such factors and the corresponding element of $\mathbf{a}_j$, or as the limit of a sequence of products of this type.

2. The vector $\mathbf{b}_j$ is nonnegative.

3. The sum of elements of $\mathbf{b}_j$ in the ith subset of the jth partition is equal to u_i^j.

There exists a unique nonnegative vector $\mathbf{b}_j$ that is multiproportional to the nonnegative vector $\mathbf{a}_j$. To construct the vector $\mathbf{b}_j$ that is multiproportional to a vector $\mathbf{a}_j$, we employ the method of iterative proportional fitting. The first iteration requires as many steps as there are partitions of the vector $\mathbf{a}_j$. At the jth step we multiply the elements in the ith subset of the jth partition by a scalar, say $\mathbf{r}_i^{j1}$, such that the sum of elements in the subset is equal to the given total u_i^j. The result of this process is a new nonnegative vector, say $\mathbf{a}_j^1$, that serves as the starting point of the next iteration. Successive iterations of the process define a sequence of vectors $\{\mathbf{a}_j^t\}$ such that each element is the product of the scalars $\{\mathbf{r}_i^{jt}\}$ and the corresponding element from the preceding iteration, where $\mathbf{a}_j^0 = \mathbf{a}_j$. This process converges to the unique vector $\mathbf{b}_j$.[4]

As an illustration of the method of iterative proportional fitting, consider the case where one has available information separately classified by each of two characteristics and wishes to construct a matrix cross-classified by these characteristics. Both marginal distributions can be used as input into the iterative procedure outlined above. Alternatively, if a three-way cross-classification is the objective and the available data set includes all three possible two-way cross-classifications, the method of iterative proportional fitting can be applied in four ways. Any pair of two-way cross-classifications can be employed, or all three can be used simultaneously. Fortunately, the appropriate choice can be made on elementary grounds. The number of degrees of freedom can be reduced to a minimum by using as much overlapping marginal information as is available. In this example all three two-way cross-classifications would be employed as marginal distributions.

Sectoral Hours Worked

The task of developing measures of labor input for each industry, cross-classified by sex, age, education, employment status, and occupation, can be divided between compiling data on annual hours worked and compiling data on labor compensation. In this section we present our methodology and data sources for constructing annual data on hours worked; we discuss the development of data on labor compensation in the following section.

The first step in measuring annual hours worked is to construct employment matrices for the civilian work force for each postwar year, cross-classified by sex, age, education, employment class, occupation, and industry of employment. Marginal totals for employment are based on the decennial *Census of Population* for the last three decades and the postwar *Current Population Survey*. We combine data from these sources by the method of iterative proportional fitting presented in the preceding section. The resulting employment matrices are adjusted to employment totals by industry from the U.S. national income and product accounts.

The second step in measuring annual hours worked is to incorporate differences in hours worked by different groups of workers. Since establishment-based surveys provide data on hours paid rather than hours worked, hours paid often have been substituted for hours worked in measuring labor input. The latter is clearly the appropriate measure of labor input. If data on hours paid are substituted for hours worked, the rising proportion of hours that are paid but not worked, due to vacations, illness, personal leaves, and holidays, leads to an upward bias in the growth of hours worked.

To avoid the deficiencies of establishment-based data on hours paid we employ data on hours worked from household surveys reported in the decennial censuses and the *Current Population Survey*. We employ the method of iterative proportional fitting to construct matrices of hours worked per week, cross-classified by sex, age, employment class, occupation, and industry for each year. The resulting hours-worked matrices are adjusted to industry totals from the national accounts. We define annual hours worked for each category of labor input as the product of employment, hours worked per week, and the number of weeks in the calendar year.

Employment

The first step in constructing employment matrices for the civilian work force for each postwar year is to assign each worker to one of 81,600 cells of the cross-classification. Information for the years of the decennial *Census of Population*—1950, 1960, and 1970—is considerably more detailed than information available for other years from the *Current Population Survey*. We employ two-way, three-way, and four-way cross-classifications of employment, from the census to generate the full six-way cross-classification for each census year.

The value of employment for each cell in the detailed cross-classification is initialized at unity; all available marginal totals from each *Census of Population* are used in the method of iterative proportional fitting to control the distribution of employment among cells for the corresponding year. We then rank intermediate years by the detail available for marginal totals in each year. We initialize the employment matrix for each intermediate year by a weighted average of employment matrices from the nearest years for which employment matrices are already available, beginning with a weighted average of matrices based on the decennial censuses. All available marginal totals for each year are incorporated by means of the method of iterative proportional fitting. For the years 1948, 1949, and 1971–1979, this process is initialized with the nearest year for which an employment matrix is available.

The addition of Alaska and Hawaii to U.S. census data, in 1960, and the redefinition of the census labor force concepts,[5] beginning with the 1967 household survey, necessitate special approaches to the labor input data for these years. The resolution of the discontinuity between 1959 and 1960 is straightforward. We construct two employment matrices for 1960—one defined on a comparable basis with earlier years, the other with later years. Since the 1960 census was the first survey to incorporate data for Alaska and Hawaii, we create a separate employment matrix for those two states, by the method of iterative proportional fitting, and subtract the matrix for the two states from the matrix for all 50 states, to create a second 1960 matrix that is comparable with 1959 and earlier years.

Fortunately, most of the definitional changes introduced by the Bureau of the Census in January 1967 affected the distinction between the unemployed and those who are not in the labor force, rather than data on the employed labor force. Three changes did affect the employment data. First, employed persons who were not at work during the survey week and were looking for jobs had their classification changed from unemployed to employed: "Up to now [January 1967] the small group of persons absent from their jobs the entire survey week because of vacations, illness, strikes, bad weather, etc., who were looking for other jobs was classified as unemployed. Starting in January 1967, such persons are classified as employed—that is, among other 'with a job but not at work' (Stein, 1967, p. 7). This definitional change shifted approximately 80,000 persons from the unemployed to the employed category (Stein, 1967, p. 10).

Given our methodology, we make no separate adjustment for this redefinition. We ultimately control our employment data to totals based on establishment surveys. Since these totals include all workers who received pay during the survey period, whether or not they actually worked during the period, the establishment survey classifies workers receiving pay from one job as employed, though they were physically absent and looking for another job. Consequently, the control totals for our employment data are unaffected by the first census redefinition. Since there is no evidence to suggest that the industrial, occupational, and demographic characteristics of the 80,000 persons reclassified from unemployed to employed are different from the characteristics of the employed population, we make no adjustment to the household-based distribution of workers in our employment matrices.

The second census redefinition involved a more accurate classification of employed persons between wage and salary workers and the self-employed and unpaid family workers. Prior to January 1967 a person simply was asked in which of the two classes he or she belonged. By the early sixties it had become clear that some proprietors who had incorporated their businesses were still reporting that they were self-employed when they should have been classified as employees of a corporate business. After January 1967, whenever a census-taker received the response "self-employed," an additional question was asked to determine whether the "proprietor's" business was incorporated. The respondent then was classified properly into one of the two employment classes. The Census Bureau estimates that this question accounted for a shift of approximately 750,000 workers from the self-employed to the wage and salary class (Stein, 1976, p. 10).

To provide a basis for constructing continuous time series, the Census Bureau conducted a separate survey of 17,500 households, the *Monthly*

Labor Survey, during 1966. This survey was based on the new questionnaire that was to become effective in January 1967. Paralleling this was the traditional *Current Population Survey* of 35,000 households. We could have treated the shift of 750,000 laborers in the same manner as the introduction of Alaska and Hawaii. We could have constructed a second 1966 matrix based on the *Monthly Labor Survey,* defined in terms consistent with 1967 and all later years. Unlike the addition of new states at a point in time, which left all prior labor matrices unaffected, the reallocation of the "corporate self-employed" affects labor matrices in all years prior to 1967. The annual totals of wage and salary workers and self-employed persons, as well as each year's demographic and occupational distribution of employees, require adjustment.

The national income and product account totals, fortunately, incorporate the necessary adjustment. The Bureau of Economic Analysis used the two 1966 census surveys to estimate the number of workers misclassified as self-employed in each industry in 1966. The Bureau then linearly extrapolated each industry's corporate self-employed back to 1948, assuming that such workers were one-third the 1966 total in 1958 and zero in 1948. All the post-1947 employment totals reported in the national accounts were adjusted to reflect this reclassification. No further adjustment to our control totals is required.

Although our employment matrices are controlled to adjusted totals from the Bureau of Economic Analysis, we still require estimates of the demographic and occupational characteristics of the corporate self-employed. Since these workers are more likely to share the characteristics of the self-employed than those of wage and salary workers, distributions based on census reports that misallocate the corporate self-employed are biased estimates of the true distributions.

We find it necessary to adjust the 1948–1966 matrices. For each industry and each year from 1948 to 1966 we distribute the corporate self-employed by sex, age, education, and occupation characteristics, by allocating totals from the Bureau of Economic Analysis in proportion to the distribution of the self-employed and unpaid family workers from the household survey.[6] We then subtract this matrix for each industry and each year from the corresponding household employment matrix for self-employed workers and add it to the employment matrix for wage and salary workers. This procedure not only accounts for the definitional shift occurring in 1967 but also corrects the misallocations that affect the measure of labor input in each year from 1948 to 1966.

The final and most perplexing change introduced in 1967 was a decision to drop all employed 14- and 15-year-old persons from the census definition of the labor force. Since these workers contribute to industrial output, their input must be recorded. The Department of Commerce no longer provides data on these young workers cross-classified by the demographic characteristics previously reported. Limited demographic data on employed 14- and 15-year-old laborers still are collected by the Census Bureau, however, and reported separately from the usual labor force data. This information, together with employment matrices representing workers 16 years old and over, is used to construct a complete time series for all employed persons 14 years of age and older for the period 1948–1979.

While census data based on household surveys provide the best source of data on labor input cross-classified by industrial, occupational, and demographic characteristics, industry totals must be reconciled with data based on establishment surveys. First, census reports suffer from a slight undercount. Part of the undercount can be attributed to the Bureau's decision to classify a holder of multiple jobs only in the industry where he or she works the most hours. A valid measure of annual hours worked necessitates counting each laborer holding multiple jobs as employed in each industry in which he works, no matter how insignificant the number of hours in secondary jobs. Establishment-based surveys meet this requirement. Second, industry totals from establishment surveys include employed workers who are less than 14 years old. Since these workers' contribution to output is captured in production measures, their labor input must be incorporated into a measure of total labor input.

The last, but perhaps most important discrepancy between establishment surveys and household surveys is that establishment surveys enumerate jobs rather than persons at work. The resulting employment data are based on annual average job counts from surveys of establishments. These data include workers who received pay but were not at work during the survey week. This establishment-based concept of employment has an important implication for the measurement of average hours worked. Average weekly and annual hours worked must be calculated on a ''per job'' basis, not ''per person at work.'' The assignment of average annual hours worked per job to an establishment-based count of jobs held by paid employees results in a consistent measure of annual hours worked.

Both the Bureau of Economic Analysis and the Bureau of Labor Statistics publish annual establishment-based estimates of the number of employed persons, by industry. Integration of our measure of labor input with the U.S. national income and product accounts requires that we use the Bureau of Economic Analysis estimates. These estimates are based on annual averages of the employment returns by individual establishments to state unemployment insurance bureaus. The payroll data account for nearly 80 percent of all wages and salaries and almost 95 percent of wages and salaries in private industry. While the Bureau of Labor Statistics also benchmarks its employment series to state unemployment insurance data, it controls its industry totals to the March returns rather than to annual averages. In addition, the Bureau of Labor Statistics data do not include agricultural and private household sectors, while data from the national income and product accounts include these sectors.

Each year's census matrices serve as marginal totals for the method of iterative proportional fitting. The resulting household data are adjusted to control totals by industry from the national accounts. The result is a complete time series of matrices that cross-classifies all employed persons by industrial, occupational, and demographic characteristics for the period 1948–1979.

Hours

Measures of labor input must incorporate differences in hours worked by different groups of workers. The Bureau of Labor Statistics publishes estimates of hours paid, from establishment surveys. For nonmanufacturing industries, hours data are compiled only for production workers, and hours worked by supervisory, self-employed, and unpaid family workers are unavailable. A more important limitation is that hours data by industry are not cross-classified by demographic characteristics. To avoid the deficiencies of establishment-based hours data from the Bureau of Labor Statistics, we use the hours data collected and published by the Bureau of the Census. The Census reports only hours that were actually *worked* during the survey week, and thus automatically excludes vacations, holidays, illness, personal leave, and all other circumstances during which an employed person may be paid for hours he or she did not work.

The census provides data on hours worked, cross-classified by most of the demographic, occupational, and industrial characteristics listed in Table 3.1. An analysis of the hours-worked data published by the Census Bureau reveals that the total hours worked per week associated with individuals in each cell has a distribution that can be accurately represented by the lognormal distribution. We therefore assume that the hours worked by the individuals in each cell have a lognormal distribution with unknown location and dispersion parameters. Assigning each employed person to the appropriate cell of the cross-classification by sex, age, employment status, occupation, and industry[7] and imposing the lognormality assumption on the distribution of hours worked, we estimate the two unknown parameters by the method of maximum likelihood.

The method of maximum likelihood cannot be applied directly to census data on hours worked, since the data are not presented as individual observations but as empirical frequency distributions. For example, for a given set of labor input characteristics the census presents the number of laborers who fall within each of the following discrete hour classes: 0 hours worked, 1–14, 15–26, 27–34, 35–40, 40, and 41 or more.

Gjeddebaek (1949) has provided an adaptation of the method of maximum likelihood that is directly applicable to data in frequency form.[8] The raw frequency data are interpreted as drawings from a multinomial model, where the units within any given cell are divided into mutually exclusive groups corresponding to the census intervals. Using the lognormal distribution to describe the probabilities of observing individuals in each interval, the likelihood of observing any given empirical distribution of hours worked can be maximized.

It is important to emphasize that the frequency distributions of hours worked obtained directly from the Census Bureau household surveys include workers "with a job but not at work" as reporting zero hours worked in the survey week. These laborers are included in our multinomial model estimates of average hours worked, so that we obtain weekly hours worked *per job* for each category of laborers.

The multinomial model provides estimates of the average hours worked for each cell in each marginal distribution provided by the census. These averages and the ultimate industry totals will be biased, however, unless they are adjusted for holders of multiple jobs. This bias arises from the census classification of a person holding more than one job as employed only in the industry in which he or she works the most hours. Furthermore, the census allocates to that industry the multiple-job-holder's total hours worked at all jobs, regardless of the industry in which the hours were actually worked. This accounting framework incorrectly assigns the total number of hours to the primary job while neglecting to assign the appropriate number of hours worked by multiple-job-holders to their secondary jobs.

The separate effects of the census procedure of assigning employed persons and their hours worked solely to primary industries reinforce each other. Consider two industries, A and B, that together employ three workers. The first employee works five hours in A, the second works 20 hours in industry A and 15 in industry B, and the third works five hours in A and ten hours in B. The true mean hours worked in each industry are:

	Mean hours	Total hours
Industry A :	$\dfrac{(5 + 20 + 5)}{3} = 10$	$3 \times 10 = 30$
Industry B :	$\dfrac{(15 + 10)}{2} = 12.5$	$2 \times 12.5 = 25$

Calculating hours worked on the basis of raw data reported by the census would lead to the following estimates:

	Mean hours	Total hours
Industry A :	$\dfrac{(5 + 35)}{2} = 20$	$2 \times 20 = 40$
Industry B :	15	$1 \times 15 = 15.$

While the total of hours worked at industries A and B is fixed at 55, failure to adjust for multiple-job-holders clearly leads to a biased distribution of total hours worked among industries.

We redistribute the hours worked by multiple-job-holders before applying the method of iterative proportional fitting. Combining our estimates of employment and average hours worked, we first convert each cell in the marginal data matrices from an estimate of average hours worked to an estimate of total hours worked. Using data on hours for multiple-job-holders published in the *Special Labor Force Reports,* we then subtract from each cell the hours worked in other industries. Finally, we add these hours to the appropriate secondary industries. This completes the required redistribution.

We next apply the method of iterative proportional fitting to construct a matrix of total weekly hours worked by laborers, cross-classified by sex, age, employment class, occupation, and industry (data for education are not available). We first construct matrices of hours worked for the years of the decennial *Census of Population,* initializing the matrix for each year with the corresponding employment matrix and incorporating all available marginal totals. Dividing the resulting hours matrix by the corresponding employment matrix yields a matrix of mean hours worked per job. For intermediate years the method of iterative proportional fitting is initialized by a matrix with entries equal to the product of the entries from the corresponding employment matrix and a weighted average of the entries from matrices of average hours worked from the nearest years for which these matrices are available.

The household survey data on employment and hours worked for the 1948–1966 period are based on a set of definitions allocating the corporate self-employed to the class of the self-employed and unpaid family workers. Applying the multinomial model to the frequency distributions of hours worked by the self-employed as reported in both the *Current Population Survey* and the *Monthly Labor Survey* for 1966, we determined that weekly hours worked in 1966 by the corporate self-employed are not statistically different from the weekly hours worked by all self-employed workers; they are different, however, from the weekly hours worked by wage and salary workers. In most cases, the corporate self-employed worked more hours per week than their wage and salary counterparts.

We estimate average weekly hours worked by the corporate self-employed from data on average weekly hours worked by self-employed workers in comparable demographic, occupational, and industrial groups. We adjust each entry in our matrices of average weekly hours for wage and salary workers for the years from 1948 to 1966 to reflect the weekly hours worked by the corporate self-employed. No adjustment of the matrices of average weekly hours worked by self-employed workers is required.

We control our estimates of annual hours worked within each industry to industry totals for hours worked, available in the national accounts. Our first step is to convert the national accounts estimates of annual hours worked for each industry to weekly hours worked, by dividing by the number of weeks in a calendar year. Controlling our weekly hours matrices to these totals and dividing by our employment matrices enumerating jobs, we obtain estimates of average hours worked per job. Consequently, we control our estimates of weekly hours worked per job for each industry to estimates of weekly hours worked per job from the national accounts data on hours worked and employment. The result is an annual series of matrices of average weekly hours worked per job, cross-classified by the demographic, occupational, and industrial characteristics presented in Table 3.1.

Sectoral Labor Compensation

The choice of an appropriate accounting framework for measuring the total and hourly compensation of labor input is important for at least two reasons. First, labor compensation is required to weight hours worked in forming an index of labor input for each industry. Second, the total wage bill determines labor's share of total cost in the measurement of productivity.

Our approach to the measurement of labor compensation is based on data for average compensation for the civilian work force from the *Census of Population* for the last three decades. These data provide estimates of average compensation per person; our employment data provide estimates of the number of jobs. Our first step in measuring labor compensation is to provide a basis for converting average compensation per person to average compensation per job. For this purpose we need estimates of the number of jobs per person. We use the method of iterative proportional fitting to construct matrices of weeks paid per year for workers, cross-classified by sex, age, employment class, occupation, and industry (data for education are not available). The average number of weeks paid per year for each category of workers, divided by fifty-two, provides an estimate of the number of jobs per person in each category.

The second step in our measurement of labor compensation is to construct matrices for each postwar year giving average hourly compensation earned by laborers, cross-classified by sex, age, education, employment class, occupation, and industry of employment. Marginal totals for average annual compensation per person in benchmark years are based on data on wage and salary income from the *Censuses of Population* for the last three decades. The wage and salary data are adjusted to incorporate employers' contributions to Social Security, unemployment compensation, and other supplements to wages and salaries. We divide average compensation per person by the ratio of the average number of weeks paid per year to fifty-two, to obtain average compensation per job for each category of workers. We then apply the method of iterative proportional fitting; the resulting compensation matrices are adjusted to industry control totals for labor compensation gross of supplements from the U.S. national income accounts.

We estimate average hourly wages in each intermediate year by first eliminating all tax and nontax supplements for each of the benchmark years. These benchmark estimates are interpolated and extrapolated to obtain initial hourly wage estimates for each intermediate year from 1948 to 1979. Annual compensation per person is estimated from data on hours and weeks paid for each intermediate year. Estimations of supplements based on the tax laws and other supplementary payments are added in each year.

Using the weeks-paid matrices in each intermediate year, average compensation per job is calculated for each category of workers. Compensation gross of supplements is controlled to U.S. national income accounts totals for each year. Average hourly compensation is determined by dividing total compensation in each labor category by the number of annual hours worked by workers in that category. Annual hours worked is calculated as the product of jobs, hours worked per week per job, and the number of weeks in the calendar year.

Weeks

In estimating labor compensation from census data, it is essential to recall that the Census provides an enumeration of persons on the basis of household surveys, while data on employment from establishment surveys provide an enumeration of jobs. If a job is filled by two persons during a given year, each paid for twenty-six weeks, employment data from establishment surveys will report one job, while compensation data from household surveys will report the average compensation received by each person. Multiplying average compensation per person in a given category by the number of jobs in that category would produce a downward bias in the resulting estimate of labor compensation. To eliminate this source of bias, we divide average compensation per person by the number of jobs per person. We estimate jobs per person as the ratio of the number of weeks paid for each person to 52. In our example, we would divide average compensation for each of the two persons by the ratio of twenty-six weeks paid for each person to fifty-two, for average compensation per job equal to twice the average compensation per person.

The Bureau of the Census provides the only source of data on weeks of employment cross-classified by demographic, occupational, and industrial characteristics of the work force. As indicated in the following census definition, these data are compiled on a weeks-paid basis rather than on a weeks-worked basis: "The data on weeks worked pertain to the number of different weeks in which a person did any work for pay or profit (including paid vacation and sick leave) or worked without pay on a family farm or in a family business" (Bureau of the Census, 1973b). Census data on weeks paid from household surveys thus are compiled on the same basis as data on employment from establishment surveys. Recall that these surveys include all jobs for which payment is made, rather than the number of persons actually at work during the survey period.

The census assigns all weeks for which a worker was paid during the past year to the cell representing that worker's present demographic, occupational, and industry characteristics. This may introduce a bias if the worker has crossed occupation, class, or industry boundaries during the past year. The data constrain our options and allow us to do little more than acknowledge this limitation, but two qualifying notes can be appended. First, according to Bancroft (1963 tables F and 15), fewer than six percent of all employed persons actually crossed such boundaries in 1961. While this percentage may shift over time, a second and more important finding of this same study is that 96.7 percent of the job changes were self-canceling— except for 3.3 percent of the sample, job shifts away from each class–occupation–industry category were fully offset by employment shifts into the same category. Consequently, unless the cumulative weeks paid to workers leaving a particular job differ substantially from the weeks paid to incoming laborers, little bias is introduced by the census procedure.

Since the census reports weeks paid in the form of empirical frequency distributions, we construct weeks matrices by methods very similar to those used to derive the hours-worked matrices. First, we assign each person to the appropriate cell. Assuming that weeks paid to the individuals in each cell has a lognormal distribution, we estimate the unknown parameters of this distribution from the empirical frequency distributions reported by the Bureau of the Census. No data are available on the weeks paid to multiple-job-holders in primary and secondary jobs, but Perrella (1970, p. 3) reports that almost half of all multiple-job-holders worked at both primary and secondary jobs in all twelve months preceding a survey taken in May 1969. Accordingly, we assume that the average weeks paid to multiple-job-holders is equal to the average number of weeks paid in each industry of employment. No separate adjustment for multiple-job-holders is required.

The method of iterative proportional fitting is used to construct a matrix of weeks paid to employed persons, cross-classified by sex, age, employment class, occupation, and industry. The matrix for each census year is initialized by means of the corresponding employment matrix. We incorporate all available marginal totals of weeks paid for each year. Matrices for intermediate years are initialized by a matrix with entries equal to the product of the entries from the corresponding employment matrix and a weighted average of entries from matrices of average weeks paid from the nearest years for which weeks matrices are available. Since no marginal totals are available for 1948, we employ the matrix for average weeks paid for 1949 to represent the corresponding matrices for 1948. Similarly, since no marginal totals are available for 1971, we use an average of the matrices for average weeks paid for 1970 and 1972 to represent the matrix for 1971. A procedure identical to that applied to hours worked is used to adjust the 1948–1966 data on weeks paid for the reallocation of the corporate self-employed to the wage and salary class.

Compensation

Our objective is to construct measures of labor compensation for each category of workers described in Table 3.1. Our model of production maintains equality between the elasticity of output with respect to each input and the share of that input in the value of output. Factor payments are used to measure marginal products.

The first problem in measuring labor compensation is the selection of an appropriate concept of compensation. The available census data on compensation include total income, earnings, and wage or salary income. Total income represents the sum of incomes received from all sources: "Total income is the algebraic sum of amounts received as wage or salary income, self-employment income, and income other than earnings... Income other than earnings includes money income received from such sources as interest, dividends, net rental income, Social Security benefits, pensions, veterans' payments, unemployment insurance, and public assistance or other governmental payments, and periodic receipts from insurance policies and annuities" (Bureau of the Census, 1963, p. xvi). Differences in total income are determined by a number of factors in addition to differences in marginal products.

Similarly, earnings is not the correct concept. Earnings include the return to capital invested by self-employed workers in their private businesses, as the following definition indicates: "Earnings are the sum of wage and salary income and self-employment income. Self-employment income is defined as net money income (gross receipts minus operating expenses) from a business, farm, or professional enterprise in which the person was engaged on his own account" (Bureau of the Census, 1963, p. xvi). Earnings reflect differences in marginal products of workers, but also incorporate differences in income from the use of capital.

The wage and salary income of wage and salary workers is the appropriate starting point for the measurement of labor compensation: "Wage or salary income is defined as the total money earnings received for work performed as an employee. It represents the amount received before deductions for personal income taxes, Social Security, bond purchases, union dues, etc." (Bureau of the Census, 1963, p. xvi).

A second problem in measuring labor compensation is that the cost of labor input from the point of view of the firm is the sum of wages and salaries and payments that take the form of supplements. The Bureau of the Census reports compensation from the point of view of the household, so that the incomes reported are measures of wage or salary income rather than the total of wages, salaries, and supplements. Household surveys exclude employers' contributions to Social Security, pension plans, unemployment insurance, and all the other programs that are combined under the heading of supplements. Differentials in the proportion of supplements in labor compensation are sufficient to make the assumption of proportionality of wages and salaries to total labor cost inappropriate. For example, employers' contributions to Social Security and unemployment insurance are calculated by applying a percentage to each worker's annual earnings, but only up to a fixed maximum.

A third problem in measuring labor compensation concerns the appropriate time period for comparing marginal productivities among distinct labor groups. A worker's average compensation per hour provides a good approximation to the worker's marginal product. Annual compensation, even based on labor earnings for each worker, is hardly an adequate proxy for compensation per hour, since annual labor compensation is the product of annual hours and hourly compensation. Annual hours may differ widely among groups and over time. If annual hours worked vary over demographic and industrial groups, then differences in labor compensation based on variations in annual earnings do not parallel differences in marginal productivity. An appropriate measure of labor compensation requires estimates of average compensation per hour for each category of labor input.

The fourth problem in measuring labor compensation is whether weights based on compensation per hour worked should be fixed over the whole time period or should vary from year to year. To account for shifting demand conditions, changing production techniques, and the impact of constraints on labor supply, the best approach is to construct a set of weights based on compensation per hour worked for each year.

We have undertaken the construction of measures of hourly compensation for each of the postwar years 1948 through 1979. Just as for data on hours and weeks, annual compensation data are presented in the form of empirical frequency distributions for the three benchmark years—1949, 1959, and 1969. Since economists investigating the distribution of labor income in the United States have long observed that the distributions can be approximated by a lognormal probability distribution, we employ Gjeddebaek's adaptation of the method of maximum likelihood to estimate the parameters of this distribution. We use this method to estimate average wage and salary income for each category of labor input in each benchmark year. It is important to note that this estimate refers to the wage and salary income of persons and not to the sum of wage payments to all workers occupying a given job.

Estimates based on Bureau of the Census data identify the amount of income workers receive and not the total labor cost incurred by the firm. To estimate labor cost we have distributed employers' contributions to Social Security among employees by adding to wage and salary income the appropriate dollar amount as determined by the worker's annual wage or salary and the year's Social Security tax laws as described by Pechman (1983). Similarly, we add unemployment compensation contributions by employers to the wage and salary income matrices. These two adjustments account for nearly 70 percent of all earnings supplements.

Up to this point it has been necessary to define average labor compensation per person. This, rather than average compensation per job, is the appropriate definition to be used in assigning employers' supplementary labor payments. Two persons reporting $10,000 each for twenty-six weeks of employment earn a different sum of supplements than a single worker reporting $20,000 income for a full year's employment. Distributing supplements on the basis of average compensation per job of $20,000 would introduce a bias. Once supplements have been assigned, however, average compensation per person must be converted to average compensation per job.

Application of the method of iterative proportional fitting requires forming marginal data distributions with each cell represented by the total labor income earned by workers assigned to that cell. This total is the product of employment and average annual labor compensation. Since establishment surveys enumerate jobs rather than persons, average compensation must be defined on the basis of jobs. To convert the census data on average compensation per person to average compensation per job, we divide average compensation for each category of workers by the ratio of the number of weeks paid to the number of weeks in a calendar year.

Control totals for annual labor compensation by industry are taken directly from Table 6.1 in the national income issue of the *Survey of Current Business*. These labor compensation data provide the basis for distributing the 30 percent of labor supplements not accounted for explicitly. Establishment-based control totals also assure that the compensation of multiple-job-holders is appropriately distributed among each worker's industries of employment. Finally, the national income accounts provide a continuous time series of labor compensation from 1948 through 1979.

The method of iterative proportional fitting results in a matrix giving labor compensation for each benchmark year, controlled to totals from the national accounts. Each cell in this matrix is divided by the number of hours worked by laborers in that cell—that is, by the product of employment, hours worked per paid week per job, and fifty-two. The results are matrices for 1949, 1959, and 1969 of mean hourly compensation for labor categories cross-classified by sex, age, education, employment class, occupation, and industry.

The labor compensation matrix for each intermediate year is initialized by a matrix with entries equal to a weighted average of wage rates for benchmark years with weights given by log-linear interpolation. The hourly wage estimates for the benchmark years include employers' contributions to Social Security and unemployment insurance, as well as all payments to employee pension funds and similar programs. These payments vary from year to year, depending on current tax laws, union contracts, and so on. Failure to account for these changes would introduce a bias when using data reported for census years to initialize the matrix of wage rates for intermediate years.

To adjust benchmark wage data so that the wage rates do not reflect the employers' tax contributions and other indirect payments, we generate a matrix of annual labor compensation with all nontax supplements excluded. Second, we generate a matrix of benchmark wage rates, exclusive of each year's Social Security and unemployment insurance taxes paid by employers. We initialize the matrix of wage rates for each intermediate year with estimates of hourly wages, excluding all supplements.

Given initial estimates of wages excluding supplements, we estimate wage rates for each intermediate year based on the work patterns, tax laws, and nontax supplements unique to that year. We first estimate annual compensation per person, based on hours worked and weeks-paid data for each intermediate year. Persons are distinguished by sex, age, education, occupation, employment class, and industry of employment. We adjust the annual earnings estimates to reflect wage and salary totals, exclusive of employer supplements, as published for each industry in the national income accounts.

We next estimate the appropriate level of employer contributions to Social Security and unemployment insurance for each cell. To account for the remaining supplements, we adjust data from all cells to control totals for each industry from the national income accounts. Using the weeks-paid matrix for each intermediate year, average compensation per job is calculated for each category of laborers. Each cell's estimate is determined by the product of average compensation per person in that cell and the ratio of fifty-two to the number of average paid weeks for laborers assigned to that cell.

To obtain wages earned per hour worked, where wages represent the sum of wages and salaries and supplements, we divide labor compensation by hours worked, defined as the product of employment, weekly hours worked, and the number of weeks per calendar year. Together with the decennial census matrices described above, these estimates for intermediate years form a complete time series of employers' hourly payments to labor from 1948–1979.

Since earnings reported to the census by self-employed laborers are a combination of labor income and the return to noncorporate capital, the procedure we have described for estimating labor compensation can be applied only to wage and salary workers. Measures of the effective labor earnings of the self-employed and unpaid family workers require imputations of labor compensation.

Given the compensation of employees and noncorporate income, by industry, from the national income and product accounts, two options present themselves. Holding sex, age, education, occupation, and industry constant, we could assume that both classes of workers earn identical hourly wages.

Using the estimates of annual hours generated above for all categories of the self-employed and unpaid family workers, an estimated wage bill for nonwage-and-salary laborers could be calculated for each industry. Subtracting this total from noncorporate income, we would obtain property compensation. Alternatively, we could assume that both corporate and noncorporate capital earn the same rate of return after taxes. Noncorporate property income for each industry could then be subtracted from total noncorporate income, to obtain labor compensation. The residual would represent the total labor return to that industry's self-employed and unpaid family workers. This wage bill would be distributed among the self-employed so as to preserve the wage differentials observed among that industry's wage and salary workers.

We have chosen to assume that after-tax rates of return are the same for corporate and noncorporate business. Differences in individual preferences and barriers to entry that prevent some wage and salary workers from moving into the self-employed category are sufficient to make suspect any claim that wages are equal, even controlling for labor characteristics. By contrast, there is less reason to expect immobility of capital resulting in differential after-tax rates of return in the corporate and noncorporate sectors for a particular industry. The cost of incorporating a noncorporate business is relatively modest, and small corporations can be treated in the same manner as noncorporate businesses from the point of view of the corporate income tax. The legal form of organization, corporate or noncorporate, can be altered with little impact on the use of capital, so that capital is freely mobile between legal forms of organizations.

Indices of Sectoral Labor Input

We have outlined the development of data on annual hours worked and labor compensation per hour for each industrial sector. Both annual hours and compensation data are cross-classified by sex, age, education, employment class, and occupation of workers. To construct an index of labor input for each industrial sector, we assume that sectoral labor input, say $\{L_i\}$, can be expressed as a translog function of its individual components, say $\{L_{li}\}$. The corresponding index of sectoral labor input is a translog quantity index of individual labor inputs:

$$\ln L_i(T) - \ln L_i(T-1) = \sum \bar{v}_{Ll}^i \left[\ln L_{li}(T) - \ln L_{li}(T-1) \right],$$

$$(i=1,2,...,n),$$

where weights are given by the average share of each component in the value of sectoral labor compensation:

$$\bar{v}^i_{Ll} = \frac{1}{2}[v^i_{Ll}(T) + v^i_{Ll}(T-1)], \qquad (i = 1, 2,..., n\,;\, l = 1, 2,..., q),$$

and:

$$v^i_{Ll} = \frac{p^i_{Ll}\,L_{li}}{\sum p^i_{Ll}\,L_{li}}\,, \qquad (i = 1, 2,..., n\,;\, l = 1, 2,..., q).$$

The value shares are computed from data on hours worked $\{L_{li}\}$ and compensation per hour $\{p^i_{Ll}\}$ for each component of sectoral labor input, cross-classified by sex, age, education, employment class, and occupation of workers. Labor compensation for the sector as a whole, $\sum p^i_{Ll}\,L_{li,}$ is controlled to labor compensation by industry, from the U.S. national income accounts.

For each of the components of labor input into an industrial sector, $\{L_{li}(T)\}$, the flow of labor services is proportional to hours worked, say $\{H_{li}(T)\}$:

$$L_{li}(T) = Q^i_{Ll}\,H_{li}(T), \qquad (i = 1, 2,..., n\,;\, l = 1, 2,..., q),$$

where the constants of proportionality $\{Q^i_{Ll}\}$ transform hours worked into a flow of labor services. The translog quantity indices of sectoral labor input $\{L_i\}$ can be expressed in terms of their components $\{L_{li}\}$ or in terms of the components of hours worked $\{H_{li}\}$:

$$\ln L_i(T) - \ln L_i(T-1) = \sum \bar{v}^i_{Ll}\,[\ln L_{li}(T) - \ln L_{li}(T-1)]$$

$$= \sum \bar{v}^i_{Ll}\,[\ln H_{li}(T) - \ln H_{li}(T-1)],$$

$$(i = 1, 2,..., n).$$

We form sectoral indices of labor input from data on hours worked by industry, cross-classified by sex, age, education, employment class, and occupation. Changes in the logarithms of hours worked for each component are weighted by average shares in sectoral labor compensation.

We define sectoral hours worked, say $\{H_i(T)\}$, as the unweighted sum of its components,

$$H_i(T) = \sum H_{li}(T)\,, \qquad (i = 1, 2,..., n).$$

Similarly, we define sectoral indices of the quality of hours worked, say $\{Q_L^i(T)\}$, that transform sectoral measures of hours worked into the translog indices of labor input:

$$L_i(T) = Q_L^i(T)H_i(T), \qquad\qquad (i = 1, 2,..., n).$$

The sectoral indices of the quality of hours worked can be expressed in the form

$$\ln Q_L^i(T) - \ln Q_L^i(T-1) = \sum \bar{v}_{Ll}^i \, [\ln H_{li}(T) - \ln H_{li}(T-1)]$$

$$= [\ln H_i(T) - \ln H_i(T-1)], \qquad (i = 1, 2,..., n),$$

so that these indices reflect changes in the composition of hours worked within each sector.[9] Sectoral labor quality remains unchanged if all components of hours worked within a sector are growing at the same rate. Sectoral quality rises if components with higher flows of labor input per hour worked are growing more rapidly and falls if components with lower flows per hour worked are growing more rapidly.

We have generated translog indices of labor input, based on the employment, hours, weeks, and labor compensation data described in the preceding sections for each industrial sector listed in Table 3.1. There are 1600 categories of labor input for each industry, and a total of fifty-one industries. Average annual rates of growth of the translog indices of sectoral labor input are presented in Table 3.2 for seven subperiods between 1948 and 1979 for all fifty-one industries. Price and quantity indices of labor input and indices of the quality of hours worked are presented, in Appendix B, on an annual basis for the period 1948–1979, for each industry. Annual data for employment, weekly hours per person, hourly compensation, hours worked, and labor compensation are also presented for each industry in Appendix B.

In order to more precisely identify differences among subperiods in patterns of growth in labor input, we classify rates of growth by subperiod as shown in Table 3.3. The overall pattern of labor input within and across all subperiods conforms well to general impressions of economic activity in the postwar period. In every subperiod more than half of the fifty-one industries experienced positive average annual growth in labor input. The pattern varies over time and depends on the relative strength of growth during the period. Considering the subperiods in chronological order, the numbers of industries with positive average annual changes in quality-adjusted hours worked are 41, 29, 27, 41, 40, 32, and 39.

Table 3.2. Sectoral labor input: rates of growth

Industry	Translog index of labor input (average annual rates of growth)						
	1948–1953	1953–1957	1957–1960	1960–1966	1966–1969	1969–1973	1973–1979
Agricultural production	−0.0320	−0.0505	−0.0251	−0.0495	−0.0241	−0.0077	−0.0260
Agricultural services	0.0177	−0.0098	−0.0350	0.0492	0.0400	0.0411	0.0429
Metal mining	0.0220	0.0034	−0.0454	−0.0069	0.0158	−0.0186	0.0225
Coal mining	−0.1040	−0.0569	−0.1224	−0.0189	−0.0119	0.0498	0.0869
Crude petroleum and natural gas	0.0491	0.0332	−0.0318	−0.0046	0.0123	−0.0030	0.0999
Nonmetallic mining and quarrying	0.0319	0.0159	−0.0137	0.0178	−0.0145	−0.0028	0.0217
Contract construction	0.0224	−0.0003	−0.0020	0.0325	0.0285	0.0235	0.0231
Food and kindred products	0.0027	−0.0081	−0.0014	0.0025	0.0048	−0.0121	0.0029
Tobacco manufacturers	0.0129	−0.0165	0.0079	−0.0084	−0.0198	0.0042	−0.0226
Textile mill products	−0.0259	−0.0392	−0.0087	0.0159	0.0076	0.0075	−0.0258
Apparel and other fabricated textile products	0.0069	−0.0120	0.0102	0.0228	−0.0017	0.0024	−0.0113
Paper and allied products	0.0327	0.0174	0.0231	0.0264	0.0244	−0.0052	0.0001
Printing and publishing	0.0217	0.0137	0.0362	0.0139	0.0253	−0.0023	0.0175
Chemicals and allied products	0.0452	0.0234	0.0210	0.0271	0.0327	−0.0070	0.0225
Petroleum and coal products	0.0252	0.0045	−0.0306	−0.0161	0.0160	0.0043	0.0321
Rubber and misc. plastic products	0.0402	0.0138	0.0121	0.0566	0.0457	0.0307	0.0160
Leather and leather products	−0.0070	−0.0113	−0.0101	0.0045	−0.0277	−0.0313	−0.0322
Lumber and wood products except furniture	−0.0175	−0.0427	−0.0034	0.0121	0.0098	0.0213	0.0050
Furniture and fixtures	0.0177	−0.0040	−0.0013	0.0370	0.0015	0.0183	−0.0042
Stone, clay and glass products	0.0144	0.0055	0.0193	0.0176	0.0082	0.0130	0.0060

Table 3.2 continued

Industry	Translog index of labor input (average annual rates of growth)						
	1948–1953	1953–1957	1957–1960	1960–1966	1966–1969	1969–1973	1973–1979
Primary metal industries	0.0216	–0.0055	–0.0309	0.0284	0.0005	–0.0047	–0.0013
Fabricated metal industries	0.0520	–0.0033	–0.0132	0.0378	0.0253	–0.0039	0.0060
Machinery except electrical	0.0354	–0.0045	–0.0184	0.0548	0.0131	0.0076	0.0313
Elec. machinery, eqpt., and supplies	0.0727	0.0074	0.0396	0.0434	0.0141	0.0015	0.0160
Trans. eqpt. and ordnance, except motor vehicles	0.1923	–0.0004	–0.0545	0.0454	0.0029	–0.0684	0.0280
Motor vehicles and equipment	0.0540	–0.0420	–0.0148	0.0393	0.0044	0.0234	–0.0004
Prof. photographic eqpt. and watches	0.0850	0.0165	0.0150	0.0364	0.0266	0.0080	0.0372
Misc. manufacturing industries	0.0079	–0.0213	0.0030	0.0233	–0.0010	0.0047	0.0058
Railroads and rail express services	–0.0421	–0.0408	–0.0714	–0.0174	–0.0269	–0.0273	–0.0106
Street rail., bus lines, and taxicabs	–0.0205	–0.0325	–0.0184	–0.0116	–0.0006	–0.0202	–0.0067
Trucking services and warehousing	0.0474	0.0184	0.0195	0.0339	0.0258	0.0218	0.0181
Water transportation	–0.0128	0.0070	–0.0355	0.0097	–0.0217	–0.0301	0.0189
Air transportation	0.0617	0.0851	0.0440	0.0461	0.1042	0.0041	0.0318
Pipelines, except natural gas	–0.0030	–0.0070	–0.0307	–0.0329	0.0097	–0.0292	0.0369
Transportation services	0.0150	–0.0148	0.0140	0.0470	0.0417	0.0241	0.0705
Telephone, telegraph, and misc. communication services	0.0222	0.0289	–0.0084	0.0226	0.0440	0.0254	0.0146
Radio and television broadcasting	0.0702	0.0409	0.0306	0.0341	0.0509	0.0297	0.0419
Electric utilities	0.0207	0.0102	0.0110	0.0108	0.0253	0.0179	0.0189
Gas utilities	0.0261	0.0178	0.0197	0.0144	0.0252	0.0179	0.0171
Water supply and sanitary services	0.0168	0.0063	0.0046	0.0189	0.0246	0.0288	0.0104

Table 3.2 continued

Industry	Translog index of labor input (average annual rates of growth)						
	1948–1953	1953–1957	1957–1960	1960–1966	1966–1969	1969–1973	1973–1979
Wholesale trade	0.0151	0.0128	0.0269	0.0233	0.0202	0.0215	0.0271
Retail trade	0.0118	0.0015	0.0143	0.0074	0.0130	0.0177	0.0171
Finance, insurance, and real estate	0.0421	0.0334	0.0392	0.0292	0.0390	0.0340	0.0400
Services, exc. private households and institutions	0.0181	0.0262	0.0335	0.0328	0.0350	0.0310	0.0382
Private households	−0.0257	0.0068	−0.0002	−0.0285	−0.0401	−0.0366	−0.0310
Institutions	0.0470	0.0428	0.0878	0.0458	0.0528	0.0013	0.0336
Federal public administration	0.0539	−0.0060	0.0055	0.0280	0.0263	−0.0169	0.0159
Federal government enterprises	0.0282	0.0091	0.0287	0.0226	0.0268	−0.0087	−0.0015
State and local educational services	0.0535	0.0586	0.0629	0.0535	0.0432	0.0374	0.0209
State and local public admin.	0.0434	0.0430	0.0270	0.0394	0.0334	0.0409	0.0253
State and local enterprises	0.0647	0.0023	0.0648	0.0204	0.0408	0.0314	0.0379

The immediate postwar period (1948–1953), the two periods that capture the surge of economic activity relating to the Vietnam War (1960–1966 and 1966–1969), and the final period (1973–1979) stand out. So does the 1957–1960 subperiod, when twenty-four of fifty-one industries experienced declines in labor input. Both agricultural sectors, all four mining industries, construction, seven of eleven durable goods industries, and four of seven transportation sectors led the downward trend. This contrasts with the 1948–1953, 1960–1966, and 1966–1969 subperiods, when construction and nearly all durable goods sectors experienced increases in labor input. In the 1960–1966 subperiod, construction and all eleven durable goods industries experienced positive average annual rates of growth.

Comparative analysis of the economic activity in the seven subperiods generates much sharper conclusions when we narrow our focus to the sectors that experienced annual rates of growth in labor input greater than six percent or rates of decline less than minus four percent. The period as a whole was characterized by a dramatic decline in the dispersion of growth rates of labor

Table 3.3. Classification of rates of growth of sectoral labor input by sub-period, 1948–1979

Average annual rate of growth of labor input	1948–1953	1953–1957	1957–1960	1960–1966	1966–1969	1969–1973	1973–1979
Less than −4%	2	5	4	1	1	1	0
−4% to −2%	4	3	7	2	4	6	5
−2% to 0	4	14	13	7	6	12	7
0 to 2%	14	12	19	13	12	15	17
2% to 4%	12	5	10	20	16	14	16
4% to 6%	11	4	1	9	8	3	3
More than 6%	6	1	3	0	1	0	3

input. During the subperiods 1948–1953, 1953–1957, and 1957–1960, a total of eight, six, and seven industries, respectively, experienced declines in labor input at rates exceeding four percent or positive growth at rates greater than six percent. By contrast, only one, two, and one industries exceeded these limits in the 1960–1966, 1966–1969, 1969–1973, and 1973–1979 subperiods, respectively. It is important to emphasize that both rapid gains and rapid losses in sectoral labor input took place during the period ending in 1960 as the U.S. economy was reshaped to meet postwar conditions.

Considering specific sectors that underwent rapid declines in labor input, we find that labor input declined at 10.4 percent annually in coal mining and at 4.21 percent annually in railroads in the subperiod 1948–1953. During the subperiod 1953–1957, labor input declined at rates exceeding four percent in agriculture, coal mining, lumber and wood products, motor vehicles, and railroads. From 1957 to 1960, declines exceeded four percent in metal mining, coal mining, transportation equipment excluding motor vehicles, and railroads. From 1960 to 1966 only agriculture experienced a decline in labor input at a rate exceeding four percent; from 1966 to 1969 only private households declined more rapidly than four percent, and transportation equipment excluding motor vehicles was the only industry to decline at this rate in the 1969–1973 period. The overall conclusion is that very rapid reductions in labor input were concentrated in coal mining and railroads.

Turning to increases in labor input at rates of growth exceeding six percent annually, there were six industries that showed rapid growth during the subperiod 1948–1953—electrical machinery, transportation equipment excluding motor vehicles, professional equipment, air transportation, broadcasting, and state and local government enterprises. Labor input in air transportation grew at 8.51 percent during the subperiod 1953–1957 and at 10.42 percent during the subperiod 1966–1969. During the subperiod 1957–1960, nonprofit institutions, state and local educational services, and state and local government enterprises all experienced annual growth rates in excess of six percent. Coal mining, crude petroleum and natural gas extraction, and transportation services had growth rates greater than six percent annually in the 1973–1979 period. Our overall conclusion is that very rapid growth in labor input over the full 1948–1979 period was limited to air transportation and state and local government enterprises. Transportation equipment excluding motor vehicles grew rapidly during the Korean mobilization and declined rapidly during Korean and Vietnam demobilizations. Coal mining declined rapidly through 1960 and began to grow rapidly during the subperiod 1969–1973.

Our earlier observation of strong economic growth during the subperiods 1948–1953 and 1960–1966 is born out by the number of industries with rates of growth in labor input in excess of two percent—twenty-nine in each subperiod. The 1966–1969 subperiod follows with 25 industries. By contrast, labor grew at rates exceeding two percent in only ten industries from 1953 to 1957. During the subperiods 1957–1960, 1969–1973, and 1973–1979, fourteen, seventeen, and twenty-two industries, respectively, surpassed this limit. Our overall conclusion from the data presented in Tables 3.2 and 3.3 is that the postwar period was characterized by persistent growth in labor input; growth rates were high in 1948–1953 and 1960–1966 and low in 1953–1957; and there was a sharp decline in dispersion of sectoral growth rates after 1960.

The growth rates of labor input for most of the fifty-one industries listed in Table 3.2 exhibit no continuous postwar trend. Labor input increased over some periods and decreased over others. The exceptions, however, are notable. Labor input has persistently declined in agriculture, railroads, and local transportation sectors. The rates of decline vary over the periods but are consistently negative. The leather and private household sectors follow closely, with declining labor input over six of the seven subperiods. The full list includes no surprises. The principal explanations are changes in technology and tastes, the rising availability of domestic and imported substitute goods, and the reorganization of some sectors as part of government enterprises.

The list of industries with persistent positive trends is much longer. The following sectors had positive average annual growth in labor input over all seven subperiods: rubber, stone, clay and glass, electrical machinery, professional equipment, trucking, air transportation, broadcasting, electric utilities, gas utilities, water supply and sanitary services, wholesale trade, retail trade, finance, insurance and real estate, services, nonprofit institutions, and all three state and local government sectors. Not surprisingly, all service sectors except private households had persistent growth. Noticeably absent are agriculture, construction, all mining, and most manufacturing industries.

Not only has labor input in some industries persistently increased over the full 1948–1979 period, but it has done so at average annual rates consistently exceeding two percent. This distinction is shared by the broadcasting industry, finance, insurance and real estate, state and local educational services, and state and local public administration. Four other sectors—air transportation, services, nonprofit institutions, and state and local government enterprises—had increases in labor input in all seven subperiods and increases greater than two percent in six of seven subperiods.

Second, trends in two industries have been significantly reversed. After experiencing a rather stagnant period from 1948 to 1960, labor input in agricultural services increased at an average annual rate of more than four percent between 1960 and 1979. More dramatically, the long decline in labor input in the coal mining industry, which reached ten- and twelve-percent annual rates in the 1948–1953 and 1957–1960 periods, was reversed in both the 1969–1973 period, when labor input increased at a 4.98 percent annual rate, and in the 1973–1979 period, when the increase was 8.69 percent.

Third, the food and kindred products industry appears to have had the most stable level of employment from peak to peak, while the transportation equipment industry appears to be the most volatile. Growth rates in the former oscillate between positive and negative values but change by more than one percent only during the 1969–1973 period. Indeed, the absolute average annual rate of growth is less than 0.5 percent in five of six periods. In the transportation equipment industry, the level of labor input exhibits severe changes. The subperiod averages, in chronological order, are 19.23%, −0.04%, −5.45%, 4.54%, 0.29%, −6.84%, and 2.80%. Interestingly, the positive average annual rate in 1948–1953 is more than twice the positive growth rate during that period in any other industry. Similarly, the negative rate in the 1969–1973 period is more than twice the negative rate reported for private households, the next most rapidly declining sector.

The results presented in Table 3.2 provide the basic framework against which we will compare similar analyses for capital and intermediate inputs and output. Of principal interest is identifying sectors whose output and inputs exhibit either substantially similar or significantly contrasting patterns of growth. These comparative analyses are developed in Chapters 4 and 5.

Alternative Measures of Sectoral Labor Input

To provide additional perspective on our approach to measuring labor input, we find it useful to compare our methodology and data sources with those of the Bureau of Labor Statistics, Denison and Kendrick. Our comparative analysis covers both labor hours and compensation. We evaluate the alternative approaches against both the constraints of the data set selected and the requirements of economic theory. Wherever possible, we test the assumptions implicit in the competing models.

Our comparison begins with the measurement of hours. The Bureau of Labor Statistics (1983, 66–68) measures of multifactor productivity employ the same data for hours as the traditional Bureau of Labor Statistics (1973b) measures of output per hour. About 85 percent of total prime business hours are based on establishment surveys that collect information on hours paid rather than hours worked. Kendrick (1961a; 1973; 1983) and Kendrick and Grossman (1980) present a strong case for an hours-worked series, but use Bureau of Labor Statistics (1973b) establishment data on hours paid for some industrial sectors.[10] As is evident from his earliest works, Denison (1961, 352) shares Kendrick's view that hours worked are more appropriate than hours paid. In his subsequent works, Denison (1967; 1974; 1979; 1985) begins from an hours-paid series when constructing his hours estimates for wage and salary workers. He converts the average hours paid for per job to average hours worked per job, using unpublished BLS ratios of ''hours at work'' to ''hours paid for.'' These ratios, extrapolated from data for a single year, 1966, were developed by BLS for the 1952–1974 period. Based on the trends in the 1952–1974 series, Denison (1985) further extrapolates his hours-worked series back to 1947 and forward to 1982.[11]

While one might criticize Kendrick for mixing census estimates of hours worked with Bureau of Labor Statistics estimates of hours paid and Denison for extrapolating estimates beyond the boundaries of the BLS survey, they do attempt to measure annual hours worked rather than annual hours paid. A bias, however, underlies their use of the hours paid series published by the Bureau of Labor Statistics. The description in the *BLS Handbook of Methods* (1971) makes it clear that separate hours series are developed for production and nonproduction workers only in the manufacturing sectors. According to the *Handbook,* (pp. 214–215), manufacturing production worker hours are taken directly from the data in the *BLS Area Wage Surveys* and the study of *Employer Expenditures* published by the Bureau of Labor Statistics (1963). For the nonmanufacturing industries the hours-paid series collected in the *Census Employment Survey* program relate to nonsupervisory workers only. The Bureau of Labor Statistics assumes that these hours apply to all wage and salary workers.

The different demographic mixes of the supervisory and nonsupervisory occupations and the different average hours worked recorded for the demographic classes make suspect the assumption that supervisory workers in each nonmanufacturing industry are paid for the same average number of hours per week as are nonsupervisory workers. For example, according to the *Census of Population,* the 1970 female-to-male ratio was 0.87 in nonsupervisory occupations in the non-manufacturing sector and only 0.22 in supervisory occupations.[12] Furthermore, female nonsupervisory workers in 1970 worked, on average, 34.5 hours while their male counterparts worked 41.5 hours. (Bureau of the Census, 1973a, Table 45; Kendrick, 1973, 156).

Given that women work fewer weekly hours than men and are proportionately underrepresented in supervisory occupations, it is highly unlikely that supervisory laborers are paid for the same number of weekly hours as are nonsupervisory laborers, an assumption implicit in Kendrick's and Denison's use of BLS hours-paid totals. A similar analysis could be based on age or education compositions; the conclusion would be the same.

The evidence suggests that both Kendrick's and Denison's annual hours series are biased downward in all nonmanufacturing sectors for which they rely on BLS estimates. More important, shifts in the demographic composition of the supervisory and nonsupervisory occupational groups over time bias any estimates of the rate of productivity change.[13]

Differences in the measurement of annual hours aside, the final labor input indices generated by Kendrick and Denison differ significantly from those presented in the last section. In constructing indices of sectoral labor input, Kendrick considers all workers within each industry to be homogeneous. Hours worked by all laborers represent equal contributions to total labor input. In short, Kendrick totally eliminates the influence of changing labor quality on his measure of an industry's labor input.[14] In fairness to Kendrick, it should be noted that he purposefully designs his index of labor input to conform to a very strict and, we believe, overly narrow interpretation of labor as an input into a production process. For Kendrick, any difference in the productive value of an hour's work by an electrical engineer and a truck driver should be caught, not in a measure of labor input but rather in an index of productivity growth.

It is evident that, given Kendrick's definition, the appropriate index of labor input for each industrial sector is an unweighted index of hours worked. Viewing Kendrick's model in terms of our own theoretical framework, Kendrick does not distinguish among the marginal products of various categories of laborers within a given industry. This makes unnecessary the construction of distinct compensation measures for each group of laborers, classified by demographic and occupational characteristics.

Denison cross-classifies workers by demographic characteristics such as age, sex, and education, in deriving indices of labor input. Denison uses Bureau of the Census data on earnings to construct weights for use in aggregating his education and sex–age hours series, both in his original *Sources of Economic Growth* (1962) and in his more recent work on productivity (1974; 1979; 1985). The principal problem with using census earnings data to measure marginal productivity is that reported earnings exclude all supplements to wages and salaries and include the return to capital invested by self-employed workers. Denison makes no adjustment to the census data to exclude returns to capital.[15]

As Denison correctly points out, earnings can be used only if the average earnings for workers cross-classified by education or by age and sex are proportional to the corresponding marginal products. Given the way supplements, particularly Social Security and unemployment insurance, are charged to employers, reported earnings do not proportionately reflect employers' labor outlay. If supplements are neglected, only the ratios of hourly labor earnings among groups of laborers with annual incomes below the lowest base for supplements will be unbiased estimates of relative wages as viewed by employers.

If, using Denison's example, the average male 35 to 64 years old has an annual labor income above the Social Security or unemployment insurance tax base, while the average 20 to 24-year-old female's labor earnings are below either base, then Denison's estimate of 2.3 for the relative valuation of an average hour's work by males and females is clearly upward biased. Supplements add to the employers' outlay for both males and females but, in this example, supplements add proportionately more to the employers' outlay for females than for males. Based on 1969 earnings reported in the decennial census, employed 35 to 64-year-old males had mean annual earnings ($10,008) well above either the Social Security ($7800) or unemployment insurance ($3000) tax base in 1969. Females 18 to 24 years of age, however, had mean labor income of $2960. (Bureau of the Census, 1973c, Tables 1 and 11.) Ratios of male (35 to 64 years old) to female (18 to 24 years old) hourly wage costs excluding supplements are upward biased estimates of relative labor costs experienced by employers.

Inclusion of the return to noncorporate capital in earnings leads to an additional bias in the same direction. Denison's assumption of proportionality between earnings and labor outlay is valid only if the ratio of noncorporate property income to total earnings is constant across sex–age and across education groups. If the representative 35 to 64-year-old male has a larger fraction of his earnings being generated from capital invested in noncorporate enterprises than does the representative 20 to 24-year-old female, then

Denison's earnings-based estimate of 2.3 for the relative valuation of an hour's work by males to an hour's work by females is upward biased. Unfortunately, we cannot test this hypothesis directly. Data measuring the noncorporate property income of workers classified by demographic characteristics are not available. The reasonableness of Denison's assumption can be evaluated by comparing the distribution of employment in wage and salary versus self-employed activities across sex and age groups.

We refer to data published in the 1970 census to evaluate Denison's assumption. We construct ratios of self-employed persons to total employment in both wage and salary and self-employed activities. The ratios, reported in Table 3.4, vary significantly across sex–age groups. For both males and females, the ratios generally increase with age; for any given age group, the ratio for males is more than twice the ratio for females; and, with particular reference to Denison's example, the ratios for older males are considerably higher than the similar ratios for young females. The ratio for males 35 to 64 years old is 0.130; the corresponding ratio for females 20 to 24 years old is 0.011. Compared to young females, older males apparently allocate a greater proportion of their labor effort to self-employed activities.

We infer that earnings for a representative male include a higher percentage of returns to noncorporate capital than do the earnings for a representative female, even after controlling for age. In short, relative earnings are inadequate measures of relative marginal products. The wage and salary income of wage and salary workers, adjusted for supplements, is a more appropriate starting point for a measure of labor compensation.

We have already emphasized that the appropriate compensation measure of labor's marginal product is the hourly wage. Denison would agree, yet his final earnings estimates depend crucially on the initial assumption that year-round, full-time-employed males and females, regardless of age, each work an identical number of annual hours. To the extent that annual hours vary across age groups within each sex, Denison's hourly earnings estimates are further biased. Differences in hourly wages ultimately based only on variations in annual earnings do not parallel differences in marginal productivity. The *Current Population Survey* (CPS) data for May 1966 do not permit us to test the reasonableness of Denison's assumption; beginning in late 1967, however, the Bureau of Labor Statistics decomposes its CPS mean hours estimate for each sex into age classes. We reproduce the CPS-based table for May 1968 as Table 3.5.

We assume that the mean weekly hours differentials in May 1968 reflect the differentials existing in May 1966. From inspection of Table 3.5, under Denison's method any year-round, full-time-employed age group within each sex that has average weekly hours below the mean for that sex will be

Table 3.4. Ratios of self-employed persons to total employment by age
and sex, 1970 [a]

	Ratio to total employment	
Age	Males	Females
14–15 years	0.044	0.026
16–17 years	0.016	0.009
18–19 years	0.014	0.005
20–24 years	0.029	0.011
25–29 years	0.052	0.024
30–34 years	0.078	0.033
35–39 years	0.101	0.038
40–44 years	0.114	0.041
45–49 years	0.124	0.045
50–59 years	0.154	0.060
60–62 years	0.166	0.062
63–64 years	0.183	0.073
65–69 years	0.243	0.093
70–74 years	0.300	0.118
75 years and over	0.336	0.133

[a] Total employed excludes unpaid family workers.
Source: Bureau of the Census (1973b), Table 47.

assigned a downward-biased hourly compensation rate. Males 16 and 17 years old are a striking example. In contrast, any age group with mean hours above the average over all age groups will be assigned an upward-biased compensation weight. Females over 65 years of age would, according to Table 3.5, have the estimates with the greatest upward bias.

The final issue concerns the intertemporal pattern of hourly earnings, and therefore weights for each labor category. Denison (1974; 1979; 1985) does weight by sex–age and education categories but holds weights constant over various subperiods. Denison (1974, p. 187) assumes that the sex–age earnings weights he creates for males and females from 1966 and 1967 data, respectively, and the education weights from 1959 data, are constant over and thus representative of all postwar years. Denison (1979, 44–45, 158;

Table 3.5. Average weekly hours for workers on full-time schedules, 1968

	Average weekly hours	
Age	Males	Females
16 years and over	45.1	41.0
16 to 21 years	42.5	39.7
16 to 19 years	41.7	39.4
16 and 17 years	38.5	38.2
18 and 19 years	42.5	39.5
20 years and over	45.2	41.1
20 to 24 years	45.3	40.3
25 years and over	45.3	41.2
25 to 44 years	45.7	40.7
45 to 64 years	44.9	41.5
65 years and over	44.5	45.7

Source: Bureau of Labor Statistics (1968), Table A-25.

1985, 157–158) constructs two sets of weights for both sex–age and education cohorts.

Relative wages across industries and among demographic groups have shifted over time, due to shifting demand conditions, altered production techniques, and the changing impact of constraints on labor supply. If relative hourly wages are the appropriate estimates of relative marginal products, the labor earnings weights must be allowed to change over time. If the weights are held constant, annual changes in marginal products would not be reflected. Estimates of year-to-year productivity change would be biased.

The discussion so far has focused on a comparison of data, assumptions, and measurement techniques. We close this section by emphasizing an important conceptual difference between Kendrick's sectoral measures of labor input and ours. Kendrick (1973, p. 146) purposefully defines any growth in sectoral output due to shifts in the demographic composition of the labor force as part of productivity change. For Kendrick, any shift in labor's sex, age, and education mix that leads to greater levels of sectoral output reflects an advance in knowledge and is therefore part of productivity change.

Our position differs greatly from Kendrick's. Shifts in the sex, age, education, occupation, and employment-class composition of labor hours in any sector do not reflect productivity change. All that is changing is the composition of labor hours and therefore the effective labor input available to the sector. In our view, quality change is an important component of measuring the growth of sectoral labor input. It accounts for much of the difference between Kendrick's series and our indices of sectoral labor input.

Conclusion

In this chapter we have developed measures of labor input that conform to our theoretical specification. Components of labor input that differ in marginal productivity are treated separately in measuring labor input for each of fifty-one industrial sectors. To achieve this objective we have constructed data on hours worked and labor compensation for 1600 types of labor input for each sector in each year from 1948 to 1979.

We have measured labor compensation from the producers' point of view, including wages and salaries, payroll taxes, and supplements paid by producers. We have employed data on labor compensation based on establishment surveys from the U.S. national income and product accounts to provide control totals for labor compensation in each sector. Finally, we have allocated labor compensation among components of labor input on the basis of household surveys from the *Census of Population* and the *Current Population Survey*.

Similarly, we have controlled hours worked for each industrial sector to total employment and hours worked from establishment surveys. Hours worked have been distributed among components of labor input on the basis of household surveys. For both labor compensation and hours worked we have allocated data from establishment-based surveys by the method of iterative proportional fitting, applied to data from household surveys.

On the basis of data from establishment and household surveys we have allocated labor compensation and hours worked among the two sexes, eight age groups, five education groups, two employment classes, and ten occupational groups for each industrial sector in each year from 1948 to 1979. Measurement of labor input from multiple-job-holders, self-employed individuals, and unpaid family workers has necessitated the use of supplementary survey data on hours worked and labor compensation for these workers.

Our data on labor input have been compiled to facilitate the incorporation of new data from establishment and household surveys as they become available. Our classification of hours worked and labor compensation is consistent with the most recent reports from the *Current Population Survey*. We have reconciled the classifications of data on labor input from earlier surveys with the classification used in current reports. Our control totals for hours worked and labor compensation are consistent with data from the current version of the U.S. national income and product accounts.

We have employed our data on hours worked and labor compensation to construct price and quantity indices of labor input for each of the fifty-one industrial sectors included in our study. Our data can also be employed to construct indices of labor input for aggregates of these sectors or components of labor input within industrial sectors. For example, it would be possible to construct price and quantity indices of labor input for each of the ten occupational groups within an industrial sector. These indices can be employed in studies of the impact of relative wages on the composition of demand for labor input by occupational groups.

The absence of data for industrial sectors that treat differently the components of labor input that differ in marginal productivity has been a major barrier to the study of economic growth in the United States. After constructing analogous measures of capital and intermediate input in Chapters 4 and 5, we will incorporate our new measures of labor input into an analysis of the growth of sectoral output, in Chapter 6, and an analysis of aggregate economic growth, in Chapter 9.

4 Sectoral Capital Input

Our next objective is to construct measures of capital input by industrial sector for the U.S. economy, in current and constant prices. Our measures of capital input are index numbers constructed from data on the services of the capital stocks and rental prices for capital services. At a conceptual level these indices are strictly analogous to the measures of labor input presented in the preceding chapter. Capital input takes the form of services of the capital stock in the same way that labor input involves the services of the work force. Capital services are compensated at rental rates, just as labor services are compensated at wage rates.

A possible approach to the construction of capital input measures would be to compile data on rental transactions in capital services. This method provides the basis for measuring capital services associated with the use of dwellings in the U.S. national income and product accounts. Data on the rental prices for tenant-occupied dwellings are used to impute rental prices for owner-occupied dwellings. Data on the stock of both tenant-occupied and owner-occupied dwellings are used in constructing estimates of the rental value of housing.

Capital goods with active rental markets are a substantial portion of the assets employed in the U.S. economy. Most types of land and structures can be rented, and a rental market exists for many types of equipment—transportation equipment, construction equipment, electronic computers, office equipment and furniture, and so on. Unfortunately, very little effort has been devoted to compiling data from rental transactions, so that the construction of measures of capital input based on sources precisely analogous to those employed for labor input is not feasible.

Our approach to measuring capital input is to infer the level of capital stocks at each point of time from data on flows of investment up to that point.

Rental prices required for indices of capital input can be inferred from data on investment goods prices and on property compensation. To construct measures of capital input that are consistent with the U.S. national income and product accounts data on investment are controlled to totals for all sectors from the national product accounts. Similarly, data on property compensation are controlled to totals from the national income accounts.

We have cross-classified the capital input of each industrial sector by six types of assets and four legal forms of organization, listed in Table 4.1. The classification by asset class corresponds to the breakdown of investment flows in the U.S. national product accounts. The classification by legal form of organization corresponds to the breakdown of property compensation in the U.S. national income accounts.

Data on property compensation are available for forty-six of the fifty-one industry groups in Table 3.1 (data on property compensation for the five sectors of federal, state, and local governments are not available). We have constructed indices of capital input for these forty-six sectors of private industry. For two of these sectors—private households and nonprofit institutions—there is no further breakdown by legal form of organization. The remaining forty-four sectors are divided between corporate and noncorporate business.

Our first task is to construct estimates of capital stock by type of asset and legal form of organization for each of the forty-six sectors of private industry on an annual basis for the period 1948–1979. For depreciable assets—equipment and structures—we employ the perpetual inventory method to estimate capital stocks from data on investment. For inventories and land our estimates are based on balance sheet data. We describe our data sources and the resulting estimates of capital stock below.

Consumers' durable equipment is used only by private households, while producers' durable equipment is employed in every sector except private households. Residential structures are allocated between owner-occupied and tenant-occupied dwellings. We assign owner-occupied dwellings to the private household sector. Tenant-occupied residential and nonresidential structures are available as an aggregate by industry for each of the remaining forty-five sectors. Inventories are employed in every sector except private households and nonprofit institutions, while land is utilized in all forty-six sectors.

Our second task is to construct estimates of rental prices by industrial sector for each type of asset and each legal form of organization for the period 1948–1979. Our approach is based on the dual to the perpetual inventory method proposed by Jorgenson (1980) and implemented by Fraumeni and Jorgenson (1980, 1986). This approach was originated by Christensen and Jorgenson (1969, 1973b). The dual to the perpetual inventory method is

Table 4.1. Characteristics of capital input

Asset class
(1) Producers' durable equipment
(2) Consumers' durable equipment
(3) Tenant-occupied residential or nonresidential structure
(4) Owner-occupied residential structure
(5) Inventory
(6) Land

Legal form
(1) Corporate business
(2) Noncorporate business
(3) Household
(4) Institution

based on the relationship between the price of an investment good at a point of time and rental prices of capital services from that point forward.

The rental price of capital services involves rates of return, depreciation, and capital gain or loss for each type of asset. It incorporates the tax structure for property compensation. We assume that the nominal rate of return after taxes is the same for all assets within a given sector, and that the sum of rental payments for all assets is equal to total property compensation. On the basis of these assumptions we can allocate property compensation for each industry among types of assets and legal forms of organization. We describe our data sources and the resulting estimates of rental prices for capital services in a later section.

Data on capital input cross-classified by characteristics such as legal form of organization and industry are required for studies of capital demand and investment behavior; data cross-classified by asset class are required for studies of investment goods supply. Later in this chapter we present indices of capital input for the forty-six industry groups included in our study. Our data base can be used to generate indices of capital input cross-classified by class of asset, by legal form of organization (for industrial sectors), or both.

The desirability of disaggregating capital input by industrial sector, class of asset, and legal form of organization has been recognized by the Bureau of Labor Statistics (1983), Christensen and Jorgenson (1969), Denison (1972), Griliches and Jorgenson (1966), Jorgenson and Griliches (1967, 1972a), Kendrick (1973), and others. Kendrick has developed measures of capital input, disaggregated by industry, for much of the postwar period, but his measures do not incorporate a cross-classification by class of asset or legal form of organization. Denison has developed measures of capital input, disaggregated by class of asset, legal form of organization, and by farm, nonfarm, and residential categories. The Bureau of Labor Statistics has developed measures of capital input disaggregated by class of asset and three major industrial sectors—farm, manufacturing, nonfarm-nonmanufacturing—but not by legal form of organization.

Sectoral Capital Stock

We construct estimates of capital stock by industry for each of the six asset classes and four legal forms of organization listed in Table 4.1. For equipment and structures we employ the perpetual inventory method, assuming that the capital stock is a weighted sum of past investments, with weights given by relative efficiencies of capital goods of different ages.

Producers' durable equipment, nonresidential structures, and tenant-occupied residential structures represent the largest portion of investment by individual industries in the U.S. Our primary data source is the work of Jack Faucett Associates (1973b) and the Bureau of Labor Statistics (1979) estimates compiled by Kenneth Rogers. These data are available in current and constant dollars for 156 manufacturing industries and thirty-two non-manufacturing industries. The manufacturing series are available through 1976. The nonmanufacturing series are available through 1974. Data on structures begin in 1890, and data on equipment begin in 1921. Tenant-occupied nonhousekeeping residential structures—hotels, motels, and dormitories—are included, while tenant-occupied housekeeping residential structures owned by nonprofit institutions and the real estate industry, are excluded.

We have extended current-dollar manufacturing investment through 1978, using growth rates from the Bureau of the Census *Annual Survey of Manufactures* (1978, 1980) for 1976 and 1978, and from the *Census of Manufactures* (Bureau of the Census, 1981) for 1977. We extend current-dollar nonmanufacturing investment series through 1978, using growth rates from the Bureau of Economic Analysis plant and equipment expenditure surveys published in the *Survey of Current Business* (no date). These data are available only for the sum of plant and equipment on a company basis.

We extend the deflators employed in the Faucett–BLS study through 1979, using the same methodology. We combine implicit deflators for investment expenditures from the U.S. national income and product accounts, Tables 7.19 and 7.20 from the *Survey of Current Business* (no date). For this purpose we employ weights developed by averaging the shares of investment expenditures by class of asset from the 1963 and 1967 capital transactions matrices constructed by the Bureau of Economic Analysis (1975a).

For nonresidential structures the weights are aggregated to correspond to the eleven U.S. national income and product account investment deflators from Table 7.19 of the *Survey of Current Business*. For producers' durable equipment the weights correspond precisely to twenty-two U.S. national income and product accounts deflators from Table 7.20 of the *Survey of Current Business*.

Information on tenant-occupied housekeeping residential structures investment is taken directly from the Bureau of Economic Analysis study, *Fixed Nonresidential Business and Residential Capital in the United States, 1925–1975* (1976a, henceforward, capital stock study). Except for the portion originating in nonprofit institutions, this investment is allocated to the real estate industry. Unpublished capital stock study data are available for 1890–1980, in both current and constant prices.

We divide investment in agriculture between agricultural production and agricultural services in proportion to capital consumption allowances in each industry. Capital consumption allowances by industry in current dollars are available from the Bureau of Economic Analysis study, *Fourteen Current Dollar Components of Gross Product Originating by Industry* (1981a).

Control totals for structures and producers' durable equipment are constructed in two stages. First, investment in structures and equipment is controlled to the totals for structures and producers' durable equipment from the Bureau of Economic Analysis *The U.S. National Income and Product Accounts of the United States, 1929–1976: Statistical Tables* (1981b). The Bureau of Economic Analysis capital stock study includes information on investment by type of asset and legal form of organization for both manufacturing and nonmanufacturing industries. Control totals for investment in these categories are derived by applying capital stock study shares to totals from the U.S. national income and product accounts. Second, the distribution of investment among nonmanufacturing industries is adjusted to reflect capital consumption allowances in those industries.

Shares of investment in producers' durable equipment in current and constant prices for households, institutions, manufacturing industries, and nonmanufacturing industries are obtained from the capital stock study. Shares of investment in structures in current and constant prices are obtained for the following categories of investment: owner-occupied residential structures assigned to households; tenant-occupied housekeeping and nonhousekeeping residential structures, nonresidential structures assigned to institutions; nonresidential structures assigned to manufacturing industries; and tenant-occupied housekeeping and nonhousekeeping residential structures, and nonresidential structures assigned to nonmanufacturing industries. Tenant occupied nonhousekeeping residential structures investments are allocated among several industries. We assign tenant-occupied housekeeping residential structures investment to investment in the finance, insurance, and real estate industries.[1] All investment in residential structures is included in our accounts.

Institutional investment from the capital stock study includes only nonprofit institutions serving persons, while the Bureau of Labor Statistics (1979) category "medical and educational services and nonprofit organizations" includes social and fraternal clubs and excludes residential structures. To reconcile these classifications, we deducted institutional investment (from the capital stock study, net of residential structures) from the sum of the BLS nonprofit institutional and service-industry investment, to generate service-industry investment as a residual. Household and institutional investment by the asset classes listed in Table 4.1 are generated in the same manner as the investment series included in the Christensen–Jorgenson national income accounting system (1969, 1970, 1973b).

The second step in imposing control totals is to distribute plant and equipment investment among the nonmanufacturing industries. We distribute investment among all industries except households and institutions, and among all types of plant and equipment, except for tenant-occupied housekeeping residential structures. We first estimate capital consumption allowances for each nonmanufacturing industry at historical cost, on the basis of our initial estimates of investment for that industry.[2] To redistribute investment among industries we multiply investment for each industry by the ratio of capital consumption allowances from the Bureau of Economic Analysis study of gross product originating to our estimate of capital consumption allowances at historical cost for the period 1948–1979. Finally, we control investment for all nonmanufacturing industries to the same totals as before.

Data on the transfer of assets between the public and private sectors can be obtained from two alternative sources. In the U.S. national income and product accounts, assets are valued at the price actually paid for the asset at the time of the transfer. In the capital stock study the value of government assets not well suited to private use is estimated. The value of other assets is based on the cost of acquisition. Government-owned, privately operated assets are transferred to the private sector at the time of sale.

We use Jack Faucett Associates' data (1973b) for government-owned, privately operated investment. This investment is transferred to private industry at acquisition cost on the date it was first leased. Jack Faucett Associates did not separate nonmanufacturing, government-owned, privately operated investment from investment originating and remaining in the private sector. We control private investment, including government-owned, privately operated investment, to private investment as reported in the U.S. national income and product accounts. To obtain estimates of the quantity of government-owned, privately operated investment, we apply investment deflators from the Bureau of Labor Statistics study (1979) to the corresponding current-dollar investment series.

Inventory investment for all industries except farming is constructed in two stages. First we estimate the quantity of corporate and noncorporate inventory stocks for all industries. Second we control the quantity of corporate and noncorporate inventory investment to totals derived from unpublished Bureau of Economic Analysis data. We obtain prices and quantities of corporate and noncorporate capital stocks, for twenty-one manufacturing industries and nine nonmanufacturing industries, from John Hinrichs of the Bureau of Economic Analysis. Four industries require further disaggregation;[3] for this purpose we use constant-dollar capital stock distributions, available from the report of Jack Faucett Associates, *Measures of Working Capital* (1973c), and constant-dollar value-added distributions available from Table 6.2 of the *Survey of Current Business*. Aggregate inventory stocks for each sector are then allocated between corporate and noncorporate components.

We estimate inventory investment by taking the first differences of inventory stocks. We employ control totals for the quantity of corporate and noncorporate nonfarm inventory investment, from the Christensen–Jorgenson aggregate national income accounts (1969, 1970, 1973b). Christensen and Jorgenson derive noncorporate inventory investment by taking the first differences of stock figures available from Shirley Loftus (1972), as updated by John Hinrichs. Corporate inventory investment is obtained by taking the change in nonfarm business inventories from Table 1.2 of the *Survey of Current Business*, less the estimated noncorporate investment.

Aggregate inventory stock from Hinrichs and Loftus are not equal to stocks generated from the U.S. national income and product accounts data. This is due to small discrepancies in the inventory valuation adjustment component of inventory investment. Farm inventory investment is taken directly from Table 1.1 and Table 1.2 of the *Survey of Current Business* and allocated to the noncorporate sector. Implicit investment deflators are derived from the unpublished Bureau of Economic Analysis data. The deflators are scaled such that the value of inventory investment is equal to data available from Table 1.1 of the *Survey of Current Business*.[4]

Land investment is derived from data on land stocks. The value of land for the economy as a whole, by legal form of organization, is based on estimates by Christensen and Jorgenson (1969, 1970, 1973b). Christensen and

Jorgenson employ earlier estimates by Goldsmith (1962) and Manvel (1968). Land stock is allocated among seven industry categories, in proportion to estimates for 1952–1966 on a corporate and noncorporate basis by Grace Milgrim (1973, Tables II-2, II-11, II-14). We assume that the relative distribution of land by corporate and noncorporate sectors among the seven industry aggregates remains constant at the 1952 distribution for earlier years and at the 1966 distribution for later years. Estimates of tenant-occupied residential and nonresidential structures stock by industry are used to allocate industry aggregates among the forty-six industries of our study. Sectoral land investment is then derived by taking the first differences of the sectoral land stocks.

We employ a single land deflator for all industries, taken from Christensen and Jorgenson (1969, 1970, 1973b). They use Goldsmith's (1962) private land stock in current and constant dollars for 1946 and 1947. The flow of funds accounts balance sheet data on the market value of land, from the Board of Governors of the Federal Reserve System (1981), is the current-dollar estimate for all subsequent years. Constant-dollar estimates and the deflator are derived from the assumption that the total stock of land is constant.

We allocate investment in consumer durables and owner-occupied residential structures to households. Investment in land associated with owner-occupied residential structures is zero, since we assume that the stock of such land is constant. We treat expenditures on consumer durables as investment, following Christensen and Jorgenson (1969, 1973b). This treatment differs from that in the U.S. national income and product accounts. Owner-occupied residential structures investment is generated by applying shares from the capital stock study to residential structures investment totals from the U.S. national income and product accounts. We do not allocate producers' durable equipment, nonresidential structures, or inventory investment to the household.

We allocate producers' durable equipment associated with residential and nonresidential structures investment and with nonresidential and tenant-occupied housekeeping and nonhousekeeping residential structures investment to nonprofit institutions serving persons. Land investment is zero, since we assume that the stock of such land is constant. We assume that institutions do not hold inventories.

To estimate capital stocks in the form of equipment and structures, we require data on investment and relative efficiencies of capital goods of different ages for each industrial sector. We assume that capital goods in the form of inventories and land do not decline in efficiency with age, so that the change in capital stock from period to period is equal to investment. For these assets we require only data on investment and on the initial levels of capital stock for each sector.

To derive replacement by industry for all sectors except households and institutions, we begin by creating an annual matrix of sectoral investment by detailed asset class: twenty-two producers' durable equipment and ten private nonresidential structures categories.[5] For manufacturing and nonmanufacturing sectors, we use an RAS procedure,[6] where the column controls are sectoral investment levels and the row controls are investment levels by asset type, from the capital stock study. The matrix of sectoral investment by asset class is initialized in 1965 by investment data from the Bureau of Labor Statistics (1979). Initial values for years other than 1965 are taken from the final investment matrix for the adjacent year. These matrices are used to create investment by industry by detailed asset class. Sectoral investment flows for total equipment and total structures separately are sums of entries by asset class across each industry. Constant-dollar investment for household consumer durables[7] are taken from Table 2.5 of the *Survey of Current Business*. Household and institutional investment data are controlled to totals from the capital stock study.

Capital stock benchmarks are taken to be zero in 1890 for tenant-occupied residential structures and nonresidential structures, and zero in 1921 for producers' durable equipment. Capital stocks are allocated between noncorporate and corporate components of each industry in proportion to the capital consumption allowances in each component. Data on capital consumption allowances are obtained from the Bureau of Economic Analysis study of gross product originating.

Investment deflators are used as asset deflators, except for inventory stocks.[8] For the farm inventory asset deflator we employ the Bureau of Labor Statistics wholesale price index for farm products, following Christensen and Jorgenson (1969, 1970, 1973b). For the nonfarm inventory asset deflator we employ the Bureau of Labor Statistics wholesale price index for industrial commodities, again following Christensen and Jorgenson. We scale the Bureau of Economic Analysis sectoral asset deflators to produce sectoral asset deflators, so that the Bureau of Labor Statistics wholesale price index is the aggregate nonfarm inventory asset deflator.[9]

The perpetual inventory method provides the theoretical framework for our measures of capital input in current and constant prices. We employ estimates of the relative efficiencies of capital goods of different ages, derived from a comprehensive study of acquisition prices of assets of different ages by Hulten and Wykoff (1981a, 1981b, 1981c). These estimates of relative efficiencies are used to weight past investments in compiling data on capital stocks. They are also used to estimate the rental prices of capital goods of different ages, given the rental price of a new capital good.

We outline the methodology employed by Hulten and Wykoff by first considering vintage price systems under geometric decline in efficiency of a durable good with age. Under geometric decline in efficiency, both the rental price of capital services and the acquisition price of a capital asset decline geometrically with the age of a durable good. The rate of decline in efficiency can be estimated from a sample of prices for acquisition of capital goods of different ages.

The econometric model for vintage price functions gives the price of acquisition of a capital good as a function of the age of the capital good and the time-period of observation. This model can be generalized by introducing appropriate transformations of the prices of acquisition, the ages of capital goods, and the time-period of observation. Hulten and Wykoff (1981b) employ a Box–Cox transformation of all three variables and estimate separate parameters for each variable from a sample of prices for acquisition of capital goods.

A further generalization of the econometric model of vintage price functions has been proposed by Hall (1971). This generalization is appropriate for durable goods with a number of varieties that are perfect substitutes in production. Each variety is characterized by a number of characteristics that affect relative efficiency.[10] As an illustration, Hall analyzes a sample of prices for half-ton pickup trucks with characteristics such as wheelbase, shipping weight, displacement, ratio of bore to stroke, horsepower, torque, and tire width.

Hulten and Wykoff (1981b) have implemented an econometric model of vintage price functions for eight categories of assets in the United States: tractors, construction machinery, metalworking machinery, general industrial equipment, trucks, autos, industrial buildings, and commercial buildings. In 1977 these categories included fifty-five percent of investment expenditures on producers' durable equipment and forty-two percent of expenditures on nonresidential structures.

With perfect substitutability among durable goods of different ages market equilibrium implies the existence of a vintage price function for each durable good. This function gives the price of acquisition as a function of age and the price of a new durable good of the same type, expressed as a function of time. Vintage price functions for each category of assets can be estimated from annual observations on used asset prices.

In the estimation of econometric models based on vintage price functions, the sample of used asset prices is "censored" by the retirement of assets from service. The price of acquisition for assets that have been retired from service is equal to zero. If only surviving assets are included in a sample of used asset prices, the sample is censored by excluding assets that have been retired. In order to correct the resulting bias in estimates of vintage price functions, Hulten and Wykoff (1981b) multiply the prices of surviving assets of each vintage by the probability of survival, expressed as a function of age.[11]

Vintage price functions for commercial and industrial buildings are summarized in Table 4.2. For each class of assets the rate of economic depreciation is tabulated as a function of the age of the asset. The natural logarithm of the price is regressed on age and time to obtain an average rate of depreciation, which Hulten and Wykoff refer to as the best geometric rate (BGA). The square of the multiple correlation coefficient (R^2) is given as a measure of the goodness of fit of the geometric approximation to the fitted vintage price function for each asset. Vintage price functions are estimated with and without the correction for censored sample bias described above.

The first conclusion that emerges from the data presented in Table 4.2 is that a correction for censored sample bias is extremely important in the estimation of vintage price functions. The Hulten-Wykoff study is the first to employ such a correction. The second conclusion reached by Hulten and Wykoff (1981b) is that " *a constant rate of depreciation can serve as a reasonable statistical approximation to the underlying Box-Cox rates even though the latter are not geometric.* [Their italics.] This result, in turn, supports those who use the single parameter depreciation approach in calculating capital stocks using the perpetual inventory method."

In Table 4.3 we present rates of economic depreciation derived from the best geometric approximation approach of Hulten and Wykoff for all assets employed in the U.S. national income and product accounts. Hulten and Wykoff have compared the best geometric depreciation rates presented in Table 4.3 with depreciation rates employed by the Bureau of Economic Analysis in perpetual inventory estimates of capital stock. The Hulten-Wykoff rate for equipment averages 0.133, while the BEA rate averages .141, so that the two rates are very similar. The Hulten-Wykoff rate for structures is 0.037, while the BEA rate is 0.060; these rates are substantially different.

Hulten and Wykoff (1981b) have summarized studies of economic depreciation completed prior to their own study. The most common methodology for such studies is based on vintage price functions. This methodology was first employed by Terborgh (1954) and has been used for studies of automobiles by Ackerman (1973), Cagan (1965), Chow (1957, 1960), Ohta and Griliches (1976), Ramm (1970), and Wykoff (1970). The vintage price approach

Table 4.2.   Rates of economic depreciation (annual percentage rates)

Age	With censored sample correction		Without censored sample correction	
	Commercial	Industrial	Commercial	Industrial
5	2.85	2.99	2.66	2.02
10	2.64	3.01	1.84	1.68
15	2.43	3.04	1.48	1.50
20	2.30	3.07	1.27	1.39
30	2.15	3.15	1.02	1.25
40	2.08	3.24	0.88	1.17
50	2.04	3.34	0.79	1.11
60	2.02	3.45	0.72	1.06
70	2.02	3.61	1.05	1.28
BGA	2.47	3.61	1.05	1.28
R^2	0.985	0.997	0.971	0.995

Source: Hulten and Wykoff (1981a), Table 5, p. 387; commercial corresponds to office and industrial corresponds to factory. "BGA" is the best geometric average of depreciation rates in each column.

is used in studies of prices of tractors by Griliches (1960), pick-up trucks by Hall (1971), machine tools by Beidleman (1976), ships by Lee (1978), and residential housing by Chinloy (1977). Unfortunately, none of these studies correct for censored sample bias; the results presented in Table 4.2 above demonstrate the importance of such a correction.

An alternative to the vintage price approach is to employ rental prices rather than prices of acquisition to estimate the pattern of decline in efficiency. This approach has been employed by Malpezzi, Ozanne, and Thibodeau (1980) to analyze rental price data on residential structures and by Taubman and Rasche (1969) to study rental price data on commercial structures. While leases on residential property are very frequently one year or less in duration, leases on commercial property are typically for much longer periods of time. Since the rental prices are constant over the period of the lease, estimates based on annual rental prices for commercial property are biased toward the one-hoss-shay pattern found by Taubman and Rasche; Malpezzi, Ozanne, and Thibodeau find rental price profiles for residential property that decline geometrically.

A second alternative to the vintage price approach is to analyze investment for replacement purposes. This approach was originated by Meyer and Kuh (1957) and has been employed by Eisner (1972), Feldstein and Foot (1974)

Table 4.3. Asset classes and rates of economic depreciation (annual percentage rates)

Producers durable equipment

1. Furniture and fixtures	11.00
2. Fabricated metal products	9.17
3. Engines and turbines	7.86
4. Tractors	16.33
5. Agricultural machinery (except tractors)	9.71
6. Construction machinery (except tractors)	17.22
7. Mining and oilfield machinery	16.50
8. Metalworking machinery	12.25
9. Special industry machinery (not elsewhere classified)	10.31
10. General industrial equipment	12.25
11. Office, computing, and accounting machinery	27.29
12. Service industry machinery	16.50
13. Electrical machinery	11.79
14. Trucks, buses, and truck trailers	25.37
15. Autos	33.33
16. Aircraft	18.33
17. Ships and boats	7.50
18. Railroad equipment	6.60
19. Instruments	14.73
20. Other	14.73

Private nonresidential structures

1. Industrial	3.61
2. Commercial	2.47
3. Religious	1.88
4. Educational	1.88
5. Hospital and institutional	2.33
6. Other	4.54
7. Railroads	1.76
8. Telephone and telegraph	3.33
9. Electric light and power	3.00
10. Gas	3.00
11. Other public utilities	4.50
12. Farm	2.37
13. Mining exploration, shafts, and wells	5.63
14. Other	2.90

Source: Jorgenson and Sullivan (1981), Table 1, p. 179.

and Coen (1976, 1980). Coen (1980) compares the explanatory power of alternative patterns of decline in efficiency in a model of investment behavior that also includes the price of capital services. For equipment he finds that eleven of twenty-one two-digit manufacturing industries are characterized by geometric decline in efficiency, three by sum of the years' digits and seven by straight-line. For structures he finds that fourteen industries are characterized by geometric decline, five by straight-line and two by one-hoss-shay patterns. Hulten and Wykoff (1981b) conclude that: "The weight of Coen's study is evidently on the side of the geometric and near-geometric forms of depreciation."

Sectoral Property Compensation

For an asset with a geometrically declining pattern of efficiency, the rental price of capital services takes the form

$$p_K(T) = p_I(T-1)r(T) + \delta p_I(T) - [p_I(T) - p_I(T-1)].$$

Given the level of capital stock, the price of investment goods, and the rate of depreciation, the rate of return on capital is the only variable that remains to be determined in the rental price of capital services.

For a sector not subject to direct or indirect taxes on property income, the value of property compensation is equal to the value of capital services. We can solve for the rate of return, given data on property compensation for the sector:

$$r(T) =$$

$$\frac{property\ compensation - \{\ \delta p_I(T) - [p_I(T) - p_I(T-1)]\ \}\ A(T-1)}{p_I(T-1)A(T-1)}$$

The rate of return is the ratio of property compensation, less depreciation and plus capital gains, to the value of assets at the beginning of the period. For a sector with more than one type of asset the value of property compensation is equal to the sum of the values of capital services over all assets. We assume that the rate of return is the same for all assets.

We have constructed estimates of capital stock by industry, cross-classified by the four legal forms of organization and six types of assets listed in Table 4.1. Private households and nonprofit institutions are treated as separate sectors; capital stocks for the remaining forty-four industrial sectors are divided between noncorporate and corporate business. In measuring rates of return we must take into account differences among legal forms of organization in the tax treatment of property compensation. Households and institutions are not subject to direct taxes, but they are subject to property taxes. Noncorporate business is subject to direct taxation, through the personal income tax. Corporate business is subject to both personal and corporate income taxes. Both noncorporate and corporate businesses are subject to property taxes.

The expression for the rental price of capital services can be modified to incorporate property taxes, by adding the rate of taxation, say $\tau(T)$, multiplied by the price of investment goods:

$$p_K(T) = p_I(T-1)r(T) + \delta p_I(T)\,[p_I(T) - p_I(T-1)] + p_I(T)\tau(T).$$

To estimate the rate of return, set property compensation equal to the value of capital services, as before. The rate of return is the ratio of property compensation, less depreciation, plus capital gains, and less property taxes, to the value of assets at the beginning of the period. Depreciation, capital gains, property taxes, and the value of assets are sums over all assets.

For forty-four of the industrial sectors listed in Table 3.1, property compensation is the sum of corporate and noncorporate property compensation. Both components of property compensation are obtained from the Bureau of Economic Analysis (1981a) study of gross product origins. Property compensation for a typical industrial sector takes the form given in Table 4.4.

To estimate rental prices for the corporate sector of each industry we must take into account the taxation of corporate income. For producers' durable equipment, the rental price of capital services, modified to take into account the corporate income tax and indirect business taxes, takes the form

$$p_K(T) = \left[\frac{1-u(T)z(T)-k(T)+y(T)}{1-u(T)}\right]\left[p_I(T-1)r(T)+\delta p_I(T)-[p_I(T)] - p_I(T-1)\right]$$

$$+ p_I(T)\tau(T),$$

where $u(T)$ is the corporate income tax rate, $z(T)$ is the present value of capital consumption allowances on one dollar's worth of investment, and $k(T)$ is the rate of the investment tax credit. The variable $y(T)$ is used to account for deduction of the investment tax credit from the value of an asset in calculating depreciation for tax purposes in 1962 and 1963:

$$y(T) = \begin{cases} k(T)u(T)z(T), & (T = 1962,\ 1963), \\ 0, & (T \neq 1962,\ 1963). \end{cases}$$

Table 4.4. Sectoral property compensation: current prices

Corporate property compensation

1. Corporate net interest
2. + Corporate capital consumption allowances
3. + Corporate inventory valuation adjustment
4. + Business transfer payments
5. + Corporate profits before tax
6. + Indirect business taxes allocated to corporate capital assets
7. = Corporate property compensation

Noncorporate property compensation

1. Noncorporate net interest
2. + Noncorporate capital consumption allowances
3. + Noncorporate inventory valuation adjustment
4. + Rental income of persons
5. + Indirect business taxes allocated to noncorporate capital assets
6. + Return to capital of self-employed persons
7. + Subsidies
8. + Statistical discrepancy allocated to property compensation
9. = Noncorporate property compensation

For tenant-occupied residential and nonresidential structures the equation for the rental price of capital services is the same as for producers' durable equipment. For inventories and land the depreciation rate δ, the present value of capital consumption allowances $z(T)$, and the rate of investment tax credit $k(T)$ are all equal to zero.

We first present the sources of data on property compensation for corporate and noncorporate business by industrial sector. Our primary data source is the Bureau of Economic Analysis study of gross product originating. We have supplemented this study with additional data on indirect business taxes allocated to capital assets. Finally, we have allocated noncorporate income between property compensation and the labor compensation of self-employed persons. To estimate rates of return by sector, we combined data on sectoral property compensation with data on depreciation and revaluation of assets.

In our sectoral production accounts, property compensation is defined from the point of view of the producer. The components of sectoral property compensation are taken directly from the Bureau of Economic Analysis study of gross product originating. This study presents information only for public utilities as a whole. We allocate property compensation before taxes among electric utilities, gas utilities, and water and sanitary services, in proportion to the value added in these industries, from a study by Jack Faucett Associates (1973a).[12]

Indirect business taxes allocated to capital assets are estimated from unpublished worksheet data by industry from the Bureau of Economic Analysis. These taxes include property taxes, motor vehicle taxes, and other taxes such as corporate franchise, occupational and business, and severance taxes. Data on the income of self-employed persons are available only as the sum of labor and property compensation. The methodology for dividing the total between labor and property compensation is presented in the discussion of the nominal rate of return.

The statistical discrepancy allocated to property compensation is determined as a by-product of the rate of return calculations. We distribute the total statistical discrepancy across all producing industries in proportion to each industry's share of the income of self-employed persons. The division of the statistical discrepancy between property compensation and labor compensation is determined in measuring the rate of return.[13] The statistical discrepancy must be allocated to outlay, to satisfy the identity that the value of input is equal to the value of output for each sector.

For each industrial sector the sum of corporate plus noncorporate property compensation is equal to total property compensation. Several components of property compensation are allocated either to corporate or to noncorporate property compensation. We assume that all business transfer payments originate in the corporate sector. We allocate to the noncorporate sector all rental income of persons,[14] return to capital of self-employed persons, subsidies, and the statistical discrepancy allocated to property compensation. Net interest and indirect business taxes allocated to capital assets are not available for corporate and noncorporate business separately. We allocate these components of property compensation in proportion to capital consumption allowances for the two legal forms of organization.[15]

We employ totals for corporate financial and corporate nonfinancial net interest from Table 1.13 of the *Survey of Current Business,* to control our estimates of net interest. It is important to control financial and nonfinancial net interest separately, as the control totals for the two categories are opposite in sign. We include the following financial industries in the finance, insurance, and real estate industry: banks, credit agencies, holding and investment companies, security and commodity dealers, insurance carriers, and insurance agents.

We employ the totals for corporate and noncorporate indirect business taxes allocated to capital assets from the Christensen–Jorgenson national income accounting system (1969, 1970, 1973b) to control our estimates. Christensen and Jorgenson use unpublished estimates from the Bureau of Economic Analysis for the value of corporate property taxes from 1948 to the present. Other indirect business taxes are allocated in proportion to the value of beginning-of-period capital stock in the corporate and noncorporate sectors.

Our measures of household and institutional property compensation are derived by using a methodology parallel to that of the Christensen–Jorgenson national accounting system. Property compensation before taxes is calculated by using our own estimates of household and institutional capital stocks and replacement. Household property compensation before taxes is defined by the formula

      space rental value of owner-occupied farm residential structures
+   space rental value of owner-occupied nonfarm residential structures
−   associated purchases of goods and services, owner-occupied farm residential structures
−   associated purchases of goods and services, owner-occupied nonfarm residential structures
+   service flow from consumers durables.

Institutional property compensation before taxes is defined to be the sum of

      space rental value of institutional structures
      equity return on implicit rental of institutional real estate
      service flow from institutional producers' durable equipment.

The income components related to nonfarm residential structures and the space rental value of owner-occupied farm residential structures, including a net rent value, are taken from Table 8.8 of the *Survey of Current Business*. The data for associated purchases of goods and services for owner-occupied farm residential structures are generated by Christensen and Jorgenson under the assumption that such purchases are proportional to space rental value. The space rental value includes the value of property taxes on owner-occupied residential structures, which are included in outlay.

We transfer household property compensation components from the real estate industry to the household industry, to maintain consistency between capital accounts and production accounts. The service flow from consumer durables is imputed from the rate of return on real estate held by households and from the value of total personal property taxes. The rate of return derivation will be discussed in a later section. Personal property taxes include the following state and local taxes, listed in Table 3.3 of the *Survey of Current Business:* personal motor vehicle licenses, personal property, and other personal taxes.

The space rental figures are taken from Table 8.8 of the *Survey of Current Business.* Net rent is not included in the imputation of space rental value by the Bureau of Economic Analysis. We impute space rental value from the rate of return on real estate held by households. The service flow from institutional producers' durable equipment is also imputed from the rate of return on real estate held by households.

To maintain consistency between capital accounts and production accounts, we reallocate income components not associated with institutions serving persons from nonprofit institutions to the service industry in the Bureau of Economic Analysis study of gross product originating. We also reallocate income representing space rental value from the real estate industry to institutions.[16]

Following Christensen and Jorgenson (1969, 1970, 1973b), the nominal rate of return on corporate capital assets, after corporate profits taxes and indirect business taxes are allocated to corporate capital assets for each sector, can be defined as follows:

$r(T) =$ (corporate property compensation before taxes

　　　　− corporate indirect business taxes allocated to property compensation

　　　　− corporate depreciation

　　　　+ corporate revaluation

　　　　− corporate profits tax liability)

　　　　/ current value of corporate capital stock at the beginning of the period.

The sectoral rates of return are defined from the point of view of the producer. The value of capital service flows is equal to property compensation before taxes.

We have discussed the derivation of all components of the nominal rate of return, except for the corporate profits tax liability. To construct corporate profits tax liabilities for all producing industries we begin with data from Table 6.22 of the *Survey of Current Business.* Data on corporate profit tax liabilities for 1979 are available only for the following aggregates: agriculture, forestry and fisheries; mining; construction; manufacturing nondurables; manufacturing durables; transportation; communication; utilities; trade; finance; insurance and real estate; and services. We allocate corporate tax liabilities among individual industries in proportion to the 1978 distribution of these liabilities.

To translate the corporate tax liability in Table 6.22 (*Survey of Current Business*) from a company to an establishment basis, we first calculate the ratio of corporate profits before taxes on an establishment basis, from the Bureau of Economic Analysis study of gross product originating, to corporate profits before taxes on a company basis, from Table 6.21 of the *Survey of Current Business*. Corporate tax liability estimates are then multiplied by these ratios to obtain an initial estimate of the value of corporate profits tax liability on an establishment basis. As a final step these estimates are controlled to total corporate profits tax liability.

The income of self-employed persons must be divided between property compensation and labor compensation. We could assume that self-employed workers earn the same wages per hour as wage and salary workers, or that corporate and noncorporate nominal rates of return on capital assets are equal. We select the second of these two alternatives and employ the corporate rates of return to obtain noncorporate property compensation before taxes, including the income of self-employed persons allocated to property compensation. The portion of the income of self-employed persons allocated to labor compensation is determined as a residual.[17]

Due to the high degree of vertical integration of the petroleum and primary metal industries, we assume that capital assets are correctly allocated within these industries but that property income is not appropriately allocated to the capital assets that generate the income. We calculate the corporate nominal rate of return and income tax rate jointly for the crude and refined petroleum industries and for the metal mining and primary metal industries. The company-to-establishment ratio applied to corporate profits tax liability is calculated for the sum of the crude and refined petroleum industries and for the sum of metal mining and primary metal industries.

The nominal rate of return on residential structures and land held by households after property taxes is employed as the household and institutional rate of return for all types of assets. Our derivation follows that of Christensen and Jorgenson (1969, 1970, 1973b). The rate of return on residential structures and land held by households is defined as follows:

$r(T)$ = (space rental value for owner-occupied residential property
  − property taxes, owner-occupied residential property
  − depreciation, owner-occupied residential property
  + revaluation, owner-occupied residential property)
  / current value of beginning-of-period capital stock,
    owner-occupied residential property.

Space rental value is defined as the sum of the components of household property compensation, excluding services from consumer durables. Property taxes on owner-occupied residential structures and the associated land are obtained from Table 8.8 of the *Survey of Current Business*. It is assumed that all indirect business taxes and nontaxes reported in that table are property taxes. Depreciation, revaluation, and capital stock values include the values of owner-occupied residential structures and the associated land.

We have already discussed the derivation of the nominal rate of return $r(T)$ and replacement. Under geometric deterioration in efficiency of assets, depreciation is equal to replacement, so that the rate of depreciation is equal to the rate of replacement. The investment tax credit rate for equipment and structures $k(T)$ is taken from estimates by Jorgenson and Sullivan (1981).[18]

To calculate the present value of depreciation deductions on one dollar's worth of investment, $z(T)$, we create a weighted average of the present values for depreciation under the different methods used for tax purposes. The weights are taken from the annual matrix of sectoral investment by asset class, described above. We calculate the share of investment in each asset class by industry. The present value of depreciation deductions on one dollar's worth of investment, $z(T)$, by industry for plant and equipment, is equal to the sum of the products of the shares and present values by asset class, as developed by Jorgenson and Sullivan (1981).

We have discussed the generation of the corporate profits tax liability on an establishment basis by industry. Corporate profits tax liability is adjusted for the investment tax credit. The effective corporate income tax rate is calculated on a base of corporate property compensation, net of indirect business taxes allocated to capital assets, and adjusted for the value of imputed depreciation deductions and the investment tax credit. The parameter $y(T)$ adjusts the value of the investment tax credit rate to account for the calculation in 1962 and 1963 of the value of an asset for depreciation purposes, net of the value of the investment tax credit.

We assume that the rate of indirect business taxes allocated to capital assets, $\tau(T)$, is equal across all types of assets for a particular industry and legal form of organization. This rate is computed as the ratio of the value of indirect business taxes allocated to capital assets, to the value of beginning-of-period capital stock.

The capital service prices for household owner-occupied residential structures and for consumer durables are analogous to those for noncorporate business. The rate of return on all household and institutional assets is assumed to be equal to the rate of return on residential structures and the associated land held by households. We assume that the rate of indirect business taxes allocated to capital assets, $\tau(T)$, is equal for owner-occupied residential structures and the associated land. We calculate this rate as the ratio of the value of property taxes to the current value of beginning-of-period capital stocks. The rate for consumer durables is the ratio of total personal property taxes to the current value of beginning-of-period capital stock of consumer durables. The prices of capital services for all institutional assets are analogous to those for households, except that no indirect business taxes are paid on assets.

Indices of Sectoral Capital Input

We have outlined the development of data on capital stock and the rental price of capital services for each industrial sector, cross-classified by asset class and legal form of organization. To construct an index of capital input for each industrial sector, we assume that sectoral capital input, say $\{K_i\}$, can be expressed as a translog function of its individual components, say $\{K_{ki}\}$. The corresponding index of sectoral capital input is a translog quantity index of individual capital inputs:

$$\ln K_i(T) - \ln K_i(T-1) = \sum \bar{v}^i_{Kk} [\ln K_{ki}(T) - \ln K_{ki}(T-1)],$$

$$(i=1, 2,..., n),$$

where weights are given by average shares of each component in the value of sectoral property compensation:

$$\bar{v}^i_{Kk} = \frac{1}{2} [v^i_{Kk}(T) + v^i_{Kk}(T-1)], \qquad (i = 1, 2,..., n; k = 1, 2,..., p),$$

and

$$v^i_{Kk} = \frac{p^i_{Kk} K_{ki}}{\sum p^i_{Kk} K_{ki}}, \qquad (i = 1, 2,..., n; k = 1, 2,..., p).$$

The value shares are computed from data on capital services $\{K_{ki}\}$ and the rental price of capital services $\{p^i_{Kk}\}$, cross-classified by asset class and legal form of organization. Property compensation for the sector as a whole, $\sum p^i_{Kk} K_{ki,}$ is controlled to property compensation by industry from the U.S. national income accounts.

The flow of capital services for each of the components of capital input $\{K_{ki}(T)\}$ is proportional to capital stock, say $\{A_{ki}(T-1)\}$:

$$K_{ki}(T) = Q^i_{Kk} A_{ki}(T-1), \qquad\qquad (i = 1, 2,..., n; k = 1, 2,..., p).$$

The constants of proportionality $\{Q^i_{Kk}\}$ transform capital stock into a flow of capital services. The translog quantity indices of sectoral capital input $\{K_i\}$ can be expressed in terms of their components $\{K_{ki}\}$ or in terms of the components of sectoral capital stock $\{A_{ki}\}$:

$$\ln K_i(T) - \ln K_i(T-1) = \sum \bar{v}^i_{Kk}[\ln K_{ki}(T) - \ln K_{ki}(T-1)],$$

$$= \sum \bar{v}^i_{Kk}[\ln A_{ki}(T-1) - \ln A_{ki}(T-2)],$$

$$(i=1, 2,..., n).$$

We form sectoral indices of capital input from data on capital stock by industry, cross-classified by asset class and legal form of organization. Changes in the logarithms of capital stock for each component are weighted by shares in sectoral property compensation.

We can define sectoral capital stock, say $\{A_i(T-1)\}$, as the unweighted sum of its components:

$$A_i(T-1) = \sum A_{ki}(T-1), \qquad\qquad (i = 1, 2,..., n).$$

Similarly, we can define *sectoral indices of the quality of capital stock,* say $Q^i_K(T)$, that transform sectoral measures of capital stock into the translog indices of capital input:

$$K_i(T) = Q^i_K(T) \cdot A_i(T-1), \qquad\qquad (i = 1, 2,..., n).$$

The sectoral indices of the quality of capital stock can be expressed in the form

$$\ln Q^i_K(T) - \ln Q^i_K(T-1) = \sum \bar{v}^i_{Kk}[\ln A_{ki}(T-1) - \ln A_{ki}(T-2)]$$

$$- [\ln A_i(T-1) - \ln A_i(T-2)], \qquad\qquad (i=1, 2,..., n).$$

These indices reflect changes in the composition of capital stock within each sector. Sectoral capital quality remains unchanged if all components of capital stock within a sector are growing at the same rate. Sectoral quality rises if components with higher flows of capital input per unit of capital stock are growing more rapidly. Quality falls if components with lower flows per unit are growing more rapidly.

We have generated translog indices of capital input, based on the capital stock and property compensation data described in the preceding sections, for forty-six of the fifty-one industrial sectors listed in Table 3.1. There are as many as eight categories of capital input for each industry, corresponding to our breakdown by asset class and legal form of organization. Average annual rates of growth of the translog indices of sectoral capital input are presented for six subperiods over the 1948–1979 period for all forty-six industries, in Table 4.5. Price and quantity indices of capital input and indices of the quality of capital stock are presented on an annual basis for the period 1948–1979 for each industry, in Appendix C. Annual data for the price and quantity of capital stock and total property compensation are also presented for 1948–1979 in Appendix C.

To identify differences in patterns of growth in capital input among sub-periods from 1948 to 1979, we present a classification of rates of growth by subperiod in Table 4.6. Considering the subperiods in chronological order, forty, thirty-four, twenty-five, thirty-four, forty, thirty-two, and thirty-two industries, respectively, are characterized by rates of growth in capital input greater than two percent per year. The third subperiod, 1957–1960, experienced relatively weak growth in capital input, while the first subperiod, 1948–1953, and the fifth subperiod, 1966–1969, experienced relatively strong growth. The subperiod 1957–1960 also corresponds to weak growth in labor input, while the subperiods 1948–1953 and 1966–1969 are closely comparable to the subperiod 1960–1966 in the growth of labor input. The variation in the number of industries exceeding growth in capital input at two percent per year is very similar to the variation in the number of industries with positive rates of growth of labor input.

To sharpen the comparison among subperiods, we narrow our focus to industries with annual rates of growth in capital input greater than eight percent or rates of decline more than two percent. There is a decline in the dispersion of growth rates of capital input over the period as a whole. During the subperiods 1948–1953, 1953–1957, 1957–1960, 1966–1969, and 1973–1979, eight, seven, eight, nine, and six industries, respectively, experienced decline in capital input at rates exceeding two percent or growth at rates greater than eight percent. By contrast, a total of three and four industries exceeded these limits in 1960–1966 and 1969–1973, respectively. The reduction in variability is less dramatic for capital input than for labor input, due largely to the surge of investment in the subperiod 1966–1969. Overall, growth in capital input is similar to growth of labor input in variability among subperiods.

We find it informative to consider the specific sectors that underwent rapid decline in capital input. There was no industry with a rate of decline in

Table 4.5. Sectoral capital input: rates of growth

Industry	Translog index of capital input (average annual rates of growth)						
	1948–1953	1953–1957	1957–1960	1960–1966	1966–1969	1969–1973	1973–1979
Agricultural production	0.0556	0.0162	0.0243	0.0383	0.0204	0.0196	0.0434
Agricultural services	0.1890	0.1153	−0.0227	0.0119	0.0384	0.0606	0.0650
Metal mining	0.0549	0.0369	0.0379	0.1203	0.1990	0.1087	0.0572
Coal mining	0.0833	−0.0805	−0.0276	0.0133	0.0290	0.1411	0.0601
Crude petroleum and natural gas	0.0227	0.0478	0.0415	0.0363	0.0323	0.0169	0.0163
Nonmetallic mining and quarrying	0.0190	0.0597	0.0518	0.0445	0.0798	0.1014	0.1010
Contract construction	0.0311	0.0477	0.0909	0.0778	0.0240	0.0238	−0.0073
Food and kindred products	0.0322	0.0134	0.0198	0.0234	0.0351	0.0328	0.0341
Tobacco manufacturers	0.0255	0.0151	0.0255	0.0175	−0.0200	0.0002	0.0275
Textile mill products	0.0705	0.0096	−0.0204	0.0382	0.0568	0.0264	0.0047
Apparel and other fabricated textile products	0.0345	0.0147	0.0086	0.0552	0.0666	0.0591	0.0234
Paper and allied products	0.0565	0.0679	0.0339	0.0362	0.0585	0.0186	0.0058
Printing and publishing	0.0086	0.0189	0.0146	0.0306	0.0512	0.0238	0.0075
Chemicals and allied products	0.0815	0.0501	0.0317	0.0518	0.0686	0.0309	0.0432
Petroleum and coal products	0.0267	0.0364	0.0035	−0.0032	0.0375	0.0329	0.0269
Rubber and misc. plastic products	0.0663	0.0611	0.0295	0.0605	0.0878	0.0579	0.0498
Leather and leather products	0.0427	0.0088	−0.0810	0.0186	0.0360	−0.0038	0.0068
Lumber and wood products except furniture	0.0545	0.0289	−0.0006	0.0174	0.0183	0.0489	0.0362
Furniture and fixtures	0.0290	0.0375	0.0210	0.0408	0.0608	0.0577	0.0360
Stone, clay, and glass products	0.0616	0.0670	0.0355	0.0236	0.0269	0.0227	0.0321

Table 4.5 continued

Industry	Translog index of capital input (average annual rates of growth)						
	1948–1953	1953–1957	1957–1960	1960–1966	1966–1969	1969–1973	1973–1979
Primary metal industries	0.0358	0.0240	0.0171	0.0142	0.0474	0.0038	0.0056
Fabricated metal industries	0.0488	0.0411	0.0146	0.0382	0.0574	0.0167	0.0472
Machinery except electrical	0.0707	0.0408	0.0191	0.0429	0.0718	0.0348	0.0487
Elec. machinery, eqpt., and supplies	0.0798	0.0527	0.0187	0.0689	0.0928	0.0267	0.0491
Trans. eqpt. and ordnance, except motor vehicles	0.0019	0.0340	0.0060	0.0188	0.1486	−0.0001	0.0127
Motor vehicles and equipment	0.0590	0.0530	−0.0013	0.0377	0.0228	0.0206	0.0834
Prof. photographic eqpt. and watches	0.1504	0.0887	0.0419	0.0418	0.0955	0.0444	0.0562
Misc. manufacturing industries	0.0265	0.0433	0.0100	0.0457	0.0569	0.0576	0.0452
Railroads and rail express services	0.0485	−0.0042	−0.0086	0.0100	0.0246	0.0079	0.0241
Street rail., bus lines, and taxicabs	0.0363	0.0318	−0.0290	0.0236	0.0092	0.0492	0.1347
Trucking services and warehousing	0.0213	0.0436	0.0301	0.0571	0.0928	0.0251	0.1919
Water transportation	0.0428	0.0083	0.0542	−0.0168	−0.0159	0.0183	0.0278
Air transportation	0.0302	0.0646	0.1583	0.1027	0.2883	0.0683	−0.0365
Pipelines, except natural gas	0.0970	0.0521	0.0272	0.0298	0.0205	0.0155	0.2531
Transportation services	0.1069	0.0965	0.0080	0.0198	0.0467	−0.0164	0.0443
Telephone, telegraph and misc. communication services	0.0730	0.0969	0.0958	0.0580	0.0596	0.0665	0.0360
Radio and television broadcasting	0.0223	0.0804	0.0460	0.0946	0.1328	0.0566	0.0703
Electric utilities	0.1195	0.0818	0.0445	0.0293	0.0670	0.1125	0.0728
Gas utilities	0.1075	0.0566	0.0433	0.0351	0.0504	0.0298	0.0057
Water supply and sanitary services	−0.0103	0.0186	0.0044	0.0011	0.0122	0.0060	−0.0182

Table 4.5 continued

Industry	Translog index of capital input (average annual rates of growth)						
	1948–1953	1953–1957	1957–1960	1960–1966	1966–1969	1969–1973	1973–1979
Wholesale trade	0.0440	0.0357	0.0252	0.0449	0.0730	0.0572	0.0490
Retail trade	0.0250	0.0655	0.0208	0.0392	0.0332	0.0390	0.0234
Finance, insurance, and real estate	−0.0014	0.0089	0.0080	0.0258	0.0163	0.0329	0.0149
Services excluding private households and institutions	0.0184	0.0438	0.0450	0.0667	0.0980	0.0563	0.0175
Private households	0.0799	0.0573	0.0367	0.0413	0.0511	0.0502	0.0456
Institutions	0.0439	0.0387	0.0442	0.0549	0.0288	−0.0090	0.0018

Table 4.6. Classification of rates of growth of sectoral capital input by subperiod, 1948–1979

Average rate of growth of capital input	1948–1953	1953–1957	1957–1960	1960–1966	1966–1969	1969–1973	1973–1979
Less than −2%	0	1	5	0	0	0	1
−2% to 0	2	1	3	2	2	4	2
0 to 2%	4	10	13	10	4	10	11
2% to 4%	14	9	13	15	14	14	11
4% to 6%	11	14	9	12	10	11	12
6% to 8%	7	5	0	4	7	3	4
More than 8%	8	6	3	3	9	4	5

excess of two percent from 1948–1953. During the subperiod 1953–1957, only coal mining experienced such a rate of decline. From 1957 to 1960 there were declines in excess of two percent per year in agricultural services, coal mining, textiles, leather, and local transportation. No industry underwent a decline in capital input at a rate exceeding two percent from 1960 to 1973. During the period 1973–1979, such a rate of decline occurred only in air transportation.

Many more industries experienced significant increases than declines in capital input. Growth in capital input at rates exceeding eight percent per year took place in eight industries in the subperiod 1948–1953—agricultural services, coal mining, chemicals, professional equipment, pipelines, transportation services, electric utilities, and gas utilities. During the subperiod 1953–1957, rapid growth in capital input occurred in agricultural services, professional equipment, transportation services, telecommunications, broadcasting, and electric utilities. The corresponding industries for the subperiod 1957–1960 were construction, air transportation, and telecommunications. The three industries characterized by very rapid growth in capital input during the subperiod 1960–1966 were metal mining, air transportation, and broadcasting. The subperiod 1966–1969 was characterized by very rapid growth in nine industries—metal mining, rubber, electrical machinery, transportation equipment excluding motor vehicles, professional equipment, trucking, air transportation, broadcasting, and services.

Four industries grew at rates in excess of eight percent per year during the subperiod 1969–1973: metal mining, coal mining, nonmetallic mining, and electric utilities. The subperiod 1973–1979 was characterized by rapid growth in nonmetallic mining, motor vehicles, local transportation, trucking, and pipelines. Agricultural services, metal mining, coal mining, nonmetallic mining, professional equipment, trucking, air transportation, pipelines, transportation services, telecommunications, broadcasting, and electric utilities stand out as industries with very rapid growth in capital input during more than one subperiod. Professional equipment, trucking, air transportation, broadcasting, and electric utilities were also characterized by very rapid growth in labor input in more than one subperiod.

Persistent growth in capital input at rates in excess of two percent per year for all seven subperiods characterizes thirteen of the industries included in Table 4.5. Metal mining experienced sustained growth in capital input. Within manufacturing, chemicals, rubber, furniture, stone, clay and glass, and professional equipment had rates of growth in capital input exceeding two percent in every subperiod. Trucking had substantial positive rates of growth of capital input in all seven subperiods. Finally, telecommunications, broadcasting, electric utilities, wholesale trade, retail trade, and private households all had substantial positive growth rates of capital input for all seven subperiods. Persistent growth in both capital input and labor input for all seven subperiods characterizes only the broadcasting industry. The only industry that experienced persistently low rates of growth in capital input, rates less than two percent per year in all seven subperiods, was water supply.

Alternative Measures of Sectoral Capital Input

For additional perspective on our approach to measuring capital input, compare our methodology and data sources with those of the Bureau of Labor Statistics, Denison, and Kendrick. Our measures of capital input are index numbers constructed from data on services of capital stocks and rental prices of capital services. For each type of capital input the appropriate concept of capital stock is a weighted sum of past investments, with weights given by the relative efficiencies of capital goods of different ages in production. The corresponding concept of the rental price of capital services is based on the relationship of the price of investment goods to future rental prices of capital services. The price of investment goods is a weighted sum of future service prices, with weights given by relative efficiencies.

Internal consistency of a measure of capital input requires that the same pattern of relative efficiency is employed in measuring both capital stock and the rental price of capital services. Any decline in efficiency affects the level of capital stock and the corresponding rental price of capital services symmetrically. Our estimates of capital stocks and the rental prices of capital services are based on geometrically declining relative efficiency. We have used the same pattern for both capital stock and the rental price of each asset, so that the requirement for internal consistency of our measures of capital input is met. In comparing our approach with those of the Bureau of Labor Statistics, Denison, and Kendrick, we first describe their methods and data sources for estimating capital stock. We then present their methods and sources for estimating the rental price of capital services, and attempt to determine whether the resulting measures of capital input are internally consistent.

Our estimates of capital stock in the form of equipment and structures are derived by the perpetual inventory method. This method is applied to investment data by industry, reconciled to control totals for the economy as a whole from the U.S. national product accounts. Denison and Kendrick employ estimates of capital stock for equipment and structures from the Bureau of Economic Analysis capital stock study. These estimates are also derived by the perpetual inventory method, using investment data from the U.S. national product accounts. The Bureau of Labor Statistics utilizes the perpetual inventory method to derive estimates of capital stock for equipment and structures, based on investment data from the U.S. national product accounts.

The perpetual inventory method is employed in our study and by the Bureau of Labor Statistics, Denison, and Kendrick. All four studies also utilize investment data from the U.S. national product accounts. The studies differ substantially, however, in their treatment of relative efficiencies of capital goods of different ages. In *Accounting for U.S. Economic Growth 1929–1969* (1974, 53) Denison employs Bureau of Economic Analysis estimates of capital stocks, gross and net of depreciation, based on Bulletin F service lines and straight-line depreciation. In *Accounting for Slower Economic Growth* (1979, 50), Denison utilizes Bureau of Economic Analysis estimates based on Bulletin F service lines less fifteen percent. This same set of estimates is employed in his book *Trends in American Economic Growth, 1929–1982* (1985, 65). Kendrick (1973, 29) uses Bureau of Economic Analysis estimates of capital stock, gross and net of depreciation, based on Bulletin F lines less fifteen percent, and straight-line depreciation. Kendrick (1976, 20) and Kendrick and Grossman (1980, 26) employ Bureau of Economic Analysis estimates based on Bulletin F lines less fifteen percent and double-declining-balance depreciation. This same set of estimates is utilized by Kendrick (1983, 56). The Bureau of Labor Statistics (1983, 41–45) employs relative efficiencies of capital goods of different ages, obtained by fitting hyperbolic functions to the Box–Cox functions estimated by Hulten and Wykoff (1981a, 1981b, 1981c).[22] We use the best-geometric-average (BGA) rates, fitted by Hulten and Wykoff, as described above.

At the level of individual industries, Kendrick's (1973) estimates for farming, railroads, nonrail transportation, contract construction, wholesale and retail trade, communications, and public utilities are based on the perpetual inventory method; however, his estimates for mining and manufacturing are based on balance sheet data. Moreover, Kendrick (1973) does not attempt to provide estimates of capital stock for finance, insurance, and real estate, or for services, including government enterprises, or agricultural services, forestry, and fisheries. Kendrick (1973) ultimately compares his estimates of capital stock for the sectors included in his study with estimates for the economy as a whole, but since his study does not include all private domestic economy industries, he finds it impossible to control the investment data for individual industries implied by his estimates of capital stock to totals from the U.S. national product accounts. Kendrick (1976, 21), Kendrick and Grossman (1980, 26), and Kendrick (1983, 56) utilize estimates of capital stock by Jack Faucett Associates (1973b) for sectors not covered in the earlier Kendrick (1973, 198–200) study. The investment data for individual industries, however, are not controlled to totals from the U.S. national product accounts. We exclude only the government sectors, and are thus able to control our investment data by industry to private domestic economy totals available in the U.S. national product accounts.

Our sectoral estimates of capital stock in the form of land for the economy as a whole are based on the studies by Milgrim (1973). Milgrim gives land by seven industrial aggregates, for corporate and noncorporate separately.

We further disaggregate to the forty-six industry level, according to the distribution of tenant-occupied and residential structures stock held by individual industries, maintaining aggregate control totals based on information from Goldsmith (1962) and Manvel (1968). The Bureau of Labor Statistics (1983, 47–48) employs estimates of land stocks in farming from the Department of Agriculture and in manufacturing and nonfarm-nonmanufacturing based on Manvel (1968). Denison (1974, 58) assumes that the stock of land for the nonresidential business sector is constant. Kendrick's estimate of the stock of land for nonfarm nonresidential business is based on the assumption that stocks of site land, forest land, and mineral land are proportional to the stock of structures; the stock of structures is used to extrapolate the stocks of land, using 1958 benchmark ratios from Goldsmith (1962). For farm land Kendrick uses estimates based on farm acreage, weighted by 1958 values per acre. Finally, Kendrick (1973, 159–162) assumes that residential site land is proportional to the stock of nonfarm residential structures, again using a 1958 benchmark ratio from Goldsmith (1962). To derive estimates of stocks of land for individual industries, Kendrick assumes that site land for manufacturing is proportional to the stock of structures in each industry, using 1958 benchmark ratios from *Statistics of Income* (1974). Balance sheet data for mining include land, as well as equipment and structures (Kendrick, 1973, 198–208).

Our estimates of inventory stocks are based on unpublished estimates from the Bureau of Economic Analysis and are consistent with data on net inventory investment from the U.S. national product accounts. The Bureau of Labor Statistics, Denison, and Kendrick employ BEA inventory stock estimates for the economy as a whole. Kendrick's estimates of inventory stocks at the level of individual industries are based on balance sheet data for mining and manufacturing and on BEA estimates for trade. Kendrick (1973, 31) does not include inventories in his estimates of capital stock for sectors other than mining, manufacturing, and trade.

This completes the comparison of our methods and sources for estimating capital stock with those employed by the Bureau of Labor Statistics, Denison, and Kendrick. An internally consistent measure of capital input must employ the same pattern of relative efficiency of capital goods of different ages for both capital stocks and rental prices. The requirement that estimates of rental prices of capital services must be consistent with the corresponding estimates of capital stock is very stringent. In addition, rental prices must reflect differences in the treatment of different types of assets and different legal forms of organization for tax purposes. First, the theory of investment behavior implies that nominal rates of return after taxes are equalized across assets.

Second, the tax laws require that rental prices must incorporate differences in tax treatment among assets and legal forms of business organization.

We begin our comparison with an elementary characterization of the rental price of capital services. In the absence of taxation the rental price of capital services at time T takes the form

$$p_K(T) = p_I(T-1)r(T) + p_D(T) - [p_I(T) - p_I(T-1)],$$

where depreciation, $p_D(T)$, depends on the pattern of relative efficiency. The value of the services of capital stock is the product of the rental price and the quantity of capital stock:

$$p_K(T)A(T-1) = \{ p_I(T-1)r(T) + p_D(T) - [p_I(T) - p_I(T-1)] \} \cdot A(T-1).$$

Finally, the value of capital services is equal to property compensation, so we can solve for the rate of return, given data on property compensation:

$$r(T) = \frac{\text{Property compensation} - \{ p_D(T) - [p_A(T) - p_A(T-1)] \} \cdot A(T-1)}{p_A(T-1) \cdot A(T-1)}.$$

The first and most important criterion for internal consistency of a measure of capital input is that the same pattern of relative efficiency must underlie both the estimates of capital stock and the estimates of rental prices for each class of assets. Our study employs geometric relative efficiency functions estimated by Hulten and Wykoff (1981a, 1981b, 1981c). They have shown that the best-geometric-average (BGA) rates of depreciation provide an accurate description of the decline in the price of acquisition of capital goods with age. The geometric relative efficiency functions are also consistent with evidence from studies of rental prices of capital goods and patterns of replacement investment. We utilize the same geometric rates for our estimates of capital stock and our estimates of rental prices.

The Bureau of Labor Statistics (1983, 57–59) also employs relative efficiency functions estimated by Hulten and Wykoff, but does not utilize the geometric relative efficiency functions fitted by Hulten and Wykoff. Instead, the Bureau of Labor Statistics has fitted a set of hyperbolic functions to the Box–Cox relative efficiency functions estimated by Hulten and Wykoff. Consistency between the resulting estimates of capital stocks and rental prices is preserved by implementing a full-blown system of vintage accounts for each class of assets. This set of accounts includes prices for acquisition and quantities of investment goods of all ages at each point in time. Measures of capital input based on hyperbolic and geometric relative efficiency functions are very similar.

For each class of assets, Denison's estimates of capital stock are based on a linearly declining pattern of relative efficiency. In *Sources of Economic Growth* (1962, 97–98), Denison employs a measure of capital input for equipment and structures with relative efficiency constant over the lifetime of the capital good, the "one-hoss-shay" pattern of relative efficiency we have described above. In *Why Growth Rates Differ* (1967, 140–141), Denison uses a measure of capital input with relative efficiency given by an unweighted average of the "one-hoss-shay" and straight-line patterns:

$$
d(\tau) = \begin{cases} 1 - \dfrac{\tau}{2L}, & (\tau = 0,\, 1, ..., L-1), \\[2ex] 0, & (\tau = L,\, L+1, ...,). \end{cases}
$$

In *Accounting for United States Economic Growth 1929–1969* (1974, 54–55), Denison introduces yet another measure of capital input, based on a weight of one fourth for straight-line and three fourths for "one-hoss-shay" patterns:

$$
d(\tau) = \begin{cases} 1 - \dfrac{\tau}{4L}, & (\tau = 0,\, 1, ..., L-1), \\[2ex] 0, & (\tau = L,\, L+1, ...,). \end{cases}
$$

This measure of capital input is employed by Denison in *Accounting for Slower Economic Growth* (1979, 50–52), and in *Trends in American Economic Growth, 1929–1982* (1985, 65).

For a linearly declining pattern of relative efficiency the mortality distribution can be represented in the form

$$
m(\tau) = \begin{cases} \dfrac{1}{\Theta}L & (\tau = 1,\, 2, ..., L-1), \\[2ex] 1 - \dfrac{1}{\Theta}\left[1 - \dfrac{1}{L}\right] & (\tau = L), \\[2ex] 0 & (\tau) = L+1,\, L+2, ...,), \end{cases}
$$

where Θ is unity for straight-line replacement, positive infinity for "one-hoss-shay" replacement, and two and four respectively for Denison's two averages of straight-line and "one-hoss shay." To derive the method of depreciation appropriate for this pattern, we first express depreciation for an asset of age V at time T, say p_D (T,V), in the form

$$p_D(T, V) = \sum_{\tau=1}^{\infty} m(\tau+V) \prod_{S=1}^{\tau} \frac{1}{1 + r(T+S)} \, p_K(T+\tau)$$

$$= \frac{1}{\Theta L} \sum_{\tau=1}^{L-V-1} \prod_{S=1}^{\tau} \frac{1}{1 + r(T+S)} \, p_K(T+\tau)$$

$$+ \left[1 - \frac{1}{\Theta}\left(1 - \frac{1}{L}\right)\right] \prod_{S=1}^{L-V} p_K(T+L-V).$$

Assuming that the rates of return $\{r(T+S)\}$ and the prices of capital services $\{p_K(T+\tau)\}$ are constant, we obtain the following expression for depreciation on an asset of age V:

$$p_D(V) = \frac{1}{r\Theta L} - \left[\frac{1}{r\Theta L} - 1 + \frac{1}{\Theta}\right]\left[\frac{1}{1+r}\right]^{L-V} p_K, \qquad (V = 0,\ 1,...,\ L-1).$$

Similarly, the value of a new asset is equal to the sum of depreciation over all ages,

$$p_I = \sum_{V=0}^{L-1} p_D(V),$$

$$= \frac{1}{r}\left\{\frac{1}{\Theta} - \left[\frac{1}{r\Theta L} - 1 + \frac{1}{\Theta}\right]\left[1 - \left(\frac{1}{1+r}\right)^{L}\right]\right\} p_K,$$

so that depreciation allowances appropriate for a linearly declining pattern of relative efficiency are given for each age by the formula

$$\frac{p_D(V)}{p_I} = \frac{\dfrac{1}{\Theta L} - r\left[\dfrac{1}{r\Theta L} - 1 + \dfrac{1}{\Theta}\right]\left[\dfrac{1}{1+r}\right]^{L-V}}{\dfrac{1}{\Theta} - \left[\dfrac{1}{r\Theta L} - 1 + \dfrac{1}{\Theta}\right]\left[1 - \left(\dfrac{1}{1+r}\right)^{L}\right]} \qquad (V = 0,\ 1,...,\ L-1).$$

The value of depreciation at time T for linearly declining patterns of relative efficiency is the sum over assets of all ages

$$\sum_{V=0}^{L-1} p_D(T, V) I (T-V-1) =$$

$$p_I(T) \sum_{V=0}^{L-1} \frac{\dfrac{1}{\Theta L} - r\left[\dfrac{1}{r\Theta L} - 1 + \dfrac{1}{\Theta}\right]\left[\dfrac{1}{1+r}\right]^{L-V}}{\dfrac{1}{\Theta} - \left[\dfrac{1}{r\Theta L} - 1 + \dfrac{1}{\Theta}\right]\left[1 - \left[\dfrac{1}{1+r}\right]^{L}\right]} I(T-V-1).$$

Denison employs linearly declining relative efficiency in measuring capital stock; in his three studies he employs three different weighted averages of the straight-line and "one-hoss-shay" patterns. In all three studies Denison employs the straight-line method of depreciation. For linearly declining patterns of relative efficiency, depreciation allowances are increasing, constant, or decreasing with age for values of the parameter Θ greater than, equal to, or less than $1 + 1/rL$, respectively. For the straight-line pattern depreciation allowances are decreasing with age; for the "one-hoss-shay" pattern, depreciation allowances are increasing with age. There is no value of the parameter Θ for which depreciation allowances are independent of age for investment goods of varying lifetimes, as Denison assumes. The straight-line method of depreciation is not appropriate for any of his methods of measuring capital stock, so that the resulting measures of capital input are internally inconsistent.

Kendrick (1973) employs capital stock estimates based on linearly declining relative efficiency in allocating property compensation among assets on the basis of "net earnings." Kendrick's measure of "net earnings" is based on capital consumption allowances from the U.S. national income accounts, as an estimate of depreciation. These estimates are based in turn on depreciation allowances for tax purposes and do not reflect a consistent valuation of assets over time or a consistent method of depreciation. The method of depreciation appropriate for Kendrick's estimates of capital stock based on linearly declining relative efficiency is the same as that we have given above for Denison, with the parameter Θ equal to unity:

$$\frac{p_D(V)}{p_I} = \frac{\dfrac{1}{L}\left[1 - \left[\dfrac{1}{1+r}\right]^{L-V}\right]}{1 - \dfrac{1}{rL}\left[1 - \left[\dfrac{1}{1+r}\right]^{L}\right]}, \qquad (V = 0, 1,..., L-1).$$

The value of depreciation at time T for linearly declining relative efficiency is the sum over assets of all ages:

$$\sum_{V=0}^{L-1} p_D(T, V)\, I(T-V-1) = p_I(T) \sum_{V=0}^{L-1} \frac{\dfrac{1}{L}\left[1 - \left(\dfrac{1}{1+r}\right)^{L-V}\right]}{1 - \dfrac{1}{rL}\left[1 - \left(\dfrac{1}{1+r}\right)^{L}\right]}\, I(T-V-1).$$

Kendrick (1973, 27–29) also employs alternative capital stock estimates based on constant relative efficiency in allocating property compensation among assets on the basis of "gross earnings." This is the "one-hoss-shay" pattern described above. Constant relative efficiency is also utilized by Kendrick and Grossman (1980, 26) and Kendrick (1983, 56–57). For constant relative efficiency, the appropriate method of depreciation is given, not by the declining balance pattern as assumed by Kendrick, but by the formula described above, with Θ equal to positive infinity:

$$\frac{P_D(V)}{p_I} = \frac{r\left(\dfrac{1}{1+r}\right)^{L-V}}{1 - \left(\dfrac{1}{1+r}\right)^{L}}, \quad (V = 0, 1, ..., L-1).$$

The value of depreciation at time T for constant relative efficiency is the sum

$$\sum_{V=0}^{L-1} p_D(T, V)\, I(T-V-1) = p_I(T) \sum_{V=0}^{L-1} \frac{r\left(\dfrac{1}{1+r}\right)^{L-V}}{1 - \left(\dfrac{1}{1+r}\right)^{L}}\, I(T-V-1).$$

Our overall conclusion is that none of Denison's measures of capital input satisfy the elementary criterion that the same pattern of relative efficiency must be employed in estimating capital stock and in estimating the rental price of capital services. In allocating property compensation among assets, Denison uses the straight-line method of depreciation, so that his estimates of rental prices of capital services are based on this method of depreciation. In estimating capital stocks Denison uses three different linearly declining patterns of relative efficiency. None of these patterns results in a pattern of depreciation allowances as given by the straight-line method, as Denison assumes. Similarly, neither of Kendrick's two measures of capital input is based on an internally consistent treatment of capital stock and the rental price of capital services. In estimating capital stocks Kendrick uses straight-line and "one-hoss-shay" patterns of relative efficiency. His weights based on "gross earnings" ignore differences among assets in rates of depreciation as a component of the rental price of capital services; his weights based on "net earnings" employ depreciation as calculated for tax purposes, so that neither the method for depreciation nor the valuation of assets is consistent over time.

For a sector with more than one type of asset the value of property compensation is equal to the sum of the values of capital services over all assets. The rate of return is equal to the value of property compensation, less depreciation and plus capital gains for all assets, divided by the value of all assets at the beginning of the period. This expression implies that the nominal rate of return $r(T)$, the rate of return net of depreciation and gross of capital gains on assets, is the same for all assets. It is with respect to each asset's nominal rate of return that economic agents choose the optimal mix of capital stocks, altering the composition of capital input until all nominal rates of return are equalized across asset classes. Consequently, measured property compensation should be allocated among assets on the basis of equality of the nominal rate of return for all assets. In contrast, capital service prices of individual assets are based on own rates of return for each asset, that is, the nominal rate of return less capital gains for that asset. Differences in own rates of return among assets reflect differences in rates of growth of the prices of the corresponding investment goods. The above describes our model of capital service prices and our method of allocating property compensation.

The Bureau of Labor Statistics (1983, 49–51) allocates property compensation among assets by assuming that the nominal rate of return is equalized among assets. Denison allocates property compensation on the basis of the assumption that the own rate of return is the same for all assets. This is consistent with optimizing producer behavior only if rates of growth of investment goods prices are the same for all assets. Denison's procedure ignores differences among assets in rates of growth of investment goods prices.[23]

Kendrick (1973, 31), like Denison, assumes that the own rate of return is the same for all assets, but Kendrick employs an alternative set of weights for capital input, based on property compensation gross of depreciation. Kendrick's "gross capital weights" are based on the assumption that the own rate of return, gross of depreciation, is the same for all assets within each sector. Like Denison, Kendrick ignores differences among rates of growth of investment goods prices. The capital service prices implicit in Kendrick's "gross weights" also ignore differences among rates of depreciation for all assets, depreciable and nondepreciable. Kendrick allocates depreciation to nondepreciable assets in proportion to the value of these assets in the value of total assets. This approach is also utilized by Kendrick and Grossman (1980, 26), and Kendrick (1983, 56).

Our estimates of capital services prices for each type of asset incorporate differences in property tax rates among types of assets, differences in the tax treatment of corporate and noncorporate income due to the corporate income tax, and differences between the tax treatment of equipment and structures due to differences in depreciation practices and to the investment tax credit for equipment. The Bureau of Labor Statistics (1983, 50) employs data on depreciation practices and the investment tax credit and data on differences in property tax rates among types of assets. Corporate and noncorporate assets, however, are assumed to have the same capital services prices, so the effect of the corporate income tax is ignored.

Denison and Kendrick ignore differences in property tax rates among types of assets and differences in the tax treatment of corporate and noncorporate income. In *Sources of Economic Growth* (1962) and *Why Growth Rates Differ* (1967), Denison ignores differences in the tax treatment of corporate and noncorporate income (see Denison, 1969, 10). In *Accounting for United States Economic Growth 1929–1969* (1974, 267–271), Denison employs separate estimates of corporate and noncorporate capital stock for the non-farm business sector. He derives weights for these assets from data on corporate and noncorporate income, by allocating noncorporate income between labor compensation of the self-employed and property compensation, but his procedures ignore the effect of the corporate income tax. These procedures are also utilized in *Accounting for Slower Economic Growth* (1979, 171) and *Trends in American Economic Growth, 1929–1982* (1985, 65).

Kendrick (1973) allocates noncorporate income between property compensation and labor compensation of the self-employed, on the basis of the assumption that the self-employed within each sector receive the same hourly compensation as employees. (1973, 30). He does not separate corporate and noncorporate assets in measuring capital input. This approach is also employed by Kendrick and Grossman (1980, 26) and Kendrick (1983, 56). Like Denison, Kendrick ignores the effect of corporate income tax. Both Denison and Kendrick ignore the impact of depreciation allowances for tax purposes and the investment tax credit in allocating property compensation among assets within a sector.

Conclusion

In this chapter we have developed measures of capital input that satisfy the conceptual requirements outlined in Chapter 2. Components of capital input that differ in marginal productivity are separately distinguished in measuring capital input for each of forty-six industrial sectors. Toward this end we have constructed data on capital stock and property compensation for eight types of capital input for each sector in each year from 1948 to 1979.

We have measured property compensation from the producers' point of view, including capital consumption allowances, business transfer payments, profits before taxes, net interest paid, inventory valuation adjustment, and indirect business taxes for corporations. Property compensation for noncorporate enterprises encompasses capital consumption allowances, income of unincorporated enterprises less labor compensation of the self-employed and unpaid family workers, net interest paid, rental income of persons, inventory valuation adjustment, subsidies, a statistical discrepancy, and indirect business taxes. Property compensation for households and institutions is imputed from data on rates of return, depreciation, and taxes.

Corporate income taxes are included in corporate profits before taxes, business property and other taxes are included in both corporate and noncorporate property compensation, and personal property and other taxes are included in the property compensation of households and institutions. Property compensation is allocated among assets within each sector so that all assets receive the same nominal rate of return. Allocation of property compensation among assets requires estimates of capital gains and losses for individual assets based on changes in the prices of these assets within each time period.

Our estimates of capital stock for plant and equipment are based on the perpetual inventory method, which requires historical data on investment and rates of replacement for structures and equipment for each industrial sector. We have controlled investment for all industrial sectors to totals from the U.S. national income and product accounts. Our estimates of capital stock for inventories and land are based on balance sheet data for each sector. The data on inventory stocks are based on estimates that underlie the U.S. national income and product accounts. Our estimates of capital stock for inventories and land are based on estimates that underlie the U.S. national income and product accounts and are consistent with inventory valuation adjustments for corporate and noncorporate sectors.

Our estimates of property compensation for all assets are based on the dual to the perpetual inventory method. The rates of replacement employed in our estimates of capital stock are derived from patterns of relative efficiency of investment goods of different ages for each class of asset for each industrial sector. The same patterns of relative efficiency are employed in measuring economic depreciation. Economic depreciation is used in allocating property compensation within each sector among assets employed in that sector.

Our data on capital input, like our data on labor input, have been constructed to readily incorporate new data on investment and stocks of inventories and land as they become available. Our classification of assets corresponds to the classification of investment employed in the U.S. national income and product accounts. Similarly, our classification of property compensation corresponds to the income classification employed in the U.S. national income and product accounts.

We have utilized our data on capital stock and property compensation to construct price and quantity indices of capital input for each of forty-six industrial sectors. Our data can also be employed to construct indices of capital input for aggregates of these sectors or components of capital input within sectors. For example, it would be possible to construct price and quantity indices of capital input by legal form of organization within each industrial sector. These indices can be employed in studies of the impact of differential taxation of corporate business, noncorporate business, and households and institutions, on the allocation of capital input.

Lack of data on capital input for industrial sectors that treats separately components of capital input that differ in marginal productivity has been a significant obstacle to the study of economic growth in the United States. In Chapter 3 we presented measures of labor input that conform to similar specifications. After constructing analogous measures of intermediate input in Chapter 5, we incorporate our new measure of capital input into an analysis of the growth of sectoral and aggregate output in Chapters 6 and 9.

5 Sectoral Output and Intermediate Input

One of the features that distinguishes our approach to productivity from its predecessors is the definition of output at the sectoral level. Capital and labor inputs are combined with inputs of intermediate goods to produce output. At the sectoral level the value of output includes the value of intermediate input, as well as the value of capital and labor inputs. In the preceding chapters we have described our approach to the measurement of capital and labor inputs. In this chapter we focus on the measurement of output and intermediate input.

The need to include intermediate goods and services in a study of sectoral productivity is easily demonstrated. For example, a supermarket manager may choose to have his own employee display ice cream products in the frozen foods cabinet, or he may contract with the supplier to have their delivery person display the product. The former results in labor cost to the supermarket; the latter is an expense related to intermediate inputs. The store manager makes this choice so that the ratio of marginal products is equal to the corresponding ratio of factor prices. Productivity change will be measured accurately only if all inputs are treated symmetrically.

For the period 1959–1979 we based our output estimates on interindustry data from the Bureau of Labor Statistics (1979). We adjusted the BLS series to be consistent with national income accounting conventions. This adjustment reflects reallocation of secondary products and redefinitions of certain types of activity from one industry to another. The Office of Economic Growth compiled data on 155 Economic Growth Sectors for this period. Sectors are aggregated as necessary to conform with the list of fifty-one industries in Table 3.1.

For the earlier period, 1948–1958, consistent time series data on output for the manufacturing industries listed in Table 3.1 are available from the Inter-industry Economics Division of the Bureau of Economic Analysis (1974b). These data incorporate the value of shipments and the cost of goods sold from the *Annual Survey of Manufactures*. The data are based on industry definitions from the U.S. national income and product accounts.

For the earlier period, 1948–1958, Jack Faucett Associates (1975) has developed data on output for nonmanufacturing industries for two classifications of these industries—the 160-order Economic Growth Sector-ing Plan of the Bureau of Labor Statistics and the 80-order sectoring of inter-industry transactions by the Bureau of Economic Analysis. These classifications are far more detailed than the breakdown of nonmanufacturing industries given in Table 3.1, but, the data are based on the industry definitions employed in interindustry accounts rather than the definitions used in the national income and product accounts.

For the twenty-one manufacturing industries listed in Table 3.1, we have used the BEA data on output in current and constant prices from 1948 to 1958. For twenty nonmanufacturing sectors, 1948–1958, we have employed the data on output in current and constant prices developed by Faucett, adjusted to conform with industry definitions used in the national income and product accounts. For the remaining ten nonmanufacturing sectors for the same period, our estimates of output in current and constant prices are derived from data provided by the Bureau of Economic Analysis. By recon-ciling industry definitions for nonmanufacturing sectors used by Faucett, BEA, and BLS, we are able to make our estimates conform with national accounting concepts. A number of adjustments are required. Principal among these are reallocation of each sector's output of secondary products and reconciliation of interindustry and national accounts with industry definitions.

Activity redefinitions and Standard Industrial Classification (SIC) reclassifications account for the major differences between the interindustry and the national income and product accounts industry definitions. While the national accounts adhere strictly to SIC conventions, sectors in the interin-dustry accounts are defined to achieve more homogeneous product group-ings. An example of an SIC reclassification initiated for interindustry accounts is the reallocation of veterinary services from the agricultural sector to the services sector; an example of interindustry activity redefinitions is reallocation, from the railroad to the construction sector, of all construction and installation work performed by railroad employees in the railroad sector.

With the aid of unpublished 80-order data on sectoral input, provided by the Bureau of Economic Analysis[1] and covering in part the earlier period, 1948–1958, we are able to reallocate the output associated with each interindustry activity redefinition and industry reclassification in Faucett's data to the appropriate national accounts sector. This reallocation brings our industry definitions into consistency with those that underlie the national accounts.

A second adjustment required to make our estimates conform to national accounting conventions involves the reallocation of each sector's production of secondary products. In the national accounts all primary and secondary products are allocated to the sector in which they are produced; there are no transfers in or out. By contrast, the interindustry data follow the convention of transferring into each sector the goods that are secondary to other industries but primary to the receiving sector. "The secondary output is treated as if sold by the producing industry to the industry to which it is primary, and it is added to the output of the primary industry for distribution to users" (Bureau of Economic Analysis, 1974c).

Fortunately, the data required to eliminate transfers of output are available from the current-dollar transactions tables. Faucett's output data for non-manufacturing sectors (adjusted for transfers and redefinitions), together with manufacturing data from the Bureau of Economic Analysis, form a consistent set of time series for sectoral output for the period 1948–1958, conforming to national income and product accounts industry definitions.

For the latter period, 1959–1979, for which similar detail are not available to bring about reclassification and redefinition of interindustry BLS data, we assume that the changes for 1959–1979 are proportional to the reclassifications and redefinitions in 1958, our one year of overlapping data from the earlier and later time periods. We therefore adjust the 1959–1979 data by the ratio of the 1958 redefined and reclassified data to the 1958 interindustry data. The adjusted price series are renormalized to 1.0 in 1972.

We derive an estimate of intermediate input in current prices for both manufacturing and nonmanufacturing industries by subtracting estimates of value added in current prices from the corresponding estimates of output in current prices. In converting these current-price estimates into constant prices we take account of the composition of the intermediate inputs in each industry. Interindustry transactions in current prices as published by the Bureau of Economic Analysis are used to allocate intermediate inputs among the industries supplying each sector. Sectoral output deflators, inclusive of indirect business taxes to the producing sectors, are used to convert the receiving sector's intermediate inputs to constant prices.

Sectoral Output

A measure of output in current and constant prices is essential to productivity measurement. The value of output is also indispensable for generating a measure of intermediate input. For 1948–1958, data on output in current and constant prices for manufacturing sectors are available from the Interindustry Economics Division of the Bureau of Economic Analysis (1974b); for non-manufacturing industries these data are available from a study undertaken by Jack Faucett Associates (1975) for the Bureau of Labor Statistics. In the Jack Faucett Associates study (1975), data on output in current and constant prices for nonmanufacturing sectors are classified according to the BLS Economic Growth Sectoring Plan, a 160-order classification of industries, and the BEA 80-order interindustry classification of industries. We directly employ data from the BEA study of manufacturing industries for 1948–1958. We adjust data from the Faucett study of nonmanufacturing industries to conform to industry definitions used in the national income and product accounts. For 1959–1979 we proportionally adjust Bureau of Labor Statistics (1979) inter-industry data on output in current and constant prices to reflect the industry definitions used in the national income and product accounts. These later BLS data are based on a 155-order classification of industries.

The value of production in government and household sectors is equal to value added. Output in constant prices is a translog index of inputs. The Bureau of Economic Analysis prepares annual value-added estimates for the household and government sectors, according to industry definitions from the national income and product accounts (1981). Our annual value-added esti-mates for the household sector represent the sum of labor compensation, an imputation for the rental value of owner-occupied dwellings, and an estimate of the service flow of consumer durables, as described in Chapter 3 and Chapter 4.

Output in constant prices is a translog index of labor and capital inputs. In the five government sectors (federal public administration, state and local public administration, state and local educational services, federal govern-ment enterprises, and state and local government enterprises), value added equals labor compensation. Output in constant prices is identical to the labor index described in Chapter 3. Since the value of output is defined wholly in terms of the value of inputs in government and household sectors 45, 47, 48, 49, 50, and 51, productivity change is zero.

Table 5.1 presents a detailed cross-classification of industry definitions employed in the national income and product accounts, the interindustry accounts, and the 155-order BLS Economic Growth Sectoring Plan. Stan-dard Industrial Classification (SIC) codes corresponding to each of the three industrial classifications are given together with details on industrial

Table 5.l.   Industrial classification

National income[a]	Inter-industry[a]	BLS[a]	SIC[b]
1	1, 2	1–5	01, 02[c]
2	3, 4	6, 7	07, 08, 09[c,d]
3	5, 6	8–10	10[e]
4	7	11	11, 12[f]
5	8	12	13[g]
6	9, 10	13, 14	14[h]
7	11, 12	15, 152	15–17[e,f,g,h,i]
8	14	18–27	20
9	15	28	21
10	16, 17, 18.01–18.03	29–32	22
11	18.04, 19	33–34	23[j]
12	24, 25	41–42	26
13	26	43–45	27
14	27–30	46–53	28[k]
15	31	54	29
16	32	55–59	30
17	33, 34	58, 59	31
18	20, 21	35–38	24[l]
19	22, 23	39–40	25
20	35, 36	60–64	32
21	37, 38	65–69	33[k,m]
22	13, 39–42	16, 70–76	34[m,n,o]
23	43–52	77–87	35
24	53–58	88–96	36[p]
25	60, 61	17, 98–102	37,(excludes 371)[l,n,o]
26	59	97	371
27	62, 63	103–107	38[k,p]
28	64	108–110	39[j]
29	65.01	111	40[q]
30	65.02	112	41
31	65.03	113	42[q]
32	65.04	114	44
33	65.05	115	45
34	65.06	116	46
35	65.07	117	47[q]
36	66	119	48 (excludes 483)
37	67	118	483
38	68.01	120	491, 493 (in part)[r]
39	68.02	121	492, 493 (in part)
40	68.03	122	49 (excludes 491, 492, part of 493)
41	69.01	123	50, 51[s]
42	69.02, 74	124, 125	52–59[t,u]
43	70, 71	126–130	60–67[i,v,w]

Table 5.1 continued

National income[a]	Inter-industry[a]	BLS[a]	SIC[b]
44	72, 73, 75–77 (except 77.05) 70, 72, 73, 75, 76, 78–82, 84, 89[d,t,u,x,y,z,*]	131–143	
46	77.05	144	83, 86[x,*]

(a) Industry titles for the national accounts sectors are as listed in Table 3.1; the interindustry codes are described in the *Survey of Current Business* (May, 1979); BLS codes are from Faucett (1975).

(b) SIC codes are from Executive Office of the President (1972) and correspond to national accounts definitions; definitional differences are noted. Unless noted otherwise, all references to interindustry reclassifications apply to the corresponding BLS sectors.

(c) Interindustry (I/O) sector 1 excludes 0254; I/O 4 includes 0254.

(d) I/O 4 excludes 074, I/O 77 includes 074.

(e) I/O 6 excludes part of 108; I/O 11 includes part of 108. BLS 8–10 includes all of 108.

(f) I/O 7 excludes part of 1112 and part of 1213; I/O 11 includes part of 1112 and part of 1213.

(g) I/O 8 excludes part of 138; I/O 11 includes part of 138; BLS 12 excludes all of 138, BLS 15, 152 includes all of 138.

(h) I/O 9 excludes part of 148; I/O 11 includes part of 148.

(i) I/O 11, 12 excludes part of 1531; I/O 71 includes part of 1531.

(j) I/O 64 excludes 39996; I/O 18.04 includes 39996.

(k) I/O 27 excludes 28195; I/O 38 includes 28195.

(l) I/O 20 excludes 2451; I/O 61 includes 2451.

(m) I/O 41 excludes 3462, 3463; I/O 37 includes 3462; I/O 38 includes 3463.

(n) I/O 60 excludes 3761; I/O 13 includes 3761. BLS 16, 70–76 includes 3761.

(o) I/O 61 excludes 3795; I/O 13 includes 3795.

(p) I/O 62 excludes 3825; I/O 53 includes 3825.

(q) I/O 65.07 excludes 474 and part of 4789; I/O 65.01 includes 474 and part of 4789; I/O 65.03 includes part of 4789.

(r) BLS 120 includes public utilities.

(s) I/O 69.01 excludes manufacturers' sales offices; BLS 120 includes manufacturers' sales offices.

(t) I/O 73 excludes 7396; I/O 69.02 includes 7396.

(u) I/O 77 excludes 8042; I/O 69.02 includes 8042.

(v) BLS 126–130 includes owner–occupied real estate.

(w) I/O 70 excludes part of 613; I/O 78 includes part of 613.

Table 5.1 continued

(x) I/O 77.01–77.04, 77.06–77.09 includes 83 and 89, except for 8922; BLS 131–143 includes 83, except for 832 and 839, and includes 89, except for 8922; I/O 77.05 includes 8922; BLS 144 includes 832, 839, and 8922; I/O 77.01–77.04, 77.06–77.09 and BLS 131–143 excludes 84; I/O 77.05 and BLS 144 include 84.

(y) BLS 131–143 includes part of 99.

(z) I/O 72 excludes dining from SIC 70.

* I/O 72, 73, 75–77 (except 77.05) includes 074, 70 (except dining), 72, 73 (except 7396), 75, 76, 78, 79, 80 (except 8042), 81, 82, 83, and 89 (except 8922); BLS 131–143 includes 074, 70, 72, 73 (except 7396), 75, 76, 78, 79, 80 (except 8042), 81, 82, 83 (except 832, 839), 89 (except 8922), and part of 99; I/O 77.05 includes 84, 86 and 8922; BLS 144 includes 832, 839, 84, 86, and 8922.

---

classifications that do not exactly correspond with the SIC codes. The first step in our procedure is to identify the BLS and interindustry classifications corresponding most closely to each industry from the national income and product accounts.

For the remaining forty-five industries, interindustry data was specifically modified to account for reclassifications and redefinitions for 1948–1958. As the 1959–1979 output series are proportionally adjusted using a 1958 scalar factor, the output series for all years 1948–1959 depend upon the modifications made in the earlier period.

For 1948–1958, if a particular national accounts sector (for example, industry 4) maps exactly into one or more of Faucett's 80-order interindustry sectors (in this case, industry 7), we choose the output series from that inter-industry sector as a first approximation to the desired national accounts series. If, however, a national accounts sector (for example, industry 34) maps into only some disaggregated part of an interindustry sector's boundaries (in this example, industry 65.06), but into one or more BLS sectors (BLS industry 116), we use Faucett's data for the BLS sectors as the initial estimate for the national accounts sector. In Table 5.1, an asterisk identifies which of the two Faucett series is chosen as the initial estimate of output for each industry in the national accounts for the earlier period.

After initial estimates for each nonmanufacturing sector are identified from the interindustry and BLS classifications, we adjust data on the value of output, in current prices, to eliminate transfers among disaggregated BLS sectors within a single industry in the interindustry accounts. Eight of the sectors included in the interindustry accounts are the same as the corresponding sectors in the more detailed BLS accounts. For all but six sectors in the interindustry accounts the value of output is the sum of the values of output of the component sectors in the BLS accounts. For six sectors in the interindustry accounts,[2] however, the value of output is not equal to the sum of component sectors, due to transfers within industries. We adjust data on the value of output for components of these six sectors to eliminate transfers, so that the value of output for each interindustry accounts sector is equal to the sum of the values of output of its components. Finally, for a number of nonmanufacturing sectors (those lines in Table 5.1 without an asterisk), we construct estimates of output from sources other than the Faucett report. First, the Faucett report publishes no results for the following nonmanufacturing sectors from the interindustry accounts:

Interindustry accounts sector	Name
11	New construction
12	Maintenance and repair construction
66	Communications, except radio and TV
67	Radio and TV broadcasting
84	Government industry
86	Household industry

We obtained unpublished data on output for contract construction, in current and constant prices, from the Interindustry Economics Division of the Bureau of Economic Analysis. These data are constructed according to conventions used in the national income and product accounts, so no further adjustments are required.

For the two communications sectors we constructed estimates of output in current and constant prices by extrapolating the six current and constant price benchmarks from BEA studies of interindustry transactions[3] by the gross-product-originating series published annually in the *Survey of Current Business* (1976b). By interpolating the ratios of gross product originating to output between benchmark years, and using the intermediate year figures, we obtained output for the communications sectors.

As previously noted, for the government and household sectors we defined output in current and constant prices in terms of labor and capital inputs. Faucett's output estimates for nonprofit institutions are equivalent to value added. In place of the Faucett series, we applied a procedure like the one used for the communications sectors to derive annual current and constant-dollar estimates for nonprofit institutions.

The BEA output estimates for the manufacturing and contract construction sectors are used directly for 1948–1958, since they are constructed by conventions and industry definitions consistent with the national income and product accounts. The value of output in these sectors includes all primary and secondary products originating in the sector. By contrast, our estimates of output for the communications sectors and for nonprofit institutions and Faucett's output estimates for the remaining nonmanufacturing industries are derived according to interindustry accounting conventions. Goods that are secondary to other industries but primary to a given sector are transferred to that sector. This results in double counting of transferred output and would result in upward-biased estimates of intermediate inputs into each sector. Current-dollar transactions tables available from the interindustry accounts make it possible to correct the Faucett series for transfers.

Faucett controls all output data presented in his report to the value of output reported in the benchmark tables in the interindustry accounts. In particular, Faucett's output in current prices equals the output reported in the transactions table, minus imports that are allocated to that industry as substitute goods and import margins. To eliminate the secondary product transfers we employ the ratio of transfers to sector output reported in the 80-order or 367-order input–output tables.[4] Defining this ratio in terms consistent with Faucett's definition of output, a time series of output for each sector, adjusted for transfers, is formed by eliminating transfers from Faucett's unadjusted output series. We interpolate and extrapolate these ratios for the two benchmark years to obtain ratios for nonbenchmark years.

In addition to secondary output transfers, activity redefinitions and SIC reclassifications account for important differences between the interindustry or BLS accounts and the national income and product accounts. Walderhaug (1973, 42–43) describes the two sets of differences:

> The GPO (national accounts gross product originating) estimates adhere strictly to the Standard Industrial Classification (SIC). In the I-0 (interindustry accounts) system, however, some industries are reclassified in order to achieve industry groups that are more homogeneous and that thus have a more stable input structure. [A sample of] these reclassifications consists of shifting veterinary services from the agricultural sector to the services sector, oil and gas field drilling services from mining to construction, and trading stamp companies from services to wholesale and retail trade.
>
> [There are also] differences between the GPO and I-0 value-added estimates that are due to the "redefinition" of certain activities (rather than whole SIC industries) from one industry to another. [Most] differences are due to the fact that in the I-0 system all construction and installation work performed by employees in establishments not in the construction industry (i.e., force account construction) is redefined to be in the construction industry. [Other redefinitions include:] manufacturing and service activities that occur in the trade and transportation

industries are shifted to the appropriate manufacturing and service industries; trade activities occurring in other industries are shifted to wholesale and retail trade; and manufacturer's sales offices are shifted from wholesale trade to manufacturing.

Walderhaug kindly prepared and made available a full 80-order interindustry national accounts reconciliation of 1963 industry value added that is similar to the more aggregated appendix table that appears in his contribution to the April 1973 issue of the *Survey of Current Business*. With this table we calculate the fraction of net output (measured in current prices) of each interindustry sector that must be added to or subtracted from the Faucett interindustry or BLS sectors. If we had data on redefined and reclassified output rather than value added, we would require only the net addition or subtraction to the output of each sector caused by redefinitions and reclassifications. Beginning with data on value added, however, we observe that the ratio of output to value added varies considerably across industries.

We first identify the value added that is redefined or reclassified from each industrial sector. We then adjust it to reflect shifts in output, using the ratios of output adjusted for transfers to value added, as reported in the interindustry accounts. Since the Walderhaug table applies only to 1963, we are compelled to assume that the addition or deduction reported by Walderhaug remains a constant proportion of value added for all years.[5] After adjusting the Faucett data series for transfers, redefinitions, and reclassifications, we obtain output series in current prices on the basis of industry definitions consistent with the national income and product accounts.

The derivation of output in constant prices from the BLS and interindustry series reported by Faucett is straightforward. In fact, we make no adjustment to the Faucett series, except for the redefinitions and reclassifications described above. Our elimination of secondary product transfers leaves each sector's output deflator unaffected. Transfers are treated as comparable to the primary output of the receiving sector. In assigning deflators to secondary products, Faucett chose price indices calculated from output in current and constant prices for goods produced in the receiving sector. Eliminating these transfers therefore requires no adjustment to the output deflators. The same conclusion applies to the shifts of redefined and reclassified industry output. The products within each sector have a common deflator. Reclassifying some of the sector's output elsewhere leaves the sector's deflator unaffected. Transfers of redefined or reclassified output into a given sector, however, do affect the output deflator for the receiving sector. We adjust Faucett's price index for output in each sector to reflect the price movements in the industries from which the redefined or reclassified goods originate.

One final adjustment to 1948–1958 output in current prices is required; output must be valued in producers' prices—that is, exclusive of trade and transportation margins and all indirect business taxes, but inclusive of all subsidies received by the sector. The current-dollar series for manufacturing and construction, taken directly from the national accounts and estimated for nonmanufacturing sectors from Faucett's data, are net of trade and transportation margins but gross of subsidies and sales and excise taxes. We thus subtract from the value of each industry's output the dollar value of sales and excise taxes reported in the national income and product accounts by the Bureau of Economic Analysis. This implies a corresponding adjustment to each sector's output deflator. While taxes do not affect the measure of constant-dollar output, the elimination of indirect business taxes alters the producers' prices for output. The adjusted deflator is calculated by dividing the original deflator gross of sales and excise taxes by unity plus the indirect tax rate for the sector.

For the period 1959–1979 we first aggregate the 155 BLS Economic Growth Sectors to the forty-five-industry level, as indicated in Table 5.1, in current and constant prices. The output estimates for the six government and household sectors depend upon input estimates in current and constant prices, as described earlier. We convert the aggregated BLS current and constant price series to series consistent with national income accounting conventions, by means of scalar adjustments. These conversions reflect the detailed 1948–1958 reallocation of secondary products and redefinition of certain types of activity from one industry to another. We assume that the changes for 1959–1979 are proportional to the reclassifications and redefinitions in 1958, our one year of overlapping data from the earlier and later time periods. As a result, we adjust the 1959–1979 data for forty-five industries by the ratio of the 1958 redefined and reclassified data to the 1958 interindustry data. The derived price series are renormalized to 1.0 for 1972.

Sectoral Intermediate Input

We construct estimates of intermediate input in current prices for all industries by subtracting value added from output, both in current prices. For the fifty-one industries listed in Table 3.1 we construct estimates of output in current and constant prices as described above. Value added in current prices is equal to the sum of labor and capital value added in current prices, constructed as described in Chapter 3 and Chapter 4, respectively.

Our first step in constructing intermediate input in constant prices is to develop an interindustry matrix in current prices for each year, 1948–1979, that conform to national income accounting definitions. The eleven 80-order interindustry benchmark matrices are the basis for determining the share of intermediate output from a particular producer in the intermediate input used by each of the forty-five industries for which we measure intermediate input.[6] Households and government industries are excluded. The 1963 367-order interindustry matrix was used to provide additional detail, as indicated in the interindustry column of Table 5.1 (Bureau of Economic Analysis, 1969). The share of 367-order intermediate output from a producer in intermediate input used by each of forty-five industries is assumed to be constant for all years. We interpolated the shares between benchmark years. The 1972 shares were used for all subsequent years. At this point we have a complete set of interindustry matrices, 1948–1979, with information on current-price intermediate inputs, by sector of origin and destination, on a basis conforming to national income accounting conventions.

The next step is to derive equivalent matrices in constant prices. We employ output deflators in purchasers' prices for each industry, to convert deliveries of intermediate input into constant prices. It is important to note that the output deflator used in evaluating the value of a sector's output is not the same as the deflator used in evaluating that sector's deliveries to intermediate demand. The former is measured in producers' prices; the latter is measured in purchasers' prices. The former is gross of all subsidies received by the producing sectors but net of all sales and excise taxes and trade and transportation margins. The latter is net of subsidies but gross of sales and excise taxes attributed to the output of the sector supplying the intermediate input. The trade and transportation margins paid by the consuming sector are captured in the intermediate input flows from the trade and transportation sectors.

Given both the decomposition of each sector's intermediate input into constant-price deliveries from all supplying sectors, and the purchasers' prices associated with each of those deliveries, a measure of aggregate intermediate input in the purchasing sector is constructed using the translog index described in the following section.

Indices of Sectoral Output and Intermediate Input

We have described the development of data on prices and quantities of output for each industrial sector. We have also outlined the development of data on intermediate input and the corresponding input price for each producing sector. To construct an index of intermediate input for each industrial sector, we assume that sectoral intermediate input $\{X_i\}$ can be expressed as a translog function of its components $\{X_{ji}\}$. The corresponding index of sectoral intermediate input is a translog quantity index of individual intermediate inputs:

$$\ln X_i(T) - \ln X_i(T-1) = \sum \bar{v}_{Xj} \left[\ln X_{ji}(T) - \ln X_{ji}(T-1)\right], \qquad (i = 1, 2, ..., n),$$

where weights are given by average shares of each component in the value of sectoral intermediate outlay:

$$\bar{v}_{Xj}^i = \frac{1}{2} \, [v_{Xj}^i(T) + v_{Xj}^i(T-1)], \qquad\qquad (i, \, j = 1, \, 2,..., \, n),$$

$$v_{Xj}^i = \frac{p_{Xj}^i \, X_{ji}}{\sum_j p_{Xj}^i \, X_{ji}}, \qquad\qquad (i, \, j = 1, \, 2,..., \, n).$$

The value shares are computed from data on intermediate input $\{X_{ji}\}$ and the corresponding prices paid by the receiving sectors $\{p_{Xj}^i\}$ for each component of sectoral intermediate input. Intermediate outlay for the sector as a whole, $\sum_j p_{Xj}^i X_{ji}$, is controlled to the value of intermediate input by industry as described earlier.

We can define an unweighted measure of sectoral intermediate input, $I_i(T)$, as the unweighted sum of its components,

$$I_i(T) = \sum_j X_{ji}(T), \qquad\qquad (i = 1, \, 2,..., \, n).$$

Similarly, we can define *sectoral indices of the quality of intermediate input* $\{Q_X^i(T)\}$ that transform unweighted sectoral measures of intermediate input into the translog indices of intermediate input:

$$X_i(T) = Q_X^i(T) \cdot I_i(T).$$

The sectoral indices of the quality of intermediate input can be expressed in the form

$$\ln Q_X^i(T) - \ln Q_X^i(T-1) = \sum_j \bar{v}_{Xj}^j \, [\ln X_{ji}(T) - \ln X_{ji}(T-1)]$$

$$- [\ln I_i(T) - \ln I_i(T-1)], \qquad\qquad (i = 1, \, 2,..., \, n),$$

so that these indices reflect changes in the composition of intermediate input within each sector. Sectoral intermediate input quality remains unchanged if all components of intermediate input are growing at the same rate. Sectoral quality rises if components with higher prices grow more rapidly than intermediate input components with lower prices; quality falls if components with lower prices grow more rapidly.

Table 5.2. Sectoral intermediate input: rates of growth

Industry	Translog index of intermediate input (average annual rates of growth)						
	1948–1953	1953–1957	1957–1960	1960–1966	1966–1969	1969–1973	1973–1979
Agricultural production	0.0256	0.0171	0.0189	0.0138	0.0119	0.0157	0.0432
Agricultural services	0.0554	0.0329	0.1076	−0.0037	−0.0320	0.0602	0.0603
Metal mining	−0.0436	0.0215	−0.0051	0.0259	0.0381	0.0159	0.0379
Coal mining	−0.0649	−0.0053	−0.0616	0.0232	0.0596	0.0412	0.1197
Crude petroleum and natural gas	−0.0015	0.0799	−0.0519	0.0262	0.0202	0.0562	0.1643
Nonmetallic mining and quarrying	0.0641	0.1007	0.0344	0.0622	−0.0513	−0.0409	0.0593
Contract construction	0.0473	0.0426	0.0489	0.0194	0.0101	0.0408	0.0062
Food and kindred products	−0.0073	−0.0118	0.0157	0.0245	0.0424	0.0699	0.0039
Tobacco manufacturers	0.0413	−0.0108	0.0734	0.0043	−0.0702	0.0207	0.0682
Textile mill products	0.0630	−0.0062	0.0075	0.0402	0.0215	0.0306	0.0059
Apparel and other fabricated textile products	0.0310	0.0403	−0.0030	0.0375	0.0493	0.0246	−0.0261
Paper and allied products	0.0981	0.0590	0.0239	0.0469	0.0232	0.0248	0.0637
Printing and publishing	0.0630	0.0636	0.0552	0.0351	0.0114	−0.0084	0.0273
Chemicals and allied products	0.0783	0.0441	0.0357	0.0705	0.0173	0.0241	0.0707
Petroleum and coal products	0.0083	0.0109	0.0059	0.0254	0.0253	0.0628	0.1690
Rubber and misc. plastic products	0.0636	0.0185	0.0519	0.0514	0.0402	0.0601	0.0391
Leather and leather products	−0.0287	−0.0161	0.0075	0.0116	0.0049	−0.0074	0.0025
Lumber and wood products except furniture	0.0888	−0.0183	0.0133	0.0379	0.0735	0.1233	0.0253
Furniture and fixtures	0.0938	0.0379	0.0034	0.0430	0.0706	0.0846	0.0164
Stone, clay, and glass products	0.1561	0.0587	0.0310	0.0451	0.0008	0.0496	0.0359

Table 5.2 continued

Industry	Translog index of intermediate input (average annual rates of growth)						
	1948–1953	1953–1957	1957–1960	1960–1966	1966–1969	1969–1973	1973–1979
Primary metal industries	0.0239	−0.0216	−0.0143	0.0716	−0.0012	0.0496	0.0183
Fabricated metal industries	0.0925	0.0100	0.0178	0.0537	0.0535	0.0113	0.0190
Machinery except electrical	0.0938	0.0035	−0.0052	0.0921	0.0294	0.0616	0.0289
Elec. machinery, eqpt., and supplies	0.1183	−0.0226	0.0466	0.0914	0.0176	0.0346	0.0248
Trans. eqpt. and ordnance, except motor vehicles	0.3393	−0.0319	−0.0620	0.0616	0.0576	−0.0252	0.0438
Motor vehicles and equipment	0.1139	−0.0007	0.0108	0.0574	−0.0040	0.0758	0.0192
Prof. photographic eqpt. and watches	0.0715	−0.0014	0.0443	0.0251	0.0698	0.1177	0.0832
Misc. manufacturing industries	0.0565	−0.0125	0.0654	0.0611	0.0338	0.0384	0.0492
Railroads and rail express services	−0.0179	−0.0341	−0.0277	0.0014	0.0043	0.0258	−0.0144
Street rail., bus lines, and taxicabs	−0.0291	−0.0280	−0.0107	−0.0035	0.0240	0.0279	−0.0280
Trucking services and warehousing	0.0895	0.0182	0.0310	0.0387	0.0517	0.0602	−0.0211
Water transportation	0.0295	0.0196	−0.1220	0.0026	−0.0733	0.1123	0.0311
Air transportation	0.0876	0.0787	0.1061	0.0966	0.1325	0.0119	0.0361
Pipelines except natural gas	0.0556	0.0596	0.0025	0.0118	0.0167	0.0053	0.0384
Transportation services	0.0433	0.1055	0.0585	0.0868	0.1263	0.0312	0.0314
Telephone, telegraph, and misc. communication services	0.0470	0.0290	0.0684	0.0554	0.0543	0.0168	−0.0029
Radio and television broadcasting	0.0824	0.0326	0.0173	−0.1960	−0.2047	−0.4274	0.0044
Electric utilities	0.0277	0.0414	0.0173	0.0768	0.0562	0.0783	0.0651
Gas utilities	0.1283	0.0842	0.0961	0.0585	0.0527	0.0114	0.0253
Water supply and sanitary services	0.0077	0.0006	−0.0312	0.0342	−0.3515	0.1543	−0.1327

Table 5.2 continued

Industry	Translog index of intermediate input (average annual rates of growth)						
	1948–1953	1953–1957	1957–1960	1960–1966	1966–1969	1969–1973	1973–1979
Wholesale trade	0.0187	0.0354	0.0304	0.0437	0.0495	0.0666	–0.0067
Retail trade	–0.0097	0.0147	0.0176	0.0356	0.0473	0.0259	0.0311
Finance, insurance, and real estate	0.0714	0.0940	0.0813	0.0664	0.0647	0.0686	0.0213
Services, excluding private households and institutions	0.0348	0.0507	0.0409	0.0598	0.0622	0.0527	0.0324
Institutions	0.0445	0.0126	0.0282	0.1338	0.0065	0.2088	0.0008

Average annual rates of growth of the translog indices of sectoral inter-mediate input for each of forty-five sectors, and a summary classification across sectors are presented for seven subperiods of the 1948–1979 period in Tables 5.2 and 5.3, respectively. The unweighted index of intermediate input, the index of the quality of intermediate input, and data for the value of intermediate input outlay are presented on an annual basis for the period 1948–1979 for each industry in Appendix D.

Classifying rates of growth by subperiod in Table 5.3, we can identify patterns of growth in intermediate input among industries over the period 1948–1979. Considering the subperiods in chronological order, we find thirty-four, twenty-one, twenty-one, thirty-five, twenty-seven, thirty-three, and twenty-eight industries, respectively, that are characterized by rates of growth in intermediate input greater than two percent per year. We have already seen that the third subperiod, 1957–1960, showed relatively weak growth in capital and labor input; growth in intermediate input was also relatively weak during this period. The subperiod 1966–1969 witnessed relatively strong growth in capital and labor input but relatively weak growth in intermediate input. The most rapid growth in intermediate input occurred during the period 1960–1966, when labor input also grew very rapidly. This subperiod was not characterized by unusually rapid growth in capital input. Our overall conclusion is that the subperiod 1966–1969 stands out as a period of relatively rapid growth in capital and labor inputs, while the subperiod 1960–1966 was a period of rapid growth of labor and intermediate inputs.

We find it useful to focus attention on industries with annual rates of growth in intermediate input greater than eight percent or rates of decline

Table 5.3. Rates of growth of sectoral intermediate input, by subperiod, 1948–1979

Average annual rate of growth of labor input	1948– 1953	1953– 1957	1957– 1960	1960– 1966	1966– 1969	1969– 1973	1973– 1979
Less −4%	4	5	6	1	6	3	4
−4% to −2%	4	9	5	2	2	2	3
0 to 2%	3	10	13	7	10	7	10
2% to 4%	6	6	7	12	8	11	15
4% to 6%	8	8	7	11	12	6	4
6% to 8%	7	3	3	7	5	10	5
More than 8%	13	4	4	5	2	6	4

greater than two percent. We observed a dramatic decline in variability of rates of growth of labor input from the subperiods before 1960 to those after 1960. There was a less dramatic but still definite decline in variability of rates of growth of capital input between the two periods. The tendency toward reduced variability is also evident for rates of growth of intermediate input. During the subperiods 1948–1953, 1953–1957, and 1957–1960, seventeen, nine, and ten industries, respectively, had rates of growth of intermediate input greater than eight percent or rates of decline greater than two percent. These limits were exceeded by six industries in 1960–1966, by eight industries in each of the two subperiods 1966–1969 and 1973–1979, and by nine industries in 1969–1973.

Considering specific sectors that underwent rapid declines in intermediate input, we find that metal mining, coal mining, leather, and local transportation experienced declines at rates greater than two percent during the subperiod 1948–1953. Five industries—primary metals, electrical machinery, transportation equipment excluding motor vehicles, railroads, and local transportation—had rapid declines during the subperiod 1953–1957. From 1957–1960 coal mining, crude petroleum and natural gas, transportation equipment excluding motor vehicles, railroads, water transportation, and water supply and sanitary services experienced rapid declines. For the subperiod 1960–1966 a rate of decline greater than two percent was recorded for broadcasting. Six industries had rapid declines in intermediate input during the period 1966–1969: agricultural services; nonmetallic mining; tobacco; water transportation; broadcasting, and water supply and sanitary services. From 1969–1973 rapid declines took place in nonmetallic mining, transportation equipment excluding motor vehicles, and broadcasting.

Finally, from 1973–1979 four industries had rapid declines: apparel; local transportation; trucking; and water supply and sanitary services.

Rates of decline in intermediate input exceeding two percent occurred in more than one subperiod in eight industrial sectors: coal mining; nonmetallic mining; transportation equipment excluding motor vehicles; railroads; local transportation; water transportation; broadcasting; and water supply and sanitary services. For coal mining, rapid declines in labor and capital inputs occurred during more than one subperiod, while for railroads there were negative growth rates for labor input in more than one subperiod. Coal mining and railroads can be identified as industries that experienced rapid declines in input during the period 1948–1979.

Growth in intermediate input at rates in excess of eight percent occurred in thirteen industries during the period 1948–1953: paper; lumber; furniture; stone, clay, and glass; fabricated metals; machinery except electrical; electrical machinery; transportation equipment, excluding motor vehicles; motor vehicles; trucking; air transportation; broadcasting; and gas utilities. The number of industries with rapid growth in intermediate input dipped to four during the subperiod 1953–1957: nonmetallic mining; transportation services; gas utilities; and finance, insurance and real estate. Rapid growth in intermediate input during the subperiod 1957–1960 occurred in agricultural services; air transportation; gas utilities; and finance, insurance, and real estate. During the subperiod 1960–1966 rapid growth was experienced by machinery except electrical; electrical machinery; air transportation; transportation services; and nonprofit institutions. Only two industries were characterized by rapid growth of intermediate input during the subperiod 1966–1969: air transportation and transportation services. During the period 1969–1973 lumber, furniture, professional equipment, water transportation, water supply and sanitary services, and nonprofit institutions had rates of growth of intermediate input exceeding eight percent per year. Finally, four industries had rapid growth during the period 1973–1979: coal mining; crude petroleum and natural gas; petroleum refining; and professional equipment.

Industries experiencing rapid growth in intermediate input during at least one subperiod are distributed broadly across the economy. Five manufacturing industries experienced annual growth rates exceeding eight percent in two subperiods: lumber; furniture; machinery except electrical; electrical machinery; and professional equipment. Other industries experiencing rapid growth rates for two subperiods include air transportation; transportation services; gas utilities; finance, insurance, and real estate; and nonprofit institutions. Professional equipment, air transportation, and transportation services also experienced rapid growth in capital input during more than one subperiod. Professional equipment and air transportation were characterized by rates of growth of labor input exceeding six percent per year in more than one subperiod. Trucking, broadcasting, and electric utilities underwent rapid growth of capital and labor input, but not rapid growth of intermediate input in more than two subperiods. We conclude that professional equipment, air transportation, transportation services, broadcasting, and electric utilities stand out as industries that experienced rapid growth in input during the period 1948 to 1979.

Average annual rates of growth of output for all fifty-one sectors included in our study are presented in Table 5.4. Price and quantity of output are presented on an annual basis for the period 1948–1979 for each industry in Appendix D. Annual data for the value of output and the effective rate of sales and excise taxes are also presented, for 1948–1979 for each industry, in Appendix D.

To identify patterns among industries of growth in output over the period 1948 to 1979, we classify rates of growth by subperiod, shown in Table 5.5. Considering the subperiods in chronological order, we found forty-one, thirty, thirty-three, forty-four, thirty-five, thirty-nine, and twenty-seven industries, respectively, that are characterized by annual rates of growth of output greater than two percent. The subperiod 1948–1953 showed relatively strong growth in output; we have already observed that this period witnessed strong growth in intermediate and labor input. The following subperiod, 1953–1957, showed relatively weak growth in output; this was also a period of weak growth in intermediate input. While 1966–1969 was characterized by strong growth in input and 1957–1960 by weak growth, these subperiods do not stand out as exceptionally strong or weak in the growth of output. The period 1973–1979 is the weakest in growth of output of the post-war era.

Considering industries with annual rates of growth of output greater than eight percent or rates of decline greater than two percent, we find that the subperiod 1948–1953 was characterized by the greatest variability in growth rates, with thirteen industries outside these limits. The subperiod 1973–1979 was characterized by the least variability, with only one industry exceeding the limits. Otherwise, there is little perceptible trend in variability of growth rates among industries over the period 1948 to 1979. The subperiods 1953–1957, 1957–1960, 1960–1966, 1966–1969, and 1969–1973 had annual rates of growth of output exceeding eight percent or rates of decline exceeding two percent for four, six, four, four, and three industries, respectively.

Coal mining declined at an annual rate of 6.27 percent, and local transportation declined at 6.22 percent during the subperiod 1948–1953, while metal mining declined at 2.87 percent. Local transportation continued its rapid decline during the period 1953–1957; rapid declines in output also took place in primary metals and in transportation equipment excluding motor

Table 5.4. Sectoral output: rates of growth

Industry	Output (average annual rates of growth)						
	1948–1953	1953–1957	1957–1960	1960–1966	1966–1969	1969–1973	1973–1979
Agricultural production	0.0191	0.0223	0.0220	0.0176	0.0216	0.0166	0.0304
Agricultural services	0.0455	0.0110	0.0411	0.0127	−0.0287	0.0369	0.0648
Metal mining	−0.0287	0.0241	−0.0077	0.0417	0.0245	0.0663	−0.0130
Coal mining	−0.0627	0.0122	−0.0592	0.0365	0.0150	−0.0072	0.0541
Crude petroleum and natural gas	0.0307	0.0480	−0.0044	0.0279	0.0404	0.0366	−0.0181
Nonmetallic mining and quarrying	0.0529	0.0720	0.0372	0.0506	−0.0023	0.0341	0.0282
Contract construction	0.0510	0.0411	0.0461	0.0329	0.0120	0.0206	−0.0057
Food and kindred products	0.0365	0.0294	0.0273	0.0226	0.0352	0.0209	0.0276
Tobacco manufacturers	0.0126	−0.0017	0.0531	0.0014	−0.0168	0.0240	−0.0075
Textile mill products	0.0457	0.0061	0.0234	0.0563	0.0341	0.0359	0.0272
Apparel and other fabricated textile products	0.0403	0.0293	0.0079	0.0409	0.0349	0.0253	0.0039
Paper and allied products	0.0639	0.0285	0.0292	0.0552	0.0415	0.0350	0.0212
Printing and publishing	0.0392	0.0432	0.0364	0.0359	0.0359	0.0214	0.0192
Chemicals and allied products	0.0885	0.0610	0.0432	0.0733	0.0557	0.0537	0.0326
Petroleum and coal products	−0.0027	0.0105	0.0408	0.0356	0.0491	0.0038	0.0522
Rubber and misc. plastic products	0.0546	0.0113	0.0493	0.0701	0.0651	0.0593	0.0264
Leather and leather products	−0.0030	0.0038	−0.0145	0.0112	0.0019	−0.0308	−0.0086
Lumber and wood products except furniture	0.0364	0.0046	0.0237	0.0361	0.0131	0.0472	0.0296
Furniture and fixtures	0.0585	0.0245	0.0065	0.0511	0.0377	0.0559	0.0174
Stone, clay, and glass products	0.0848	0.0340	0.0291	0.0459	0.0092	0.0408	0.0119

Table 5.4 continued

Industry	Output (average annual rates of growth)						
	1948–1953	1953–1957	1957–1960	1960–1966	1966–1969	1969–1973	1973–1979
Primary metal industries	0.0226	−0.0288	−0.0236	0.0653	−0.0105	0.0380	−0.0069
Fabricated metal industries	0.0763	0.0085	0.0120	0.0592	0.0510	0.0109	0.0133
Machinery except electrical	0.0704	−0.0062	−0.0071	0.0856	0.0242	0.0513	0.0326
Elec. machinery, eqpt., and supplies	0.1129	−0.0048	0.0532	0.0948	0.0400	0.0402	0.0403
Trans. eqpt. and ordnance, except motor vehicles	0.2789	−0.0249	−0.0525	0.0690	0.0313	−0.0239	0.0307
Motor vehicles and equipment	0.1089	−0.0021	0.0167	0.0675	0.0180	0.0628	0.0170
Prof. photographic eqpt. and watches	0.1008	0.0138	0.0475	0.0547	0.0654	0.0582	0.0511
Misc. manufacturing industries	0.0447	0.0052	0.0461	0.0539	0.0409	0.0359	0.0138
Railroads and rail express services	−0.0140	−0.0021	−0.0214	0.0349	−0.0008	0.0222	0.0019
Street rail., bus lines, and taxicabs	−0.0622	−0.0360	−0.0241	−0.0079	0.0034	−0.0150	−0.0082
Trucking services and warehousing	0.1234	0.0393	0.0381	0.0482	0.0198	0.0558	0.0086
Water transportation	−0.0130	0.0511	−0.1126	−0.0189	−0.0351	0.1253	0.0069
Air transportation	0.1621	0.1204	0.0761	0.1063	0.1465	0.0105	0.0547
Pipelines except natural gas	0.0698	0.0654	0.0053	0.0643	0.0690	0.0524	0.0167
Transportation services	−0.0026	0.0319	0.0151	0.0425	0.0667	0.0524	0.0009
Telephone, telegraph, and misc. communication services	0.0613	0.0564	0.0573	0.0702	0.0835	0.0747	0.0764
Radio and television broadcasting	0.1133	0.0658	0.0256	−0.0492	0.0155	−0.0122	−0.0333
Electric utilities	0.0764	0.0673	0.0573	0.0710	0.0674	0.0651	0.0390
Gas utilities	0.1199	0.0745	0.0699	0.0566	0.0627	0.0125	−0.0066
Water supply and sanitary services	0.0606	0.0228	0.0449	0.0382	0.0100	0.0361	0.0141

Table 5.4 continued

Industry	Output (average annual rates of growth)						
	1948–1953	1953–1957	1957–1960	1960–1966	1966–1969	1969–1973	1973–1979
Wholesale trade	0.0310	0.0442	0.0429	0.0551	0.0558	0.0548	0.0236
Retail trade	0.0275	0.0294	0.0194	0.0400	0.0260	0.0354	0.0226
Finance, insurance, and real estate	0.0433	0.0613	0.0602	0.0504	0.0488	0.0590	0.0336
Services, except private households and institutions	0.0236	0.0368	0.0338	0.0486	0.0425	0.0424	0.0354
Private households	0.0732	0.0547	0.0349	0.0385	0.0482	0.0480	0.0442
Institutions	0.0375	0.0329	0.0353	0.0394	0.0447	0.0419	0.0323
Federal public administration	0.0539	–0.0060	0.0055	0.0280	0.0263	–0.0169	0.0159
Federal government enterprises	0.0282	0.0091	0.0287	0.0226	0.0268	–0.0087	–0.0015
State and local educational services	0.0535	0.0586	0.0629	0.0535	0.0432	0.0374	0.0209
State and local public admin.	0.0434	0.0430	0.0270	0.0394	0.0334	0.0409	0.0253
State and local enterprises	0.0647	0.0023	0.0648	0.0204	0.0408	0.0314	0.0379

vehicles. Rapidly declining industries during the subperiod 1957–1960 included coal mining, primary metals, transportation equipment excluding motor vehicles, railroads, local transportation, and water transportation. Broadcasting underwent rapid decline during the subperiod 1960–1966. Agricultural services declined at 2.87 percent per year during 1966–1969, and water transportation declined at 3.51 percent during this period. Leather and transportation equipment excluding motor vehicles declined rapidly during 1969–1973, while broadcasting declined rapidly from 1973–1979. Local transportation and transportation equipment excluding motor vehicles stand out as rapidly declining industries for three subperiods. Coal mining, primary metals, water transportation, and broadcasting declined at rapid rates in more than one subperiod.

Turning to industries with annual rates of growth of output exceeding eight percent for one or more subperiods, we find ten industries with rapid growth in output during the subperiod 1948–1953: chemicals; stone, clay and glass; electrical machinery; transportation equipment excluding motor vehicles;

Table 5.5. Classification of rates of growth of sectoral output by sub-period, 1948–1979

Average annual rate of growth of labor input	1948–1953	1953–1957	1957–1960	1960–1966	1966–1969	1969–1973	1973–1979
Less than −2%	3	3	6	1	2	2	1
−2% to 0	5	6	4	2	4	5	9
0 to 2%	2	12	8	4	10	5	14
2% to 4%	10	13	15	15	13	17	19
4% to 6%	12	9	13	18	14	17	6
6% to 8%	9	7	5	8	6	4	2
More than 8%	10	1	0	3	2	1	0

motor vehicles; professional equipment; trucking; air transportation; broadcasting; and gas utilities. Air transportation grew at 12.04 percent per year during the subperiod 1953–1957. Machinery excluding electrical, electrical machinery, and air transportation grew at annual rates exceeding eight percent during the subperiod 1960–1966. Rapid growth took place in air transportation and telephones during 1966–1969. During 1969–1973 water transportation grew at an annual rate of 11.88 percent. Air transportation stands out as a rapidly growing industry for four subperiods. Electrical machinery grew at rapid rates in two subperiods.

Alternative Measures of Sectoral Output, Intermediate Input, and Productivity

We can provide additional perspective on our approach to measuring sectoral output, intermediate input, and productivity by comparing our methods and sources with those of Kendrick and other studies of sectoral productivity. Our measure of the value of sectoral output includes the value of intermediate input, as well as the value of capital and labor inputs into each sector. We treat intermediate input symmetrically with capital input and labor input in measuring productivity at the sectoral level. Our measure of productivity is an index number constructed from data on prices and quantities of output, intermediate input, capital input, and labor input. This measure of productivity is based on a model of production and technical change for each industrial sector, with output represented as a function of the three inputs and time. The production function is combined with necessary conditions for producer equilibrium and the rate of technical change for each sector.

The first study of productivity for individual industrial sectors based on a value of output including the value of intermediate input is that of Leontief (1953). Leontief compares interindustry transactions among fourteen industries for the United States for 1919, 1929, and 1939, in constant prices of 1939. For each industry he tabulates relative changes in the ratios of intermediate inputs and labor input to output; the ratio of capital input to output is omitted because he lacked appropriate data. Relative changes between 1919 and 1929 and between 1929 and 1939 are weighted, by averages of the quantities of inputs for each pair of years, to obtain an index of productivity change for each sector. The weights sum to the average value of input into each sector in constant prices of 1939, excluding capital input. The corresponding measure of productivity based on our model of production and technical change involves weights based on average value shares of individual inputs, including capital input. If these weights were applied to relative changes in the ratios of individual inputs to output, measured as differences in logarithms of these ratios, we would obtain the negative of the translog index of technical change described in Chapter 2.

Watanabe (1971) presents measures of productivity for individual industrial sectors in Japan, based on the value of output including the value of intermediate input. Watanabe compares interindustry transactions accounts for 1955, 1960, and 1965, in constant prices of 1960, for seventeen industries. He tabulates the difference between the rate of growth of output and a weighted average of rates of growth of intermediate input, capital input, and labor input for each sector. Quantities of intermediate input for each sector are obtained from interindustry transactions tables. The weights are ratios of the value of each input to the value of output for 1960; these weights add to unity and are equal to the value shares of individual inputs for 1960. If average weights for each pair of years were applied to rates of growth measured as differences in logarithms, we would obtain the translog index of technical change for each sector.

Watanabe also derives measures of value added for each sector and tabulates the difference between the rate of growth of value added and a weighted average of rates of growth of primary factor inputs; weights are given by the share of each primary factor input in value added. Again, if average weights were applied to rates of growth measured as differences in logarithms, we would obtain the translog index of technical change for value added for each sector.

Kendrick (1961a, 1973) advocates an approach to sectoral productivity measurement based on value added, where value added is defined as the sum of the value of capital input and the value of labor input. The corresponding measure of productivity is an index number constructed from data on prices and quantities of value added, capital input, and labor input. The price and quantity of value added are index numbers constructed from data on prices and quantities of output and intermediate input. Kendrick's approach to productivity measurement is based on a model of production for each individual sector, with output represented as a function of intermediate input and the quantity of value added. Value added is represented as a function of capital input, labor input, and time. Production and value-added functions for each sector are combined with necessary conditions for value added. The rate of productivity growth for value added is an appropriate measure of productivity if output can be represented as a function of intermediate input and value added.

In fact, Kendrick (1973, 17) does not use value added as a measure of output at the level of individual industries included in his study. He employs output to measure productivity at the level of individual industries, and simply ignores the growth of intermediate input. The resulting rates of productivity growth are measures of the rate of productivity growth for value added, as defined in Chapter 2, only if rates of growth of output and intermediate goods are identical. To provide further perspective on Kendrick's approach, we represent the accounting identity between the value of output, say $q(T)Z(T)$, and the sum of the values of intermediate input $p_X(T)X(T)$, capital input $p_K(T)K(T)$, and labor input $p_L(T)L(T)$ in the form

$$q(T)Z(T) = p_X(T)X(T) + p_K(T)K(T) + p_L(T)L(T).$$

Value added, say $p_V(T)V(T)$, is defined as the difference between the value of output and the value of intermediate input:

$$p_V(T)V(T) = q(T)Z(T) - p_X(T)X(T)$$

$$= p_K(T)K(T) + p_L(T)L(T).$$

Value added is therefore equal to the sum of the values of capital and labor inputs. By employing output in place of value added and setting the value of input equal to the sum of the values of capital and labor inputs, Kendrick has based his measures of productivity for individual industries on quantity data that fail to satisfy the accounting identity between output and the sum of the values of inputs.

The same problem arises in Kendrick's analysis of aggregate sectors. For aggregates over individual industries Kendrick employs data from the Bureau of Economic Analysis on gross product originating. For approximately fifty percent of the business economy these data are based on output rather than value added, so Kendrick's (1973, 22) measures of productivity for aggregates over individual industries ignore the growth of intermediate input. The condition required for validity of his measures of the rate of productivity growth for aggregates is precisely equivalent to the condition we have given for individual industries: rates of growth of output and intermediate inputs must be identical.   ⸮

We can test Kendrick's assumption directly, using the output and intermediate input data and the indices described and constructed earlier in this chapter. Table 5.6 presents the average annual rates of growth of output and intermediate input in each of forty-five sectors over the 1948–1969 period, the period analyzed by Kendrick (1973). The ratio of the average annual rate of growth of intermediate input to the corresponding growth rate of output is reported for each sector in the last column. The data in Table 5.6 illustrate that Kendrick's assumption is both inappropriate and, more importantly, a significant source of bias. Not only are the ratios not equal to unity, but ratios greater than unity suggest that Kendrick's resulting measures of productivity growth are upward-biased; ratios less than unity imply downward-biased measures. Even if one chooses to restrict the sectoral model of productivity by excluding intermediate input, the growth rate of real value added cannot be measured by the growth rate of gross output.

In defining output, Kendrick (1973, 17) considers whether or not to exclude the value of depreciation from the value of output. At the sectoral level, depreciation would be excluded along with the value of intermediate goods in the measurement of output. Kendrick considers two measures of productivity, one based on value added gross of depreciation, and the other based on value added net of depreciation. He associates the gross measure with gross capital stock, as a measure of capital input, and the net measure with net capital stock, as a measure of capital input. In Chapter 4 we have seen that the selection of an appropriate concept of capital input depends on the relative efficiency of capital goods of different vintages. Associated with a concept of capital input, there is a corresponding measure of depreciation; for any measure of depreciation, there is a measure of value added net of depreciation. Kendrick (1973, 18) indicates that he would have preferred to use a measure of output net of depreciation. Kendrick is able to implement an approach based on value added net of depreciation only at the economywide level, where he uses net national product in place of gross national product as a measure of value added.

To evaluate Kendrick's approach to the measurement of value added net of depreciation, we can decompose the value of capital input into the value of return to capital, evaluated at the own rate of return, and the value of depreciation:

Table 5.6. Sectoral intermediate input and output: rates of growth, 1948–1969

Industry	Average annual rates of growth		Ratio of growth of intermediate input to growth of output
	Intermediate input	Output	
Agricultural production	0.0177	0.0201	0.8814
Agricultural services	0.0292	0.0183	1.5931
Metal mining	0.0058	0.0121	0.4835
Coal mining	−0.0101	−0.0085	1.1933
Crude petroleum and natural gas	0.0178	0.0296	0.6030
Nonmetallic mining and quarrying	0.0498	0.0458	1.0888
Contract construction	0.0333	0.0377	0.8850
Food and kindred products	0.0113	0.0297	0.3814
Tobacco manufacturers	0.0095	0.0082	1.1468
Textile mill products	0.0295	0.0363	0.8103
Apparel and other fabricated textile products	0.0324	0.0330	0.9817
Paper and allied products	0.0547	0.0465	1.1767
Printing and publishing	0.0467	0.0381	1.2232
Chemicals and allied products	0.0548	0.0677	0.8084
Petroleum and coal products	0.0158	0.0244	0.6472
Rubber and misc. plastic products	0.0465	0.0515	0.9024
Leather and leather products	−0.0048	0.0014	−3.3906
Lumber and wood products except furniture	0.0409	0.0251	1.6285
Furniture and fixtures	0.0524	0.0395	1.3274
Stone, clay, and glass products	0.0658	0.0452	1.4544

Table 5.6 continued

Industry	Average annual rates of growth		Ratio of growth of intermediate input to growth of output
	Intermediate input	Output	
Primary metal industries	0.0198	0.0137	1.4509
Fabricated metal industries	0.0495	0.0457	1.0824
Machinery except electrical	0.0528	0.0425	1.2427
Elec. machinery, eqpt., and supplies	0.0591	0.0664	0.8911
Trans. equipment except motor vehicles	0.0917	0.0783	1.1705
Motor vehicles and equipment	0.0444	0.0498	0.8911
Prof. photographic eqpt. and watches	0.0402	0.0584	0.6891
Misc. manufacturing industries	0.0427	0.0395	1.0822
Railroads and rail express services	−0.0137	0.0031	−4.4393
Street rail., bus lines, and taxicabs	−0.0114	−0.0269	0.4237
Trucking services and warehousing	0.0476	0.0589	0.8082
Water transportation	−0.0164	−0.0199	0.8254
Air transportation	0.0975	0.1237	0.7884
Pipelines except natural gas	0.0307	0.0581	0.5287
Transportation services	0.0816	0.0293	2.7863
Telephone, telegraph and misc. communication services	0.0501	0.0655	0.7644
Radio and television broadcasting	−0.0569	0.0313	−1.8189
Electric utilities	0.0469	0.0691	0.6788
Gas utilities	0.0846	0.0779	1.0862
Water supply and sanitary services	−0.0430	0.0375	−1.1443
Wholesale trade	0.0351	0.0456	0.7692
Retail trade	0.0199	0.0300	0.6640

Table 5.6 continued

Industry	Average annual rates of growth		Ratio of growth of intermediate input to growth of output
	Intermediate input	Output	
Finance, insurance, and real estate	0.0747	0.0519	1.4388
Services, excl. private households and institutions	0.0498	0.0374	1.3291
Institutions	0.0562	0.0379	1.4831

$$p_K(T) = p_I(T-1) \left[r(T) - \frac{p_I(T) - p_I(T-1)}{p_I(T-1)} \right] A(T-1)$$

$$+ p_D(T)A(T-1).$$

As before, we have simplified this expression by ignoring the impact of taxation. Value added net of depreciation is defined as the difference between value added and the value of depreciation:

$$p_V(T)V(T) - p_D(T)A(T-1)$$

$$= p_I(T-1) \left[r(T) - \frac{p_I(T) - p_I(T-1)}{p_I(T-1)} \right] A(T-1) + p_L(T)L(T).$$

Capital stock $A(T-1)$ appears on both the left side, where it is associated with depreciation, and on the right-hand side, where it is associated with the own rate of return on capital or, using Kendrick's terminology, the net earnings of capital.

Kendrick's approach to the measurement of net value added could be rationalized on the basis of a model of production, by treating the quantity of net value added as an aggregate that depends on the quantities of gross value added, which depends on the quantities of output and intermediate input. If we were to attempt to represent this aggregate as a function of capital input, labor input, and time, however, both net value added and the inputs would involve the quantity of capital input. A model of production involving net value added would confound outputs and inputs by including capital input in both categories. By contrast, gross value added can be represented as a function of capital input, labor input, and time, so that outputs and inputs are distinct. We conclude that the quantity of net value added cannot serve as an appropriate point of departure for productivity measurement. Only at the economy-wide level do Kendrick's measures of productivity based on gross value added avoid the confounding of outputs and inputs. Fortunately, only gross value added is used for Kendrick's sectoral aggregates of individual industries, so that his measures of productivity for these aggregates avoid the confounding of outputs and inputs. As we have already pointed out, only output is used at the level of individual industries; again, outputs and inputs are distinct.

For individual industries Kendrick's measures of productivity are based on output; for sectoral aggregates his measures are based on gross value added. At the economy-wide level Kendrick presents measures of productivity based on both gross and net value added. At all three levels Kendrick employs two alternative measures of input. The first is based on the "net earnings" of capital, that is, property compensation excluding capital consumption allowances. The second is based on "gross earnings" of capital including capital consumption allowances. For measures of input based on the "net earnings" of capital, the value of output and gross value added include capital consumption allowances, but the value of input excludes capital consumption allowances. The price and quantity data on outputs and inputs fail to satisfy the accounting identity between the value of output and the value of input. At the economy-wide level Kendrick's measure of net value added is based on net national product. The corresponding measure of input based on "net earnings" excludes indirect business taxes, while the measure of output includes these taxes. Similarly, for the measure for input based on "gross earnings" of capital, the value of output includes indirect business taxes, but the value of input excludes these taxes. Again, the value of output is not equal to the value of input for either of these measures.

Kendrick and Grossman (1980, 22–25) and Kendrick (1983, 56) employ measures of output at the level of individual industries, based on data from the Bureau of Economic Analysis on gross product originating in each industrial sector. Both studies drop the concept of value added net of depreciation, employed by Kendrick (1973). This important change in methodology has the advantage that the confounding of output and capital input in Kendrick's (1973) study is entirely avoided, but, the Bureau of Economic Analysis data on the growth of gross product originating omit the growth of intermediate input for fifty percent of the business economy. The data presented in Table 5.6 indicate that the productivity measures of Kendrick and Grossman (1980) and Kendrick (1983) are subject to very significant biases.

An important issue in the measurement of output and intermediate input involves the use of energy consumption to adjust potential capital services for capacity utilization. This issue can be analyzed by means of a modified form of our sectoral models of production and technical change. As before, these models are based on production functions $\{F^i\}$ for all sectors, characterized by constant returns to scale:

$$Z_i = F^i (E_i, M_i, K_i, L_i, T), \qquad\qquad (i = 1, 2,..., n),$$

where $\{Z_i\}$ is the set of outputs, $\{E_i\}$, $\{M_i\}$, $\{K_i\}$, and $\{L_i\}$ are the sets of energy inputs, nonenergy intermediate inputs, capital inputs, and labor inputs, respectively, and T is time. For convenience we refer to nonenergy intermediate inputs as materials inputs, even though these intermediate inputs include services and semifinished goods, as well as raw materials. We denote the prices of energy inputs and materials by $\{p_E^i\}$ and $\{p_M^i\}$, respectively.

In the sectoral models of production and technical change presented in Chapter 2, we have represented output as a function of intermediate, capital, and labor inputs and time:

$$Z_i = F^i (X^i(E^i, M_i), K_i, L_i, T), \qquad\qquad (i = 1, 2,..., n),$$

where intermediate input $\{X_i\}$ is an aggregate of energy and materials inputs. If we specialize the models by representing output as a function of utilized capital input $\{U_i\}$ where utilized capital input is an aggregate of energy and capital inputs, we obtain

$$Z_i = F^i (U_i(E_i, K_i), M_i, L_i, T), \qquad\qquad (i = 1, 2,..., n).$$

Constant returns to scale in all inputs implies that the utilized capital input is characterized by constant returns to scale in energy and capital inputs. Proportional increases in capital input and energy consumption result in a proportional increase in utilized capital input. Using constant returns to scale of utilized capital input in energy and capital inputs, we can rewrite utilized capital input in the form

$$U_i = U_i\,(E_i,\,K_i)$$

$$= K_i \cdot u_i \left[\frac{E_i}{K_i},\, 1 \right]$$

$$= K_i \cdot u_i \left[\frac{E_i}{K_i} \right] \qquad\qquad (i = 1,\, 2,...,\, n),$$

so that utilized capital input is the product of capital input and a function u_i of the ratio of energy consumption to capital. The sectoral functions $\{u_i\}$ represent utilization adjustments for capital inputs in each sector. By choosing specific forms for the sectoral utilized capital functions we can define index numbers for utilization adjustments in terms of price and quantity data at discrete points of time.

An approach to productivity measurement that incorporates an explicit relative utilization adjustment would require a model of production and technical change for each industrial sector with output represented as a function of utilized capital, materials, and labor inputs and time. Utilized capital input would be represented as a function of energy and capital inputs not involving changes in technology. Production and utilized capital functions for each sector would be combined with necessary conditions for producer equilibrium and the rate of technical change. We employ a model of production and technical change that incorporates energy, materials, capital, and labor inputs and time, so that we have implicitly incorporated any necessary adjustment for the relative utilization of capital at the sectoral level. No further adjustment of capital inputs for relative utilization is required.

An adjustment for relative utilization of capital input was originally introduced at the aggregate level by Griliches and Jorgenson (1966; 1967; 1972) and was subsequently withdrawn by Christensen and Jorgenson (1973b). Denison (1974, 56) has argued that a relative utilization adjustment is inappropriate at the aggregate level. We conclude that Denison is correct. From our present viewpoint, his ''other output determinants'' are inputs of intermediate goods, including energy. These inputs are properly incorporated into our economy-wide framework through the process of aggregation over sectors.

Kendrick (1973, 26), Kendrick and Grossman, (1980), and Kendrick (1983) do not employ relative utilization adjustment at the sectoral level. These studies utilize productivity measures based on quantities of value added and quantities of primary factor input. From our perspective, relative utilization of capital is implicitly incorporated into this model through the construction of index numbers for value added from price and quantity data on output and intermediate input, including energy input. As Kendrick suggests, no further adjustment for relative utilization is appropriate.

Conclusion

In this chapter we have developed measures of output and intermediate input that incorporate the methodological principles presented in Chapter 2. Components of intermediate input that differ in marginal productivity are accounted for separately in measuring intermediate input for each of forty-five industrial sectors. To accomplish this goal we have constructed data on intermediate input by sector of origin for each producing sector in each year from 1948 to 1979.

We have measured output and intermediate input from the producers' point of view, excluding from the value of output excise and sales taxes and including subsidies paid to producers. We include taxes and exclude subsidies from the value of intermediate input. The purchasers' prices employed in measuring intermediate input are consistent with the producers' prices used in measuring output, adjusted for taxes and subsidies. Both output and intermediate input conform to the Standard Industrial Classification of economic activities.

Our data on output and intermediate input, like our data on capital and labor inputs, have been assembled so as to assimilate available data on output and intermediate input, their prices, and excise and sales taxes and subsidies paid to producers. Our classification of economic activities corresponds to the classification employed in the U.S. national income and product accounts. For each industrial sector the value of output is equal to the sum of the values of labor, capital, and intermediate inputs.

We have used our data on prices and quantities of intermediate input to construct price and quantity indices of intermediate input for each of the fifty-one industrial sectors included in our study. Our data can also be employed to construct indices of intermediate input for aggregates of these sectors, or components of intermediate input within sectors. For example, it would be possible to construct price and quantity indices of energy and nonenergy intermediate inputs within each industrial sector. These indices can be employed in studies of the impact of the prices of labor, capital, and nonenergy inputs, as well as the price of energy input on the demand for energy by sector.

Data on intermediate input for industrial sectors have been employed in past studies of economic growth in the United States. Lack of capital and labor input data compiled on a comparable basis and treating separately components of each type of input that differ in marginal productivity has, however, made it impossible to treat all three inputs symmetrically to analyze growth at the sectoral level. In Chapters 3 and 4 we have presented appropriate measures of labor and capital inputs. We incorporate our new measures of output and intermediate input into an analysis of sectoral and aggregate growth in Chapters 6 and 9, respectively.

6 Growth in Sectoral Output

The purpose of this chapter is to analyze the sources of growth in output for industrial sectors of the U.S. economy. Sources of growth in output can be divided between productivity growth and growth in intermediate, capital, and labor inputs. We have presented data on growth in output and inputs in Chapters 3, 4, and 5. In this chapter we construct measures of productivity growth.

Our initial objective is to measure the rate of sectoral productivity growth. We combine the data on output and intermediate, capital, and labor inputs from Chapters 3, 4, and 5 into a production account for each of the sectors listed in Table 3.1. The value of output from the point of view of the producing sector is equal to the sum of intermediate outlay, property compensation, and labor compensation.

To construct rates of productivity growth, we employ a model of producer behavior based on the translog production function. From this model we derive the translog index of the rate of productivity growth, and we present these indices for forty-five of the fifty-one industries listed in Table 3.1. Productivity change is by definition equal to zero for the remaining six industries, since output is defined in terms of an index of inputs.

We then analyze patterns of change in levels of productivity among industries for seven subperiods of the period 1948–1979. We present rates of productivity growth for the period as a whole for the forty-five industries for which we have measures of productivity change. Using these data, we analyze patterns of change among industries for the whole period.

Our next objective is to allocate the growth in output between changes in productivity and the contributions of growth in intermediate, capital, and labor inputs. The contribution of each input is the product of that input's growth rate and its share in the value of output. The rate of growth of output is the sum of the rate of productivity growth and the contributions of all three inputs.

We present average rates of growth in output and in intermediate, capital, and labor inputs for the period 1948–1979. In Chapters 3, 4, and 5 we have analyzed patterns of growth in output and in the three inputs for seven subperiods of the period 1948–1979. Using data on growth in output and the three inputs presented in this chapter, we analyze patterns of growth among sectors for the period as a whole.

We compare the rate of productivity growth for each industry with the contributions of intermediate, capital, and labor inputs for the period 1948–1979. The results of this comparison provide the basis for an analysis of the relative contribution of the two sources of growth. We also analyze the association between output growth rates and rates of productivity growth for the period as a whole. This analysis provides indirect evidence about the importance of economies of scale as a source of growth.

We also present the contributions of intermediate, capital, and labor inputs to output growth for the period 1948–1979. We compare the contribution of each input with the contributions of the other inputs. This comparison provides the basis for an analysis of the relative importance of the contributions of intermediate, capital, and labor inputs to output growth.

To provide additional detail on sources of output growth we decompose the growth of intermediate input into the growth of an unweighted index of intermediate input and growth in intermediate input quality. We also decompose capital and labor input growth into growth of capital stock and hours worked, and growth in the quality of capital stock and hours worked.

We analyze the contribution of growth in input quality to the growth of intermediate, capital, and labor inputs. We also analyze the contribution of growth in input quality and growth in unweighted indices of input to output growth. The contribution of each of the two components of input growth is the product of the average share of the input in the value of output and the growth rate of the component.

Using this decomposition of input growth into the growth of an unweighted input index and input quality, we compare our analysis of sources of growth in output with an analysis that fails to incorporate changes in input quality. Omission of input quality change would affect measures of intermediate, capital, and labor inputs and levels of productivity. It would have substantial effects on the allocation of output growth among its sources.

Indices of Sectoral Productivity

The starting point for the measurement of productivity is a production account in current prices for each producing sector of the U.S. economy.

The fundamental accounting identity for each sector is that the value of output is equal to the value of input. We define the values of output and input from the point of view of the producer. For each sector of the economy we measure revenue as proceeds to the sector and outlay as expenditures of the sector.

The value of output includes the value of primary factor inputs, capital and labor, and the value of intermediate input. The value of output excludes indirect business taxes on output and sales and excise taxes, and includes subsidies received by the sector. The value of output also excludes trade and transportation margins associated with deliveries of output to consuming sectors. The value of input includes all taxes on intermediate, capital, and labor inputs and all trade and transportation costs incurred in taking delivery of intermediate input.

Given our definitions of output and inputs, the accounting identity for each sector can be written

$$q_i \, Z_i = p_X^i \, X_i + p_K^i \, K_i + p_L^i \, L_i, \qquad\qquad (I = 1, 2,..., n).$$

The value of output from the point of view of the producing sector $\{q_i \, Z_i\}$ is equal to the sum of intermediate outlay $\{p_X^i \, X_i\}$, property compensation $\{p_K^i \, K_i\}$, and labor compensation $\{p_L^i \, L_i\}$. The production account for a typical industrial sector takes the form given in Table 6.1. Data on the value of output and intermediate outlay are presented for each industry in Appendix D. Data on the value of labor and property compensation for each industry are presented in Appendices B and C, respectively.

To construct an index of productivity for each industrial sector, we assume that sectoral output $\{Z_i\}$ can be expressed as a translog function of sectoral intermediate input $\{X_i\}$, capital input $\{K_i\}$, labor input $\{L_i\}$, and time T. The corresponding index of productivity is the translog index of the rate of productivity growth $\{\overline{v}_T^i\}$:[1]

$$\overline{v}_T^i = [\ln Z_i(T) - \ln Z_i(T-1)] - \overline{v}_X^i \, [\ln X_i(T) - \ln X_i(T-1)]$$

$$- \overline{v}_K^i \, [\ln K_i(T) - \ln K_i(T-1)] - \overline{v}_L^i \, [\ln L_i(T) - \ln L_i(T-1)],$$

$$(i=1, 2,..., n),$$

where weights are given by average shares of sectoral intermediate input, capital input, and labor input in the value of sectoral output:

Table 6.1.   Sectoral production account: current prices

Revenue

1. Value of output from the point of view of consuming sectors
2. − Sales and excise taxes
3. − Trade and transportation margins
4. + Subsidies received by the producing sector
5. = Value of output from the point of view of the producing sector

Outlay

1. Intermediate outlay
2. + Property compensation
3. + Labor compensation
4. = Value of input from the point of view of the producing sector

---

$$\overline{v}_T^i = \frac{1}{2}\ [v_T^i(T) + v_T^i(T-1)],$$

$$\overline{v}_X^i = \frac{1}{2}\ [v_X^i(T) + v_X^i(T-1)],$$

$$\overline{v}_K^i = \frac{1}{2}\ [v_K^i(T) + v_K^i(T-1)],$$

$$\overline{v}_L^i = \frac{1}{2}\ [v_L^i(T) + v_L^i(T-1)], \qquad\qquad (i = 1, 2,..., n);$$

$$v_X^i = \frac{p_X^i\ X_i}{q_i\ Z_i}\ ,$$

$$v_K^i = \frac{p_K^i\ K_i}{q_i\ Z_i}\ ,$$

$$v_L^i = \frac{p_L^i\ L_i}{q_i\ Z_i}\ , \qquad\qquad (i = 1, 2,..., n).$$

For the five government sectors listed in Table 3.1, output is equal to labor input, so productivity growth is zero. For private households, output is equal to an index of capital and labor inputs; again, productivity growth is zero. Translog indices of productivity growth for the remaining forty-five sectors are presented for seven subperiods in the 1948–1979 period in Table 6.2. Translog indices of productivity growth for each industry are presented on an annual basis for the period 1948–1979 in Appendix D.

To identify patterns of productivity change among industries over the period 1948–1979, we classify rates of productivity growth by subperiod, as shown in Table 6.3. Considering the subperiods in chronological order, we find fourteen, fifteen, eleven, eight, seventeen, fifteen, and twenty-eight industries, respectively, with negative rates of productivity growth. The subperiod 1960–1966 stands out as a period of widespread growth in the level of productivity, while 1973–1979 is a period of widespread decline. The remaining five subperiods have almost the same number of industries with declining levels of productivity—almost one-third of the forty-five industries in each of the five periods. Recalling that the subperiods 1948–1953 and 1966–1969 were characterized by strong growth of output, and 1957–1960 and 1973–1979 by weak growth, there is no close relationship between rates of productivity growth and rates of growth of output.

Focusing on industries with annual rates of productivity growth greater than four percent and less than minus two percent, seven industries fell outside these limits for the subperiod 1948–1953. This period is also characterized by the highest variability in rates of growth of output and input. The subperiod 1953–1957 has four industries with rates of productivity growth greater than four percent or less than minus two percent. Two of the six remaining subperiods—1957–1960 and 1960–1966—have five industries outside these limits. The subperiods 1966–1969, 1969–1973, and 1973–1979 have seven, nine, and fifteen industries with very high or very low rates of productivity growth.

The level of productivity in transportation services declined at 4.36 percent per year and in local transportation declined at 4.08 percent per year during the subperiod 1948–1953. The level of productivity also declined at a rate of two percent per year in tobacco manufacturing. The productivity level in transportation services continued declining at the rate of 4.59 percent per year during the subperiod 1953–1957. From 1957–1960 three industries had annual rates of productivity growth less than minus two percent—water transportation, transportation services, and nonprofit institutions. For all three industries, rapid declines continued during the period 1960–1966, and productivity declined in that subperiod at 4.05 percent per year in broadcasting.

For seven industries—agricultural services, metal mining, lumber and wood products, trucking, transportation services, and broadcasting—annual

Table 6.2. Sectoral rates of productivity growth

Industry	Translog index of productivity growth (average annual rates of growth)						
	1948– 1953	1953– 1957	1957– 1960	1960– 1966	1966– 1969	1969– 1973	1973– 1979
Agricultural production	0.0123	0.0237	0.0152	0.0205	0.0197	0.0074	0.0064
Agricultural services	0.0011	−0.0033	0.0038	−0.0083	−0.0408	−0.0153	0.0098
Metal mining	−0.0077	0.0059	0.0037	0.0125	−0.0338	0.0478	−0.0558
Coal mining	0.0000	0.0533	0.0242	0.0314	−0.0122	−0.0694	−0.0404
Crude petroleum and natural gas	0.0166	−0.0135	0.0111	0.0022	0.0176	0.0008	−0.1323
Nonmetallic mining and quarrying	0.0150	0.0118	0.0148	0.0065	0.0002	0.0240	−0.0307
Contract construction	0.0139	0.0136	0.0123	0.0052	−0.0066	−0.0118	−0.0176
Food and kindred products	0.0398	0.0390	0.0142	0.0021	−0.0001	−0.0335	0.0219
Tobacco manufacturers	−0.0200	0.0040	0.0068	−0.0040	0.0255	0.0170	−0.0446
Textile mill products	0.0089	0.0206	0.0224	0.0226	0.0131	0.0121	0.0297
Apparel and other fabricated textile products	0.0168	0.0060	0.0065	0.0072	0.0015	0.0063	0.0228
Paper and allied products	−0.0124	−0.0221	0.0041	0.0151	0.0133	0.0193	−0.0198
Printing and publishing	−0.0004	0.0045	−0.0070	0.0097	0.0144	0.0240	−0.0019
Chemicals and allied products	0.0170	0.0206	0.0117	0.0159	0.0264	0.0359	−0.0243
Petroleum and coal products	−0.0154	−0.0027	0.0401	0.0179	0.0234	−0.0500	−0.0941
Rubber and misc. plastic products	−0.0058	−0.0108	0.0139	0.0159	0.0174	0.0116	−0.0051
Leather and leather products	0.0148	0.0170	−0.0122	0.0020	0.0072	−0.0152	−0.0002
Lumber and wood products except furniture	−0.0076	0.0267	0.0184	0.0104	−0.0291	−0.0297	0.0079
Furniture and fixtures	−0.0009	0.0017	0.0034	0.0102	−0.0066	−0.0039	0.0069
Stone, clay, and glass products	0.0013	−0.0076	0.0014	0.0133	0.0025	0.0081	−0.0132

Table 6.2 continued

Industry	Translog index of productivity growth (average annual rates of growth)						
	1948– 1953	1953– 1957	1957– 1960	1960– 1966	1966– 1969	1969– 1973	1973– 1979
Primary metal industries	−0.0004	−0.0164	−0.0106	0.0108	−0.0157	0.0052	−0.0204
Fabricated metal industries	0.0046	0.0010	0.0063	0.0132	0.0078	0.0050	−0.0026
Machinery, except electrical	0.0036	−0.0115	0.0005	0.0149	−0.0048	0.0132	0.0016
Elec. machinery, eqpt., and supplies	0.0156	−0.0007	0.0124	0.0242	0.0152	0.0196	0.0181
Trans. eqpt. and ordnance, except motor vehicles	0.0096	−0.0060	0.0037	0.0159	−0.0122	0.0162	−0.0065
Motor vehicles and equipment	0.0151	0.0014	0.0139	0.0170	0.0163	0.0048	−0.0018
Prof. photographic eqpt. and watches	0.0136	−0.0057	0.0194	0.0223	0.0119	0.0069	−0.0084
Misc. manufacturing industries	0.0106	0.0164	0.0103	0.0076	0.0171	0.0074	−0.0224
Railroads and rail express services	0.0042	0.0306	0.0198	0.0390	0.0028	0.0160	0.0119
Street rail., bus lines, and taxicabs	−0.0408	−0.0115	−0.0089	−0.0058	−0.0117	−0.0318	0.0032
Trucking services and warehousing	0.0525	0.0186	0.0106	0.0088	−0.0288	0.0097	−0.0023
Water transportation	−0.0334	0.0355	−0.0262	−0.0213	0.0134	0.0717	−0.0206
Air transportation	0.0901	0.0417	−0.0156	0.0244	0.0017	−0.0047	0.0278
Pipelines, except natural gas	0.0179	0.0224	0.0019	0.0534	0.0518	0.0472	−0.0936
Transportation services	−0.0436	−0.0459	−0.0308	−0.0328	−0.0433	0.0244	−0.0367
Telephone, telegraph, and misc. communication services	0.0207	0.0069	0.0139	0.0261	0.0303	0.0349	0.0564
Radio and television broadcasting	0.0450	0.0221	−0.0027	−0.0405	−0.0274	−0.0301	−0.0827
Electric utilities	0.0169	0.0169	0.0301	0.0285	0.0133	−0.0132	−0.0195
Gas utilities	0.0147	0.0064	−0.0044	0.0081	0.0135	−0.0032	−0.0275
Water supply and sanitary services	0.0585	0.0125	0.0467	0.0273	0.0263	0.0141	0.0310

Table 6.2 continued

Industry	Translog index of productivity growth (average annual rates of growth)						
	1948–1953	1953–1957	1957–1960	1960–1966	1966–1969	1969–1973	1973–1979
Wholesale trade	0.0096	0.0230	0.0158	0.0240	0.0198	0.0173	−0.0018
Retail trade	0.0222	0.0157	0.0030	0.0173	−0.0034	0.0118	−0.0010
Finance, insurance, and real estate	0.0023	0.0062	0.0077	0.0012	−0.0006	0.0040	0.0092
Services excl. private households and institutions	−0.0050	−0.0072	−0.0060	−0.0057	−0.0173	−0.0049	0.0029
Institutions	−0.0077	−0.0017	−0.0263	−0.0255	0.0107	−0.0170	0.0215

Table 6.3. Classification of sectoral rates of productivity growth by sub-period, 1948–1979

Average rate of productivity growth	1948–1953	1953–1957	1957–1960	1960–1966	1966–1969	1969–1973	1973–1979
Less than −4%	2	1	0	1	2	2	7
−4% to −2%	1	1	3	3	4	4	7
−2% to 0	11	13	8	4	11	9	14
0 to 2%	24	18	29	25	22	22	10
2% to 4%	3	10	3	11	5	5	6
4% to 6%	3	2	2	1	1	2	1
More than 6%	1	0	0	0	0	1	0

rates of productivity growth fell below minus two percent during the sub-period 1966–1969. For the subperiod 1969–1973, annual rates of productivity growth below this limit were experienced by coal mining, food, petroleum and coal, lumber, local transportation, and broadcasting. Finally, the subperiod 1973–1979 saw rapid declines in productivity growth for four-teen industries: metal mining, coal mining, crude petroleum and natural gas, nonmetallic mining, tobacco, chemicals, petroleum and coal, primary metal, miscellaneous manufacturing, water transportation, pipelines, transportation services, broadcasting, and gas utilities.

During the subperiod 1948–1953 the rate of productivity growth in air transportation was 9.01 percent. Other industries with rates of productivity growth exceeding four percent during this period are trucking, broadcasting, and water supply and sanitary services. Rapid productivity growth continued in air transportation during the subperiod 1953–1957. Coal mining was also characterized by rapid productivity growth during this period. During 1957–1960 only petroleum and coal products and water supply and sanitary services had rates of productivity growth in excess of four percent.

Productivity continued to grow rapidly only in pipelines during the periods 1960–1966 and 1966–1969. The rate of productivity growth in water transportation from 1969–1973 reached the level of 7.17 percent; high rates of productivity growth also characterized metal mining and pipelines. Only telecommunications stands out as an industry undergoing rapid improvement in productivity during the period 1973 to 1979.

Positive rates of productivity growth during all seven subperiods took place in only two manufacturing industries—textiles and apparel—and four industries outside manufacturing—agriculture, railroads, telecommunications, and water supply and sanitary services. The list of industries with positive rates of productivity growth in six of the seven subperiods is nearly as long, including five manufacturing industries—chemicals, fabricated metals, electrical machinery, motor vehicles, and miscellaneous manufacturing—and four nonmanufacturing industries—nonmetallic mining, pipelines, wholesale trade, and finance, insurance, and real estate. Only three industries experienced negative rates of productivity growth during six of the seven subperiods—local transportation, transportation services, and services. Railroads were characterized by persistent decline in output but positive rates of productivity growth, while local transportation had declining output and negative rates of productivity growth.

Sources of Growth in Sectoral Output

Our next objective is to allocate the growth in output between growth in inputs and change in productivity. The growth rate of output is the sum of a weighted average of the growth rates of intermediate, capital, and labor inputs, and the rate of productivity growth. The weights for input growth rates are the shares of the inputs in the value of output. Table 6.4 presents rates of growth of output and of intermediate, capital, and labor inputs, and the rate of productivity growth for each of the fifty-one industrial sectors listed in Table 3.1, for the period 1948–1979.

Table 6.5 summarizes the patterns of output, input, and productivity growth by subperiod. Positive growth in output predominates; only leather

Table 6.4. Sectoral output, inputs, and productivity: rates of growth, 1948–1979

	Average annual rates of growth				
Industry	Output	Intermediate input	Capital input	Labor input	Rate of productivity growth
Agricultural production	0.0216	0.0224	0.0337	−0.0320	0.0146
Agricultural services	0.0297	0.0392	0.0696	0.0252	−0.0055
Metal mining	0.0142	0.0133	0.0849	0.0017	−0.0056
Coal mining	0.0038	0.0216	0.0356	−0.0175	−0.0027
Crude petroleum and natural gas	0.0213	0.0511	0.0293	0.0284	−0.0214
Nonmetallic mining and quarrying	0.0409	0.0400	0.0647	0.0117	0.0038
Contract construction	0.0271	0.0290	0.0390	0.0199	0.0006
Food and kindred products	0.0281	0.0174	0.0276	−0.0008	0.0131
Tobacco manufacturers	0.0072	0.0223	0.0153	−0.0066	−0.0068
Textile mill products	0.0345	0.0250	0.0278	−0.0103	0.0192
Apparel and other fabricated textile products	0.0264	0.0201	0.0376	0.0029	0.0109
Paper and allied products	0.0401	0.0526	0.0373	0.0166	−0.0016
Printing and publishing	0.0323	0.0358	0.0206	0.0170	0.0058
Chemicals and allied products	0.0591	0.0539	0.0517	0.0242	0.0121
Petroleum and coal products	0.0271	0.0515	0.0218	0.0069	−0.0179
Rubber and misc. plastic products	0.0477	0.0468	0.0587	0.0319	0.0043
Leather and leather products	−0.0047	−0.0037	0.0081	−0.0156	0.0025
Lumber and wood products, except furniture	0.0288	0.0485	0.0309	−0.0017	0.0009
Furniture and fixtures	0.0373	0.0496	0.0397	0.0111	0.0026

Table 6.4 continued

	Average annual rates of growth			
Industry	Output	Intermediate input	Capital input	Labor input	Rate of productivity growth
Stone, clay, and glass products	0.0383	0.0579	0.0383	0.0119	0.0007
Primary metal industries	0.0128	0.0234	0.0194	0.0045	−0.0059
Fabricated metal industries	0.0350	0.0387	0.0388	0.0171	0.0050
Machinery, except electrical	0.0417	0.0493	0.0477	0.0223	0.0036
Elec. machinery, eqpt., and supplies	0.0580	0.0493	0.0568	0.0296	0.0158
Trans. eqpt. and ordnance, except motor vehicles	0.0559	0.0673	0.0257	0.0313	0.0039
Motor vehicles and equipment	0.0451	0.0436	0.0445	0.0128	0.0091
Prof. photographic eqpt. and watches	0.0569	0.0585	0.0737	0.0351	0.0081
Misc. manufacturing industries	0.0340	0.0434	0.0414	0.0050	0.0046
Railroads and rail express services	0.0053	−0.0087	0.0164	−0.0305	0.0187
Street rail., bus lines, and taxicabs	−0.0217	−0.0095	0.0450	−0.0155	−0.0147
Trucking services and warehousing	0.0488	0.0359	0.0724	0.0273	0.0116
Water transportation	0.0040	0.0094	0.0162	−0.0050	−0.0009
Air transportation	0.0957	0.0746	0.0780	0.0509	0.0281
Pipelines, except natural gas	0.0493	0.0289	0.0837	−0.0064	0.0093
Transportation services	0.0268	0.0654	0.0453	0.0317	−0.0304
Telephone, telegraph, and misc. communication services	0.0688	0.0355	0.0661	0.0212	0.0290
Radio and television broadcasting	0.0132	−0.0929	0.0705	0.0430	−0.0205
Electric utilities	0.0628	0.0545	0.0749	0.0162	0.0092
Gas utilities	0.0531	0.0636	0.0455	0.0193	−0.0001

Table 6.4 continued

	Average annual rates of growth				
Industry	Output	Intermediate input	Capital input	Labor input	Rate of productivity growth
Water supply and sanitary services	0.0328	−0.0349	−0.0002	0.0157	0.0312
Wholesale trade	0.0425	0.0311	0.0468	0.0212	0.0145
Retail trade	0.0293	0.0229	0.0349	0.0118	0.0103
Finance, insurance, and real estate	0.0493	0.0636	0.0154	0.0364	0.0044
Services, except private households and institutions	0.0377	0.0468	0.0460	0.0307	−0.0052
Private households	0.0491	0.0000	0.0521	−0.0234	0.0000
Institutions	0.0373	0.0652	0.0290	0.0423	−0.0059
Federal public administration	0.0173	0.0000	0.0000	0.0174	0.0000
Federal government enterprises	0.0141	0.0000	0.0000	0.0125	0.0000
State and local educational services	0.0457	0.0000	0.0000	0.0455	0.0000
State and local public admin.	0.0362	0.0000	0.0000	0.0346	0.0000
State and local enterprises	0.0363	0.0000	0.0000	0.0361	0.0000

and local transportation had negative output growth for the whole period. Air transportation had the highest rate of output growth for the period 1948–1979, 9.57 percent per year.

Patterns of growth of intermediate input were summarized by subperiod in Chapter 5. Positive growth in intermediate input predominates data for 1948–1979 given in Table 6.4. Only leather, railroads, local transportation, broadcasting, and water supply and sanitary services experienced negative growth in intermediate input for the period as a whole. Leather and local transportation also had negative growth in output for this period. No industries had growth rates in intermediate input over eight percent per year. The highest growth rate is for air transportation, at 7.46 percent.

Patterns of growth of capital input by subperiod are summarized in

Table 6.5. Rates of growth of sectoral output, inputs, and productivity, 1948–1979

Average rates of growth	Output	Intermediate input	Capital input	Labor input	Rate of productivity growth
Less than −4%	0	1	0	0	0
−4% to −2%	1	1	0	3	3
−2% to 0	1	3	1	9	12
0 to 2%	9	3	6	19	27
2% to 4%	21	15	17	16	3
4% to 6%	16	16	12	4	0
6% to 8%	2	6	8	0	0
More than 8%	1	0	2	0	0

Chapter 4. Positive growth in capital input also predominates for the period 1948–1979. For metal mining, capital input grew at a rate of 8.49 percent for the period as a whole. For pipelines the corresponding growth rate is 8.37 percent. Only water supply and sanitary services had a negative growth rate for capital input for the period 1948–1979. This industry also had a negative growth rate for intermediate input.

Patterns of growth of labor input were summarized by subperiod in Chapter 3. For twelve of the fifty-one industries listed in Table 3.1 the growth rate of labor input for the period 1948–1979 was negative. The rate of decline of labor input in agriculture was 3.20 percent per year. For railroads the rate of decline was 3.05 percent, and for private households the rate was 2.34 percent. Agriculture had positive growth rates of output, intermediate input, and capital input, and railroads and private households had positive growth rates for output and capital input. The highest growth rate for labor input was for air transportation, at 5.09 percent; the rates for broadcasting, nonprofit institutions, and state and local education services also exceeded four percent.

In the preceding section we summarized productivity change for subperiods within the period 1948–1979. From data presented in Table 6.4 we conclude that one-third of the industries experienced productivity declines, while two-thirds underwent productivity growth. Water supply and sanitary services had the highest rate of productivity growth, at 3.12 percent, while telecommunications had the second-highest rate, at 2.90 percent. Air transportation, at 2.81 percent, completes the list of industries with rates of productivity growth exceeding two percent.

Although positive productivity growth rates predominate for the period 1948–1979, there are three industries with rates of decline greater than two percent for the period as a whole—crude petroleum and natural gas, transportation services, and broadcasting. The remaining industries with negative productivity growth include agricultural services, metal and coal mining, tobacco manufacturers, paper, petroleum and coal products, primary metals manufacturing, local transportation, water transportation, gas utilities, services, and nonprofit institutions.

The association between output growth and productivity growth for the period 1948–1979 is weak. To characterize this association in greater detail, Table 6.6 presents a cross-classification of rates of productivity growth and output growth rates. Of the thirty industries with positive rates of productivity growth, twenty-nine had positive output growth rates and only leather had a negative output growth rate. Of the fifteen industries with negative rates of productivity growth, fourteen had positive output growth rates and only local transportation had a negative output growth rate. We conclude that there is no evidence of pervasive economies of scale at the industry level for the period 1948–1979; this does not rule out economies of scale at the plant or firm level, or the possibility of economies of scale at the industry level for some industries.

Economies of scale at the industry level could be constant, even if individual plants or firms within an industry are characterized by increasing returns, provided that expansion of industry output occurs, through expansion in the number of plants or firms, with no change in the average size of the plant or firm. Economies of scale at the industry level would result from increasing returns for plants and firms and growth in the average size of the plant or firm. The weak association between growth of output and productivity growth is consistent with constant returns to scale at the industry level for most industries.

Contributions of Growth in Sectoral Inputs

Our next objective is to analyze the contributions of inputs to output growth for the period 1948–1979. The output growth rate is the sum of the contributions of intermediate, capital, and labor inputs, and productivity growth. The contribution of each input is the product of its growth rate and its share in the value of output. We begin by comparing the productivity growth for each industry with the sum of the contributions of all three inputs.

Table 6.6. Rates of growth of sectoral output by rates of sectoral productivity growth, 1948–1979

Average rate of productivity growth	Average rate of growth of output							
	Less than −2%	−2% to 0	0 to 2%	2% to 4%	4% to 6%	6% to 8%	More than 8%	Total
Less than −2%	0	0	1	2	0	0	0	3
−2% to 0	1	0	5	4	2	0	0	12
0 to 2%	0	1	1	12	12	1	0	27
2% to 4%	0	0	0	1	0	1	1	3
4% to 6%	0	0	0	0	0	0	0	0
Total	1	1	7	19	14	2	1	45

From Table 6.4, productivity growth accounts for a predominant part of output growth for only five industries—agriculture, textiles, leather, railroads, and water supply and sanitary services. The sum of the contributions of sectoral intermediate, capital, and labor inputs is the predominant source of growth in sectoral output for the remaining forty-six industries, as indicated by Table 6.7. We conclude that productivity growth is a much less important source of output growth than the growth of intermediate, capital, and labor inputs.

To analyze sources of output growth for the period 1948–1979, Table 6.7 includes the contribution of growth in each input. The shares of intermediate and capital inputs in the value of output are given in the first two columns. The shares of labor, intermediate, and capital inputs sum to unity. The share of labor input is the largest among the shares of all three inputs for twelve of the fifty-one industries, including five government sectors, where the value of labor input is equal to the value of output. Other industries where the share of labor input predominates are agricultural services, professional equipment, telecommunications, broadcasting, wholesale trade, retail trade, and nonprofit institutions. The share of capital input is the largest of the input shares in only two industries: water supply and sanitary services, and private households. The share of intermediate input predominates in thirty-seven of the fifty-one industries.

The contributions to output growth of growth in intermediate, capital, and labor inputs are presented in the third, fourth, and fifth columns of the table,

Table 6.7. Contributions to growth in sectoral output: rates of growth, 1948–1979

| | Average annual rates of growth | | | | | |
| | Average value shares | | Contributions to growth in output | | | |
Industry	Intermediate input	Capital input	Intermediate input	Capital input	Labor input	Rate of productivity growth
Agricultural production	0.5688	0.1277	0.0128	0.0040	−0.0097	0.0146
Agricultural services	0.4361	0.1182	0.0173	0.0068	0.0111	−0.0055
Metal mining	0.5914	0.1518	0.0075	0.0127	−0.0004	−0.0056
Coal mining	0.4309	0.1570	0.0112	0.0069	−0.0116	−0.0027
Crude petroleum and natural gas	0.5221	0.3482	0.0291	0.0104	0.0031	−0.0214
Nonmetallic mining and quarrying	0.3957	0.2731	0.0153	0.0178	0.0039	0.0038
Contract construction	0.5630	0.0605	0.0169	0.0022	0.0074	0.0006
Food and kindred products	0.7716	0.0641	0.0134	0.0018	−0.0002	0.0131
Tobacco manufacturers	0.5059	0.2928	0.0116	0.0039	−0.0015	−0.0068
Textile mill products	0.6440	0.0809	0.0157	0.0026	−0.0030	0.0192
Apparel and other fabricated textile products	0.6416	0.0410	0.0130	0.0016	0.0009	0.0109
Paper and allied products	0.6128	0.1375	0.0322	0.0054	0.0041	−0.0016
Printing and publishing	0.4955	0.1096	0.0176	0.0023	0.0066	0.0058
Chemicals and allied products	0.6110	0.1731	0.0329	0.0091	0.0050	0.0121
Petroleum and coal products	0.7787	0.1062	0.0422	0.0024	0.0005	−0.0179
Rubber and misc. plastic products	0.5432	0.0990	0.0259	0.0062	0.0113	0.0043
Leather and leather products	0.6041	0.0517	−0.0023	0.0005	−0.0054	0.0025
Lumber and wood products, except furniture	0.5108	0.1380	0.0245	0.0045	−0.0011	0.0009
Furniture and fixtures	0.5725	0.0720	0.0281	0.0029	0.0038	0.0026

Table 6.7 continued

| | Average annual rates of growth | | | | | |
| | Average value shares | | Contributions to growth in output | | | |
Industry	Intermediate input	Capital input	Intermediate input	Capital input	Labor input	Rate of productivity growth
Stone, clay, and glass products	0.5114	0.1439	0.0281	0.0057	0.0038	0.0007
Primary metal industries	0.6572	0.1077	0.0154	0.0023	0.0011	−0.0059
Fabricated metal industries	0.5246	0.0944	0.0200	0.0037	0.0062	0.0050
Machinery, except electrical	0.4891	0.1261	0.0240	0.0062	0.0080	0.0036
Elec. machinery, eqpt., and supplies	0.5329	0.1003	0.0262	0.0058	0.0102	0.0158
Trans. eqpt. and ordnance, except motor vehicles	0.6064	0.0537	0.0408	0.0013	0.0100	0.0039
Motor vehicles and equipment	0.6684	0.1271	0.0285	0.0053	0.0022	0.0091
Prof. photographic eqpt. and watches	0.3559	0.1432	0.0217	0.0102	0.0170	0.0081
Misc. manufacturing industries	0.5487	0.0940	0.0243	0.0037	0.0015	0.0046
Railroads and rail express services	0.5395	0.1137	−0.0046	0.0019	−0.0108	0.0187
Street rail., bus lines, and taxicabs	0.6184	0.1011	−0.0063	0.0036	−0.0044	−0.0147
Trucking services and warehousing	0.6097	0.1020	0.0222	0.0072	0.0078	0.0116
Water transportation	0.6141	0.0831	0.0058	0.0011	−0.0019	−0.0009
Air transportation	0.5691	0.1244	0.0421	0.0103	0.0153	0.0281
Pipelines, except natural gas	0.4731	0.3508	0.0133	0.0282	−0.0014	0.0093
Transportation services	0.7496	0.0732	0.0488	0.0034	0.0049	−0.0304
Telephone, telegraph, and misc. communication services	0.2074	0.3664	0.0077	0.0234	0.0087	0.0290
Radio and television broadcasting	0.2362	0.2484	−0.0064	0.0185	0.0216	−0.0205

Table 6.7 continued

	Average annual rates of growth					
	Average value shares		Contributions to growth in output			
Industry	Intermediate input	Capital input	Intermediate input	Capital input	Labor input	Rate of productivity growth
Electric utilities	0.4120	0.3754	0.0227	0.0275	0.0034	0.0092
Gas utilities	0.6646	0.2133	0.0403	0.0106	0.0024	−0.0001
Water supply and sanitary services	0.1549	0.5424	−0.0031	−0.0001	0.0048	0.0312
Wholesale trade	0.2030	0.1908	0.0064	0.0090	0.0127	0.0145
Retail trade	0.3950	0.1264	0.0091	0.0043	0.0056	0.0103
Finance, insurance, and real estate	0.5559	0.2344	0.0341	0.0031	0.0076	0.0044
Services, except private households and institutions	0.6124	0.1390	0.0286	0.0064	0.0078	−0.0052
Private households	0.0000	0.9605	0.0000	0.0499	−0.0008	0.0000
Institutions	0.2338	0.3415	0.0146	0.0105	0.0182	−0.0059
Federal public administration	0.0000	0.0000	0.0000	0.0000	0.0173	0.0000
Federal government enterprises	0.0000	0.0000	0.0000	0.0000	0.0141	0.0000
State and local educational services	0.0000	0.0000	0.0000	0.0000	0.0457	0.0000
State and local public admin.	0.0000	0.0000	0.0000	0.0000	0.0362	0.0000
State and local enterprises	0.0000	0.0000	0.0000	0.0000	0.0363	0.0000

and the rate of productivity growth is given in the sixth column. From these data we conclude that the contribution of intermediate input is by far the most significant source of growth in output.

The contribution of intermediate input alone exceeds the rate of productivity growth for thirty-six of the forty-five industries for which we have a measure of intermediate input. The nine industries where the rate of productivity growth exceeds the contribution of intermediate input are agriculture, textiles, leather, railroads, telecommunications, broadcasting, water supply and sanitary services, wholesale trade, and retail trade.

If we focus attention on capital and labor inputs, excluding intermediate input from consideration, we find that the sum of the contributions of capital and labor inputs exceeds the rate of productivity growth for twenty-nine of the forty-five industries for which we have a measure of productivity growth. For sixteen of these industries the rate of productivity growth is greater than the contributions of capital and labor inputs together.

For twenty-five of the forty-five industries the contribution of capital input or labor input alone is more important than productivity growth as a source of growth in output. Our overall conclusion is that the predominant contributions to output growth are those of intermediate, capital, and labor inputs. By far the most important contribution is that of intermediate input. Even excluding the contribution of intermediate input, either the contribution of capital input or the contribution of labor input exceeds the rate of productivity growth for a majority of industries.

Contributions of Growth in Quality of Sectoral Inputs

We have decomposed output growth into the sum of a weighted average of growth rates of indices of sectoral intermediate, capital, and labor inputs, and the rate of productivity growth. We can provide additional perspective on sources of output growth by comparing our results with those based on measures of intermediate, capital, and labor inputs that fail to incorporate changes in input quality.

Recall that the rate of growth of intermediate input is the sum of rates of growth of an unweighted index of intermediate input and the quality of intermediate input. Similarly, the rate of growth of capital input is the sum of rates of growth of capital stock and the quality of capital stock. Finally, the rate of growth of sectoral labor input is the sum of rates of growth of hours worked and the quality of hours worked.

Using indices of the quality of intermediate input, capital stock, and hours worked, we can decompose the rate of growth of output as follows:

$$\ln Z_i(T) - \ln Z_i(T-1)$$

$$= \bar{v}_X^i \left[\ln X_i(T) - \ln X_i(T-1)\right] + \bar{v}_K^i \left[\ln K_i(T) - \ln K_i(T-1)\right]$$

$$+ \bar{v}_L^i \left[\ln L_i(T) - \ln L_i(T-1)\right] + \bar{v}_T^i$$

$$= \bar{v}_X^i \left[\ln Q_X^i(T) - \ln Q_X^i(T-1)\right] + \bar{v}_X^i \left[\ln I_i(T) - \ln I_i(T-1)\right]$$

$$+ \bar{v}_K^i \left[\ln Q_K^i(T) - \ln Q_K^i(T-1)\right] + \bar{v}_K^i \left[\ln A_i(T-1) - \ln A_i(T-2)\right]$$

$$+ \bar{v}_L^i \left[\ln Q_L^i(T) - \ln Q_L^i(T-1) \right] + \bar{v}_L^i \left[\ln H_i(T) - \ln H_i(T-1) \right]$$

$$+ \bar{v}_T, \qquad\qquad\qquad (i = 1, 2, ..., n).$$

The output growth rate is the sum of three terms. The first is a weighted average of the growth rates of unweighted intermediate input, capital stock, and hours worked. The second is a weighted average of growth rates of quality of intermediate input, capital stock, and hours worked. The third is the rate of productivity growth. Table 6.8 presents the growth rates of the quality of sectoral intermediate, capital, and labor inputs for the period 1948–1979, and growth rates of indices of intermediate input, capital stock, and hours worked.

Our first conclusion from Table 6.8 is that growth in input quality is not an important source of growth in intermediate input. Except for the five industrial sectors where the growth of sectoral intermediate input is negative— leather, railroads, local transportation, broadcasting, and water supply and sanitary services—the growth of an unweighted index of intermediate input exceeds the growth of intermediate input quality. For most industrial sectors the growth rate of the unweighted index greatly exceeds the growth of intermediate input quality.

Our second conclusion from Table 6.8 is that growth in capital input quality is an important but not predominant source of growth in capital input. For five industrial sectors—agriculture, agricultural services, railroads, water transportation, and transportation services—the growth of capital quality actually exceeds the growth of capital stock. For forty of the forty-six industries for which we have data on capital input, the quality of capital stock increased during the period 1948–1979. For all forty-six industries the level of capital stock is increasing. For most industries growth in capital quality is much greater as a proportion of growth in capital input than growth in intermediate input quality as a proportion of intermediate input growth.

Finally, we conclude from Table 6.8 that growth in the quality of hours worked is a very important source of growth in labor input. For sixteen of the fifty-one industries the growth rate of labor quality exceeds the rate of growth of hours worked. Eight of these industries are in manufacturing: food, tobacco, textiles, petroleum and coal, leather, lumber and wood, primary metals, and miscellaneous manufacturing. The eight industries outside manufacturing are agriculture, metal mining, coal mining, railroads, local transportation, water transportation, pipelines, and private households.

The average growth rate of the quality of hours worked is positive for forty-nine of the fifty-one industries included in our study; private households and state and local government enterprises are the only exceptions. By

Table 6.8. Sectoral input quality: rates of growth, 1948–1979

Industry	Average annual rates of growth					
	Quality of intermediate input	Unweighted intermediate input	Quality of capital stock	Capital stock	Quality of hours worked	Hours worked
Agricultural production	0.0008	0.0216	0.0293	0.0044	0.0050	−0.0370
Agricultural services	−0.0006	0.0398	0.0548	0.0148	0.0075	0.0177
Metal mining	−0.0002	0.0136	−0.0014	0.0863	0.0055	−0.0036
Coal mining	0.0004	0.0212	−0.0020	0.0376	0.0039	−0.0214
Crude petroleum and natural gas	−0.0013	0.0524	−0.0032	0.0325	0.0083	0.0201
Nonmetallic mining and quarrying	−0.0002	0.0402	0.0018	0.0629	0.0035	0.0083
Contract construction	0.0003	0.0288	0.0055	0.0335	0.0032	0.0167
Food and kindred products	0.0010	0.0164	0.0068	0.0208	0.0030	−0.0038
Tobacco manufacturers	−0.0003	0.0226	0.0014	0.0139	0.0071	−0.0137
Textile mill products	0.0014	0.0236	0.0095	0.0183	0.0023	−0.0127
Apparel and other fabricated textile products	0.0019	0.0182	0.0046	0.0330	0.0013	0.0016
Paper and allied products	0.0008	0.0518	−0.0038	0.0412	0.0051	0.0114
Printing and publishing	−0.0003	0.0361	0.0028	0.0178	0.0034	0.0136
Chemicals and allied products	0.0000	0.0539	0.0025	0.0492	0.0071	0.0171
Petroleum and coal products	−0.0002	0.0517	0.0066	0.0152	0.0073	−0.0004
Rubber and misc. plastic products	0.0008	0.0460	0.0056	0.0532	0.0030	0.0288
Leather and leather products	0.0005	−0.0042	0.0033	0.0048	0.0010	−0.0166
Lumber and wood products, except furniture	0.0014	0.0471	0.0085	0.0224	0.0034	−0.0051
Furniture and fixtures	0.0002	0.0495	0.0075	0.0322	0.0030	0.0081
Stone, clay, and glass products	0.0010	0.0570	0.0066	0.0317	0.0053	0.0067

Table 6.8 continued

	Average annual rates of growth					
Industry	Quality of intermediate input	Unweighted intermediate input	Quality of capital stock	Capital stock	Quality of hours worked	Hours worked
Primary metal industries	−0.0002	0.0235	0.0063	0.0131	0.0042	0.0002
Fabricated metal industries	−0.0002	0.0388	0.0076	0.0312	0.0037	0.0135
Machinery, except electrical	−0.0001	0.0494	0.0035	0.0442	0.0049	0.0174
Elec. machinery, eqpt., and supplies	0.0006	0.0487	0.0102	0.0466	0.0057	0.0239
Trans. eqpt. and ordnance, except motor vehicles	0.0009	0.0664	0.0054	0.0203	0.0055	0.0259
Motor vehicles and equipment	−0.0003	0.0438	0.0110	0.0335	0.0042	0.0086
Prof. photographic eqpt. and watches	0.0002	0.0583	0.0075	0.0662	0.0059	0.0292
Misc. manufacturing industries	0.0008	0.0426	0.0022	0.0391	0.0042	0.0008
Railroads and rail express services	−0.0014	−0.0073	0.0123	0.0041	0.0051	−0.0356
Street rail., bus lines, and taxicabs	−0.0024	−0.0071	0.0197	0.0254	0.0020	−0.0175
Trucking services and warehousing	−0.0003	0.0362	0.0134	0.0590	0.0042	0.0230
Water transportation	0.0012	0.0082	0.0086	0.0076	0.0032	−0.0083
Air transportation	−0.0002	0.0748	0.0054	0.0726	0.0018	0.0491
Pipelines, except natural gas	−0.0008	0.0298	0.0233	0.0605	0.0077	−0.0139
Transportation services	−0.0004	0.0657	0.0399	0.0053	0.0054	0.0263
Telephone, telegraph, and misc. communication services	−0.0002	0.0357	0.0225	0.0436	0.0054	0.0158
Radio and television broadcasting	−0.0006	−0.0923	0.0036	0.0669	0.0021	0.0408
Electric utilities	−0.0010	0.0555	0.0125	0.0624	0.0041	0.0121
Gas utilities	−0.0003	0.0639	0.0022	0.0432	0.0050	0.0143
Water supply and sanitary services	0.0008	−0.0357	−0.0004	0.0002	0.0034	0.0124

Table 6.8 continued

Industry	Average annual rates of growth					
	Quality of intermediate input	Unweighted intermediate input	Quality of capital stock	Capital stock	Quality of hours worked	Hours worked
Wholesale trade	0.0003	0.0307	0.0081	0.0386	0.0037	0.0175
Retail trade	−0.0003	0.0232	0.0076	0.0273	0.0015	0.0103
Finance, insurance, and real estate	−0.0002	0.0638	−0.0002	0.0156	0.0053	0.0312
Services, except private households and institutions	0.0007	0.0460	0.0106	0.0355	0.0005	0.0302
Private households			0.0110	0.0411	−0.0027	−0.0207
Institutions	−0.0005	0.0657	0.0002	0.0287	0.0034	0.0388
Federal public administration					0.0056	0.0117
Federal government enterprises					0.0016	0.0125
State and local educational services					0.0038	0.0419
State and local public admin.					0.0036	0.0326
State and local enterprises					−0.0005	0.0367

contrast, the rate of growth of hours worked is positive for only thirty-seven of the fifty-one industries. For most industries growth in labor quality as a proportion of growth in labor input is much greater than growth in the quality of intermediate and capital inputs as proportions of growth in intermediate or capital input, respectively.

The contributions to output growth of the quality of intermediate, capital, and labor inputs are presented for the period 1948–1979 in Table 6.9. The contribution of input quality is equal to the product of its growth rate and the share of the corresponding input in the value of output. The table also shows the contributions of unweighted intermediate input, capital stock, and hours worked; again, the contribution of each index is the product of its growth rate and the value share of the corresponding input. For convenience, productivity growth rates are included in the table.

An analysis of sources of output growth that fails to incorporate changes in input quality would lead to results that differ from those of our analysis in a number of respects. First, the omission of changes in input quality would

Table 6.9.   Contributions of input quality to growth in sectoral output: rates of growth, 1948–1979

Industry	Quality of intermediate input	Unweighted intermediate input	Quality of capital stock	Capital stock	Quality of hours worked	Hours worked	Rate of productivity growth
	Average annual rates of growth						
Agricultural production	0.0004	0.0124	0.0035	0.0005	0.0016	−0.0113	0.0146
Agricultural services	−0.0002	0.0176	0.0044	0.0024	0.0030	0.0081	−0.0055
Metal mining	−0.0001	0.0076	0.0000	0.0128	0.0014	−0.0017	−0.0056
Coal mining	0.0002	0.0110	−0.0002	0.0071	0.0015	−0.0130	−0.0027
Crude petroleum and natural gas	−0.0007	0.0298	−0.0011	0.0116	0.0011	0.0020	−0.0214
Nonmetallic mining and quarrying	−0.0001	0.0154	0.0005	0.0173	0.0011	0.0028	0.0038
Contract construction	0.0002	0.0167	0.0003	0.0019	0.0012	0.0062	0.0006
Food and kindred products	0.0008	0.0126	0.0004	0.0014	0.0005	−0.0006	0.0131
Tobacco manufacturers	−0.0002	0.0119	0.0003	0.0035	0.0015	−0.0029	−0.0068
Textile mill products	0.0009	0.0148	0.0008	0.0018	0.0007	−0.0037	0.0192
Apparel and other fabricated textile products	0.0012	0.0117	0.0002	0.0014	0.0004	0.0005	0.0109
Paper and allied products	0.0005	0.0318	−0.0004	0.0058	0.0013	0.0028	−0.0016
Printing and publishing	−0.0002	0.0177	0.0003	0.0020	0.0014	0.0052	0.0058
Chemicals and allied products	0.0000	0.0329	0.0005	0.0085	0.0015	0.0035	0.0121
Petroleum and coal products	−0.0001	0.0423	0.0006	0.0017	0.0009	−0.0004	−0.0179
Rubber and misc. plastic products	0.0005	0.0254	0.0007	0.0055	0.0011	0.0102	0.0043
Leather and leather products	0.0003	−0.0025	0.0002	0.0003	0.0004	−0.0058	0.0025
Lumber and wood products, except furniture	0.0007	0.0239	0.0012	0.0033	0.0012	−0.0022	0.0009
Furniture and fixtures	0.0001	0.0280	0.0006	0.0023	0.0011	0.0027	0.0026

Table 6.9 continued

	Average annual rates of growth						
Industry	Quality of intermediate input	Unweighted intermediate input	Quality of capital stock	Capital stock	Quality of hours worked	Hours worked	Rate of productivity growth
Stone, clay and glass products	0.0005	0.0276	0.0009	0.0047	0.0018	0.0020	0.0007
Primary metal industries	−0.0001	0.0155	0.0008	0.0015	0.0010	0.0001	−0.0059
Fabricated metal industries	−0.0001	0.0201	0.0007	0.0030	0.0014	0.0048	0.0050
Machinery, except electrical	−0.0001	0.0241	0.0005	0.0056	0.0019	0.0061	0.0036
Elec. machinery, eqpt., and supplies	0.0003	0.0259	0.0010	0.0047	0.0021	0.0081	0.0158
Trans. eqpt. and ordnance, except motor vehicles	0.0005	0.0402	0.0002	0.0011	0.0018	0.0082	0.0039
Motor vehicles and equipment	−0.0002	0.0287	0.0010	0.0043	0.0009	0.0013	0.0091
Prof. photographic eqpt. and watches	0.0000	0.0217	0.0008	0.0094	0.0029	0.0140	0.0081
Misc. manufacturing industries	0.0004	0.0239	0.0002	0.0035	0.0015	−0.0001	0.0046
Railroads and rail express services	−0.0008	−0.0038	0.0014	0.0006	0.0018	−0.0125	0.0187
Street rail., bus lines, and taxicabs	−0.0015	−0.0048	0.0017	0.0020	0.0006	−0.0050	−0.0147
Trucking services and warehousing	−0.0002	0.0224	0.0013	0.0059	0.0012	0.0065	0.0116
Water transportation	0.0008	0.0050	0.0006	0.0005	0.0010	−0.0029	−0.0009
Air transportation	−0.0001	0.0422	0.0007	0.0096	0.0005	0.0148	0.0281
Pipelines, except natural gas	−0.0005	0.0138	0.0081	0.0201	0.0015	−0.0029	0.0093
Transportation services	−0.0003	0.0490	0.0029	0.0005	0.0009	0.0040	−0.0304
Telephone, telegraph, and misc. communication services	0.0000	0.0077	0.0079	0.0155	0.0023	0.0064	0.0290
Radio and television broadcasting	−0.0003	−0.0061	0.0005	0.0180	0.0010	0.0206	−0.0205
Electric utilities	−0.0008	0.0235	0.0044	0.0231	0.0009	0.0024	0.0092
Gas utilities	−0.0004	0.0407	0.0005	0.0101	0.0006	0.0017	−0.0001

Table 6.9 continued

	Average annual rates of growth						
Industry	Quality of intermediate input	Unweighted intermediate input	Quality of capital stock	Capital stock	Quality of hours worked	Hours worked	Rate of productivity growth
Water supply and sanitary services	0.0003	−0.0034	−0.0002	0.0001	0.0010	0.0038	0.0312
Wholesale trade	0.0001	0.0063	0.0015	0.0075	0.0022	0.0105	0.0145
Retail trade	−0.0001	0.0093	0.0009	0.0034	0.0007	0.0049	0.0103
Finance, insurance, and real estate	−0.0001	0.0342	−0.0001	0.0033	0.0011	0.0065	0.0044
Services, except private households and institutions	0.0005	0.0282	0.0016	0.0049	0.0001	0.0076	−0.0052
Private households			0.0105	0.0394	−0.0001	−0.0006	
Institutions	−0.0002	0.0148	0.0003	0.0102	0.0014	0.0167	−0.0059
Federal public administration					0.0056	0.0117	
Federal government enterprises					0.0016	0.0125	
State and local educational services					0.0038	0.0419	
State and local public admin.					0.0036	0.0326	
State and local enterprises					−0.0005	0.0367	

affect the measure of productivity growth. The contributions of input quality would be allocated to changes in productivity. For all but one of the forty-five industries for which we have measures of productivity growth—the exception being crude petroleum and natural gas—the omission of changes in input quality would increase measured productivity growth. Failure to include changes in input quality would lead to overestimation of the role of productivity growth in the growth of output.

We could compare the rate of productivity growth with the contribution of intermediate input, based on measures that exclude changes in input quality. We would still find that the contribution of this input alone exceeds the rate of productivity growth for thirty-five of the forty-five industries for which we have a measure of intermediate input. For apparel, leather, and pipelines the role of productivity growth would exceed that of intermediate input on the basis of measures that exclude input quality. Our inferences about intermediate input as a source of output growth would be only modestly affected by omission of input quality change.

Excluding intermediate input from consideration, we could compare the rate of productivity growth with the sum of the contributions of capital and labor inputs on the basis of measures that exclude changes in input quality. We would find that the measured rate of productivity growth exceeds the sum of the measured contributions of capital and labor inputs for six additional industries. Four of these are manufacturing industries: chemicals, electrical machinery, motor vehicles, and miscellaneous manufacturing; the other two industries are water transportation and air transportation.

We have found that the sum of the contributions of capital and labor inputs exceeds productivity growth for twenty-nine of forty-five industries. For measures excluding input quality, the role of productivity growth and the contributions of capital and labor inputs would be reversed. We conclude that failure to incorporate changes in input quality leads to a drastic change in inferences about the relative importance of productivity change and the contributions of capital and labor inputs.

Conclusion

In this chapter we have analyzed sources of growth for each sector of the U.S. economy listed in Table 3.1, for the period 1948–1979. We presented growth rates in output and in intermediate, capital, and labor inputs, together with rates of productivity growth for each sector. We find that positive rates of growth predominate among the forty-five sectors for which our measures of output are independent of measures of input. Only leather products and local transportation have negative rates of output growth for the period as a whole.

Similarly, we find that positive growth rates of intermediate input characterize industrial sectors for the period 1948–1979. Among the forty-five industrial sectors for which we have measures of intermediate input only five industries had negative growth rates for the period as a whole. As for output and intermediate input, positive growth in capital input predominated for the period 1948–1979. Among the forty-six industries for which we have measures of capital input, only water supply and sanitary services had negative growth rates for the whole period.

We have measures of labor input for the period 1948–1979 for all fifty-one industries listed in Table 3.1. For twelve of these industries the rate of growth of labor input for the period as a whole was negative. For forty-five industries we have measures of the productivity growth rate. Rates of productivity growth for the period 1948–1979 were negative for fifteen of these industries. We conclude that patterns of growth among industries are different for output, intermediate input, and capital input on the one hand and for labor input and the rate of productivity growth on the other.

Comparing rates of growth of output with rates of productivity growth, we find that the association between these measures is weak. We conclude that there is no evidence of pervasive economies of scale at the industry level. This conclusion does not rule out economies of scale at the plant or firm level or the possibility of economies of scale at the industry level for some industries.

We have compared productivity growth for each industry with the contributions of all three inputs. We find that productivity growth accounts for a predominant portion of output growth for only five of the forty-five industries for which we measure growth in productivity. We conclude that productivity is a much less important source of growth than the contributions of intermediate, capital, and labor inputs.

Analyzing sources of growth in output in greater detail, we have found that the contribution of intermediate input is the single most important source of growth in output. The contribution of this input exceeds the rate of productivity growth for thirty-six of the forty-five industries for which we have a measure of intermediate input. The sum of the contributions of capital and labor inputs exceeds the rate of productivity growth for twenty-nine of the forty-five industries for which we have a measure of productivity growth.

We have decomposed the growth in intermediate, capital, and labor inputs into components corresponding to growth in an unweighted index of each input and an index of input quality. We find that growth in input quality is not an important source of growth in intermediate input. Growth in the quality of capital input contributes more substantially to the growth of capital input. Finally, growth in the quality of labor input is a very important source of growth in labor input.

If we omitted changes in input quality, we would find the contribution of growth in intermediate input still predominant as a source of output growth. The relative importance of the contributions of capital and labor inputs would decrease substantially, while the growth in the level of productivity would increase significantly in most industries. We conclude that an analysis of sources of output growth must incorporate input measures that reflect the growth in input quality.

7 Sectoral Substitution and Technical Change

In Chapters 3, 4, 5, and 6 we presented measures of output, of intermediate, capital, and labor inputs, and of productivity. In this chapter our objective is to analyze growth in productivity and the distribution of the value of output among the three inputs. Our methodology for productivity measurement is based on a model of producer behavior that incorporates a production function. We employ this model to characterize substitution among inputs and productivity growth.

We describe the relative distribution of the value of output in terms of the value shares of the three inputs. The value share of each input is defined as the ratio of the value of that input to the value of output. Necessary conditions for producer equilibrium are given by equalities between the value shares and the elasticities of output with respect to the three inputs. Under constant returns to scale the elasticities and the value shares for all three inputs sum to unity.

To describe the implications of patterns of substitution for the distribution of the value of output, we introduce *share elasticities,* defined as changes in value shares with respect to proportional changes in quantities of the three inputs. Share elasticities are invariant with respect to changes in the dimensions for measurement of the prices and quantities of inputs and output. The share elasticities of inputs for each sector are parameters in our econometric model of production.

Our second objective is to characterize the rate of productivity growth and its changes over time. For this purpose we define rates of productivity growth as rates of growth of output with respect to time, holding intermediate input, capital input, and labor input constant. Under constant returns to scale, the rate of productivity growth can be expressed as the rate of growth of output less a weighted average of the rates of growth of the three inputs, where the weights are given by the corresponding value shares.

To describe the implications of changes in productivity for patterns of substitution, we introduce biases of productivity growth, defined as changes in the value shares with respect to time. To describe changes in the rate of productivity growth, we introduce its acceleration. The rate of productivity growth, acceleration, and the biases all depend on the units for measurement of time. The biases of productivity growth and acceleration are fixed parameters in our econometric model.

Finally, we consider restrictions on patterns of substitution and productivity growth implied by Hicks neutrality of productivity growth and by the existence of a value-added aggregate. These restrictions imply that the production function, originally represented in terms of intermediate, capital, and labor inputs and time, can be represented in terms of a smaller number of variables. Under Hicks neutrality, substitution among inputs is independent of productivity growth; the existence of a value-added aggregate implies that productivity growth does not involve intermediate input.

We derive restrictions on the shares and share elasticities corresponding to Hicks neutrality and the existence of a value-added aggregate for the production function. Similarly, we derive the corresponding restrictions on the rate of productivity growth, acceleration, and the biases. Interpreting the parameters of the production function as share elasticities, biases, and acceleration, we derive restrictions on these parameters. We present the results of empirical tests of these restrictions, by industrial sector.

Sectoral Distribution

Our analysis of the distribution of the value of output is based on estimates of share elasticities and the biases and acceleration of productivity growth. Share elasticities measure the impact of changes in quantities of inputs on shares of inputs in the value of output. Biases measure the effect of productivity growth on value shares. Acceleration describes increases or decreases in the rate of productivity growth. To introduce these measures we first extend our model of producer behavior.

Our model of production is based on production functions $\{F^i\}$ for each of the n sectors, characterized by constant returns to scale:

$$Z_i = F^i(X_i, K_i, L_i, T), \qquad\qquad (i = 1, 2,..., n)$$

where $\{Z_i\}$ is the set of outputs, $\{X_i\}$, $\{K_i\}$, and $\{L_i\}$ are the sets of intermediate, capital, and labor inputs, and T is time. Where $\{q_i\}$, $\{p_X^i\}$, $\{p_K^i\}$, and $\{p_L^i\}$ denote the prices of outputs and intermediate, capital, and labor inputs, we can define the shares of intermediate input, capital input, and labor input, say $\{v_X^i\}$, $\{v_K^i\}$, and $\{v_L^i\}$, in the value of output for each of the sectors, as before, by

$$v_X^i = \frac{p_X^i X_i}{q_i Z_i},$$

$$v_K^i = \frac{p_K^i K_i}{q_i Z_i},$$

$$v_L^i = \frac{p_L^i L_i}{q_i Z_i}, \qquad\qquad (i = 1, 2,..., n).$$

Necessary conditions for producer equilibrium are given by equalities between the value shares of each input and the elasticity of output with respect to that input:

$$v_X^i = \frac{\partial \ln Z_i}{\partial \ln X_i} (X_i, K_i, L_i, T),$$

$$v_K^i = \frac{\partial \ln Z_i}{\partial \ln X_i} (X_i, K_i, L_i, T),$$

$$v_L^i = \frac{\partial \ln Z_i}{\partial \ln L_i} (X_i, K_i, L_i, T) \qquad\qquad (i = 1, 2,..., n).$$

Under constant returns to scale, both the elasticities and the value shares for all three inputs sum to unity.

Finally, we can define rates of productivity growth, say $\{v_T^i\}$ for all n sectors, as rates of growth of output with respect to time, holding intermediate input, capital input, and labor input constant:

$$v_T^i = \frac{\partial \ln Z_i}{\partial T} (X_i, K_i, L_i, T), \qquad\qquad (i = 1, 2,..., n).$$

Given the production functions $\{F^i\}$, we can differentiate logarithmically a second time with respect to the logarithms of intermediate, capital, and labor inputs, to obtain the second-order logarithmic derivatives as functions of these inputs and time

$$u_{XX}^i = \frac{\partial^2 \ln Z_i}{\partial \ln X_i^2} \quad (X_i, K_i, L_i, T),$$

$$u_{XK}^i = \frac{\partial^2 \ln Z_i}{\partial \ln X_i \, \partial \ln K_i} \quad (X_i, K_i, L_i, T),$$

$$u_{XL}^i = \frac{\partial^2 \ln Z_i}{\partial \ln X_i \, \partial \ln L_i} \quad (X_i, K_i, L_i, T),$$

$$u_{KK}^i = \frac{\partial^2 \ln Z_i}{\partial \ln K_i^2} \quad (X_i, K_i, L_i, T),$$

$$u_{KL}^i = \frac{\partial^2 \ln Z_i}{\partial \ln K_i \, \partial \ln L_i} \quad (X_i, K_i, L_i, T),$$

$$u_{LL}^i = \frac{\partial^2 \ln Z_i}{\partial \ln L_i^2} \quad (X_i, K_i, L_i, T), \qquad\qquad (i = 1, 2,..., n).$$

Setting the elasticity of output with respect to each input equal to the corresponding value share, we can define the *share elasticities* with respect to quantity as the derivatives of the value shares with respect to the logarithms of intermediate, capital, and labor inputs:[1]

$$u_{XX}^i = \frac{\partial v_X^i}{\partial \ln X_i} \quad (X_i, K_i, L_i, T),$$

$$u_{XK}^i = \frac{\partial v_X^i}{\partial \ln K_i} \quad (X_i, K_i, L_i, T),$$

$$u_{XL}^i = \frac{\partial v_X^i}{\partial \ln L_i} \quad (X_i, K_i, L_i, T),$$

$$u_{KK}^i = \frac{\partial v_K^i}{\partial \ln K_i} \quad (X_i, K_i, L_i, T),$$

$$u_{KL}^i = \frac{\partial v_K^i}{\partial \ln L_i} \quad (X_i, K_i, L_i, T),$$

$$u_{LL}^i = \frac{\partial v_L^i}{\partial \ln L_i} \quad (X_i, K_i, L_i, T), \qquad\qquad (i = 1, 2,..., n).$$

Share elasticities can be employed to derive the implications of patterns of substitution for the relative distribution of the value of output among the three inputs. If a share elasticity is positive, the value share increases with an increase in the quantity of the corresponding input. If a share elasticity is negative, the value share decreases with the corresponding quantity. Finally, if a share elasticity is zero, the value share is independent of the quantity. The share elasticities are second-order logarithmic derivatives of the production function with respect to the logarithms of intermediate, capital, and labor inputs. They are invariant with respect to changes in the dimensions for measurement of the prices and quantities of output and inputs.

Interchanging the order of differentiation, we can observe that the share elasticities with respect to quantity are symmetric

$$u_{XK}^i = \frac{\partial^2 \ln Z_i}{\partial \ln X_i \, \partial \ln K_i} = \frac{\partial^2 \ln Z_i}{\partial \ln K_i \, \partial \ln X_i} = u_{KX}^i \,,$$

$$u_{XL}^i = \frac{\partial^2 \ln Z_i}{\partial \ln X_i \, \partial \ln L_i} = \frac{\partial^2 \ln Z_i}{\partial \ln L_i \, \partial \ln X_i} = u_{LX}^i \,,$$

$$u_{KL}^i = \frac{\partial^2 \ln Z_i}{\partial \ln K_i \, \partial \ln L_i} = \frac{\partial^2 \ln Z_i}{\partial \ln L_i \, \partial \ln K_i} = u_{LK}^i \,, \qquad\qquad (i = 1, 2,..., n).$$

These restrictions hold for all values of intermediate, capital, and labor inputs and time.

Second, the sum of the share elasticities for a given value share, defined by the corresponding second-order logarithmic derivatives, is equal to zero under constant return to scale

$$u_{XX}^i + u_{XK}^i + u_{XL}^i = 0 \,,$$

$$u_{KX}^i + u_{KK}^i + u_{KL}^i = 0 \,,$$

$$u_{LX}^i + u_{LK}^i + u_{LL}^i = 0 \,, \qquad\qquad (i = 1, 2,..., n) \,.$$

Like symmetry restrictions, these restrictions hold for all values of intermediate, capital, and labor inputs and time.

Similarly, given the production functions $\{F^i\}$ we can differentiate logarithmically with respect to the logarithms of intermediate, capital, and labor inputs and with respect to time to obtain the second-order logarithmic derivatives as functions of these inputs and time:

$$u_{XT}^i = \frac{\partial^2 \ln Z_i}{\partial \ln X_i \, \partial T} \quad (X_i, K_i, L_i, T) \,,$$

$$u_{KT}^i = \frac{\partial^2 \ln Z_i}{\partial \ln K_i \, \partial T} \quad (X_i, K_i, L_i, T) \,,$$

$$u_{LT}^i = \frac{\partial^2 \ln Z_i}{\partial \ln L_i \, \partial T} \quad (X_i, K_i, L_i, T) \,, \qquad\qquad (i = 1, 2,..., n).$$

Setting the elasticity of output with respect to each input equal to the corresponding value share, we can define the *biases of productivity growth* with respect to quantity as derivatives of the value shares with respect to time:[2]

$$u_{XT}^i = \frac{\partial v_X^i}{\partial T} \quad (X_i, K_i, L_i, T) \,,$$

$$u_{KT}^i = \frac{\partial v_K^i}{\partial T} \quad (X_i, K_i, L_i, T) \,,$$

$$u_{LT}^i = \frac{\partial v_L^i}{\partial T} \quad (X_i, K_i, L_i, T) \,, \qquad\qquad (i = 1, 2,..., n).$$

Biases of productivity growth can be employed to derive the implications of productivity growth for the relative distribution of the value of output among the three inputs. If a bias is positive, the corresponding value share increases with time. If a bias is negative, the value share decreases with time. Finally, if a bias is zero, the value share is independent of time.

Alternatively, we can define the biases of productivity growth as derivatives of the rate of productivity growth with respect to the logarithms of intermediate, capital, and labor inputs:

$$u_{TX}^i = \frac{\partial v_T^i}{\partial \ln X_i} \quad (X_i, K_i, L_i, T) \,,$$

$$u_{TK}^i = \frac{\partial v_T^i}{\partial \ln K_i} \quad (X_i, K_i, L_i, T) \,,$$

$$u_{TL}^i = \frac{\partial v_T^i}{\partial \ln L_i} \quad (X_i, K_i, L_i, T) \,, \qquad\qquad (i = 1, 2,..., n).$$

Interchanging the order of differentiation, we observe that the two definitions of biases of productivity growth are equivalent

$$u_{TX}^i = \frac{\partial^2 \ln Z_i}{\partial T \, \partial \ln X_i} = \frac{\partial^2 \ln Z_i}{\partial \ln X_i \, \partial T} = u_{XT}^i \,,$$

$$u_{TK}^i = \frac{\partial^2 \ln Z_i}{\partial T \, \partial \ln K_i} = \frac{\partial^2 \ln Z_i}{\partial \ln K_i \, \partial T} = u_{KT}^i \,,$$

$$u_{TL}^i = \frac{\partial^2 \ln Z_i}{\partial T \, \partial \ln L_i} = \frac{\partial^2 \ln Z_i}{\partial \ln L_i \, \partial T} = u_{LT}^i \,, \qquad (i = 1, 2,..., n).$$

These restrictions hold for all values of intermediate, capital, and labor inputs and time.

Under constant returns to scale, the sum of the biases of productivity growth, defined by the corresponding second-order logarithmic derivatives, is equal to zero:

$$u_{XT}^i + u_{KT}^i + u_{LT}^i = 0 \,, \qquad\qquad (i = 1, 2,..., n).$$

Like symmetry restrictions, these restrictions hold for all values of the three inputs and time.

Finally, given the production functions $\{F^i\}$, we can differentiate twice with respect to time to obtain the second-order logarithmic derivative with respect to time as a function of intermediate, capital, and labor inputs and time

$$u_{TT}^i = \frac{\partial^2 \ln Z_i}{\partial T^2} \quad (X_i, K_i, L_i, T) \,, \qquad\qquad (i = 1, 2,..., n) \,.$$

Setting the logarithmic derivative equal to the rate of productivity growth, we define the *acceleration of productivity growth* as the derivative of the rate of productivity growth with respect to time:

$$u_{TT}^i = \frac{\partial v_T^i}{\partial T} \quad (X_i, K_i, L_i, T) \,, \qquad\qquad (i = 1, 2,..., n) \,.$$

The biases and the acceleration of productivity growth are second-order logarithmic derivatives of the production function with respect to the logarithms of the quantities of intermediate, capital, and labor inputs and with respect to time. They are invariant with respect to changes in dimensions for measurement of the prices and quantities of output and the inputs, but vary with changes in the dimension for measurement of time.

For each of the n sectors the value shares can be expressed in terms of the first-order partial derivatives of the production functions $\{F^i\}$ with respect to the inputs

$$v_X^i = \frac{\partial \ln F^i}{\partial \ln X_i} = \frac{X_i}{F^i} \cdot \frac{\partial F^i}{\partial X_i},$$

$$v_K^i = \frac{\partial \ln F^i}{\partial \ln K_i} = \frac{K_i}{F^i} \cdot \frac{\partial F^i}{\partial K_i},$$

$$v_L^i = \frac{\partial \ln F^i}{\partial \ln L_i} = \frac{L_i}{F^i} \cdot \frac{\partial F^i}{\partial L_i}, \qquad (i = 1, 2,..., n).$$

Similarly, the rate of productivity growth is a function of the three inputs and time and can be expressed in terms of the derivative of the production function with respect to time:

$$v_T^i = \frac{\partial \ln F^i}{\partial T} = \frac{1}{F^i} \cdot \frac{\partial F^i}{\partial T}, \qquad (i = 1, 2,..., n).$$

If the production function is increasing in all three inputs, the value shares must be nonnegative. To check these restrictions for particular values of the inputs and time, we can compute the value shares and verify that they have the appropriate sign.

The share elasticities can be expressed in terms of the second-order partial derivatives of the production functions $\{F^i\}$ with respect to the inputs:[3]

$$u_{XX}^i = \frac{\partial^2 \ln F^i}{\partial \ln X_i^2} = \frac{X_i^2}{F^i} \cdot \frac{\partial^2 F^i}{\partial X_i^2} - v_X^i (v_X^i - 1),$$

$$u_{XK}^i = \frac{\partial^2 \ln F^i}{\partial \ln X_i \, \partial \ln K_i} = \frac{X_i K_i}{F^i} \frac{\partial^2 F^i}{\partial X_i \, \partial K_i} - v_X^i v_K^i,$$

$$u_{XL}^i = \frac{\partial^2 \ln F^i}{\partial \ln X_i \, \partial \ln L_i} = \frac{X_i L_i}{F^i} \frac{\partial^2 F^i}{\partial X_i \, \partial L_i} - v_X^i v_L^i,$$

$$u_{KK}^i = \frac{\partial^2 \ln F^i}{\partial \ln K_i^2} = \frac{K_i^2}{F^i} \cdot \frac{\partial^2 F^i}{\partial K_i^2} - v_K^i (v_K^i - 1),$$

$$u^i_{KL} = \frac{\partial^2 \ln F^i}{\partial \ln K_i\, \partial \ln L_i} = \frac{K_i\, L_i}{F^i} \cdot \frac{\partial^2 F^i}{\partial K_i\, \partial L_i} - v^i_K\, v^i_L \,,$$

$$u^i_{LL} = \frac{\partial^2 \ln F^i}{\partial \ln L_i^{\,2}} = \frac{L_i^{\,2}}{F^i} \cdot \frac{\partial^2 F^i}{\partial L_i^{\,2}} - v^i_L\, (v^i_L - 1) \,, \qquad (i = 1, 2,..., n).$$

Denoting the Hessian matrices of second-order partial derivatives of the production functions $\{F^i\}$ by $\{H^i\}$, we can represent the matrices of share elasticities, say $\{U^i\}$, in the form

$$U^i = \frac{1}{F^i} \cdot N^i \cdot H^i \cdot N^i - v^i\, v^{i'} + V^i, \qquad (i = 1, 2,..., n),$$

where

$$N^i = \begin{bmatrix} X_i & 0 & 0 \\ 0 & K_i & 0 \\ 0 & 0 & L_i \end{bmatrix} ,$$

$$V^i = \begin{bmatrix} v^i_X & 0 & 0 \\ 0 & v^i_K & 0 \\ 0 & 0 & v^i_L \end{bmatrix} , \quad v^i = \begin{bmatrix} v^i_X \\ v^i_K \\ v^i_L \end{bmatrix} , \qquad (i = 1, 2,..., n).$$

Under concavity of the production functions $\{F^i\}$ the Hessian matrices $\{H^i\}$ are negative semidefinite for all values of the three inputs and time. To check these restrictions for particular values of the inputs and time, we observe that the matrices

$$\frac{1}{F^i} \cdot N^i \cdot H^i \cdot N^i = U^i + v^i v^{i'} - V^i, \qquad (i = 1, 2,..., n),$$

are negative semidefinite if and only if the Hessian matrices $\{H^i\}$ are negative semidefinite.

We first compute the matrices $\{U^i\}$ of share elasticities. Using the computed value shares, we can evaluate the matrices $\{U^i + v^i v^{i'} - V^i\}$. These matrices are negative semidefinite under concavity of the production function, so that they can be represented in terms of their Cholesky factorizations

$$U^i + v^i v^{i'} - V^i = L^i \cdot D^i \cdot L^{i'}, \qquad (i = 1, 2,..., n),$$

where $\{\mathbf{L}^i\}$ are unit lower triangular matrices and $\{\mathbf{D}^i\}$ are diagonal matrices.

If the matrices of share elasticities are negative semidefinite, the diagonal elements of the matrices $\{\mathbf{D}^i\}$ must be nonpositive. To check these restrictions for particular values of the three inputs and time we can represent the matrices $\{\mathbf{U}^i + \mathbf{v}^i\mathbf{v}^{i'} - \mathbf{V}^i\}$ in terms of their Cholesky factorizations and verify that the diagonal elements of the matrices $\{\mathbf{D}^i\}$ are nonpositive.

Next consider restrictions on the production functions $\{\mathbf{F}^i\}$ associated with Hicks neutrality of productivity growth and the existence of value-added functions. First, a production function that is homogeneous of degree one in intermediate, capital, and labor inputs is Hicks neutral if and only if it can be represented in the form

$$Z_i = A_i(T) \cdot W_i(X_i, K_i, L_i) , \qquad\qquad (i = 1, 2,..., n),$$

where W_i is a sectoral aggregate for input, homogeneous of degree one in the three inputs, and A_i is a function of time (see Chapter 2).

To derive restrictions on the biases of productivity growth implied by Hicks neutrality, we first observe that the rate of productivity growth depends only on time:

$$v_T^i = \frac{d \ln A_i(T)}{dT} , \qquad\qquad (i = 1, 2,..., n),$$

so the biases are zero for all three inputs:

$$u_{XT}^i = u_{KT}^i = u_{LT}^i = 0, \qquad\qquad (i = 1, 2,..., n).$$

Similarly, a value-added function exists if and only if the production function can be represented in the form

$$Z_i = F^i[X_i, G^i(K_i, L_i, T)], \qquad\qquad (i = 1, 2,..., n),$$

where G^i is a value-added function, homogeneous of degree one in capital and labor inputs (see Chapter 2). To derive restrictions on the shares and share elasticities and on the rate and biases of productivity growth, we first express the value shares of capital and labor inputs and the rate of productivity growth in the form

$$v_K^i = \frac{\partial \ln Z_i}{\partial \ln K_i} = \frac{\partial \ln F^i}{\partial \ln G^i} \cdot \frac{\partial \ln G^i}{\partial \ln K_i} ,$$

$$v_L^i = \frac{\partial \ln Z_i}{\partial \ln L_i} = \frac{\partial \ln F^i}{\partial \ln G^i} \cdot \frac{\partial \ln G^i}{\partial \ln L_i} \, ,$$

$$v_T^i = \frac{\partial \ln Z_i}{\partial T} = \frac{\partial \ln F^i}{\partial \ln G^i} \cdot \frac{\partial \ln G^i}{\partial T} \, , \qquad\qquad (i = 1, 2,..., n).$$

Next we express the share elasticities of capital and labor inputs and the bias of productivity growth with respect to intermediate input in the form

$$u_{XK}^i = \frac{\partial^2 \ln F^i}{\partial \ln X_i \, \partial \ln G^i} \cdot \frac{\partial \ln G^i}{\partial \ln K_i} = r^i \cdot v_K^i \, ,$$

$$u_{XL}^i = \frac{\partial^2 \ln F^i}{\partial \ln X_i \, \partial \ln G^i} \cdot \frac{\partial \ln G^i}{\partial \ln L_i} = r^i \cdot v_L^i \, ,$$

$$u_{XT}^i = \frac{\partial^2 \ln F^i}{\partial \ln X_i \, \partial \ln G^i} \cdot \frac{\partial \ln G^i}{\partial T} = r^i \cdot v_T^i \, , \qquad\qquad (i = 1, 2,..., n),$$

where r^i is a function of all three inputs and time

$$r^i = \frac{\dfrac{\partial^2 \ln F^i}{\partial \ln \mathbf{X}_i \, \partial \ln \mathbf{G}^i}}{\dfrac{\partial \ln F^i}{\partial \ln G^i}} \quad [X_i, G^i(K_i, L_i, T)], \qquad\qquad (i = 1, 2,..., n).$$

A value-added function exists if and only if there is a common factor of proportionality between the two share elasticities and the bias of productivity growth and the corresponding value shares and the rate of productivity growth.

This completes the development of our model of producer behavior. We have introduced measures of substitution and productivity growth based on share elasticities and the biases and acceleration of productivity growth. We have expressed monotonicity and concavity conditions for the production functions in terms of shares and share elasticities. Finally, we have derived restrictions on shares and share elasticities and the rate and biases of productivity growth implied by Hicks neutrality and the existence of a value-added function. Next we present a framework for estimating the parameters of the underlying production function.

Econometric Models

The development of our econometric model of production proceeds through three stages. We first specify a functional form for the production functions $\{F^i\}$, taking into account restrictions on the parameters implied by the theory of production. Second, we derive parametric restrictions required for Hicks neutrality and the existence of a value-added function. Finally, we formulate an error structure for the econometric model and discuss procedures for estimating the unknown parameters.

Our first step in formulating an econometric model of producer behavior is to consider specific forms of the production functions $\{F^i\}$

$$
\begin{aligned}
Z_i = \exp[&\alpha_0^i + \alpha_X^i \ln X_i + \alpha_K^i \ln K_i + \alpha_L^i \ln L_i + \alpha_T^i \cdot T \\
&+ \frac{1}{2} \beta_{XX}^i (\ln X_i)^2 + \beta_{XK}^i \ln X_i \ln K_i + \beta_{XL}^i \ln X_i \ln L_i \\
&+ \beta_{XT}^i \ln X_i \cdot T + \frac{1}{2} \beta_{KK}^i (\ln K_i)^2 + \beta_{KL}^i \ln K_i \ln L_i \\
&+ \beta_{KT}^i \ln K_i \cdot T + \frac{1}{2} \beta_{LL}^i (\ln L_i)^2 + \beta_{LT}^i \ln L_i \cdot T \\
&+ \frac{1}{2} \beta_{TT}^i \cdot T^2], \qquad\qquad (i = 1, 2,..., n) .
\end{aligned}
$$

We have referred to these forms as translog production functions.[4] Since the share elasticities and the biases and acceleration of productivity growth are constant, we can also characterize these forms as *constant share elasticity* or CSE production functions, to indicate the interpretation of the fixed parameters.[5]

The translog production function for an industrial sector is characterized by constant returns to scale if and only if the parameters satisfy the conditions

$$\alpha_X^i + \alpha_K^i + \alpha_L^i = 1,$$

$$\beta_{XX}^i + \beta_{XK}^i + \beta_{XL}^i = 0,$$

$$\beta_{XK}^i + \beta_{KK}^i + \beta_{KL}^i = 0,$$

$$\beta_{XL}^i + \beta_{KL}^i + \beta_{LL}^i = 0,$$

$$\beta_{XT}^i + \beta_{KT}^i + \beta_{LT}^i = 0, \qquad\qquad (i = 1, 2,..., n).$$

The share elasticities and the biases of productivity growth are symmetric, so that the parameters satisfy the conditions

$$\beta_{XK}^i = \beta_{KX}^i ,$$

$$\beta_{XL}^i = \beta_{LX}^i ,$$

$$\beta_{KL}^i = \beta_{LK}^i ,$$

$$\beta_{XT}^i = \beta_{TX}^i ,$$

$$\beta_{KT}^i = \beta_{TK}^i ,$$

$$\beta_{LT}^i = \beta_{TL}^i , \qquad\qquad (i = 1, 2,..., n).$$

The value shares of intermediate, capital, and labor inputs can be expressed as

$$v_X^i = \alpha_X^i + \beta_{XX}^i \ln X_i + \beta_{XK}^i \ln K_i + \beta_{XL}^i \ln L_i + \beta_{XT}^i \cdot T ,$$

$$v_K^i = \alpha_K^i + \beta_{XK}^i \ln X_i + \beta_{KK}^i \ln K_i + \beta_{KL}^i \ln L_i + \beta_{KT}^i \cdot T ,$$

$$v_L^i = \alpha_L^i + \beta_{XL}^i \ln X_i + \beta_{KL}^i \ln K_i + \beta_{LL}^i \ln L_i + \beta_{LT}^i \cdot T , \qquad (i = 1, 2,..., n).$$

The rate of productivity growth takes the form

$$v_T^i = \alpha_T^i + \beta_{XT}^i \ln X_i + \beta_{KT}^i \ln K_i + \beta_{LT}^i \ln L_i + \beta_{TT}^i \cdot T, \qquad (i = 1, 2,..., n).$$

Our final step in considering specific forms of the production functions $\{F^i\}$ is to derive restrictions on the parameters implied by the condition that the production functions are increasing and concave in the three inputs. First, setting the inputs equal to unity and time equal to zero, we obtain necessary conditions for the production functions to be increasing:

$$\alpha_X^i \geq 0 ,$$

$$\alpha_K^i \geq 0 ,$$

$$\alpha_L^i \geq 0 , \qquad\qquad (i = 1, 2,..., n).$$

Concavity of the sectoral production functions $\{\mathbf{F}^i\}$ implies that the matrices of second-order partial derivatives $\{\mathbf{H}^i\}$ are negative semidefinite, so that the matrices $\{\mathbf{U}^i + \mathbf{v}^i\mathbf{v}^{i'} - \mathbf{V}^i\}$ are negative semidefinite, where[6]

$$\frac{1}{\mathbf{F}^i} \cdot \mathbf{N}^i \cdot \mathbf{H}^i \cdot \mathbf{N}^i = \mathbf{U}^i + \mathbf{v}^i\mathbf{v}^{i'} - \mathbf{V}^i, \qquad\qquad (i = 1, 2,..., n).$$

For translog production functions the matrices of share elasticities $\{\mathbf{U}^i\}$ are constant. Since the production functions are increasing in each of the three inputs, the value shares are nonnegative:

$$v_X^i \geq 0,$$

$$v_K^i \geq 0,$$

$$v_L^i \geq 0, \qquad\qquad (i = 1, 2,..., n).$$

Under constant returns to scale these value shares sum to unity:

$$v_X^i + v_K^i + v_L^i = 1, \qquad\qquad (i = 1, 2,..., n).$$

Without violating the nonnegativity restrictions on value shares we can set the matrices $\{\mathbf{v}^i\mathbf{v}^{i'} - \mathbf{V}^i\}$ equal to zero, for example, by choosing the value shares

$$v_X^i = 1,$$

$$v_K^i = 0,$$

$$v_L^i = 0, \qquad\qquad (i = 1, 2,..., n).$$

Necessary conditions for the matrices $\{\mathbf{U}^i + \mathbf{v}^i\mathbf{v}^{i'} - \mathbf{V}^i\}$ to be negative semidefinite are that the matrices of share elasticities $\{U^i\}$ are negative semidefinite. These conditions are also sufficient, since the matrices $\{\mathbf{v}^i\mathbf{v}^{i'} - \mathbf{V}^i\}$ are negative semidefinite for all nonnegative value shares summing to unity.

To impose concavity on the translog production functions, the matrices $\{\mathbf{U}^i\}$ of constant share elasticities can be represented in terms of their Cholesky factorizations

$$
\begin{bmatrix} \beta^i_{XX} & \beta^i_{XK} & \beta^i_{XL} \\ \beta^i_{KX} & \beta^i_{KK} & \beta^i_{KL} \\ \beta^i_{LX} & \beta^i_{KL} & \beta^i_{LL} \end{bmatrix} = \begin{bmatrix} 1 & 0 & 0 \\ \lambda^i_{21} & 1 & 0 \\ \lambda^i_{31} & \lambda^i_{32} & 1 \end{bmatrix} \begin{bmatrix} \delta^i_l & 0 & 0 \\ 0 & \delta^i_2 & 0 \\ 0 & 0 & \delta^i_3 \end{bmatrix} \begin{bmatrix} 1 & \lambda^i_{21} & \lambda^i_{31} \\ 0 & 1 & \lambda^i_{32} \\ 0 & 0 & 1 \end{bmatrix},
$$

$$
= \begin{bmatrix} \delta^i_1 & \lambda^i_{21}\delta^i_1 & \lambda^i_{31}\delta^i_1 \\ \lambda^i_{21}\delta^i_1 & \lambda^i_{21}\lambda^i_{21}\delta^i_1 + \delta^i_2 & \lambda^i_{31}\lambda^i_{21}\delta^i_1 + \lambda^i_{32}\delta^i_2 \\ \lambda^i_{31}\delta^i_1 & \lambda^i_{31}\lambda^i_{21}\delta^i_1 + \lambda^i_{32}\delta^i_2 & \lambda^i_{31}\lambda^i_{31}\delta^i_1 + \lambda^i_{32}\lambda^i_{32}\delta^i_2 + \delta^i_3 \end{bmatrix}
$$

$$(i = 1, 2, ..., n).$$

Under constant returns to scale the constant share elasticities satisfy symmetry restrictions and restrictions implied by homogeneity of degree one of the production function. These restrictions imply that the parameters of the Cholesky factorizations $\{\lambda^i_{21}, \lambda^i_{31}, \lambda^i_{32}, \delta^i_1, \delta^i_2, \delta^i_3\}$ must satisfy the following conditions

$$1 + \lambda^i_{21} + \lambda^i_{31} = 0,$$

$$1 + \lambda^i_{32} = 0,$$

$$\delta^i_3 = 0, \qquad\qquad\qquad\qquad (i = 1, 2, ..., n).$$

Under these conditions there is a one-to-one transformation between the constant share elasticities $\{\beta^i_{XX}, \beta^i_{XK}, \beta^i_{XL}, \beta^i_{KK}, \beta^i_{KL}, \beta^i_{LL}\}$ and the parameters of the Cholesky factorizations. The matrices of share elasticities are negative semidefinite if and only if the diagonal elements $\{\delta^i_1, \delta^i_2\}$ of the matrices $\{D^i\}$ are nonpositive. This completes the specification of our model of production.

Using the interpretation of the parameters of the translog production functions as share elasticities and biases of productivity growth, we can derive restrictions on these parameters associated with Hicks neutrality of productivity growth and the existence of value-added functions.[7] Under Hicks neutrality the biases are zero for all three inputs

$$\beta^i_{XT} = \beta^i_{KT} = \beta^i_{LT} = 0, \qquad\qquad (i = 1, 2, ..., n).$$

The existence of value-added functions implies that shares and share elasticities and the rate and biases of productivity growth satisfy the restrictions

$$u_{XK}^i = r^i \cdot v_K^i \,,$$

$$u_{XL}^i = r^i \cdot v_L^i \,,$$

$$u_{XT}^i = r^i \cdot v_T^i \,, \qquad\qquad\qquad (i = 1, 2,..., n),$$

where the functions $\{r^i\}$ depend on all three inputs and time.

Two alternative sets of restrictions are jointly necessary and sufficient for the existence of value-added functions. Evaluating the functions $\{r^i\}$ and the value shares where the three inputs are equal to unity and time is equal to zero, we obtain the first set of necessary conditions for the existence of value-added functions[8]

$$\beta_{XK}^i = \rho^i \cdot \alpha_K^i \,,$$

$$\beta_{XL}^i = \rho^i \cdot \alpha_L^i \,,$$

$$\beta_{XT}^i = \rho^i \cdot \alpha_T^i \,, \qquad\qquad\qquad (i = 1, 2,..., n).$$

The first set of sufficient restrictions consists of the necessary conditions given above, together with the restriction

$$\rho^i = 0 \,, \qquad\qquad\qquad (i = 1, 2,..., n).$$

The value-added functions can be made explicit by observing that the sectoral production functions $\{F^i\}$ take the form

$$Z_i = \exp[\alpha_0^i + \alpha_X^i \ln X_i + \alpha_K^i \ln K_i + \alpha_L^i \ln L_i + \alpha_T^i \cdot T$$

$$+ \frac{1}{2} \beta_{KK}^i (\ln K_i)^2 + \beta_{KL}^i \ln K_i \ln L_i + \beta_{KT}^i \ln K_i \cdot T$$

$$+ \frac{1}{2} \beta_{LL}^i (\ln L_i)^2 + \beta_{LT}^i \ln L_i \cdot T + \frac{1}{2} \beta_{TT}^i \cdot T^2] \,, \qquad (i = 1, 2,..., n),$$

so the value-added functions take the form

$$\alpha_V^i \ln V_i = \alpha_K^i \ln K_i + \alpha_L^i \ln L_i + \alpha_T^i \cdot T$$

$$+ \frac{1}{2} \beta_{KK}^i (\ln K_i)^2 + \beta_{KL}^i \ln K_i \ln L_i + \beta_{KT}^i \ln K_i \cdot T$$

$$+ \frac{1}{2} \beta^i_{LL} (\ln L_i)^2 + \beta^i_{LT} \ln L_i \cdot T + \frac{1}{2} \beta^i_{TT} \cdot T^2 , \qquad (i = 1, 2,..., n),$$

and the production functions take the form

$$Z_i = \exp[\alpha^i_0 + \alpha^i_X \ln X_i + \alpha^i_V \ln V_i], \qquad (i = 1, 2,..., n).$$

We conclude that output is a linear logarithmic function of intermediate input and value-added.

A second set of restrictions that implies the existence of value-added functions is that the value shares of capital and labor inputs $\{v^i_K, v^i_L\}$ and the rates of productivity growth $\{v^i_T\}$ are in fixed ratios to each other

$$\frac{v^i_K}{v^i_L} = \frac{\beta^i_{XK}}{\beta^i_{XL}} ,$$

$$\frac{v^i_K}{v^i_T} = \frac{\beta^i_{XK}}{\beta^i_{XT}} ,$$

$$\frac{v^i_L}{v^i_T} = \frac{\beta^i_{XL}}{\beta^i_{XT}} , \qquad (i = 1, 2,..., n).$$

These restrictions imply that the parameters in the equations for the value shares of capital and labor inputs and the rates of productivity growth are in fixed proportions

$$\alpha^i_K \beta^i_{XL} = \alpha^i_L \beta^i_{XK} ,$$

$$\alpha^i_K \beta^i_{KL} = \alpha^i_L \beta^i_{KK} ,$$

$$\alpha^i_K \beta^i_{LL} = \alpha^i_L \beta^i_{KL} ,$$

$$\alpha^i_K \beta^i_{LT} = \alpha^i_L \beta^i_{KT} ,$$

$$\alpha^i_K \beta^i_{XT} = \alpha^i_T \beta^i_{XK} ,$$

$$\alpha^i_K \beta^i_{KT} = \alpha^i_T \beta^i_{KK} ,$$

$$\alpha^i_K \beta^i_{LT} = \alpha^i_T \beta^i_{KL} ,$$

$$\alpha^i_K \beta^i_{TT} = \alpha^i_T \beta^i_{KT} , \qquad (i = 1, 2,..., n).$$

Under these restrictions the value-added functions take the form

$$\alpha_V^i \ln V_i = \alpha_K^i \ln K_i + \alpha_L^i \ln L_i + \alpha_T^i \cdot T, \qquad\qquad (i = 1, 2,..., n),$$

and the production functions take the form

$$Z_i = \exp[\alpha_0^i + \alpha_X^i \ln X_i + \alpha_V^i \ln V_i$$

$$+ \frac{1}{2} \beta_{XX}^i (\ln X_i)^2 + \beta_{XV}^i \ln X_i \ln V_i + \frac{1}{2} \beta_{VV}^i (\ln V_i)^2],$$

$$(i = 1, 2,..., n).$$

We conclude that value-added is a linear logarithmic function of capital input, labor input, and time.

We obtain data on the value shares $\{v_X^i, v_K^i, v_L^i\}$ from the price and quantity data on output and intermediate, capital, and labor inputs presented in Chapters 3–5. The average rates of productivity growth in any two periods, say $\{\bar{v}_T^i\}$, can be computed from these price and quantity data, using the translog index number

$$\bar{v}_T^i = \ln Z_i(T) - \ln Z_i(T-1) - \bar{v}_X^i [\ln X_i(T) - \ln X_i(T-1)]$$

$$- \bar{v}_K^i [\ln K_i(T) - \ln K_i(T-1)] - \bar{v}_L^i [\ln L_i(T) - \ln L_i(T-1)],$$

$$(i = 1, 2,..., n),$$

where

$$\bar{v}_T^i = \frac{1}{2}[v_T^i(T) + v_T^i(T-1)], \qquad\qquad (i = 1, 2,..., n),$$

and the average value shares in the two periods are given by

$$\bar{v}_X^i = \frac{1}{2}[v_X^i(T) + v_X^i(T-1)],$$

$$\bar{v}_K^i = \frac{1}{2}[v_K^i(T) + v_K^i(T-1)],$$

$$\bar{v}_L^i = \frac{1}{2}[v_L^i(T) + v_L^i(T-1)], \qquad\qquad (i = 1, 2,..., n).$$

The rates of productivity growth $\{v_T^i\}$ are not directly observable. Using the translog index numbers for the average rates of productivity growth $\{\bar{v}_T^i\}$ and the average value shares $\{\bar{v}_X^i, \bar{v}_K^i, \bar{v}_L^i\}$, the value shares and the rate of productivity growth can be written in the form

$$\bar{v}_X^i = \alpha_X^i + \beta_{XX}^i \, \overline{\ln X_i} + \beta_{XK}^i \overline{\ln K_i} + \beta_{XL}^i \, \overline{\ln L_i} + \beta_{XT}^i \cdot \bar{T},$$

$$\bar{v}_K^i = \alpha_K^i + \beta_{XK}^i \, \overline{\ln X_i} + \beta_{KK}^i \overline{\ln K_i} + \beta_{KL}^i \, \overline{\ln L_i} + \beta_{KT}^i \cdot \bar{T},$$

$$\bar{v}_L^i = \alpha_L^i + \beta_{XL}^i \, \overline{\ln X_i} + \beta_{KL}^i \overline{\ln K_i} + \beta_{LL}^i \, \overline{\ln L_i} + \beta_{LT}^i \cdot \bar{T},$$

$$\bar{v}_T^i = \alpha_T^i + \beta_{XT}^i \, \overline{\ln X_i} + \beta_{KT}^i \overline{\ln K_i} + \beta_{LT}^i \, \overline{\ln L_i} + \beta_{TT}^i \cdot \bar{T}, \qquad (i = 1, 2,..., n),$$

where the average values of intermediate, capital, and labor inputs and time in the two periods are given by

$$\overline{\ln X_i} = \frac{1}{2}[\ln X_i(T) + \ln X_i(T-1)] ,$$

$$\overline{\ln K_i} = \frac{1}{2}[\ln K_i(T) + \ln K_i(T-1)] ,$$

$$\overline{\ln L_i} = \frac{1}{2}[\ln L_i(T) + \ln L_i(T-1)] ,$$

$$\bar{T} = \frac{1}{2}[T + (T-1)] = T - \frac{1}{2} ,$$

and $\{\alpha_X^i, \alpha_K^i, \alpha_L^i, \alpha_T^i; \beta_{XX}^i, \beta_{XK}^i, \beta_{XL}^i, \beta_{XT}^i, \beta_{KK}^i, \beta_{KL}^i, \beta_{KT}^i, \beta_{LL}^i, \beta_{LT}^i, \beta_{TT}^i\}$ are fixed parameters.

To formulate an econometric model of producer behavior, we add a stochastic component to the equations for the value shares and the rate of productivity growth. We assume that each of these equations has two additive components.[9] The first is a nonrandom function of intermediate, capital, and labor inputs and time; the second is an unobservable random disturbance that is functionally independent of these variables. We obtain an econometric model of producer behavior corresponding to the translog production function by adding random disturbances to all four equations

$$v_X^i = \alpha_X^i + \beta_{XX}^i \ln X_i + \beta_{XK}^i \ln K_i + \beta_{XL}^i \ln L_i + \beta_{XT}^i \cdot T + \varepsilon_X^i ,$$

$$v_K^i = \alpha_K^i + \beta_{XK}^i \ln X_i + \beta_{KK}^i \ln K_i + \beta_{KL}^i \ln L_i + \beta_{KT}^i \cdot T + \varepsilon_K^i ,$$

$$v_L^i = \alpha_L^i + \beta_{XL}^i \ln X_i + \beta_{KL}^i \ln K_i + \beta_{LL}^i \ln L_i + \beta_{LT}^i \cdot T + \varepsilon_L^i \,,$$

$$v_T^i = \alpha_T^i + \beta_{XT}^i \ln X_i + \beta_{KT}^i \ln K_i + \beta_{LT}^i \ln L_i + \beta_{TT}^i \cdot T + \varepsilon_T^i \,,$$

$$(i = 1, 2,..., n) \,,$$

where $\{ \alpha_X^i, \alpha_K^i, \alpha_L^i, \alpha_T^i; \beta_{XX}^i, \beta_{XK}^i, \beta_{XL}^i, \beta_{XT}^i, \beta_{KK}^i, \beta_{KL}^i, \beta_{KT}^i, \beta_{LL}^i, \beta_{LT}^i, \beta_{TT}^i \}$ are unknown parameters and $\{\varepsilon_X^i, \varepsilon_K^i, \varepsilon_L^i, \varepsilon_T^i\}$ are unobservable random disturbances. Since the value shares sum to unity, the unknown parameters satisfy the same restrictions as before, and the random disturbances corresponding to the three value shares sum to zero

$$\varepsilon_X^i + \varepsilon_K^i + \varepsilon_L^i = 0 \,, \qquad\qquad (i = 1, 2,..., n).$$

We assume that the random disturbances for all four equations have expected value equal to zero for all observations

$$E \begin{bmatrix} \varepsilon_X^i \\ \varepsilon_K^i \\ \varepsilon_L^i \\ \varepsilon_T^i \end{bmatrix} = 0 \,, \qquad\qquad (i = 1, 2,..., n).$$

We also assume that the random disturbances have a covariance matrix that is the same for all observations; since the random disturbances corresponding to the three value shares sum to zero, this matrix is positive semidefinite with rank at most equal to three. We assume that the covariance matrix of the random disturbances corresponding to the first two value shares and the rate of productivity growth, say Σ^i, has rank three, where

$$V \begin{bmatrix} \varepsilon_X^i \\ \varepsilon_K^i \\ \varepsilon_T^i \end{bmatrix} = \Sigma^i \,, \qquad\qquad (i = 1, 2,..., n),$$

so Σ^i is a positive definite matrix. Finally, we assume that the random disturbances corresponding to distinct observations in the same or distinct equations are uncorrelated. Under this assumption the matrix of random disturbances for the first two value shares and the rate of productivity growth for all observations has the Kronecker product form

$$V \begin{bmatrix} \varepsilon_X^i(1) \\ \varepsilon_X^i(2) \\ \vdots \\ \varepsilon_T^i(N) \end{bmatrix} = \Sigma^i \otimes I , \qquad (i = 1, 2, \dots, n).$$

Since the rates of productivity growth $\{v_T^i\}$ are not directly observable, the equation for productivity growth can be written

$$\bar{v}_T^i = \alpha_T^i + \beta_{XT}^i \overline{\ln X_i} + \beta_{KT}^i \overline{\ln K_i} + \beta_{LT}^i \overline{\ln L_i} + \beta_{TT}^i \cdot \bar{T} + \bar{\varepsilon}_T^i , \quad (i = 1, 2, \dots, n),$$

where $\bar{\varepsilon}_T^i$ is the average disturbance in the two periods

$$\bar{\varepsilon}_T^i = \frac{1}{2}[\varepsilon_T^i(T) + \varepsilon_T^i(T-1)], \qquad (i = 1, 2, \dots, n).$$

Similarly, the equations for the value shares of intermediate, capital, and labor inputs can be written

$$\bar{v}_X^i = \alpha_X^i + \beta_{XX}^i \overline{\ln X_i} + \beta_{XK}^i \overline{\ln K_i} + \beta_{XL}^i \overline{\ln L_i} + \beta_{XT}^i \cdot \bar{T} + \bar{\varepsilon}_X^i ,$$

$$\bar{v}_K^i = \alpha_K^i + \beta_{XK}^i \overline{\ln X_i} + \beta_{KK}^i \overline{\ln K_i} + \beta_{KL}^i \overline{\ln L_i} + \beta_{KT}^i \cdot \bar{T} + \bar{\varepsilon}_K^i ,$$

$$\bar{v}_L^i = \alpha_L^i + \beta_{XL}^i \overline{\ln X_i} + \beta_{KL}^i \overline{\ln K_i} + \beta_{LL}^i \overline{\ln L_i} + \beta_{LT}^i \cdot \bar{T} + \bar{\varepsilon}_L^i , \quad (i = 1, 2, \dots, n),$$

where

$$\bar{\varepsilon}_X^i = \frac{1}{2}[\varepsilon_X^i(T) + \varepsilon_X^i(T-1)],$$

$$\bar{\varepsilon}_K^i = \frac{1}{2}[\varepsilon_K^i(T) + \varepsilon_K^i(T-1)],$$

$$\bar{\varepsilon}_L^i = \frac{1}{2}[\varepsilon_L^i(T) + \varepsilon_L^i(T-1)], \qquad (i = 1, 2, \dots, n).$$

As before, the average value shares $\{\bar{v}_X^i, \bar{v}_K^i, \bar{v}_L^i\}$ sum to unity, so the average disturbances $\{\bar{\varepsilon}_X^i, \bar{\varepsilon}_K^i, \bar{\varepsilon}_L^i\}$ sum to zero:

$$\bar{\varepsilon}_X^i + \bar{\varepsilon}_K^i + \bar{\varepsilon}_L^i = 0, \qquad (i = 1, 2, \dots, n).$$

The covariance matrix of the average disturbances corresponding to the equation for technical change for all observations, say Ω, is a Laurent matrix:

$$V \begin{bmatrix} \bar{\varepsilon}_T^i(2) \\ \bar{\varepsilon}_T^i(3) \\ \vdots \\ \bar{\varepsilon}_T^i(N) \end{bmatrix} = \Omega, \qquad (i = 1, 2,..., n).$$

where

$$\Omega = \begin{bmatrix} \frac{1}{2} & \frac{1}{4} & 0 & \cdots & 0 \\ \frac{1}{4} & \frac{1}{2} & \frac{1}{4} & \cdots & 0 \\ 0 & \frac{1}{4} & \frac{1}{2} & \cdots & 0 \\ \vdots & \vdots & \vdots & & \vdots \\ 0 & 0 & 0 & \cdots & \frac{1}{2} \end{bmatrix}$$

The covariance matrix of the average disturbances corresponding to each equation for the three value shares is the same, so the covariance matrix of the average disturbances for the first two value shares and the rate of productivity growth for all observations has the Kronecker product form

$$V \begin{bmatrix} \bar{\varepsilon}_X^i(2) \\ \bar{\varepsilon}_X^i(3) \\ \vdots \\ \bar{\varepsilon}_X^i(N) \\ \bar{\varepsilon}_K^i(2) \\ \vdots \\ \bar{\varepsilon}_T^i(N) \end{bmatrix} = \Sigma^i \otimes \Omega, \qquad (i = 1, 2,..., n).$$

Although disturbances in equations for the average rate of productivity growth and the average value shares are autocorrelated, the data can be transformed to eliminate the autocorrelation. The matrix Ω is positive definite, so there is a matrix T such that

$$T \Omega T' = I,$$

$$T'T = \Omega^{-1}.$$

To construct the matrix T we can first invert the matrix Ω, to obtain the inverse matrix Ω^{-1}, a positive definite matrix. We then calculate the

Cholesky factorization of the inverse matrix Ω^{-1}:

$$\Omega^{-1} = LDL',$$

where L is a unit lower triangular matrix and D is a diagonal matrix with positive elements along the main diagonal. Finally, we can write the matrix T in the form

$$T = D^{1/2}L',$$

where $D^{1/2}$ is a diagonal matrix with elements along the main diagonal equal to the square roots of the corresponding elements of D.

We can transform the equations for the average rates of productivity growth by the matrix $T = D^{1/2}L'$ to obtain equations with uncorrelated random disturbances:

$$
D^{1/2}L'
\begin{bmatrix}
\overline{v}_T^i(2) \\
\overline{v}_T^i(3) \\
\vdots \\
\overline{v}_T^i(N)
\end{bmatrix}
= D^{1/2}L'
\begin{bmatrix}
l\ \overline{\ln X_i(2)} \ldots 2 - 1/2 \\
l\ \overline{\ln X_i(3)} \ldots 3 - 1/2 \\
\vdots \quad \vdots \quad \vdots \\
l\ \overline{\ln X_i(N)} \ldots N - 1/2
\end{bmatrix}
\begin{bmatrix}
\alpha_T^i \\
\beta_{XT}^i \\
\vdots \\
\beta_{TT}^i
\end{bmatrix}
+ D^{1/2}L'
\begin{bmatrix}
\overline{\varepsilon}_T^i(2) \\
\overline{\varepsilon}_T^i(3) \\
\vdots \\
\overline{\varepsilon}_T^i(N)
\end{bmatrix},
$$

$$(i = 1, 2,..., n),$$

since

$$T\,\Omega\,T' = (D^{1/2}L')\,\Omega\,(D^{1/2}L')' = I.$$

The transformation $T = D^{1/2}L'$ was applied to data on the average rates of productivity growth $\{\overline{v}_T^i\}$ and data on the average values of the variables that appear on the right side of the corresponding equation.

We can apply the transformation $T = D^{1/2}L'$ to the first two equations for average value shares, to obtain equations with uncorrelated disturbances. As before, the transformation is applied to data on the average value shares and the average values of variables that appear on the right side of the corresponding equations. The covariance matrices of the transformed disturbances from the first two equations for the average value shares and the equation for the average rate of productivity growth have the Kronecker product form

$$(I \otimes D^{1/2}L')(\Sigma^i \otimes \Omega)(I \otimes D^{1/2}L')' = \Sigma^i \otimes I, \qquad\qquad (i = 1, 2,..., n).$$

To estimate the unknown parameters of the translog production function, combine the first two equations for the average value shares with the equation for the average rate of productivity growth, to obtain a complete econometric model. We estimate the parameters of the equations for the remaining average value shares from estimates of the parameters of the first two average value shares, using the restrictions on these parameters given above. The complete model involves nine unknown parameters. A total of eleven additional parameters can be estimated as functions of these parameters, given the restrictions.

Our estimator for the unknown parameters of the econometric model of producer behavior is based on the nonlinear three-stage least squares estimator introduced by Jorgenson and Laffont (1974). To test the validity of restrictions implied by Hicks neutrality of productivity growth and the existence of value-added functions, we employ test statistics introduced by Gallant and Jorgenson (1979). These statistics are based on the difference between the estimated covariance matrix of the disturbances for the complete econometric model of production Ω without restriction, say $\hat{\Sigma}_\Omega^i$, and the corresponding matrices for the econometric models ω with restrictions, say $\hat{\Sigma}_\omega^i$. The test statistics take the form

$$(X_p^i)^2 = (N-1)[tr(\hat{\Sigma}_\omega^i - \hat{\Sigma}_\Omega^i)], \qquad\qquad (i = 1, 2,..., n),$$

where N is the number of observations and p is the number of restrictions. Under the null hypothesis these test statistics are distributed, asymptotically, as chi-squared with p degrees of freedom. These test statistics reduce to

$$(X_p^i)^2 = (N-1)[tr(\hat{\Sigma}_\Omega^i)^{-1} \hat{\Sigma}_\omega - 3], \qquad\qquad (i = 1, 2,..., n).$$

In the following section these statistics are constructed for tests of Hicks neutrality and the existence of a value-added function for all industrial sectors.

Empirical Results

We have generated an econometric model of producer behavior from a production function for each sector. In this model the rate of productivity growth and the distributive shares of productive inputs are determined endogenously. While the rate of productivity growth is endogenous within our econometric model, this model must be carefully distinguished from models of induced productivity growth, such as those analyzed by Hicks

(1932), Kennedy (1964), Samuelson (1965), von Weizsacker (1962), and many others. In those models the biases of productivity growth are determined endogenously. As Samuelson (1965) has pointed out, models of induced productivity growth require intertemporal optimization, since productivity growth at any point in time affects future production possibilities.[10]

We next present estimates of the unknown parameters for our complete econometric model of producer behavior. These estimates are based on annual time series data for forty-five of the fifty-one industries listed in Table 3.1. The data are described in Chapters 3 through 6 and cover the period 1948–1979. There are thirty observations for each behavioral equation, since unweighted two-period moving averages of all data are employed. Nine unknown parameters are estimated for each industrial sector, so eighty-one degrees of freedom are available for tests of the restrictions on parameters implied by Hicks neutrality of productivity growth or by the existence of value-added functions.

Under Hicks neutrality the biases of productivity growth are equal to zero

$$\beta^i_{XT} = \beta^i_{KT} = \beta^i_{LT} = 0, \qquad\qquad (i = 1, 2,..., n).$$

Each set of restrictions involves only two independent restrictions, since the sum of the biases is equal to zero. Under these restrictions there are seven unknown parameters to be estimated.

One of the two alternative sets of restrictions that are jointly necessary and sufficient for the existence of a value-added function involves the necessary conditions

$$\beta^i_{XK} = \rho^i \cdot \alpha^i_K ,$$

$$\beta^i_{XL} = \rho^i \cdot \alpha^i_L ,$$

$$\beta^i_{XT} = \rho^i \cdot \alpha^i_T , \qquad\qquad (i = 1, 2,..., n).$$

Each set of restrictions involves a set of three restrictions with the introduction of one new parameter, so seven parameters remain to be estimated. Sufficient conditions take the form

$$\rho^i = 0 , \qquad\qquad (i = 1, 2,..., n).$$

Under this additional restriction six parameters remain to be estimated.

The second set of jointly necessary and sufficient conditions for the existence of a value-added function implies that the equations for the value shares of capital and labor inputs and the rate of productivity growth are in fixed proportions

$$\alpha_K^i \beta_{XL}^i = \alpha_L^i \beta_{XK}^i ,$$

$$\alpha_K^i \beta_{KL}^i = \alpha_L^i \beta_{KK}^i ,$$

$$\alpha_K^i \beta_{LL}^i = \alpha_L^i \beta_{XL}^i ,$$

$$\alpha_K^i \beta_{LT}^i = \alpha_L^i \beta_{KT}^i ,$$

$$\alpha_K^i \beta_{XT}^i = \alpha_T^i \beta_{XK}^i ,$$

$$\alpha_K^i \beta_{KT}^i = \alpha_T^i \beta_{KK}^i ,$$

$$\alpha_K^i \beta_{LT}^i = \alpha_T^i \beta_{KL}^i ,$$

$$\alpha_K^i \beta_{TT}^i = \alpha_T^i \beta_{KT}^i , \qquad\qquad (i = 1, 2,..., n).$$

Each set of restrictions involves a set of five independent restrictions, so there are only four unknown parameters to be estimated.

Our test procedure is presented in diagrammatic form in Figure 7.1. We first test the restrictions derived from Hicks neutrality of productivity growth. Next we test the necessary conditions for the existence of value-added functions; given these restrictions, we test the additional restriction implied by a linear logarithmic production function in terms of value-added. Finally, we test the restrictions implied by a linear logarithmic value-added function. To control the overall level of significance for our four tests for each industry, we set the level of significance for each set of four tests at 0.05. We then allocate the overall level of significance among the four tests in each set, assigning a level of significance of .0125 to each test. The probability of a false rejection for one test among each set of four tests is less than or equal to 0.05 by the Bonferroni inequality (Savin, 1984). Critical values for our test statistics based on the distribution of chi-squared are given in Table 7.1. With the aid of these critical values, the reader can evaluate the results of our tests for alternative levels of significance or alternative allocations of the overall level of significance among tests. Test statistics for each industry for all four hypotheses are given in Table 7.2.

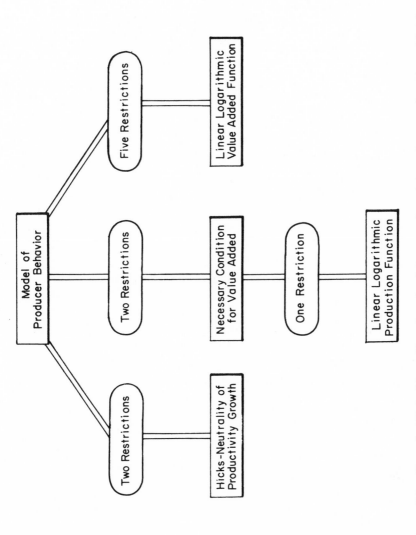

Figure 7.1. Tests for Hicks-Neutrality of productivity growth and the existence of a value-added function

Table 7.1. Critical values, chi-squared

Degrees of freedom	Level of significance					
	0.10	0.05	0.0125	0.01	0.005	0.001
1	2.71	3.84	6.36	6.63	7.88	10.83
2	4.60	6.00	8.90	9.22	10.60	13.82
5	9.25	11.05	14.72	15.10	16.75	20.50

For the test statistics for Hicks neutrality of productivity growth we employ the critical value 8.90 for chi-squared with two degrees of freedom at a level of significance of 0.0125. At this level of significance we reject Hicks neutrality for thirty-nine of the forty-five industries listed in Table 7.2. Hicks neutrality cannot be rejected for two manufacturing industries: furniture and professional equipment. Outside manufacturing Hicks neutrality is not rejected for four industries: coal mining, railroads, local transportation, and air transportation. Under Hicks neutrality all biases of productivity growth are zero. Biases of productivity growth are significant for thirty-nine of the forty-five industries listed in Table 7.2.

Recall from Chapter 2 that under Hicks neutrality the rate of productivity growth depends only on time; an alternative and equivalent interpretation of Hicks neutrality is that there exists an aggregate input that depends on intermediate, capital, and labor inputs and is independent of time. The measures of the rate of productivity growth we presented in Chapter 6 should not be regarded as functions depending only on time. Neither should sums of the contributions of intermediate, capital, and labor inputs to growth in output be treated as rates of growth of an input aggregate depending only on intermediate, capital, and labor inputs.

We next test the implications of the existence of a value-added function for each sector. The first step is to test the necessary condition for the production function to give output as a function of quantities of intermediate input and value-added. This condition implies proportionality between the elasticities of the share of intermediate input with respect to quantities of capital and labor inputs and the bias of productivity growth with respect to intermediate input on the one hand and shares of capital and labor inputs and the rate of productivity growth on the other. The proportionality restrictions require two degrees of freedom, so we employ the critical value 8.90 for chi-squared with

Table 7.2. Test statistics for Hicks neutrality and value-added

Industry	Hypothesis			
	Hicks neutrality	Value-added	Linear logarithmic production	Linear logarithmic value-added
Agricultural production	13.57744	2.64298	56.37679	3.55835
Agricultural services	87.18799	4.32311	217.19255	43.99791
Metal mining	53.77558	5.84981	594.58167	143.99590
Coal mining	7.80862	0.11741	113.14082	34.82356
Crude petroleum and natural gas	115.61687	101.65751		439.14655
Nonmetallic mining and quarrying	31.87799	18.48956		40.45981
Contract construction	40.35053	16.18092		24.03429
Food and kindred products	202.10265	10.31050		50.12397
Tobacco manufacturers	341.23721	2.97736	402.54575	48.26852
Textile mill products	66.42392	73.97914		33.85308
Apparel and other fabricated textile products	18.45301	0.98496	80.22119	52.27906
Paper and allied products	74.09027	0.43699	181.85878	55.44430
Printing and publishing	25.59909	6.91850	10.83237	42.41746
Chemicals and allied products	70.06010	10.37972		92.29266
Petroleum and coal products	12.38201	40.75902		41.63322
Rubber and misc. plastic products	19.90396	6.90673	30.71129	11.05953
Leather and leather products	118.05912	13.73001		16.59960
Lumber and wood products, except furniture	108.91556	56.99397		107.47490
Furniture and fixtures	2.52354	3.17142	52.37727	11.79638
Stone, clay, and glass products	35.82701	0.09173	110.01637	44.70860

Table 7.2 continued

	Hypothesis			
Industry	Hicks neutrality	Value-added	Linear logarithmic production	Linear logarithmic value-added
Primary metal industries	43.43753	3.42956	271.38806	112.44886
Fabricated metal industries	9.63434	13.49313		16.01762
Machinery, except electrical	11.62228	4.34444	173.94717	15.68269
Elec. machinery, eqpt., and supplies	45.27106	13.27333		17.40074
Trans. eqpt. and ordnance, except motor vehicles	99.06059	3.65807	115.07674	15.61398
Motor vehicles and equipment	72.09034	98.79008		63.30442
Prof. photographic eqpt. and watches	3.19310	29.03769		31.94822
Misc. manufacturing industries	16.41284	3.21363	267.41782	21.29054
Railroads and rail express services	3.39583	4.17953	373.97614	45.13210
Street rail., bus lines, and taxicabs	7.83315	12.50228		43.989774
Trucking services and warehousing	22.64095	3.95077	70.62433	47.53611
Water transportation	327.65210	6.56898	868.56451	17.29881
Air transportation	1.80194	0.92803	29.45816	1.99761
Pipelines, except natural gas	66.88699	77.54673		393.50027
Transportation services	63.34061	16.13122		83.79382
Telephone, telegraph, and misc. communication services	76.09354	3.48541	1086.09863	114.14265
Radio and television broadcasting	40.99236	6.48545	549.47766	32.55209
Electric utilities	58.46849	4.68787	235.97801	121.64507
Gas utilities	124.82802	30.68885		189.71628

Table 7.2 continued

Industry	Hypothesis			
	Hicks neutrality	Value-added	Linear logarithmic production	Linear logarithmic value-added
Water supply and sanitary services	100.70554	2.98534	276.37747	43.37103
Wholesale trade	23.72135	12.25310		58.67421
Retail trade	22.74431	16.64033		34.89933
Finance, insurance, and real estate	28.22812	0.35815	1543.31470	122.96541
Services, except private households and institutions	80.08928	5.04299	156.37421	932.30579
Institutions	15.59493	3.74159	633.43951	8.23915

two degrees of freedom at a level of significance of 0.0125.

We reject the necessary condition for the existence of a value-added function for nineteen of the forty-five industries listed in Table 7.2. The existence of a value-added function is rejected for ten manufacturing industries: food, textiles, chemicals, petroleum and coal, leather, lumber and wood products, fabricated metals, electrical machinery, motor vehicles, and professional equipment. Outside manufacturing the existence of a value-added function is rejected for nine industries: crude petroleum and natural gas, nonmetallic mining, construction, local transportation, pipelines, transportation services, gas utilities, wholesale trade, and retail trade. For these industries we terminate the test procedure at this point; for the remaining twenty-six industries we test additional restrictions.

Two sets of conditions are jointly necessary and sufficient for the existence of a value-added function. The first is that output is a linear logarithmic function of intermediate input and value-added. Under this condition the elasticities of the shares of capital and labor inputs and the bias of productivity growth with respect to quantities of intermediate input are zero. These restrictions are obtained by setting the factor of proportionality in the necessary condition for the existence of a value-added function equal to zero. Given proportionality, the test for a linear logarithmic production function requires one degree of freedom. We employ the critical value of 6.36 for chi-squared with one degree of freedom at a level of significance of 0.0125.

We reject the hypothesis that the production function is linear logarithmic, given proportionality, for all twenty-six of the industries for which we have not rejected the proportionality condition.

The final step in testing for the existence of a value-added function is to test the second of two sets of conditions that are jointly necessary and sufficient, that value-added is a linear logarithmic function of capital input, labor input, and time. Under this condition the equations for value shares of capital and labor inputs and the rate of productivity growth are in fixed proportions to each other. These restrictions require five degrees of freedom, so we employ the critical value of 14.7 for chi-squared with five degrees of freedom at a level of significance of 0.0125. We reject the hypothesis that the value-added function is linear logarithmic for forty of the forty-five industries listed in Table 7.2. The existence of a linear logarithmic value-added function is not rejected for only two manufacturing industries, rubber and furniture. Outside manufacturing the existence of a linear logarithmic value-added function is not rejected for only three industries: agriculture, air transportation, and nonprofit institutions.

Overall, conditions that are jointly necessary and sufficient for the existence of a value-added function are rejected for forty of the forty-five industries listed in Table 7.2. We reject the hypothesis that the production function is linear logarithmic in all forty-five industries; for five industries we do not reject the hypothesis that the value-added function is linear logarithmic. We conclude that intermediate input should be treated symmetrically with capital and labor inputs. The existence of a sectoral value-added function is not supported by the empirical evidence. The measures of productivity growth we presented in Chapter 6 are based on a symmetric treatment of all three inputs.

The final step to implement the econometric models of production developed in Section 7.3 is to present estimates of the unknown parameters. Table 7.3 presents estimates of these parameters for forty-five of the fifty-one industries listed in Table 3.1. The parameters $\{\alpha_X^i, \alpha_K^i, \alpha_L^i\}$ can be interpreted as average value shares of intermediate input, capital input, and labor input, respectively. Similarly, the parameter $\{\alpha_T^i\}$ can be interpreted as average rates of productivity growth. The parameters $\{\beta_{XX}^i, \beta_{XK}^i, \beta_{XL}^i, \beta_{KK}^i, \beta_{KL}^i, \beta_{LL}^i\}$ can be interpreted as constant share elasticities, the parameters $\{\beta_{XT}^i, \beta_{KT}^i, \beta_{LT}^i\}$ can be interpreted as constant biases of productivity growth. Finally, the parameter $\{\beta_{TT}^i\}$ can be interpreted as the constant acceleration of productivity growth.

Table 7.3. Parameter estimates, sectoral models of production, and technical change

Parameter	Industry			
	Agricultural production	Agricultural services	Metal mining	Coal mining
α_X^i	0.581	0.402	0.559	0.466
	(0.00380)	(0.00473)	(0.00690)	(0.00478)
α_K^i	0.125	0.166	0.189	0.169
	(0.00689)	(0.0106)	(0.00976)	(0.00951)
α_L^i	0.294	0.432	0.253	0.365
	(0.00932)	(0.00804)	(0.00342)	(0.00832)
α_T^i	0.0276	−0.0339	−0.0478	−0.0189
	(0.0373)	(0.0775)	(0.0660)	(0.0263)
β_{XX}^i	0.000	0.000	0.000	0.000
	(0.000)	(0.000)	(0.000)	(0.000)
β_{XK}^i	0.000	0.000	0.000	0.000
	(0.000)	(0.000)	(0.000)	(0.000)
β_{XL}^i	0.000	0.000	0.000	0.000
	(0.000)	(0.000)	(0.000)	(0.000)
β_{XT}^i	0.00140	−0.00434	−0.00413	0.00433
	(0.000326)	(0.000405)	(0.000591)	(0.000409)
β_{KK}^i	−0.158	0.000	0.000	−0.0224
	(0.0712)	(0.000)	(0.000)	(0.0458)
β_{KL}^i	0.158	0.000	0.000	0.0224
	(0.0712)	(0.000)	(0.000)	(0.0458)
β_{KT}^i	0.00974	0.00634	0.00478	0.00297
	(0.00444)	(0.000906)	(0.00836)	(0.00199)
β_{LL}^i	−0.158	0.000	0.000	−0.0224
	(0.0712)	(0.000)	(0.000)	(0.0458)
β_{LT}^i	−0.0111	−0.00199	−0.000653	−0.00730
	(0.00447)	(0.000688)	(0.000293)	(0.00195)
β_{TT}^i	0.000111	−0.00338	−0.00416	−0.00357
	(0.00320)	(0.00663)	(0.00565)	(0.00226)

Table 7.3 continued

	Industry			
Parameter	Crude petroleum and natural gas	Nonmetallic mining and quarrying	Contract construction	Food and kindred products
α_X^i	0.571 (0.00464)	0.407 (0.00412)	0.540 (0.00267)	0.775 (0.00195)
α_K^i	0.303 (0.00555)	0.272 (0.00659)	0.0650 (0.00146)	0.0651 (0.00193)
α_L^i	0.126 (0.00108)	0.321 (0.00356)	0.395 (0.00298)	0.160 (0.000741)
α_T^i	−0.0522 (0.0622)	−0.000143 (0.0313)	−0.00922 (0.00680)	0.00704 (0.0273)
β_{XX}^i	0.000 (0.000)	0.000 (0.000)	0.000 (0.000)	0.000 (0.000)
β_{XK}^i	0.000 (0.000)	0.000 (0.000)	0.000 (0.000)	0.000 (0.000)
β_{XL}^i	0.000 (0.000)	0.000 (0.000)	0.000 (0.000)	0.000 (0.000)
β_{XT}^i	0.00618 (0.000397)	0.00132 (0.000353)	−0.00301 (0.000229)	0.000433 (0.000167)
β_{KK}^i	−0.0413 (0.00211)	−0.126 (0.0172)	0.000 (0.000)	0.000 (0.000)
β_{KL}^i	0.0413 (0.00211)	0.126 (0.0172)	0.000 (0.000)	0.000 (0.000)
β_{KT}^i	−0.00380 (0.000475)	0.00767 (0.00122)	0.000589 (0.000125)	0.000147 (0.000166)
β_{LL}^i	−0.0413 (0.00211)	−0.126 (0.0172)	0.000 (0.000)	0.000 (0.000)
β_{LT}^i	−0.00238 (0.0000923)	−0.00900 (0.00112)	0.00242 (0.000256)	−0.000580 (0.0000634)
β_{TT}^i	−0.00377 (0.00533)	−0.00145 (0.00269)	−0.00124 (0.000581)	−0.000422 (0.00234)

Table 7.3 continued

	Industry			
Parameter	Tobacco manufacturers	Textile mill products	Apparel and other fabricated textile products	Paper and allied products
α_X^i	0.459 (0.00551)	0.649 (0.00268)	0.628 (0.00220)	0.619 (0.00153)
α_K^i	0.333 (0.00576)	0.0841 (0.00269)	0.0486 (0.00146)	0.115 (0.00338)
α_L^i	0.208 (0.00165)	0.267 (0.00153)	0.323 (0.00179)	0.266 (0.00341)
α_T^i	0.0336 (0.0627)	0.0360 (0.0278)	0.0113 (0.00827)	−0.00508 (0.0221)
β_{XX}^i	0.000 (0.000)	0.000 (0.000)	0.000 (0.000)	0.000 (0.000)
β_{XK}^i	0.000 (0.000)	0.000 (0.000)	0.000 (0.000)	0.000 (0.000)
β_{XL}^i	0.000 (0.000)	0.000 (0.000)	0.000 (0.000)	0.000 (0.000)
β_{XT}^i	−0.00591 (0.000472)	0.000352 (0.000230)	−0.00168 (0.000189)	0.000743 (0.000131)
β_{KK}^i	0.000 (0.000)	−0.0515 (0.0222)	0.000 (0.000)	−0.155 (0.0331)
β_{KL}^i	0.000 (0.000)	0.0515 (0.0222)	0.000 (0.000)	0.155 (0.0331)
β_{KT}^i	0.00508 (0.000493)	0.00206 (0.000684)	0.000977 (0.000125)	0.00188 (0.000678)
β_{LL}^i	0.000 (0.000)	−0.0515 (0.0222)	0.000 (0.000)	−0.155 (0.0331)
β_{LT}^i	0.000825 (0.000141)	−0.00241 (0.000657)	0.000705 (0.000154)	−0.00262 (0.000679)
β_{TT}^i	0.000597 (0.00537)	0.00144 (0.00238)	0.000214 (0.000708)	−0.000273 (0.00190)

Table 7.3 continued

Parameter	Industry			
	Printing and publishing	Chemicals and allied products	Petroleum and coal products	Rubber and misc. plastics products
α_X^i	0.498 (0.00313)	0.635 (0.00319)	0.811 (0.00388)	0.533 (0.00523)
α_K^i	0.114 (0.00259)	0.152 (0.00339)	0.0900 (0.00410)	0.0964 (0.00461)
α_L^i	0.388 (0.00350)	0.213 (0.00180)	0.0988 (0.000803)	0.371 (0.00407)
α_T^i	0.0118 (0.0315)	0.00421 (0.0307)	−0.0884 (0.0945)	0.0228 (0.0423)
β_{XX}^i	−0.0614 (0.0232)	0.000 (0,000)	0.000 (0.000)	0.000 (0.000)
β_{XK}^i	−0.0309 (0.0150)	0.000 (0.000)	0.000 (0.000)	0.000 (0.000)
β_{XL}^i	0.0922 (0.0285)	0.000 (0.000)	0.000 (0.000)	0.000 (0.000)
β_{XT}^i	0.00184 (0.000450)	0.00293 (0.000273)	0.00417 (0.000332)	−0.00141 (0.000448)
β_{KK}^i	−0.0155 (0.0158)	−0.00889 (0.0249)	−0.167 (0.0142)	−0.0137 (0.0320)
β_{KL}^i	0.0464 (0.0302)	0.00889 (0.0249)	0.167 (0.0142)	0.0137 (0.0320)
β_{KT}^i	0.00136 (0.000396)	−0.00230 (0.000690)	0.00130 (0.000434)	0.000119 (0.00101)
β_{LL}^i	−0.139 (0.0494)	−0.00889 (0.0249)	−0.167 (0.0142)	−0.0137 (0.0320)
β_{LT}^i	−0.00320 (0.000617)	−0.000629 (0.000645)	−0.00547 (0.000264)	0.00130 (0.000992)
β_{TT}^i	0.000577 (0.00270)	−0.000614 (0.00263)	−0.00232 (0.00809)	0.00933 (0.00362)

Table 7.3 continued

	Industry			
Parameter	Leather and leather products	Lumber and wood products, except furniture	Furniture and fixtures	Stone, clay, and glass products
α^i_X	0.597 (0.00298)	0.523 (0.00270)	0.594 (0.00454)	0.534 (0.00324)
α^i_K	0.0507 (0.00338)	0.154 (0.00377)	0.0653 (0.00228)	0.127 (0.00354)
α^i_L	0.352 (0.00336)	0.323 (0.00393)	0.341 (0.00342)	0.340 (0.00215)
α^i_T	−0.00289 (0.0337)	−0.0105 (0.0388)	0.00677 (0.0150)	−0.00437 (0.0299)
β^i_{XX}	0.000 (0.000)	0.000 (0.000)	0.000 (0.000)	0.000 (0.000)
β^i_{XK}	0.000 (0.000)	0.000 (0.000)	0.000 (0.000)	0.000 (0.000)
β^i_{XL}	0.000 (0.000)	0.000 (0.000)	0.000 (0.000)	0.000 (0.000)
β^i_{XT}	−0.000943 (0.000255)	0.00130 (0.000231)	0.00259 (0.000389)	0.00251 (0.000277)
β^i_{KK}	0.000 (0.000)	−0.0859 (0.0311)	−0.0235 (0.0178)	0.000 (0.000)
β^i_{KL}	0.000 (0.000)	0.0859 (0.0311)	0.0235 (0.0178)	0.000 (0.000)
β^i_{KT}	−0.0000538 (0.000289)	0.00375 (0.000875)	−0.000103 (0.000595)	−0.00215 (0.000304)
β^i_{LL}	0.000 (0.000)	00.0859 (0.0311)	−0.0235 (0.0178)	0.000 (0.000)
β^i_{LT}	0.000997 (0.000287)	−0.00506 (0.000880)	−0.00248 (0.000634)	−0.000362 (0.000184)
β^i_{TT}	−0.00118 (0.00288)	−0.00123 (0.00332)	0.000291 (0.00128)	−0.000158 (0.00256)

Table 7.3 continued

Parameter	Industry			
	Primary metal industries	Fabricated metal industries	Machinery, except electrical	Elec. machinery, equipment supplies
α_X^i	0.674 (0.00293)	0.533 (0.00256)	0.511 (0.00303)	0.532 (0.0360)
α_K^i	0.0719 (0.00321)	0.0941 (0.00300)	0.110 (0.00329)	0.0977 (0.00398)
α_L^i	0.254 (0.00178)	0.373 (0.00276)	0.379 (0.00250)	0.370 (0.00235)
α_T^i	−0.00287 (0.0358)	0.00936 (0.0170)	0.00237 (0.0157)	0.0259 (0.0227)
β_{XX}^i	0.000 (0.000)	0.000 (0.000)	0.000 (0.000)	0.000 (0.000)
β_{XK}^i	0.000 (0.000)	0.000 (0.000)	0.000 (0.000)	0.000 (0.000)
β_{XL}^i	0.000 (0.000)	0.000 (0.000)	0.000 (0.000)	0.000 (0.000)
β_{XT}^i	0.00222 (0.000251)	0.000963 (0.000219)	0.00270 (0.000260)	−0.000134 (0.000308)
β_{KK}^i	−0.169 (0.0125)	0.000 (0.000)	−0.0597 (0.0160)	0.000 (0.000)
β_{KL}^i	0.169 (0.0125)	0.000 (0.000)	0.0597 (0.0160)	0.000 (0.000)
β_{KT}^i	0.0000270 (0.000321)	0.00000736 (0.000257)	0.000234 (0.000467)	−0.000375 (0.000341)
β_{LL}^i	−0.169 (0.0125)	0.000 (0.000)	−0.0597 (0.0160)	0.000 (0.000)
β_{LT}^i	−0.00225 (0.000225)	−0.000971 (0.000236)	−0.00294 (0.000429)	0.000509 (0.000201)
β_{TT}^i	0.000941 (0.00306)	0.000128 (0.00146)	−0.000280 (0.00134)	0.00111 (0.00194)

Table 7.3 continued

Parameter	Industry			
	Trans. equipment except motor vehicles	Motor vehicles and equipment	Prof. photographic equipment and watches	Misc. manufacturing industries
α_X^i	0.608 (0.00306)	0.680 (0.00503)	0.373 (0.00449)	0.582 (0.00313)
α_K^i	0.0505 (0.00238)	0.115 (0.00631)	0.116 (0.00580)	0.0894 (0.00334)
α_L^i	0.342 (0.00252)	0.205 (0.00191)	0.512 (0.00271)	0.329 (0.00257)
α_T^i	0.00153 (0.0127)	0.0216 (0.0851)	0.00955 (0.0259)	−0.00456 (0.0293)
β_{XX}^i	0.000 (0.000)	0.000 (0.000)	0.000 (0.000)	0.000 (0.000)
β_{XK}^i	0.000 (0.000)	0.000 (0.000)	0.000 (0.000)	0.000 (0.000)
β_{XL}^i	0.000 (0.000)	0.000 (0.000)	0.000 (0.000)	0.000 (0.000)
β_{XT}^i	−0.000145 (0.000262)	0.00131 (0.000431)	0.00210 (0.000385)	0.00397 (0.000268)
β_{KK}^i	0.000 (0.000)	0.000 (0.000)	−0.344 (0.0208)	0.000 (0.000)
β_{KL}^i	0.000 (0.000)	0.000 (0.000)	0.344 (0.0208)	0.000 (0.000)
β_{KT}^i	−0.000393 (0.000204)	−0.00149 (0.000540)	0.0126 (0.000901)	−0.000463 (0.000286)
β_{LL}^i	0.000 (0.000)	0.000 (0.000)	−0.344 (0.0208)	0.000 (0.000)
β_{LT}^i	0.000538 (0.000216)	0.000173 (0.000163)	−0.0147 (0.000787)	−0.00351 (0.000221)
β_{TT}^i	−0.000637 (0.00109)	0.00200 (0.00729)	−0.000551 (0.00221)	−0.00114 (0.00251)

Table 7.3 continued

Parameter	Railroads and rail express services	Street rail., bus lines, taxi cabs	Trucking services and warehousing	Water transportation
α_X^i	0.560	0.604	0.599	0.577
	(0.00174)	(0.00898)	(0.00210)	(0.00291)
α_K^i	0.0977	0.119	0.101	0.0970
	(0.00291)	(0.00205)	(0.00183)	(0.00265)
α_L^i	0.342	0.277	0.300	0.326
	(0.00220)	(0.00950)	(0.00172)	(0.00326)
α_T^i	0.0170	−0.00684	−0.00339	−0.00951
	(0.0139)	(0.0199)	(0.0355)	(0.0432)
β_{XX}^i	0.000	−0.112	0.000	0.000
	(0.000)	(0.0219)	(0.000)	(0.000)
β_{XK}^i	0.000	0.0863	0.000	0.000
	(0.000)	(0.0234)	(0.000)	(0.000)
β_{XL}^i	0.000	0.0258	0.000	0.000
	(0.000)	(0.00957)	(0.000)	(0.000)
β_{XT}^i	0.00269	−0.00186	−0.00140	−0.00473
	(0.000149)	(0.00111)	(0.000180)	(0.000249)
β_{KK}^i	−0.0435	−0.0665	−0.0167	0.000
	(0.0309)	(0.0247)	(0.00405)	(0.000)
β_{KL}^i	0.0435	−0.0199	0.0167	0.000
	(0.0309)	(0.00536)	(0.00405)	(0.000)
β_{KT}^i	−0.000119	0.00228	0.000430	0.00177
	(0.00122)	(0.00115)	(0.000240)	(0.000227)
β_{LL}^i	−0.0435	−0.00593	−0.0167	0.000
	(0.0309)	(0.00449)	(0.00405)	(0.000)
β_{LT}^i	−0.00257	−0.000418	0.000966	0.00296
	(0.00120)	(0.000206)	(0.000234)	(0.000279)
β_{TT}^i	−0.000348	0.000874	−0.00251	−0.00121
	(0.00119)	(0.00171)	(0.00305)	(0.00370)

Table 7.3 continued

	Industry			
Parameter	Air transportation	Pipelines, except natural gas	Transportation services	Telephone, telegraph, and misc. communication services
α_X^i	0.578 (0.00388)	0.483 (0.00814)	0.791 (0.00177)	0.188 (0.000848)
α_K^i	0.113 (0.00620)	0.380 (0.0109)	0.0614 (0.00231)	0.404 (0.00639)
α_L^i	0.308 (0.00402)	0.137 (0.00309)	0.147 (0.00143)	0.407 (0.0680)
α_T^i	0.0182 (0.0420)	−0.0195 (0.0287)	−0.0855 (0.187)	0.0420 (0.0140)
β_{XX}^i	0.000 (0.000)	0.000 (0.000)	0.000 (0.000)	0.000 (0.000)
β_{XK}^i	0.000 (0.000)	0.000 (0.000)	0.000 (0.000)	0.000 (0.000)
β_{XL}^i	0.000 (0.000)	0.000 (0.000)	0.000 (0.000)	0.000 (0.000)
β_{XT}^i	0.00119 (0.000333)	0.00131 (0.000697)	0.00533 (0.000152)	−0.00237 (0.0000727)
β_{KK}^i	−0.0162 (0.00795)	−0.0261 (0.00421)	0.000 (0.000)	0.000 (0.000)
β_{KL}^i	0.0162 (0.00795)	0.0261 (0.00421)	0.000 (0.000)	0.000 (0.000)
β_{KT}^i	0.000306 (0.000653)	0.00441 (0.000969)	−0.0152 (0.000198)	(0.00476) (0.000548)
β_{LL}^i	−0.0162 (0.00795)	−0.0261 (0.00421)	0.000 (0.000)	0.000 (0.000)
β_{LT}^i	−0.00150 (0.000514)	−0.00571 (0.000377)	−0.00381 (0.000123)	−0.00239 (0.000582)
β_{TT}^i	−0.000817 (0.00359)	−0.00403 (0.00245)	−0.00720 (0.0160)	0.00175 (0.00120)

Table 7.3 continued

Parameter	Industry			
	Radio and television broadcasting	Electric utilities	Gas utilities	Water supply and sanitary services
α_X^i	0.0776	0.474	0.717	0.0913
	(0.0102)	(0.00786)	(0.00376)	(0.00568)
α_K^i	0.315	0.344	0.185	0.594
	(0.00614)	(0.00930)	(0.00224)	(0.00497)
α_L^i	0.608	0.182	0.0978	0.315
	(0.00968)	(0.00217)	(0.00189)	(0.00342)
α_T^i	0.0000306	0.00585	−0.00371	0.0343
	(0.0945)	(0.0230)	(0.0107)	(0.0177)
β_{XX}^i	0.000	0.000	0.000	0.000
	(0.000)	(0.000)	(0.000)	(0.000)
β_{XK}^i	0.000	0.000	0.000	0.000
	(0.000)	(0.000)	(0.000)	(0.000)
β_{XL}^i	0.000	0.000	0.000	0.000
	(0.000)	(0.000)	(0.000)	(0.000)
β_{XT}^i	−0.0201	0.00785	0.00655	−0.00790
	(0.000874)	(0.000673)	(0.000322)	(0.000486)
β_{KK}^i	−0.0785	0.000	0.000	0.000
	(0.0344)	(0.000)	(0.000)	(0.000)
β_{KL}^i	0.0785	0.000	0.000	0.000
	(0.0344)	(0.000)	(0.000)	(0.000)
β_{KT}^i	0.0116	−0.00405	−0.00355	0.00634
	(0.00143)	(0.000797)	(0.000192)	(0.000425)
β_{LL}^i	−0.0785	0.000	0.000	0.000
	(0.0344)	(0.000)	(0.000)	(0.000)
β_{LT}^i	0.00854	−0.00380	−0.00300	0.00155
	(0.00156)	(0.000186)	(0.000162)	(0.000293)
β_{TT}^i	−0.00431	−0.000974	−0.000415	0.000444
	(0.00810)	(0.00197)	(0.000918)	(0.00151)

Table 7.3 continued

	Industry				
Parameter	Wholesale trade	Retail trade	Finance, insurance, and real estate	Services, except private households and institutions	Institutions
α_X^i	0.206 (0.000870)	0.403 (0.00151)	0.614 (0.00220)	0.606 (0.000945)	0.278 (0.00411)
α_K^i	0.202 (0.00397)	0.116 (0.00501)	0.178 (0.00383)	0.117 (0.00177)	0.323 (0.0106)
α_L^i	0.592 (0.00349)	0.481 (0.00548)	0.208 (0.00359)	0.277 (0.00129)	0.400 (0.00718)
α_T^i	0.0155 (0.0273)	0.00481 (0.0133)	0.00940 (0.0356)	−0.00765 (0.0105)	0.0184 (0.0476)
β_{XX}^i	0.000 (0.000)	−0.0454 (0.0238)	0.000 (0.000)	−0.00230 (0.00368)	0.000 (0.000)
β_{XK}^i	0.000 (0.000)	−0.0725 (0.0204)	0.000 (0.000)	−0.00744 (0.00445)	0.000 (0.000)
β_{XL}^i	0.000 (0.000)	0.118 (0.0388)	0.000 (0.000)	0.00974 (0.00808)	0.000 (0.000)
β_{XT}^i	0.000357 (0.0000745)	0.00379 (0.000810)	0.00730 (0.000189)	−0.000416 (0.000184)	0.00563 (0.000352)
β_{KK}^i	0.000 (0.000)	−0.116 (0.0607)	−0.0904 (0.0506)	−0.0240 (0.0119)	−0.172 (0.0765)
β_{KL}^i	0.000 (0.000)	0.188 (0.0737)	0.0904 (0.0506)	0.0315 (0.00915)	0.172 (0.0765)
β_{KT}^i	0.00147 (0.000340)	0.00308 (0.00180)	−0.00855 (0.000892)	−0.00159 (0.000260)	−0.00391 (0.00125)
β_{LL}^i	0.000 (0.000)	−0.306 (0.0916)	−0.0904 (0.0506)	−0.0412 (0.00824)	−0.172 (0.0765)
β_{LT}^i	−0.00183 (0.000299)	−0.00687 (0.00217)	0.00124 (0.000885)	0.00200 (0.000203)	−0.00173 (0.00105)
β_{TT}^i	−0.0000643 (0.00233)	−0.00102 (0.00114)	0.000299 (0.00305)	0.0000165 (0.000899)	0.00216 (0.00408)

In estimating the parameters model of production, we retain the biases of productivity growth as parameters to be estimated for all forty-five industries. Our tests of Hicks neutrality have shown that these biases are significant for thirty-nine of the forty-five industries. Estimates of the share elasticities are obtained under the restrictions implied by the necessary and sufficient conditions for concavity of the production functions presented earlier in this chapter. Under these restrictions the matrices of constant share elasticities $\{U^i\}$ must be negative semidefinite for all industries. To impose concavity restrictions, we represent the matrices of constant share elasticities for all sectors in terms of their Cholesky factorizations. The necessary and sufficient conditions are that the diagonal elements $\{\delta_1^i, \delta_2^i\}$ of the matrices $\{D^i\}$ that appear in the Cholesky factorizations must be nonpositive.

Our interpretation of the parameter estimates reported in Table 7.3 begins with an analysis of estimates of the parameters $\{\alpha_X^i, \alpha_K^i, \alpha_L^i, \alpha_T^i\}$. It is useful to recall that if the production functions are increasing in intermediate, capital, and labor inputs, the average value shares are nonnegative for each sector. These conditions are satisfied for all forty-five sectors included in our study. Not all the production functions are increasing in time. The estimated average rate of productivity growth is positive in twenty-five sectors and negative in twenty industries.

In Chapter 6 we reported that fifteen of the forty-five industries have negative average rates of productivity growth for the period 1948–1979. There is a positive but far from perfect association between the signs of the average rates of productivity growth and the signs of the estimated values of the parameter $\{\alpha_T^i\}$. For thirty-four of the forty-five industries the signs are the same—for twenty-two industries both signs are positive and for twelve both signs are negative. Three industries had positive estimates of the parameter $\{\alpha_T^i\}$ and negative average rates of productivity growth for the period as a whole. Eight industries had negative parameter estimates and positive average rates of productivity growth.

The estimated share elasticities $\{\beta_{XX}^i, \beta_{XK}^i, \beta_{XL}^i, \beta_{KK}^i, \beta_{KL}^i, \beta_{LL}^i\}$ describe the implications of patterns of substitution for the relative distribution of the value of output among intermediate, capital, and labor inputs. Positive share elasticities imply that the corresponding value shares increase with an increase in quantity; negative share elasticities imply that the value shares decrease with an increase in quantity; share elasticities equal to zero imply that the value shares are independent of quantity. It is important to keep in mind that we have fitted these parameters subject to the restrictions implied by concavity of the production function. These restrictions require that all the share elasticities be set equal to zero for twenty of the forty-five industries listed in Table 7.3. It is important to note that these conditions are neither necessary nor sufficient for the existence of a value-added function. The two sets of conditions that are jointly necessary and sufficient for the existence of a value-added function also involve restrictions on the biases of productivity growth. We do not impose these additional restrictions in estimating the parameters of our models of producer behavior.

Our interpretation of the parameter estimates given in Table 7.3 continues with the estimated elasticities of the share of each input with respect to the quantity of the input itself $\{\beta_{XX}^i, \beta_{KK}^i, \beta_{LL}^i\}$. Under the necessary and sufficient conditions for concavity of the production function for each sector, these share elasticities are nonpositive. The share of each input is nonincreasing in the quantity of the input itself. This condition, together with the condition that the sum of all the share elasticities with respect to a given input is equal to zero, implies that only one of the elasticities of the shares of each input with respect to the quantities of the other two inputs $\{\beta_{XK}^i, \beta_{XL}^i, \beta_{KL}^i\}$ can be negative. All three of these share elasticities can be nonnegative; this condition holds for forty-one of the forty-five industries listed in Table 7.3. For twenty of these industries all three share elasticities are set equal to zero by imposing the conditions for concavity of the production function. The four industries with exactly one negative share elasticity are printing and publishing, local transportation, retail trade, and services.

The estimated elasticities of the share of labor with respect to the quantity of capital $\{\beta_{KL}^i\}$ are nonnegative for forty-four of forty-five sectors. Except for local transportation, the share of labor does not decrease with an increase in the quantity of capital, holding quantities of labor and intermediate inputs and time constant. Of course, this parameter can also be interpreted as the elasticity of the share of capital with respect to the quantity of labor, so the share of capital does not decrease with an increase in the quantity of labor. The estimated elasticity of the share of intermediate input with respect to the quantity of capital $\{\beta_{XK}^i\}$ is negative for three industries: printing, retail trade, and services. This parameter can also be interpreted as the elasticity of the share of capital with respect to the quantity of intermediate input. The estimated elasticity of the share of intermediate input with respect to the quantity of labor $\{\beta_{XL}^i\}$, also interpreted as the elasticity of the share of labor with respect to the quantity of intermediate input, is nonnegative for all forty-five industries.

The estimated biases of productivity growth $\{\beta_{XT}^i, \beta_{KT}^i, \beta_{LT}^i\}$. can be interpreted as the change in the share of each input with respect to time, holding all inputs constant. The sum of the three biases of productivity growth is equal to zero, so we can rule out the possibility that the three biases are either all negative or all positive. Each of the remaining six logical possibilities— any two biases negative or any two biases positive—occurs among the results presented in Table 7.3.

If the estimated value of the bias of productivity growth with respect to labor input $\{\beta_{LT}^i\}$ is positive, productivity growth is labor using; if the value is negative, productivity growth is labor saving. Productivity growth is labor using for fourteen of the forty-five industries listed in Table 7.3 and labor saving for the remaining thirty-one.

Considering the biases of productivity growth with respect to capital input $\{\beta_{KT}^i\}$ and intermediate input $\{\beta_{XT}^i\}$, that productivity growth is capital using for twenty-nine of the forty-five industries listed in Table 7.3 and capital saving for the remaining sixteen industries. Finally, productivity growth is intermediate input using for twenty-nine of the forty-five industries and intermediate input saving for the remaining sixteen. These same conclusions characterize the overall pattern of productivity growth across sectors in each broadly defined industry group.

There are industry groups for which a particular pattern of productivity growth holds for all or nearly all sectors within the industry division. In particular, productivity growth is capital using in both agriculture sectors, three of four mining industries, construction, thirteen of twenty-one manufacturing sectors, five of seven transportation sectors, and three of five utility industries. Productivity growth is intermediate input using in fifteen of twenty-one manufacturing industries but is intermediate input saving in three of four mining industries and construction. Productivity growth is labor saving in both agriculture sectors, all four mining industries, fourteen of twenty-one manufacturing sectors, five of seven transportation sectors, and three of five utilities.

A classification of industries by their patterns of the biases of productivity growth is given in Table 7.4. The pattern that occurs with greatest frequency is labor saving in combination with capital using and intermediate-input-using productivity growth. This pattern characterizes seventeen industries. Labor saving together with capital using and intermediate-input-saving productivity growth occurs for four industries. Labor-saving, capital-saving, and intermediate-input-using growth takes place in ten industries. Productivity growth is labor using, capital saving, and intermediate input saving for four industries. Productivity growth is labor using, capital saving, and intermediate input using for two industrial sectors. Finally, productivity growth is labor using, capital using, and intermediate input saving for eight industries.

An alternative and equivalent interpretation of biases of productivity growth is that they represent changes in the rate of productivity growth with respect to proportional changes in input quantities. For example, if the bias with respect to labor input $\{\beta_{LT}^i\}$ is positive, the rate of productivity growth increases with respect to the quantity of labor input. If the bias is negative, the rate of productivity growth decreases with respect to the quantity of labor input. The rate of productivity growth increases in the quantity of labor input for fourteen of the forty-five industries listed in Table 7.3 and decreasing for

Table 7.4. Classification of industries by biases of productivity growth

Pattern of biases	Industries
Labor-saving Capital-using Intermediate-using	Agriculture, coal mining, nonmetallic mining, food, textiles, paper, printing, petroleum and coal, lumber and wood, primary metals, fabricated metals, machinery except electrical, professional equipment, air transportation, pipelines, wholesale trade, retail trade.
Labor-saving Capital-using Intermediate-saving	Agricultural services, metal mining, local transportation, telephones.
Labor-saving Capital-saving Intermediate-using	Crude petroleum and natural gas, chemicals, furniture, stone, clay, and glass, miscellaneous manufacturing, railroads, transportation services, electric utilities, gas utilities, institutions.
Labor-using Capital-saving Intermediate-saving	Leather, electrical machinery, transportation equipment, services.
Labor-using Capital-saving Intermediate-using	Motor vehicles, finance, insurance, and real estate.
Labor using Capital using Intermediate-saving	Construction, tobacco, apparel, rubber, trucking, water transportation, broadcasting, water supply.

the remaining thirty-one. The rate of productivity growth increases in the quantity of capital input for twenty-nine of the forty-five industries and decreasing for sixteen. Finally, the rate of productivity growth increases in the quantity of intermediate input for twenty-nine industries and decreases for sixteen. The relative frequency of labor saving productivity growth, where the rate decreases with the quantity of labor input, gives some credence to theories of induced innovation, though no simple theory of induced innovation accounts for the observed patterns of productivity growth for all forty-five industries.

If the estimated value of the acceleration of productivity growth $\{\beta_{TT}^i\}$ is positive, the rate of productivity growth increases over time; if the value is negative the rate decreases. For seventeen industries the estimated value is positive; for the remaining twenty-eight industries the estimated value is negative. Positive estimates dominate finance, insurance, and real estate, and the service industries; negative estimates are clustered in mining, construction, transportation, and trade. Deceleration rather than acceleration of productivity growth predominates.

Conclusion

In this Chapter we have analyzed the implications of patterns of producer behavior for productivity growth and for the relative distribution of the value of sectoral output among intermediate, capital, and labor inputs. We have characterized substitution possibilities among inputs and productivity growth in terms of share elasticities, biases of productivity growth, and the acceleration of the rate of productivity growth.

We have defined share elasticities with respect to quantity as changes in the value shares of each input with respect to proportional changes in input quantities. Share elasticities can be employed to derive the implications of patterns of substitution for the distribution of the value of output. We have estimated share elasticities as fixed parameters of our econometric models of producer behavior. These models are based on the translog production function.

The estimated elasticities of the share of each input with respect to its own quantity are nonpositive under necessary and sufficient conditions for concavity of the sectoral production functions. Only one of the elasticities of the shares of each input with respect to the quantities of the other two inputs can be negative. All three of these share elasticities are nonnegative for forty-one of the forty-five industries included in our study.

The elasticities of the share of labor with respect to the quantity of capital are nonnegative for all industries for which we have estimates, except local transportation. The shares of labor do not decrease with an increase in the quantity of capital, in all sectors except local transportation. These parameters can also be interpreted as elasticities of the share of capital with respect to the quantity of labor; equivalently, we can say that the capital share does not decrease with the quantity of labor for forty-four of the forty-five industries.

For forty-four of the forty-five industries for which we have estimates, the elasticity of the share of intermediate input with respect to capital input is nonpositive. The exception is local transportation. These parameters can also be interpreted as elasticities of the shares of capital with respect to intermediate input. The elasticity of the share of intermediate input with respect to labor is nonnegative for all forty-five industries.

We have defined biases of productivity growth with respect to quantity as changes in the value shares of each input with respect to time. An alternative and equivalent definition of these biases is changes in the rate of productivity growth with respect to proportional changes in input quantities. Biases of productivity growth can be employed to derive the implications of patterns of productivity growth for the distribution of the value of output.

We have estimated biases of productivity growth with respect to intermediate input, capital input, and labor input as fixed parameters of our econometric models. We find that biases with respect to labor input are negative for thirty-one industries and positive for the remaining fourteen. We conclude that labor-saving productivity growth predominates among the forty-five industries included in our study. Alternatively, we can say that the rate of productivity growth decreases with labor input for more than two-thirds of the forty-five industries.

Biases with respect to capital input are positive for twenty-nine of the forty-five industries and negative for the remaining sixteen. Capital-using productivity growth predominates among these industries; alternatively, increases in the rate of productivity growth with capital input are more frequent than decreases. Finally, biases with respect to intermediate input are positive for twenty-nine industries and negative for sixteen, so intermediate-input-using productivity growth predominates.

We have also estimated accelerations of productivity growth as fixed parameters of our econometric models. We find that the estimated values of these parameters are negative for twenty-eight industries and positive for the remaining seventeen industries. We conclude that productivity growth at the sectoral level is decelerating.

We have derived restrictions on shares and share elasticities corresponding to the existence of a value-added aggregate for our models of production. We also have derived the corresponding restrictions on the rate and biases of productivity growth. Interpreting the share elasticities and biases of productivity growth as fixed parameters of econometric models, we have derived tests for the existence of a value-added aggregate for each sector.

We have presented empirical tests of the existence of a value-added function for forty-five industries. We find that conditions necessary and sufficient for the existence of a sectoral value-added function are rejected for forty of the forty-five industries included in our study. We conclude that intermediate, capital, and labor inputs should be treated symmetrically in modeling production at the sectoral level. This treatment is employed in our analysis of the sources of growth in Chapter 6 and our analysis of the distribution of the value of output in this Chapter.

Finally, we have derived restrictions on the biases of productivity growth corresponding to Hicks neutrality of productivity growth. Interpreting the biases as fixed parameters, these restrictions imply that the biases are equal to zero, so the rate of productivity growth is independent of the quantities of intermediate, capital, and labor inputs, and the value shares are independent of time. We have presented tests of Hicks neutrality. This hypothesis is rejected for thirty-nine of the forty-five industries included in our study.

8 Aggregate Labor and Capital Inputs

We next turn our attention to the aggregate production account. We employ a multisectoral model of production to generate the production account for the economy as a whole. This account includes measures of aggregate value-added, capital input, and labor input. Deliveries to intermediate demand offset intermediate input. In this chapter we present measures of aggregate capital and labor inputs. In the following chapter we develop measures of the aggregate quantity of value-added and aggregate productivity.

Our multisectoral model of production includes production functions for each sector. In addition, it includes market equilibrium conditions. These conditions equate the supply of each type of capital and labor input and the sum of demands for that type of input by all sectors. We assume that aggregate capital and labor inputs can be expressed as translog functions of their individual components, so that measures of these inputs can be constructed as translog index numbers.

Labor input for each sector is cross-classified by sex, age, education, employment class, and occupation. The flow of labor services is proportional to hours worked for each of the components of labor input. Defining aggregate hours worked as an unweighted sum of its components, we can treat the quality of hours worked as an index that transforms hours worked into the translog index of aggregate labor input. This quality index reflects changes in the composition of hours worked by sex, age, education, employment class, and occupation.

Similarly, capital input for each sector is cross-classified by asset class and legal form of organization. The flow of capital services is proportional to capital stock for each of the components of capital input. Defining aggregate capital stock as an unweighted sum of its components, we can treat the quality of capital stock as an index that transforms capital stock into the translog index of capital input. This quality index reflects changes in the composition of aggregate capital stock by asset class and legal form of organization.

Our next objective is to analyze the sources of quality change in aggregate capital and labor inputs. For this purpose we introduce partial indices of labor input, obtained by adding hours worked and the corresponding shares of labor compensation over some characteristics of the labor force, and constructing a translog index over the remaining characteristics. We also introduce partial indices of capital input, obtained by adding capital stocks and the corresponding shares of property compensation over some characteristics of the capital stock, and constructing a translog index over the remaining characteristics.

To analyze the sources of change in the quality of labor input, we introduce the contribution of each characteristic of labor input. This contribution is defined as the difference between the rate of growth of the corresponding partial index of labor input and the rate of growth of hours worked. Similarly, we define the contribution of each characteristic of capital input as the difference between the rate of growth of the corresponding partial index of capital input and the rate of growth of capital stock.

Aggregate Inputs

We have introduced indices of aggregate capital and labor inputs in Chapter 2. In this section we implement these indices empirically. The treatment of capital and labor inputs is symmetrical; we begin with the implementation of labor input. In Chapter 3 we have described data on annual hours worked and labor compensation per hour, cross-classified by sex, age, education, employment class, and occupation of workers. Our multisectoral model of production includes market equilibrium conditions that take the form of equalities between the supply of each type of labor and the sum of demands for that type of labor by all sectors:

$$L_l = \sum L_{li} , \qquad\qquad\qquad (l = 1, 2,..., q),$$

where $\{L_l\}$ is the set of supplies of labor input.

We can define the prices of labor inputs for the economy as a whole $\{p_{Ll}\}$ in terms of prices paid in all sectors $\{p_{Ll}^i\}$:

$$p_{Ll}L_l = p_{Ll}\sum L_{li}$$

$$= \sum p_{Ll}^i L_{li} , \qquad\qquad (l = 1, 2,..., q).$$

The value of each of the labor inputs for the economy as a whole is equal to the sum of the values over all sectors. Labor compensation for the economy as a whole is controlled to labor compensation from the U.S. national income accounts.

We construct an index of aggregate labor input consistent with the methodology presented in Chapter 2. We assume that aggregate labor input, say $L(T)$, can be expressed as a translog function of its individual components, so that the growth rate of the translog quantity index of labor input takes the form

$$\ln L(T) - \ln L(T-1) = \sum \bar{v}_{Ll}[\ln L_l(T) - \ln L_l(T-1)],$$

where weights are given by the average shares of the individual components in the value of labor compensation:

$$\bar{v}_{Ll} = \frac{1}{2} [v_{Ll}(T) + v_{Ll}(T-1)], \qquad\qquad (l = 1, 2,..., q),$$

$$v_{Ll} = \frac{p_{Ll}L_l}{\sum p_{Ll}L_l}, \qquad\qquad (l = 1, 2,..., q).$$

The value shares are computed from data on hours worked $\{L_l\}$ and compensation per hour $\{p_{Ll}\}$ for all components of labor input, cross-classified by sex, age, education, employment class, and occupation of workers.

To quantify the effect of changes in the composition of hours worked we begin by recognizing that the relationship between labor services and hours worked is not the same for all categories of labor input. For each of the components of aggregate labor input $\{L_l(T)\}$ the flow of labor services is proportional to hours worked, say $\{H_l(T)\}$:

$$L_l(T) = Q_{Ll} \cdot H_l(T), \qquad\qquad (l = 1, 2,..., q),$$

where the constants of proportionality $\{Q_{Ll}\}$ transform hours worked into flows of labor services.

Each of the scalars $\{Q_{Ll}\}$ is specific to a given category of labor input but is independent of time. It follows that the translog quantity index of labor input can be expressed either in terms of its components $\{L_l\}$ or in terms of the components of hours worked $\{H_l\}$:

$$\ln L(T) - \ln L(T-1) = \sum \bar{v}_{Ll}[\ln L_l(T) - \ln L_l(T-1)],$$

$$= \sum \bar{v}_{Ll} [\ln H_l(T) - \ln H_l(T-1)].$$

We form the index of labor input from data on hours worked, with workers cross-classified by sex, age, education, employment class, and occupation. Changes in the logarithms of hours worked for each component are weighted by average shares in the value of aggregate labor compensation.

The relation between labor input and hours worked is a function of the changing composition of hours worked. More precisely, it depends on the factor of proportionality that transforms hours worked into labor input. We can define *aggregate hours worked,* say $H(T)$, as the unweighted sum of its components,

$$H(T) = \sum H_l(T).$$

We can then define the aggregate index of the *quality of hours worked,* say $Q_L(T)$, as an index that transforms hours worked into the translog index of labor input:

$$L(T) = Q_L(T) \cdot H(T).$$

It follows that the growth rate of the index of the quality of hours worked can be expressed in the form

$$\ln Q_L(T) - \ln Q_L(T-1) = \sum \bar{v}_{Ll}[\ln H_l(T) - \ln H_l(T-1)]$$

$$- [\ln H(T) - \ln H(T-1)] .$$

The quality index reflects changes in the composition of hours worked, classified by sex, age, education, employment class, and occupation, but not by industry.

The aggregate index of labor input, the corresponding price index, and the index of the quality of hours worked are presented for the period 1948–1979 in Table 8.1. Annual data for employment, weekly hours per person, hourly compensation, and total labor compensation and hours worked are also reported. Thirty-five percent of the average annual rate of growth of labor input can be attributed to a shift in the composition of hours worked. The

Table 8.1. Aggregate labor input

Year	Labor input			Quality	Employment	Weekly hours per person	Hourly compensation	Hours worked
	Price	Quantity	Outlay					
1948	0.337	506.116	170.641	0.837	61622	39.4	1.35	126155
1949	0.329	489.268	160.956	0.838	60131	38.9	1.32	121779
1950	0.351	508.512	178.391	0.849	61669	39.0	1.43	125006
1951	0.385	535.993	206.562	0.859	64258	39.0	1.59	130168
1952	0.389	549.172	213.647	0.875	64963	38.8	1.63	130908
1953	0.402	559.805	225.151	0.884	65962	38.5	1.70	132188
1954	0.415	543.107	225.184	0.887	64426	38.1	1.76	127732
1955	0.434	560.179	242.838	0.889	66144	38.2	1.85	131407
1956	0.456	572.535	261.031	0.894	67737	37.9	1.95	133564
1957	0.484	573.358	277.527	0.905	67917	37.4	2.10	132188
1958	0.497	558.083	277.344	0.909	66331	37.1	2.17	128031
1959	0.516	578.450	298.767	0.917	67959	37.3	2.27	131679
1960	0.532	597.919	318.345	0.943	68715	37.0	2.41	132350
1961	0.548	590.057	323.231	0.935	68796	36.8	2.45	131682
1962	0.567	612.296	347.125	0.952	70102	36.8	2.59	134198
1963	0.591	619.709	366.351	0.955	70786	36.8	2.71	135408
1964	0.622	636.632	396.042	0.965	72269	36.6	2.88	137661
1965	0.638	658.722	419.982	0.968	74557	36.6	2.96	141995
1966	0.678	687.626	466.157	0.981	77494	36.3	3.19	146297
1967	0.698	697.959	487.110	0.989	78978	35.9	3.31	147304
1968	0.769	714.658	549.685	0.995	81012	35.6	3.67	149894
1969	0.825	734.201	605.735	0.995	83381	35.5	3.94	153884
1970	0.875	730.832	639.146	1.005	83476	35.0	4.21	151760
1971	0.938	731.880	686.211	1.006	83678	34.9	4.52	151846
1972	1.000	748.803	748.803	1.000	86103	34.9	4.79	156231
1973	1.092	780.627	852.644	1.004	89587	34.8	5.25	162258
1974	1.183	785.569	929.372	1.009	91138	34.3	5.72	162398
1975	1.258	770.668	969.664	1.019	89582	33.9	6.15	157797
1976	1.369	792.608	1085.264	1.022	91855	33.9	6.71	161779
1977	1.473	817.768	1204.910	1.019	95236	33.8	7.19	167479
1978	1.601	858.203	1374.150	1.025	99557	33.7	7.87	174713
1979	1.787	865.392	1546.140	1.009	102540	33.5	8.64	178861

remaining growth in labor input is due to growth in unweighted annual hours, reported in the last column of Table 8.1. Labor input increases at an average rate of 1.73 percent per year. The aggregate quality and unweighted hours indices increase at average annual rates of 0.60 and 1.13 percent, respectively. Sources of the changing quality of labor input will be identified later in this chapter.

In Chapter 4 we have described the development of sectoral data on capital stocks and rental prices, cross-classified by asset class and legal form of organization. Our multisectoral model of production includes market equilibrium conditions that take the form of equalities between the supply of each type of capital and the sum of demands for that type of capital by all sectors:

$$K_k = \sum K_{ki} , \qquad\qquad (k = 1, 2,..., p),$$

where $\{K_k\}$ is the set of supplies of capital input.

We can define the prices of capital inputs for the economy as a whole $\{p_{Kk}\}$ in terms of prices paid in all sectors $\{p_{Kk}^i\}$:

$$p_{Kk}K_k = p_{Kk}\sum K_{ki} ,$$

$$= \sum p_{Kk}^i K_{ki} , \qquad\qquad (k = 1, 2,..., p).$$

The value of each of the capital inputs for the economy as a whole is equal to the sum of the values over all sectors. Consistent with our treatment of labor compensation, property compensation for the economy as a whole is controlled to property compensation from the U.S. national income accounts.

To construct an index of aggregate capital input, we assume that capital input, say $K(T)$, can be expressed as a translog function of its individual components, so that the translog quantity index of capital input takes the form

$$\ln K(T) - \ln K(T-1) = \sum \bar{v}_{Kk} [\ln K_k(T) - \ln K_k(T-1)] ,$$

where weights are given by the average shares of individual components in the value of property compensation:

$$\bar{v}_{Kk} = \frac{1}{2} [v_{Kk}(T) + v_{Kk}(T-1)] , \qquad\qquad (k = 1, 2,..., p),$$

$$v_{Kk} = \frac{p_{Kk}K_k}{\sum p_{Kk}K_k}, \qquad\qquad (k = 1, 2,..., p).$$

The value shares are computed from data on capital stocks $\{K_k\}$ and rental prices $\{p_{Kk}\}$ for all components of capital input, cross-classified by asset class and legal form of organization.

For each of the components of aggregate capital input $\{K_k(T)\}$, the flow of capital services is proportional to capital stock, say $\{A_k(T-1)\}$:

$$K_k(T) = Q_{Kk} \cdot A_k(T-1), \qquad\qquad (k = 1, 2, ..., p),$$

where the constants of proportionality $\{Q_{Kk}\}$ transform capital stock into a flow of capital services. The translog quantity index of capital input can be expressed either in terms of its components $\{K_k\}$ or in terms of the components of capital stock $\{A_k\}$:

$$\ln K(T) - \ln K(T-1) = \sum \bar{v}_{Kk} \, [\ln K_k(T) - \ln K_k(T-1)] \, ,$$

$$= \sum \bar{v}_{Kk} \, [\ln A_k(T-1) - \ln A_k(T-2)] \, .$$

We form the aggregate index of capital input from data on capital stocks, cross-classified by asset class and legal form of organization. Changes in the logarithms of capital stock for each component are weighted by average shares in the value of aggregate property compensation.

We can define *aggregate capital stock,* say $A(T-1)$, as the unweighted sum of its components:

$$A(T-1) = \sum A_k(T-1) \, .$$

Similarly, we can define the aggregate index of the *quality of capital stock,* say $Q_K(T)$, as an index that transforms capital stock into the translog index of capital input:

$$K(T) = Q_K(T) \cdot A(T-1).$$

The growth rate of the index of the quality of capital stock can be expressed in the form

$$\ln Q_K(T) - \ln Q_K(T-1) = \sum \bar{v}_{Kk} \, [\ln A_k(T-1) - \ln A_k(T-2)]$$

$$- [\ln A(T-1) - \ln A(T-2)],$$

so that this index reflects changes in the composition of capital stock by asset class and legal form of organization, but not by industry.

The aggregate index of capital input, the corresponding price index, and the index of the quality of capital stock are presented for the period 1948–1979 in Table 8.2. Annual data for property compensation and the

Table 8.2.   Aggregate capital input

	Capital input				Capital stock		
Year	Price	Quantity	Outlay	Quality	Price	Quantity	Value
1948	0.070	1305.551	91.625	0.769	0.430	1698.266	730.750
1949	0.071	1389.125	98.227	0.788	0.438	1762.570	771.632
1950	0.077	1443.025	110.573	0.799	0.459	1806.634	829.066
1951	0.080	1544.629	122.956	0.821	0.505	1880.726	949.464
1952	0.083	1634.266	136.226	0.840	0.521	1946.081	1013.656
1953	0.083	1690.210	139.928	0.847	0.529	1995.356	1054.830
1954	0.085	1752.328	149.685	0.856	0.536	2047.939	1097.737
1955	0.091	1801.970	163.539	0.860	0.556	2095.348	1164.328
1956	0.090	1895.862	170.298	0.874	0.594	2169.209	1289.248
1957	0.086	1974.786	169.519	0.884	0.621	2233.899	1386.912
1958	0.090	2036.169	183.363	0.890	0.635	2289.113	1452.728
1959	0.094	2071.313	195.611	0.890	0.653	2327.963	1519.012
1960	0.094	2140.852	201.263	0.895	0.661	2391.676	1581.384
1961	0.097	2203.394	212.871	0.899	0.671	2449.706	1643.235
1962	0.100	2255.367	224.655	0.902	0.684	2501.459	1711.579
1963	0.100	2332.820	233.712	0.908	0.693	2570.222	1781.738
1964	0.103	2424.248	250.277	0.916	0.708	2647.478	1874.087
1965	0.114	2530.103	288.338	0.926	0.727	2732.704	1987.393
1966	0.116	2666.613	308.036	0.939	0.752	2839.391	2136.139
1967	0.116	2821.108	327.189	0.955	0.778	2954.582	2300.065
1968	0.115	2947.736	339.728	0.965	0.815	3053.858	2488.332
1969	0.117	3085.869	360.530	0.976	0.857	3161.693	2708.225
1970	0.116	3231.705	373.537	0.987	0.899	3273.677	2943.877
1971	0.122	3338.149	405.943	0.993	0.942	3360.610	3164.523
1972	0.136	3466.490	472.587	1.000	1.000	3466.489	3466.490
1973	0.143	3641.102	521.235	1.012	1.092	3598.504	3930.665
1974	0.139	3847.979	534.779	1.026	1.232	3751.569	4622.961
1975	0.149	3989.837	595.192	1.034	1.355	3860.294	5229.177
1976	0.163	4066.135	663.890	1.036	1.450	3923.164	5687.090
1977	0.190	4195.751	798.570	1.043	1.575	4022.948	6334.997
1978	0.199	4374.290	871.078	1.053	1.749	4154.980	7265.061
1979	0.207	4568.473	947.793	1.063	1.940	4296.380	8334.971

price, quantity, and value of capital stock are also presented. The shifting composition of capital stock has been a significant source of growth in capital input. Capital stock has increased at an average annual rate of 2.99 percent. This accounts for more than seventy-four percent of the average annual growth of capital input, at 4.04 percent per year. Changes in the composition of capital stock are responsible for the remaining twenty-six percent of capital input growth. Later in this chapter we will decompose the contribution of capital input to economic growth into its sources.

Partial Indices of Labor Input

The principal objective of this and the following section is to analyze the effects of changes in the composition of total hours worked.[1] For this purpose we consider the components of hours worked, say $\{H_{saecoi}(T)\}$, cross-classified by sex, age, education, employment class, occupation, and industry. Previously, we have used a single subscript l to represent categories of labor input cross-classified by all characteristics except for industry. The subscript has represented 1600 categories of labor input.

In our new notation labor input is cross-classified by two sexes, represented by the subscript s; eight age groups, represented by a, five education classes, represented by e; two employment classes, represented by c; ten occupational groups, represented by o; and fifty-one industry groups, represented by i. Similarly, we consider the shares of the components of labor input in the value of labor compensation for the economy as a whole, say $\{v_{saecoi}(T)\}$ cross-classified by sex, age, education, employment class, occupation, and industry.

Our analysis begins with the construction of "partial" indices of labor input. We define a partial index of labor input by adding hours worked and the corresponding value shares over some characteristics of the labor force, and constructing a translog index over the remaining characteristics. More specifically, we define a first-order index of labor input, corresponding to each characteristic of labor input, by adding hours worked and the corresponding value shares over all other characteristics of labor input and constructing a translog index on the single characteristic of interest. Since there are six characteristics of labor input—sex, age, education, employment class, occupation, and industry—there are six first-order indices of labor input.

As an illustration, the first-order index of labor input corresponding to sex, say L_s, can have its growth rate expressed in the form

$$\Delta \ln L_s = \sum_s \bar{v}_s \, \Delta \ln H_s \, ,$$

$$= \sum_s \bar{v}_s \, \Delta \ln \sum_a \sum_e \sum_c \sum_o \sum_i H_{saecoi} \, ,$$

where

$$\bar{v}_s = \frac{1}{2} [v_s(T) + v_s(T-1)],$$

$$v_s = \sum_a \sum_e \sum_c \sum_o \sum_i v_{saecoi},$$

and the Δ notation signifies first differences in the associated variable, for example:

$$\Delta \ln L_s = \ln L_s(T) - \ln L_s(T-1) .$$

The resulting first-order index corresponds to sex, but not to age, education, employment class, occupation, or industry. There are six first-order indices.

We can define a second-order index of labor input, corresponding to any two characteristics of labor input, by adding hours worked and the corresponding value shares over other characteristics and constructing a translog index. The second-order index corresponding to sex and age, for example, reflects changes in the composition of aggregate hours worked by sex and age, but not by education, employment class, occupation, or industry. There are fifteen second-order indices of labor input generated by combinations of two of the six characteristics of labor input. An example second-order index is defined in Table 8.3, together with the first-order index.

Similarly, we can define twenty third-order, fifteen fourth-order, six fifth-order indices, and one sixth-order index of labor input to correspond to three, four, five, or all six characteristics of labor input. Continuing our example, the third-order index corresponding to sex, age, and education reflects changes in the composition of aggregate hours worked by these characteristics, but not by employment class, occupation, and industry. The fourth-order index corresponding to sex, age, education, and class of employment, reflects changes in the composition of aggregate hours worked by these four characteristics. Each fifth-order index captures compositional changes among all but the excluded characteristic. Third-, fourth-, fifth- and sixth-order indices are defined in Table 8.3. The sixth-order index reflects compositional shifts among all characteristics of labor input.

Special attention must be focused on the fifth-order index of labor input that corresponds to all characteristics of labor input except industry. This index corresponds to the index of aggregate labor input $L(T)$ defined earlier in this chapter. Recall that the growth rate of the index can be expressed in terms of the components of hours worked $\{H_l\}$:

$$\ln L(T) - \ln L(T-1) = \sum \bar{v}_{Ll} [\ln H_l(T) - \ln H_l(T-1)].$$

Table 8.3. Partial indices of labor input

Hours worked (one index):

$$\Delta\ln H = \Delta\ln \sum_{s}\sum_{a}\sum_{e}\sum_{c}\sum_{o}\sum_{i} H_{saecoi}$$

First-order (six indices):

$$\Delta\ln L_{s} = \sum_{s} \bar{v}_{s} \ln H_{s}$$
$$= \sum_{s} \bar{v}_{s} \Delta\ln \sum_{a}\sum_{e}\sum_{c}\sum_{o}\sum_{i} H_{saecoi}$$

Second-order (fifteen indices):

$$\Delta\ln L_{sa} = \sum_{s}\sum_{a} \bar{v}_{sa} \Delta\ln H_{sa}$$
$$= \sum_{s}\sum_{a} \bar{v}_{sa} \Delta\ln \sum_{e}\sum_{c}\sum_{o}\sum_{i} H_{saecoi}$$

Third-order (twenty indices):

$$\Delta\ln L_{sae} = \sum_{s}\sum_{a}\sum_{e} \bar{v}_{sae} \Delta\ln H_{sae}$$
$$= \sum_{s}\sum_{a}\sum_{e} \bar{v}_{sae} \Delta\ln \sum_{c}\sum_{o}\sum_{i} H_{saecoi}$$

Fourth-order (fifteen indices):

$$\Delta\ln L_{saec} = \sum_{s}\sum_{a}\sum_{e}\sum_{c} \bar{v}_{saec} \Delta\ln H_{saec}$$
$$= \sum_{s}\sum_{a}\sum_{e}\sum_{c} \bar{v}_{saec} \Delta\ln \sum_{o}\sum_{i} H_{saecoi}$$

Fifth-order (six indices):

$$\Delta\ln L_{saeco} = \sum_{s}\sum_{a}\sum_{e}\sum_{c}\sum_{o} \bar{v}_{saeco} \Delta\ln H_{saeco}$$
$$= \sum_{s}\sum_{a}\sum_{e}\sum_{c}\sum_{o} \bar{v}_{saeco} \Delta\ln \sum_{i} H_{saecoi}$$

Sixth-order (one index):

$$\Delta\ln L_{saecoi} = \sum_{s}\sum_{a}\sum_{e}\sum_{c}\sum_{o}\sum_{i} \bar{v}_{saecoi} \Delta\ln H_{saecoi}$$

In our new notation, this expression has the equivalent form

$$\Delta\ln L = \sum_{s}\sum_{a}\sum_{e}\sum_{c}\sum_{o} \bar{v}_{saeco} \Delta\ln H_{saeco} ,$$

$$= \sum_{s}\sum_{a}\sum_{e}\sum_{c}\sum_{o} \bar{v}_{saeco} \Delta\ln \sum_{i} H_{saecoi} .$$

To construct the index of aggregate labor input, add hours worked over industries, to obtain hours worked, cross-classified by all characteristics except industry. Similarly, add value shares over industries, obtaining

$$v_{saeco} = \sum_i v_{saecoi} \cdot$$

This index must be contrasted with the sixth-order index of labor input, which reflects changes in the composition of labor input by industry as well as the five remaining characteristics.

To complete the set of partial indices of labor input, add hours worked over all characteristics of the labor force, to obtain an index of aggregate hours worked. This index does not reflect any change in the composition of labor input. The single index of aggregate hours worked is defined in Table 8.3.

There are sixty-four partial indices of labor input, corresponding to the six characteristics of the labor force. We have calculated these sixty-four partial indices of labor input annually for the period 1948–1979; and the results are presented in Table 8.4. These indices form the basis for our analysis of the effects of changes in the postwar composition of aggregate hours worked, in the following section.

The Quality of Labor Input

Our next objective is to identify the contributions to economic growth of the changing composition of total hours worked by sex, age, education, employment class, occupation, and industry. For this purpose, we first construct an index of labor quality that captures the effect of all changes in the composition of hours worked. This index is defined in terms of the aggregate hours worked and sixth-order partial indices described in the preceding section.

The rate of growth of the index of labor quality is defined as the difference between the rate of growth of the sixth-order partial index of labor input and the rate of growth of aggregate hours worked. To analyze the effects of changes in the quality of hours worked, we can decompose the index of labor quality into specific components. Each component corresponds to the contribution of changes in the composition of labor input by one or more characteristics of the labor force.

The index of labor quality must not be confused with the aggregate index of labor quality introduced earlier in this chapter. The latter incorporates the effects of changes in the composition of labor input among all characteristics except industry. This is consistent with the requirements of our aggregate model of production. As indicated in Chapter 2, our analysis of sources of economic growth accounts separately for the contribution to economic growth of reallocations of labor input among sectors.

The index of labor quality incorporates the effects of changes in the distribution of hours worked across all labor characteristics, including industry.

Table 8.4.   Translog indices of labor input

Year	Hours worked	s	a	e	c	o	i	sa
1948	0.808	0.847	0.817	0.691	0.775	0.738	0.759	0.853
1949	0.780	0.815	0.792	0.669	0.747	0.712	0.729	0.823
1950	0.800	0.837	0.821	0.691	0.772	0.739	0.753	0.853
1951	0.833	0.868	0.851	0.719	0.807	0.775	0.795	0.882
1952	0.838	0.872	0.862	0.728	0.812	0.787	0.805	0.892
1953	0.846	0.881	0.871	0.739	0.821	0.795	0.818	0.902
1954	0.818	0.849	0.845	0.719	0.792	0.768	0.785	0.872
1955	0.841	0.871	0.869	0.741	0.818	0.792	0.812	0.893
1956	0.855	0.882	0.881	0.757	0.834	0.810	0.831	0.903
1957	0.846	0.871	0.873	0.756	0.828	0.808	0.826	0.893
1958	0.820	0.841	0.847	0.739	0.802	0.785	0.792	0.863
1959	0.843	0.864	0.870	0.763	0.827	0.811	0.819	0.885
1960	0.847	0.878	0.884	0.774	0.834	0.823	0.826	0.907
1961	0.843	0.859	0.865	0.777	0.828	0.813	0.821	0.879
1962	0.859	0.875	0.882	0.803	0.846	0.834	0.841	0.895
1963	0.867	0.882	0.889	0.809	0.856	0.842	0.852	0.901
1964	0.881	0.895	0.901	0.830	0.872	0.862	0.869	0.912
1965	0.909	0.922	0.926	0.861	0.901	0.889	0.900	0.936
1966	0.936	0.948	0.952	0.894	0.932	0.929	0.936	0.962
1967	0.943	0.952	0.958	0.906	0.939	0.937	0.945	0.967
1968	0.959	0.966	0.973	0.929	0.957	0.958	0.963	0.980
1969	0.985	0.989	0.994	0.959	0.983	0.986	0.990	0.999
1970	0.971	0.980	0.995	0.948	0.969	0.969	0.974	1.004
1971	0.972	0.974	0.977	0.965	0.970	0.978	0.971	0.980
1972	1.000	1.000	1.000	1.000	1.000	1.000	1.000	1.000
1973	1.039	1.038	1.034	1.048	1.040	1.042	1.041	1.033
1974	1.040	1.037	1.034	1.059	1.041	1.046	1.045	1.032
1975	1.010	1.003	1.007	1.046	1.011	1.019	1.011	1.001
1976	1.036	1.027	1.031	1.078	1.039	1.046	1.037	1.022
1977	1.072	1.060	1.064	1.119	1.075	1.083	1.075	1.053
1978	1.118	1.105	1.109	1.173	1.123	1.134	1.124	1.096
1979	1.145	1.107	1.117	1.181	1.131	1.148	1.154	1.097
Average annual rate of growth	0.0113	0.0086	0.0101	0.0173	0.0122	0.0143	0.0135	0.0081

	se	sc	so	si	ae	ac	ao	ai
1948	0.712	0.806	0.752	0.778	0.696	0.777	0.747	0.765

Table 8.4 continued

	se	sc	so	si	ae	ac	ao	ai
1949	0.689	0.775	0.726	0.746	0.677	0.752	0.723	0.737
1950	0.710	0.799	0.751	0.770	0.705	0.785	0.756	0.767
1951	0.737	0.834	0.785	0.811	0.732	0.818	0.790	0.807
1952	0.747	0.839	0.797	0.820	0.747	0.830	0.807	0.822
1953	0.758	0.848	0.808	0.833	0.759	0.841	0.817	0.836
1954	0.736	0.816	0.780	0.799	0.742	0.814	0.791	0.805
1955	0.757	0.840	0.802	0.825	0.765	0.840	0.815	0.832
1956	0.772	0.854	0.820	0.843	0.780	0.855	0.831	0.850
1957	0.770	0.846	0.818	0.837	0.000	0.850	0.830	0.845
1958	0.750	0.816	0.794	0.802	0.763	0.824	0.807	0.813
1959	0.775	0.842	0.818	0.830	0.787	0.850	0.832	0.840
1960	0.794	0.859	0.840	0.846	0.805	0.866	0.849	0.853
1961	0.787	0.841	0.822	0.829	0.801	0.849	0.835	0.840
1962	0.814	0.859	0.843	0.850	0.827	0.868	0.854	0.860
1963	0.819	0.869	0.851	0.860	0.834	0.878	0.863	0.871
1964	0.841	0.884	0.869	0.876	0.854	0.892	0.880	0.886
1965	0.870	0.913	0.897	0.907	0.881	0.918	0.905	0.915
1966	0.903	0.942	0.935	0.941	0.913	0.947	0.941	0.948
1967	0.914	0.948	0.944	0.950	0.924	0.955	0.950	0.957
1968	0.935	0.963	0.963	0.966	0.946	0.971	0.969	0.974
1969	0.963	0.986	0.988	0.990	0.973	0.993	0.994	0.998
1970	0.955	0.977	0.977	0.978	0.970	0.993	0.987	0.992
1971	0.967	0.972	0.980	0.973	0.972	0.976	0.982	0.976
1972	1.000	1.000	1.000	1.000	1.000	1.000	1.000	1.000
1973	1.047	1.039	1.039	1.040	1.043	1.034	1.037	1.037
1974	1.056	1.038	1.043	1.041	1.052	1.035	1.040	1.039
1975	1.039	1.005	1.014	1.006	1.037	1.008	1.014	1.007
1976	1.069	1.030	1.039	1.030	1.069	1.033	1.040	1.031
1977	1.107	1.064	1.071	1.065	1.107	1.067	1.075	1.067
1978	1.159	1.109	1.121	1.112	1.160	1.112	1.124	1.114
1979	1.161	1.111	1.133	1.113	1.168	1.121	1.138	1.127
Average annual rate of growth	0.0158	0.0104	0.0132	0.0116	0.0167	0.0118	0.0136	0.0125

	ec	eo	ei	co	ci	oi	sae	sac
1948	0.667	0.677	0.697	0.714	0.756	0.749	0.718	0.808
1949	0.646	0.654	0.670	0.689	0.726	0.720	0.696	0.779
1950	0.670	0.679	0.695	0.714	0.750	0.746	0.724	0.812
1951	0.700	0.712	0.732	0.752	0.793	0.786	0.751	0.845
1952	0.709	0.725	0.744	0.764	0.803	0.799	0.765	0.856
1953	0.720	0.735	0.758	0.773	0.815	0.811	0.778	0.867
1954	0.700	0.711	0.729	0.746	0.783	0.777	0.759	0.837
1955	0.724	0.735	0.755	0.771	0.810	0.803	0.780	0.861

Table 8.4 continued

	ec	eo	ei	co	ci	oi	sae	sac
1956	0.741	0.753	0.774	0.789	0.829	0.820	0.793	0.874
1957	0.741	0.752	0.772	0.787	0.824	0.815	0.792	0.867
1958	0.724	0.733	0.745	0.765	0.790	0.785	0.772	0.837
1959	0.750	0.758	0.772	0.794	0.818	0.815	0.796	0.862
1960	0.763	0.772	0.783	0.808	0.825	0.827	0.821	0.887
1961	0.766	0.771	0.782	0.798	0.818	0.815	0.808	0.860
1962	0.793	0.798	0.810	0.822	0.839	0.837	0.835	0.879
1963	0.801	0.806	0.816	0.831	0.850	0.845	0.841	0.889
1964	0.824	0.830	0.837	0.853	0.868	0.864	0.861	0.901
1965	0.856	0.860	0.870	0.881	0.900	0.893	0.888	0.927
1966	0.892	0.901	0.908	0.924	0.936	0.936	0.920	0.957
1967	0.904	0.911	0.920	0.934	0.945	0.945	0.931	0.964
1968	0.928	0.935	0.942	0.956	0.964	0.966	0.951	0.978
1969	0.959	0.966	0.971	0.984	0.990	0.992	0.977	0.998
1970	0.947	0.950	0.957	0.967	0.974	0.974	0.977	1.000
1971	0.964	0.970	0.966	0.978	0.971	0.979	0.974	0.978
1972	1.000	1.000	1.000	1.000	1.000	1.000	1.000	1.000
1973	1.049	1.049	1.049	1.043	1.042	1.043	1.043	1.033
1974	1.061	1.060	1.060	1.048	1.044	1.048	1.049	1.033
1975	1.046	1.042	1.038	1.020	1.010	1.016	1.032	1.002
1976	1.080	1.075	1.071	1.049	1.036	1.043	1.060	1.025
1977	1.121	1.117	1.113	1.085	1.073	1.078	1.095	1.055
1978	1.175	1.171	1.168	1.137	1.123	1.131	1.148	1.099
1979	1.184	1.192	1.176	1.143	1.129	1.137	1.149	1.101
Average annual rate of growth	0.0185	0.0182	0.0169	0.0152	0.0129	0.0135	0.0152	0.0100

	sao	sai	sec	seo	sei	sco	sci	soi
1948	0.763	0.785	0.685	0.691	0.705	0.728	0.770	0.761
1949	0.737	0.755	0.661	0.667	0.677	0.703	0.739	0.732
1950	0.769	0.785	0.685	0.690	0.701	0.724	0.763	0.756
1951	0.802	0.824	0.715	0.723	0.737	0.763	0.804	0.795
1952	0.818	0.838	0.724	0.736	0.749	0.775	0.813	0.807
1953	0.830	0.853	0.736	0.747	0.764	0.785	0.826	0.820
1954	0.804	0.820	0.714	0.723	0.735	0.757	0.793	0.786
1955	0.825	0.845	0.737	0.746	0.761	0.781	0.819	0.811
1956	0.841	0.861	0.753	0.763	0.779	0.798	0.837	0.828
1957	0.839	0.856	0.752	0.763	0.777	0.797	0.831	0.823
1958	0.815	0.821	0.733	0.742	0.749	0.773	0.797	0.792
1959	0.838	0.848	0.760	0.767	0.777	0.801	0.825	0.821
1960	0.865	0.870	0.781	0.789	0.796	0.823	0.842	0.839
1961	0.843	0.848	0.774	0.780	0.787	0.807	0.825	0.822
1962	0.863	0.868	0.803	0.808	0.815	0.831	0.846	0.845

Table 8.4 continued

	sao	sai	sec	seo	sei	sco	sci	soi
1963	0.871	0.878	0.811	0.815	0.822	0.839	0.857	0.852
1964	0.887	0.893	0.833	0.838	0.843	0.860	0.874	0.870
1965	0.912	0.921	0.865	0.869	0.875	0.888	0.905	0.899
1966	0.946	0.953	0.900	0.908	0.913	0.929	0.940	0.940
1967	0.957	0.963	0.912	0.919	0.924	0.941	0.949	0.950
1968	0.975	0.978	0.933	0.941	0.944	0.961	0.966	0.970
1969	0.997	0.999	0.962	0.970	0.972	0.986	0.990	0.994
1970	0.996	0.997	0.953	0.958	0.960	0.974	0.978	0.978
1971	0.984	0.978	0.965	0.972	0.967	0.979	0.972	0.980
1972	1.000	1.000	1.000	1.000	1.000	1.000	1.000	1.000
1973	1.034	1.036	1.048	1.046	1.048	1.041	1.040	1.041
1974	1.037	1.036	1.058	1.056	1.056	1.044	1.041	1.045
1975	1.010	1.003	1.039	1.036	1.033	1.016	1.005	1.012
1976	1.033	1.025	1.071	1.066	1.063	1.041	1.029	1.037
1977	1.063	1.057	1.109	1.103	1.102	1.073	1.063	1.069
1978	1.111	1.103	1.162	1.156	1.155	1.124	1.112	1.120
1979	1.123	1.109	1.164	1.173	1.156	1.127	1.110	1.124
Average annual rate of growth	0.0125	0.0112	0.0171	0.0171	0.0160	0.0141	0.0118	0.0126

	aec	aeo	aei	aco	aci	aoi	eco	eci
1948	0.664	0.682	0.694	0.722	0.757	0.752	0.659	0.691
1949	0.646	0.660	0.669	0.699	0.729	0.724	0.636	0.664
1950	0.676	0.690	0.699	0.729	0.760	0.755	0.659	0.689
1951	0.706	0.724	0.735	0.766	0.801	0.794	0.695	0.726
1952	0.722	0.741	0.752	0.784	0.816	0.811	0.708	0.738
1953	0.735	0.753	0.768	0.795	0.831	0.825	0.718	0.752
1954	0.717	0.732	0.743	0.769	0.800	0.793	0.694	0.725
1955	0.742	0.756	0.769	0.793	0.828	0.818	0.719	0.751
1956	0.759	0.773	0.787	0.810	0.845	0.834	0.736	0.769
1957	0.760	0.773	0.786	0.809	0.840	0.830	0.737	0.767
1958	0.744	0.754	0.759	0.786	0.807	0.800	0.718	0.739
1959	0.770	0.780	0.787	0.815	0.836	0.829	0.746	0.767
1960	0.790	0.797	0.802	0.834	0.849	0.845	0.761	0.778
1961	0.786	0.792	0.798	0.820	0.836	0.830	0.760	0.778
1962	0.815	0.819	0.826	0.842	0.857	0.852	0.790	0.806
1963	0.824	0.828	0.834	0.853	0.869	0.861	0.799	0.813
1964	0.845	0.850	0.854	0.872	0.884	0.878	0.824	0.835
1965	0.875	0.878	0.885	0.898	0.913	0.905	0.855	0.868
1966	0.909	0.915	0.921	0.937	0.947	0.945	0.898	0.907
1967	0.922	0.926	0.933	0.947	0.957	0.955	0.910	0.919
1968	0.944	0.949	0.955	0.968	0.975	0.975	0.935	0.942
1969	0.972	0.977	0.981	0.993	0.998	0.999	0.965	0.971

Table 8.4 continued

	aec	aeo	aei	aco	aci	aoi	eco	eci
1970	0.969	0.968	0.973	0.986	0.993	0.988	0.950	0.957
1971	0.971	0.975	0.972	0.982	0.976	0.983	0.970	0.965
1972	1.000	1.000	1.000	1.000	1.000	1.000	1.000	1.000
1973	1.044	1.045	1.045	1.038	1.037	1.039	1.050	1.049
1974	1.053	1.053	1.053	1.042	1.038	1.042	1.061	1.060
1975	1.038	1.035	1.031	1.015	1.006	1.012	1.042	1.037
1976	1.071	1.067	1.063	1.042	1.030	1.037	1.076	1.070
1977	1.109	1.106	1.102	1.075	1.065	1.070	1.117	1.111
1978	1.163	1.160	1.157	1.126	1.113	1.122	1.172	1.167
1979	1.172	1.181	1.171	1.133	1.123	1.133	1.184	1.172
Average annual rate of growth	0.0183	0.0177	0.0169	0.0145	0.0127	0.0132	0.0189	0.0171

	eoi	coi	saec	saeo	saei	saco	saci	saoi
1948	0.701	0.735	0.683	0.697	0.706	0.737	0.775	0.766
1949	0.674	0.707	0.661	0.673	0.680	0.713	0.745	0.738
1950	0.698	0.731	0.690	0.702	0.708	0.741	0.775	0.767
1951	0.736	0.773	0.720	0.735	0.744	0.778	0.815	0.805
1952	0.750	0.786	0.736	0.752	0.761	0.795	0.830	0.821
1953	0.763	0.798	0.750	0.766	0.777	0.807	0.845	0.836
1954	0.733	0.765	0.730	0.744	0.751	0.781	0.813	0.804
1955	0.758	0.791	0.753	0.766	0.776	0.803	0.838	0.827
1956	0.775	0.808	0.768	0.783	0.793	0.819	0.855	0.843
1957	0.773	0.804	0.769	0.783	0.792	0.817	0.849	0.839
1958	0.745	0.774	0.749	0.762	0.764	0.793	0.815	0.808
1959	0.774	0.805	0.775	0.787	0.791	0.820	0.842	0.835
1960	0.788	0.818	0.803	0.812	0.814	0.847	0.865	0.858
1961	0.783	0.807	0.791	0.800	0.802	0.827	0.842	0.838
1962	0.812	0.831	0.821	0.828	0.831	0.850	0.864	0.860
1963	0.818	0.839	0.830	0.836	0.839	0.860	0.875	0.868
1964	0.840	0.860	0.851	0.857	0.859	0.878	0.890	0.884
1965	0.871	0.889	0.881	0.886	0.889	0.904	0.919	0.911
1966	0.914	0.934	0.916	0.921	0.925	0.942	0.952	0.949
1967	0.925	0.944	0.929	0.934	0.938	0.954	0.962	0.960
1968	0.948	0.965	0.950	0.955	0.958	0.974	0.978	0.979
1969	0.976	0.991	0.976	0.981	0.983	0.996	0.999	1.001
1970	0.960	0.974	0.974	0.977	0.977	0.994	0.998	0.994
1971	0.972	0.980	0.973	0.977	0.974	0.984	0.978	0.984
1972	1.000	1.000	1.000	1.000	1.000	1.000	1.000	1.000
1973	1.049	1.044	1.043	1.042	1.044	1.036	1.036	1.037
1974	1.059	1.048	1.050	1.048	1.050	1.038	1.035	1.039
1975	1.035	1.016	1.032	1.029	1.026	1.011	1.001	1.008
1976	1.067	1.043	1.062	1.058	1.055	1.035	1.023	1.031

Table 8.4 continued

	eoi	coi	saec	saeo	saei	saco	saci	saoi
1977	1.106	1.078	1.097	1.09	1.091	1.064	1.055	1.061
1978	1.162	1.132	1.151	1.145	1.146	1.113	1.102	1.111
1979	1.171	1.132	1.152	1.163	1.153	1.117	1.105	1.120
Average annual rate of growth	0.0166	0.0139	0.0169	0.0165	0.0159	0.0134	0.0115	0.0122

	seco	seci	seoi	scoi	aeco	aeci	aeoi	acoi
1948	0.673	0.697	0.711	0.747	0.661	0.683	0.699	0.737
1949	0.649	0.669	0.683	0.718	0.640	0.659	0.674	0.711
1950	0.669	0.693	0.706	0.740	0.668	0.689	0.703	0.740
1951	0.706	0.730	0.744	0.782	0.704	0.726	0.741	0.781
1952	0.719	0.742	0.757	0.794	0.723	0.744	0.759	0.798
1953	0.730	0.756	0.771	0.807	0.735	0.759	0.774	0.812
1954	0.706	0.729	0.741	0.773	0.714	0.735	0.746	0.780
1955	0.729	0.755	0.766	0.798	0.738	0.761	0.771	0.806
1956	0.747	0.773	0.783	0.815	0.755	0.779	0.788	0.822
1957	0.747	0.771	0.780	0.811	0.756	0.778	0.786	0.818
1958	0.727	0.743	0.752	0.781	0.737	0.751	0.760	0.789
1959	0.755	0.771	0.781	0.810	0.766	0.780	0.789	0.819
1960	0.777	0.790	0.800	0.830	0.785	0.795	0.805	0.837
1961	0.770	0.781	0.790	0.813	0.781	0.791	0.798	0.822
1962	0.800	0.811	0.819	0.838	0.000	0.821	0.826	0.846
1963	0.808	0.818	0.825	0.846	0.820	0.830	0.834	0.855
1964	0.832	0.840	0.846	0.865	0.843	0.851	0.855	0.874
1965	0.863	0.873	0.877	0.894	0.873	0.882	0.885	0.901
1966	0.905	0.911	0.919	0.937	0.913	0.920	0.925	0.943
1967	0.918	0.923	0.930	0.948	0.924	0.932	0.936	0.954
1968	0.941	0.944	0.952	0.969	0.948	0.955	0.959	0.975
1969	0.969	0.971	0.978	0.993	0.976	0.981	0.985	0.999
1970	0.957	0.960	0.964	0.977	0.968	0.974	0.974	0.988
1971	0.972	0.966	0.973	0.980	0.975	0.972	0.977	0.983
1972	1.000	1.000	1.000	1.000	1.000	1.000	1.000	1.000
1973	1.048	1.048	1.047	1.042	1.046	1.045	1.045	1.040
1974	1.056	1.056	1.055	1.045	1.053	1.052	1.052	1.042
1975	1.036	1.032	1.030	1.012	1.035	1.030	1.028	1.011
1976	1.066	1.063	1.059	1.037	1.068	1.062	1.059	1.037
1977	1.103	1.101	1.096	1.069	1.106	1.100	1.097	1.069
1978	1.157	1.155	1.150	1.121	1.161	1.157	1.152	1.122
1979	1.165	1.152	1.156	1.119	1.174	1.168	1.167	1.128
Average annual rate of growth	0.0177	0.0162	0.0157	0.0130	0.0185	0.0173	0.0165	0.0137

Table 8.4 continued

	ecoi	saeco	saeci	saeoi	sacoi	secoi	aecoi	saecoi
1948	0.689	0.676	0.693	0.711	0.751	0.699	0.686	0.698
1949	0.663	0.653	0.667	0.684	0.723	0.672	0.661	0.672
1950	0.686	0.679	0.696	0.712	0.751	0.693	0.689	0.698
1951	0.726	0.716	0.733	0.750	0.791	0.733	0.729	0.737
1952	0.740	0.733	0.750	0.767	0.807	0.746	0.747	0.755
1953	0.752	0.748	0.767	0.783	0.822	0.760	0.762	0.771
1954	0.722	0.725	0.741	0.755	0.790	0.730	0.735	0.743
1955	0.748	0.748	0.766	0.779	0.814	0.755	0.760	0.768
1956	0.765	0.765	0.784	0.796	0.830	0.772	0.777	0.784
1957	0.763	0.766	0.782	0.794	0.826	0.770	0.775	0.782
1958	0.736	0.745	0.755	0.766	0.796	0.743	0.749	0.755
1959	0.766	0.773	0.783	0.794	0.824	0.772	0.779	0.784
1960	0.781	0.799	0.806	0.816	0.848	0.792	0.797	0.807
1961	0.776	0.788	0.794	0.804	0.829	0.783	0.790	0.795
1962	0.806	0.818	0.824	0.833	0.853	0.813	0.820	0.826
1963	0.814	0.828	0.834	0.840	0.862	0.820	0.829	0.834
1964	0.837	0.850	0.855	0.860	0.879	0.843	0.851	0.856
1965	0.868	0.880	0.886	0.890	0.907	0.874	0.881	0.886
1966	0.913	0.918	0.923	0.928	0.947	0.917	0.923	0.927
1967	0.924	0.932	0.937	0.941	0.959	0.929	0.935	0.940
1968	0.948	0.954	0.958	0.962	0.979	0.951	0.958	0.962
1969	0.976	0.981	0.983	0.987	1.001	0.978	0.985	0.987
1970	0.960	0.976	0.978	0.979	0.993	0.964	0.974	0.978
1971	0.973	0.977	0.973	0.978	0.984	0.973	0.977	0.978
1972	1.000	1.000	1.000	1.000	1.000	1.000	1.000	1.000
1973	1.050	1.043	1.044	1.043	1.038	1.048	1.046	1.044
1974	1.058	1.049	1.049	1.049	1.039	1.055	1.052	1.049
1975	1.034	1.029	1.025	1.024	1.007	1.029	1.027	1.023
1976	1.066	1.059	1.055	1.052	1.030	1.059	1.059	1.052
1977	1.105	1.092	1.090	1.087	1.060	1.095	1.095	1.085
1978	1.162	1.146	1.145	1.141	1.111	1.150	1.152	1.141
1979	1.165	1.156	1.150	1.154	1.115	1.151	1.163	1.150
Average annual rate of growth	0.0169	0.0173	0.0163	0.0156	0.0128	0.0161	0.0170	0.0161

This index is the sum of the effects captured in the aggregate index of labor quality and the mutually exclusive term measuring the effect of reallocations among industries. Since our present objective is to identify all labor-related characteristics contributing to economic growth, the appropriate index is the index of labor quality. It is this index we decompose.

The partial indices of labor input derived in the last section and reported in Table 8.4 are instrumental for identifying the first- and higher-order contributions of the six characteristics of labor input. We can define the first-order contribution of each characteristic of labor input to the rate of growth of labor quality as the difference between the rate of growth of the corresponding partial index of labor input and the rate of growth of hours worked.

As an illustration, the first-order contribution of sex to the rate of growth of labor quality, say Q_{Ls}, takes the form

$$\Delta \ln Q_{Ls} = \Delta \ln L_s - \Delta \ln H.$$

This index reflects the effect of changes in the composition of hours worked by sex on the rate of growth of labor quality. There are six first-order contributions to the rate of growth of labor quality, corresponding to the six characteristics of labor input.

We can define the second-order contribution of each pair of characteristics to the rate of growth of labor quality as the difference between the rate of growth of the corresponding partial index of labor input and the rate of growth of hours worked, less the sum of the two first-order contributions of these characteristics to the rate of growth of labor quality. For example, the second-order contribution of sex and age, say Q_{Lsa}, takes the form

$$\Delta \ln Q_{Lsa} = \Delta \ln L_{sa} - \Delta \ln H - \Delta \ln Q_{Ls} - \Delta \ln Q_{La},$$

$$= \Delta \ln L_{sa} - \Delta \ln L_a - \Delta \ln L_s + \Delta \ln H.$$

This index reflects the effect of changes in the composition of hours worked by sex and age on the rate of growth of labor quality, exclusive of the effects already reflected in the first-order contributions of sex and age.

There are fifteen second-order contributions to the rate of growth of labor quality. These second-order contributions, together with the six first-order contributions, are defined in Table 8.5. Similarly, we can define third-, fourth-, fifth-, and sixth-order contributions of characteristics of hours worked to the rate of growth of the quality of labor input, by extension of our definitions of first- and second-order contributions. There are twenty third-order indices, fifteen fourth-order indices, six fifth-order indices, and one sixth-order index. All are defined in Table 8.5.

By summing the contributions of all orders corresponding to a given set of characteristics of labor input, we obtain the partial index of labor quality corresponding to those characteristics. For example, our aggregate index of labor quality presented in column 4 of Table 8.1 is the partial index of labor

Table 8.5.   Contributions to the growth of labor quality

First-order (six indices):

$$\Delta \ln Q_{Ls} = \Delta \ln L_s - \Delta \ln H$$

Second-order (fifteen indices):

$$\Delta \ln Q_{Lsa} = \Delta \ln L_{sa} - \Delta \ln L_a - \Delta \ln L_s + \Delta \ln H$$

Third-order (twenty indices):

$$\Delta \ln Q_{Lsae} = \Delta \ln L_{sae} - \Delta \ln L_{sa} - \Delta \ln L_{se} - \Delta \ln L_{ae}$$
$$+ \Delta \ln L_s + \Delta \ln L_a + \Delta \ln L_e - \Delta \ln H$$

Fourth-order (fifteen indices):

$$\Delta \ln Q_{Lsaec} = \Delta \ln L_{saec} - \Delta \ln L_{sae} - \Delta \ln L_{sac} - \Delta \ln L_{sec}$$
$$- \Delta \ln L_{aec} + \Delta \ln L_{sa} + \Delta \ln L_{se} + \Delta \ln L_{sc}$$
$$+ \Delta \ln L_{ae} + \Delta \ln L_{ac} + \Delta \ln L_{ec} + \Delta \ln L_s$$
$$- \Delta \ln L_a - \Delta \ln L_e - \Delta \ln L_c + \Delta \ln H$$

Fifth-order (six indices):

$$\Delta \ln Q_{Lsaeco} = \Delta \ln L_{saeco} - \Delta \ln L_{saec} - \Delta \ln L_{saeo} - \Delta \ln L_{saco}$$
$$- \Delta \ln L_{seco} - \Delta \ln L_{aeco} + \Delta \ln L_{sae} + \Delta \ln L_{sac}$$
$$+ \Delta \ln L_{sao} + \Delta \ln L_{sec} + \Delta \ln L_{seo} + \Delta \ln L_{sco}$$
$$+ \Delta \ln L_{aec} + \Delta \ln L_{aeo} + \Delta \ln L_{aco} + \Delta \ln L_{eco}$$
$$- \Delta \ln L_{sa} - \Delta \ln L_{se} - \Delta \ln L_{sc} - \Delta \ln L_{so}$$
$$- \Delta \ln L_{ae} - \Delta \ln L_{ac} - \Delta \ln L_{ao} - \Delta \ln L_{ec}$$
$$- \Delta \ln L_{eo} - \Delta \ln L_{co} + \Delta \ln L_s + \Delta \ln L_a$$
$$+ \Delta \ln L_e + \Delta \ln L_c + \Delta \ln L_o - \Delta \ln H$$

Six-order (one index):

$$\Delta \ln Q_{Lsaecoi} = \Delta \ln L_{saecoi} - \Delta \ln L_{saeco} - \Delta \ln L_{saeci} - \Delta \ln L_{saeoi}$$
$$- \Delta \ln L_{sacoi} - \Delta \ln L_{secoi} - \Delta \ln L_{aecoi} + \Delta \ln L_{saec}$$
$$+ \Delta \ln L_{saeo} + \Delta \ln L_{saei} + \Delta \ln L_{saco} + \Delta \ln L_{saci}$$
$$+ \Delta \ln L_{saoi} + \Delta \ln L_{seco} + \Delta \ln L_{seci} + \Delta \ln L_{seoi}$$
$$+ \Delta \ln L_{scoi} + \Delta \ln L_{aeco} + \Delta \ln L_{aeci} + \Delta \ln L_{aeoi}$$
$$+ \Delta \ln L_{acoi} + \Delta \ln L_{ecoi} - \Delta \ln L_{sae} - \Delta \ln L_{sac}$$
$$- \Delta \ln L_{sao} - \Delta \ln L_{sai} - \Delta \ln L_{sec} - \Delta \ln L_{seo}$$
$$- \Delta \ln L_{sei} - \Delta \ln L_{sco} - \Delta \ln L_{sci} - \Delta \ln L_{soi}$$
$$- \Delta \ln L_{aec} - \Delta \ln L_{aeo} - \Delta \ln L_{aei} - \Delta \ln L_{aco}$$
$$- \Delta \ln L_{aci} - \Delta \ln L_{aoi} - \Delta \ln L_{eco} - \Delta \ln L_{eci}$$
$$- \Delta \ln L_{eoi} - \Delta \ln L_{coi} + \Delta \ln L_{sa} + \Delta \ln L_{ae}$$
$$+ \Delta \ln L_{sc} + \Delta \ln L_{so} + \Delta \ln L_{si} + \Delta \ln L_{ae}$$
$$+ \Delta \ln L_{ac} + \Delta \ln L_{ao} + \Delta \ln L_{ai} + \Delta \ln L_{ec}$$
$$+ \Delta \ln L_{eo} + \Delta \ln L_{ei} + \Delta \ln L_{co} + \Delta \ln L_{ci}$$

Table 8.5 continued

$$+ \Delta \ln L_{oi} - \Delta \ln L_s - \Delta \ln L_a - \Delta \ln L_e$$
$$- \Delta \ln L_c - \Delta \ln L_o - \Delta \ln L_i - \Delta \ln H$$

---

quality corresponding to all characteristics of labor input except industry. We can represent this index in the form:

$$\Delta \ln Q_L = \Delta \ln Q_{Ls} + \Delta \ln Q_{La} + \Delta \ln Q_{Le} + \Delta \ln Q_{Lc}$$

$$+ \Delta \ln Q_{Lo} + \Delta \ln Q_{Lsa} + \Delta \ln Q_{Lse} + \Delta \ln Q_{Lsc}$$

$$+ \Delta \ln Q_{Lso} + \Delta \ln Q_{Lae} + \Delta \ln Q_{Lac} + \Delta \ln Q_{Lao}$$

$$+ \Delta \ln Q_{Lec} + \Delta \ln Q_{Leo} + \Delta \ln Q_{Lco} + \Delta \ln Q_{Lsae}$$

$$+ \Delta \ln Q_{Lsac} + \Delta \ln Q_{Lsao} + \Delta \ln Q_{Lsec} + \Delta \ln Q_{Lseo}$$

$$+ \Delta \ln Q_{Lsco} + \Delta \ln Q_{Laec} + \Delta \ln Q_{Laeo} + \Delta \ln Q_{Laco}$$

$$+ \Delta \ln Q_{Leco} + \Delta \ln Q_{Lsaec} + \Delta \ln Q_{Lsaeo} + \Delta \ln Q_{Lsaco}$$

$$+ \Delta \ln Q_{Lseco} + \Delta \ln Q_{Laeco} + \Delta \ln Q_{Lsaeco} \; .$$

This index is the sum of five first-order contributions, ten second-order contributions, ten third-order contributions, five fourth-order contributions, and one fifth-order contribution to the rate of growth of labor quality. The index incorporates the effects of changes in the composition of hours worked among all characteristics of labor input except industry.

We apply the formulas of Table 8.5 to the disaggregated labor data described in Chapter 3. The resulting quality indices for each year in the period 1948–1979 are presented in the second through last columns in Table 8.6. The first column of this table reports the quality index that represents the total contribution made by all sources. It is formed by summing over all first- and higher-order contributions, corresponding to all six characteristics of labor input.

The analysis of variance provides an analogy that is useful for interpreting the first- and higher-order contributions of the characteristics of labor input to the rate of growth of labor quality. Each of the characteristics of hours worked corresponds to a factor in the analysis of variance. Decomposition of

Table 8.6. Decomposition of labor quality

Labor year	Quality	s	a	e	c	o	i	sa
1948	0.864	1.048	1.012	0.855	0.960	0.914	0.940	0.995
1949	0.862	1.046	1.016	0.859	0.959	0.914	0.936	0.995
1950	0.872	1.046	1.026	0.863	0.964	0.923	0.942	0.994
1951	0.885	1.042	1.022	0.863	0.968	0.930	0.955	0.995
1952	0.901	1.041	1.028	0.869	0.969	0.939	0.961	0.994
1953	0.911	1.041	1.029	0.873	0.971	0.940	0.966	0.994
1954	0.909	1.039	1.033	0.879	0.969	0.940	0.960	0.994
1955	0.932	1.035	1.033	0.881	0.973	0.942	0.965	0.994
1956	0.917	1.032	1.031	0.886	0.976	0.948	0.972	0.994
1957	0.924	1.030	1.032	0.893	0.978	0.955	0.976	0.994
1958	0.921	1.026	1.033	0.902	0.978	0.958	0.967	0.993
1959	0.930	1.025	1.032	0.905	0.981	0.962	0.972	0.992
1960	0.952	1.036	1.043	0.914	0.985	0.972	0.975	0.991
1961	0.944	1.019	1.027	0.921	0.982	0.965	0.974	0.997
1962	0.961	1.019	1.027	0.935	0.984	0.971	0.979	0.997
1963	0.963	1.017	1.026	0.933	0.987	0.971	0.983	0.997
1964	0.971	1.015	1.023	0.942	0.989	0.978	0.986	0.997
1965	0.975	1.014	1.018	0.947	0.991	0.979	0.991	0.997
1966	0.989	1.012	1.016	0.955	0.995	0.992	0.999	0.998
1967	0.997	1.010	1.016	0.961	0.996	0.994	1.002	1.000
1968	1.003	1.007	1.014	0.968	0.997	0.998	1.004	1.000
1969	1.002	1.004	1.009	0.974	0.998	1.001	1.005	1.001
1970	1.007	1.009	1.024	0.976	0.997	0.997	1.003	1.000
1971	1.006	1.002	1.005	0.993	0.998	1.006	0.999	1.000
1972	1.000	1.000	1.000	1.000	1.000	1.000	1.000	1.000
1973	1.005	0.999	0.995	1.009	1.001	1.003	1.003	1.000
1974	1.009	0.997	0.995	1.019	1.001	1.006	1.005	1.000
1975	1.013	0.993	0.997	1.035	1.001	1.009	1.001	1.001
1976	1.016	0.992	0.995	1.041	1.003	1.010	1.001	1.000
1977	1.013	0.989	0.993	1.044	1.003	1.010	1.002	1.000
1978	1.020	0.988	0.992	1.049	1.004	1.014	1.005	1.000
1979	1.004	0.967	0.975	1.031	0.988	1.003	1.008	1.017
Average annual rate of growth	0.0048	−0.0026	−0.0012	0.0060	0.0009	0.0030	0.0022	0.0007

	se	sc	so	si	ae	ac	ao	ai
1948	0.984	0.992	0.973	0.977	0.996	0.991	1.000	0.995
1949	0.984	0.991	0.974	0.979	0.996	0.991	0.999	0.994
1950	0.983	0.990	0.972	0.977	0.995	0.992	0.997	0.992
1951	0.984	0.992	0.973	0.978	0.997	0.993	0.998	0.993
1952	0.985	0.992	0.974	0.978	0.998	0.994	0.997	0.993
1953	0.986	0.992	0.976	0.979	0.999	0.994	0.998	0.994

Table 8.6 continued

	se	sc	so	si	ae	ac	ao	ai
1954	0.986	0.991	0.978	0.980	0.999	0.995	0.997	0.994
1955	0.987	0.992	0.979	0.982	0.999	0.995	0.996	0.993
1956	0.988	0.900	0.981	0.983	1.000	0.995	0.996	0.993
1957	0.989	0.993	0.983	0.985	1.000	0.995	0.995	0.992
1958	0.990	0.992	0.985	0.987	0.999	0.995	0.994	0.993
1959	0.991	0.993	0.984	0.988	0.999	0.996	0.994	0.994
1960	0.990	0.994	0.985	0.989	0.996	0.996	0.989	0.990
1961	0.995	0.997	0.992	0.992	1.004	1.000	1.000	0.996
1962	0.996	0.998	0.993	0.992	1.003	1.000	0.998	0.996
1963	0.996	0.998	0.993	0.993	1.005	1.000	0.999	0.996
1964	0.997	0.999	0.993	0.994	1.005	1.000	0.999	0.997
1965	0.997	0.999	0.994	0.994	1.005	1.000	1.000	0.997
1966	0.998	1.000	0.994	0.994	1.004	1.000	0.997	0.997
1967	0.999	1.000	0.998	0.995	1.004	1.001	0.998	0.997
1968	0.999	1.000	0.998	0.996	1.004	1.001	0.998	0.998
1969	1.000	1.000	0.999	0.997	1.004	1.001	0.999	0.999
1970	0.998	0.999	0.999	0.996	0.999	1.001	0.995	0.995
1971	1.000	1.000	1.000	1.000	1.002	1.000	0.999	1.000
1972	1.000	1.000	1.000	1.000	1.000	1.000	1.000	1.000
1973	1.000	1.000	0.999	1.000	1.000	1.000	1.000	1.000
1974	1.000	1.000	1.000	0.999	0.998	1.000	1.000	1.000
1975	1.000	1.000	1.002	1.001	0.995	1.000	0.999	0.999
1976	1.000	1.000	1.001	1.002	0.996	0.999	0.999	0.999
1977	1.000	1.000	1.000	1.002	0.996	0.999	0.999	1.000
1978	1.001	1.000	1.001	1.002	0.998	0.999	1.000	1.000
1979	1.018	1.016	1.021	0.999	1.015	1.016	1.017	1.001
Average annual rate of growth	0.0011	0.0008	0.0016	0.0007	0.0006	0.0008	0.0005	0.0002

	ec	eo	ei	co	ci	oi	sae	sac
1948	1.006	1.074	1.073	1.008	1.037	1.080	1.005	1.005
1949	1.006	1.070	1.070	1.009	1.038	1.080	1.005	1.005
1950	1.006	1.064	1.069	1.001	1.033	1.072	1.005	1.005
1951	1.005	1.066	1.067	1.003	1.029	1.063	1.005	1.005
1952	1.005	1.060	1.063	1.002	1.029	1.057	1.005	1.005
1953	1.005	1.058	1.061	1.002	1.027	1.055	1.005	1.005
1954	1.004	1.053	1.057	1.002	1.030	1.054	1.004	1.005
1955	1.004	1.052	1.056	1.000	1.026	1.050	1.004	1.004
1956	1.003	1.049	1.052	0.998	1.023	1.042	1.004	1.004
1957	1.003	1.042	1.047	0.996	1.020	1.035	1.004	1.004
1958	1.002	1.035	1.043	0.996	1.019	1.034	1.004	1.004
1959	1.002	1.033	1.041	0.997	1.017	1.033	1.003	1.004
1960	1.001	1.026	1.037	0.996	1.014	1.030	1.003	1.003

Table 8.6 continued

	ec	eo	ei	co	ci	oi	sae	sac
1961	1.004	1.029	1.033	1.000	1.015	1.028	0.999	1.000
1962	1.004	1.024	1.030	1.001	1.013	1.026	0.999	1.000
1963	1.004	1.026	1.027	1.000	1.011	1.021	0.999	1.000
1964	1.003	1.022	1.023	1.000	1.009	1.017	0.999	1.000
1965	1.003	1.021	1.020	1.000	1.008	1.014	0.999	1.000
1966	1.002	1.015	1.016	1.000	1.005	1.008	0.999	1.000
1967	1.002	1.012	1.013	1.000	1.004	1.006	0.999	1.000
1968	1.001	1.008	1.010	1.001	1.003	1.005	1.000	1.000
1969	1.001	1.006	1.007	1.000	1.003	1.001	1.000	1.000
1970	1.001	1.005	1.007	1.000	1.002	1.003	1.000	1.000
1971	1.000	0.999	1.001	1.001	1.001	1.002	1.000	1.000
1972	1.000	1.000	1.000	1.000	1.000	1.000	1.000	1.000
1973	1.000	0.998	0.998	1.001	0.999	0.999	1.000	1.000
1974	1.000	0.994	0.996	1.000	0.998	0.997	1.000	1.000
1975	0.999	0.988	0.992	1.000	0.998	0.996	1.000	1.000
1976	0.999	0.987	0.992	0.999	0.996	0.996	1.000	1.000
1977	0.999	0.988	0.992	0.999	0.995	0.993	1.000	1.000
1978	0.999	0.985	0.991	0.999	0.996	0.993	1.000	1.000
1979	1.015	1.007	0.989	1.007	0.991	0.983	0.983	0.984
Average annual rate of growth	0.0003	−0.0021	−0.0026	0.0000	−0.0015	−0.0030	−0.0007	−0.0007

	sao	sai	sec	seo	sei	sco	sci	soi
1948	1.007	1.007	1.004	1.017	1.003	1.009	1.003	1.020
1949	1.007	1.007	1.004	1.017	1.004	1.010	1.003	1.019
1950	1.007	1.007	1.004	1.018	1.004	1.009	1.005	1.021
1951	1.007	1.007	1.004	1.017	1.004	1.009	1.003	1.020
1952	1.007	1.007	1.004	1.016	1.004	1.009	1.003	1.020
1953	1.006	1.006	1.004	1.016	1.004	1.008	1.003	1.018
1954	1.006	1.006	1.004	1.015	1.004	1.009	1.004	1.017
1955	1.006	1.006	1.004	1.015	1.004	1.008	1.003	1.016
1956	1.006	1.005	1.004	1.014	1.004	1.008	1.003	1.015
1957	1.006	1.005	1.004	1.014	1.004	1.007	1.003	1.013
1958	1.006	1.005	1.004	1.013	1.004	1.008	1.003	1.011
1959	1.006	1.005	1.004	1.013	1.004	1.007	1.003	1.011
1960	1.007	1.005	1.004	1.012	1.002	1.005	1.002	1.006
1961	1.002	1.003	1.001	1.007	1.002	1.003	1.001	1.006
1962	1.002	1.003	1.001	1.006	1.001	1.002	1.001	1.006
1963	1.003	1.003	1.001	1.005	1.001	1.001	1.000	1.005
1964	1.003	1.002	1.000	1.005	1.001	1.001	1.000	1.005
1965	1.002	1.002	1.000	1.004	1.001	1.001	1.000	1.005
1966	1.001	1.001	1.000	1.004	1.001	1.000	1.000	1.004
1967	1.000	1.001	1.000	1.003	1.001	1.000	1.000	1.002

Table 8.6 continued

	sao	sai	sec	seo	sei	sco	sci	soi
1968	1.000	1.001	1.000	1.002	1.001	1.000	1.000	1.003
1969	1.000	1.000	1.000	1.001	1.001	1.000	1.000	1.003
1970	1.001	1.001	1.000	1.002	1.001	1.001	1.001	1.000
1971	1.000	1.000	1.000	1.001	1.000	1.000	1.000	0.999
1972	1.000	1.000	1.000	1.000	1.000	1.000	1.000	1.000
1973	1.000	1.000	1.000	0.999	1.000	1.000	1.000	1.001
1974	1.000	1.000	1.000	0.999	1.000	1.000	1.000	1.001
1975	0.999	1.000	1.000	0.998	1.000	1.000	1.000	0.999
1976	1.000	1.000	1.000	0.998	0.999	1.000	1.000	0.999
1977	1.000	1.000	1.000	0.998	0.999	1.000	1.000	1.000
1978	1.000	1.000	1.000	0.997	0.999	1.000	1.000	1.000
1979	0.983	1.003	0.984	0.981	1.001	0.984	1.002	1.003
Average annual rate of growth	−0.0008	−0.0001	−0.0007	−0.0012	−0.0001	−0.0008	0.0000	−0.0005

	aec	aeo	aei	aco	aci	aoi	eco	eci
1948	0.997	0.998	0.993	1.008	1.004	0.997	1.000	0.989
1949	0.997	0.998	0.992	1.008	1.003	0.997	1.000	0.989
1950	0.998	1.000	0.993	1.008	1.003	0.998	1.000	0.990
1951	0.998	1.000	0.993	1.007	1.003	0.998	1.000	0.991
1952	0.998	0.999	0.993	1.007	1.003	0.997	1.001	0.991
1953	0.998	1.000	0.993	1.006	1.002	0.996	1.001	0.991
1954	0.998	1.000	0.993	1.006	1.002	0.997	1.001	0.991
1955	0.999	1.001	0.993	1.006	1.002	0.998	1.002	0.992
1956	0.999	1.001	0.994	1.005	1.001	0.998	1.002	0.993
1957	0.999	1.002	0.994	1.005	1.001	0.999	1.003	0.993
1958	0.999	1.003	0.995	1.005	1.001	0.999	1.003	0.994
1959	1.000	1.003	0.995	1.005	1.001	0.999	1.003	0.994
1960	1.000	1.004	0.996	1.005	1.001	1.001	1.004	0.995
1961	0.997	0.998	0.993	1.001	0.999	0.997	1.000	0.994
1962	0.997	0.999	0.995	1.001	0.999	0.997	1.000	0.995
1963	0.998	0.998	0.995	1.001	0.999	0.997	1.001	0.995
1964	0.998	0.998	0.996	1.000	0.999	0.998	1.001	0.996
1965	0.998	0.998	0.996	1.001	0.999	0.998	1.001	0.996
1966	0.999	0.999	0.998	1.001	0.999	1.000	1.000	0.997
1967	0.999	0.999	0.998	1.000	0.999	1.000	1.000	0.998
1968	0.999	0.999	0.999	1.000	0.999	1.000	1.000	0.998
1969	0.999	0.998	0.999	1.000	0.999	1.000	1.000	0.999
1970	1.000	1.001	1.000	1.000	1.000	1.001	1.000	0.999
1971	1.000	0.999	0.999	1.000	1.000	1.000	1.000	1.000
1972	1.000	1.000	1.000	1.000	1.000	1.000	1.000	1.000
1973	1.000	1.000	1.000	1.000	1.000	1.000	1.000	1.000
1974	1.000	1.001	1.001	1.000	1.000	1.001	1.000	1.001

Table 8.6 continued

	aec	aeo	aei	aco	aci	aoi	eco	eci
1975	1.001	1.003	1.002	1.000	1.000	1.000	0.999	1.001
1976	1.001	1.002	1.002	1.000	1.001	1.001	0.999	1.002
1977	1.001	1.002	1.002	1.000	1.001	1.001	0.999	1.002
1978	1.001	1.001	1.002	1.000	1.001	1.001	0.999	1.002
1979	0.985	0.985	1.005	0.984	1.002	1.003	0.983	1.004
Average annual rate of growth	−0.0004	−0.0004	0.0004	−0.0008	0.0000	0.0002	−0.0005	0.0005

	eoi	coi	saec	saeo	saei	saco	saci	saoi
1948	0.949	0.978	0.995	0.994	0.998	0.995	0.998	0.994
1949	0.952	0.977	0.995	0.994	0.998	0.995	0.998	0.994
1950	0.953	0.983	0.995	0.995	0.999	0.995	0.998	0.994
1951	0.955	0.985	0.995	0.994	0.999	0.995	0.998	0.994
1952	0.958	0.985	0.995	0.995	0.999	0.995	0.998	0.995
1953	0.960	0.986	0.995	0.995	0.999	0.995	0.998	0.995
1954	0.963	0.984	0.995	0.995	0.999	0.995	0.998	0.995
1955	0.965	0.987	0.995	0.995	0.999	0.995	0.998	0.996
1956	0.968	0.990	0.995	0.995	0.999	0.995	0.998	0.996
1957	0.972	0.992	0.995	0.995	0.999	0.995	0.998	0.996
1958	0.976	0.993	0.995	0.995	0.999	0.995	0.999	0.997
1959	0.977	0.993	0.995	0.996	0.999	0.996	0.999	0.997
1960	0.980	0.995	0.995	0.996	0.999	0.996	0.999	0.997
1961	0.981	0.994	0.999	0.999	1.001	0.999	1.000	0.999
1962	0.983	0.994	0.999	1.000	1.000	0.999	1.000	0.999
1963	0.985	0.996	0.999	1.000	1.000	0.999	1.000	0.999
1964	0.988	0.996	1.000	1.000	1.000	1.000	1.000	0.999
1965	0.989	0.997	1.000	1.000	1.000	1.000	1.000	0.999
1966	0.992	0.998	1.000	1.000	1.000	1.000	1.000	0.999
1967	0.994	0.998	1.000	1.000	1.000	1.000	1.000	1.000
1968	0.995	0.998	1.000	1.000	1.000	1.000	1.000	1.000
1969	0.997	0.999	1.000	1.000	1.000	1.000	1.000	1.000
1970	0.998	0.999	1.000	1.000	1.000	1.000	1.000	1.000
1971	1.000	0.999	1.000	1.000	1.000	1.000	1.000	1.000
1972	1.000	1.000	1.000	1.000	1.000	1.000	1.000	1.000
1973	1.000	1.000	1.000	1.000	1.000	1.000	1.000	1.000
1974	1.001	1.001	1.000	1.000	1.000	1.000	1.000	1.000
1975	1.004	1.001	1.000	1.000	1.000	1.000	1.000	1.000
1976	1.003	1.002	1.000	1.000	1.000	1.000	1.000	1.000
1977	1.003	1.002	1.000	1.000	1.000	1.000	1.000	1.000

Table 8.6 continued

	eoi	coi	saec	saeo	saei	saco	saci	saoi
1978	1.003	1.002	1.000	1.000	1.000	1.000	1.000	1.000
1979	1.003	1.010	1.016	1.017	0.999	1.016	0.998	0.997
Average annual rate of growth	0.0018	0.0010	0.0007	0.0007	0.0000	0.0007	0.0000	0.0001

	seco	seci	seoi	scoi	aeco	aeci	aeoi	acoi
1948	0.996	0.966	0.995	0.997	1.001	1.002	1.008	0.997
1949	0.996	0.971	0.994	0.996	1.000	1.002	1.008	0.997
1950	0.996	0.974	0.994	0.995	1.000	1.002	1.007	0.997
1951	0.996	0.968	0.994	0.996	1.000	1.002	1.007	0.997
1952	0.996	0.971	0.994	0.996	1.000	1.002	1.007	0.997
1953	0.996	0.969	0.994	0.996	1.000	1.002	1.007	0.998
1954	0.996	0.975	0.994	0.996	1.000	1.002	1.007	0.998
1955	0.996	0.971	0.994	0.996	1.000	1.002	1.006	0.998
1956	0.996	0.972	0.994	0.996	0.999	1.002	1.005	0.999
1957	0.996	0.976	0.994	0.997	0.999	1.001	1.004	0.999
1958	0.996	0.988	0.994	0.996	0.999	1.001	1.004	0.999
1959	0.996	0.985	0.994	0.997	0.999	1.001	1.004	0.999
1960	0.996	0.992	0.996	0.998	0.999	1.001	1.003	0.999
1961	0.997	0.999	1.002	1.002	1.005	1.000		
1962	1.000	0.992	0.997	0.999	1.001	1.002	1.004	1.000
1963	1.000	0.989	0.997	1.000	1.001	1.002	1.004	1.000
1964	1.000	0.992	0.997	1.000	1.001	1.001	1.003	1.000
1965	1.000	0.988	0.997	1.000	1.000	1.001	1.003	1.000
1966	1.000	0.993	0.998	1.000	1.000	1.001	1.002	1.000
1967	1.000	0.995	0.998	1.000	1.000	1.001	1.001	1.000
1968	1.000	0.997	0.998	1.000	1.000	1.000	1.001	1.000
1969	1.000	0.998	0.998	1.000	1.000	1.000	1.001	1.001
1970	1.000	0.998	0.999	0.999	1.000	1.000	1.000	1.000
1971	1.000	1.007	1.000	1.000	1.000	1.000	1.000	1.000
1972	1.000	1.000	1.000	1.000	1.000	1.000	1.000	1.000
1973	1.000	0.999	1.000	1.000	1.000	1.000	1.000	1.000
1974	1.000	1.002	1.001	1.000	1.000	1.000	1.000	1.000
1975	1.000	1.009	1.001	1.000	1.000	1.000	0.999	1.000
1976	1.000	1.009	1.002	1.000	1.000	1.000	0.999	1.000
1977	1.000	1.007	1.002	1.000	1.000	1.000	0.999	1.000
1978	1.000	1.008	1.002	1.000	1.000	1.000	0.999	1.000
1979	1.017	1.015	1.000	0.998	1.016	0.998	0.997	0.998
Average annual rate of growth	0.0007	0.0016	0.0002	0.0000	0.0005	−0.0001	−0.0003	0.0000

Table 8.6 continued

	ecoi	saeco	saeci	saeoi	sacoi	secoi	aecoi	saecoi
1948	1.007	1.005	1.002	1.071	1.003	1.001	0.999	0.998
1949	1.007	1.005	1.002	1.066	1.002	1.001	0.999	0.998
1950	1.007	1.006	1.002	1.072	1.002	1.001	0.999	0.998
1951	1.006	1.005	1.002	1.087	1.002	1.001	0.999	0.998
1952	1.006	1.005	1.002	1.096	1.002	1.001	0.999	0.998
1953	1.005	1.005	1.002	1.098	1.002	1.001	0.999	0.998
1954	1.005	1.005	1.002	1.085	1.002	1.002	0.999	0.998
1955	1.004	1.005	1.002	1.085	1.002	1.002	0.999	0.998
1956	1.004	1.005	1.002	1.084	1.002	1.002	0.999	0.998
1957	1.003	1.005	1.002	1.081	1.002	1.002	0.999	0.998
1958	1.003	1.005	1.002	1.069	1.002	1.002	0.999	0.998
1959	1.002	1.005	1.002	1.074	1.001	1.002	1.000	0.998
1960	1.002	1.005	1.002	1.076	1.001	1.001	1.000	0.998
1961	1.003	1.001	1.000	1.058	1.000	1.000	0.998	1.000
1962	1.002	1.001	1.000	1.051	1.000	1.000	0.999	1.000
1963	1.002	1.001	1.000	1.054	1.000	1.000	0.999	1.000
1964	1.002	1.001	1.000	1.049	1.000	1.000	0.999	1.000
1965	1.002	1.001	1.000	1.043	1.000	1.000	0.999	1.000
1966	1.001	1.000	1.000	1.051	1.000	1.000	1.000	1.000
1967	1.001	1.000	1.000	1.050	1.000	1.000	1.000	1.000
1968	1.001	1.000	1.000	1.048	1.000	1.000	1.000	1.000
1969	1.001	1.000	1.000	1.040	1.000	1.000	1.000	1.000
1970	1.000	1.000	1.000	1.035	1.000	1.000	1.000	1.000
1971	1.000	1.000	1.000	1.022	1.000	1.000	1.000	1.000
1972	1.000	1.000	1.000	1.000	1.000	1.000	1.000	1.000
1973	1.000	1.000	1.000	0.991	1.000	1.000	1.000	1.000
1974	1.000	1.000	1.000	0.983	1.000	1.000	1.000	1.000
1975	1.000	1.000	1.000	0.967	1.000	1.000	1.000	1.000
1976	1.000	1.000	1.000	0.961	1.000	1.000	1.000	1.000
1977	1.000	1.000	1.000	0.955	1.000	1.000	1.000	1.000
1978	1.000	1.000	1.000	0.956	1.000	1.000	1.000	1.000
1979	0.998	0.984	1.002	0.969	1.003	1.002	1.002	0.998
Average annual rate of growth	−0.0003	−0.0007	0.0000	−0.0032	0.0000	0.0000	0.0001	0.000

the rate of growth of labor quality by all six characteristics corresponds to a six-way layout. The first-order contribution of each of the six characteristics corresponds to the main effect of the factor. The second-order contribution of any two of the six characteristics corresponds to the interaction effect of the two factors. The third-, fourth-, fifth-, and sixth-order contributions to the rate of growth of labor quality correspond to higher-order interactions.

The indices reported in Tables 8.4 and 8.6 imply that the shifting demographic, occupational, and industrial composition of the labor force has been a very significant source of postwar economic growth. The sixth-order partial index of labor input given in the last column of Table 8.4 increases at an average annual rate of 1.61 percent for the period 1948–1979. This represents the sum of the growth rates of hours worked and the index of quality change. Fifty-one percent of this growth was due to quality change; the quality index given in the first column of Table 8.6 increases at an average annual rate of 0.48 percent.

If the postwar period is partitioned at 1966, we observe that the importance of quality change has declined in both absolute and relative terms. On average, the total quality index increased 0.75 percent per year over the 1948–1966 period and 0.11 percent per year between 1966 and 1979. At the same time, the importance of compositional change declined substantially relative to increases in hours worked. Between 1948 and 1966, hours worked increased at an average 0.82 percent annual rate; quality change accounted for nearly forty-eight percent of the growth in the partial index of labor input. After 1966, the economy experienced a surge in hours worked. The unweighted hours index increased at an average rate of 1.55 percent; labor quality is responsible for approximately five percent of the growth in the sixth-order partial index of labor input.

The sources of the postwar change in aggregate labor input can be determined from the quality indices reported in Table 8.6. Comparing the main effects, only sex and age have negative effects over the 1948–1979 period. The former, reflecting the high rate of entry of women into low-paying jobs, has a negative effect averaging −0.26 percent per year. The effect of age, from the increasing proportion of relatively young laborers after 1960, decreases at an average annual rate of −0.12 percent. The main effects of employment class, education, occupation, and industry are all positive— 0.09 percent, 0.60 percent, 0.30 percent, and 0.22 percent per year, respectively.

The postwar shift of laborers to high-paying occupations slows down considerably by the end of the 1960–1966 subperiod, so this characteristic has little effect on total quality change after 1966. The main effect of age reverses itself after 1960. The effect is positive through 1960, averaging 0.25 percent per year; after 1960, the effect turns negative, declining at an average annual rate of −0.35 percent. This reversal reflects the entry into the employed labor force of a large number of young laborers who were born immediately following World War II. Their low wages and low imputed productivity account for the negative effect of age on labor quality.

Although the second- and higher-order interactive effects are small, their aggregate effect is quantitatively important. The annual average rate of growth of the sum of the interactive effects is −0.15 percent over the full 1948–1979 period. Had these effects not been considered, the quality index would have been found to increase at a 0.63 percent annual rate. This compares to 0.48 percent when all main and interaction effects are considered.

Failure to consider interaction effects would increase the calculated contribution of changing labor quality as a source of economic growth by almost one third. Relative to the 1.73 percent average annual rate of growth in labor input, neglecting interaction effects would bias the calculated contribution upward by nine percent. To identify the sources of economic growth, the interaction effects among demographic, occupational, and industrial characteristics must be explicitly incorporated into the analysis.

While second- and higher-order effects are quantitatively significant, their inclusion does not affect the qualitative interpretation of the sources of economic growth. The sex and age factors are still the dominant causes of slowing growth of the quality index. The interaction effects of age and sex with each other and other factors are generally positive and consequently reduce the negative effect of −0.38 percent that would be inferred by simply summing the main effects of sex and age, −0.26 percent and −0.12 percent, respectively.

The positive interaction between sex and occupation suggests that women increasingly enter high-paying occupation groups, yet even when all interaction effects are taken into account, the conclusion remains that the changing sex-age composition of the employed labor force has had a negative impact on labor input per hour worked. The increasing entry of women and young workers into low-paying jobs increases hours worked proportionately more than it increases labor input.

Taken as a whole, the reported quality indices suggest that changes in the composition of aggregate hours worked are important sources of economic growth. Moreover, the decomposition of aggregate quality change demonstrates that the contributions of specific characteristics of the labor force to aggregate economic growth can be quantified. We also find it important to emphasize that changes in the composition of hours worked are not confounded with productivity growth.

Our measure of aggregate labor input incorporates the effect of changes in the sex, age, education, employment class, and occupation composition of hours worked. Our method for measuring aggregate productivity growth includes a separate adjustment for the contribution of the reallocation of labor input among sectors. We identify shifts in the demographic, occupational, and industrial composition of the labor force as sources of economic growth distinct from advances in productivity at the sectoral level.

Partial Indices of Capital Input

Our next objective is to analyze the effects of changes in the postwar composition of capital stock. Our methodology for capital is analogous to that described for labor so the discussion can be brief. In this section we derive the partial indices of capital input. We construct and evaluate the quality indices in the next section. The derivation of the partial indices begins with identifying the components of capital stock, say $\{A_{aoi}(T-1)\}$, cross-classified by asset class, legal form of organization, and industry.

Previously we have used a single subscript k to represent categories of capital input cross-classified by all characteristics except industry. The subscript k has represented twelve categories of capital input. In our new notation capital input is cross-classified by four asset classes, represented by the subscript a; three legal forms of organization, represented by o; and forty-six industries, represented by i. Similarly, we consider the shares of the components of capital input in the value of property compensation for the economy as a whole, say $\{v_{aoi}(T)\}$, cross-classified by asset class, legal form of organization, and industry.

As before, we construct a partial index of capital input by adding capital stocks and the corresponding value shares over some characteristics of the capital stock. We then construct a translog index over the remaining characteristics. More specifically, we can define a first-order index of capital input, corresponding to each characteristic of capital input, by adding stocks and the corresponding value shares over all other characteristics of capital input and constructing a translog index over the single characteristic of interest.

Since there are three characteristics of capital input—asset class, legal form of organization, and industry—there are three first-order indices of capital input. For example, the growth rate of the first-order index of capital input corresponding to asset class, say K_a, can be expressed in the form

$$\Delta \ln K_a = \sum_a \bar{v}_a \, \Delta \ln A_a \,,$$

$$= \sum_a \bar{v}_a \, \Delta \ln \sum_o \sum_i A_{aoi} \,,$$

where

$$\bar{v}_a = \frac{1}{2}[v_a(T) + v_a(T-1)],$$

$$v_a = \sum_o \sum_i v_{aoi}.$$

This first-order index reflects changes in the composition of capital stock by asset class, but not by legal form of organization or industry.

We can define a second-order index of capital input, corresponding to any two characteristics of capital input, by adding capital stocks and the corresponding value shares over the remaining characteristic and constructing a translog index. There are three second-order indices of capital input generated by combinations of two of the three characteristics of capital input. An example second-order index is defined in Table 8.7.

The second-order index corresponding to asset class and legal form of organization corresponds to the index of capital input presented earlier in this chapter. Using our new notation, we can represent the growth rate of this index in the form

$$\Delta \ln K = \sum_a \sum_o \bar{v}_{ao} \, \Delta \ln K_{ao}$$

$$= \sum_a \sum_o \bar{v}_{ao} \, \Delta \ln \sum_i K_{aoi}.$$

To construct this index we add capital stocks over industries to obtain capital stock cross-classified by all characteristics except industry. Similarly, we add value shares over industries, obtaining

$$v_{ao} = \sum_i v_{aoi}.$$

Table 8.7 also defines a third-order index and an unweighted capital stock index. The third-order index of capital input corresponds to all three characteristics of capital input. This index reflects changes in the composition of capital input by industry as well as all three characteristics. To complete the set of partial indices of capital input we add capital stock over all characteristics of the capital stock to obtain an index of aggregate capital stock. This index does not reflect changes in the composition of capital input.

There are eight partial indices of capital input, over the three characteristics of capital stock. Using the formulas in Table 8.7 and the disaggregated data described in Chapter 4, we calculate annual values over the 1948–1979 period for each of the eight partial indices. The results, reported in Table 8.8,

Table 8.7. Partial indices of capital input

Capital stock (one index):

$$\Delta \ln A = \Delta \ln \sum_a \sum_o \sum_i A_{aoi}$$

First-order (three indices):

$$\Delta \ln K_a = \sum_a \bar{v}_a \Delta \ln A_a$$
$$= \sum_a \bar{v}_a \Delta \ln \sum_o \sum_i A_{aoi}$$

Second-order (three indices):

$$\Delta \ln K_{ao} = \sum_a \sum_o \bar{v}_{ao} \Delta \ln A_{ao}$$
$$= \sum_a \sum_o \bar{v}_{ao} \Delta \ln \sum_i A_{aoi}$$

Third-order (one index):

$$\Delta \ln K_{aoi} = \sum_a \sum_o \sum_i \bar{v}_{aoi} \Delta \ln A_{aoi}$$

---

are used in the following section to identify the sources of quality change in aggregate capital stock.

The Quality of Capital Input

To evaluate the contributions to economic growth of changes in the composition of capital stock, we first define a quality index that incorporates the effects of all changes. The quality index of capital input described earlier in this chapter and reported in Table 8.2 incorporates the effects of changes in the composition of capital stock among asset classes and legal forms of organization, but not among industries. Our analysis of sources of economic growth takes separate account of the contribution to economic growth due to the reallocation of capital stock among sectors.

For present purposes we require an index of capital quality that captures the effects of all three characteristics of capital input. We can define this index in terms of the third-order partial index of capital input and the aggregate index of capital stock. The rate of growth of the quality index is defined as the difference between the rate of growth of the third-order partial index of capital input and the rate of growth of capital stock. To analyze the effects of changes in the quality of capital stock, we decompose the total quality index into components corresponding to first- and higher-order effects of changes in the composition of capital input by asset class, legal form of organization, and industry.

Table 8.8.   Translog indexes of capital input

Year	Capital stock	a	o	i	ao	ai	oi	aoi
1948	0.490	0.376	0.460	0.433	0.377	0.357	0.425	0.352
1949	0.508	0.401	0.479	0.452	0.401	0.379	0.444	0.374
1950	0.521	0.417	0.492	0.461	0.416	0.391	0.453	0.387
1951	0.543	0.446	0.514	0.483	0.446	0.419	0.475	0.415
1952	0.561	0.471	0.535	0.504	0.471	0.445	0.497	0.440
1953	0.576	0.487	0.550	0.518	0.488	0.459	0.510	0.455
1954	0.591	0.506	0.566	0.535	0.506	0.477	0.527	0.473
1955	0.604	0.521	0.580	0.548	0.520	0.492	0.541	0.487
1956	0.626	0.548	0.603	0.572	0.547	0.521	0.566	0.517
1957	0.644	0.571	0.622	0.594	0.570	0.546	0.588	0.542
1958	0.660	0.590	0.639	0.612	0.587	0.565	0.606	0.561
1959	0.672	0.601	0.650	0.621	0.598	0.575	0.616	0.572
1960	0.690	0.621	0.670	0.641	0.618	0.597	0.637	0.595
1961	0.707	0.640	0.687	0.660	0.636	0.616	0.655	0.614
1962	0.722	0.655	0.703	0.676	0.651	0.633	0.673	0.631
1963	0.741	0.677	0.724	0.701	0.673	0.659	0.698	0.657
1964	0.764	0.703	0.747	0.724	0.699	0.685	0.722	0.684
1965	0.788	0.733	0.772	0.753	0.730	0.717	0.752	0.717
1966	0.819	0.772	0.805	0.790	0.769	0.760	0.789	0.759
1967	0.852	0.816	0.841	0.831	0.814	0.807	0.831	0.806
1968	0.881	0.852	0.872	0.864	0.850	0.844	0.864	0.843
1969	0.912	0.891	0.906	0.901	0.890	0.886	0.901	0.886
1970	0.944	0.932	0.942	0.939	0.932	0.930	0.939	0.930
1971	0.969	0.963	0.968	0.967	0.963	0.962	0.967	0.962
1972	1.000	1.000	1.000	1.000	1.000	1.000	1.000	1.000
1973	1.038	1.050	1.039	1.042	1.050	1.053	1.042	1.053
1974	1.082	1.109	1.086	1.092	1.110	1.116	1.094	1.117
1975	1.114	1.149	1.120	1.128	1.151	1.155	1.129	1.155
1976	1.132	1.171	1.138	1.144	1.173	1.175	1.144	1.172
1977	1.161	1.208	1.167	1.174	1.210	1.210	1.175	1.207
1978	1.199	1.259	1.207	1.214	1.262	1.260	1.215	1.257
1979	1.239	1.314	1.249	1.257	1.318	1.317	1.257	1.312
Average annual rate of growth	0.0299	0.0403	0.0322	0.0344	0.0404	0.0421	0.0350	0.0424

We define the first-order contribution of each characteristic of capital input to the rate of growth of capital quality as the difference between the rate of growth of the corresponding partial index of capital input and the rate of growth of capital stock. For example, the first-order contribution of asset class to the rate of growth of capital quality, say Q_{Ka}, takes the form

$$\Delta \ln Q_{Ka} = \Delta \ln K_a - \Delta \ln A.$$

This index reflects the effect of changes in the composition of capital stock by asset class on the rate of growth of capital quality. There are three first-order contributions to the rate of growth of capital quality, corresponding to the three characteristics of capital input.

We define the second-order contribution of each pair of characteristics to the rate of growth of capital quality as the difference between the rate of growth of the corresponding partial index of capital input and the rate of growth of capital stock, less the sum of the two first-order contributions of these characteristics to the rate of growth of capital quality. For example, the second-order contribution of asset class and legal form of organization, say Q_{Kao}, takes the form

$$\Delta \ln Q_{Kao} = \Delta \ln K_{ao} - \Delta \ln A - \Delta \ln Q_{Ka} - \Delta \ln Q_{Ko} ,$$

$$= \Delta \ln K_{ao} - \Delta \ln K_a - \Delta \ln K_o + \Delta \ln A .$$

The index reflects the effect of changes in the composition of capital stock by asset class and legal form of organization on the rate of growth of capital quality. This index is the net of effects already reflected in the first-order contributions of each of the two characteristics. There are three second-order contributions to the rate of growth of total capital quality. These second-order contributions, together with the three first-order and one third-order contributions, are defined in Table 8.9.

By summing the contributions of all orders corresponding to a given set of characteristics of capital input, we obtain the partial index of capital quality corresponding to those characteristics. For example, the aggregate index of capital quality is the partial index of capital quality corresponding to all characteristics of capital input except industry. We can represent the growth rate of this index in the form

$$\Delta \ln Q_K = \Delta \ln Q_{Ka} + \Delta \ln Q_{Ko} + \Delta \ln Q_{Kao} .$$

This index is the sum of the two first-order and one second-order contributions to the rate of growth of capital quality, corresponding to asset class and

Table 8.9.   Contributions to the growth of capital quality

First-order (three indices):

$$\Delta \ln Q_{Ka} = \Delta \ln K_a - \Delta \ln A$$

Second-order (three indices):

$$\Delta \ln Q_{Kao} = \Delta \ln K_{ao} - \Delta \ln K_a - \Delta \ln K_o + \Delta \ln A$$

Third-order (one index):

$$\Delta \ln Q_{Kaoi} = \Delta \ln K_{aoi} - \Delta \ln K_{ao} - \Delta \ln K_{ai} - \Delta \ln K_{oi}$$
$$+ \Delta \ln K_a + \Delta \ln K_o + \Delta \ln K_i - \Delta \ln A$$

---

legal form of organization. This index incorporates the effects of changes in the composition of capital stock among all characteristics of capital input except industry.

Using the partial indices and formulas presented in Tables 8.8 and 8.9, respectively, we construct the seven indices corresponding to the partial first- and higher-order contributions of all three characteristics of capital input; the indices are reported in Table 8.10. The other index reported in the table is the index of capital quality. This index corresponds to the effect of changes in all characteristics of capital input. As before, the analysis of variance provides a useful analogy for interpreting the contribution of each characteristic of capital input to the rate of growth of capital quality. First-order contributions correspond to main effects, while second- and third-order contributions correspond to higher-order interactions.

The decomposition of capital input growth provides an interesting contrast to the parallel analysis of labor input. While unweighted hours worked increased by only 0.82 percent per year in the 1948–1966 period and surged to 1.55 percent per year growth in the 1966–1979 subperiod, we observe no change in trend rates of growth in aggregate capital stock. Over the full 1948–1979 period, capital stock increased at an annual rate of 2.99 percent. The rates in the 1948–1966 and 1966–1979 subperiods differ little from this postwar mean. In 1948–1966, capital stock increased at a 2.85 percent average annual rate. It increased, on average, by 3.18 percent between 1966 and 1979.

Second, while the rate of growth in the sixth-order partial index of labor input increased substantially from its average 1.58-percent level in 1948–1966 to a 1.66-percent rate over 1966–1979, the rate of growth in the third-order partial index of capital input exhibits the opposite trend. It declines from a 4.27 percent annual rate in the first subperiod to 4.21 percent

Table 8.10. Decomposition of capital quality

Year	Capital quality	a	o	i	ao	ai	oi	aoi
1948	0.719	0.768	0.939	0.884	1.066	1.072	1.046	0.944
1949	0.736	0.789	0.942	0.888	1.061	1.063	1.042	0.948
1950	0.742	0.799	0.945	0.884	1.058	1.062	1.040	0.951
1951	0.764	0.821	0.947	0.891	1.056	1.056	1.039	0.953
1952	0.784	0.838	0.952	0.899	1.052	1.051	1.034	0.956
1953	0.790	0.846	0.955	0.900	1.048	1.047	1.032	0.959
1954	0.800	0.856	0.958	0.906	1.044	1.041	1.029	0.963
1955	0.806	0.862	0.960	0.907	1.040	1.041	1.028	0.966
1956	0.827	0.876	0.963	0.914	1.036	1.040	1.027	0.969
1957	0.841	0.886	0.965	0.922	1.034	1.036	1.025	0.971
1958	0.849	0.893	0.968	0.926	1.029	1.034	1.023	0.975
1959	0.851	0.895	0.968	0.925	1.027	1.035	1.024	0.976
1960	0.862	0.901	0.971	0.930	1.024	1.034	1.023	0.979
1961	0.869	0.905	0.973	0.933	1.022	1.032	1.022	0.981
1962	0.874	0.907	0.975	0.937	1.020	1.031	1.021	0.982
1963	0.886	0.913	0.977	0.945	1.018	1.029	1.019	0.984
1964	0.895	0.920	0.978	0.948	1.017	1.028	1.020	0.984
1965	0.910	0.929	0.980	0.955	1.017	1.025	1.019	0.985
1966	0.927	0.942	0.983	0.964	1.014	1.020	1.017	0.987
1967	0.946	0.957	0.987	0.975	1.011	1.014	1.012	0.989
1968	0.957	0.967	0.990	0.981	1.008	1.010	1.010	0.992
1969	0.971	0.977	0.993	0.988	1.006	1.007	1.007	0.994
1970	0.985	0.987	0.997	0.994	1.003	1.004	1.003	0.997
1971	0.992	0.993	0.999	0.997	1.002	1.002	1.001	0.999
1972	1.000	1.000	1.000	1.000	1.000	1.000	1.000	1.000
1973	1.014	1.011	1.001	1.004	0.999	0.999	0.999	1.001
1974	1.032	1.025	1.004	1.009	0.997	0.997	0.998	1.003
1975	1.037	1.032	1.006	1.013	0.996	0.993	0.996	1.002
1976	1.035	1.035	1.005	1.010	0.996	0.993	0.995	1.001
1977	1.040	1.041	1.006	1.012	0.996	0.990	0.995	1.001
1978	1.049	1.050	1.007	1.013	0.995	0.988	0.994	1.001
1979	1.058	1.060	1.008	1.014	0.995	0.988	0.992	1.001
Average annual rate of growth	0.0125	0.0104	0.0023	0.0044	−0.0022	−0.0026	−0.0017	0.0019

in the second subperiod. It is important to emphasize however, that capital input increases considerably faster than labor input. In the 1966–1979 subperiod the growth rate is 4.21 percent for capital, compared with 1.66 percent for labor. In the 1948–1966 subperiod the capital and labor growth rates are 4.27 percent and 1.58 percent, respectively.

The similarities and differences in the intertemporal patterns of the labor and capital quality indices are highly informative. For the full 1948–1979 period, labor quality is responsible for twenty-eight percent of the observed growth in labor input. The corresponding percentage for capital quality is thirty-one percent. The contribution of labor quality as a source of economic growth declined over time, in absolute terms as well as relative to the growth of labor input. A similar pattern emerges for capital.

The annual growth rate of capital quality fell from 1.41 percent in the subperiod 1948–1966 to 1.02 percent in the subperiod 1966–1979. The ratio of growth in capital quality to growth in capital input declined from thirty-three percent to twenty-four percent between the two subperiods. The quality indices presented in Table 8.10 reveal that all three characteristics of capital are positive sources of quality change. Although the three main effects are positive, asset type exhibits the largest main effect and legal form of organization the smallest.

Accounting for the second- and third-order interaction effects does not alter the qualitative description of the sources of growth due to capital input, but does affect the magnitude of the changing quality of capital stock. The negative trend in each second-order effect implies that components of quality change are positively correlated. The main effect of asset type, for example, captures positive quality contributions that are due in part to changes in legal form of organization and industry. These same contributions are also captured in the main effects of the two remaining characteristics.

Ignoring the interaction effects would lead to double counting.[2] Specifically, simply summing over the average annual rates of growth of the main effects would imply that quality increased at 1.71 percent per year over 1948–1979. In actuality, the quality index increased at a 1.25-percent rate. The difference of 0.46 percent per year reflects the upward bias in the growth of the contribution of capital input to economic growth if interaction effects are neglected. This bias amounts to a thirty-seven percent upward bias in the estimate of capital's contribution over the 1948–1979 period.

Conclusion

The analysis presented in this chapter suggests three important conclusions. Our primary conclusion is that the changing compositions of hours worked and capital stocks are important components in the contribution of primary inputs to economic growth. Twenty-eight percent of labor input's total contribution is due to changes in the sex, age, education, employment class, occupation, and industry distribution of labor input. The corresponding share of capital quality in the contribution of capital input is thirty-one percent. This source of economic growth is due to the changing composition of capital stock among asset classes, legal forms of organization, and industries.

Our second conclusion is that adjusting for the first-order effects of input characteristics is insufficient to account for input quality. Failure to include second- and higher-order quality effects would bias upward the total contribution of both labor and capital inputs. The sum total of labor's contribution through hours worked, aggregate quality, and the reallocation of hours among industries would be biased upward by nine percent. Ignoring second- and third-order contributions for capital's characteristics would lead to a thirty-seven percent upward bias in the growth rate of capital's total contribution to economic growth.

Third, the most important result of the research reported in this chapter is that the contributions of primary inputs to economic growth explain much of what has been previously unexplained and therefore attributed to productivity growth. Ignoring the changing composition of primary inputs biases the estimate of aggregate productivity growth and prevents the identification of important sources of economic growth; moreover, the impact of specific characteristics of capital and labor inputs can be measured separately within an economic analysis of aggregate productivity change. The proportion of the economy's growth explained by the growth of the labor and capital quality and by the industrial redistribution of primary inputs is one of the subjects of the following chapter.

9 Growth in Aggregate Output

In this final chapter we analyze the sources of U.S. economic growth over the period 1948 to 1979. Sources of growth in output for the economy as a whole can be divided between aggregate productivity growth and the contributions of aggregate capital and labor inputs. We have presented data on growth in capital and labor inputs in Chapter 8. In this chapter we construct measures of growth in output, the rate of productivity growth, and the contributions of capital and labor inputs.

Our initial objective is to measure value added for the economy as a whole. We first specialize the sectoral models of production employed in Chapters 6 and 7 by introducing value-added functions for each sector. These functions give quantities of value added as functions of capital inputs, labor inputs, and time. We utilize this more restrictive methodology to generate index numbers of the quantity of value added for each sector. The quantity of aggregate value added is defined as the sum of quantities of value added over all sectors.

The existence of sectoral value-added functions is consistent with the assumptions that underlie the sectoral models of production we have employed in Chapters 6 and 7. It is important to emphasize, however, that we did not use sectoral value-added functions in analyzing the sources of growth in sectoral output, in Chapter 6, or in analyzing sectoral distribution and productivity growth, in Chapter 7. Accordingly, the results we have presented in those chapters do not depend on the existence of value-added functions.

To construct the rate of productivity growth we employ the model of aggregate producer behavior from Chapter 2. This model includes a production function and necessary conditions for producer equilibrium. In Chapter 2 we have pointed out that the existence of an aggregate production function imposes very stringent conditions on sectoral models of production. All sectoral value-added functions must be identical to the aggregate production function. Capital and labor inputs must be identical functions of their components for all sectors.

The measures of value added and the rate of productivity growth presented in this chapter and the measures of capital and labor inputs presented in Chapter 8 depend on the existence of an aggregate production function. It is important to reemphasize that we did not incorporate the restrictions implied by the existence of an aggregate production function in analyzing sectoral production patterns in Chapters 6 and 7.

Comparing sectoral and aggregate models of production in Chapter 2, we found that the analysis of sources of economic growth differs between the two unless the assumptions of the aggregate model are met. The differences can be identified with the contributions of reallocations of value added and primary factor inputs among sectors to the rate of aggregate productivity growth. These contributions can be regarded as a measure of the significance of departures from the assumptions that underlie the existence of an aggregate production function.

We have discussed the measurement of aggregate capital and labor inputs, in Chapter 8. In this chapter we present estimates of aggregate value added, and allocate the growth of value added among its components—the contributions of capital and labor inputs and the rate of productivity growth. Further, we decompose the contribution of capital input into the contributions of capital stock and the quality of capital stock. Similarly, we decompose the contribution of labor input into the contributions of hours worked and the quality of hours worked.

We allocate the rate of aggregate productivity growth among a weighted sum of sectoral productivity growth rates and reallocations of value added and the primary factor inputs among sectors. Tests for the existence of sectoral value added functions in Chapter 7 have cast considerable doubt on the separability of value added at the sectoral level. Reallocations of value added and the primary factor inputs among sectors are measures of departure from the separability of value added at the sectoral level and the stringent conditions implied by the existence of an aggregate production function. We find that the departures are quite sizable. The contribution of sectoral productivity growth rates, however, greatly predominates over the reallocations in accounting for aggregate productivity growth.

We compare our approach to the analysis of U.S. economic growth with alternative approaches. Models of aggregate production have been implemented for the United States by the Bureau of Labor Statistics (1983), by Christensen and Jorgenson (1969; 1970; 1973a; 1973b) and Christensen,

Cummings, and Jorgenson (1980; 1981), by Denison (1962; 1967; 1974; 1979; 1985), by Kendrick (1961; 1973), Kendrick and Grossman (1980), and Kendrick (1983), and by many others. Sectoral models of production have been implemented for the United States by Fraumeni and Jorgenson (1980; 1986) and Gollop and Jorgenson (1980; 1983), by Kendrick (1961; 1973), by Kendrick and Grossman (1980), and Kendrick (1983), by Leontief (1953), by Star (1974), and by Wolff (1985); for Germany by Conrad (1985) and Conrad and Jorgenson (1985), and by Frohn, Krengel, Kubier, Oppenlander, and Uhlmann (1973); for Japan by Ezaki (1978), by Jorgenson, Kuroda, and Nishimizu (1986), by Nishimizu and Hulten (1978), and by Watanabe (1971); and for the United Kingdom by Armstrong (1975).

We extend our model of aggregate production to characterize possibilities for substitution between capital and labor inputs and changes in these substitution possibilities over time. We describe the relative distribution of value added in terms of the value of capital and labor inputs. Necessary conditions for producer equilibrium are given by equalities between the value shares of each input and the elasticity of value added with respect to that input. Under constant returns to scale both the elasticities and the value shares sum to unity.

To describe the implications of patterns of substitution for the distribution of value added, we employ share elasticities, as in Chapter 7. We take the share elasticities of capital and labor inputs as parameters in an econometric model of production. To describe the implications of changes in productivity for patterns of substitution, we employ biases of productivity growth and the acceleration of productivity growth, again as in Chapter 7. We take the biases and acceleration of productivity growth as parameters in an econometric model that is based on a translog production function.[1]

Finally, we consider restrictions on patterns of substitution and productivity growth implied by Harrod neutrality, Hicks neutrality, and Solow neutrality of productivity growth.[2] Under Harrod neutrality labor input and time are separable from capital input; under Hicks neutrality capital and labor input are separable from time; under Solow neutrality capital input and time are separable from labor input. Each of these restrictions implies that the aggregate production function, originally represented in terms of capital input, labor input, and time, can be represented in terms of a smaller number of variables.

We derive restrictions on the shares and share elasticities corresponding to Harrod neutrality, Hicks neutrality, and Solow neutrality for the aggregate production function. We also derive restrictions on the rate of productivity growth, its acceleration, and the biases of productivity growth. We also derive restrictions on these parameters, associated with restrictions on patterns of substitution and productivity growth. Finally, we present the results of empirical tests of these restrictions.

Aggregate Output

The starting point for the measurement of aggregate productivity is a production account for the U.S. economy in current prices.[3] The fundamental identity for the production account is that the value of output is equal to the value of input. We define the value of output and input from the point of view of the producer. We measure revenue as proceeds to the producing sector of the economy and outlay as expenditures of the sector.

The value of output is equal to the value of deliveries to final demand—personal consumption expenditures, gross private domestic investment, government purchases, and net exports—excluding indirect business taxes on output and excise and sales taxes, and including subsidies paid to producers. The value of input includes the value of primary factors of production—capital and labor inputs—including indirect business taxes on input, property taxes, and other taxes on property compensation.

Our concept of aggregate output is intermediate between output at market prices and output at factor cost, as these terms are conventionally employed. Given our definitions of output and input, the accounting identity for the economy as a whole can be written

$$\sum P_V^j V_j = \sum P_{Kk} K_k + \sum P_{Ll} L_l \ .$$

The sum of value added in all sectors, $\sum P_V^j V_j$, is equal to the sum of property compensation, $\sum P_{Kk} K_k$, and labor compensation, $\sum P_{Ll} L_l$.

In implementing the production account for the U.S. economy we included value added in the fifty-one sectors listed in Table 3.1. These sectors include forty-six private domestic sectors and five civilian government sectors: federal public administration, state and local public administration, federal government enterprises, state and local government enterprises, and state and local educational services.

In the U.S. national income and product accounts, aggregate value added includes the services of owner-occupied dwellings and the output of new residential housing. Value added includes the output of consumers' durables utilized by households and producers' durables utilized by nonprofit institutions, but excludes the value of the services of these durables. The services of owner-occupied residential real estate, including structures and land, are imputed from market rental prices of tenant-occupied residential real estate.

The value of the services of owner-occupied real estate is allocated among net rent, interest, taxes, and capital consumption allowances. A similar imputation is made for the services of real estate used by nonprofit institutions, but the imputed value excludes net rent. We treat the services of producers' durables and real estate utilized by nonprofit institutions and the services of consumers' durables utilized by households symmetrically with the services of owner-occupied housing. For this purpose we include these services in aggregate value added.

Given our definition of output and input from the point of view of the producer, the aggregate production account takes the form given in Table 9.1. The value of output from the point of view of the producing sector is equal to the sum of gross domestic civilian product, as defined in the U.S. national income and product accounts, the services of consumers' durables, the services of durables held by institutions, and net rent on institutional real estate.

The value of indirect business taxes on output, net of subsidies, is excluded from the value of output from the point of view of the producing sector. The net value of these taxes is equal to the sum of federal and state and local business tax and nontax accruals, less the federal capital stock tax, state and local business motor vehicle licenses, property taxes and other taxes, and federal subsidies.

As an accounting identity, the value of output is equal to the value of input from the point of view of the producing sector. The value of input includes income originating in business, households and institutions, and civilian government, as defined in the U.S. national income and product accounts. The value of input also includes capital consumption allowances, business transfer payments, the statistical discrepancy, and certain indirect business taxes on property and property compensation. Finally, the value of input includes the imputed value of services of consumers' durables and durables held by institutions, and net rent on institutional real estate.

Revenue and outlay accounts are linked through capital formation and the corresponding compensation of capital services. To make this link explicit, we divide the value of input from the point of view of the producer between labor and property compensation. Property compensation also includes profits, rentals, net interest, capital consumption allowances, business transfer payments, part of the statistical discrepancy, subsidies, the property compensation of self-employed workers, and direct taxes included in outlay on capital services, including business motor vehicle licenses, property taxes, and other taxes. Labor compensation includes the compensation of employees, the labor compensation of the self-employed, and the remainder of the statistical discrepancy.

Table 9.1.   Aggregate production account: current prices

Revenue

1.   Gross domestic civilian product
2.   + Services of consumer durables
3.   + Services of durables held by institutions
4.   + Net rent on institutional real estate
5.   − Federal indirect business tax and nontax accruals
6.   + Capital stock tax
7.   − State and local indirect business tax and nontax accruals
8.   + Business motor vehicle licenses
9.   + Business property taxes
10.   + Other business taxes
11.   + Subsidies
12.   = Value of output from the point of view of the producing sector

Outlay

1.   Income originating in business
2.   + Income originating in households and institutions
3.   + Income originating in civilian government
4.   + Capital consumption allowances
5.   + Business transfer payments
6.   + Statistical discrepancy
7.   + Services of consumer durables
8.   + Services of durables held by institutions
9.   + Net rent on institutional real estate
10.   + Certain indirect business taxes (revenue account above,
        lines 6 + 8 + 9 + 10)
11.   = Value of input from the point of view of the producing sector

To construct a quantity index for aggregate output we first measure the prices and quantities of value added in each of the fifty-one producing sectors included in our study. Value added, in all forty-six private domestic sectors except households, equals the value of output less the value of intermediate input. The quantity of value added is an index formed from quantities of output and intermediate input, as described in Chapter 2.

The value of the services of the five civilian government sectors—federal administration, state and local public administration, federal enterprises, state and local enterprises, and state and local educational services—is equal to the value of labor compensation. The quantity of deliveries of these services is equal to the quantity of labor input, described in Chapter 3. For the household sector the quantity of value added is equal to an index of capital and labor inputs. Capital input into the household sector includes the services of owner-occupied residential real estate and consumers' durables. For this sector we employ the measure of labor input described in Chapter 3 and the measure of capital input described in Chapter 4.

The quantity of aggregate value added is the sum of the quantities of value added in all sectors:

$$V = \sum V_i .$$

We can define the price of value added for the economy as a whole, P_V, in terms of prices of value added in all sectors, $\{p_V^i\}$:

$$p_V V = p_V \sum V_i ,$$

$$= \sum p_V^i V_i .$$

Value added for the economy as a whole is the sum of value added over all sectors. The quantity index of value added, the corresponding price index, and value added in all sectors are presented for the period 1948–1979 in Table 9.2.

Aggregate Productivity Index

We have presented an index of productivity for the economy as a whole, in Chapter 2. Our next objective is to implement this index empirically. We assume that value added V can be expressed as a translog function of capital input K, labor input L, and time T. The corresponding index of productivity growth is the translog index $\bar{v}_T$:

$$\bar{v}_T = \ln V(T) - \ln V(T-1) - \bar{v}_K[\ln K(T) - \ln K(T-1)]$$

$$- \bar{v}_L[\ln L(T) - \ln L(T-1)] ,$$

where weights are given by average shares of capital and labor inputs, $\bar{v}_K$ and $\bar{v}_L$, in value added:

$$\bar{v}_K = \frac{1}{2}[v_K(T) + v_K(T-1)] ,$$

$$\bar{v}_L = \frac{1}{2}[v_L(T) + v_L(T-1)] ,$$

Table 9.2.   Aggregate value-added

Year	Price	Quantity	Value-added
1948	0.500	524.265	262.271
1949	0.497	521.783	259.183
1950	0.511	565.513	288.966
1951	0.549	600.755	329.518
1952	0.565	619.089	349.875
1953	0.569	641.503	365.080
1954	0.587	638.219	374.868
1955	0.597	680.612	406.380
1956	0.610	707.349	431.330
1957	0.618	723.745	447.048
1958	0.637	722.925	460.704
1959	0.642	769.668	494.381
1960	0.661	785.726	519.609
1961	0.669	801.803	536.103
1962	0.683	837.036	571.778
1963	0.684	877.198	600.064
1964	0.699	924.156	646.319
1965	0.727	973.978	708.320
1966	0.755	1025.453	774.195
1967	0.775	1050.043	814.301
1968	0.810	1098.022	889.411
1969	0.854	1130.867	966.263
1970	0.898	1127.214	1012.683
1971	0.943	1158.060	1092.155
1972	1.000	1221.389	1221.389
1973	1.074	1279.095	1373.877
1974	1.158	1264.618	1464.148
1975	1.242	1260.177	1564.853
1976	1.316	1329.082	1749.155
1977	1.416	1415.118	2003.478
1978	1.524	1473.305	2245.231
1979	1.645	1515.618	2493.933

$$\bar{v}_T = \frac{1}{2}[v_T(T) + v_T(T-1)] \,,$$

$$v_K = \frac{p_K K}{p_V V} \,,$$

$$v_L = \frac{p_L L}{p_V V} \,.$$

The value shares are computed from data on the quantities of value added, capital input, and labor input and the corresponding prices, p_V, p_K, and p_L.

We assume that capital input and labor input can be expressed as translog functions of individual capital inputs $\{K_k\}$ and individual labor inputs $\{L_l\}$:

$$\ln K(T) - \ln K(T-1) = \sum \bar{v}_{Kk}[\ln K_k(T) - \ln K_k(T-1)] \,,$$

$$\ln L(T) - \ln L(T-1) = \sum \bar{v}_{Ll}[\ln L_l(T) - \ln L_l(T-1)] \,,$$

where weights are given by average shares of individual capital, and labor inputs in the value of the corresponding aggregates:

$$\bar{v}_{Kk} = \frac{1}{2}\,[v_{Kk}(T) + v_{Kk}(T-1)], \qquad\qquad (k = 1, 2, ..., p),$$

$$\bar{v}_{Ll} = \frac{1}{2}\,[v_{Ll}(T) + v_{Ll}(T-1)], \qquad\qquad (l = 1, 2, ..., q),$$

$$v_{KK} = \frac{p_{Kk}K_k}{\sum p_{Kk}K_k} \,, \qquad\qquad (k = 1, 2, ..., p),$$

$$v_{Ll} = \frac{p_{Ll}L_l}{\sum p_{Ll}L_l} \,, \qquad\qquad (l = 1, 2, ..., q).$$

The value shares are computed from data on capital inputs and their prices $\{p_{Kk}\}$ and labor inputs and their prices $\{p_{Ll}\}$. We have presented quantity indices for capital and labor inputs for the period 1948–1979, in Tables 8.1 and 8.2. We have presented a quantity index for value added for this period in Table 9.2.

Our next objective is to compare productivity growth and the contributions of capital and labor inputs as sources of economic growth. Annual growth rates for value added, capital input, and labor input for the period 1948–1979 are shown in Table 9.3. The growth rate of value added is the sum of the average rate of productivity growth and a weighted average of growth rates of capital and labor inputs, with weights given by the average value shares of the inputs. The share of capital input in value added is also shown; the value share of labor input is equal to unity less the value share of capital input. The weighted growth rates of capital and labor inputs and the rate of productivity growth are presented in Table 9.3.

Value added grew rapidly throughout the period. Declines were recorded only in 1949, 1954, 1958, 1970, 1974, and 1975. Only the downturn in 1974–1975 lasted for more than one year; all declines except for 1970 were followed by sharp recoveries. Turning to the growth of capital input, each decline in value added is followed by a reduction in the growth rate of capital input the following year. By comparison with the growth of capital input, the growth of labor input was considerably more uneven. While the growth rate of capital input was positive throughout the period, substantial declines in labor input coincided with declines in value added in 1949, 1954, 1958, 1970, and 1975; a decline in labor input also took place in 1961. Finally, the pattern of productivity growth, like that of labor input, was relatively uneven, with declines in the level of productivity in 1949, 1952, 1954, 1960, 1967, 1969, 1970, 1974, 1975, and 1978. Rapid growth in productivity is associated with recoveries in the growth of value added in 1950, 1955, and 1959. Rapid growth in productivity also took place during the subperiod 1960–1966; this period was characterized by unusually rapid growth of value added, capital input, and labor input.

The average value share of capital input was very stable over the period 1948–1979, ranging from 0.3642 in 1949 to 0.4025 in 1966. Accordingly, the cyclical patterns of the contributions of capital and labor inputs are virtually identical to the patterns of the growth rates of capital and labor inputs. The contribution of capital input was positive throughout the period from 1948 to 1979, and relatively even. By contrast, the contributions of labor input and the rate of productivity growth were negative for six and ten of the thirty-one years, respectively, and relatively uneven.

The contribution of capital input provides the largest single contribution to output growth in fourteen of the thirty-one years. The contribution of labor input provides the largest single contribution in seven years. Finally, the rate of productivity growth provides the largest contribution in ten periods. The contribution of capital input is greater than that of labor input in eighteen of the thirty-one years. The contribution of capital input is greater than the rate

Table 9.3. Contributions to growth in aggregate output, 1949–1979

Year	Value-added	Capital input	Labor input	Average share of capital input	Contributions to growth in aggregate value-added		
					Capital input	Labor input	Productivity growth
1949	−0.0047	0.0620	−0.0339	0.3642	0.0226	−0.0215	−0.0058
1950	0.0805	0.0381	0.0386	0.3808	0.0145	0.0239	0.0421
1951	0.0605	0.0680	0.0526	0.3779	0.0257	0.0327	0.0020
1952	0.0301	0.0564	0.0243	0.3812	0.0215	0.0150	−0.0065
1953	0.0356	0.0337	0.0192	0.3863	0.0130	0.0118	0.0108
1954	−0.0051	0.0361	−0.0303	0.3913	0.0141	−0.0184	−0.0008
1955	0.0643	0.0279	0.0310	0.4009	0.0112	0.0185	0.0346
1956	0.0385	0.0508	0.0218	0.3986	0.0202	0.0131	0.0052
1957	0.0229	0.0408	0.0014	0.3870	0.0158	0.0009	0.0062
1958	−0.0011	0.0306	−0.0270	0.3886	0.0119	−0.0165	0.0035
1959	0.0627	0.0171	0.0358	0.3968	0.0068	0.0216	0.0342
1960	0.0206	0.0330	0.0331	0.3915	0.0129	0.0201	−0.0124
1961	0.0203	0.0288	−0.0132	0.3922	0.0113	−0.0080	0.0170
1962	0.0430	0.0233	0.0370	0.3950	0.0092	0.0224	0.0114
1963	0.0469	0.0338	0.0120	0.3912	0.0132	0.0073	0.0263
1964	0.0521	0.0384	0.0269	0.3884	0.0149	0.0165	0.0207
1965	0.0525	0.0427	0.0341	0.3972	0.0170	0.0206	0.0150
1966	0.0515	0.0525	0.0429	0.4025	0.0211	0.0257	0.0047
1967	0.0237	0.0563	0.0149	0.3998	0.0225	0.0090	−0.0078
1968	0.0447	0.0439	0.0236	0.3919	0.0172	0.0144	0.0131
1969	0.0295	0.0458	0.0270	0.3775	0.0173	0.0168	−0.0046
1970	−0.0032	0.0462	−0.0046	0.3710	0.0171	−0.0029	−0.0175
1971	0.0270	0.0324	0.0014	0.3703	0.0120	0.0009	0.0141
1972	0.0532	0.0377	0.0229	0.3793	0.0143	0.0142	0.0247
1973	0.0462	0.0491	0.0416	0.3832	0.0188	0.0257	0.0017
1974	−0.0114	0.0553	0.0063	0.3723	0.0206	0.0040	−0.0359
1975	−0.0035	0.0362	−0.0191	0.3728	0.0135	−0.0120	−0.0050
1976	0.0532	0.0189	0.0280	0.3799	0.0072	0.0174	0.0286
1977	0.0627	0.0314	0.0312	0.3891	0.0122	0.0190	0.0314
1978	0.0403	0.0417	0.0483	0.3933	0.0164	0.0293	−0.0054
1979	0.0283	0.0434	0.0083	0.3840	0.0167	0.0051	0.0065

of productivity growth in twenty years. Finally, the contribution of labor input is greater than the rate of productivity growth in fifteen of the thirty-one years.

We have allocated the sources of growth in value added among the contributions of capital and labor inputs and the rate of productivity growth. We next decompose the rate of growth of capital input between rates of growth of capital stock and capital quality. Similarly, we decompose the rate of growth of labor input between rates of growth of hours worked and labor quality. Using indices of the quality of capital stock and hours worked, we can decompose the rate of growth of value added as follows:

$$\ln V(T) - \ln V(T-1) = \bar{v}_K[\ln Q_K(T) - \ln Q_K(T-1)]$$

$$+ \bar{v}_K[\ln A(T) - \ln A(T-2)]$$

$$+ \bar{v}_L[\ln Q_L(T) - \ln Q_L(T-1)]$$

$$+ \bar{v}_L[\ln H(T) - \ln H(T-1)] + \bar{v}_T.$$

The rate of growth of value added is the sum of a weighted average of growth rates of capital stock and hours worked, a weighted average of the growth rates of capital and labor quality, and the rate of productivity growth. Table 9.4 presents weighted rates of growth of the quality of capital stock and hours worked for the period 1948–1979 and weighted rates of growth of capital stock and hours worked.

The growth of capital quality is an important source of growth of capital input, but it is dominated by the growth of capital stock. Both components of the growth of capital input show positive rates of growth throughout the period 1948–1979. Growth in the quality of hours worked is an important source of growth in labor input, with positive rates of growth in every year except 1961, 1972, 1977, and 1979. By comparison, the growth in hours worked is considerably more erratic, with declines in 1949, 1954, 1957, 1958, 1961, 1970, and 1975. Only the decline that took place in 1957 failed to coincide with a decline in labor input (Table 9.3). The growth in hours worked exceeded the growth in the quality of hours worked as a source of growth in labor input in twenty of the thirty-one years from 1948 to 1979.

In Chapter 2 we decomposed the translog index of the rate of productivity growth into a weighted sum of sectoral productivity growth rates and weighted sums of rates of growth of value added, capital input, and labor input, reflecting the contributions of the reallocations of these outputs and inputs among sectors:

$$\bar{v}_T = \sum \frac{\bar{w}_j}{\bar{v}_V^j} \cdot \bar{v}_T^j + [\ln V(T) - \ln V(T-1)] - \sum \bar{w}_j [\ln V_j(T) - \ln V_j(T-1)]$$

$$+ \sum \bar{w}_j \cdot \frac{\bar{v}_K^j}{\bar{v}_V^j} \sum \bar{v}_{Kk}^j [\ln K_{kj}(T) - \ln K_{kj}(T-1)]$$

Table 9.4. Contributions to growth in aggregate input and the aggregate rate of productivity growth, 1948–1979

| Year | Quality of capital stock | Capital stock | Quality of Hours worked | Sectoral hours worked | Rates of productivity growth | Reallocations of: | | |
						Value-added	Capital input	Labor input
1949	0.0091	0.0135	0.0009	-0.0224	0.0087	-0.0112	-0.0005	-0.0027
1950	0.0051	0.0094	0.0077	0.0162	0.0583	-0.0141	-0.0017	-0.0004
1951	0.0105	0.0152	0.0075	0.0252	-0.0058	0.0053	0.0007	0.0017
1952	0.0085	0.0130	0.0115	0.0035	0.0014	-0.0090	0.0015	-0.0004
1953	0.0033	0.0097	0.0058	0.0060	0.0258	-0.0152	-0.0005	0.0008
1954	0.0039	0.0102	0.0024	-0.0209	0.0045	-0.0028	0.0012	-0.0037
1955	0.0020	0.0092	0.0016	0.0170	0.0466	-0.0142	0.0011	0.0010
1956	0.0064	0.0138	0.0033	0.0098	0.0050	-0.0029	0.0037	-0.0005
1957	0.0044	0.0114	0.0072	-0.0063	0.0027	0.0038	0.0021	-0.0023
1958	0.0024	0.0095	0.0030	-0.0195	0.0019	0.0050	0.0017	-0.0051
1959	0.0001	0.0067	0.0047	0.0169	0.0389	-0.0067	0.0007	0.0012
1960	0.0024	0.0106	0.0170	0.0031	-0.0063	-0.0031	0.0023	-0.0052
1961	0.0019	0.0094	-0.0050	-0.0030	0.0150	-0.0003	0.0017	0.0006
1962	0.0010	0.0083	0.0109	0.0114	0.0135	-0.0036	0.0015	-0.0001
1963	0.0026	0.0106	0.0019	0.0054	0.0264	-0.0017	0.0026	-0.0010
1964	0.0034	0.0115	0.0064	0.0101	0.0233	-0.0025	0.0009	-0.0009
1965	0.0044	0.0126	0.0018	0.0187	0.0159	-0.0033	0.0021	0.0003
1966	0.0057	0.0154	0.0078	0.0178	0.0033	-0.0020	0.0022	0.0012
1967	0.0066	0.0159	0.0048	0.0042	-0.0090	0.0000	0.0017	-0.0004
1968	0.0043	0.0130	0.0038	0.0105	0.0170	-0.0043	0.0005	0.0000
1969	0.0042	0.0131	0.0004	0.0164	-0.0040	-0.0013	0.0015	-0.0009
1970	0.0042	0.0129	0.0059	-0.0087	-0.0163	0.0001	0.0013	-0.0026
1971	0.0023	0.0097	0.0006	0.0003	0.0152	-0.0003	0.0006	-0.0014
1972	0.0025	0.0118	-0.0035	0.0177	0.0255	-0.0011	0.0005	-0.0002
1973	0.0045	0.0143	0.0023	0.0234	-0.0069	0.0068	0.0011	0.0006
1974	0.0051	0.0155	0.0034	0.0005	-0.0512	0.0144	0.0019	-0.0010
1975	0.0028	0.0107	0.0060	-0.0181	-0.0058	0.0049	-0.0008	-0.0034
1976	0.0011	0.0061	0.0019	0.0155	0.0310	-0.0006	-0.0017	-0.0001
1977	0.0024	0.0098	-0.0021	0.0212	0.0175	0.0144	-0.0005	0.0001
1978	0.0037	0.0127	0.0036	0.0257	-0.0092	0.0026	0.0001	0.0011
1979	0.0038	0.0129	-0.0093	0.0145	-0.0256	0.0163	0.0002	0.0157

$$-\bar{v}_K \cdot \sum \bar{v}_{Kk}[\ln K_k(T) - \ln K_k(T-1)]$$

$$+\sum \bar{w}_j \cdot \frac{\bar{v}_L^j}{\bar{v}_V^j} \sum \bar{v}_{Ll}^j [\ln L_{lj}(T) - \ln L_{lj}(T-1)]$$

$$- \bar{v}_L \cdot \sum \bar{v}_{Ll} [\ln L_l(T) - \ln L_l(T-1)].$$

Table 9.4 presents annual growth rates for the weighted sum of sectoral productivity growth and the weighted sums reflecting the contributions of the reallocations of value added, capital input, and labor input among sectors for the period 1948–1979.

The weighted sum of sectoral productivity growth rates is by far the most important component of the rate of aggregate productivity growth over the period 1948–1979. The impact of the reallocation of value added among sectors is negative for twenty of the thirty-one years, and exceeds the impact of the weighted sum of sectoral productivity growth rates in four of the thirty-one years. The impact of the reallocation of capital input on the aggregate productivity growth rate is very small in every year and is negative for only six of the thirty-one years. The impact of the reallocation of labor input is small, but not negligible, and is negative for nineteen of the thirty-one years.

We can interpret the contributions of reallocations of value added and the primary-factor inputs as measures of departures from the assumptions that underlie our model of aggregate production. These assumptions include the existence of value-added functions, for each sector, that are identical to the aggregate production function. In addition, capital and labor inputs are identical functions of their components for all sectors. Finally, all sectors pay the same prices for capital and labor inputs, so that the prices of sectoral value added are identical. The departures from these very stringent assumptions have a sizable impact on the aggregate productivity growth rate. The impact of the reallocation of value added among sectors is significant; but the contribution of the weighted sum of sectoral productivity growth rates far outweighs the effects of departures from the aggregate model.

We have analyzed the sources of growth in aggregate value added in the U.S. economy over the period 1948–1979, on the basis of annual data from the aggregate production account as presented in Tables 9.3 and 9.4. These data are summarized for the period as a whole and for seven subperiods— 1948–1953, 1953–1957, 1957–1960, 1960–1966, 1966–1969, 1969–1973, and 1973–1979—in Table 9.5. The first part of the table provides data from Table 9.3, on growth in output and inputs. The second part summarizes data, again from Table 9.3, on the contributions of capital input, labor input, and the rate of productivity growth to the growth of output. The third part presents decompositions of the contributions of capital input and labor input. The final part contains a decomposition of the aggregate productivity growth rate.

Table 9.5. Aggregate output, inputs, and productivity: rates of growth, 1948–1979

Variable	1948– 1979	1948– 1953	1953– 1957	1957– 1960	1960– 1966	1966– 1969	1969– 1973	1973– 1979
Value-added	0.0342	0.0404	0.0302	0.0274	0.0444	0.0326	0.0308	0.0283
Capital input	0.0404	0.0516	0.0389	0.0269	0.0366	0.0487	0.0414	0.0378
Labor input	0.0173	0.0202	0.0060	0.0140	0.0233	0.0218	0.0153	0.0172
Contribution of capital input	0.0156	0.0195	0.0153	0.0105	0.0145	0.0190	0.0156	0.0144
Contribution of labor input	0.0105	0.0124	0.0035	0.0084	0.0141	0.0134	0.0095	0.0105
Rate of productivity growth	0.0081	0.0085	0.0113	0.0084	0.0159	0.0002	0.0058	0.0034
Contribution of capital quality	0.0040	0.0073	0.0042	0.0016	0.0032	0.0050	0.0034	0.0031
Contribution of capital stock	0.0115	0.0122	0.0111	0.0089	0.0113	0.0140	0.0122	0.0113
Contribution of labor quality	0.0037	0.0067	0.0036	0.0083	0.0040	0.0030	0.0013	0.0006
Contribution of hours worked	0.0068	0.0057	–0.0001	0.0002	0.0101	0.0104	0.0082	0.0099
Rates of sectoral productivity growth	0.0083	0.0177	0.0147	0.0115	0.0162	0.0013	0.0044	–0.0072
Reallocation of value added	–0.0009	–0.0088	–0.0040	–0.0016	–0.0022	–0.0019	0.0014	0.0087
Reallocation of capital input	0.0009	–0.0001	0.0020	0.0015	0.0018	0.0012	0.0009	–0.0001
Reallocation of labor input	–0.0002	–0.0002	–0.0014	–0.0030	0.0000	–0.0004	–0.0009	0.0021

For the period 1948–1979, aggregate value added grew at 3.42 percent per year, and capital input grew at 4.04 percent per year, indicating that the ratio of capital input to output rose during the period. By contrast, labor input grew at only 1.73 percent per year, and the aggregate productivity growth rate averaged 0.81 percent per year. The average annual rate of growth of value added reached its maximum at 4.44 percent, during the period 1960–1966 and fell to a minimum of 2.74 percent per year during the period 1957–1960. The average annual rate of growth of capital input reached a maximum of 5.16 percent, from 1948–1953, and fell to a minimum of 2.69 percent per year in 1957–1960. The rate of growth of labor input reached its maximum during the period 1960–1966, at 2.33 percent per year and fell to a minimum of 0.60 percent per year in 1953–1957.

To analyze the sources of U.S. economic growth for the period 1948–1979, we next considered the contributions of capital and labor inputs, and the rate of productivity growth as sources of growth in value added. For the period as a whole the contribution of capital input averaged 1.56 percent per year, the contribution of labor input averaged 1.05 percent per year, and the rate of productivity growth averaged 0.81 percent per year. Capital input is the most important source of growth in six of the seven subperiods— 1948–1953, 1953–1957, 1957–1960, 1966–1969, 1969–1973, and 1973– 1979. Productivity growth is the most important source of growth during the subperiod 1960–1966. Our overall conclusion is that capital input is the most important source of growth in value added, labor input is the next most important, and productivity growth is the least important. This conclusion is supported by our analysis of growth for the period as a whole, by the data for subperiods given in Table 9.5, and by the annual data presented in Table 9.3.

We next analyze the contributions of capital and labor inputs in more detail. Data on the contributions of capital stock and its quality, and on hours worked and their quality, are presented for the period as a whole and for the subperiods in Table 9.5. For the period 1948–1979 the contribution of capital stock accounts for almost three-fourths of the contribution of capital input. This quantitative relationship between capital stock and its quality character-izes most of the period. The average contribution of capital quality reached its maximum at 0.73 percent per year in 1948–1953, and fell to a minimum of 0.16 percent per year in 1957–1960. The contribution of capital stock reached its maximum at 1.40 percent per year in 1966–1969, and fell to a minimum of 0.89 percent per year in 1957–1960.

For the period as a whole the contribution of hours worked exceeded the contribution of labor quality. For the first three subperiods—1948–1953, 1953–1957, and 1957–1960—the contribution of hours worked fell below the contribution of the quality of hours worked. For the last four subperiods the contribution of hours worked greatly exceeded the contribution of labor qual-ity. The average contribution of labor quality reached its maximum at 0.83 percent per year in 1957–1960 and declined steadily to a minimum of 0.06 percent per year in 1973–1979. The contribution of hours worked reached its maximum of 1.04 percent per year in 1966–1969, and fell to a negative 0.01 percent per year during the period 1957–1960.

Finally, to analyze the sources of the aggregate productivity growth rate, we decompose this rate into the four components given in Table 9.5—a weighted sum of sectoral productivity growth rates and reallocations of value added, capital input, and labor input among sectors. For the period 1948–1979 sectoral productivity growth rates are the predominant component of the aggregate productivity growth rate. This component averaged 0.83 percent per year, slightly exceeding the average rate of aggregate productivity growth of 0.81 percent per year. The reallocation of value added averaged a negative 0.09 percent per year, while reallocations of capital and labor inputs averaged a positive 0.09 percent per year and a negative 0.02 percent per year, respectively. Sectoral productivity growth rates reached a maximum during the period 1948–1953, at 1.77 percent per year, and fell to a negative 0.72 percent per year in 1973–1979. Reallocations of value added were negative for the first five subperiods and then became positive in 1969–1973 and 1973–1979. Reallocations of capital input were positive for every subperiod except 1948–1953 and 1973–1979, when they were negligible, and reallocations of labor input were negative for five subperiods and positive for two subperiods.

The decline in the rate of growth in value added between 1960–1966 and 1966–1969 resulted from a dramatic fall in the rate of productivity growth, from 1.59 percent during the period 1960–1966 to 0.02 percent per year during the period 1966–1969. The contribution of capital input increased substantially in these two periods, while the growth in contribution of labor input slowed slightly. The decline in aggregate productivity growth mirrored the precipitous decline in sectoral productivity growth, from an annual rate of 1.62 percent in 1960–1966 to 0.13 percent in 1966–1969.

The revival of the rate of productivity growth in 1969–1973 was offset by slower growth in the contributions of capital and labor inputs, leaving the rate of growth of value added slightly lower. The recovery of sectoral productivity growth rates, to an average annual rate of 0.44 percent per year, in 1969–1973, still well below the average of 0.83 percent per year for the period 1948–1979, was an important component of the recovery of aggregate productivity growth. Almost equally important was the change in the reallocation of value added, from −0.19 percent per year during the period 1966–1969 to 0.14 percent per year during the period 1969–1973. After 1973, sectoral productivity growth turned negative, resulting in a further reduction in aggregate productivity growth. We conclude that the decline in the aggregate productivity growth after 1966 can be attributed to a corresponding decline in sectoral productivity growth rates.

Alternative Measures of Aggregate Productivity

We provide additional perspective on our approach to measuring aggregate productivity growth by comparing our sources and methods with those of other studies. Our measure of the quantity of aggregate output is based on quantities of value added in each producing sector. Our measures of the quantities of aggregate primary-factor inputs are based on all types of primary-factor inputs. Finally, our measure of aggregate productivity growth is an index number constructed from data on prices and quantities of value added in all sectors, all types of capital input, and all types of labor input. This measure of productivity growth is based on a model of production for the economy as a whole, with the quantity of value added represented as a function of capital input, labor input, and time.

For the U.S. economy as a whole, Christensen and Jorgenson (1969; 1970; 1973a; 1973b) have employed an approach to productivity measurement that is broadly similar to ours. Their study of aggregate productivity covers the period 1929–1969 for the private sector of the U.S. economy. Christensen, Cummings, and Jorgenson (1978; 1980; 1981) have extended the estimates of Christensen and Jorgenson through 1973. As in our study, aggregate value added is defined from the producers' point of view, including the value of sales and excise taxes and including the value of subsidies. The quantity of value added, however, is measured as an index of deliveries to final demand rather than the sum of quantities of value added over industrial sectors. The quantity of labor input is divided among categories of the labor force, broken down by educational attainment but not by sex, age, employment class, or occupation.

The empirical results of Christensen, Cummings, and Jorgenson (1980) for the period 1948–1973 are very similar to ours. For this period their estimate of the average growth rate of value added for the private domestic sector of the U.S. economy is 3.95 percent per year; by comparison our estimate of the rate of growth for the civilian sector of the U.S. economy is 3.56 percent per year. The two estimates are not precisely comparable, since Christensen, Cummings, and Jorgenson do not include government sectors in their measure of value added. They estimate the average growth rate of capital input at 4.10 percent per year for the period 1948–1973; our estimate for this period is 4.18 percent per year. These estimates are for the same sectors of the U.S. economy, since neither set of estimates includes capital input for the government sectors. Christensen, Cummings, and Jorgenson estimate the average growth rate of labor input at 1.61 percent per year, while our estimate is 1.73 percent per year. Finally, their estimate of the rate of productivity growth is 1.33 percent per year, while our estimate is 0.93 percent per year. Again, the two estimates for labor input and the rate of productivity growth are not precisely comparable, since we include labor input for the government sectors and they do not.

Christensen, Cummings, and Jorgenson (1980) have presented estimates of aggregate productivity growth for Canada, France, Germany, Italy, Japan, Korea, the Netherlands, and the United Kingdom, as well as for the United States. Their estimates cover various periods beginning after 1947 and ending in 1973; the estimates cover the period 1960–1973 for all countries. Groes and Bjerregaard (1978) have developed comparable data for Denmark for the period 1950–1972. On the basis of the close correspondence between our results for the U.S. economy as a whole and those of Christensen, Cummings, and Jorgenson, we conclude that it is appropriate to compare our aggregate results with those for the other countries presented in their study.

The Bureau of Labor Statistics (1983) has employed private business product as a measure of value added in the U.S. economy as a whole. This measure is obtained from the gross national product by excluding output originating in general government, government enterprises, owner-occupied housing, the rest of the world, and households and institutions, as well as the statistical discrepancy. The resulting measure of value added is gross of depreciation. This has the important advantage of avoiding the confounding of measures of output and capital input that we analyzed in Chapter 5. We have summarized the differences between our methodology for measuring labor and capital inputs and that of the Bureau of Labor Statistics in Chapters 3 and 4.

Denison (1985) employs an approach to production based on value added at the economy-wide level. He uses national income as a measure of value added. This measure excludes capital consumption allowances and indirect business taxes. His measure of capital input is based on the "net earnings" of capital, also excluding business taxes. The prices and quantities of inputs and outputs employed in Denison's measure of productivity satisfy the accounting identity between the value of output and the value of input, but the corresponding model of production involves net value added, so that outputs and inputs are confounded by including capital input in both categories. We conclude that the quantity of net value added employed by Denison cannot serve as an appropriate starting point for productivity measurement at the aggregate level.

Denison (1985) has provided estimates of aggregate productivity for the U.S. economy, covering the period 1929–1982. Earlier, Denison (1967) presented comparable estimates at the aggregate level for Belgium, Denmark, France, Germany, the Netherlands, Norway, the United Kingdom, and the United States, for the period 1950–1962. Walters (1968, 1970) has given estimates for Canada for the period 1950–1967, Dholakis (1974) has given estimates for India for the period 1948–1969, Denison and Chung (1976) have given estimates for Japan for the period 1952–1971, and Kim and Park (1985) have given estimates for Korea for the period 1963–1982 that are closely comparable to Denison's estimates for the United States. We have summarized differences between our methodology and that of Denison in Chapters 3–5. A detailed comparison of the results of Christensen and Jorgenson (1969, 1970, 1973a, 1973b) and those of Denison (1967) is given by Jorgenson and Griliches (1972a).

For the U.S. economy as a whole, Kendrick (1961, 1973), Grossman and Kendrick (1980), and Kendrick (1983) have employed an approach to the measurement of value added through summation over the growth rates of quantities of value added in all sectors, with weights that change periodically. Similarly, the corresponding estimates of the growth rates of capital and labor inputs are constructed by summing the corresponding quantities over all sectors, with periodically changing weights, and by taking unweighted sums of the growth rates of quantities for all industrial sectors. We have compared our methodology at the sectoral level with that of Kendrick in Chapters 3–5. Kendrick employs unweighted sums of capital stock and hours worked as measures of capital and labor inputs at the sectoral level. At the aggregate level he employs unweighted sums as a variant of his principal estimates, which are based on weighted sums that depend on property and labor compensation by sector. Christensen and Jorgenson and Denison disaggregate capital and labor inputs for the economy as a whole, by categories of capital stock and hours worked, but not by sector.

Christensen, Cummings, and Jorgenson (1980), the Bureau of Labor Statistics (1983), and Kendrick (1983) all employ measures of value added for the U.S. economy as a whole that are gross of depreciation. These measures avoid the confounding of output and capital input that characterizes the measures used in Kendrick's (1973) earlier work and in all of Denison's studies. We conclude that Denison's (1985) concept of value added net of depreciation has been displaced by value added gross of depreciation as a starting point for studies of productivity at the aggregate level. A detailed comparison of our results with those of the Bureau of Labor Statistics, Denison, and Kendrick is presented by the Bureau of Labor Statistics (1983).

A very important difference between our methodology at the sectoral level and Kendrick's (1973, 17) methodology is that his approach is based on the existence of a value-added function for each sector. Kendrick employs identical functions to represent capital inputs for all sectors—unweighted sums of capital stocks in each sector. Similarly, he represents labor inputs for all sectors as unweighted sums of hours worked in each sector. Under these assumptions there exists an aggregate production function with the quantity of value added represented as a function of capital and labor inputs. Capital and labor inputs, in turn, are represented as unweighted sums of capital stocks and hours worked in all sectors, respectively. This is one of the two variant measures of capital and labor inputs employed by Kendrick (1973) at the aggregate level. This variant is consistent with his sectoral measures of capital and labor inputs.

Our measure of the rate of aggregate productivity growth depends on sectoral productivity growth rates and on terms that reflect changes in the distribution of value added, capital input, and labor input among sectors. Sectoral productivity growth rates are weighted by ratios of the value of output in the corresponding sector to the sum of value added in all sectors. This formula was originally proposed by Domar (1961) for a model with two producing sectors, each characterized by a linear logarithmic production function with output as a function of intermediate input from the other sector, capital input, labor input, and time. Domar's approach has been extended by Hulten (1978) to an arbitrary number of producing sectors without using the assumption that the production function in each sector is linear logarithmic. Both Domar and Hulten assume that prices of intermediate inputs are the same for producing and receiving sectors and that the prices of capital and labor inputs are the same for all sectors. Under these assumptions the rate of productivity growth for the economy as a whole does not depend on the distribution of inputs among sectors. Hulten's formula has been implemented for ten sectors of the Japanese economy for the period 1955–1971 by Nishimizu (1974) and by Nishimizu and Hulten (1978).

Domar has analyzed an approach to aggregate productivity measurement introduced by Leontief (1953). In Chapter 5 we have described Leontief's approach to the measurement of sectoral productivity. It is based on an average of weighted relative changes in ratios of intermediate and labor inputs to output, with weights that depend on quantities of intermediate and labor inputs. For the economy as a whole, Leontief averages the weighted relative changes over all sectors. Domar points out that the appropriate measure of the aggregate rate of productivity growth is a weighted sum, rather than a weighted average; Leontief's approach fails to eliminate deliveries to intermediate demand in the process of aggregating over sectors.

One of the curiosities of the literature on productivity measurement is that Leontief's approach has been reintroduced by the Statistical Office of the United Nations (1968), Watanabe (1971), Star (1974), and Ezaki (1978). Watanabe advocates weights for sectoral productivity growth rates based on the ratio of the value of output in each sector to the sum of the values of outputs in all sectors. Star (1974, 128–129) advocates the use of this same weighting system. Ezaki, Star, and Watanabe have failed to implement correctly the approach to aggregation over sectors we have presented in Chapter 2.

Our measure of the rate of aggregate productivity growth depends on changes in the distribution of value added, capital input, and labor input among sectors, as well as sectoral productivity growth rates. The contribution of changes in the distribution of capital and labor inputs among sectors to the rate of productivity growth for the U.S. economy as a whole has been measured by Kendrick (1973) for thirty-four industry groups for the period 1948 to 1966. The contribution of these changes to the rate of productivity growth for the U.S. manufacturing sector has been measured by Massell (1961) for seventeen industry groups for the period 1946 to 1957. Denison (1985) has measured the contribution of changes in the distribution of capital and labor inputs between farm and nonfarm sectors of the U.S. economy for the period 1929 to 1982 and of labor input between self-employment and other employment within the nonfarm sector for the same period.

Aggregate Substitution

In previous sections we have presented a measure of the rate of aggregate productivity growth based on a model of production for the economy. The point of departure for this model is a translog production function. Our next objective is to characterize the distribution of the value of output between capital and labor inputs and changes in this distribution over time. To describe the distribution of the value of output, we first describe the relative distribution in terms of the value shares of capital and labor inputs. Necessary conditions for producer equilibrium are given by equalities between the value shares of each input and the elasticity of aggregate output with respect to that input. Under constant returns to scale the elasticities and the value shares for capital and labor inputs sum to unity.

As before, we characterize the implications of patterns of substitution, for the distribution of the value of output in terms of share elasticities, defined as changes in value shares with respect to proportional changes in quantities of inputs. If a share elasticity is positive, the value share increases with an increase in the quantity of the corresponding input; if a share elasticity is negative, the value share decreases with the quantity of the input; if a share elasticity is zero, the value share is independent of the quantity of the input.

To characterize the changes in patterns of substitution, we first introduce the rate of productivity growth, defined as the rate of growth of value added, holding capital and labor inputs constant. To describe the implications of changes in productivity for patterns of substitution, we introduce biases of productivity growth, defined as changes in the value shares of capital and labor inputs with respect to time. If a bias is positive, the corresponding value share increases with time; if a bias is negative, the value share decreases with time; if a bias is zero, the value share is independent of time. Finally, to describe changes in the rate of productivity growth we introduce its acceleration. If the acceleration is positive, negative, or zero, the rate of productivity growth respectively increases with time, decreases with time, or is independent of time.

Our aggregate model of production is based on a production function, say F, characterized by constant returns to scale:

$$V = F(K, L, T),$$

where V, K, and L are value added, capital input, and labor input, and T is time. Capital and labor inputs are functions of supplies of capital and labor inputs that are characterized by constant returns to scale:

$$K = K(K_1, K_2,..., K_p),$$

$$L = L(L_1, L_2,..., L_q).$$

Where p_V, p_K, and p_L denote the prices of value added, capital input, and labor input, we can define the shares of capital and labor inputs, say v_K and v_L, in value added by

$$v_K = \frac{p_K K}{p_V V},$$

$$v_L = \frac{p_L L}{p_V V}.$$

Necessary conditions for producer equilibrium are given by equalities between value shares of capital and labor input and elasticities of the quantity of value added with respect to each input:

$$v_K = \frac{\partial \ln V}{\partial \ln K} (K, L, T),$$

$$v_L = \frac{\partial \ln V}{\partial \ln L} (K, L, T).$$

Under constant returns to scale both the elasticities and the value shares sum to unity. Finally, we can define the rate of productivity growth v_T as the rate of growth of the quantity of value added with respect to time, holding capital and labor inputs constant:

$$v_T = \frac{\partial \ln V}{\partial T} \ (K, L, T).$$

Given the production function F, we can differentiate logarithmically a second time with respect to the logarithms of capital and labor inputs to obtain share elasticities with respect to quantity as functions of these inputs and time:

$$u_{KK} = \frac{\partial^2 \ln V}{\partial \ln K^2} \ (K, L, T) = \frac{\partial v_K}{\partial \ln K} \ ,$$

$$u_{KL} = \frac{\partial^2 \ln V}{\partial \ln K \, \partial \ln L} \ (K, L, T) = \frac{\partial v_K}{\partial \ln L} \ ,$$

$$= \frac{\partial^2 \ln V}{\partial \ln L \, \partial \ln K} \ (K, L, T) = \frac{\partial v_L}{\partial \ln K} \ ,$$

$$u_{LL} = \frac{\partial^2 \ln V}{\partial \ln L^2} \ (K, L, T) = \frac{\partial v_L}{\partial \ln L} \ ,$$

where share elasticities with respect to quantity are symmetric. Under constant returns to scale the sum of the share elasticities for a given value share is equal to zero:

$$u_{KK} + u_{KL} = 0 \ ,$$

$$u_{LK} + u_{LL} = 0 \ ,$$

Like the symmetry restrictions, these restrictions hold for all values of capital and labor inputs and time.

Similarly, given the production function, we can differentiate logarithmically a second time with respect to time and with respect to the logarithms of capital and labor inputs. We obtain biases of productivity growth with respect to quantity as functions of these inputs and time:

$$u_{TK} = \frac{\partial^2 \ln V}{\partial T \, \partial \ln K} \ (K, L, T) = \frac{\partial v_K}{\partial T} \ ,$$

$$= \frac{\partial^2 \ln V}{\partial \ln K \, \partial T} \ (K, L, T) = \frac{\partial v_T}{\partial \ln K} \ ,$$

$$u_{TL} = \frac{\partial^2 \ln V}{\partial T \, \partial \ln L} \; (K, L, T) = \frac{\partial v_L}{\partial T} \, ,$$

$$= \frac{\partial^2 \ln V}{\partial \ln L \, \partial T} \; (K, L, T) = \frac{\partial v_T}{\partial \ln L} \, .$$

The biases with respect to quantity are symmetric. Under constant returns to scale the sum of the biases is equal to zero:

$$u_{TK} + u_{TL} = 0.$$

Like the symmetry restrictions, this restriction holds for all values of capital and labor inputs and time.

Finally, given the production function, we can differentiate a second time with respect to time to obtain the acceleration of productivity growth as a function of capital input, labor input, and time:

$$u_{TT} = \frac{\partial^2 \ln V}{\partial T^2} \; (K, L, T) = \frac{\partial v_T}{\partial T} \; (K, L, T).$$

The value shares and rate of productivity growth are functions of capital and labor inputs and time. These functions can be expressed in terms of the first-order partial derivatives of the production function:

$$v_K = \frac{\partial \ln F}{\partial \ln K} = \frac{K}{F} \frac{\partial F}{\partial K} \, ,$$

$$v_L = \frac{\partial \ln F}{\partial \ln L} = \frac{L}{F} \frac{\partial F}{\partial L} \, ,$$

$$v_T = \frac{\partial \ln F}{\partial \ln T} = \frac{T}{F} \frac{\partial F}{\partial T} \, .$$

If the production function F is increasing in capital and labor inputs, the value shares are nonnegative. To check these restrictions for particular values of capital and labor inputs and time, we can compute the value shares and verify that they have the right sign.

Similarly, the share elasticities can be expressed in terms of the second-order partial derivatives of the production function with respect to capital and labor inputs:[4]

$$u_{KK} = \frac{\partial 2 \ln F}{\partial \ln K^2} = \frac{K^2}{F} \cdot \frac{\partial^2 F}{\partial K^2} - v_K(v_K - 1) \, ,$$

$$u_{KL} = \frac{\partial^2 \ln F}{\partial \ln K \, \partial \ln L} = \frac{K \cdot L}{F} \cdot \frac{\partial^2 F}{\partial K \, \partial L} - v_K v_L \, ,$$

$$u_{LL} = \frac{\partial 2 \ln F}{\partial \ln L^2} = \frac{L^2}{F} \frac{\partial^2 F}{\partial L^2} - v_L(v_L - 1) \, .$$

Denoting the Hessian matrix of second-order partial derivatives of the production function by H, we can represent the matrix of share elasticities, say U, in the form

$$U = \frac{1}{F} \, N \cdot H \cdot N - vv' + V \, ,$$

where

$$N = \begin{bmatrix} K & 0 \\ 0 & L \end{bmatrix}, \quad V = \begin{bmatrix} v_K & 0 \\ 0 & v_L \end{bmatrix}, \quad v = \begin{bmatrix} v_K \\ v_L \end{bmatrix} .$$

Under concavity of the production function the Hessian matrix H is negative semidefinite for all values of capital and labor inputs and time. The matrix

$$\frac{1}{F} \cdot N \cdot H \cdot N = U + vv' - V$$

is negative semidefinite if and only if the Hessian matrix is negative semidefinite. This matrix can be expressed in terms of its Cholesky factorization:

$$U + vv' - V = L \cdot D \cdot L' \, ,$$

where L is a unit lower triangular matrix and D is a diagonal matrix with nonpositive elements. To check these restrictions for particular values of capital and labor inputs and time, we compute the matrix of share elasticities; using the corresponding computed value shares we can represent the matrix U + vv'−V in terms of its Cholesky factorization and verify that the diagonal elements of the matrix D are nonpositive.

Finally, consider restrictions on the form of the production function associated with restrictions on patterns of productivity growth. Under Hicks neutrality the production function can be represented in the form

$$V = A(T) \cdot W(K, L) \, ,$$

where W is aggregate input, homogeneous of degree one in capital and labor inputs, and A is a function of time. The rate of productivity growth is independent of capital and labor inputs, depending only on time:

$$v_T = \frac{d \ln A(T)}{dT} \, ,$$

so that biases of productivity growth are zero for both inputs:

$$u_{KT} = u_{LT} = 0 \, .$$

Under Harrod neutrality the production function can be represented in the form

$$V = F[K, \ G(L, \ T)] = F[K, \ A(T) \cdot L] \, ,$$

where F is homogeneous of degree one in capital and labor inputs and, as before, A is a function of time. To derive restrictions on value shares and the rate and biases of productivity growth, we first express the value share of labor input and the rate of productivity growth in the form

$$v_L = \frac{\partial \ln V}{\partial \ln L} = \frac{\partial \ln F}{\partial \ln G} \cdot \frac{\partial \ln G}{\partial \ln L} \, ,$$

$$v_T = \frac{\partial \ln V}{\partial T} = \frac{\partial \ln F}{\partial \ln G} \cdot \frac{\partial \ln G}{\partial T} \, .$$

Second, we express the share elasticity and the bias of productivity growth with respect to capital input in the form

$$u_{KL} = \frac{\partial^2 \ln F}{\partial \ln K \, \partial \ln G} \cdot \frac{\partial \ln G}{\partial \ln L} = r_K v_L \, ,$$

$$u_{KT} = \frac{\partial^2 \ln F}{\partial \ln K \, \partial \ln G} \cdot \frac{\partial \ln G}{\partial T} = r_K v_T \, ,$$

where r_K is a function of capital and labor inputs and time:

$$r_K = \frac{\dfrac{\partial^2 \ln F}{\partial \ln K \, \partial \ln G}}{\dfrac{\partial \ln F}{\partial \ln G}} \, .$$

Under Solow neutrality the production function can be represented in the form

$$v = F[G(K, T), L] = F[A(T) \cdot K, L] \,,$$

where F is homogeneous of degree one in capital and labor inputs and A is a function of time. The elasticity of the share of capital with respect to labor and the bias of productivity growth with respect to labor take the form

$$u_{LK} = r_L v_K \,,$$

$$u_{LT} = r_L v_T \,,$$

where r_L is a function of capital and labor inputs and time:

$$r_L = \frac{\dfrac{\partial^2 \ln F}{\partial \ln L \, \partial \ln G}}{\dfrac{\partial \ln F}{\partial \ln G}} \,.$$

Any two of the three types of neutrality of productivity growth—Hicks neutrality, Harrod neutrality, Solow neutrality—imply the third; under these restrictions the production function is linear logarithmic in value added, capital input, and labor input, with an arbitrary function of time representing the level of productivity:

$$\ln V = \alpha_K \ln K + \alpha_L \ln L + \ln A(T) \,.$$

Aggregate Econometric Model

To formulate an econometric model of aggregate production, we consider a specific form of the production function F:

$$V = \exp[\alpha_0 + \alpha_K \ln K + \alpha_L \ln L + \alpha_T T + \frac{1}{2} \beta_{KK} (\ln K)^2$$

$$+ \beta_{KL} \ln K \cdot \ln L + \beta_{KT} \ln K \cdot T + \frac{1}{2} \beta_{LL} (\ln L)^2$$

$$+ \beta_{LT} \ln \cdot L \cdot T + \frac{1}{2} \beta_{TT} T^2] \,.$$

We refer to this form as the translog production function. Since the share elasticities and the biases and acceleration of productivity growth are constant, we can also characterize this function as the constant share elasticity, or CSE, production function, indicating the interpretation of the fixed parameters.

The translog production function is characterized by constant returns to scale if and only if the parameters satisfy the conditions

$$\alpha_K + \alpha_L = 1 \;,$$

$$\beta_{KK} + \beta_{KL} = 0 \;,$$

$$\beta_{KL} + \beta_{LL} = 0 \;,$$

$$\beta_{KT} + \beta_{LT} = 0 \;.$$

The value shares of capital and labor can be expressed as

$$v_K = \alpha_K + \beta_{KK} \ln K + \beta_{KL} \ln L + \beta_{KT} T \;,$$

$$v_L = \alpha_L + \beta_{KL} \ln K + \beta_{LL} \ln L + \beta_{LT} T \;.$$

Similarly, the rate of productivity growth can be expressed as

$$v_T = \alpha_T + \beta_{KT} \ln K + \beta_{LT} \ln L + \beta_{TT} T \;.$$

Our final step in considering a specific form for the production function F is to derive restrictions on the parameters implied by the fact that the production function is increasing and concave in capital and labor inputs. Setting the inputs equal to unity and time equal to zero, we obtain necessary conditions for the production function to be increasing:

$$\alpha_K \geq 0 \;,$$

$$\alpha_L \geq 0 \;.$$

Concavity of the production function F implies that the matrix of second-order partial derivatives with respect to the two inputs is negative semidefinite, so that the matrix $\mathbf{U} + \mathbf{v v'} - \mathbf{V}$ is negative semidefinite, where[5]

$$\frac{1}{\mathbf{F}} \cdot \mathbf{N} \cdot \mathbf{H} \cdot \mathbf{N} = \mathbf{U} + \mathbf{v v'} - \mathbf{V} \;.$$

For the translog production function the matrix of share elasticities $\mathbf{U}$ is constant. Since the production function is increasing in both inputs, the value shares are nonnegative and sum to unity. Without violating these conditions we can set the matrix $\mathbf{vv'} - \mathbf{V}$ equal to zero. Since this matrix is negative semidefinite, a necessary and sufficient condition for the matrix $\mathbf{U} + \mathbf{vv'} - \mathbf{V}$ to be negative semidefinite is that the matrix $\mathbf{U}$ is negative semidefinite.

To impose concavity on the translog production function the matrix $\mathbf{U}$ of constant share elasticities can be represented in terms of its Cholesky factorization. Under constant returns to scale there is a one-to-one transformation between the constant share elasticities and the parameter describing the Cholesky factorization. This factorization takes the form

$$
\begin{bmatrix} \beta_{KK} & \beta_{KL} \\ \beta_{KL} & \beta_{LL} \end{bmatrix} = \begin{bmatrix} 1 & 0 \\ -1 & 1 \end{bmatrix} \begin{bmatrix} \delta & 0 \\ 0 & 0 \end{bmatrix} \begin{bmatrix} 1 & -1 \\ 0 & 1 \end{bmatrix} ,
$$

$$
= \delta \begin{bmatrix} 1 & -1 \\ -1 & 1 \end{bmatrix} .
$$

The matrix of share elasticities is negative semidefinite if and only if the parameter δ is nonpositive.

Using the interpretation of the parameters of the translog production function as share elasticities and biases of productivity growth, we can derive restrictions on these parameters associated with restrictions on patterns of productivity growth. Under Hicks neutrality the biases are zero for both inputs:

$$
\alpha_{KT} = \alpha_{LT} = 0 .
$$

To derive the restrictions corresponding to Harrod neutrality, we can set both inputs equal to unity and time equal to zero. Evaluating the share elasticity of labor and the bias with respect to capital input, we obtain necessary conditions for Harrod neutrality:

$$
\beta_{KL} = \rho_K \alpha_L ,
$$

$$
\beta_{KT} = \rho_K \alpha_T ,
$$

where the parameter ρ_K is constant. The necessary and sufficient condition for Harrod neutrality is that the production function is linear logarithmic in capital and labor inputs, so that

$$
\ln V = \alpha_0 + \alpha_K \ln K + \alpha_L \ln L + \alpha_T T + \beta_{TT} T^2
$$

Similarly, necessary conditions for Solow neutrality are

$$\beta_{KL} = \rho_L \, \alpha_K \, ,$$

$$\beta_{LT} = \rho_L \, \alpha_T \, ,$$

where the parameter ρ_L is constant. The necessary and sufficient condition for Solow neutrality is that the production function is linear logarithmic. Under this condition productivity growth is Hicks neutral, Harrod neutral, and Solow neutral.

We can also consider specific forms for capital and labor inputs as functions of supplies of capital and labor inputs. For example, the quantity of capital input can be expressed as a translog function of all types of capital input:

$$K = \exp[\alpha_1 \ln K_1 + \alpha_2 \ln K_2 + ... + \alpha_p \ln K_p$$

$$+ \frac{1}{2} \beta_{11}(\ln K_1)^2 + \beta_{12} \ln K_1 \ln K_2 + ... + \frac{1}{2} \beta_{pp}(\ln K_p)^2] \, .$$

The quantity of capital input is characterized by constant returns to scale if and only if the parameters satisfy the conditions

$$\alpha_1 + \alpha_2 + ... + \alpha_p = 1,$$

$$\beta_{11} + \beta_{12} + ... + \beta_{1p} = 0,$$

...

$$\beta_{1p} + \beta_{2p} + ... + \beta_{pp} = 0.$$

The shares of each type of capital input in aggregate capital input can be expressed as

$$v_{Kk} = \alpha_k + \beta_{1k} \ln K_1 + ... + \beta_{kp} \ln K_p \, , \qquad (k = 1, 2,..., p).$$

Considering data on capital input at any two discrete points of time, we can express the growth rate of capital input as a weighted average of growth rates of each type of capital input, with weights given by average value shares:

$$\ln K(T) - \ln K(T-1) = \sum \bar{v}_{Kk} [\ln K_k(T) - \ln K_k (T-1)],$$

where

$$\bar{v}_{Kk} = \frac{1}{2}[v_{Kk}(T) + v_{Kk}(T-1)], \qquad\qquad (k = 1, 2,..., p).$$

Similarly, if labor input is a translog function of its components, we can express the growth rate of labor input in the form

$$\ln L(T) - \ln L(T-1) = \sum \bar{v}_{Ll} [\ln L_l(T) - \ln L_l(T-1)] ,$$

where

$$\bar{v}_{Ll} = \frac{1}{2}[v_{Ll}(T) + v_{Ll}(T-1)], \qquad\qquad (l = 1, 2,..., q).$$

We refer to these expressions for capital and labor inputs, K and L, as translog indices of capital and labor inputs.

The product of price and quantity indices must be equal to the corresponding values. For example, we can define the price index of capital input as the ratio of the value of capital input to the translog quantity index. The price index of labor input can be defined in a strictly analogous way. The resulting price indices of capital and labor inputs can be determined from data on prices and quantities at any two discrete points of time.

We obtain data on the value shares of capital and labor inputs $\{v_{Kk}, v_{Ll}\}$ from the price and quantity data on capital and labor inputs presented in Chapter 8. Data on the quantity of capital and labor inputs K and L, the corresponding prices, p_K and p_L, and the value shares, v_K and v_L, are obtained from these same price and quantity data. The average rate of productivity growth for any two periods, $\bar{v}_T$, can be computed from the price and quantity data, using the translog index number:

$$\bar{v}_T = \ln V(T) - \ln V(T-1) - \bar{v}_K [\ln K(T) - \ln K(T-1)]$$

$$- \bar{v}_L [\ln L(T) - \ln (T-1)] ,$$

where

$$\bar{v}_T = \frac{1}{2}[v_T(T) + v_T(T-1)] ,$$

and where the average value shares in the two periods are given by

$$\bar{v}_K = \frac{1}{2}[v_K(T) + v_K(T-1)] ,$$

$$\bar{v}_L = \frac{1}{2}[v_L(T) + v_L(T-1)] .$$

The rate of productivity growth v_T is not directly observable. The average rate of productivity growth $\bar{v}_T$ and the average value shares $\bar{v}_K$ and $\bar{v}_L$ can be written in the form

$$\bar{v}_K = \alpha_K + \beta_{KK} \overline{\ln K} + \beta_{KL} \overline{\ln L} + \beta_{KT} \cdot \bar{T} ,$$

$$\bar{v}_L = \alpha_L + \beta_{KL} \overline{\ln K} + \beta_{LL} \overline{\ln L} + \beta_{LT} \cdot \bar{T} ,$$

$$\bar{v}_T = \alpha_T + \beta_{KT} \overline{\ln K} + \beta_{LT} \overline{\ln L} + \beta_{TT} \cdot \bar{T} ,$$

where the average values of capital and labor inputs and time in the two periods are given by

$$\overline{\ln K} = \frac{1}{2}[\ln K(T) + \ln K(T-1)] ,$$

$$\overline{\ln L} = \frac{1}{2}[\ln L(T) + \ln L(T-1)] ,$$

$$\bar{T} = \frac{1}{2}[T + (T-1)] = T - \frac{1}{2} ,$$

and $\{\alpha_K, \alpha_L, \alpha_T; \beta_{KK}, \beta_{KL}, \beta_{LL,} \beta_{KT}, \beta_{LT}, \beta_{TT}\}$ are fixed parameters.

To formulate an econometric model of production, we add unobservable random disturbances to the equations for the value shares and rate of productivity growth, treating the fixed parameters as unknowns to be estimated.[6]

We assume, as before, that the disturbances in all four equations have expected value zero and that the covariance matrix of the disturbances is the same for all observations. Since the two value shares sum to unity, the corresponding disturbances sum to zero and the rank of the covariance matrix is at most two. We assume that the matrix corresponding to the value share of capital and the rate of productivity growth has rank two. Finally, we assume that the disturbances corresponding to distinct observations in the same or distinct equations are uncorrelated.

Since the rate of productivity growth v_T is not directly observable, the equation for productivity growth can be written

$$\bar{v}_T = \alpha_T + \beta_{KT}\overline{\ln K} + \beta_{LT}\overline{\ln L} + \beta_{TT} \cdot \bar{T} + \bar{\varepsilon}_T \, ,$$

where ε_T is the disturbance in the equation for the rate of productivity growth and $\bar{\varepsilon}_T$ is the average disturbance in two periods:

$$\bar{\varepsilon}_T = \frac{1}{2}[\varepsilon_T(T) + \varepsilon_T(T-1)] \, .$$

Similarly, the equations for the value shares of capital and labor inputs can be written

$$\bar{v}_K = \alpha_K + \beta_{KK}\overline{\ln K} + \beta_{KL}\overline{\ln L} + \beta_{KT} \cdot \bar{T} + \bar{\varepsilon}_K \, ,$$

$$\bar{v}_L = \alpha_L + \beta_{KL}\overline{\ln K} + \beta_{LL}\overline{\ln L} + \beta_{LT} \cdot \bar{T} + \bar{\varepsilon}_L \, ,$$

where ε_K and ε_L are the disturbances in the equations for the value shares of capital and labor inputs and

$$\bar{\varepsilon}_K = \frac{1}{2}[\varepsilon_K(T) + \varepsilon_K(T-1)] \, ,$$

$$\bar{\varepsilon}_L = \frac{1}{2}[\varepsilon_L(T) + \varepsilon_L(T-1)] \, .$$

The average value shares $\bar{v}_K$ and $\bar{v}_L$ sum to unity, so that the average disturbances, $\bar{\varepsilon}_K$ and $\bar{\varepsilon}_L$, sum to zero.

The covariance matrix of the average disturbances for the value share of capital and the rate of productivity growth for all observations has the Kronecker product form

$$V \begin{bmatrix} \bar{\varepsilon}_K(2) \\ \bar{\varepsilon}_K(3) \\ \vdots \\ \bar{\varepsilon}_K(N) \\ \bar{\varepsilon}_T(2) \\ \vdots \\ \bar{\varepsilon}_T(N) \end{bmatrix} = \Sigma \otimes \Omega \, ,$$

where Ω is a Laurent matrix, as before, and Σ is a positive definite matrix. Since Ω is a positive definite matrix, we can transform the data on the average rate of productivity growth, average value shares, and average values of the variables that appear on the right side of each equation to obtain equations with uncorrelated disturbances. The covariance matrix of the transformed disturbances has the Kronecker product form

$$(I \otimes D^{1/2}L')(\Sigma \otimes \Omega)(I \otimes D^{1/2}L')' = \Sigma \otimes I .$$

To estimate the unknown parameters of the translog production function, we combine the equation for the value share of capital with the equation for the rate of productivity growth. We derive estimates of the parameters of the equation for the share of labor, using the restrictions on these parameters given above. The complete model involves five unknown parameters. A total of five additional parameters can be estimated as functions of these parameters, given the restrictions. As before, we use an estimator based on the nonlinear three-stage least squares estimator introduced by Jorgenson and Laffont (1974) and test statistics introduced by Gallant and Jorgenson (1979).

Our estimates of the unknown parameters of the econometric model of production and productivity growth for the economy as a whole are based on annual time series data, given in Chapter 8 and earlier in this chapter for the period 1948–1979. There are thirty observations for each behavioral equation, as before, so that the number of degrees of freedom available for tests of restrictions implied by patterns of productivity growth is fifty-five.

Under Hicks neutrality the biases of productivity growth are zero, so that

$$\beta_{KT} = \beta_{LT} = 0.$$

This set of restrictions involves only one independent restriction, since the sum of the biases is zero. Under this restriction there are four unknown parameters to be estimated. Necessary conditions for Harrod neutrality take the form

$$\beta_{KL} = \rho_K \, \alpha_L \, ,$$

$$\beta_{KT} = \rho_K \, \alpha_T \, .$$

Similarly, necessary conditions for Solow neutrality take the form

$$\beta_{KL} = \rho_L \, \alpha_K \, ,$$

$$\beta_{LT} = \rho_L \, \alpha_T \, .$$

Each set of restrictions involves a set of two restrictions with the introduction of one new parameter, so that four parameters remain to be estimated. Given these restrictions the necessary and sufficient condition for Harrod neutrality is

$$\rho_K = 0 \, .$$

Under this restriction the production function is linear logarithmic in capital and labor inputs, so that productivity growth is also Hicks neutral and Solow neutral. Only three unknown parameters remain to be estimated.

Our proposed test procedure is presented in diagrammatic form in Figure 9.1. We first propose to test restrictions derived from Hicks neutrality, Harrod neutrality, and Solow neutrality. Next we propose to test the condition implied by a linear logarithmic aggregate production function. To control the overall level of significance among the four tests, we assign a level of significance of 0.0125 to each test. The probability of a false rejection for one test among the set of four tests is less than or equal to 0.05, by the Bonferroni inequality.[7] Critical values for our test statistics, based on the distribution of chi-squared, are given in Table 9.6. With the aid of these critical values, the reader can evaluate the results of our tests, as before, for alternative levels of significance or for alternative allocations of the overall level of significance among tests. Test statistics for all four hypotheses are given in Table 9.7.

Considering the test statistics for Hicks neutrality, Harrod neutrality, and Solow neutrality, we employ a critical value of 6.46 for chi-squared with one degree of freedom at a level of significance of 0.0125. The second step in our procedure is to test the condition that the aggregate production function is linear logarithmic. This condition implies that the share elasticities and the biases are equal to zero. We employ the same critical value for chi-squared with one degree of freedom as before. At the level of significance of 0.0125 we cannot reject the hypothesis that the aggregate production function is linear logarithmic. Our overall conclusion is that the aggregate production function can be represented in the form proposed by Cobb and Douglas (1928). Aggregate technical change can be regarded, equivalently, as Hicks neutral, Harrod neutral, or Solow neutral.

Table 9.8 presents estimates of the parameters of the aggregate model of production. The parameters α_K and α_L can be interpreted as average value

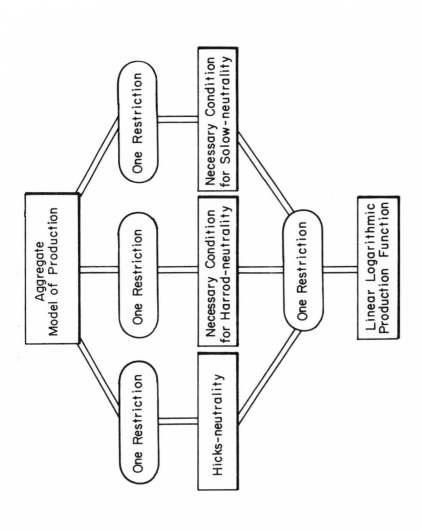

Figure 9.1. Tests of restrictions on aggregate productivity growth

Table 9.6. Critical values of chi-squared

Degrees of freedom	Level of significance				
	0.10	0.05	0.01	0.005	0.001
1	2.71	3.84	6.63	7.88	10.83

Table 9.7. Test statistics for restrictions on aggregate productivity growth

	Hypothesis			
	Hicks neutrality	Harrod neutrality	Solow neutrality	Linear logarithmic production
Test statistic	0.0402	0.1896	0.0109	1.4044

shares of capital and labor inputs. Similarly, the parameter α_T can be interpreted as the average rate of productivity growth. To interpret the estimates of these parameters it is useful to recall that if the production function is increasing in capital input and labor input, the average value shares are nonnegative. These conditions are satisfied by our estimates.

The parameters β_{KK}, β_{KL}, and β_{LL} can be interpreted as constant share elasticities. These parameters describe the implications of patterns of substitution for the relative distribution of output between capital and labor inputs. A positive share elasticity implies that the corresponding value share increases with an increase in quantity; a negative share elasticity implies that the value share decreases with an increase in quantity; a share elasticity equal to zero implies that the corresponding value share is independent of quantity. Estimates of these parameters are derived by representing the matrix of constant share elasticities U in terms of its Cholesky factorization and imposing the necessary and sufficient condition for concavity, namely that the parameter δ from the Cholesky factorization is nonpositive. This restriction requires that all share elasticities be set equal to zero for the aggregate production function. We conclude that the value shares of capital and labor inputs are independent of the input quantities. It is important to note that this condition

Table 9.8. Parameter estimates, aggregate model of production

	Hypothesis parameter	Estimate
α_K	0.385	(0.00246)
α_L	0.615	(0.00246)
α_T	0.0113	(0.0211)
β_{KK}	0.000	(0.000)
β_{KL}	0.000	(0.000)
β_{KT}	−0.000266	(0.000211)
β_{LL}	0.000	(0.000)
β_{LT}	0.000266	(0.000211)
β_{TT}	0.000338	(0.00180)

is necessary but not sufficient for the production function to be linear logarithmic. A linear logarithmic production function also requires that biases be set equal to zero.

We continue interpretation of the parameter estimates given in Table 9.6 with the estimated biases, β_{KT} and β_{LT}. These biases describe the implications of patterns of productivity growth for the distribution of the value of output. A positive bias implies that the corresponding value share increases with time; a negative bias implies that the value share decreases with time; a zero bias implies that the value share is independent of time. The sum of the two biases is zero. The estimated value of the bias with respect to labor input is positive, so that aggregate productivity growth is labor using and capital saving. An alternative and equivalent interpretation of the biases is that they represent changes in the rate of productivity growth with respect to proportional changes in the input quantities. We conclude that the rate of productivity growth is decreasing with respect to the quantity of capital input and increasing with respect to the quantity of labor input.

We conclude the interpretation of the parameter estimates given in Table 9.6 with the acceleration of productivity growth, β_{TT}. This parameter describes increases or decreases in the rate of productivity growth with time. The estimated value is positive, so that the rate of productivity growth is increasing with time, holding capital and labor inputs constant.

Conclusion

In this chapter we have developed measures of value added and its quantity based on the model of aggregate production presented in Chapter 2. To accomplish this objective we have introduced value-added functions for each of the sectors listed in Table 3.1, imposing additional restrictions on the sectoral models of production employed in Chapters 6 and 7. We have presented measures of value added and its price and quantity for the period 1948–1979. We have measured value added from the producer's point of view, excluding sales and excise taxes and including subsidies paid to producers.

We have analyzed sources of growth in output for the U.S. economy for the period 1948–1979. We have presented annual rates of growth of value added, capital input, and labor input, together with rates of productivity growth. We have found that the contribution of capital input to the growth of value added was positive throughout the period from 1948 to 1979, and relatively even. By contrast the contribution of labor input and the rate of productivity growth were negative for six and ten of the thirty-one years, respectively, and relatively uneven.

Analyzing the sources of growth in aggregate value added in greater detail, we have found that the contribution of capital input exceeded the rate of productivity growth in twenty of thirty-one years. The contribution of capital input was greater than that of labor input in eighteen of the thirty-one years. Finally, the contribution of labor input was greater than the rate of productivity growth in only fifteen of the thirty-one years. For the period as a whole the contribution of capital input averaged 1.56 percent per year, the contribution of labor input averaged 1.05 percent per year, and the rate of productivity growth averaged 0.81 percent per year. We concluded that the contribution of capital input was the most important source of growth in value added, the contribution of labor input was the next most important, and the rate of productivity growth was the least important.

We have analyzed the growth in capital input into components corresponding to capital stock and capital quality, where capital quality is defined as capital input per unit of capital stock. Similarly, we have analyzed the growth in labor input into components corresponding to hours worked and labor quality, where labor quality is defined as labor input per hour worked. For the period 1948–1979 the contribution of capital stock accounted for almost three-fourths of the contribution of capital input. For the subperiod from 1948 to 1960 the contribution of hours worked fell below the contribution of labor quality. For the subperiod from 1960 to 1979 the contribution of hours worked greatly exceeded the contribution of labor quality.

Finally, we decomposed the rate of productivity growth into a weighted sum of sectoral productivity growth rates and reallocations of value added, capital input, and labor input among sectors. For the period 1948–1979 sectoral productivity growth rates were the predominant component of aggregate productivity growth. This component averaged 0.83 percent per year, while the reallocation of value added averaged −0.09 percent per year and reallocations of capital and labor inputs averaged 0.09 percent per year and −0.02 percent per year, respectively. The decline in the growth of value added after 1966 can be attributed to a decline in sectoral productivity growth rates. We conclude that recovery of U.S. economic growth to levels that prevailed before 1966 will require accelerated development and implementation of new technology at the level of individual industrial sectors.

Our measure of aggregate productivity growth is based on a model of production that includes a translog production function and necessary conditions for producer equilibrium. The reallocations of value added and the primary factor inputs among sectors are measures of departures from the assumptions that underlie this model of aggregate production. We find that the contribution of the weighted sum of sectoral productivity growth rates far outweighs the effects of departures from the aggregate model. While the assumptions underlying the aggregate model are clearly inappropriate for an analysis of growth of output at the sectoral level, they do not seriously distort an analysis of growth of aggregate output.

Using a model of aggregate production based on the translog production function, we have analyzed the implications of patterns of substitution for the relative distribution of value added for the economy between capital and labor inputs. We have characterized substitution possibilities between inputs and changes in these possibilities over time in terms of share elasticities, biases of productivity growth, and the acceleration of productivity growth. These measures are fixed parameters of our econometric model of production.

We derived restrictions on shares and share elasticities and the rate and biases of productivity growth corresponding to Harrod neutrality, Hicks neutrality, and Solow neutrality. Interpreting the share elasticities and biases as fixed parameters, we derived corresponding tests of these restrictions. We found that none of the three types of neutrality can be rejected. The conjunction of all three types implies that the aggregate production function is linear logarithmic; this set of restrictions also cannot be rejected. We conclude that the aggregate production function can be represented in linear logarithmic form.

The final step in our implementation of an aggregate model of production is to estimate the fixed parameters of the model under necessary and sufficient conditions for concavity of the production function. We find that the estimated share elasticities are equal to zero under these restrictions. We have also estimated biases of productivity growth; we find the bias with respect to labor input to be positive—that labor-using productivity growth predominates for the U.S. economy as a whole. Alternatively, we can say that the rate of productivity growth increases with labor input and decreases with capital input. Finally, we have estimated the acceleration of productivity growth; the estimated value of this parameter is positive, implying that the rate of productivity growth at the aggregate level is increasing with time, holding capital and labor inputs constant.

Appendixes

Notes

References

Index

Data Sources for Labor Input

This appendix lists the sources of the detailed labor data used to construct the sectoral measures of labor input described in Chapter 3. Tables are presented in sections to identify the particular sources of the employment, hours worked, weeks paid, and compensation data, respectively. The tables within each section are ordered similarly. Tables describing the data sources relevant to each benchmark year are presented first; a summary table for all intermediate years follows. Additional tables that identify the sources of various supporting data conclude each section.

Employment

Tables A.1 through A.6 list the sources of the employment data used to generate the cross-classified employment matrices described in Chapter 3. All data for each of the benchmark years are taken from the decennial censuses conducted by the Bureau of the Census, U.S. Department of Commerce. Identifying publication codes for the population subject reports and detailed table titles and numbers are presented for the 1950, 1960, and 1970 data in Tables A.1 through A.3, respectively.

The data sources for the nonbenchmark or intermediate years are arranged in Table A.4, so that the subscripted variables at the head of each column indicate the extent of cross-classification available in the data sources listed directly below. Each variable derives its name from the first letter of the labor dimension it represents: industry (i), sex (s), employment class (c), age (a), education (e), and occupation (o). Each subscript indicates the maximum number of discrete divisions available in the data tables. Absence of a subscript suggests that the divisions for the variable match exactly with the characteristic groups listed in Table 3.1. Blank lines within any column imply that the particular data series are not available for the corresponding years. Note that, while entries appear in Table A.4 for the three benchmark years, these sources are listed only for completeness' sake. The data reported in Tables A.1 through A.3 were used to generate the 1950, 1960, and 1970 employment matrices.

The three-part entry for each data source listed in Table A.4 should be interpreted as follows. The first entry indicates the parent publication series, the second identifies the relevant volume within the series, and the third specifies the number of the appropriate table. For convenience, publication titles have been abbreviated as follows:

SLFR   *Special Labor Force Reports*
                Bureau of Labor Statistics
                U.S. Department of Labor

E/E   *Employment and Earnings*
                Division of Manpower and Employment Statistics
                Bureau of Labor Statistics
                U.S. Department of Labor

P-20   *Series P-20, Current Population Reports—*
                Population Characteristics
                Bureau of the Census
                U.S. Department of Commerce

P-50   *Series P-50, Current Population Reports—*
                Labor Force
                Bureau of the Census
                U.S. Department of Commerce

P-60   *Series P-60, Current Population Reports—*
                Consumer Income
                Bureau of the Census
                U.S. Department of Commerce

The employment model described in Chapter 3 requires two additional sets of employment data. The data tables necessary to build the second 1960 labor matrix based on the employed U.S. population, exclusive of those working in either Alaska or Hawaii are listed separately under their state titles in Table A.5. Table A.6 identifies the published sources of the data compiled by the Monthly Labor Survey's 1966 study of employed persons under the then newly conceived Census definitions.

Table A.1. U.S. Census employment data: 1950

Population subject report	Table number	Title
P-E No. 1B	4	Age of the experienced civilian labor force, by detailed occupation and sex, for the U.S.: 1950.
P-E No. 1B	5	Age of wage and salary workers in the experienced civilian labor force, by detailed occupation and sex, for the U.S.: 1950.
P-E No. 1B	6	Age of employed persons, by detailed occupation and sex, for the U.S.: 1950.
P-E No. 1C	2	Detailed occupation of employed persons, by detailed industry and sex, for the U.S.: 1950.
P-E No. 1D	3	Age of employed persons, by detailed industry and sex, for the U.S.: 1950.
P-E No. 1D	4	Age of employed wage and salary workers, by detailed industry and sex, for the U.S.: 1950.
P-E No. 1D	6	Major occupation group of employed persons, by detailed industry and sex, for the U.S.: 1950.
P-E No. 1D	7	Major occupation group of employed wage and salary workers, by detailed industry and sex, for the U.S.: 1950.
P-E No. 5B	11	Major occupation group: persons 14 years old and over, by years of school completed, age, color, and sex, for the U.S., by regions: 1950.

Hours Worked

The sources of the data required to apply the model of hours worked described in Chapter 3 are listed in Tables A.7 through A.12. Sources of the data for each decennial census year are presented in Tables A.7 through A.9. The format for presentation of the data sources for each intermediate year, in Table A.10, is the same as for Table A.4.

Using a format similar to that used in Table A.10, Tables A.11 and A.12 list the data sources relating to the hours and employment series, respectively, for multiple job holders. The letter enclosed in parentheses and appended to the variable list at the head of each column indicates whether the recorded sources report data referring to the multiple job holders' employment characteristics in their primary (P) or secondary (S) industry of employment.

Weeks Paid

As described in Chapter 3, we require data on weeks paid per person to convert data measuring average compensation per person to estimates of average compensation per job. The sources of these data are listed in Tables A.13 through A.16. The weeks-paid data used to construct the benchmark year series for this research are taken from the 1950, 1960, and 1970 decennial censuses. Since the "weeks paid" responses of those interviewed are based on their work experience during the previous year, the benchmark years for the weeks data are those immediately preceding the decennial census years. The specific data sources are listed in Tables A.13 through A.15.

The abbreviations and format used in Table A.16 to present the sources for the weeks data of the intermediate years are identical to those for Table A.4.

Compensation

Tables A.17 through A.21 identify data sources for labor compensation. All the compensation tables for the benchmark years 1949, 1959, and 1969 presented in Tables A.17 through A.19 are derived from the 1950, 1960, and 1970 decennial censuses, respectively. The one-year lag is explained by the fact that the census respondent declares his annual compensation for the previous year. The payroll tax tables, A.20 and A.21, are taken directly from Social Security Administration (1980) and Pechman (1977).

Table A.2. U.S. Census employment data: 1960

Population subject report	Table number	Title
PC(2)-5B	8	Major occupation group—Persons 14 years old and over in the experienced civilian labor force, by years of school completed, age, color, and sex, for the U.S., by type of residence, and by regions: 1960.
PC(2)-7A	4	Age of the experienced civilian labor force, by detailed occupation and sex, for the U.S.: 1960.
PC(2)-7A	5	Age of wage and salary workers in the experienced civilian labor force, by detailed occupation and sex, for the U.S.: 1960.
PC(2)-7A	6	Age of employed persons, by detailed occupation and sex, for the U.S.: 1960.
PC(2)-7A	36	Industry group of employed persons, by occupation, color, and sex, for the U.S.: 1960.
PC(2)-7C	1	Major occupation group of employed persons, by major industry group, age, and sex, for the U.S.: 1960.
PC(2)-7C	2	Detailed occupation of employed persons, by detailed industry and sex, for the U.S.: 1960.
PC(2)-7F	4	Age of employed persons, by detailed industry and sex, for the U.S.: 1960.

Table A.2 continued

| PC(2)-7F | 21 | Years of school completed by the experienced civilian labor force, by detailed industry and sex, for the U.S.: 1960. |
| PC(2)-7F | 28 | Class of workers and color of the experienced civilian labor force, by agricultural and nonagricultural industries, years of school completed, and sex, for the U.S.: 1960. |

Table A.3.   U.S. Census employment data: 1970

Population subject report	Table number	Title
PC(2)-5B	11	Major occupation group of employed persons 14 years old and over, by years of school completed, age, race, and sex: 1970.
PC(2)-7B	3	Years of school completed by the experienced civilian labor force by detailed industry, and sex: 1970.
PC(2)-7B	34	Age of employed persons by detailed industry, and sex: 1970.
PC(2)-7B	37	Class of worker of employed persons by detailed industry, and sex: 1970.
PC(2)-7B	47	Age of employed persons by class of worker, agricultural and nonagricultural industries, race, Spanish origin, and sex: 1970.
PC(2)-7C	1	Industry group of employed persons by occupation, age and sex: 1970.
PC(2)-7C	5	Industry group of employed wage and salary workers by occupation, race, and sex: 1970.
PC(2)-7C	6	Industry group of self-employed workers by occupation, race, and sex: 1970.
PC(2)-7C	8	Detailed occupation and employed persons by detailed industry and sex: 1970.

Table A.4. Employment data for nonbenchmark years

Year	sci_2	sc_1i_{37}	sci_2a	si_{17}
1948	P-50,#13,T-9,10			
1949	P-50,#19,T-9			
1950	P-50,#31,T-9			
1951	P-50,#40,T-9			
1952	P-50,#45,T-9			
1953	P-50,#59,T-C9			P-50,#50,T-5
1954	P-50,#59,T-A9			
1955	P-50,#67,T-12			
1956	P-50,#72,T-12			
1957	P-50,#85,T-12			
1958	P-50,#89,T-13			
1959	SLFR,#23,T-C4	SLFT,#11,T-B		
1960	SLFR,#23,T-C4	SLFR,#19,T-A.2		
1961	SLFR,#23,T-C4	SLFR,#25,T-A.2		
1962	SLFR,#69,T-C4	SLFR,#38,T-A.2		
1963	SLFR,#69,T-C4	SLFR,#48,T-A.2		
1964	SLFR,#69,T-C4	SLFR,#62,T-A.2		
1965	SLFR,#69,T-C4	SLFR,#76,T-A.2		
1966	E/E,Jan'67,T-14	SLFR,#91,T-A.2		
1967		SLFR,#107,T-A.2	E/E,Jan'68,T-A.16	
1968		SLFR,#115,T-A.2	E/E,Jan'69,T-A.18	
1969		SLFR,#127,T-A.2	E/E,Jan'70,T-A.18	
1970		SLFR,#141,T-A.2	E/E,Jan'71,T-A.18	
1971			E/E,Jan'72,T-A.18	
1972		SLFR,#162,T-A.2	SLFR,#152,T-A.19	
1973			SLFR,#163,T-A.21	
1974			SLFR,#178,T-A.20	
1975			SLFR,#185,T-20	
1976			SLFR,#199,T-21	
1977			SLFR,#212,T-24	
1978			SLFR,#218,T-24	
1979			SLFR,#234,T-24	

	$si_{18}a_5$	si_7a	si_6a_6	si_2a
1948				P-50,#13,T-5,6
1949				P-50,#19,T-5,6
1950		P-50,#31,T-E		P-50,#31,T-5,6
1951		P-50,#40,T-E		P-50,#40,T-5,6

Table A.4 continued

	$si_{18}a_5$	si_7a	si_6a_6	si_2a
1952		P-50,#45,T-E		P-50,#45,T-5,6
1953				P-50,#59,T-C5,6
1954		P-50,#67,T-F		P-50,#59,T-A.5,6
1955		P-50,#67,T-F		P-50,#67,T-8,9
1956		P-50,#72,T-G		P-50,#72,T-8,9
1957				P-50,#85,T-9,10
1958			P-50,#89,T-18	P-50,#89,T-9,10
1959	SLFR,#4,T-C10			SLFR,#31,T-C2,3
1960				SLFR,#31,T-C2,3
1961	SLFR,#23,T-C10			SLFR,#31,T-C2,3
1962	SLFR,#31,T-C10			SLFR,#31,T-C2,3
1963	SLFR,#43,T-C10			SLFR,#69,T-C2,3
1964	SLFR,#52,T-C10			SLFR,#69,T-C2,3
1965	SLFR,#69,T-C10			SLFR,#69,T-C2,3
1966				E/E,Jan'67,T-A.13
1967				
1968				
1969				
1970				
1971				
1972				
1973				
1974				
1975				
1976				
1977				
1978				
1979				

	$s_1i_{13}a_t$	$si_{42}e$	$i_{12}o$	sae
1948	P-50,#75,T-4			
1949				
1950	P-50,#75,T-4			
1951				
1952	P-50,#75,T-4			
1953				
1954	P-50,#75,T-4			
1955				
1956	P-50,#75,T-4			

Table A.4 continued

	$s_1i_{13}a_t$	$si_{42}e$	$i_{12}o$	sae
1957				
1958				
1959			SLFR,#4,T-C9	SLFR,#1,T-D
1960			SLFR,#14,T-C9	
1961			SLFR,#23,T-C9	
1962			SLFR,#31,T-C9	SLFR,#30,T-D
1963			SLFR,#43,T-C9	
1964			SLFR,#52,T-C9	SLFR,#53,T-D
1965			SLFR,#69,T-C9	SLFR,#65,T-D
1966				SLFR,#83,T-D
1967				SLFR,#92,T-D
1968		SLFR,#103,T-N		SLFR,#103,T-D
1969		SLFR,#125,T-N		SLFR,#125,T-D
1970		SLFR,#125,T-N		SLFR,#125,T-D
1971		SLFR,#140,T-N		SLFR,#140,T-D
1972		SLFR,#148,T-N		SLFR,#148,T-D
1973				SLFR,#161,T-D
1974				SLFR,#175,T-D
1975				SLFR,#186,T-D
1976				SLFR,#193,T-D
1977				SLFR,#209,T-E,T-L,
1978				SLFR,#225,T-E,
				SLFR,#218,T-3
1979				SLFR,#240,T-E,
				SLFR,#234,T-3

	sa_5e	sao	sa_6o	sa_5o
1948				
1949				
1950				
1951				
1952	P-50,#49,T-2			
1953				
1954				
1955				
1956				
1957	P-50,#78,T-2			P-20,#80,T-4
1958			P-50,#89,T-16	
1959		SLFR,#4,T-C8		

Table A.4 continued

	sa_5e	sao	sa_6o	sa_5o
1960		SLFR,#14,T-C8		
1961		SLFR,#23,T-C8		
1962		SLFR,#31,T-C8		
1963		SLFR,#43,T-C8		
1964		SLFR,#52,T-C8		
1965		SLFR,#69,T-C8		
1966				
1967				
1968				
1969				
1970				
1971				
1972				
1973				
1974				
1975				
1976				
1977				
1978				
1979				

	sa_2o	s_1a_6o	seo	so
1948			P-50,#14,T-5	P-50,#13,T-15
1949				P-50,#19,T-14
1950	P-50,#32,T-4			P-50,#31,T-14
1951	P-50,#41,T-4			P-50,#40,T-14
1952			P-50,#49,T-4	P-50,#45,T-14
1953	P-50,#51,T-4			P-50,#67,T-25
1954	P-50,#58,T-3			P-50,#59,T-A.10
1955	P-50,#64,T-3			P-50,#67,T-13
1956	P-50,#71,T-3			P-50,#72,T-13
1957	P-50,#83,T-3		P-50,#78,T-7	P-50,#85,T-13
1958	P-50,#90,T-3			P-50,#89,T-14
1959	SLFR,#6,T-G	P-0,#104,T-8	SLFR,#1,T-1	
1960	SLFR,#16,T-G			
1961	SLFR,#22,T-G			
1962	SLFR,#34,T-G		SLFR,#30,T-I	
1963	SLFR,#42,T-G			
1964	SLFR,#55,T-G		SLFR,#53,T-I	

Table A.4 continued

	sa_2o	s_1a_6o	seo	so
1965	SLFR,#68,T-F		SLFR,#65,T-I	
1966	SLFR,#87,T-F	.	SLFR,#83,T-I	
1967	SLFR,#98,T-G	P-20,#171,T-10	SLFR,#92,T-I	
1968	SLFR,#111,T-E	P-20,#188,T-9	SLFR,#103,T-I	
1969	SLFR,#124,T-E	P-20,#193,T-9	SLFR,#125,T-I	
1970	SLFR,#135,T-E	P-20,#210,T-9	SLFR,#125,T-I	
1971	SLFR,#147,T-E	P-20,#235,T-9	SLFR,#140,T-I	
1972	SLFR,#158,T-E		SLFR,#148,T-I	
1973	SLFR,#163,T-E		SLFR,#161,T-I	
1974	SLFR,#178,A-18		SLFR,#175,T-I	
1975	SLFR,#185,A-18		SLFR,#186,T-I	
1976	SLFR,#199,A-18		SLFR,#193,T-I	
1977	SLFR,#211,T-21,T-38		SLFR,#209,T-J	
1978	SLFR,#218,T-21,T-38		SLFR,#225,T-J	
1979	SLFR,#234,T-21,T-38		SLFR,#240,T-J	

Table A.5. U.S. Census employment data for Alaska: 1960

Characteristics of the population	Table number	Title
Vol. 1, Pt. 3	122	Occupation of the experienced civilian labor force Alaska by color, of the employed by race and class of worker, and of persons not in labor force with work experience, by sex, for the State: 1960.
Vol. 1, Pt. 3	123	Age of employed persons, by occupation, color, and sex, for the State, 1960.
Vol. 1, Pt. 3	125	Industry group of the employed, by occupation and sex, for the State: 1960.
Vol. 1, Pt. 3	126	Detailed industry of the experienced civilian labor force and of the employed, by sex, for the State: 1960.
Vol. 1, Pt. 3	128	Age of employed persons, by industry and sex, for the State: 1960.

Table A.6. U.S. Census employment data for Hawaii: 1960

Characteristics of the population	Table number	Title
Vol. 1, Pt. 3	122	Occupation of the experienced civilian labor force by color, of the employed by race and class of worker, and of persons not in labor force with work experience, by sex, for the State and for standard metropolitan statistical areas of 250,000 or more: 1960.
Vol. 1, Pt. 13	123	Age of employed persons, by occupation, color, and sex, for the State and for standard metropolitan statistical areas of 250,000 or more: 1960.
Vol. 1, Pt. 13	125	Industry group of the employed by occupation and sex, for the State and for standard metropolitan areas of 250,000.
Vol. 1, Pt. 13	127	Detailed industry of the employed, by sex, for the State and for standard metropolitan statistical areas of 100,000 or more: 1960.
Vol. 1, Pt. 13	128	Age of employed persons, by industry and sex, for the State and for standard metropolitan statistical areas of 250,000 or more: 1960.
	8	Employed persons by age and sex, Monthly Labor Survey—Current Population Survey comparisons, annual average 1966.
	11	Employed persons by class of worker and occupation group, Monthly Labor Survey—Current Population Survey comparisons, annual average 1966.

Source: Stein [1967].

Table A.7.   U.S. Census hours worked data: 1950

Population subject report	Table number	Title
P-E No. 1A	13	Hours worked during census week by persons by age, color, and sex, for the U.S., urban and rural: 1950.
P-E No. 1B	14	Hours worked during the census week by employed persons, by detailed occupation and sex, for the U.S.: 1950.
P-E No. 1B	15	Hours worked during the census week by employed wage and salary workers, by detailed occupation and sex, for the U.S.: 1950.
P-E No. 1D	10	Hours worked during the census week by employed persons, by detailed industry and sex, for the U.S.: 1950.
P-E No. 1D	11	Hours worked during the census week by employed wage and salary workers, by detailed industry and sex, for the U.S.: 1950.

Table A.8. U.S. Census hours worked data: 1960

Population subject report	Table number	Title
PC(2)-6A	12	Hours worked by employed persons, by marital status, presence of own children, age, color, and sex, for the U.S., urban and rural: 1960.
PC(2)-7A	13	Hours worked by employed persons, by detailed occupation and sex, for the U.S.: 1960.
PC(2)-7F	9	Hours worked by employed persons, by detailed industry and sex, for the U.S.: 1960.
PC(2)-7F	10	Hours worked by employed wage and salary workers, by detailed industry and sex, for the U.S.: 1960.
PC(2)-7F	23	Hours worked and color of employed persons, by class of worker, agricultural and nonagricultural industries, and sex, for the U.S.: 1960.

Table A.9. U.S. Census hours worked data: 1970

Population subject report	Table number	Title
PC(2)-6A	17	Hours worked by employed persons by marital status, presence of own children, age, race, and sex: 1970.
PC(2)-7A	45	Employed persons by hours worked, detailed occupation, and sex: 1970.
PC(2)-7B	39	Employed persons by hours worked, detailed industry, and sex: 1970.
PC(2)-7B	48	Hours worked by employed persons by class of worker, agricultural and nonagricultural industries, race, Spanish origin, and sex: 1970.

Table A.10. Hours worked data for nonbenchmark years

Year	$si_{18}a_5$	si_7a	si_6a_6	si_2a
1948				
1949				
1950				
1951				
1952				
1953				
1954				
1955				
1956	P-50,#72,T-18			
1957	P-50,#85,T-18			
1958	P-50,#89,T-24			
1959		SLFR,#4,T-D7		
1960		SLFR,#14,T-D7		
1961		SLFR,#23,T-D7		
1962		SLFR,#31,T-D7		
1963		SLFR,#43,T-D7		
1964		SLFR,#52,T-D7		
1965		SLFR,#69,T-D7		
1966		E/E,Jan'67,T-22		
1967			E/E,Jan'68,T-A.21	E/E,Jan'68,T-A.22
1968			E/E,Jan'69,T-A.23	E/E,Jan'69,T-A.24
1969			SLFR,#116,T-A.24	SLFR,#116,T-A.25
1970			SLFR,#129,T-A.24	SLFR,#129,T-A.25
1971			SLFR,#142,T-A.24	SLFR,#142,T-A.27
1972			SLFR,#152,T-A.24	SLFR,#163,T-A.27
1973			SLFR,#163,T-A.26	SLFR,#163,T-A.27
1974			SLFR,#178,T-A.25,T-20	SLFR,#178,T-A.26
1975			SLFR,#185,T-A.25,T-20	SLFR,#185,T-A.26
1976			SLFR,#199,T-31,T-21	SLFR,#199,T-32
1977			SLFR,#212,T-35,T-24	SLFR,#212,T-36,T-22
1978			SLFR,#218,T-35,T-24	SLFR,#218,T-36,T-24
1979			SLFR,#234,T-35,T-24	SLFR,#234,T-36,T-21

	c	ci_2	c_1i_9	c_1i_8
1948				
1949				
1950				
1951				P-50#40,T-G
1952				P-50#45,T-H
1953				
1954				
1955				
1956				

Table A.10 continued

	c	ci_2	c_1i_9	c_1i_8
1957				
1958		P-50#89,T-22		
1959		SLFR#4,T-D2		
1960		SLFR#23,T-D2		
1961		SLFR#23,T-D2		
1962		SLFR#31,T-D2		
1963		SLFR#43,T-D2		
1964		SLFR#52,T-D2		
1965		SLFR#69,T-D2		
1966		E/E,Jan'67,T-22		
1967	E/E,Jan'68,T-A.20		E/E,Jan'68,T-A.20	
1968	E/E,Jan'69,T-A.22		E/E,Jan'69,T-A.22	
1969	SLFR#116,T-A.23		SLFR#116,T-A.23	
1970	SLFR#129,T-A.23		SLFR#129,T-A.23	
1971	SLFR#142,T-A.23		SLFR#152,T-A.23	
1972	SLFR#152,T-A.23		SLFR#152,T-A.23	
1973	SLFR#163,T-A.25		SLFR#163,T-A.25	
1974	SLFR#234,T-34		SLFR#178,T-A.24	
1975			SLFR#185,T-A.24	
1976			SLFR#199,T-30,T-24	
1977			SLFR#212,T-31,T-27	
1978			SLFR#218,T-34,T-27	
1979			SLFR#234,T-34,T-27	

	c_1i_6	c_1i_5	i_2	o	o_8
1948		P-50#61,T-8			
1949		P-50#61,T-8			
1950					
1951					
1952				P-50#45,T-H	
1953		P-50#61,T-8			
1954		P-50#61,T-8			
1955		P-50#67,T-17	P-50#67,T-16		
1956		P-50#67,T-17	P-50#72,T-17		
1957		P-50#85,T-21	P-50#85,T-17		
1958	P-50#89,T-2			P-50#89,T-27	
1959	SLFR#4,T-D3			SLFR#4,T-D6	
1960	SLFR#14,T-D3			SLFR#14,T-D6	
1961	SLFR#23,T-D3			SLFR#23,T-D6	
1962	SLFR#31,T-D3			SLFR#31,T-D6	
1963	SLFR#43,T-D3			SLFR#43,T-D6	
1964	SLFR#52,T-D3			SLFR#52,T-D6	
1965	SLFR#69,T-D3			SLFR#69,T-D6	
1966	E/E,Jan'67,T-19				E/E,Jan'67,T-20

Table A.10 continued

	c_1i_6	c_1i_5	i_2	o	o_8
1967			E/E,Jan'68T-A.18		
1968			E/E,Jan'69T-A.20		
1969			SLFR#116,T-A.21		
1970			SLFR#129,T-A.21		
1971			SLFR#142,T-A.21		
1972			SLFR#152,T-A.21		
1973			SLFR#163,T-A.21		
1974			SLFR#178,T-A.22		
1975			SLFR#185,T-A.22		
1976			SLFR#199,T-30		
1977			SLFR#212,T-32		
1978			SLFR#218,T-32		
1979			SLFR#234,T-32		

Table A.11. Hours worked data for multiple job holders

Year	$ci_2(P)$	$ci_2(S)$	$c_1i_{12}(P)$
1948			
1949			
1950			
1951			
1952			
1953			
1954			
1955			
1956			
1957			
1958			
1959			
1960	SLFR#18,T-G	SLFR#18,T-H	
1961			
1962	SLFR#29,T-F	SLFR#29,T-G	
1963	SLFR#39,T-F	SLFR#39,T-G	
1964	SLFR#51,T-F	SLFR#51,T-G	
1965	SLFR#63,T-G	SLFR#63,T-H	
1966	SLFR#90,T-G	SLFR#90,T-H	
1967			
1968			
1969	SLFR#123,T-H	SLFR#123,T-I	SLFR#123,T-H
1970	SLFR#139,T-H	SLFR#139,T-I	SLFR#139,T-H
1971	SLFR#139,T-H	SLFR#139,T-I	SLFR#139,T-H

Table A.11 continued

Year	$ci_2(P)$	$ci_2(S)$	$c_1i_{12}(P)$
1972	SLFR#166,T-H	SLFR#166,T-I	SLFR#166,T-H
1973	SLFR#166,T-H	SLFR#166,T-I	SLFR#166,T-H
1974	SLFR#177,T-H	SLFR#177,T-I	SLFR#177,T-H
1975	SLFR#182,T-H	SLFR#182,T-I	SLFR#182,T-H
1976	SLFR#194,T-B8	SLFR#194,T-B9	SLFR#194,T-B8
1977	SLFR#194,T-B8	SLFR#211,T-H	SLFR#194,T-B8
1978	SLFR#194,T-B8	SLFR#211,T-H	SLFR#194,T-B8
1979	SLFR#194,T-B8	SLFR#239,T-H	SLFR#194,T-B8

Year	$c_1i_{12}(S)$	$c_1i_{11}(P)$	$c_1i_{11}(S)$
1948			
1949			
1950			
1951			
1952			
1953			
1954			
1955			
1956			
1957			
1958			
1959			
1960		SLFR,#18,T-G	SLFR,#18,T-H
1961			
1962		SLFR,#29,T-F	SLFR,#29,T-G
1963		SLFR,#39,T-F	SLFR,#39,T-G
1964		SLFR,#51,T-F	SLFR,#51,T-G
1965		SLFR,#63,T-G	SLFR,#63,T-H
1966		SLFR,#90,T-G	SLFR,#90,T-H
1967			
1968			
1969	SLFR,#123,T-I		
1970	SLFR,#139,T-I		
1971	SLFR,#139,T-I		
1972	SLFR,#166,T-I		
1973	SLFR,#166,T-I		
1974	SLFR,#177,T-I		
1975	SLFR,#182,T-I		
1976	SLFR,#194,T-B9		
1977	SLFR,#211,T-H,T-L		
1978	SLFR,#221,T-C,T-H		
1979	SLFR,#239,T-H		

Table A.12. Employment data for multiple job holders

Year	$ci_2(P)$	$ci_2(S)$	$c_1i_{16}(P)$
1948			
1949			
1950	P-50,#30,T-2	P-50,#30,T-2	
1951			
1952			
1953			
1954			
1955			
1956	P-50,#74,T-2	P-50,#74,T-2	
1957	P-50,#80,T-6	P-50,#80,T-6	P-50,#80,T-6
1958	P-50,#88,T-6	P-50,#88,T-6	P-50,#88,T-6
1959	SLFR,#9,T-2	SLFR,#9,T-B	
1960	SLFR,#18,T-3	SLFR,#18,T-3	
1961			
1962	SLFR,#29,T-2	SLFR,#29,T-2	
1963	SLFR,#39,T-2	SLFR,#39,T-2	
1964	SLFR,#51,T-4	SLFR,#51,T-4	
1965	SLFR,#63,T-3	SLFR,#63,T-3	
1966	SLFR,#90,T-3	SLFR,#90,T-3	
1967			
1968			
1969	SLFR,#123,T-B	SLFR,#123,T-B	
1970	SLFR,#139,T-B	SLFR,#139,T-B	
1971	SLFR,#139,T-B	SLFR,#139,T-B	
1972	SLFR,#166,T-B	SLFR,#166,T-B	
1973	SLFR,#166,T-B	SLFR,#166,T-B	
1974	SLFR,#177,T-C	SLFR,#177,T-C	
1975	SLFR,#182,T-C	SLFR,#182,T-C	
1976	SLFR,#194,T-B3	SLFR,#194,T-B3	
1977	SLFR,#211,T-C	SLFR,#211,T-C	
1978	SLFR,#221	SLFR,#221,T-C	
1979	SLFR,#239,T-C	SLFR,#239,T-C	

	$c_1i_{16}(S)$	$c_1i_{12}(P)$	$c_1i_{12}(S)$
1948			
1949			
1950			

Table A.12 continued

	$c_1i_{16}(S)$	$c_1i_{12}(P)$	$c_1i_{12}(S)$
1951			
1952			
1953			
1954			
1955			
1956			
1957	P-50,#80,T-6		
1958	P-50,#88,T-6		
1959			
1960			
1961			
1962			
1963			
1964			
1965			
1966			
1967			
1968			
1969		SLFR,#123,T-B	SLFR,#123,T-B
1970		SLFR,#139,T-B	SLFR,#139,T-B
1971		SLFR,#139,T-B	SLFR,#139,T-B
1972		SLFR,#166,T-B	SLFR,#166,T-B
1973		SLFR,#166,T-B	SLFR,#166,T-B
1974		SLFR,#177,T-C	SLFR,#177,T-C
1975		SLFR,#182,T-C	SLFR,#182,T-C
1976		SLFR,#194,T-B3	SLFR,#194,T-B3
1977		SLFR,#211,T-C	SLFR,#211,T-C
1978		SLFR,#221,T-C	SLFR,#221,T-C
1979		SLFR,#239,T-C	SLFR,#239,T-C

	$c_1i_{11}(P)$	$c_1i_{11}(S)$	$c_1i_9(P)$	$c_1i_9(S)$
1948				
1949				
1950				
1951				
1952				
1953				
1954				
1955				
1956				

Table A.12 continued

	$c_1i_{11}(P)$	$c_1i_{11}(S)$	$c_1i_9(P)$	$c_1i_9(S)$
1957				
1958				
1959			SLFR#9,T-2	SLFR#8,T-B
1960	SLFR#18,T-3	SLFR#18,T-3		
1961				
1962	SLFR#39,T-2	SLFR#29,T-2		
1963	SLFR#39,T-2	SLFR#39,T-2		
1964	SLFR#51,T-4	SLFR#51,T-4		
1965	SLFR#63,T-3	SLFR#63,T-3		
1966	SLFR#90,T-3	SLFR#90,T-3		
1967				
1968				
1969				
1970				
1971				
1972				
1973				
1974				
1975				
1976				
1977				
1978				
1979				

Table A.13. U.S. Census weeks paid data: 1949

Population subject report	Table number	Title
P-E No. 1A	14	Weeks worked in 1949 by labor force status: persons by age, color, and sex, for the U.S., urban and rural: 1950.
P-E No. 1B	16	Weeks worked in 1949 by the experienced civilian labor force, by detailed occupation and sex, for the U.S.: 1950.
P-E No. 1B	17	Weeks worked in 1949 by wage and salary workers in the experienced civilian labor force, by detailed occupation and sex, for the U.S.: 1950.
P-E No. 1D	12	Weeks worked in 1949 by the experienced civilian labor force, by detailed industry and sex, for the U.S.: 1950.
P-E No. 1D	13	Weeks worked in 1949 by wage and salary workers in the experienced civilian labor force, by detailed industry and sex, for the U.S.: 1950.
P-E No. 1D	21	Weeks worked in 1949 by the experienced civilian labor force, by class of worker and sex, for the U.S.: 1950.

Table A.14. U.S. Census weeks paid data: 1959

Population subject report	Table number	Title
PC(2)-6A	15	Employment status, by weeks worked in 1959, age, color, and sex, for the U.S., urban and rural: 1960.
PC(2)-7A	14	Weeks worked in 1959 by the experienced civilian labor force, by detailed occupation and sex, for the U.S.: 1960.
PC(2)-7A	17	Weeks worked in 1959 by wage and salary workers in the experienced civilian labor force, by detailed occupation and sex, for the U.S.: 1960.
PC(2)-7F	11	Weeks worked in 1959 by the experienced civilian labor force, by detailed industry and sex, for the U.S.: 1960.
PC(2)-7F	13	Weeks worked in 1959 by wage and salary workers in the experienced civilian labor force, by industry, wage or salary income in 1959, and sex, for the U.S.: 1960.
PC(2)-7F	24	Weeks worked in 1959 and color of the experienced civilian labor force, by class of worker, agricultural and nonagricultural industries, and sex, for the U.S.: 1960.

Table A.15. U.S. Census weeks paid data: 1969

Population subject report	Table number	Title
PC(2)-6A	22	Employment status by weeks worked in 1969, age, race, Spanish origin, and sex: 1970.
PC(2)-7A	11	Weeks worked in 1969 by the experienced civilian labor force by detailed occupation and sex: 1970.
PC(2)-7A	14	Weeks worked in 1969 by wage and salary workers 16 years old and over in the experienced civilian labor force by the selected occupations and sex: 1970.
PC(2)-7B	6	Weeks worked in 1969 by the experienced civilian labor force, by detailed industry, and sex: 1970.
PC(2)-7B	9	Weeks worked in 1969 by wage and salary workers in the experienced civilian labor force by industry, and sex: 1970.

Table A.16. Weeks paid data for nonbenchmark years

Year	sc_1i_{36}	c_1i_9	sc_1i_8
1948			
1949			
1950			P-50,#35, T-4
1951			P-50,#43, T-4
1952			P-50,#48, T-4
1953		P-50,#54, T-3	
1954		P-50,#59, T-B2	
1955		P-50,#68, T-2	
1956		P-50,#77, T-2	
1957		P-50,#86, T-B	
1958	P-50,#91, T-2,1		
1959	SLFR,#11, T-B-A		
1960	SLFR,#19, T-A.2,A.1		
1961	SLFR,#25, T-A.2,A.3		
1962	SLFR,#38, T-A.2,A.3		
1963	SLFR,#48, T-A.2,A.3		
1964	SLFR,#62, T-A.2,A.3		
1965	SLFR,#76, T-A.2,A.3		
1966	SLFR,#91, T-A.2,A.3		
1967	SLFR,#107, T-A.2,A.3		
1968	SLFR,#115, T-A.2,A.3		
1969	SLFR,#127, T-A.2,A.3		
1970	SLFR,#141, T-A.2,A.3		
1971	SLFR,#162, T-A.2,A.3		
1972	SLFR,#162, T-A.2,A.3		
1973	SLFR,#171, T-A.2,A.3		
1974	SLFR,#181, T-A.2,A.3		
1975	SLFR,#192, T-B2,B3		
1976	SLFR,#201, T-B2-B3		
1977	SLFR,#224, T-A.2		
1978	SLFR,#236, T-A.2		
1979			

Year	sa	so
1948		
1949		
1950	P-50,#35, T-1	P-50,#35, T-3
1951	P-50,#43, T-1	P-50,#43, T-3
1952	P-50,#48, T-1	P-50,#48, T-3

Table A.16 continued

Year	sa	so
1953	P-50,#54, T-1	
1954	P-50,#59, T-1	
1955	P-50,#68, T-1	P-50,#68, T-3
1956	P-50,#77, T-1	P-50,#77, T-3
1957	P-50,#86, T-1	P-50,#86, T-3
1958	P-50,#91, T-1	P-50,#91, T-3
1959	SLFR,#11, T-A	SLFR,#11, T-C
1960	SLFR,#19, T-A.1	SLFR,#19, T-A.4, A.1
1961	SLFR,#25, T-A.1	SLFR,#25, T-A.4, A.1
1962	SLFR,#38, T-A.1	SLFR,#38, T-A.4, A.1
1963	SLFR,#48, T-A.1	SLFR,#58, T-A.4, A.1
1964	SLFR,#62, T-A.1	SLFR,#62, T-A.5, A.1
1965	SLFR,#76, T-A.1	SLFR,#76, T-A.5, A.1
1966	SLFR,#91, T-A.1	SLFR,#91, T-A.5, A.1
1967	SLFR,#107,T-A.1	SLFR,#107,T-A.5
1968	SLFR,#115,T-A.1	SLFR,#115,T-A.5
1969	SLFR,#127,T-A.1	SLFR,#127,T-A.1
1970	SLFR,#141,T-A.1	SLFR,#141,T-A.5
1971	SLFR,#162,T-A.1	SLFR,#162,T-A.5
1972	SLFR,#162,T-A.1	SLFR,#162,T-A.5
1973	SLFR,#171,T-A.1	SLFR,#171,T-A.5
1974	SLFR,#181,T-A.1	SLFR,#181,T-A.5
1975	SLFR,#192,T-B1	SLFR,#192,T-A.5
1976	SLFR,#201,T-B1	SLFR,#201,T-B6
1977	SLFR,#224,T-A.1	SLFR,#224,T-A.4
1978	SLFR,#236,T-A.1	SLFR,#236,T-A.4
1979		

Table A.17. U.S. Census labor compensation data: 1949

Population subject report	Table number	Title
P-E No. 1B	19	Income in 1949 of the experienced civilian labor force, by detailed occupation and sex, for the U.S.: 1950.
P-E No. 1B	22	Wage and salary income in 1949 of wage and salary workers in the experienced civilian labor force, by detailed occupation and sex, for the U.S.: 1950.
P-E No. 1D	15	Income in 1949 of the experienced civilian labor force, by detailed industry and sex, for the U.S.: 1950.
P-E No. 1D	17	Wage and salary income in 1949 of wage and salary workers in the experienced civilian labor force, by detailed industry and sex, for the U.S.: 1950.
P-E No. 5B	12	Income in 1949, persons 14 years old and over, by years of school completed, age, color, and sex, for the U.S., by regions: 1950.

Table A.18. U.S. Census labor compensation data: 1959

Population subject report	Table number	Title
PC(2)-5B	6	Total income—males 14 years old and over with incomes in 1959, by years of school completed, age, and color, for the U.S., by type of residence, and by regions: 1960.
PC(2)-5B	7	Total income—females 14 years old and over with incomes in 1959, by years of school completed, age, and color, for the U.S., by type of residence, and by regions: 1960.
PC(2)-5B	9	Occupation and earnings—persons 18 to 64 years old in the experienced civilian labor force with earnings in 1959, by years of school completed, age, and sex, for the U.S.: 1960.
PC(2)-7A	25	Income in 1959 of the experienced civilian labor force, by detailed occupation and sex, for the U.S.: 1960.
PC(2)-7A	27	Wage and salary income in 1959 of wage and salary workers in the experienced civilian labor force, by detailed occupation and sex, for the U.S.: 1960.
PC(2)-7F	15	Income in 1959 of the experienced civilian labor force, by detailed industry and sex, for the U.S.: 1960.
PC(2)-7F	17	Wage or salary income in 1959 of wage and salary workers in the experienced civilian labor force, by detailed industry and sex, for the U.S.: 1960.

Table A.18 continued

Population subject report	Table number	Title
PC(2)-7F	18	Earnings in 1959 of the experienced civilian labor force, by detailed industry and sex, for the U.S.: 1960.

Table A.19. U.S. Census labor compensation data: 1969

Population subject report	Table number	Title
PC(2)-5B	7	Total income—males 14 years old and over with incomes in 1969, by years of school completed, age, and race: 1970.
PC(2)-5B	8	Total income of females 14 years old and over with income in 1969, by years of school completed, age, and race: 1970.
PC(2)-7A	24	Wage and salary earnings in 1969 of wage and salary workers, 16 years old and over, in the experienced civilian labor force, by detailed occupation and sex: 1970.
PC(2)-7B	12	Earnings in 1969 of the experienced civilian labor force by detailed industry, and sex: 1970.
PC(2)-7B	16	Earnings in 1969 of the experienced civilian labor force by years of school completed, industry, and sex: 1970.
PC(2)-7B	20	Wage and salary earnings in 1969 of wage and salary workers in the experienced civilian labor force by industry, and sex: 1970.

Table A.19 continued

Population subject report	Table number	Title
PC(2)-8B	1	Earnings and occupation of total and white males 25 to 64 years old in the experienced civilian labor force with earnings in 1969, by work experience in 1969, years of school completed, and age: 1970.
PC(2)-8B	5	Earnings and occupation of males 18 to 24 years old in the experienced civilian labor force with earnings in 1969, by work experience in 1969, years of school completed, race, and Spanish origin: 1970.
PC(2)-8B	6	Earnings and occupation of males 65 years old and over in the experienced civilian labor force with earnings in 1969, by work experience in 1969, years of school completed, race, and Spanish origin: 1970.
PC(2)-8B	7	Earnings and occupation of total and white females 25 to 64 years old in the experienced civilian labor force with earnings in 1969, by work experience in 1969, years of school completed, and age: 1970.
PC(2)-8B	11	Earnings and occupation of females 18 to 24 years old in the experienced civilian labor force with earnings in 1969, by work experience in 1969, years of school completed, race, and Spanish origin: 1970.

Table A.20. History of Social Security tax rates

Year	Maximum taxable wages[a] (dollars)	Tax rate (percent)		
		Employer	Employee	Employed
1937–49	3,000	1.0	1.0	[b]
1950	3,000	1.5	1.5	[b]
1951–53	3,600	1.5	1.5	2.25
1954	3,600	2.0	2.0	3.0
1955–56	4,200	2.0	2.0	3.0
1957–58	4,200	2.25	2.25	3.375
1959	4,800	2.5	2.5	3.75
1960–61	4,800	3.0	3.0	4.5
1962	4,800	3.125	3.125	4.7
1963–65	4,800	3.625	3.625	5.4
1966	6,600	4.2	4.2	6.15
1967	6,600	4.4	4.4	6.4
1968	7,800	4.4	4.4	6.4
1969–70	7,800	4.8	4.8	6.9
1971	7,800	5.2	5.2	7.5
1972	9,000	5.2	5.2	7.5
1973	10,800	5.85	5.85	8.0
1974	13,200	5.85	5.85	7.9
1975	14,100	5.85	5.85	7.9
1976	15,300	5.85	5.85	7.9
1977	16,500	5.85	5.85	7.9
1978	17,700	6.05	6.05	8.1
1979	22,900	6.13	6.13	8.1

The spanning header reads: "Old-age, survivors, disability, and health insurance"

Source: Social Security Administration [1980], p. 35.
[a] Maximum taxable wages is in dollars per year for OASDHI.
[b] Not covered by the program until January 1, 1951.

Table A.21. History of unemployment insurance tax rates (federal unemployment insurance[a])

Year	Covered wages (dollars per year)	Actual rate paid[b] (percent)
1936	All wages	1.0
1937	All wages	2.0
1938	All wages	3.0
1939–60	3,000	3.0
1961	3,000	3.1
1962	3,000	3.5
1963	3,000	3.35
1964–69	3,000	3.1
1970–71	3,000	3.2
1972	4,200	3.2
1973	4,200	3.28
1974–76	4,200	3.2
1977	4,200	3.4
1978	6,000	3.4
1979	6,000	3.4

Source: Pechman [1977], p. 312.

[a] Applicable to employers of 8 persons or more between 1936 and 1956, to employers of 4 persons or more from 1956 through 1971, and to employers of one person or more in 1972 and later years.

[b] Covered wages are in dollars per year for federal unemployment insurance.

[c] For federal unemployment insurance, employers are taxed by the states on the basis of an experience rating determined by past unemployment records. All employers are permitted to take the maximum credit allowed against the federal unemployment tax, even though they may, in fact, pay a lower rate because of a good experience rating. In 1969, the effective tax rate on covered wages ranged from 0.4 percent in Texas and Illinois to 2.9 percent in Alaska. *Unemployment Compensation,* Hearings before the House Committee on Ways and Means, 91 Cong. 1 sess. [1969], p. 183.

For federal unemployment insurance, credit up to 90 percent of the tax is allowed for contributions paid into a stage unemployment fund. Beginning in 1961, credits up to 90 percent are computed as if the tax rate were 3 percent.

Sectoral Production Accounts: Labor Input

Table B.1. Agricultural production

Year	Labor input				Employment	Weekly hours per person	Hourly compensation	Hours worked
	Price	Quantity	Outlay	Quality				
1948	0.337	57.737	19.473	0.884	8094	49.8	0.93	20950
1949	0.276	55.638	15.351	0.891	7900	48.7	0.77	20025
1950	0.279	55.391	15.436	0.911	7730	48.5	0.79	19500
1951	0.384	51.742	19.846	0.893	7271	49.2	1.07	18587
1952	0.299	50.603	15.150	0.908	7054	48.7	0.85	17871
1953	0.273	49.209	13.426	0.904	6814	49.3	0.77	17459
1954	0.266	48.185	12.795	0.909	6836	47.8	0.75	17006
1955	0.230	46.613	10.715	0.907	6643	47.7	0.65	16477
1956	0.269	43.547	11.699	0.909	6316	46.8	0.76	15362
1957	0.342	40.204	13.755	0.908	5988	45.6	0.97	14196
1958	0.410	38.616	15.848	0.913	5752	45.3	1.17	13561
1959	0.303	37.999	11.504	0.915	5605	45.7	0.86	13316
1960	0.396	37.293	14.765	0.950	5275	45.9	1.17	12590
1961	0.421	35.135	14.793	0.921	5218	45.1	1.21	12235
1962	0.427	34.651	14.788	0.933	5026	45.6	1.24	11908
1963	0.522	32.665	17.044	0.919	4727	46.4	1.50	11399
1964	0.496	30.773	15.260	0.930	4455	45.8	1.44	10610
1965	0.579	30.085	17.417	0.940	4242	46.5	1.70	10261
1966	0.709	27.717	19.660	0.964	3839	46.2	2.13	9218
1967	0.628	26.717	16.774	0.975	3681	45.9	1.91	8787
1968	0.688	26.527	18.259	0.978	3647	45.9	2.10	8700
1969	0.852	25.779	21.972	0.979	3501	46.4	2.60	8448
1970	0.852	26.063	22.212	1.028	3400	46.0	2.73	8130
1971	0.902	24.825	22.392	0.993	3339	46.2	2.79	8022
1972	1.000	24.813	24.813	1.000	3343	45.8	3.12	7958
1973	1.452	24.997	36.291	1.007	3323	46.1	4.56	7964
1974	1.414	24.470	34.598	0.999	3359	45.0	4.41	7852
1975	1.034	24.301	25.118	1.008	3304	45.0	3.25	7733
1976	1.218	23.538	28.677	1.004	3248	44.5	3.81	7517
1977	1.298	22.871	29.677	1.002	3106	45.3	4.05	7320
1978	2.183	22.700	49.543	1.008	3060	45.4	6.86	7223
1979	2.449	21.389	52.383	1.032	3008	42.5	7.88	6649

Table B.2.   Agricultural services

Year	Labor input				Employment	Weekly hours per person	Hourly compensation	Hours worked
	Price	Quantity	Outlay	Quality				
1948	0.338	1.752	0.593	0.856	345	37.2	0.89	668
1949	0.369	1.718	0.634	0.864	338	36.9	0.98	649
1950	0.414	1.784	0.738	0.906	337	36.7	1.15	643
1951	0.431	1.864	0.805	0.884	358	37.0	1.17	689
1952	0.451	1.945	0.878	0.899	370	36.8	1.24	707
1953	0.475	1.915	0.910	0.884	365	37.3	1.29	707
1954	0.509	1.905	0.970	0.878	368	37.0	1.37	709
1955	0.539	1.872	1.009	0.872	366	36.8	1.44	701
1956	0.558	1.859	1.038	0.866	370	36.4	1.48	701
1957	0.568	1.841	1.045	0.864	371	36.1	1.50	696
1958	0.608	1.805	1.098	0.859	365	36.1	1.60	686
1959	0.606	1.791	1.086	0.841	366	36.5	1.56	695
1960	0.642	1.658	1.064	0.771	372	36.3	1.52	702
1961	0.674	1.731	1.167	0.782	388	35.8	1.61	723
1962	0.636	1.846	1.174	0.815	395	36.0	1.59	740
1963	0.575	1.919	1.103	0.830	400	36.3	1.46	755
1964	0.666	2.018	1.343	0.854	413	35.9	1.74	771
1965	0.660	2.143	1.415	0.865	430	36.2	1.75	809
1966	0.620	2.227	1.382	0.898	433	36.0	1.71	810
1967	0.607	2.336	1.419	0.939	437	35.7	1.75	812
1968	0.713	2.445	1.743	0.964	446	35.7	2.10	828
1969	0.707	2.511	1.775	0.963	456	35.9	2.09	851
1970	0.708	2.464	1.744	0.933	460	36.0	2.02	862
1971	0.777	2.533	1.969	0.997	441	36.2	2.37	830
1972	1.000	2.725	2.725	1.000	466	36.7	3.06	890
1973	1.095	2.960	3.242	1.009	499	36.9	3.38	958
1974	0.934	2.919	2.728	1.015	512	35.3	2.90	939
1975	1.054	2.649	2.792	1.031	486	33.2	3.33	838
1976	1.356	2.984	4.045	1.072	521	33.5	4.45	909
1977	1.212	3.172	3.845	1.072	539	34.5	3.98	966
1978	1.510	3.675	5.549	1.071	629	34.2	4.95	1120
1979	1.705	3.828	6.528	1.080	662	33.6	5.64	1157

Table B.3. Metal mining

Year	Labor input				Employment	Weekly hours per person	Hourly compensation	Hours worked
	Price	Quantity	Outlay	Quality				
1948	0.298	1.193	0.355	0.872	105	39.6	1.64	216
1949	0.317	1.080	0.343	0.875	98	38.3	1.75	195
1950	0.330	1.136	0.375	0.879	100	39.3	1.84	204
1951	0.364	1.254	0.457	0.883	107	40.3	2.04	224
1952	0.395	1.287	0.508	0.894	108	40.5	2.23	228
1953	0.427	1.331	0.569	0.900	112	40.2	2.43	234
1954	0.427	1.206	0.515	0.904	106	38.3	2.44	211
1955	0.455	1.280	0.582	0.907	109	39.4	2.61	223
1956	0.483	1.370	0.662	0.912	116	39.4	2.79	237
1957	0.511	1.350	0.690	0.920	117	38.2	2.97	232
1958	0.523	1.068	0.558	0.932	95	36.7	3.08	181
1959	0.552	1.001	0.553	0.936	86	37.8	3.27	169
1960	0.555	1.178	0.654	0.936	98	39.1	3.29	199
1961	0.576	1.106	0.638	0.944	92	38.7	3.44	185
1962	0.587	1.058	0.621	0.953	87	38.8	3.54	175
1963	0.605	1.005	0.607	0.955	83	38.6	3.65	166
1964	0.640	1.018	0.651	0.962	83	38.8	3.89	167
1965	0.638	1.073	0.684	0.962	87	39.0	3.88	176
1966	0.655	1.129	0.740	0.969	90	39.4	4.01	184
1967	0.681	1.032	0.703	0.975	82	39.3	4.20	167
1968	0.715	1.093	0.781	0.986	84	40.1	4.46	175
1969	0.765	1.185	0.906	0.990	92	39.5	4.79	189
1970	0.805	1.225	0.986	0.999	96	38.9	5.08	194
1971	0.895	1.115	0.998	1.002	90	37.6	5.67	176
1972	1.000	1.062	1.062	1.000	87	37.1	6.32	168
1973	1.090	1.099	1.198	0.986	90	37.7	6.80	176
1974	1.198	1.208	1.447	1.004	97	37.7	7.61	190
1975	1.367	1.151	1.573	1.016	94	36.6	8.79	179
1976	1.555	1.141	1.774	1.018	94	36.2	10.01	177
1977	1.721	1.125	1.936	1.015	93	36.2	11.05	175
1978	1.895	1.150	2.180	1.021	94	36.4	12.23	178
1979	2.121	1.259	2.670	1.033	102	36.3	13.86	193

Table B.4. Coal mining

Year	Labor input				Employment	Weekly hours per person	Hourly compensation	Hours worked
	Price	Quantity	Outlay	Quality				
1948	0.296	6.632	1.966	0.934	544	34.9	1.99	987
1949	0.298	5.101	1.521	0.934	485	30.1	2.00	759
1950	0.318	5.431	1.729	0.939	480	32.2	2.15	804
1951	0.369	5.134	1.893	0.938	452	32.4	2.49	761
1952	0.373	4.525	1.688	0.942	408	31.5	2.53	668
1953	0.412	3.942	1.625	0.940	353	31.8	2.79	583
1954	0.425	2.943	1.252	0.935	278	30.3	2.86	438
1955	0.422	3.137	1.324	0.933	261	34.4	2.83	467
1956	0.456	3.309	1.510	0.937	272	34.7	3.08	491
1957	0.490	3.141	1.537	0.938	266	33.6	3.30	465
1958	0.509	2.474	1.259	0.941	225	31.2	3.44	365
1959	0.527	2.334	1.229	0.944	199	33.2	3.58	344
1960	0.545	2.175	1.185	0.941	185	33.4	3.69	321
1961	0.537	1.960	1.053	0.944	165	33.6	3.65	289
1962	0.541	1.938	1.048	0.953	157	34.6	3.71	283
1963	0.549	1.959	1.076	0.952	152	36.2	3.76	286
1964	0.582	1.938	1.128	0.957	149	36.3	4.01	281
1965	0.600	1.945	1.168	0.959	146	37.1	4.14	282
1966	0.629	1.942	1.222	0.965	143	37.6	4.37	280
1967	0.663	1.948	1.291	0.974	142	37.7	4.64	278
1968	0.715	1.853	1.324	0.978	136	37.2	5.03	263
1969	0.802	1.875	1.503	0.983	138	37.0	5.67	265
1970	0.883	2.065	1.823	0.990	148	37.7	6.29	290
1971	0.946	2.104	1.990	0.999	150	37.5	6.80	293
1972	1.000	2.331	2.331	1.000	163	38.2	7.19	324
1973	1.134	2.288	2.594	1.002	163	37.4	8.18	317
1974	1.441	2.457	3.540	1.007	182	35.9	10.43	339
1975	1.500	3.026	4.540	1.018	216	36.8	10.99	413
1976	1.368	3.363	4.600	1.057	230	37.0	10.40	442
1977	1.723	3.311	5.707	0.954	242	38.3	11.83	483
1978	1.739	3.487	6.064	1.063	236	37.2	13.29	456
1979	1.992	3.853	7.677	1.054	264	37.0	15.11	508

Table B.5.   Crude petroleum and natural gas

Year	Labor input				Employment	Weekly hours per person	Hourly compensation	Hours worked
	Price	Quantity	Outlay	Quality				
1948	0.403	2.478	0.998	0.801	278	38.0	1.81	550
1949	0.417	2.440	1.018	0.805	272	38.1	1.89	539
1950	0.424	2.514	1.066	0.813	275	38.5	1.94	550
1951	0.444	2.817	1.250	0.823	303	38.6	2.05	609
1952	0.467	3.062	1.430	0.843	321	38.7	2.21	646
1953	0.481	3.167	1.522	0.852	330	38.5	2.30	661
1954	0.496	3.217	1.596	0.857	336	38.2	2.39	668
1955	0.512	3.368	1.725	0.862	350	38.2	2.48	695
1956	0.537	3.554	1.909	0.871	363	38.4	2.63	726
1957	0.552	3.617	1.996	0.884	366	38.2	2.74	728
1958	0.557	3.403	1.897	0.900	339	38.1	2.82	672
1959	0.573	3.473	1.989	0.911	339	38.4	2.93	678
1960	0.593	3.288	1.948	0.914	323	38.1	3.05	640
1961	0.611	3.273	2.000	0.932	316	38.0	3.20	624
1962	0.622	3.289	2.046	0.947	311	38.2	3.31	618
1963	0.644	3.179	2.047	0.943	300	38.4	3.41	599
1964	0.658	3.218	2.118	0.955	299	38.5	3.54	599
1965	0.676	3.197	2.162	0.960	296	38.5	3.65	592
1966	0.708	3.198	2.265	0.969	292	38.7	3.86	587
1967	0.757	3.144	2.379	0.968	287	38.7	4.12	578
1968	0.794	3.181	2.526	0.973	288	38.8	4.34	582
1969	0.833	3.318	2.763	0.981	291	39.8	4.59	602
1970	0.882	3.226	2.844	0.997	280	39.5	4.94	576
1971	0.939	3.134	2.944	1.004	272	39.3	5.30	555
1972	1.000	3.176	3.176	1.000	272	39.9	5.62	565
1973	1.079	3.279	3.539	0.998	280	40.1	6.06	584
1974	1.155	3.830	4.424	1.009	310	41.9	6.55	675
1975	1.341	4.048	5.426	1.018	336	40.5	7.68	707
1976	1.451	4.240	6.152	0.995	359	40.6	8.12	758
1977	1.582	4.688	7.418	1.009	388	40.9	8.98	826
1978	1.707	5.442	9.288	1.020	444	41.1	9.79	949
1979	1.872	5.970	11.174	1.037	480	41.0	10.92	1024

Table B.6. Nonmetallic mining and quarrying

	Labor input				Weekly hours per	Hourly	Hours
Year	Price	Quantity	Outlay	Quality	Employment	person	compensation	worked
1948	0.293	1.053	0.308	0.916	102	41.0	1.42	217
1949	0.301	1.031	0.310	0.919	102	40.0	1.46	212
1950	0.334	1.072	0.358	0.921	104	40.7	1.63	220
1951	0.354	1.177	0.416	0.923	112	41.4	1.73	241
1952	0.368	1.207	0.443	0.932	114	41.3	1.81	245
1953	0.395	1.235	0.487	0.934	117	41.1	1.95	250
1954	0.410	1.218	0.500	0.933	117	40.5	2.03	247
1955	0.428	1.271	0.544	0.933	121	40.9	2.11	258
1956	0.460	1.345	0.619	0.933	128	41.0	2.27	273
1957	0.484	1.316	0.637	0.934	127	40.3	2.39	266
1958	0.513	1.274	0.654	0.941	123	40.0	2.55	256
1959	0.521	1.321	0.688	0.942	125	40.8	2.60	265
1960	0.560	1.263	0.707	0.935	122	40.2	2.77	255
1961	0.563	1.272	0.716	0.944	121	40.5	2.81	255
1962	0.576	1.288	0.743	0.956	120	40.8	2.91	255
1963	0.579	1.287	0.745	0.957	119	41.1	2.93	254
1964	0.621	1.313	0.815	0.965	119	41.6	3.17	257
1965	0.633	1.382	0.875	0.962	124	42.1	3.23	271
1966	0.659	1.405	0.926	0.971	125	42.1	3.39	273
1967	0.691	1.364	0.943	0.978	122	41.6	3.58	264
1968	0.731	1.347	0.985	0.983	120	41.5	3.80	259
1969	0.786	1.345	1.057	0.988	118	42.0	4.11	257
1970	0.844	1.323	1.117	0.988	118	41.3	4.41	253
1971	0.894	1.319	1.180	1.005	118	40.4	4.75	248
1972	1.000	1.266	1.266	1.000	115	40.0	5.29	239
1973	1.067	1.330	1.419	1.003	119	40.5	5.66	251
1974	1.140	1.407	1.604	1.000	124	41.3	6.03	266
1975	1.260	1.351	1.702	1.028	119	40.1	6.85	248
1976	1.316	1.368	1.799	1.025	120	40.4	7.13	252
1977	1.443	1.372	1.979	1.024	120	40.6	7.82	253
1978	1.539	1.452	2.235	1.028	126	40.8	8.37	267
1979	1.684	1.515	2.551	1.020	131	41.2	9.09	281

Table B.7. Contract construction

Year	Labor input				Employment	Weekly hours per person	Hourly compensation	Hours worked
	Price	Quantity	Outlay	Quality				
1948	0.296	33.648	9.967	0.910	3338	37.1	1.55	6440
1949	0.297	32.004	9.521	0.910	3202	36.8	1.56	6120
1950	0.328	34.622	11.340	0.911	3471	36.7	1.71	6616
1951	0.355	37.811	13.429	0.920	3705	37.2	1.88	7157
1952	0.371	38.758	14.397	0.930	3699	37.7	1.98	7253
1953	0.397	37.636	14.952	0.932	3643	37.1	2.13	7031
1954	0.415	36.142	15.001	0.937	3525	36.6	2.23	6717
1955	0.441	37.176	16.404	0.941	3622	36.5	2.38	6880
1956	0.453	38.961	17.639	0.939	3761	36.9	2.44	7224
1957	0.482	37.588	18.124	0.938	3680	36.4	2.60	6972
1958	0.486	36.328	17.666	0.942	3565	36.2	2.63	6712
1959	0.519	37.982	19.721	0.944	3703	36.4	2.82	7003
1960	0.541	37.363	20.196	0.941	3659	36.3	2.92	6911
1961	0.555	37.660	20.906	0.950	3635	36.5	3.03	6898
1962	0.565	39.231	22.158	0.965	3708	36.7	3.13	7076
1963	0.582	40.416	23.506	0.967	3779	37.0	3.23	7277
1964	0.613	42.040	25.756	0.977	3899	37.0	3.44	7492
1965	0.630	43.891	27.645	0.978	4050	37.1	3.54	7816
1966	0.681	45.396	30.904	0.987	4126	37.3	3.86	8004
1967	0.680	45.375	30.834	0.992	4084	37.5	3.87	7959
1968	0.760	46.764	35.521	0.999	4216	37.2	4.36	8145
1969	0.804	49.451	39.764	1.001	4409	37.5	4.62	8598
1970	0.866	47.841	41.408	0.999	4349	36.9	4.97	8338
1971	0.928	49.205	45.680	1.007	4437	36.9	5.37	8504
1972	1.000	50.455	50.455	1.000	4649	36.3	5.74	8783
1973	1.052	54.315	57.127	1.002	4969	36.5	6.05	9439
1974	1.123	53.552	60.126	1.002	4964	36.0	6.46	9305
1975	1.185	47.940	56.786	1.011	4449	35.7	6.88	8256
1976	1.306	49.321	64.424	1.010	4513	36.2	7.58	8504
1977	1.365	52.709	71.967	1.005	4871	36.0	7.89	9126
1978	1.427	59.006	84.177	1.005	5428	36.2	8.24	10220
1979	1.544	62.375	96.338	1.006	5727	36.2	8.93	10794

Table B.8. Food and kindred products

Year	Labor input				Employment	Weekly hours per person	Hourly compensation	Hours worked
	Price	Quantity	Outlay	Quality				
1948	0.327	17.516	5.725	0.933	1847	39.6	1.51	3798
1949	0.328	17.223	5.650	0.937	1827	39.2	1.52	3721
1950	0.347	17.447	6.047	0.935	1834	39.6	1.60	3775
1951	0.376	17.729	6.667	0.936	1878	39.2	1.74	3832
1952	0.392	17.814	6.980	0.945	1876	39.1	1.83	3813
1953	0.417	17.753	7.409	0.949	1877	38.8	1.96	3787
1954	0.439	17.518	7.683	0.952	1853	38.6	2.06	3723
1955	0.459	17.517	8.047	0.949	1851	38.8	2.15	3736
1956	0.488	17.536	8.549	0.946	1869	38.6	2.28	3750
1957	0.509	17.188	8.757	0.948	1844	38.2	2.39	3667
1958	0.532	16.753	8.909	0.955	1787	38.2	2.51	3551
1959	0.559	16.936	9.472	0.956	1798	38.3	2.64	3584
1960	0.579	17.113	9.903	0.958	1820	38.2	2.74	3616
1961	0.596	16.910	10.074	0.952	1805	38.3	2.80	3592
1962	0.610	17.052	10.405	0.965	1793	38.4	2.91	3576
1963	0.628	16.846	10.585	0.960	1779	38.4	2.98	3551
1964	0.662	16.945	11.221	0.965	1781	38.4	3.16	3553
1965	0.672	17.048	11.450	0.960	1796	38.5	3.19	3592
1966	0.699	17.377	12.152	0.971	1809	38.5	3.35	3622
1967	0.730	17.506	12.776	0.977	1820	38.3	3.52	3626
1968	0.773	17.595	13.603	0.982	1821	38.3	3.75	3624
1969	0.822	17.629	14.489	0.981	1827	38.3	3.98	3636
1970	0.889	17.388	15.452	0.992	1812	37.6	4.36	3547
1971	0.933	17.231	16.077	1.006	1777	37.5	4.64	3466
1972	1.000	16.919	16.919	1.000	1752	37.6	4.94	3423
1973	1.077	16.799	18.094	0.995	1746	37.6	5.30	3416
1974	1.171	16.864	19.746	1.003	1739	37.6	5.81	3401
1975	1.272	16.561	21.073	1.017	1690	37.5	6.39	3296
1976	1.405	16.679	23.428	1.015	1717	37.2	7.05	3325
1977	1.524	16.735	25.509	1.014	1739	36.9	7.64	3338
1978	1.642	16.907	27.756	1.016	1760	36.8	8.24	3368
1979	1.781	17.093	30.443	1.023	1764	36.8	9.01	3380

Table B.9. Tobacco manufacturers

| | Labor input | | | | | Weekly | | |
Year	Price	Quantity	Outlay	Quality	Employment	hours per person	Hourly compensation	Hours worked
1948	0.258	0.839	0.216	0.832	100	36.2	1.15	188
1949	0.275	0.837	0.230	0.835	102	35.2	1.23	187
1950	0.296	0.819	0.243	0.832	98	36.1	1.32	184
1951	0.313	0.895	0.280	0.835	106	36.3	1.40	200
1952	0.329	0.901	0.296	0.840	106	36.3	1.48	200
1953	0.353	0.895	0.316	0.844	106	35.9	1.60	198
1954	0.371	0.887	0.329	0.862	104	35.5	1.71	192
1955	0.383	0.894	0.342	0.864	102	36.4	1.77	193
1956	0.417	0.874	0.365	0.867	99	36.5	1.94	188
1957	0.450	0.838	0.377	0.873	95	36.2	2.11	179
1958	0.461	0.844	0.389	0.884	93	36.8	2.18	178
1959	0.475	0.858	0.408	0.889	93	37.2	2.26	180
1960	0.512	0.858	0.439	0.909	93	36.4	2.50	176
1961	0.519	0.843	0.437	0.903	90	37.2	2.51	174
1962	0.545	0.844	0.460	0.920	90	36.5	2.69	171
1963	0.569	0.834	0.474	0.920	89	36.5	2.81	169
1964	0.585	0.860	0.503	0.927	91	36.6	2.91	173
1965	0.623	0.818	0.510	0.931	88	35.8	3.11	164
1966	0.642	0.816	0.524	0.940	85	36.7	3.23	162
1967	0.662	0.831	0.550	0.951	86	36.4	3.37	163
1968	0.735	0.800	0.588	0.963	84	35.5	3.79	155
1969	0.792	0.769	0.610	0.970	81	35.1	4.12	148
1970	0.859	0.792	0.680	0.985	81	35.6	4.54	150
1971	0.928	0.762	0.707	1.001	77	35.5	4.98	142
1972	1.000	0.751	0.751	1.000	77	35.0	5.36	140
1973	1.087	0.782	0.851	1.000	79	35.5	5.83	146
1974	1.228	0.767	0.942	1.008	79	34.6	6.63	142
1975	1.398	0.720	1.006	1.0	73	34.5	7.68	131
1976	1.606	0.697	1.119	1.023	72	33.9	8.81	127
1977	1.761	0.680	1.197	1.022	70	34.1	9.65	124
1978	1.969	0.677	1.332	1.026	69	34.3	10.83	123
1979	2.194	0.683	1.498	1.037	69	34.2	12.19	123

Table B.10. Textile mill products

Year	Labor input				Employment	Weekly hours per person	Hourly compensation	Hours worked
	Price	Quantity	Outlay	Quality				
1948	0.403	8.888	3.584	0.940	1333	37.7	1.37	2612
1949	0.414	7.694	3.183	0.942	1196	36.3	1.41	2255
1950	0.431	8.516	3.669	0.942	1260	38.1	1.47	2495
1951	0.463	8.224	3.806	0.941	1243	37.3	1.58	2412
1952	0.471	7.835	3.694	0.948	1168	37.6	1.62	2283
1953	0.478	7.807	3.728	0.948	1163	37.6	1.64	2273
1954	0.479	6.998	3.354	0.957	1053	36.9	1.66	2020
1955	0.484	7.349	3.556	0.954	1064	38.5	1.67	2128
1956	0.507	7.140	3.623	0.954	1043	38.1	1.75	2067
1957	0.528	6.675	3.522	0.957	990	37.4	1.83	1927
1958	0.535	6.255	3.345	0.964	927	37.2	1.87	1792
1959	0.560	6.694	3.752	0.963	954	38.7	1.95	1920
1960	0.575	6.504	3.737	0.978	931	37.9	2.03	1836
1961	0.585	6.304	3.689	0.969	902	38.3	2.05	1796
1962	0.598	6.563	3.925	0.981	913	38.9	2.12	1847
1963	0.618	6.441	3.980	0.977	900	38.9	2.19	1821
1964	0.653	6.513	4.256	0.977	902	39.3	2.31	1841
1965	0.681	6.847	4.666	0.973	935	40.0	2.40	1943
1966	0.717	7.153	5.131	0.974	974	40.0	2.53	2028
1967	0.751	6.995	5.253	0.977	971	39.2	2.66	1978
1968	0.803	7.322	5.877	0.980	1006	39.5	2.85	2064
1969	0.858	7.317	6.276	0.978	1016	39.1	3.04	2066
1970	0.900	7.028	6.328	0.994	989	38.0	3.24	1952
1971	0.942	7.022	6.615	1.003	965	38.5	3.42	1933
1972	1.000	7.420	7.420	1.000	1005	39.2	3.62	2049
1973	1.088	7.541	8.207	0.997	1036	38.8	3.93	2089
1974	1.207	6.944	8.380	1.003	990	37.2	4.38	1913
1975	1.280	6.182	7.915	1.018	872	37.0	4.72	1676
1976	1.395	6.651	9.278	1.014	921	37.8	5.12	1811
1977	1.514	6.616	10.020	1.013	915	37.9	5.55	1804
1978	1.636	6.617	10.823	1.007	916	38.1	5.97	1814
1979	1.787	6.458	11.539	1.011	894	37.9	6.54	1764

Table B.11. Apparel and other fabricated textile products

Year	Labor input				Employment	Weekly hours per person	Hourly compensation	Hours worked
	Price	Quantity	Outlay	Quality				
1948	0.430	7.440	3.200	0.973	1234	34.9	1.43	2238
1949	0.425	7.240	3.075	0.975	1211	34.5	1.41	2175
1950	0.452	7.524	3.402	0.970	1234	35.4	1.50	2272
1951	0.490	7.405	3.631	0.967	1243	34.7	1.62	2243
1952	0.487	7.616	3.712	0.966	1258	35.3	1.61	2308
1953	0.505	7.701	3.893	0.962	1284	35.1	1.66	2344
1954	0.517	7.255	3.750	0.972	1221	34.4	1.72	2186
1955	0.524	7.575	3.968	0.964	1256	35.2	1.72	2301
1956	0.560	7.532	4.218	0.962	1260	35.0	1.84	2293
1957	0.571	7.342	4.194	0.963	1236	34.7	1.88	2233
1958	0.588	6.952	4.090	0.969	1180	34.2	1.95	2100
1959	0.599	7.481	4.481	0.966	1239	35.2	1.98	2269
1960	0.603	7.570	4.561	0.988	1252	34.5	2.03	2244
1961	0.631	7.298	4.606	0.968	1231	34.5	2.09	2207
1962	0.629	7.935	4.989	0.981	1281	35.5	2.11	2368
1963	0.646	7.944	5.133	0.974	1294	35.5	2.15	2388
1964	0.683	8.014	5.477	0.972	1314	35.3	2.27	2414
1965	0.698	8.375	5.843	0.968	1363	35.8	2.31	2534
1966	0.728	8.678	6.319	0.966	1414	35.8	2.40	2630
1967	0.776	8.569	6.650	0.968	1406	35.4	2.57	2591
1968	0.850	8.643	7.345	0.973	1421	35.2	2.83	2600
1969	0.898	8.633	7.756	0.970	1430	35.0	2.98	2605
1970	0.929	8.273	7.685	0.987	1381	34.2	3.13	2454
1971	0.957	8.343	7.986	1.004	1359	34.4	3.28	2433
1972	1.000	8.579	8.579	1.000	1389	34.8	3.42	2512
1973	1.077	8.717	9.390	0.996	1424	34.6	3.66	2564
1974	1.169	8.216	9.606	1.004	1366	33.7	4.01	2396
1975	1.225	7.727	9.463	1.023	1259	33.8	4.28	2212
1976	1.306	8.449	11.031	1.016	1346	34.8	4.53	2434
1977	1.418	8.328	11.810	1.016	1339	34.5	4.92	2400
1978	1.537	8.445	12.976	1.018	1357	34.4	5.34	2429
1979	1.674	8.146	13.634	1.014	1323	34.2	5.79	2353

Table B.12. Paper and allied products

Year	Price	Labor input			Employment	Weekly hours per person	Hourly compensation	Hours worked
		Quantity	Outlay	Quality				
1948	0.334	4.734	1.581	0.867	471	39.8	1.62	976
1949	0.346	4.478	1.550	0.870	454	39.0	1.69	920
1950	0.362	4.955	1.796	0.870	486	40.3	1.76	1018
1951	0.396	5.225	2.069	0.877	511	40.1	1.94	1065
1952	0.414	5.209	2.157	0.891	505	39.8	2.06	1045
1953	0.428	5.576	2.389	0.898	534	39.9	2.15	1109
1954	0.444	5.569	2.472	0.908	535	39.4	2.26	1096
1955	0.463	5.840	2.704	0.909	552	40.0	2.36	1148
1956	0.487	6.028	2.936	0.913	571	39.7	2.49	1180
1957	0.512	5.978	3.063	0.919	568	39.3	2.64	1162
1958	0.531	5.908	3.137	0.930	559	39.0	2.76	1135
1959	0.549	6.297	3.458	0.935	583	39.7	2.87	1204
1960	0.565	6.407	3.620	0.948	593	39.2	3.00	1208
1961	0.584	6.531	3.813	0.948	600	39.5	3.10	1231
1962	0.604	6.731	4.068	0.962	616	39.0	3.25	1250
1963	0.623	6.814	4.244	0.959	623	39.2	3.34	1269
1964	0.647	6.897	4.464	0.965	626	39.2	3.50	1277
1965	0.665	7.089	4.716	0.963	641	39.5	3.59	1315
1966	0.687	7.505	5.153	0.972	669	39.7	3.74	1380
1967	0.713	7.618	5.431	0.980	681	39.2	3.91	1389
1968	0.756	7.813	5.907	0.985	693	39.3	4.17	1417
1969	0.807	8.075	6.514	0.986	715	39.4	4.45	1464
1970	0.874	7.780	6.800	0.995	704	38.2	4.87	1397
1971	0.927	7.614	7.060	1.004	680	38.3	5.21	1354
1972	1.000	7.737	7.737	1.000	685	38.8	5.60	1382
1973	1.073	7.909	8.486	0.999	702	38.3	6.00	1415
1974	1.187	7.778	9.230	1.005	702	37.9	6.68	1382
1975	1.307	7.156	9.352	1.019	643	37.5	7.46	1254
1976	1.445	7.554	10.913	1.017	675	37.8	8.23	1327
1977	1.571	7.774	12.211	1.014	694	38.0	8.92	1370
1978	1.713	7.894	13.524	1.018	702	38.0	9.76	1386
1979	1.889	7.916	14.951	1.017	706	37.9	10.75	1391

Table B.13. Printing and publishing

Year	Labor input				Employment	Weekly hours per person	Hourly compensation	Hours worked
	Price	Quantity	Outlay	Quality				
1948	0.363	7.660	2.779	0.900	812	37.2	1.77	1572
1949	0.375	7.619	2.854	0.908	809	36.8	1.84	1549
1950	0.407	7.564	3.080	0.934	820	35.1	2.06	1495
1951	0.416	8.001	3.327	0.914	843	36.9	2.06	1616
1952	0.428	8.221	3.519	0.927	855	36.8	2.15	1638
1953	0.449	8.537	3.830	0.939	876	36.9	2.28	1679
1954	0.468	8.607	4.030	0.944	886	36.5	2.39	1683
1955	0.488	8.790	4.285	0.943	905	36.6	2.49	1721
1956	0.518	8.928	4.624	0.930	929	36.7	2.61	1772
1957	0.542	9.019	4.889	0.936	940	36.4	2.75	1780
1958	0.560	8.894	4.978	0.943	930	36.0	2.86	1741
1959	0.572	9.239	5.288	0.950	945	36.6	2.94	1796
1960	0.561	10.053	5.635	1.003	973	36.6	3.05	1850
1961	0.599	9.765	5.852	0.966	983	36.5	3.14	1866
1962	0.622	9.858	6.131	0.972	994	36.2	3.27	1873
1963	0.639	9.924	6.341	0.971	999	36.3	3.36	1887
1964	0.659	10.229	6.741	0.983	1014	36.4	3.51	1922
1965	0.678	10.503	7.122	0.979	1043	36.5	3.59	1982
1966	0.708	10.925	7.735	0.985	1074	36.7	3.78	2047
1967	0.729	11.331	8.255	0.997	1108	36.4	3.93	2099
1968	0.772	11.511	8.892	0.997	1126	36.4	4.17	2132
1969	0.827	11.787	9.742	0.993	1155	36.5	4.45	2191
1970	0.876	11.679	10.231	1.014	1147	35.7	4.81	2127
1971	0.944	11.197	10.573	1.010	1107	35.6	5.17	2046
1972	1.000	11.386	11.386	1.000	1118	36.2	5.42	2102
1973	1.062	11.677	12.400	0.993	1153	36.2	5.71	2171
1974	1.150	11.560	13.295	0.995	1155	35.7	6.20	2144
1975	1.215	11.395	13.850	1.006	1136	35.4	6.63	2091
1976	1.312	11.576	15.194	1.013	1151	35.2	7.20	2110
1977	1.384	12.009	16.619	1.004	1201	35.4	7.53	2208
1978	1.475	12.586	18.568	1.009	1253	35.3	8.07	2302
1979	1.595	12.970	20.684	1.001	1305	35.3	8.64	2393

Table B.14. Chemicals and allied products

Year	Labor input				Employment	Weekly hours per person	Hourly compensation	Hours worked
	Price	Quantity	Outlay	Quality				
1948	0.331	6.997	2.313	0.829	640	38.0	1.83	1265
1949	0.351	6.608	2.318	0.832	608	37.7	1.95	1191
1950	0.370	6.927	2.561	0.836	627	38.1	2.06	1243
1951	0.401	7.814	3.131	0.846	700	38.1	2.26	1385
1952	0.416	8.176	3.401	0.864	723	37.8	2.40	1420
1953	0.432	8.773	3.793	0.877	763	37.8	2.53	1501
1954	0.452	8.687	3.924	0.887	749	37.7	2.67	1468
1955	0.469	8.975	4.210	0.892	767	37.9	2.79	1510
1956	0.496	9.398	4.662	0.898	798	37.8	2.97	1570
1957	0.525	9.635	5.062	0.908	811	37.7	3.18	1591
1958	0.543	9.407	5.106	0.924	781	37.6	3.34	1528
1959	0.561	9.823	5.512	0.934	799	38.0	3.49	1578
1960	0.564	10.260	5.791	0.957	816	37.9	3.60	1609
1961	0.590	10.165	6.001	0.956	817	37.5	3.76	1595
1962	0.608	10.449	6.348	0.969	826	37.7	3.92	1618
1963	0.629	10.585	6.661	0.963	843	37.6	4.04	1649
1964	0.653	10.828	7.068	0.970	855	37.7	4.22	1674
1965	0.665	11.254	7.489	0.969	886	37.8	4.30	1743
1966	0.692	12.068	8.352	0.977	941	37.9	4.51	1853
1967	0.712	12.566	8.949	0.985	977	37.7	4.68	1913
1968	0.761	12.900	9.811	0.989	1007	37.4	5.01	1957
1969	0.812	13.310	10.808	0.989	1039	37.4	5.35	2019
1970	0.863	13.227	11.421	0.996	1028	37.3	5.73	1992
1971	0.917	12.853	11.792	1.006	989	37.2	6.16	1915
1972	1.000	12.542	12.542	1.000	980	36.9	6.67	1881
1973	1.067	12.943	13.806	1.000	1009	37.0	7.11	1941
1974	1.183	13.221	15.648	1.007	1028	36.8	7.94	1970
1975	1.305	13.229	17.267	1.019	1025	36.5	8.87	1947
1976	1.413	13.711	19.374	1.021	1051	36.8	9.62	2014
1977	1.535	14.071	21.593	1.016	1082	36.9	10.40	2077
1978	1.643	14.525	23.868	1.025	1105	37.0	11.23	2125
1979	1.786	14.815	26.464	1.033	1117	37.0	12.30	2151

Table B.15. Petroleum and coal products

Year	Price	Quantity	Outlay	Quality	Employment	Weekly hours per person	Hourly compensation	Hours worked
1948	0.366	2.955	1.082	0.827	222	36.5	2.57	421
1949	0.389	2.879	1.121	0.829	217	36.3	2.74	409
1950	0.391	2.942	1.149	0.834	219	36.6	2.76	416
1951	0.441	3.130	1.380	0.841	231	36.6	3.14	439
1952	0.469	3.232	1.515	0.855	235	36.4	3.40	446
1953	0.481	3.351	1.612	0.865	240	36.5	3.53	457
1954	0.505	3.334	1.682	0.873	237	36.5	3.73	450
1955	0.517	3.361	1.736	0.876	237	36.6	3.84	452
1956	0.543	3.369	1.828	0.883	236	36.6	4.06	450
1957	0.571	3.412	1.949	0.892	237	36.6	4.32	451
1958	0.584	3.296	1.924	0.906	225	36.6	4.49	429
1959	0.620	3.164	1.962	0.917	215	36.4	4.82	407
1960	0.620	3.113	1.931	0.936	208	36.3	4.93	392
1961	0.656	2.978	1.954	0.937	200	36.0	5.22	375
1962	0.658	2.929	1.927	0.947	194	36.1	5.29	364
1963	0.684	2.859	1.956	0.949	189	36.1	5.51	355
1964	0.689	2.813	1.938	0.959	184	36.2	5.60	346
1965	0.711	2.792	1.986	0.960	181	36.4	5.79	343
1966	0.724	2.826	2.047	0.969	181	36.5	5.95	344
1967	0.746	2.853	2.128	0.981	180	36.6	6.20	343
1968	0.793	2.915	2.311	0.988	185	36.2	6.64	348
1969	0.849	2.965	2.516	0.993	187	36.2	7.15	352
1970	0.869	3.050	2.649	0.992	190	36.7	7.31	362
1971	0.928	3.034	2.814	1.001	188	36.6	7.88	357
1972	1.000	2.994	2.994	1.000	184	36.9	8.48	353
1973	1.071	3.016	3.229	1.002	185	36.9	9.10	355
1974	1.206	3.222	3.887	1.005	190	38.3	10.28	378
1975	1.405	3.162	4.444	1.013	189	37.4	12.08	368
1976	1.531	3.280	5.022	1.018	194	37.7	13.22	380
1977	1.660	3.392	5.631	1.013	200	38.0	14.26	395
1978	1.776	3.554	6.311	1.022	205	38.5	15.39	410
1979	1.924	3.656	7.035	1.037	206	38.8	16.93	416

Table B.16. Rubber and miscellaneous plastic products

Year	Price	Quantity	Outlay	Quality	Employment	Weekly hours per person	Hourly compensation	Hours worked
1948	0.374	2.941	1.100	0.923	323	37.4	1.75	628
1949	0.385	2.689	1.035	0.926	299	36.8	1.81	572
1950	0.405	3.071	1.244	0.925	324	38.8	1.90	654
1951	0.441	3.308	1.460	0.930	350	38.5	2.08	701
1952	0.462	3.384	1.564	0.940	353	38.6	2.21	709
1953	0.482	3.595	1.733	0.946	376	38.3	2.31	749
1954	0.493	3.328	1.641	0.960	347	37.8	2.40	683
1955	0.516	3.766	1.942	0.958	379	39.3	2.51	775
1956	0.545	3.761	2.048	0.959	388	38.3	2.65	773
1957	0.575	3.799	2.183	0.962	389	38.5	2.81	778
1958	0.599	3.499	2.095	0.971	365	37.4	2.95	710
1959	0.607	3.964	2.405	0.972	397	38.9	2.99	804
1960	0.626	3.940	2.468	0.986	399	37.9	3.14	787
1961	0.644	3.903	2.512	0.982	393	38.3	3.21	783
1962	0.644	4.443	2.862	0.992	438	38.7	3.24	882
1963	0.668	4.484	2.994	0.985	447	38.6	3.34	897
1964	0.692	4.692	3.245	0.985	463	39.0	3.46	938
1965	0.710	5.066	3.597	0.978	497	39.5	3.52	1021
1966	0.729	5.532	4.034	0.980	541	39.5	3.63	1112
1967	0.767	5.552	4.258	0.986	546	39.1	3.84	1109
1968	0.810	5.989	4.849	0.988	587	39.1	4.06	1194
1969	0.854	6.344	5.418	0.986	628	38.8	4.27	1268
1970	0.905	6.076	5.499	0.995	611	37.9	4.57	1203
1971	0.952	6.103	5.81	0.006	607	37.9	4.86	1195
1972	1.000	6.669	6.669	1.000	656	38.5	5.08	1314
1973	1.061	7.173	7.609	0.996	710	38.4	5.36	1419
1974	1.170	7.007	8.201	1.002	706	37.5	5.96	1377
1975	1.253	6.022	7.543	1.019	603	37.1	6.48	1165
1976	1.342	6.531	8.762	1.013	654	37.4	6.90	1271
1977	1.461	7.212	10.539	1.009	721	37.6	7.48	1409
1978	1.575	7.626	12.014	1.013	760	37.5	8.10	1482
1979	1.726	7.895	13.631	1.013	791	37.3	8.88	1535

Table B.17. Leather and leather products

Year	Price	Labor input			Employment	Weekly hours per person	Hourly compensation	Hours worked
		Quantity	Outlay	Quality				
1948	0.391	2.682	1.048	0.971	411	35.6	1.38	761
1949	0.388	2.560	0.993	0.976	396	35.2	1.37	724
1950	0.403	2.658	1.070	0.976	401	36.1	1.43	751
1951	0.432	2.504	1.082	0.973	386	35.4	1.52	710
1952	0.454	2.617	1.189	0.974	388	36.7	1.61	741
1953	0.468	2.590	1.213	0.974	391	36.0	1.65	733
1954	0.481	2.454	1.182	0.982	374	35.4	1.71	689
1955	0.496	2.576	1.277	0.976	386	36.2	1.76	728
1956	0.528	2.526	1.333	0.972	383	36.0	1.86	717
1957	0.544	2.476	1.348	0.972	377	35.8	1.92	703
1958	0.564	2.333	1.315	0.976	360	35.2	2.00	659
1959	0.583	2.480	1.445	0.971	375	36.1	2.05	704
1960	0.592	2.402	1.423	0.989	364	35.4	2.12	670
1961	0.609	2.362	1.438	0.972	360	35.8	2.14	670
1962	0.622	2.410	1.500	0.984	361	36.0	2.22	676
1963	0.647	2.329	1.508	0.979	351	35.9	2.30	656
1964	0.682	2.343	1.597	0.979	350	36.3	2.42	660
1965	0.691	2.394	1.653	0.973	357	36.5	2.44	678
1966	0.722	2.468	1.781	0.973	365	36.9	2.55	699
1967	0.760	2.383	1.810	0.975	355	36.5	2.69	674
1968	0.816	2.443	1.994	0.977	361	36.7	2.89	689
1969	0.879	2.271	1.996	0.975	345	35.8	3.11	642
1970	0.922	2.123	1.956	0.989	321	35.5	3.31	592
1971	0.949	2.042	1.939	1.000	302	35.8	3.45	563
1972	1.000	2.051	2.051	1.000	300	36.3	3.63	566
1973	1.048	2.004	2.100	0.994	297	36.0	3.78	556
1974	1.164	1.825	2.123	1.001	279	34.6	4.22	503
1975	1.236	1.634	2.019	1.017	247	34.5	4.56	443
1976	1.303	1.799	2.344	1.011	267	35.3	4.78	490
1977	1.407	1.730	2.435	1.004	262	34.9	5.13	475
1978	1.511	1.758	2.657	0.998	266	35.1	5.47	486
1979	1.676	1.652	2.770	1.001	253	34.6	6.08	455

Table B.18. Lumber and wood products, except furniture

| Year | Price | Labor input | | | Employment | Weekly hours per person | Hourly compensation | Hours worked |
		Quantity	Outlay	Quality				
1948	0.295	7.194	2.124	0.932	973	38.8	1.08	1961
1949	0.307	6.228	1.911	0.931	859	38.1	1.12	1699
1950	0.335	6.791	2.273	0.936	924	38.3	1.23	1843
1951	0.374	7.161	2.677	0.931	983	38.2	1.37	1954
1952	0.386	6.869	2.650	0.938	927	38.6	1.43	1858
1953	0.398	6.593	2.621	0.937	899	38.2	1.47	1786
1954	0.416	6.029	2.505	0.936	825	38.1	1.53	1636
1955	0.438	6.387	2.800	0.939	865	38.4	1.62	1727
1956	0.487	6.199	3.018	0.935	854	37.9	1.79	1683
1957	0.496	5.557	2.757	0.934	776	37.4	1.83	1510
1958	0.491	5.276	2.591	0.935	732	37.6	1.81	1433
1959	0.537	5.722	3.071	0.939	773	38.5	1.98	1547
1960	0.545	5.501	2.999	0.945	749	38.0	2.03	1479
1961	0.557	5.169	2.879	0.943	698	38.3	2.07	1392
1962	0.577	5.329	3.075	0.958	703	38.7	2.18	1413
1963	0.615	5.397	3.316	0.960	705	38.9	2.32	1428
1964	0.639	5.649	3.610	0.966	730	39.1	2.43	1485
1965	0.652	5.794	3.776	0.966	741	39.5	2.48	1523
1966	0.694	5.914	4.104	0.977	749	39.5	2.67	1537
1967	0.709	5.761	4.085	0.984	733	39.0	2.75	1487
1968	0.750	5.926	4.444	0.993	748	39.0	2.93	1515
1969	0.817	6.090	4.978	0.992	777	38.6	3.19	1559
1970	0.883	5.901	5.212	1.004	761	37.7	3.49	1493
1971	0.934	6.133	5.728	1.003	782	38.2	3.69	1552
1972	1.000	6.419	6.419	1.000	803	39.0	3.94	1630
1973	1.080	6.631	7.162	0.994	837	38.9	4.23	1693
1974	1.227	6.112	7.500	1.003	798	37.3	4.85	1547
1975	1.343	5.202	6.988	1.017	685	36.5	5.38	1299
1976	1.431	5.940	8.502	1.011	759	37.8	5.70	1492
1977	1.575	6.307	9.931	1.010	807	37.8	6.26	1586
1978	1.715	6.619	11.351	1.011	844	37.9	6.83	1662
1979	1.822	6.832	12.448	1.035	860	37.5	7.43	1676

Table B.19. Furniture and fixtures

| Year | Labor input | | | | Employment | Weekly hours per person | Hourly compensation | Hours worked |
	Price	Quantity	Outlay	Quality				
1948	0.366	2.796	1.023	0.927	363	39.5	1.37	746
1949	0.365	2.553	0.933	0.930	338	38.7	1.37	679
1950	0.387	3.047	1.180	0.941	384	40.1	1.47	801
1951	0.427	2.945	1.256	0.939	378	39.5	1.62	776
1952	0.439	3.012	1.322	0.947	381	39.7	1.68	787
1953	0.458	3.055	1.399	0.950	389	39.4	1.76	795
1954	0.478	2.782	1.331	0.955	359	38.6	1.85	721
1955	0.506	3.049	1.541	0.956	383	39.6	1.95	789
1956	0.529	3.069	1.624	0.955	391	39.2	2.04	795
1957	0.545	3.007	1.637	0.957	389	38.5	2.11	777
1958	0.558	2.834	1.582	0.963	369	38.0	2.17	728
1959	0.592	3.038	1.797	0.964	387	38.7	2.31	779
1960	0.610	2.995	1.827	0.970	385	38.2	2.39	764
1961	0.622	2.850	1.772	0.969	366	38.2	2.44	728
1962	0.621	3.098	1.923	0.980	385	39.1	2.46	782
1963	0.638	3.119	1.990	0.977	387	39.3	2.52	790
1964	0.667	3.282	2.190	0.980	404	39.4	2.64	828
1965	0.685	3.479	2.383	0.978	426	39.7	2.71	880
1966	0.717	3.738	2.679	0.982	457	39.6	2.84	942
1967	0.744	3.618	2.690	0.981	452	38.8	2.95	912
1968	0.803	3.711	2.981	0.988	464	38.5	3.21	929
1969	0.865	3.756	3.249	0.985	473	38.3	3.45	943
1970	0.911	3.484	3.172	0.994	446	37.4	3.66	867
1971	0.940	3.530	3.318	1.002	443	37.8	3.81	872
1972	1.000	3.847	3.847	1.000	482	38.0	4.04	952
1973	1.077	4.040	4.352	0.998	514	37.5	4.35	1001
1974	1.186	3.806	4.514	0.999	497	36.5	4.79	942
1975	1.275	3.245	4.137	1.013	427	35.7	5.22	792
1976	1.351	3.558	4.807	1.015	454	36.7	5.54	867
1977	1.454	3.770	5.481	0.998	487	36.9	5.87	934
1978	1.571	4.003	6.288	1.006	510	37.1	6.39	984
1979	1.744	3.940	6.871	1.018	505	36.5	7.17	958

Table B.20. Stone, clay, and glass products

Year	Labor input				Employment	Weekly hours per person	Hourly compensation	Hours worked
	Price	Quantity	Outlay	Quality				
1948	0.326	5.494	1.792	0.874	579	38.4	1.55	1155
1949	0.335	5.027	1.686	0.877	540	37.6	1.60	1054
1950	0.357	5.489	1.957	0.878	571	38.7	1.70	1148
1951	0.391	5.934	2.318	0.883	610	38.9	1.88	1234
1952	0.396	5.800	2.299	0.896	591	38.7	1.93	1189
1953	0.425	5.905	2.512	0.904	601	38.4	2.09	1201
1954	0.443	5.640	2.499	0.911	573	38.2	2.20	1138
1955	0.463	6.063	2.806	0.913	604	38.8	2.30	1220
1956	0.491	6.192	3.041	0.915	619	38.6	2.45	1243
1957	0.517	6.037	3.123	0.921	609	38.0	2.59	1205
1958	0.530	5.747	3.048	0.930	579	37.7	2.68	1136
1959	0.548	6.353	3.483	0.936	615	39.0	2.79	1248
1960	0.558	6.396	3.568	0.948	619	38.5	2.88	1240
1961	0.571	6.170	3.520	0.949	595	38.6	2.95	1195
1962	0.596	6.306	3.756	0.963	603	38.4	3.12	1204
1963	0.610	6.445	3.928	0.961	612	38.7	3.19	1232
1964	0.635	6.690	4.249	0.968	627	38.9	3.35	1270
1965	0.651	6.869	4.474	0.966	642	39.1	3.42	1307
1966	0.677	7.110	4.813	0.975	658	39.2	3.59	1340
1967	0.701	6.972	4.886	0.980	647	38.8	3.74	1307
1968	0.757	7.002	5.302	0.986	650	38.6	4.06	1304
1969	0.803	7.285	5.851	0.986	674	38.7	4.31	1357
1970	0.855	7.112	6.084	0.994	657	38.5	4.63	1315
1971	0.915	7.050	6.450	1.005	646	38.4	5.00	1289
1972	1.000	7.211	7.211	1.000	667	38.2	5.44	1325
1973	1.060	7.675	8.135	1.000	707	38.4	5.77	1411
1974	1.160	7.549	8.753	1.006	701	37.8	6.35	1379
1975	1.262	6.867	8.665	1.020	641	37.1	7.00	1237
1976	1.378	7.078	9.756	1.018	660	37.2	7.64	1277
1977	1.497	7.312	10.945	1.015	682	37.3	8.27	1323
1978	1.623	7.748	12.573	1.021	714	37.5	9.02	1394
1979	1.753	7.956	13.951	1.030	730	37.4	9.83	1420

Table B.21. Primary metal industries

Year	Labor input				Employment	Weekly hours per person	Hourly compensation	Hours worked
	Price	Quantity	Outlay	Quality				
1948	0.302	14.517	4.385	0.905	1234	37.0	1.85	2373
1949	0.315	12.329	3.887	0.906	1088	35.6	1.93	2013
1950	0.337	14.277	4.815	0.909	1191	37.5	2.07	2324
1951	0.369	15.914	5.879	0.912	1304	38.1	2.28	2582
1952	0.391	15.016	5.877	0.923	1236	37.4	2.44	2407
1953	0.413	16.173	6.680	0.928	1319	37.6	2.59	2579
1954	0.430	13.819	5.944	0.932	1176	35.9	2.71	2194
1955	0.456	15.865	7.238	0.932	1281	37.8	2.87	2519
1956	0.486	16.250	7.892	0.935	1316	37.6	3.07	2572
1957	0.525	15.822	8.312	0.939	1313	36.5	3.33	2493
1958	0.550	13.130	7.217	0.947	1110	35.6	3.52	2052
1959	0.566	14.273	8.077	0.949	1138	37.6	3.63	2225
1960	0.587	14.422	8.468	0.959	1173	36.5	3.81	2225
1961	0.600	13.523	8.119	0.963	1094	36.5	3.91	2078
1962	0.616	14.119	8.692	0.973	1117	37.0	4.05	2147
1963	0.622	14.442	8.987	0.971	1127	37.6	4.08	2201
1964	0.644	15.475	9.972	0.977	1182	38.1	4.25	2345
1965	0.655	16.430	10.758	0.975	1249	38.4	4.31	2494
1966	0.683	17.099	11.686	0.980	1293	38.4	4.53	2581
1967	0.701	16.539	11.596	0.987	1267	37.6	4.68	2479
1968	0.757	16.582	12.548	0.991	1267	37.6	5.07	2475
1969	0.807	17.125	13.812	0.992	1303	37.7	5.41	2555
1970	0.843	16.102	13.573	0.995	1266	36.4	5.67	2394
1971	0.915	15.065	13.778	1.001	1180	36.3	6.19	2227
1972	1.000	15.436	15.436	1.000	1182	37.2	6.76	2284
1973	1.090	16.804	18.320	1.002	1266	37.7	7.38	2482
1974	1.227	17.139	21.035	1.007	1287	37.6	8.35	2519
1975	1.370	14.729	20.185	1.018	1145	36.0	9.43	2141
1976	1.526	14.991	22.880	1.019	1156	36.2	10.51	2177
1977	1.683	15.477	26.046	1.016	1189	36.5	11.55	2255
1978	1.796	16.174	29.053	1.018	1226	36.9	12.36	2351
1979	1.995	16.671	33.252	1.032	1256	36.6	13.92	2389

Table B.22. Fabricated metal industries

Year	Labor input				Employment	Weekly hours per person	Hourly compensation	Hours worked
	Price	Quantity	Outlay	Quality				
1948	0.340	11.221	3.815	0.914	1106	38.2	1.74	2195
1949	0.350	10.008	3.505	0.917	1004	37.4	1.80	1952
1950	0.373	11.442	4.269	0.918	1105	38.8	1.91	2229
1951	0.408	12.774	5.210	0.927	1215	39.0	2.11	2466
1952	0.424	13.262	5.623	0.942	1244	38.9	2.23	2519
1953	0.441	14.551	6.413	0.950	1351	39.0	2.34	2740
1954	0.454	13.097	5.944	0.958	1229	38.2	2.43	2445
1955	0.471	14.038	6.617	0.959	1294	38.9	2.53	2618
1956	0.502	14.232	7.140	0.962	1318	38.6	2.70	2646
1957	0.524	14.360	7.520	0.968	1333	38.3	2.83	2654
1958	0.541	12.761	6.898	0.979	1194	37.6	2.96	2332
1959	0.564	13.649	7.692	0.983	1248	38.3	3.10	2485
1960	0.576	13.805	7.946	0.993	1258	38.0	3.20	2486
1961	0.588	13.319	7.832	0.992	1215	38.0	3.26	2401
1962	0.601	14.258	8.575	1.000	1276	38.4	3.36	2550
1963	0.617	14.430	8.907	0.993	1294	38.6	3.43	2600
1964	0.650	14.974	9.730	0.995	1333	38.9	3.61	2693
1965	0.664	15.860	10.532	0.988	1411	39.1	3.67	2872
1966	0.690	17.319	11.955	0.991	1527	39.4	3.82	3128
1967	0.720	17.649	12.716	0.993	1579	38.7	4.00	3179
1968	0.773	18.107	13.999	0.995	1629	38.4	4.30	3256
1969	0.821	18.683	15.340	0.991	1691	38.4	4.55	3374
1970	0.889	16.981	15.088	0.994	1575	37.3	4.94	3055
1971	0.947	16.060	15.210	1.005	1482	37.1	5.32	2859
1972	1.000	16.979	16.979	1.000	1535	38.1	5.59	3037
1973	1.061	18.396	19.511	0.999	1652	38.4	5.92	3295
1974	1.183	17.955	21.250	1.004	1646	37.4	6.64	3199
1975	1.304	16.080	20.974	1.017	1476	36.8	7.42	2828
1976	1.411	16.744	23.626	1.016	1532	37.0	8.01	2949
1977	1.530	17.382	26.598	1.013	1593	37.1	8.66	3071
1978	1.634	18.431	30.107	1.016	1681	37.1	9.28	3246
1979	1.754	19.075	33.454	1.024	1729	37.1	10.04	3331

Table B.23. Machinery, except electrical

Year	Labor input				Employment	Weekly hours per person	Hourly compensation	Hours worked
	Price	Quantity	Outlay	Quality				
1948	0.328	15.515	5.094	0.886	1437	38.7	1.76	2893
1949	0.340	12.962	4.404	0.885	1240	37.5	1.82	2418
1950	0.359	13.881	4.984	0.891	1266	39.1	1.94	2574
1951	0.395	17.349	6.852	0.898	1525	40.2	2.15	3191
1952	0.417	18.318	7.632	0.910	1605	39.9	2.29	3327
1953	0.440	18.519	8.156	0.916	1628	39.4	2.44	3338
1954	0.456	16.327	7.438	0.922	1471	38.2	2.54	2925
1955	0.467	17.002	7.948	0.923	1497	39.1	2.61	3044
1956	0.502	18.433	9.253	0.926	1609	39.3	2.81	3289
1957	0.524	18.189	9.534	0.931	1614	38.5	2.95	3227
1958	0.540	15.550	8.391	0.940	1398	37.6	3.07	2733
1959	0.565	17.071	9.649	0.945	1498	38.3	3.24	2983
1960	0.584	17.215	10.047	0.954	1509	38.0	3.37	2981
1961	0.598	16.684	9.969	0.960	1454	38.0	3.47	2871
1962	0.612	18.143	11.108	0.972	1528	38.8	3.60	3084
1963	0.625	18.570	11.615	0.969	1566	38.9	3.67	3166
1964	0.651	19.824	12.905	0.976	1644	39.2	3.85	3354
1965	0.669	21.427	14.330	0.974	1780	39.3	3.94	3635
1966	0.699	23.916	16.726	0.980	1952	39.7	4.15	4033
1967	0.721	24.316	17.543	0.989	2006	38.9	4.32	4061
1968	0.782	23.842	18.656	0.993	1998	38.2	4.70	3966
1969	0.835	24.875	20.779	0.994	2070	38.4	5.03	4134
1970	0.901	23.506	21.174	0.999	2014	37.1	5.45	3885
1971	0.951	21.451	20.400	1.006	1840	36.8	5.79	3521
1972	1.000	23.018	23.018	1.000	1922	38.0	6.05	3802
1973	1.058	25.641	27.141	1.000	2119	38.4	6.41	4236
1974	1.153	26.982	31.106	1.005	2255	37.8	7.01	4435
1975	1.281	24.760	31.720	1.016	2099	36.9	7.88	4026
1976	1.390	25.125	34.926	1.017	2112	37.2	8.55	4083
1977	1.512	26.236	39.678	1.014	2203	37.3	9.28	4274
1978	1.612	28.549	46.032	1.019	2363	37.7	9.95	4627
1979	1.735	30.946	53.689	1.031	2535	37.6	10.83	4959

Table B.24. Electrical machinery, equipment, and supplies

Year	Labor input				Employment	Weekly hours per person	Hourly compensation	Hours worked
	Price	Quantity	Outlay	Quality				
1948	0.352	9.356	3.289	0.857	978	37.2	1.74	1892
1949	0.368	8.013	2.948	0.860	843	36.8	1.83	1614
1950	0.369	9.539	3.515	0.865	968	37.9	1.84	1910
1951	0.403	10.935	4.410	0.876	1093	38.0	2.04	2162
1952	0.422	12.040	5.076	0.895	1180	38.0	2.18	2332
1953	0.438	13.459	5.896	0.906	1314	37.7	2.29	2573
1954	0.450	12.064	5.434	0.920	1183	36.9	2.39	2273
1955	0.465	12.804	5.948	0.921	1231	37.6	2.47	2410
1956	0.488	13.684	6.674	0.925	1306	37.7	2.60	2563
1957	0.514	13.865	7.120	0.933	1331	37.2	2.76	2576
1958	0.549	12.784	7.021	0.947	1220	36.9	3.00	2340
1959	0.576	14.687	8.461	0.948	1379	37.4	3.15	2685
1960	0.586	15.612	9.150	0.968	1451	37.0	3.28	2794
1961	0.611	15.529	9.488	0.964	1456	36.9	3.40	2792
1962	0.619	16.935	10.489	0.977	1557	37.1	3.49	3004
1963	0.640	16.475	10.539	0.972	1530	36.9	3.59	2938
1964	0.666	16.340	10.876	0.975	1511	37.0	3.74	2906
1965	0.680	17.479	11.881	0.968	1614	37.3	3.80	3128
1966	0.685	20.252	13.866	0.971	18	37.4	3.84	3614
1967	0.720	20.757	14.951	0.983	1914	36.8	4.08	3661
1968	0.777	20.811	16.160	0.986	1933	36.4	4.42	3659
1969	0.839	21.128	17.729	0.986	1983	36.0	4.78	3712
1970	0.906	19.791	17.923	1.000	1871	35.3	5.23	3430
1971	0.961	18.463	17.742	1.008	1730	35.3	5.59	3176
1972	1.000	19.265	19.265	1.000	1782	36.0	5.77	3339
1973	1.052	21.258	22.367	0.994	1967	36.2	6.04	3706
1974	1.125	21.398	24.068	1.001	1985	35.9	6.50	3704
1975	1.264	18.636	23.548	1.019	1706	35.7	7.43	3169
1976	1.377	19.390	26.694	1.016	1783	35.7	8.07	3308
1977	1.492	20.388	30.408	1.008	1881	35.8	8.67	3506
1978	1.593	22.064	35.143	1.014	2029	35.7	9.32	3772
1979	1.709	23.400	40.003	1.023	2123	35.9	10.09	3963

Table B.25   Transportation equipment and ordnance, except motor vehicles

Year	Labor input				Employment	Weekly hours per person	Hourly compensation	Hours worked
	Price	Quantity	Outlay	Quality				
1948	0.318	5.645	1.795	0.870	473	37.0	1.97	911
1949	0.319	5.463	1.744	0.871	460	36.8	1.98	881
1950	0.327	5.510	1.800	0.875	456	37.3	2.04	884
1951	0.351	8.953	3.138	0.885	703	38.9	2.21	1422
1952	0.361	13.004	4.693	0.898	1009	38.8	2.31	2034
1953	0.386	14.762	5.700	0.906	1158	38.0	2.49	2288
1954	0.403	13.272	5.347	0.913	1050	37.4	2.62	2043
1955	0.425	12.847	5.463	0.913	1005	37.8	2.76	1976
1956	0.447	13.904	6.218	0.916	1072	38.3	2.92	2133
1957	0.471	14.737	6.946	0.922	1147	37.7	3.09	2247
1958	0.507	13.453	6.824	0.930	1044	37.4	3.36	2031
1959	0.534	13.530	7.224	0.932	1045	37.5	3.54	2040
1960	0.561	12.516	7.021	0.936	963	37.5	3.74	1879
1961	0.578	12.486	7.214	0.947	944	37.7	3.89	1853
1962	0.591	13.520	7.993	0.959	1004	37.9	4.04	1980
1963	0.630	13.629	8.589	0.959	1012	37.9	4.30	1997
1964	0.662	13.296	8.806	0.967	993	37.4	4.56	1931
1965	0.671	13.772	9.242	0.968	1021	37.7	4.62	1999
1966	0.691	16.432	11.349	0.974	1193	38.2	4.79	2370
1967	0.710	17.544	12.452	0.986	1268	37.9	4.98	2500
1968	0.763	17.450	13.316	0.992	1277	37.2	5.39	2472
1969	0.838	16.577	13.883	0.994	1228	36.7	5.92	2344
1970	0.913	13.793	12.590	0.998	1043	35.8	6.49	1941
1971	0.939	12.166	11.425	1.005	908	36.0	6.72	1700
1972	1.000	12.421	12.421	1.000	929	36.1	7.12	1745
1973	1.083	12.608	13.648	0.999	963	35.4	7.70	1773
1974	1.194	12.568	15.003	1.005	967	34.9	8.54	1757
1975	1.295	12.272	15.896	1.018	918	35.5	9.39	1694
1976	1.398	12.176	17.024	1.019	912	35.4	10.14	1679
1977	1.512	12.508	18.907	1.011	941	35.5	10.88	1737
1978	1.621	13.556	21.972	1.019	1011	35.5	11.76	1868
1979	1.767	14.918	26.356	1.031	1092	35.8	12.97	2033

Table B.26. Motor vehicles and equipment

Year	Price	Quantity	Outlay	Quality	Employment	Weekly hours per person	Hourly compensation	Hours worked
1948	0.264	10.108	2.672	0.899	758	36.6	1.85	1443
1949	0.280	9.930	2.776	0.901	736	37.0	1.96	1415
1950	0.309	11.408	3.521	0.904	802	38.8	2.17	1619
1951	0.339	11.648	3.949	0.909	843	37.5	2.40	1644
1952	0.360	11.235	4.043	0.921	787	38.2	2.58	1565
1953	0.379	13.245	5.023	0.927	911	38.7	2.74	1833
1954	0.392	11.265	4.421	0.934	777	38.3	2.86	1547
1955	0.413	13.446	5.550	0.935	890	39.9	3.01	1846
1956	0.448	11.592	5.192	0.939	800	38.1	3.28	1584
1957	0.472	11.198	5.283	0.945	772	37.9	3.47	1520
1958	0.512	8.842	4.527	0.956	617	37.0	3.81	1187
1959	0.504	10.144	5.109	0.960	686	38.0	3.77	1355
1960	0.514	10.714	5.510	0.969	719	37.9	3.88	1419
1961	0.525	9.452	4.962	0.973	643	37.3	3.98	1247
1962	0.539	10.918	5.881	0.982	701	39.2	4.12	1427
1963	0.565	11.576	6.538	0.978	745	39.2	4.30	1519
1964	0.594	11.886	7.056	0.980	769	38.9	4.53	1556
1965	0.617	13.344	8.236	0.977	846	39.8	4.70	1752
1966	0.651	13.561	8.825	0.981	879	38.8	4.97	1774
1967	0.677	12.485	8.451	0.987	835	37.4	5.21	1623
1968	0.743	13.786	10.242	0.989	891	38.6	5.73	1788
1969	0.790	13.740	10.849	0.991	922	37.1	6.10	1780
1970	0.834	11.813	9.850	0.997	816	35.8	6.48	1520
1971	0.955	12.538	11.971	1.002	848	36.4	7.45	1606
1972	1.000	13.690	13.690	1.000	887	38.1	7.79	1757
1973	1.078	15.085	16.258	0.998	970	38.4	8.38	1939
1974	1.229	13.016	15.998	1.004	911	35.1	9.62	1664
1975	1.348	11.448	15.430	1.015	787	35.4	10.66	1447
1976	1.438	13.467	19.367	1.015	878	37.3	11.37	1703
1977	1.596	14.794	23.612	1.010	954	37.9	12.56	1880
1978	1.705	15.518	26.460	1.015	1009	37.4	13.49	1962
1979	1.872	15.046	28.165	1.025	1001	36.2	14.96	1883

Table B.27. Professional photographic equipment and watches

Year	Labor input				Employment	Weekly hours per person	Hourly compensation	Hours worked
	Price	Quantity	Outlay	Quality				
1948	0.344	2.652	0.912	0.855	274	37.3	1.71	533
1949	0.361	2.416	0.873	0.858	251	37.0	1.81	483
1950	0.384	2.740	1.052	0.863	275	38.1	1.93	545
1951	0.410	3.337	1.367	0.874	325	38.8	2.09	655
1952	0.431	3.703	1.596	0.892	355	38.6	2.24	712
1953	0.450	4.056	1.825	0.905	387	38.2	2.37	769
1954	0.472	3.791	1.790	0.919	366	37.2	2.53	708
1955	0.491	3.912	1.922	0.921	371	37.8	2.64	729
1956	0.515	4.205	2.165	0.925	396	37.9	2.77	780
1957	0.545	4.332	2.361	0.933	409	37.5	2.96	797
1958	0.570	4.113	2.345	0.946	387	37.1	3.14	746
1959	0.589	4.406	2.594	0.950	406	37.7	3.26	796
1960	0.598	4.533	2.710	0.970	412	37.5	3.38	802
1961	0.623	4.420	2.754	0.963	404	37.5	3.50	788
1962	0.634	4.623	2.930	0.975	414	37.8	3.60	814
1963	0.658	4.628	3.045	0.969	418	37.7	3.71	820
1964	0.678	4.649	3.152	0.971	419	37.7	3.84	822
1965	0.691	4.967	3.433	0.968	445	38.0	3.90	880
1966	0.708	5.638	3.991	0.971	498	38.5	4.01	997
1967	0.737	5.886	4.340	0.983	520	38.0	4.22	1027
1968	0.790	5.958	4.705	0.985	538	37.1	4.53	1038
1969	0.845	6.107	5.160	0.985	556	36.8	4.85	1064
1970	0.900	5.819	5.238	0.995	535	36.1	5.22	1004
1971	0.957	5.473	5.239	1.006	500	35.9	5.61	934
1972	1.000	5.819	5.819	1.000	523	36.7	5.83	999
1973	1.060	6.306	6.686	0.995	568	36.8	6.15	1088
1974	1.131	6.613	7.477	1.003	596	36.5	6.61	1132
1975	1.240	6.149	7.624	1.020	551	36.1	7.37	1035
1976	1.348	6.457	8.704	1.017	579	36.2	7.99	1090
1977	1.451	6.934	10.062	1.010	623	36.4	8.54	1178
1978	1.537	7.414	11.398	1.019	658	36.5	9.13	1249
1979	1.664	7.882	13.115	1.027	694	36.5	9.96	1317

Table B.28. Miscellaneous manufacturing industries

	Labor input				Weekly hours per	Hourly	Hours
Year	Price	Quantity	Outlay	Quality	Employment	person	compensation	worked
1948	0.377	3.395	1.281	0.894	444	38.6	1.44	890
1949	0.373	3.074	1.148	0.896	410	37.7	1.43	804
1950	0.407	3.304	1.343	0.898	428	38.7	1.56	862
1951	0.443	3.308	1.465	0.898	432	38.5	1.70	864
1952	0.448	3.296	1.476	0.905	425	38.6	1.73	854
1953	0.466	3.530	1.646	0.909	455	38.5	1.81	911
1954	0.482	3.322	1.600	0.917	432	37.8	1.88	849
1955	0.505	3.373	1.705	0.916	434	38.2	1.97	863
1956	0.530	3.401	1.804	0.916	440	38.0	2.07	871
1957	0.565	3.243	1.833	0.919	421	37.8	2.21	828
1958	0.577	3.071	1.771	0.928	399	37.4	2.28	776
1959	0.605	3.221	1.950	0.930	412	37.9	2.40	812
1960	0.601	3.272	1.968	0.951	414	37.5	2.44	807
1961	0.615	3.177	1.954	0.944	403	37.6	2.48	789
1962	0.626	3.345	2.093	0.963	414	37.8	2.57	814
1963	0.643	3.319	2.135	0.960	413	37.7	2.63	811
1964	0.674	3.410	2.299	0.968	421	37.7	2.78	826
1965	0.683	3.589	2.453	0.967	441	38.0	2.82	870
1966	0.703	3.763	2.647	0.971	459	38.1	2.91	908
1967	0.737	3.702	2.730	0.975	455	37.6	3.07	890
1968	0.804	3.723	2.992	0.984	458	37.3	3.37	887
1969	0.856	3.752	3.210	0.985	465	37.0	3.59	894
1970	0.892	3.673	3.276	0.999	452	36.7	3.80	862
1971	0.945	3.612	3.414	1.006	444	36.5	4.06	842
1972	1.000	3.725	3.725	1.000	462	36.4	4.26	874
1973	1.064	3.824	4.068	1.001	477	36.1	4.54	896
1974	1.156	3.830	4.425	1.004	481	35.8	4.95	895
1975	1.234	3.543	4.372	1.010	442	35.8	5.31	823
1976	1.296	3.736	4.840	1.019	458	36.1	5.63	860
1977	1.412	3.808	5.377	0.998	476	36.1	6.01	894
1978	1.554	3.925	6.099	0.978	501	36.1	6.48	941
1979	1.697	3.959	6.716	1.018	485	36.1	7.37	911

Table B.29. Railroads and rail express services

Year	Labor input				Employment	Weekly hours per person	Hourly compensation	Hours worked
	Price	Quantity	Outlay	Quality				
1948	0.302	19.276	5.817	0.880	1505	41.7	1.78	3262
1949	0.327	16.437	5.382	0.881	1351	39.6	1.94	2778
1950	0.359	15.572	5.587	0.875	1375	37.1	2.11	2651
1951	0.390	16.423	6.410	0.880	1435	37.3	2.31	2779
1952	0.407	15.845	6.452	0.888	1385	36.9	2.43	2658
1953	0.414	15.615	6.458	0.890	1361	36.9	2.47	2614
1954	0.424	13.927	5.907	0.891	1207	37.1	2.54	2328
1955	0.429	14.189	6.091	0.892	1198	38.0	2.57	2369
1956	0.469	14.005	6.567	0.894	1185	37.9	2.82	2333
1957	0.500	13.263	6.626	0.897	1118	37.9	3.01	2200
1958	0.534	11.408	6.094	0.904	957	37.8	3.24	1879
1959	0.555	11.177	6.199	0.910	925	38.0	3.39	1828
1960	0.572	10.707	6.120	0.915	886	37.8	3.51	1742
1961	0.575	10.083	5.796	0.927	812	38.3	3.58	1620
1962	0.584	10.038	5.864	0.938	793	38.6	3.68	1593
1963	0.594	9.837	5.847	0.939	771	38.9	3.75	1559
1964	0.605	9.872	5.970	0.948	756	39.4	3.85	1550
1965	0.640	9.625	6.156	0.950	735	39.5	4.08	1509
1966	0.651	9.645	6.280	0.961	724	39.7	4.20	1494
1967	0.687	9.248	6.358	0.973	696	39.1	4.49	1415
1968	0.722	9.095	6.571	0.983	667	39.7	4.77	1377
1969	0.768	8.897	6.836	0.991	643	40.0	5.12	1336
1970	0.847	8.592	7.273	0.984	626	39.9	5.59	1300
1971	0.941	8.217	7.731	1.008	597	39.1	6.37	1214
1972	1.000	7.885	7.885	1.000	575	39.3	6.72	1174
1973	1.141	7.977	9.105	1.005	572	39.7	7.70	1182
1974	1.266	7.843	9.929	1.008	579	38.5	8.57	1158
1975	1.342	7.373	9.893	1.017	548	37.9	9.17	1079
1976	1.520	7.268	11.049	1.020	528	38.6	10.41	1061
1977	1.651	7.310	12.066	1.018	534	38.5	11.29	1069
1978	1.789	7.322	13.102	1.021	530	38.7	12.27	1068
1979	1.968	7.487	14.734	1.030	543	38.3	13.61	1083

Table B.30. Street railways, bus lines, and taxicabs

Year	Price	Quantity	Outlay	Quality	Employment	Weekly hours per person	Hourly compensation	Hours worked
		Labor input						
1948	0.407	3.328	1.354	0.970	426	41.1	1.49	911
1949	0.413	3.223	1.331	0.972	412	41.1	1.51	881
1950	0.431	3.069	1.323	0.969	393	41.2	1.57	842
1951	0.453	3.063	1.389	0.973	391	41.1	1.66	836
1952	0.469	3.057	1.435	0.979	388	41.1	1.73	829
1953	0.477	3.004	1.432	0.981	382	41.0	1.76	813
1954	0.494	2.851	1.409	0.984	362	40.9	1.83	770
1955	0.517	2.708	1.400	0.980	346	40.8	1.91	734
1956	0.526	2.647	1.392	0.981	338	40.8	1.94	717
1957	0.546	2.637	1.440	0.988	336	40.6	2.03	709
1958	0.541	2.534	1.371	0.993	322	40.4	2.02	677
1959	0.567	2.483	1.407	0.996	315	40.4	2.13	662
1960	0.566	2.496	1.412	1.000	316	40.3	2.13	663
1961	0.594	2.465	1.464	1.000	313	40.3	2.23	655
1962	0.606	2.437	1.477	1.005	307	40.4	2.29	644
1963	0.620	2.405	1.490	0.998	304	40.6	2.33	640
1964	0.645	2.353	1.519	1.001	301	39.9	2.43	624
1965	0.676	2.336	1.578	0.988	306	39.5	2.51	628
1966	0.732	2.328	1.705	0.996	308	38.8	2.75	621
1967	0.752	2.389	1.796	0.997	318	38.5	2.82	637
1968	0.814	2.360	1.922	0.998	319	37.9	3.06	628
1969	0.858	2.324	1.994	0.994	318	37.6	3.21	621
1970	0.889	2.393	2.128	1.008	322	37.7	3.37	631
1971	0.964	2.356	2.271	1.003	318	37.7	3.64	624
1972	1.000	2.289	2.289	1.000	310	37.7	3.76	608
1973	1.059	2.144	2.271	1.004	303	36.0	4.00	567
1974	1.174	2.105	2.472	1.011	306	34.8	4.47	553
1975	1.301	2.063	2.684	1.019	301	34.4	4.99	538
1976	1.399	1.997	2.792	1.018	298	33.6	5.36	521
1977	1.545	1.923	2.973	1.031	288	33.1	6.00	495
1978	1.656	1.907	3.158	1.022	286	33.3	6.37	496
1979	1.675	2.060	3.450	1.033	306	33.3	6.51	530

Table B.31. Trucking services and warehousing

Year	Labor input				Employment	Weekly hours per person	Hourly compensation	Hours worked
	Price	Quantity	Outlay	Quality				
1948	0.262	7.132	1.869	0.898	727	39.4	1.26	1488
1949	0.282	7.114	2.009	0.901	723	39.3	1.36	1479
1950	0.302	7.680	2.321	0.901	779	39.4	1.45	1596
1951	0.321	8.361	2.684	0.910	841	39.4	1.56	1722
1952	0.348	8.660	3.015	0.921	861	39.4	1.71	1762
1953	0.375	9.038	3.391	0.927	893	39.3	1.86	1826
1954	0.392	8.826	3.463	0.932	870	39.2	1.95	1775
1955	0.419	9.256	3.877	0.935	911	39.2	2.09	1855
1956	0.442	9.641	4.266	0.935	947	39.2	2.21	1931
1957	0.458	9.727	4.455	0.938	957	39.1	2.29	1944
1958	0.473	9.509	4.500	0.942	934	38.9	2.38	1891
1959	0.490	10.219	5.006	0.951	984	39.3	2.49	2012
1960	0.525	10.313	5.414	0.953	1002	38.9	2.67	2027
1961	0.535	10.271	5.496	0.959	989	39.0	2.74	2007
1962	0.548	10.751	5.889	0.972	1018	39.1	2.84	2072
1963	0.575	10.982	6.316	0.973	1030	39.5	2.99	2114
1964	0.590	11.364	6.699	0.980	1054	39.7	3.08	2174
1965	0.608	12.025	7.317	0.981	1097	40.3	3.19	2296
1966	0.630	12.638	7.966	0.992	1140	40.3	3.34	2388
1967	0.656	12.685	8.324	0.994	1154	39.8	3.48	2391
1968	0.715	13.191	9.430	1.001	1187	40.0	3.82	2469
1969	0.755	13.656	10.308	1.002	1227	40.0	4.04	2554
1970	0.815	13.383	10.913	1.010	1218	39.2	4.39	2483
1971	0.897	13.656	12.254	1.004	1237	39.6	4.81	2549
1972	1.000	14.065	14.065	1.000	1276	39.7	5.34	2635
1973	1.087	14.900	16.203	1.007	1342	39.7	5.84	2773
1974	1.177	14.814	17.441	1.000	1373	38.9	6.28	2777
1975	1.271	13.615	17.308	1.001	1287	38.1	6.79	2550
1976	1.395	13.976	19.495	1.005	1318	38.0	7.48	2605
1977	1.525	14.782	22.545	1.002	1397	38.0	8.16	2764
1978	1.633	15.774	25.753	0.999	1493	38.1	8.70	2959
1979	1.723	16.609	28.612	1.024	1548	37.7	9.42	3038

Table B.32. Water transportation

Year	Labor input				Employment	Weekly hours per person	Hourly compensation	Hours worked
	Price	Quantity	Outlay	Quality				
1948	0.291	3.187	0.928	0.953	274	33.9	1.92	483
1949	0.286	2.956	0.844	0.957	253	33.9	1.89	446
1950	0.318	2.776	0.883	0.939	242	34.0	2.07	427
1951	0.349	3.127	1.092	0.948	270	33.9	2.29	477
1952	0.379	3.081	1.168	0.959	263	34.0	2.51	465
1953	0.426	2.990	1.273	0.959	255	34.0	2.83	451
1954	0.425	2.751	1.168	0.955	236	33.9	2.80	416
1955	0.446	2.868	1.279	0.954	246	34.0	2.94	434
1956	0.459	2.968	1.363	0.952	255	34.0	3.03	450
1957	0.496	3.076	1.527	0.954	264	34.0	3.27	466
1958	0.489	2.713	1.325	0.959	232	33.9	3.24	409
1959	0.506	2.789	1.413	0.964	237	33.9	3.38	418
1960	0.552	2.765	1.526	0.954	237	34.0	3.64	419
1961	0.558	2.702	1.507	0.961	230	34.0	3.71	407
1962	0.584	2.707	1.581	0.974	227	34.0	3.93	402
1963	0.611	2.671	1.632	0.970	225	34.0	4.10	398
1964	0.620	2.787	1.728	0.978	233	34.0	4.19	412
1965	0.646	2.730	1.763	0.974	229	34.0	4.35	405
1966	0.685	2.930	2.008	0.988	244	33.8	4.68	429
1967	0.693	3.014	2.089	0.995	246	34.2	4.77	438
1968	0.770	2.953	2.275	1.003	245	33.4	5.34	426
1969	0.837	2.745	2.297	1.003	230	33.1	5.81	396
1970	0.908	2.646	2.401	0.993	223	33.2	6.24	385
1971	0.937	2.463	2.307	1.016	204	33.0	6.58	350
1972	1.000	2.407	2.407	1.000	208	32.2	6.92	348
1973	1.098	2.434	2.673	1.010	207	32.3	7.68	348
1974	1.182	2.438	2.882	1.017	208	32.0	8.31	347
1975	1.299	2.342	3.043	1.028	198	32.0	9.24	329
1976	1.425	2.331	3.322	1.028	198	31.8	10.14	328
1977	1.562	2.323	3.629	1.028	198	31.7	11.12	326
1978	1.644	2.574	4.233	1.037	210	32.9	11.79	359
1979	1.727	2.727	4.709	1.053	215	33.5	12.59	374

Table B.33. Air transportation

	Labor input					Weekly hours per person	Hourly compensation	Hours worked
Year	Price	Quantity	Outlay	Quality	Employment			
1948	0.243	1.415	0.344	0.958	92	36.3	1.99	173
1949	0.260	1.384	0.359	0.960	90	36.2	2.12	169
1950	0.278	1.388	0.387	0.963	90	36.3	2.29	169
1951	0.297	1.550	0.461	0.977	99	36.3	2.48	186
1952	0.310	1.802	0.559	0.986	114	36.2	2.61	214
1953	0.322	1.926	0.621	0.994	121	36.2	2.73	227
1954	0.335	1.964	0.657	0.996	123	36.2	2.84	231
1955	0.350	2.116	0.740	0.995	133	36.1	2.97	249
1956	0.361	2.435	0.878	0.993	153	36.2	3.06	287
1957	0.379	2.707	1.027	0.994	170	36.2	3.21	319
1958	0.391	2.706	1.059	0.993	170	36.2	3.31	319
1959	0.426	2.846	1.211	0.997	178	36.2	3.62	335
1960	0.441	3.089	1.363	0.987	195	36.2	3.72	367
1961	0.460	3.122	1.437	0.983	198	36.2	3.86	372
1962	0.485	3.184	1.545	0.992	200	36.2	4.11	376
1963	0.506	3.263	1.650	0.998	204	36.1	4.31	383
1964	0.538	3.412	1.834	1.005	215	35.6	4.61	398
1965	0.564	3.623	2.042	1.002	232	35.1	4.82	424
1966	0.586	4.074	2.389	1.010	258	35.2	5.05	473
1967	0.622	4.710	2.931	1.011	303	34.7	5.37	546
1968	0.666	5.217	3.474	1.014	335	34.6	5.76	603
1969	0.731	5.569	4.068	1.017	359	34.4	6.34	642
1970	0.831	5.495	4.566	1.025	357	33.8	7.27	628
1971	0.906	5.334	4.833	1.009	348	34.2	7.80	620
1972	1.000	5.345	5.345	1.000	352	34.2	8.53	626
1973	1.056	5.662	5.978	1.001	372	34.3	9.01	663
1974	1.131	5.729	6.480	0.995	375	34.6	9.60	675
1975	1.247	5.722	7.135	0.996	373	34.7	10.60	673
1976	1.375	5.762	7.924	0.997	377	34.6	11.69	678
1977	1.544	5.877	9.076	0.994	390	34.2	13.10	693
1978	1.703	6.108	10.401	0.997	411	33.6	14.49	718
1979	1.779	6.852	12.190	1.013	448	34.0	15.37	793

Table B.34. Pipelines, except natural gas

Year	Price	Labor input Quantity	Outlay	Quality	Employment	Weekly hours per person	Hourly compensation	Hours worked
1948	0.398	0.332	0.132	0.809	30	36.6	2.30	57
1949	0.405	0.321	0.130	0.812	29	36.5	2.35	55
1950	0.421	0.299	0.126	0.814	27	36.4	2.45	51
1951	0.453	0.315	0.143	0.827	28	36.4	2.68	53
1952	0.466	0.335	0.156	0.846	29	36.5	2.82	55
1953	0.486	0.327	0.159	0.860	28	36.4	2.98	53
1954	0.495	0.319	0.158	0.872	27	36.3	3.08	51
1955	0.510	0.310	0.158	0.880	26	36.2	3.21	49
1956	0.533	0.313	0.167	0.891	26	36.3	3.39	49
1957	0.547	0.318	0.174	0.904	26	36.3	3.53	49
1958	0.553	0.311	0.172	0.922	25	36.2	3.64	47
1959	0.582	0.302	0.176	0.936	24	36.1	3.89	45
1960	0.592	0.290	0.172	0.941	23	36.0	3.98	43
1961	0.620	0.279	0.173	0.948	22	35.9	4.20	41
1962	0.631	0.268	0.169	0.957	21	35.8	4.31	39
1963	0.646	0.260	0.168	0.953	20	36.6	4.40	38
1964	0.672	0.249	0.167	0.961	19	36.5	4.61	36
1965	0.662	0.249	0.165	0.963	19	36.5	4.56	36
1966	0.719	0.238	0.171	0.973	18	36.4	5.00	34
1967	0.731	0.241	0.176	0.984	18	36.4	5.14	34
1968	0.761	0.243	0.185	0.992	18	36.3	5.40	34
1969	0.787	0.245	0.193	1.000	18	36.3	5.63	34
1970	0.919	0.224	0.206	1.001	17	35.1	6.57	31
1971	0.936	0.234	0.219	1.011	17	36.2	6.76	32
1972	1.000	0.232	0.232	1.000	17	36.2	7.14	32
1973	1.079	0.218	0.235	1.005	16	36.1	7.74	30
1974	1.186	0.218	0.259	1.008	16	36.0	8.54	30
1975	1.400	0.227	0.318	1.010	17	35.0	10.10	31
1976	1.461	0.243	0.355	1.020	18	35.2	10.64	33
1977	1.607	0.242	0.389	1.015	18	35.7	11.65	33
1978	1.756	0.276	0.484	1.015	20	36.5	12.74	38
1979	2.016	0.272	0.549	1.028	20	35.7	14.80	37

Table B.35.   Transportation services

Year	Labor input				Employment	Weekly hours per person	Hourly compensation	Hours worked
	Price	Quantity	Outlay	Quality				
1948	0.316	0.760	0.240	0.880	83	36.9	1.51	159
1949	0.353	0.722	0.255	0.882	79	36.7	1.69	151
1950	0.350	0.698	0.244	0.875	77	36.7	1.67	147
1951	0.416	0.773	0.321	0.885	84	36.8	2.00	161
1952	0.412	0.806	0.332	0.895	87	36.6	2.01	165
1953	0.443	0.819	0.363	0.899	88	36.6	2.17	167
1954	0.470	0.775	0.364	0.900	83	36.7	2.30	158
1955	0.471	0.794	0.374	0.901	85	36.7	2.31	162
1956	0.498	0.792	0.394	0.898	85	36.7	2.43	162
1957	0.540	0.771	0.417	0.898	83	36.6	2.64	158
1958	0.547	0.733	0.401	0.900	79	36.5	2.68	150
1959	0.591	0.778	0.460	0.906	83	36.6	2.91	15
1960	0.610	0.805	0.491	0.901	86	36.7	2.99	164
1961	0.612	0.821	0.502	0.919	86	36.7	3.06	164
1962	0.629	0.847	0.533	0.941	87	36.6	3.22	165
1963	0.641	0.873	0.560	0.947	89	36.7	3.30	170
1964	0.647	0.926	0.599	0.959	93	36.7	3.37	178
1965	0.679	0.950	0.645	0.962	95	36.8	3.55	182
1966	0.693	1.066	0.739	0.984	105	36.5	3.71	199
1967	0.721	1.136	0.819	0.989	111	36.6	3.88	211
1968	0.779	1.137	0.885	0.995	111	36.5	4.21	210
1969	0.789	1.209	0.954	0.996	118	36.4	4.27	223
1970	0.866	1.227	1.062	0.991	122	35.9	4.66	228
1971	0.887	1.257	1.115	1.013	124	35.4	4.89	228
1972	1.000	1.251	1.251	1.000	127	34.9	5.44	230
1973	1.076	1.330	1.431	1.011	135	34.5	5.92	242
1974	1.176	1.413	1.662	1.017	141	34.9	6.51	255
1975	1.262	1.428	1.803	1.016	146	34.1	6.97	259
1976	1.406	1.489	2.093	1.025	152	33.8	7.84	267
1977	1.705	1.618	2.759	1.027	167	33.4	9.52	290
1978	1.738	1.883	3.272	1.036	189	34.0	9.79	334
1979	1.843	2.032	3.744	1.040	204	33.9	10.42	359

Table B.36. Telephone, telegraph, and miscellaneous communication
services

Year	Labor input				Employment	Weekly hours per person	Hourly compensation	Hours worked
	Price	Quantity	Outlay	Quality				
1948	0.272	7.672	2.087	0.850	694	35.4	1.63	1278
1949	0.290	7.506	2.178	0.848	690	34.9	1.74	1252
1950	0.330	7.371	2.435	0.849	671	35.2	1.98	1228
1951	0.319	7.803	2.488	0.861	698	35.3	1.94	1283
1952	0.339	8.139	2.757	0.876	725	34.9	2.10	1315
1953	0.353	8.572	3.027	0.886	752	35.0	2.21	1370
1954	0.369	8.613	3.176	0.892	747	35.2	2.32	1367
1955	0.379	8.949	3.393	0.898	760	35.7	2.40	1411
1956	0.410	9.496	3.892	0.899	807	35.6	2.60	1495
1957	0.416	9.620	4.003	0.902	823	35.3	2.65	1509
1958	0.455	8.995	4.091	0.911	772	34.8	2.93	1397
1959	0.472	8.993	4.248	0.928	745	35.4	3.10	1372
1960	0.445	9.380	4.176	0.956	748	35.7	3.01	1389
1961	0.479	9.047	4.331	0.942	735	35.6	3.19	1359
1962	0.525	9.236	4.847	0.958	730	35.9	3.55	1364
1963	0.488	9.280	4.525	0.962	729	36.0	3.31	1365
1964	0.542	9.688	5.255	0.977	747	36.1	3.74	1404
1965	0.575	10.108	5.810	0.978	775	36.3	3.97	1463
1966	0.567	10.746	6.093	0.981	818	36.4	3.93	1550
1967	0.595	10.956	6.515	0.990	849	35.5	4.16	1567
1968	0.622	11.198	6.966	0.995	856	35.8	4.37	1593
1969	0.650	12.262	7.966	0.999	923	36.2	4.58	1738
1970	0.721	13.178	9.495	1.004	993	36.0	5.11	1857
1971	0.823	12.894	10.616	1.010	992	35.0	5.87	1807
1972	1.000	13.117	13.117	1.000	1005	35.5	7.07	1856
1973	1.108	13.572	15.040	1.002	1032	35.7	7.84	1917
1974	1.170	13.592	15.898	1.001	1046	35.3	8.27	1923
1975	1.222	13.162	16.078	1.002	1023	34.9	8.65	1858
1976	1.517	12.971	19.680	1.003	1009	34.9	10.75	1831
1977	1.631	13.323	21.735	0.999	1022	35.5	11.52	1887
1978	1.778	13.978	24.856	1.002	1061	35.8	12.59	1975
1979	1.929	14.819	28.586	1.005	1123	35.7	13.70	2087

Table B.37. Radio and television broadcasting

	Labor input					Weekly hours per person	Hourly compensation	Hours worked
Year	Price	Quantity	Outlay	Quality	Employment			
1948	0.368	0.566	0.208	0.952	52	35.1	2.19	95
1949	0.379	0.605	0.229	0.957	55	35.3	2.27	101
1950	0.407	0.649	0.264	0.961	59	35.2	2.45	108
1951	0.429	0.709	0.304	0.968	64	35.1	2.60	117
1952	0.459	0.740	0.340	0.985	66	35.0	2.83	120
1953	0.478	0.804	0.384	0.996	71	34.9	2.98	129
1954	0.506	0.866	0.438	0.995	77	34.7	3.15	139
1955	0.529	0.896	0.474	0.988	80	34.8	3.27	145
1956	0.572	0.915	0.524	0.974	83	34.7	3.49	150
1957	0.588	0.947	0.557	0.976	86	34.6	3.59	155
1958	0.624	0.950	0.593	0.972	87	34.5	3.80	156
1959	0.629	0.993	0.625	0.980	90	34.6	3.86	162
1960	0.645	1.038	0.669	0.986	93	34.7	3.98	168
1961	0.663	1.058	0.702	0.988	95	34.6	4.10	171
1962	0.666	1.079	0.719	0.996	96	34.6	4.16	173
1963	0.686	1.125	0.772	0.999	99	35.0	4.29	180
1964	0.701	1.185	0.831	1.007	103	35.1	4.42	188
1965	0.732	1.224	0.896	0.994	108	35.0	4.56	197
1966	0.779	1.274	0.993	0.997	113	34.7	4.87	204
1967	0.784	1.362	1.068	1.001	121	34.5	4.92	217
1968	0.845	1.396	1.180	1.009	124	34.3	5.34	221
1969	0.829	1.484	1.230	1.005	131	34.6	5.22	236
1970	0.912	1.533	1.397	1.015	132	35.1	5.80	241
1971	0.930	1.568	1.459	1.012	136	35.0	5.89	248
1972	1.000	1.619	1.619	1.000	141	35.3	6.26	259
1973	1.056	1.671	1.765	0.998	146	35.2	6.60	268
1974	1.134	1.719	1.950	0.997	151	35.1	7.08	275
1975	1.231	1.741	2.142	1.002	156	34.2	7.72	278
1976	1.337	1.817	2.429	1.011	161	34.3	8.46	287
1977	1.464	1.893	2.771	0.998	170	34.3	9.14	303
1978	1.572	2.035	3.199	1.003	182	34.2	9.87	324
1979	1.700	2.149	3.652	1.017	189	34.3	10.82	337

Table B.38. Electric utilities

| Year | Price | Labor input | | | Employment | Weekly hours per person | Hourly compensation | Hours worked |
		Quantity	Outlay	Quality				
1948	0.291	4.174	1.216	0.890	309	37.7	2.01	606
1949	0.299	4.230	1.263	0.891	317	37.2	2.06	613
1950	0.328	4.284	1.406	0.894	321	37.1	2.27	619
1951	0.340	4.446	1.512	0.902	326	37.5	2.37	637
1952	0.365	4.494	1.642	0.915	329	37.1	2.59	635
1953	0.382	4.630	1.768	0.924	335	37.1	2.73	648
1954	0.399	4.682	1.869	0.931	336	37.2	2.87	650
1955	0.414	4.715	1.953	0.933	339	37.1	2.99	653
1956	0.434	4.807	2.088	0.936	342	37.3	3.14	664
1957	0.454	4.822	2.190	0.939	344	37.1	3.30	664
1958	0.478	4.912	2.350	0.947	352	36.7	3.50	671
1959	0.502	4.903	2.463	0.954	348	36.7	3.71	664
1960	0.517	4.984	2.578	0.965	349	36.8	3.86	667
1961	0.542	4.986	2.702	0.968	349	36.7	4.06	666
1962	0.561	5.008	2.811	0.977	347	36.7	4.24	663
1963	0.583	5.052	2.946	0.979	348	36.9	4.42	667
1964	0.616	5.133	3.162	0.989	349	36.9	4.71	671
1965	0.623	5.326	3.320	1.008	353	37.2	4.86	683
1966	0.663	5.318	3.524	0.995	357	37.3	5.10	691
1967	0.688	5.445	3.749	1.000	363	37.3	5.33	704
1968	0.732	5.529	4.048	0.999	369	37.2	5.66	715
1969	0.769	5.738	4.414	1.008	377	37.5	6.00	736
1970	0.848	5.852	4.963	0.995	387	37.8	6.53	760
1971	0.900	6.009	5.410	1.009	393	37.7	7.03	770
1972	1.000	6.013	6.013	1.000	401	37.3	7.74	777
1973	1.070	6.163	6.598	0.998	411	37.4	8.26	799
1974	1.148	6.202	7.122	1.000	416	37.1	8.88	802
1975	1.267	6.075	7.694	1.001	410	36.8	9.81	785
1976	1.428	6.018	8.594	0.999	411	36.4	11.03	779
1977	1.566	6.115	9.574	0.994	420	36.4	12.04	795
1978	1.686	6.459	10.887	1.001	435	36.9	13.05	834
1979	1.771	6.905	12.230	1.011	461	36.8	13.85	883

Table B.39. Gas utilities

Year	Labor input				Employment	Weekly hours per person	Hourly compensation	Hours worked
	Price	Quantity	Outlay	Quality				
1948	0.274	1.720	0.470	0.871	141	37.7	1.70	276
1949	0.315	1.744	0.549	0.872	144	37.2	1.96	280
1950	0.326	1.770	0.577	0.875	146	37.2	2.04	283
1951	0.365	1.852	0.676	0.883	150	37.6	2.30	293
1952	0.393	1.887	0.741	0.895	153	37.1	2.52	295
1953	0.412	1.960	0.808	0.904	157	37.2	2.67	303
1954	0.432	1.998	0.863	0.911	159	37.1	2.81	307
1955	0.445	2.027	0.901	0.913	161	37.0	2.90	310
1956	0.476	2.084	0.991	0.915	164	37.2	3.12	318
1957	0.508	2.105	1.069	0.918	167	37.0	3.34	320
1958	0.544	2.163	1.177	0.926	172	36.6	3.61	326
1959	0.569	2.179	1.240	0.933	171	36.6	3.80	326
1960	0.581	2.233	1.297	0.944	173	36.7	3.92	331
1961	0.613	2.236	1.371	0.946	173	36.6	4.15	330
1962	0.627	2.245	1.408	0.955	172	36.7	4.29	329
1963	0.652	2.265	1.476	0.957	173	36.8	4.46	331
1964	0.667	2.302	1.535	0.967	173	36.9	4.62	333
1965	0.647	2.446	1.582	1.006	176	37.0	4.66	340
1966	0.690	2.435	1.680	0.994	177	37.2	4.91	342
1967	0.724	2.493	1.804	0.999	181	37.1	5.17	349
1968	0.777	2.532	1.967	0.999	184	37.1	5.55	354
1969	0.798	2.626	2.096	1.008	188	37.3	5.76	364
1970	0.847	2.678	2.270	0.996	192	37.6	6.04	376
1971	0.901	2.749	2.477	1.009	195	37.5	6.50	381
1972	1.000	2.752	2.752	1.000	199	37.1	7.16	385
1973	1.068	2.821	3.013	0.998	204	37.3	7.62	395
1974	1.144	2.839	3.247	1.000	206	37.0	8.18	397
1975	1.271	2.781	3.534	1.001	203	36.7	9.10	388
1976	1.428	2.756	3.935	0.999	204	36.3	10.21	385
1977	1.564	2.798	4.377	0.995	209	36.2	11.14	393
1978	1.676	2.960	4.960	1.002	218	36.4	12.01	413
1979	1.785	3.127	5.581	1.016	223	37.1	12.98	430

Table B.40. Water supply and sanitary services

Year	Labor input				Employment	Weekly hours per person	Hourly compensation	Hours worked
	Price	Quantity	Outlay	Quality				
1948	0.213	0.649	0.139	0.935	88	35.5	0.85	162
1949	0.235	0.665	0.156	0.947	89	35.4	0.95	164
1950	0.224	0.671	0.150	0.945	90	35.5	0.91	166
1951	0.247	0.687	0.170	0.940	93	35.5	0.99	171
1952	0.267	0.696	0.186	0.953	93	35.4	1.09	171
1953	0.285	0.706	0.201	0.946	96	35.1	1.15	175
1954	0.307	0.697	0.214	0.928	98	34.5	1.22	176
1955	0.330	0.703	0.232	0.930	98	34.7	1.31	177
1956	0.340	0.715	0.243	0.928	99	34.9	1.35	18
1957	0.377	0.724	0.273	0.940	99	34.9	1.51	180
1958	0.407	0.734	0.299	0.941	102	34.6	1.64	182
1959	0.444	0.730	0.324	0.943	101	34.6	1.79	181
1960	0.474	0.734	0.348	0.942	101	34.6	1.91	182
1961	0.497	0.741	0.368	0.947	102	34.4	2.01	183
1962	0.505	0.757	0.382	0.967	102	34.6	2.09	183
1963	0.535	0.768	0.411	0.967	103	34.7	2.21	186
1964	0.573	0.782	0.448	0.980	103	34.7	2.40	187
1965	0.594	0.799	0.475	0.977	106	34.6	2.48	191
1966	0.629	0.822	0.517	0.988	108	34.6	2.66	195
1967	0.668	0.836	0.558	0.972	113	34.2	2.78	201
1968	0.719	0.865	0.622	0.986	115	34.3	3.03	205
1969	0.784	0.885	0.694	0.974	120	34.0	3.26	212
1970	0.840	0.946	0.795	0.988	125	34.5	3.55	224
1971	0.910	0.953	0.867	0.993	125	34.6	3.86	224
1972	1.000	0.959	0.959	1.000	125	34.5	4.28	224
1973	1.056	0.993	1.048	1.008	126	35.1	4.55	230
1974	1.140	0.998	1.137	1.003	130	34.5	4.89	233
1975	1.241	0.998	1.239	1.032	127	34.3	5.47	226
1976	1.372	1.002	1.375	1.043	125	34.7	6.12	225
1977	1.494	1.024	1.530	1.046	127	34.7	6.68	229
1978	1.614	1.068	1.724	1.041	136	33.9	7.18	240
1979	1.841	1.057	1.947	1.039	133	34.4	8.18	238

Table B.41. Wholesale trade

	Labor input					Weekly hours per person	Hourly compensation	Hours worked
Year	Price	Quantity	Outlay	Quality	Employment			
1948	0.373	31.029	11.560	0.913	3010	39.0	1.89	6111
1949	0.376	30.274	11.394	0.918	2934	38.9	1.92	5932
1950	0.400	30.283	12.102	0.914	2947	38.9	2.03	5954
1951	0.420	32.031	13.445	0.919	3100	38.9	2.14	6270
1952	0.415	32.934	13.675	0.929	3160	38.8	2.14	6375
1953	0.432	33.458	14.465	0.937	3190	38.7	2.25	6421
1954	0.452	33.200	15.006	0.941	3162	38.6	2.36	6347
1955	0.495	33.924	16.803	0.941	3220	38.7	2.59	6480
1956	0.521	35.061	18.274	0.940	3344	38.6	2.73	6705
1957	0.544	35.214	19.142	0.943	3370	38.3	2.85	6715
1958	0.539	35.232	19.006	0.950	3358	38.2	2.85	6665
1959	0.580	36.543	21.198	0.960	3424	38.4	3.10	6846
1960	0.574	38.174	21.913	0.981	3504	38.4	3.13	6999
1961	0.592	38.011	22.513	0.972	3519	38.4	3.20	7032
1962	0.610	39.072	23.822	0.983	3564	38.6	3.33	7148
1963	0.624	39.372	24.584	0.978	3610	38.6	3.40	7241
1964	0.666	40.473	26.960	0.984	3689	38.6	3.64	7397
1965	0.647	41.773	27.018	0.981	3801	38.7	3.53	7657
1966	0.719	43.892	31.538	0.992	3956	38.7	3.97	7954
1967	0.696	44.392	30.912	0.993	4031	38.4	3.84	8041
1968	0.794	45.216	35.885	0.997	4108	38.2	4.40	8158
1969	0.840	46.641	39.194	0.993	4246	38.2	4.64	8443
1970	0.868	47.466	41.221	0.998	4327	38.0	4.82	8550
1971	0.922	48.235	44.470	1.010	4360	37.9	5.18	8587
1972	1.000	48.822	48.822	1.000	4455	37.9	5.56	8778
1973	1.077	50.839	54.768	1.001	4673	37.6	6.00	9132
1974	1.209	51.197	61.917	1.005	4796	36.7	6.76	9157
1975	1.263	50.584	63.904	1.018	4706	36.5	7.15	8938
1976	1.386	52.369	72.599	1.017	4864	36.6	7.84	9257
1977	1.476	53.887	79.544	1.015	5017	36.6	8.33	9549
1978	1.571	56.982	89.538	1.022	5266	36.6	8.94	10020
1979	1.735	59.812	103.759	1.024	5526	36.5	9.88	10499

Table B.42. Retail trade

Year	Labor input				Employment	Weekly hours per person	Hourly compensation	Hours worked
	Price	Quantity	Outlay	Quality				
1948	0.338	62.243	21.044	0.981	8999	42.3	1.06	19777
1949	0.345	62.679	21.635	0.982	9009	42.5	1.09	19895
1950	0.365	63.477	23.158	0.988	9083	42.4	1.16	20025
1951	0.382	65.887	25.198	0.983	9511	42.3	1.21	20898
1952	0.384	66.297	25.426	0.987	9638	41.8	1.21	20943
1953	0.398	66.042	26.291	0.986	9738	41.2	1.26	20882
1954	0.434	65.226	28.278	0.983	9632	41.3	1.37	20685
1955	0.464	66.242	30.727	0.973	9898	41.2	1.40	21225
1956	0.470	66.755	31.384	0.958	10165	41.1	1.45	21708
1957	0.485	66.441	32.222	0.959	10260	40.5	1.49	21589
1958	0.471	65.565	30.888	0.956	10177	40.4	1.44	21377
1959	0.530	66.667	35.366	0.958	10369	40.2	1.63	21685
1960	0.512	69.351	35.538	0.990	10519	39.9	1.63	21844
1961	0.535	66.703	35.701	0.967	10465	39.5	1.66	21503
1962	0.566	67.906	38.435	0.984	10558	39.2	1.79	21502
1963	0.572	68.070	38.916	0.990	10621	38.8	1.82	21439
1964	0.641	69.688	44.687	0.992	10946	38.5	2.04	21902
1965	0.623	70.990	44.213	0.987	11332	38.0	1.97	22408
1966	0.724	72.517	52.504	1.001	11664	37.2	2.33	22577
1967	0.675	72.309	48.805	1.004	11823	36.5	2.17	22458
1968	0.805	73.719	59.371	1.010	12166	36.0	2.61	22746
1969	0.852	75.404	64.213	1.003	12672	35.6	2.74	23436
1970	0.853	77.777	66.322	1.025	12940	35.2	2.80	23657
1971	0.924	78.505	72.508	1.011	13236	35.2	3.00	24206
1972	1.000	78.910	78.910	1.000	13567	34.9	3.21	24595
1973	1.093	80.929	88.429	1.004	14050	34.4	3.52	25128
1974	1.205	80.535	97.017	1.004	14318	33.6	3.88	24995
1975	1.224	80.971	99.104	1.013	14412	33.2	3.98	24907
1976	1.371	83.352	114.243	1.019	14922	32.9	4.48	25500
1977	1.453	85.442	124.105	1.010	15628	32.5	4.71	26376
1978	1.547	88.461	136.856	1.012	16347	32.0	5.03	27234
1979	1.701	89.653	152.510	1.027	16800	31.2	5.60	27221

Table B.43.   Finance, insurance, and real estate

Year	Labor input				Employment	Weekly hours per person	Hourly compensation	Hours worked
	Price	Quantity	Outlay	Quality				
1948	0.378	20.763	7.858	0.878	1998	35.9	2.11	3732
1949	0.396	20.856	8.255	0.879	2012	35.8	2.20	3744
1950	0.404	21.354	8.631	0.871	2081	35.8	2.23	3870
1951	0.417	22.799	9.505	0.886	2188	35.7	2.34	4063
1952	0.416	24.188	10.064	0.902	2281	35.7	2.38	4232
1953	0.394	25.628	10.088	0.915	2383	35.7	2.28	4423
1954	0.387	26.962	10.436	0.924	2485	35.6	2.27	4604
1955	0.429	27.823	11.930	0.925	2569	35.6	2.51	4750
1956	0.398	28.679	11.408	0.922	2659	35.5	2.32	4912
1957	0.500	29.286	14.657	0.926	2710	35.4	2.94	4993
1958	0.481	29.854	14.357	0.932	2757	35.3	2.84	5058
1959	0.509	30.855	15.691	0.945	2813	35.2	3.05	5153
1960	0.636	32.944	20.966	0.981	2895	35.2	3.96	5300
1961	0.538	33.115	17.801	0.966	2954	35.2	3.29	5412
1962	0.604	34.346	20.748	0.981	3014	35.3	3.75	5528
1963	0.678	35.187	23.867	0.980	3087	35.3	4.21	5668
1964	0.709	36.477	25.874	0.990	3167	35.3	4.45	5815
1965	0.706	37.742	26.639	0.991	3270	35.4	4.43	6012
1966	0.724	39.243	28.410	1.001	3363	35.4	4.59	6186
1967	0.766	40.343	30.922	0.996	3488	35.3	4.83	6396
1968	0.898	42.415	38.110	0.999	3656	35.3	5.69	6702
1969	0.961	44.115	42.379	0.996	3813	35.3	6.06	6994
1970	0.982	45.210	44.408	0.998	3937	34.9	6.21	7152
1971	1.102	46.783	51.561	1.010	4028	34.9	7.05	7314
1972	1.000	47.539	47.539	1.000	4160	34.7	6.34	7504
1973	1.123	50.547	56.785	1.009	4399	34.6	7.18	7908
1974	1.208	51.664	62.408	1.009	4529	34.3	7.72	8082
1975	1.298	52.754	68.454	1.018	4600	34.2	8.37	8178
1976	1.403	54.030	75.812	1.024	4704	34.1	9.10	8331
1977	1.502	56.651	85.115	1.020	4938	34.2	9.71	8769
1978	1.604	61.019	97.847	1.028	5270	34.2	10.44	9368
1979	1.745	64.260	112.112	1.034	5551	34.0	11.43	9809

Table B.44. Services, except private households and institutions

Year	Labor input				Employment	Weekly hours per person	Hourly compensation	Hours worked
	Price	Quantity	Outlay	Quality				
1948	0.238	39.923	9.484	1.009	5753	37.5	0.84	11233
1949	0.244	39.708	9.705	1.009	5730	37.5	0.87	11166
1950	0.251	40.681	10.199	1.021	5804	37.5	0.90	11304
1951	0.272	41.467	11.278	1.009	5997	37.4	0.97	11662
1952	0.287	42.801	12.301	1.017	6147	37.4	1.03	11940
1953	0.303	43.709	13.237	1.016	6289	37.3	1.08	12207
1954	0.314	44.210	13.903	1.019	6356	37.2	1.13	12310
1955	0.331	45.130	14.928	1.010	6554	37.2	1.18	12687
1956	0.364	47.052	17.149	1.004	6855	37.3	1.29	13304
1957	0.381	48.537	18.499	1.006	7105	37.1	1.35	13699
1958	0.401	49.112	19.687	1.005	7228	36.9	1.42	13864
1959	0.426	50.506	21.521	1.004	7470	36.8	1.51	14280
1960	0.423	53.675	22.724	1.033	7730	36.7	1.54	14752
1961	0.464	53.963	25.046	1.009	7978	36.6	1.65	15174
1962	0.479	56.225	26.955	1.020	8250	36.5	1.72	15645
1963	0.502	57.992	29.137	1.016	8558	36.4	1.80	16203
1964	0.547	60.432	33.040	1.017	8922	36.3	1.96	16863
1965	0.575	62.565	35.967	1.012	9324	36.2	2.05	17539
1966	0.626	65.357	40.908	1.012	9887	35.7	2.23	18337
1967	0.666	67.400	44.896	1.012	10306	35.3	2.37	18909
1968	0.729	69.297	50.506	1.012	10717	34.9	2.60	19429
1969	0.789	72.595	57.264	1.011	11339	34.6	2.81	20374
1970	0.859	74.300	63.789	1.023	11559	34.3	3.09	20617
1971	0.920	74.904	68.878	1.009	11871	34.1	3.27	21075
1972	1.000	78.138	78.138	1.000	12535	34.0	3.52	22177
1973	1.081	82.188	88.833	1.002	13242	33.8	3.82	23284
1974	1.194	84.148	100.455	1.000	13793	33.3	4.20	23890
1975	1.307	85.272	111.463	1.002	14057	33.0	4.62	24151
1976	1.413	88.536	125.087	1.009	14568	32.9	5.02	24909
1977	1.522	93.175	141.779	1.003	15393	32.9	5.38	26374
1978	1.663	97.779	162.560	1.014	16150	32.6	5.94	27369
1979	1.831	103.342	189.171	1.025	16728	32.9	6.61	28605

Table B.45. Private households

Year	Labor input				Employment	Weekly hours per person	Hourly compensation	Hours worked
	Price	Quantity	Outlay	Quality				
1948	0.308	7.682	2.364	1.087	1936	36.1	0.65	3634
1949	0.312	7.547	2.357	1.084	1969	34.9	0.66	3578
1950	0.316	8.146	2.573	1.095	2179	33.7	0.67	3822
1951	0.340	7.833	2.662	1.089	2200	32.3	0.72	3696
1952	0.371	7.054	2.615	1.080	2088	30.9	0.78	3357
1953	0.398	6.757	2.691	1.071	2109	29.6	0.83	3241
1954	0.423	6.075	2.571	1.058	2021	28.1	0.87	2951
1955	0.444	6.875	3.053	1.046	2319	28.0	0.90	3377
1956	0.460	7.106	3.268	1.036	2479	27.3	0.93	3525
1957	0.479	6.942	3.323	1.032	2476	26.8	0.96	3456
1958	0.500	7.008	3.503	1.019	2578	26.4	0.99	3533
1959	0.527	6.737	3.553	1.005	2600	25.5	1.03	3444
1960	0.547	6.937	3.797	1.031	2577	25.8	1.10	3457
1961	0.573	6.516	3.734	0.999	2679	24.1	1.11	3354
1962	0.587	6.487	3.807	1.002	2716	23.6	1.14	3329
1963	0.598	6.407	3.831	1.004	2678	23.6	1.17	3281
1964	0.622	6.292	3.916	1.001	2704	23.0	1.21	3229
1965	0.654	6.066	3.968	0.998	2626	22.9	1.27	3123
1966	0.688	5.846	4.022	1.002	2578	22.4	1.34	2998
1967	0.729	5.739	4.182	1.002	2495	22.7	1.42	2944
1968	0.797	5.491	4.377	1.001	2464	22.0	1.55	2820
1969	0.856	5.183	4.439	0.992	2345	22.0	1.65	2686
1970	0.885	5.082	4.499	1.034	2293	21.2	1.78	2526
1971	0.963	4.723	4.550	0.998	2248	20.8	1.87	2432
1972	1.000	4.623	4.623	1.000	2207	20.7	1.95	2376
1973	1.072	4.478	4.799	0.998	2101	21.1	2.08	2306
1974	1.173	3.883	4.556	1.001	1916	20.0	2.29	1994
1975	1.262	3.625	4.575	1.003	1871	19.1	2.46	1857
1976	1.419	3.774	5.354	1.012	1874	19.7	2.79	1917
1977	1.512	3.877	5.864	1.014	1913	19.7	2.98	1965
1978	1.617	3.813	6.166	1.014	1873	19.8	3.19	1932
1979	1.711	3.717	6.359	1.000	1784	20.6	3.33	1910

Table B.46. Institutions

Year	Labor input				Employment	Weekly hours per person	Hourly compensation	Hours worked
	Price	Quantity	Outlay	Quality				
1948	0.387	3.909	1.514	0.931	727	31.2	1.28	1180
1949	0.415	4.158	1.725	0.931	774	31.2	1.37	1256
1950	0.426	4.375	1.862	0.947	799	31.2	1.43	1298
1951	0.451	4.554	2.054	0.945	833	31.2	1.52	1354
1952	0.464	4.738	2.198	0.957	856	31.3	1.58	1391
1953	0.492	4.945	2.432	0.955	895	31.3	1.67	1456
1954	0.513	5.123	2.628	0.958	925	31.3	1.75	1503
1955	0.526	5.397	2.838	0.951	979	31.3	1.78	1595
1956	0.544	5.624	3.059	0.942	1029	31.4	1.82	1677
1957	0.567	5.869	3.326	0.948	1066	31.4	1.91	1740
1958	0.587	6.159	3.616	0.953	1113	31.4	1.99	1817
1959	0.596	6.827	4.066	0.954	1234	31.4	2.02	2012
1960	0.591	7.638	4.517	0.972	1354	31.4	2.05	2208
1961	0.607	8.082	4.906	0.965	1443	31.4	2.08	2354
1962	0.614	8.717	5.351	0.980	1530	31.4	2.14	2499
1963	0.633	8.902	5.639	0.981	1562	31.4	2.21	2550
1964	0.646	9.213	5.955	0.989	1613	31.2	2.27	2619
1965	0.670	9.524	6.380	0.991	1664	31.2	2.36	2700
1966	0.703	10.052	7.068	0.992	1773	30.9	2.48	2849
1967	0.738	10.504	7.750	0.999	1859	30.6	2.62	2955
1968	0.761	10.978	8.358	1.005	1948	30.3	2.72	3071
1969	0.805	11.776	9.480	1.005	2024	31.3	2.88	3292
1970	0.879	11.307	9.940	1.004	2010	30.3	3.14	3166
1971	0.932	11.611	10.826	1.005	2047	30.5	3.33	3247
1972	1.000	11.712	11.712	1.000	2134	29.7	3.56	3292
1973	1.083	11.838	12.815	1.005	2162	29.4	3.87	3309
1974	1.157	12.028	13.917	1.009	2203	29.2	4.16	3349
1975	1.204	12.890	15.523	1.014	2343	29.3	4.34	3574
1976	1.294	12.948	16.752	1.021	2412	28.4	4.70	3566
1977	1.404	13.030	18.293	1.017	2462	28.1	5.08	3600
1978	1.484	13.776	20.450	1.027	2570	28.2	5.42	3771
1979	1.567	14.485	22.692	1.035	2669	28.3	5.77	3933

Table B.47. Federal public administration

Year	Labor input				Employment	Weekly hours per person	Hourly compensation	Hours worked
	Price	Quantity	Outlay	Quality				
1948	0.270	17.367	4.681	0.856	1428	34.7	1.82	2577
1949	0.288	17.619	5.078	0.856	1448	34.7	1.94	2613
1950	0.301	17.968	5.401	0.861	1468	34.7	2.04	2649
1951	0.318	22.518	7.161	0.872	1817	34.7	2.18	3279
1952	0.336	23.950	8.036	0.883	1910	34.7	2.33	3446
1953	0.348	22.737	7.905	0.895	1814	34.2	2.45	3226
1954	0.348	21.398	7.452	0.902	1693	34.2	2.47	3011
1955	0.374	21.625	8.080	0.908	1701	34.2	2.67	3025
1956	0.397	22.056	8.766	0.912	1727	34.2	2.85	3071
1957	0.415	22.198	9.206	0.919	1724	34.2	3.00	3066
1958	0.460	21.865	10.053	0.929	1703	33.7	3.36	2988
1959	0.465	22.190	10.314	0.931	1707	34.1	3.41	3027
1960	0.490	22.567	11.052	0.921	1755	34.1	3.55	3112
1961	0.508	23.226	11.807	0.947	1757	34.1	3.79	3116
1962	0.515	24.423	12.588	0.963	1818	34.1	3.91	3222
1963	0.542	24.750	13.408	0.966	1836	34.1	4.12	3254
1964	0.578	24.753	14.313	0.973	1823	34.1	4.43	3230
1965	0.600	25.114	15.076	0.977	1842	34.1	4.62	3265
1966	0.621	26.701	16.574	0.977	1964	34.0	4.78	3470
1967	0.625	28.737	17.975	0.987	2087	34.1	4.86	3699
1968	0.680	29.103	19.783	0.996	2098	34.0	5.33	3712
1969	0.732	28.897	21.139	0.994	2069	34.3	5.72	3693
1970	0.853	27.394	23.377	0.991	2029	33.3	6.66	3512
1971	0.915	27.724	25.366	1.008	1991	33.7	7.26	3493
1972	1.000	27.411	27.411	1.000	2005	33.4	7.87	3481
1973	1.075	27.006	29.025	1.006	1991	32.9	8.51	3409
1974	1.124	28.071	31.544	1.007	2039	33.4	8.91	3540
1975	1.234	28.357	34.992	1.010	2063	33.2	9.81	3566
1976	1.312	28.944	37.969	1.016	2074	33.5	10.49	3618
1977	1.411	29.090	41.036	1.016	2079	33.6	11.29	3636
1978	1.520	29.573	44.960	1.017	2105	33.7	12.17	3694
1979	1.601	29.712	47.570	1.017	2107	33.9	12.83	3709

Table B.48. Federal government enterprises

Year	Labor input				Employment	Weekly hours per person	Hourly compensation	Hours worked
	Price	Quantity	Outlay	Quality				
1948	0.271	6.186	1.676	0.960	570	35.2	1.61	1042
1949	0.283	6.568	1.857	0.961	605	35.1	1.68	1105
1950	0.302	6.407	1.935	0.966	587	35.2	1.80	1073
1951	0.319	6.715	2.140	0.971	612	35.1	1.91	1118
1952	0.335	7.270	2.433	0.986	656	35.0	2.04	1193
1953	0.338	7.124	2.407	0.994	644	34.6	2.08	1159
1954	0.337	7.152	2.410	0.998	644	34.6	2.08	1159
1955	0.363	7.121	2.588	0.995	643	34.6	2.24	1157
1956	0.383	7.165	2.744	0.991	650	34.6	2.35	1170
1957	0.394	7.389	2.914	0.993	669	34.6	2.42	1204
1958	0.430	7.549	3.247	0.994	659	35.8	2.64	1228
1959	0.428	7.809	3.343	1.010	695	34.6	2.67	1251
1960	0.450	8.054	3.627	1.012	715	34.6	2.82	1287
1961	0.473	8.170	3.866	1.005	734	34.5	2.94	1315
1962	0.487	8.319	4.051	1.013	746	34.2	3.05	1328
1963	0.530	8.309	4.401	1.010	750	34.1	3.31	1331
1964	0.559	8.362	4.677	1.013	756	34.0	3.50	1335
1965	0.588	8.517	5.005	1.010	776	33.8	3.67	1364
1966	0.595	9.226	5.490	1.006	849	33.6	3.70	1484
1967	0.609	9.654	5.881	1.011	887	33.5	3.81	1544
1968	0.670	9.780	6.553	1.011	896	33.6	4.19	1565
1969	0.718	9.997	7.177	1.014	907	33.8	4.50	1595
1970	0.824	10.245	8.442	1.010	924	34.1	5.15	1640
1971	0.884	10.061	8.899	1.008	918	33.8	5.51	1615
1972	1.000	9.670	9.670	1.000	888	33.9	6.18	1564
1973	1.086	9.654	10.484	1.001	884	33.9	6.72	1560
1974	1.204	9.808	11.805	1.002	897	33.9	7.46	1583
1975	1.345	9.586	12.895	1.009	880	33.6	8.39	1537
1976	1.473	9.466	13.944	1.012	853	34.1	9.22	1513
1977	1.606	9.225	14.814	1.005	841	34.0	9.98	1485
1978	1.694	9.474	16.052	1.013	846	34.4	10.62	1512
1979	1.842	9.566	17.621	1.009	868	34.0	11.50	1533

Table B.49.   State and local educational services

| Year | Labor input | | | | Employment | Weekly hours per person | Hourly compensation | Hours worked |
	Price	Quantity	Outlay	Quality				
1948	0.271	13.883	3.766	0.909	1579	28.8	1.59	2367
1949	0.286	14.621	4.176	0.910	1660	28.8	1.68	2489
1950	0.294	15.392	4.527	0.930	1718	28.7	1.77	2564
1951	0.316	15.921	5.036	0.935	1768	28.7	1.91	2639
1952	0.326	17.115	5.574	0.960	1850	28.7	2.02	2763
1953	0.336	18.143	6.096	0.973	1944	28.6	2.11	2891
1954	0.354	19.211	6.797	0.984	2043	28.5	2.25	3025
1955	0.363	20.366	7.402	0.987	2180	28.2	2.32	3197
1956	0.388	21.467	8.320	0.989	2309	28.0	2.47	3363
1957	0.409	22.938	9.373	1.004	2426	28.1	2.65	3541
1958	0.430	24.355	10.470	1.014	2552	28.1	2.81	3724
1959	0.448	25.728	11.514	1.021	2687	27.9	2.95	3905
1960	0.469	27.703	12.979	1.036	2869	27.8	3.13	4143
1961	0.498	28.746	14.321	1.026	3006	27.8	3.30	4341
1962	0.527	29.945	15.784	1.033	3163	27.3	3.51	4493
1963	0.552	31.653	17.463	1.025	3375	27.3	3.65	4784
1964	0.573	33.788	19.345	1.026	3603	27.2	3.79	5102
1965	0.592	35.936	21.285	1.025	3890	26.9	3.92	5435
1966	0.635	38.189	24.255	1.018	4251	26.3	4.17	5816
1967	0.688	39.776	27.377	1.019	4537	25.6	4.52	6051
1968	0.745	41.772	31.126	1.017	4811	25.4	4.89	6366
1969	0.807	43.472	35.086	1.012	5069	25.3	5.27	6658
1970	0.882	45.206	39.856	1.009	5313	25.1	5.74	6944
1971	0.941	46.883	44.138	1.003	5563	25.0	6.09	7244
1972	1.000	48.570	48.570	1.000	5740	25.2	6.45	7528
1973	1.063	50.485	53.665	1.004	5923	25.3	6.89	7792
1974	1.124	51.998	58.426	1.007	6151	25.0	7.30	8006
1975	1.237	53.146	65.735	1.009	6355	24.7	8.05	8165
1976	1.341	53.945	72.352	1.014	6430	24.7	8.78	8242
1977	1.437	54.652	78.556	1.013	6562	24.5	9.40	8359
1978	1.512	56.304	85.124	1.021	6690	24.6	9.96	8546
1979	1.628	57.243	93.193	1.022	6804	24.5	10.74	8680

Table B.50. State and local public administration

Year	Price	Labor input Quantity	Outlay	Quality	Employment	Weekly hours per person	Hourly compensation	Hours worked
1948	0.308	15.462	4.755	0.906	2153	32.4	1.31	3629
1949	0.313	16.828	5.266	0.905	2234	34.0	1.33	3954
1950	0.321	17.513	5.618	0.910	2311	34.0	1.37	4091
1951	0.341	17.959	6.124	0.922	2283	34.9	1.48	4139
1952	0.363	18.405	6.678	0.935	2305	34.9	1.59	4187
1953	0.377	19.211	7.238	0.943	2358	35.3	1.67	4331
1954	0.392	20.131	7.901	0.952	2469	35.0	1.76	4496
1955	0.407	20.746	8.435	0.957	2561	34.6	1.83	4611
1956	0.427	21.779	9.301	0.957	2701	34.4	1.92	4837
1957	0.446	22.813	10.185	0.965	2807	34.4	2.03	5024
1958	0.460	24.124	11.108	0.974	2945	34.4	2.11	5266
1959	0.476	24.386	11.619	0.974	2997	34.1	2.18	5321
1960	0.505	24.738	12.491	0.966	3073	34.1	2.29	5444
1961	0.513	26.539	13.613	0.986	3180	34.6	2.38	5724
1962	0.529	27.342	14.459	1.001	3229	34.6	2.49	5809
1963	0.552	27.882	15.394	0.999	3302	34.6	2.59	5935
1964	0.569	29.064	16.528	1.002	3426	34.6	2.68	6169
1965	0.597	30.156	18.009	1.001	3565	34.6	2.81	6408
1966	0.634	31.338	19.860	0.997	3765	34.1	2.97	6681
1967	0.684	32.379	22.153	1.002	3897	33.9	3.22	6873
1968	0.730	33.951	24.772	1.011	4054	33.9	3.47	7138
1969	0.794	34.643	27.515	1.004	4173	33.8	3.75	7339
1970	0.875	35.663	31.211	0.992	4349	33.8	4.08	7647
1971	0.935	37.557	35.117	1.007	4483	34.0	4.43	7929
1972	1.000	39.162	39.162	1.000	4714	34.0	4.70	8326
1973	1.079	40.802	44.032	1.006	4893	33.9	5.11	8623
1974	1.168	41.833	48.864	1.006	5020	33.9	5.53	8840
1975	1.259	43.613	54.889	1.008	5214	33.9	5.97	9196
1976	1.352	44.310	59.898	1.012	5263	34.0	6.44	9307
1977	1.461	44.829	65.486	1.012	5366	33.7	6.95	9416
1978	1.554	46.564	72.358	1.013	5610	33.5	7.40	9777
1979	1.666	47.492	79.136	1.012	5744	33.4	7.93	9979

Table B.51. State and local government enterprises

Year	Labor input				Employment	Weekly hours per person	Hourly compensation	Hours worked
	Price	Quantity	Outlay	Quality				
1948	0.267	2.394	0.640	1.023	230	37.1	1.44	444
1949	0.283	2.495	0.707	1.020	239	37.3	1.52	464
1950	0.290	2.621	0.760	1.014	252	37.4	1.55	490
1951	0.309	2.784	0.859	1.027	260	38.0	1.67	514
1952	0.327	3.233	1.056	1.036	298	38.2	1.78	592
1953	0.344	3.308	1.138	1.033	303	38.5	1.87	607
1954	0.360	3.296	1.187	1.028	305	38.3	1.95	608
1955	0.382	3.337	1.274	1.019	311	38.4	2.05	621
1956	0.395	3.320	1.310	1.010	312	38.4	2.10	623
1957	0.410	3.338	1.368	1.008	315	38.3	2.18	628
1958	0.430	3.472	1.494	1.002	337	37.5	2.27	657
1959	0.453	3.863	1.750	1.016	354	39.2	2.43	721
1960	0.477	4.054	1.934	1.011	380	38.5	2.54	760
1961	0.496	3.959	1.962	1.001	389	37.1	2.62	750
1962	0.518	4.231	2.192	1.012	402	37.9	2.76	793
1963	0.539	4.312	2.325	1.008	429	36.4	2.87	811
1964	0.567	4.543	2.574	1.009	444	37.0	3.01	854
1965	0.601	4.618	2.777	1.009	458	36.4	3.20	868
1966	0.655	4.582	3.000	1.001	451	37.0	3.46	868
1967	0.697	4.631	3.227	1.012	454	36.8	3.72	868
1968	0.735	4.977	3.658	1.014	483	37.1	3.93	931
1969	0.791	5.179	4.094	1.018	502	37.0	4.24	965
1970	0.844	5.447	4.597	1.013	530	37.0	4.51	1020
1971	0.928	5.537	5.140	1.003	546	36.9	4.91	1047
1972	1.000	5.606	5.606	1.000	547	37.4	5.27	1063
1973	1.093	5.872	6.419	1.001	579	36.9	5.77	1112
1974	1.163	6.303	7.330	1.003	623	36.8	6.15	1192
1975	1.243	6.816	8.470	1.005	674	36.7	6.59	1286
1976	1.338	6.837	9.149	1.008	676	36.6	7.11	1286
1977	1.438	6.786	9.756	1.001	679	36.4	7.59	1286
1978	1.526	7.122	10.869	1.009	703	36.6	8.12	1338
1979	1.634	7.371	12.043	1.008	734	36.3	8.68	1387

APPENDIX C

Sectoral Production Accounts: Capital Input

Table C.1. Agricultural production

	Capital input				Capital stock		
Year	Price	Quantity	Outlay	Quality	Price	Quantity	Value
1948	0.0215	189.165	4.067	0.511	0.307	369.842	113.638
1949	0.0175	204.910	3.595	0.547	0.309	374.845	115.714
1950	0.0225	211.633	4.760	0.562	0.333	376.380	125.503
1951	0.0144	231.116	3.322	0.608	0.369	379.941	140.049
1952	0.0300	242.116	7.264	0.632	0.381	382.828	145.799
1953	0.0282	249.760	7.042	0.649	0.381	384.732	146.758
1954	0.0279	253.854	7.071	0.674	0.397	376.770	149.539
1955	0.0319	259.111	8.254	0.683	0.417	379.421	158.148
1956	0.0275	267.333	7.351	0.705	0.452	379.064	171.176
1957	0.0206	266.451	5.484	0.710	0.479	375.528	179.852
1958	0.0218	266.716	5.813	0.713	0.511	374.060	191.320
1959	0.0296	274.350	8.121	0.727	0.541	377.566	204.349
1960	0.0210	286.616	6.029	0.747	0.555	383.724	212.855
1961	0.0230	291.144	6.699	0.757	0.579	384.565	222.508
1962	0.0243	294.460	7.144	0.764	0.607	385.533	234.164
1963	0.0163	301.359	4.899	0.783	0.631	385.106	242.885
1964	0.0179	329.274	5.886	0.840	0.654	391.859	256.306
1965	0.0194	341.386	6.606	0.868	0.693	393.160	272.619
1966	0.0167	360.561	6.021	0.903	0.731	399.310	291.995
1967	0.0212	376.187	7.979	0.941	0.759	399.694	303.468
1968	0.0189	386.347	7.308	0.961	0.794	401.893	319.299
1969	0.0167	383.344	6.385	0.955	0.831	401.614	333.840
1970	0.0174	391.141	6.802	0.973	0.866	402.180	348.284
1971	0.0198	400.015	7.927	0.992	0.893	403.294	360.112
1972	0.0260	405.191	10.529	1.000	1.000	405.191	405.191
1973	0.0382	414.619	15.850	1.018	1.177	407.136	479.192
1974	0.0315	431.125	13.583	1.045	1.347	412.505	555.824
1975	0.0544	449.322	24.421	1.083	1.485	414.758	615.853
1976	0.0387	460.794	17.843	1.102	1.624	418.047	678.941
1977	0.0424	459.448	19.499	1.101	1.779	417.318	742.558
1978	0.0223	494.116	11.021	1.174	2.041	421.041	859.347
1979	0.0349	537.814	18.792	1.268	2.302	424.166	976.434

Table C.2. Agricultural services

Year	Capital input				Capital stock		
	Price	Quantity	Outlay	Quality	Price	Quantity	Value
1948	0.0363	3.178	0.115	0.247	0.264	12.887	3.397
1949	0.0309	3.536	0.109	0.270	0.276	13.083	3.605
1950	0.0136	4.479	0.061	0.338	0.302	13.244	3.995
1951	0.0124	6.080	0.075	0.450	0.331	13.497	4.469
1952	0.0114	7.249	0.082	0.530	0.350	13.668	4.777
1953	0.0089	8.175	0.073	0.595	0.358	13.729	4.909
1954	0.0076	10.238	0.078	0.758	0.376	13.508	5.077
1955	0.0058	11.273	0.065	0.829	0.400	13.592	5.435
1956	0.0054	12.832	0.069	0.944	0.439	13.590	5.960
1957	0.0056	12.967	0.073	0.961	0.467	13.492	6.306
1958	0.0066	12.495	0.083	0.932	0.498	13.403	6.673
1959	0.0076	12.190	0.093	0.902	0.533	13.512	7.204
1960	0.0140	12.112	0.169	0.882	0.547	13.729	7.507
1961	0.0108	11.685	0.127	0.847	0.572	13.794	7.890
1962	0.0290	11.912	0.345	0.857	0.601	13.895	8.349
1963	0.0336	11.891	0.399	0.854	0.622	13.924	8.654
1964	0.0316	12.133	0.383	0.857	0.650	14.150	9.205
1965	0.0363	12.585	0.457	0.874	0.690	14.392	9.935
1966	0.0478	13.009	0.622	0.885	0.724	14.705	10.646
1967	0.0533	13.590	0.724	0.910	0.761	14.935	11.358
1968	0.0461	14.222	0.656	0.928	0.796	15.319	12.199
1969	0.0636	14.595	0.928	0.939	0.831	15.542	12.910
1970	0.0735	15.141	1.113	0.951	0.869	15.922	13.839
1971	0.0752	15.869	1.193	0.968	0.897	16.396	14.713
1972	0.0458	16.906	0.774	1.000	1.000	16.906	16.906
1973	0.0352	18.599	0.656	1.069	1.140	17.396	19.825
1974	0.0809	20.510	1.659	1.145	1.312	17.909	23.494
1975	0.0700	22.424	1.570	1.217	1.455	18.430	26.809
1976	0.0528	23.027	1.216	1.227	1.619	18.765	30.382
1977	0.0974	23.728	2.312	1.241	1.783	19.119	34.085
1978	0.0631	25.453	1.606	1.290	2.040	19.734	40.248
1979	0.0642	27.464	1.765	1.349	2.291	20.359	46.649

Table C.3. Metal mining

Year	Capital input				Capital stock		
	Price	Quantity	Outlay	Quality	Price	Quantity	Value
1948	0.1379	0.986	0.136	1.078	0.523	0.915	0.478
1949	0.1169	1.053	0.123	1.081	0.537	0.974	0.523
1950	0.1729	1.052	0.182	1.087	0.547	0.968	0.529
1951	0.2309	1.132	0.261	1.088	0.597	1.040	0.621
1952	0.1470	1.243	0.183	1.072	0.603	1.160	0.699
1953	0.1551	1.298	0.201	1.056	0.611	1.229	0.750
1954	0.1490	1.323	0.197	1.046	0.609	1.265	0.770
1955	0.1739	1.471	0.256	1.016	0.614	1.448	0.890
1956	0.2481	1.501	0.372	1.001	0.652	1.499	0.977
1957	0.1662	1.504	0.250	1.008	0.680	1.492	1.014
1958	0.1535	1.569	0.241	0.998	0.676	1.572	1.063
1959	0.1539	1.615	0.249	0.997	0.669	1.619	1.084
1960	0.1470	1.685	0.248	0.992	0.658	1.699	1.118
1961	0.1170	1.813	0.212	0.970	0.664	1.869	1.240
1962	0.1293	1.943	0.251	0.945	0.665	2.056	1.368
1963	0.1433	1.997	0.286	0.929	0.672	2.150	1.445
1964	0.1589	2.166	0.344	0.919	0.679	2.357	1.601
1965	0.1605	2.653	0.426	0.913	0.684	2.908	1.989
1966	0.1469	3.468	0.509	0.914	0.705	3.793	2.674
1967	0.1328	3.939	0.523	0.910	0.734	4.327	3.174
1968	0.0865	4.321	0.374	0.914	0.768	4.730	3.632
1969	0.0846	6.300	0.533	0.976	0.839	6.458	5.417
1970	0.0770	7.335	0.564	1.000	0.897	7.334	6.579
1971	0.0721	7.947	0.573	0.992	0.950	8.009	7.608
1972	0.0847	9.135	0.774	1.000	1.000	9.135	9.135
1973	0.1735	9.730	1.688	1.010	1.061	9.632	10.216
1974	0.1941	11.747	2.280	1.112	1.216	10.568	12.852
1975	0.0999	12.008	1.199	1.075	1.388	11.172	15.507
1976	0.2057	12.750	2.622	1.084	1.418	11.767	16.689
1977	0.0868	12.032	1.045	0.969	1.545	12.418	19.181
1978	0.1325	13.448	1.781	1.042	1.711	12.903	22.072
1979	0.1062	13.711	1.456	1.033	1.932	13.276	25.644

Table C.4. Coal mining

Year	Capital input				Capital stock		
	Price	Quantity	Outlay	Quality	Price	Quantity	Value
1948	0.3798	2.055	0.780	1.081	0.472	1.900	0.898
1949	0.1682	2.513	0.423	1.073	0.501	2.343	1.175
1950	0.2141	2.488	0.533	1.068	0.512	2.329	1.193
1951	0.1511	3.210	0.485	1.079	0.560	2.975	1.665
1952	0.1215	3.148	0.382	1.075	0.568	2.928	1.664
1953	0.0978	3.116	0.305	1.069	0.583	2.915	1.699
1954	0.0904	2.896	0.262	1.067	0.595	2.714	1.616
1955	0.1352	2.705	0.366	1.063	0.601	2.545	1.529
1956	0.2164	2.416	0.523	1.055	0.640	2.290	1.465
1957	0.2443	2.258	0.552	1.050	0.685	2.150	1.473
1958	0.1983	2.185	0.433	1.029	0.696	2.123	1.478
1959	0.1635	2.122	0.347	1.049	0.706	2.022	1.428
1960	0.1636	2.079	0.340	1.042	0.710	1.995	1.415
1961	0.2019	1.976	0.399	1.024	0.709	1.929	1.367
1962	0.1895	1.964	0.372	1.005	0.710	1.954	1.388
1963	0.2341	1.876	0.439	0.995	0.717	1.886	1.353
1964	0.3205	1.820	0.583	0.987	0.725	1.844	1.336
1965	0.2482	2.224	0.552	0.997	0.737	2.232	1.644
1966	0.2737	2.251	0.616	0.993	0.750	2.266	1.700
1967	0.2341	2.392	0.560	0.994	0.777	2.408	1.871
1968	0.1833	2.488	0.456	0.988	0.814	2.518	2.049
1969	0.1583	2.456	0.389	0.979	0.862	2.508	2.161
1970	0.4039	2.608	1.053	0.972	0.910	2.682	2.440
1971	0.2301	3.532	0.813	0.997	0.958	3.543	3.394
1972	0.1976	3.963	0.783	1.000	1.000	3.963	3.963
1973	0.2379	4.318	1.027	1.002	1.041	4.311	4.489
1974	0.6175	5.051	3.119	1.012	1.169	4.993	5.838
1975	0.6685	5.500	3.676	1.011	1.443	5.441	7.849
1976	0.5960	5.593	3.333	1.010	1.489	5.535	8.242
1977	0.4688	5.676	2.661	1.012	1.730	5.609	9.702
1978	0.4491	5.904	2.651	1.010	1.935	5.848	11.317
1979	0.5212	6.192	3.227	1.017	2.140	6.089	13.031

Table C.5. Crude petroleum and natural gas

Year	Capital input				Capital stock		
	Price	Quantity	Outlay	Quality	Price	Quantity	Value
1948	0.0958	36.201	3.467	1.097	0.540	32.991	17.809
1949	0.0804	36.863	2.965	1.094	0.536	33.699	18.067
1950	0.0892	37.441	3.340	1.098	0.534	34.101	18.223
1951	0.1062	38.567	4.095	1.097	0.589	35.165	20.723
1952	0.0909	39.234	3.567	1.086	0.606	36.112	21.891
1953	0.1020	40.550	4.136	1.082	0.609	37.482	22.826
1954	0.1013	41.764	4.229	1.083	0.602	38.553	23.218
1955	0.1076	43.878	4.719	1.073	0.627	40.906	25.649
1956	0.1124	46.136	5.185	1.069	0.658	43.142	28.397
1957	0.0986	49.102	4.844	1.067	0.682	46.017	31.385
1958	0.0892	51.541	4.600	1.059	0.672	48.664	32.683
1959	0.0845	53.046	4.484	1.052	0.687	50.409	34.622
1960	0.0926	55.607	5.147	1.048	0.672	53.080	35.684
1961	0.0863	57.585	4.968	1.041	0.676	55.336	37.392
1962	0.0817	59.776	4.884	1.033	0.689	57.860	39.890
1963	0.0920	62.268	5.726	1.028	0.673	60.594	40.797
1964	0.0879	64.065	5.631	1.025	0.672	62.527	42.046
1965	0.0898	66.561	5.980	1.021	0.679	65.200	44.256
1966	0.0816	69.122	5.637	1.017	0.716	67.948	48.619
1967	0.0974	71.985	7.011	1.014	0.743	70.994	52.757
1968	0.0888	73.931	6.567	1.011	0.784	73.157	57.346
1969	0.0848	76.150	6.459	1.009	0.837	75.498	63.222
1970	0.0916	78.869	7.221	1.009	0.892	78.159	69.723
1971	0.0909	79.484	7.223	1.003	0.922	79.241	73.079
1972	0.0817	80.333	6.560	1.000	1.000	80.333	80.333
1973	0.1218	81.471	9.925	0.999	1.085	81.581	88.553
1974	0.1514	82.793	12.536	0.995	1.352	83.170	112.454
1975	0.2079	85.197	17.712	0.994	1.508	85.709	129.239
1976	0.2667	86.635	23.105	0.994	1.524	87.138	132.829
1977	0.2492	87.582	21.821	0.995	1.650	87.999	145.191
1978	0.2564	88.715	22.743	0.995	1.839	89.140	163.927
1979	0.3210	89.847	28.839	0.994	2.095	90.433	189.482

Table C.6.   Nonmetallic mining and quarrying

Year	Capital input				Capital stock		
	Price	Quantity	Outlay	Quality	Price	Quantity	Value
1948	0.4632	0.573	0.266	0.967	0.500	0.593	0.297
1949	0.5113	0.551	0.282	0.973	0.526	0.566	0.298
1950	0.5925	0.549	0.325	0.979	0.537	0.561	0.301
1951	0.6630	0.555	0.368	0.986	0.585	0.563	0.329
1952	0.6076	0.598	0.364	1.000	0.598	0.598	0.358
1953	0.5611	0.630	0.354	1.008	0.610	0.625	0.381
1954	0.6380	0.649	0.414	1.006	0.619	0.646	0.399
1955	0.7134	0.692	0.494	0.994	0.624	0.696	0.434
1956	0.6962	0.736	0.512	0.973	0.666	0.757	0.504
1957	0.5819	0.801	0.466	0.983	0.708	0.814	0.576
1958	0.4780	0.865	0.413	0.977	0.717	0.885	0.635
1959	0.4960	0.897	0.445	1.009	0.730	0.888	0.648
1960	0.5534	0.935	0.518	1.010	0.730	0.926	0.677
1961	0.5264	0.913	0.481	1.005	0.727	0.909	0.661
1962	0.5909	0.935	0.552	1.001	0.724	0.934	0.676
1963	0.7227	0.944	0.683	0.999	0.729	0.946	0.689
1964	0.7291	1.061	0.774	1.010	0.736	1.051	0.773
1965	0.6209	1.104	0.686	0.997	0.746	1.107	0.826
1966	0.6495	1.221	0.793	0.997	0.756	1.224	0.926
1967	0.6430	1.490	0.958	0.998	0.784	1.493	1.170
1968	0.5260	1.629	0.857	1.002	0.816	1.626	1.326
1969	0.5466	1.551	0.848	0.992	0.869	1.563	1.358
1970	0.4710	1.580	0.744	0.992	0.915	1.593	1.457
1971	0.4809	1.801	0.866	0.994	0.962	1.812	1.744
1972	0.4314	2.207	0.952	1.000	1.000	2.207	2.207
1973	0.5810	2.327	1.352	1.000	1.056	2.327	2.457
1974	0.5560	2.883	1.603	1.016	1.183	2.839	3.358
1975	0.5049	3.117	1.574	1.016	1.413	3.069	4.337
1976	0.4299	3.347	1.439	1.016	1.464	3.294	4.822
1977	0.4629	3.623	1.677	1.017	1.658	3.564	5.909
1978	0.5054	3.928	1.985	1.018	1.806	3.857	6.966
1979	0.5601	4.267	2.390	1.023	1.986	4.171	8.283

Table C.7. Contract construction

Year	Capital input				Capital stock		
	Price	Quantity	Outlay	Quality	Price	Quantity	Value
1948	0.2290	6.555	1.501	0.844	0.418	7.764	3.245
1949	0.2981	6.640	1.979	0.850	0.424	7.816	3.316
1950	0.2585	6.388	1.652	0.841	0.439	7.599	3.336
1951	0.2735	6.962	1.904	0.858	0.488	8.113	3.960
1952	0.2871	7.479	2.147	0.872	0.505	8.581	4.331
1953	0.2682	7.660	2.054	0.878	0.507	8.727	4.429
1954	0.2899	7.283	2.111	0.853	0.506	8.538	4.317
1955	0.2499	7.950	1.987	0.879	0.539	9.042	4.870
1956	0.3396	8.334	2.830	0.879	0.584	9.482	5.539
1957	0.3449	9.270	3.197	0.908	0.627	10.207	6.402
1958	0.3094	10.353	3.204	0.929	0.647	11.149	7.212
1959	0.2754	11.055	3.045	0.941	0.684	11.753	8.038
1960	0.2434	12.175	2.964	0.958	0.689	12.712	8.756
1961	0.2256	13.410	3.026	0.984	0.698	13.632	9.510
1962	0.2294	14.808	3.396	0.987	0.704	15.007	10.561
1963	0.2389	15.619	3.731	0.992	0.711	15.744	11.199
1964	0.2404	16.437	3.951	1.000	0.736	16.430	12.087
1965	0.2819	17.803	5.019	1.005	0.746	17.714	13.216
1966	0.2469	19.416	4.794	1.010	0.780	19.222	15.000
1967	0.3165	20.447	6.472	1.007	0.784	20.301	15.911
1968	0.2583	21.273	5.495	1.001	0.840	21.258	17.849
1969	0.2958	20.864	6.172	1.006	0.868	20.747	18.004
1970	0.3332	21.171	7.055	1.004	0.891	21.081	18.774
1971	0.3475	20.960	7.284	1.002	0.949	20.918	19.853
1972	0.3808	21.289	8.106	1.000	1.000	21.289	21.289
1973	0.3620	22.948	8.307	1.006	1.068	22.818	24.359
1974	0.3419	23.446	8.015	1.002	1.215	23.404	28.428
1975	0.5174	23.130	11.969	1.003	1.385	23.056	31.944
1976	0.4901	22.234	10.898	1.000	1.450	22.245	32.249
1977	0.6124	21.666	13.269	1.002	1.662	21.624	35.938
1978	0.6607	21.261	14.047	1.004	1.844	21.185	39.061
1979	0.6740	21.968	14.807	1.003	2.060	21.911	45.132

Table C.8. Food and kindred products

Year	Capital input				Capital stock		
	Price	Quantity	Outlay	Quality	Price	Quantity	Value
1948	0.1108	21.429	2.375	0.890	0.511	24.080	12.298
1949	0.1068	22.794	2.434	0.888	0.502	25.656	12.891
1950	0.0951	23.434	2.227	0.885	0.511	26.479	13.533
1951	0.0873	24.633	2.150	0.897	0.581	27.475	15.950
1952	0.1034	25.199	2.606	0.903	0.591	27.918	16.487
1953	0.1062	25.167	2.673	0.905	0.588	27.799	16.359
1954	0.1030	25.004	2.575	0.904	0.587	27.652	16.241
1955	0.1241	25.206	3.128	0.908	0.563	27.761	15.635
1956	0.1031	26.131	2.694	0.918	0.624	28.451	17.758
1957	0.1087	26.556	2.888	0.922	0.654	28.817	18.839
1958	0.1272	26.925	3.426	0.933	0.659	28.871	19.037
1959	0.1362	27.336	3.725	0.939	0.653	29.121	19.012
1960	0.1258	28.184	3.545	0.946	0.658	29.779	19.604
1961	0.1319	28.547	3.765	0.951	0.665	30.007	19.949
1962	0.1342	29.455	3.952	0.961	0.674	30.651	20.659
1963	0.1467	30.626	4.494	0.970	0.691	31.585	21.829
1964	0.1423	31.467	4.477	0.975	0.706	32.270	22.768
1965	0.1466	32.273	4.730	0.979	0.726	32.968	23.943
1966	0.1669	32.433	5.414	0.982	0.746	33.040	24.634
1967	0.1568	33.752	5.293	0.990	0.774	34.105	26.408
1968	0.1553	35.169	5.461	0.995	0.803	35.348	28.377
1969	0.1573	36.032	5.670	0.997	0.844	36.154	30.508
1970	0.1703	36.903	6.283	0.993	0.899	37.173	33.425
1971	0.1809	37.764	6.831	0.995	0.944	37.947	35.820
1972	0.1578	38.934	6.145	1.000	1.000	38.934	38.934
1973	0.1387	41.077	5.697	1.039	1.149	39.527	45.436
1974	0.1534	42.054	6.453	1.051	1.343	40.014	53.742
1975	0.2830	43.845	12.408	1.067	1.397	41.082	57.401
1976	0.2350	45.649	10.728	1.074	1.435	42.494	60.985
1977	0.2381	47.441	11.297	1.078	1.507	43.992	66.290
1978	0.2252	48.868	11.004	1.087	1.657	44.973	74.500
1979	0.2446	50.411	12.328	1.098	1.802	45.924	82.775

Table C.9. Tobacco manufacturers

Year	Capital input				Capital stock		
	Price	Quantity	Outlay	Quality	Price	Quantity	Value
1948	0.0810	2.736	0.222	0.958	0.303	2.857	0.866
1949	0.0995	2.889	0.287	0.955	0.278	3.026	0.842
1950	0.0844	2.922	0.247	0.959	0.308	3.047	0.937
1951	0.0973	2.982	0.290	0.959	0.354	3.110	1.100
1952	0.1014	3.078	0.312	0.958	0.337	3.214	1.083
1953	0.1332	3.107	0.414	0.958	0.321	3.242	1.040
1954	0.1221	3.210	0.392	0.961	0.342	3.340	1.142
1955	0.1201	3.296	0.396	0.964	0.358	3.420	1.224
1956	0.1310	3.214	0.421	0.966	0.377	3.329	1.254
1957	0.1447	3.300	0.478	0.978	0.478	3.376	1.613
1958	0.1600	3.352	0.536	0.990	0.571	3.384	1.933
1959	0.1800	3.396	0.611	1.006	0.663	3.376	2.239
1960	0.1897	3.562	0.676	1.009	0.752	3.530	2.655
1961	0.1801	3.741	0.674	1.008	0.778	3.711	2.886
1962	0.1845	3.999	0.738	1.012	0.735	3.954	2.908
1963	0.2182	4.015	0.876	1.011	0.734	3.972	2.917
1964	0.1920	4.010	0.770	1.012	0.726	3.964	2.878
1965	0.1720	4.047	0.696	1.012	0.787	3.998	3.144
1966	0.1747	3.957	0.691	1.012	0.793	3.908	3.098
1967	0.2211	3.764	0.832	1.008	0.820	3.733	3.062
1968	0.2197	3.852	0.846	1.009	0.837	3.817	3.194
1969	0.2647	3.726	0.986	1.007	0.854	3.700	3.159
1970	0.3375	3.628	1.225	1.004	0.887	3.612	3.202
1971	0.3769	3.441	1.297	1.003	0.955	3.432	3.278
1972	0.3502	3.479	1.218	1.000	1.000	3.479	3.479
1973	0.3270	3.728	1.219	0.999	1.034	3.734	3.861
1974	0.3346	3.856	1.290	1.001	1.235	3.853	4.756
1975	0.3943	4.238	1.671	1.001	1.339	4.232	5.667
1976	0.4250	4.364	1.855	1.001	1.435	4.358	6.253
1977	0.4690	4.399	2.063	1.001	1.516	4.392	6.657
1978	0.5223	4.397	2.297	1.000	1.659	4.397	7.294
1979	0.5962	4.397	2.622	1.000	1.844	4.397	8.108

Table C.10. Textile mill products

Year	Capital input				Capital stock		
	Price	Quantity	Outlay	Quality	Price	Quantity	Value
1948	0.2364	7.036	1.664	0.742	0.533	9.480	5.057
1949	0.1301	7.832	1.019	0.741	0.530	10.573	5.601
1950	0.1065	8.613	0.917	0.780	0.544	11.048	6.014
1951	0.1568	9.139	1.433	0.797	0.635	11.471	7.283
1952	0.0926	10.381	0.961	0.855	0.626	12.136	7.598
1953	0.0767	10.008	0.768	0.835	0.617	11.992	7.397
1954	0.0555	9.970	0.553	0.838	0.609	11.893	7.247
1955	0.0849	9.915	0.841	0.845	0.602	11.730	7.062
1956	0.0852	10.142	0.864	0.859	0.658	11.808	7.773
1957	0.0734	10.400	0.763	0.873	0.686	11.909	8.175
1958	0.0747	10.229	0.765	0.876	0.686	11.674	8.013
1959	0.0970	10.060	0.975	0.879	0.699	11.440	7.998
1960	0.1036	9.783	1.013	0.862	0.696	11.352	7.896
1961	0.0948	10.520	0.997	0.921	0.704	11.426	8.046
1962	0.1039	10.711	1.113	0.929	0.717	11.534	8.267
1963	0.1084	11.059	1.198	0.942	0.734	11.742	8.621
1964	0.1316	11.219	1.476	0.949	0.746	11.816	8.814
1965	0.1537	11.563	1.777	0.954	0.758	12.117	9.190
1966	0.1508	12.300	1.855	0.968	0.767	12.713	9.751
1967	0.1278	13.354	1.707	0.975	0.804	13.703	11.018
1968	0.1397	13.934	1.947	0.980	0.830	14.222	11.810
1969	0.1375	14.584	2.005	0.989	0.862	14.739	12.708
1970	0.1399	15.032	2.103	0.992	0.895	15.154	13.568
1971	0.1326	15.425	2.045	0.995	0.953	15.510	14.781
1972	0.1351	15.814	2.137	1.000	1.000	15.814	15.814
1973	0.1260	16.206	2.043	0.996	1.094	16.265	17.791
1974	0.1527	16.028	2.448	0.974	1.192	16.450	19.601
1975	0.1261	16.585	2.091	0.978	1.379	16.955	23.381
1976	0.1608	16.385	2.636	0.987	1.436	16.593	23.835
1977	0.2172	16.377	3.557	0.988	1.504	16.571	24.922
1978	0.2510	16.736	4.200	0.992	1.645	16.875	27.752
1979	0.2758	16.670	4.597	0.996	1.787	16.743	29.928

Table C.11. Apparel and other fabricated textile products

Year	Capital input				Capital stock		
	Price	Quantity	Outlay	Quality	Price	Quantity	Value
1948	0.1761	2.672	0.470	0.877	0.788	3.046	2.399
1949	0.1590	2.807	0.446	0.880	0.747	3.188	2.383
1950	0.1072	2.787	0.299	0.873	0.759	3.191	2.422
1951	0.1183	3.190	0.377	0.897	0.871	3.556	3.096
1952	0.1305	3.153	0.411	0.889	0.804	3.546	2.852
1953	0.1178	3.174	0.374	0.891	0.801	3.563	2.853
1954	0.0997	3.211	0.320	0.892	0.783	3.598	2.819
1955	0.1071	3.286	0.352	0.912	0.773	3.603	2.784
1956	0.1131	3.448	0.390	0.902	0.808	3.823	3.087
1957	0.1040	3.367	0.350	0.889	0.818	3.786	3.096
1958	0.1388	3.330	0.462	0.895	0.802	3.719	2.985
1959	0.1178	3.327	0.392	0.892	0.825	3.728	3.074
1960	0.1432	3.455	0.495	0.901	0.811	3.836	3.111
1961	0.1531	3.518	0.539	0.904	0.811	3.893	3.156
1962	0.1643	3.510	0.577	0.901	0.820	3.894	3.192
1963	0.1661	3.872	0.643	0.918	0.826	4.217	3.482
1964	0.1485	4.158	0.617	0.936	0.849	4.443	3.774
1965	0.1933	4.391	0.849	0.976	0.836	4.499	3.760
1966	0.2107	4.811	1.014	0.986	0.833	4.877	4.061
1967	0.1939	5.237	1.015	0.990	0.865	5.290	4.577
1968	0.1863	5.466	1.018	0.991	0.903	5.516	4.978
1969	0.1837	5.875	1.079	0.989	0.918	5.943	5.457
1970	0.1911	6.410	1.225	0.994	0.930	6.450	5.997
1971	0.1649	6.683	1.102	0.996	0.984	6.707	6.603
1972	0.2172	7.013	1.523	1.000	1.000	7.013	7.013
1973	0.1601	7.442	1.191	1.001	1.093	7.433	8.126
1974	0.1413	7.871	1.112	1.005	1.173	7.828	9.183
1975	0.2126	7.810	1.660	1.005	1.334	7.773	10.370
1976	0.2083	7.714	1.607	1.009	1.388	7.645	10.614
1977	0.2887	8.007	2.311	1.008	1.441	7.945	11.450
1978	0.2883	8.303	2.394	1.009	1.534	8.225	12.618
1979	0.2858	8.564	2.447	1.010	1.692	8.476	14.339

Table C.12. Paper and allied products

Year	Capital input				Capital stock		
	Price	Quantity	Outlay	Quality	Price	Quantity	Value
1948	0.1579	6.634	1.048	0.935	0.492	7.092	3.492
1949	0.1245	7.251	0.903	0.939	0.494	7.719	3.812
1950	0.1672	7.485	1.251	0.927	0.500	8.078	4.039
1951	0.2282	7.793	1.778	0.927	0.580	8.409	4.879
1952	0.1660	8.580	1.424	0.952	0.587	9.015	5.291
1953	0.1612	8.801	1.419	0.952	0.593	9.242	5.481
1954	0.1589	9.128	1.450	0.950	0.590	9.605	5.671
1955	0.1789	9.601	1.718	0.947	0.592	10.140	6.008
1956	0.2003	10.309	2.065	0.952	0.655	10.824	7.095
1957	0.1548	11.547	1.787	0.970	0.697	11.905	8.298
1958	0.1378	12.273	1.691	0.971	0.701	12.642	8.856
1959	0.1560	12.528	1.954	0.971	0.711	12.902	9.168
1960	0.1476	12.783	1.887	0.964	0.713	13.262	9.461
1961	0.1489	13.088	1.949	0.969	0.714	13.505	9.649
1962	0.1507	13.401	2.020	0.969	0.724	13.826	10.013
1963	0.1476	13.911	2.053	0.975	0.742	14.266	10.580
1964	0.1583	14.225	2.252	0.978	0.755	14.548	10.989
1965	0.1661	14.759	2.452	0.980	0.771	15.064	11.614
1966	0.1765	15.885	2.803	0.987	0.796	16.089	12.809
1967	0.1545	17.294	2.672	0.994	0.830	17.395	14.445
1968	0.1599	18.536	2.964	0.998	0.856	18.582	15.905
1969	0.1685	18.932	3.190	0.996	0.894	19.013	16.997
1970	0.1535	19.499	2.993	0.996	0.944	19.568	18.478
1971	0.1485	20.166	2.995	0.999	0.998	20.193	20.155
1972	0.1785	20.259	3.616	1.000	1.000	20.259	20.259
1973	0.2254	20.394	4.597	1.000	1.064	20.394	21.698
1974	0.2657	20.148	5.353	0.969	1.276	20.800	26.549
1975	0.2656	18.240	4.845	0.824	1.481	22.134	32.778
1976	0.3238	18.714	6.060	0.821	1.542	22.782	35.123
1977	0.3284	19.458	6.390	0.822	1.628	23.684	38.548
1978	0.3289	20.267	6.666	0.826	1.769	24.550	43.431
1979	0.3753	21.110	7.923	0.831	1.913	25.406	48.599

Table C.13. Printing and publishing

Year	Capital input				Capital stock		
	Price	Quantity	Outlay	Quality	Price	Quantity	Value
1948	0.0691	10.418	0.720	0.905	0.442	11.507	5.084
1949	0.0791	10.486	0.829	0.907	0.447	11.564	5.166
1950	0.0748	10.562	0.790	0.912	0.457	11.586	5.290
1951	0.0749	10.835	0.812	0.923	0.524	11.740	6.154
1952	0.0821	10.849	0.890	0.910	0.538	11.927	6.422
1953	0.0874	10.873	0.950	0.908	0.544	11.968	6.512
1954	0.0866	10.811	0.936	0.909	0.543	11.891	6.459
1955	0.1042	10.998	1.146	0.918	0.528	11.980	6.321
1956	0.1042	11.252	1.173	0.913	0.598	12.320	7.365
1957	0.1078	11.728	1.265	0.913	0.626	12.846	8.042
1958	0.0957	11.786	1.127	0.915	0.625	12.883	8.050
1959	0.1149	12.059	1.386	0.930	0.633	12.970	8.206
1960	0.1181	12.253	1.448	0.939	0.634	13.043	8.269
1961	0.1084	12.567	1.362	0.952	0.640	13.204	8.448
1962	0.1152	12.818	1.477	0.956	0.651	13.413	8.731
1963	0.1218	12.929	1.574	0.954	0.667	13.558	9.047
1964	0.1557	13.448	2.094	0.962	0.687	13.979	9.608
1965	0.1564	14.009	2.190	0.977	0.706	14.344	10.133
1966	0.1689	14.723	2.487	0.974	0.729	15.123	11.025
1967	0.1502	15.772	2.370	0.984	0.764	16.036	12.252
1968	0.1595	16.618	2.650	0.988	0.795	16.819	13.373
1969	0.1684	17.167	2.890	0.991	0.843	17.328	14.610
1970	0.1455	17.853	2.597	0.995	0.903	17.943	16.203
1971	0.1670	18.033	3.011	0.996	0.952	18.113	17.251
1972	0.1766	18.449	3.258	1.000	1.000	18.449	18.449
1973	0.2006	18.884	3.788	1.009	1.069	18.721	20.019
1974	0.1652	19.107	3.156	0.997	1.235	19.174	23.675
1975	0.2257	19.029	4.294	0.980	1.401	19.418	27.206
1976	0.2579	18.985	4.895	0.983	1.443	19.304	27.851
1977	0.3202	18.928	6.061	0.980	1.528	19.309	29.501
1978	0.3631	19.320	7.016	0.985	1.670	19.616	32.756
1979	0.3855	19.752	7.614	0.987	1.806	20.005	36.124

Table C.14.   Chemicals and allied products

Year	Capital input				Capital stock		
	Price	Quantity	Outlay	Quality	Price	Quantity	Value
1948	0.1830	10.976	2.009	0.901	0.524	12.185	6.387
1949	0.1817	11.963	2.174	0.916	0.509	13.062	6.643
1950	0.2206	12.560	2.771	0.910	0.518	13.804	7.152
1951	0.2501	13.257	3.315	0.913	0.595	14.523	8.640
1952	0.1922	15.381	2.956	0.952	0.595	16.160	9.615
1953	0.1817	16.496	2.997	0.947	0.604	17.421	10.527
1954	0.1819	17.395	3.165	0.942	0.603	18.463	11.139
1955	0.2291	17.990	4.121	0.938	0.593	19.180	11.367
1956	0.2084	19.052	3.970	0.954	0.654	19.971	13.052
1957	0.2016	20.161	4.064	0.961	0.688	20.973	14.426
1958	0.1866	21.095	3.936	0.963	0.694	21.898	15.193
1959	0.2346	21.648	5.079	0.962	0.700	22.494	15.740
1960	0.2107	22.169	4.672	0.967	0.709	22.931	16.259
1961	0.2185	22.801	4.981	0.967	0.704	23.583	16.597
1962	0.2186	24.058	5.259	0.971	0.712	24.773	17.650
1963	0.2295	25.094	5.760	0.980	0.725	25.603	18.575
1964	0.2319	26.141	6.063	0.982	0.737	26.628	19.634
1965	0.2457	27.672	6.799	0.989	0.753	27.976	21.075
1966	0.2297	30.244	6.948	0.996	0.781	30.379	23.712
1967	0.1932	33.140	6.404	1.000	0.812	33.138	26.924
1968	0.2177	35.524	7.735	1.002	0.828	35.438	29.335
1969	0.1978	37.152	7.350	0.999	0.866	37.206	32.226
1970	0.1865	38.878	7.250	0.999	0.916	38.921	35.650
1971	0.2037	40.442	8.237	0.998	0.957	40.509	38.780
1972	0.2246	41.536	9.331	1.000	1.000	41.536	41.536
1973	0.2379	42.044	10.003	1.001	1.059	42.022	44.516
1974	0.2284	44.222	10.102	1.036	1.250	42.679	53.343
1975	0.2610	44.203	11.536	0.967	1.435	45.696	65.568
1976	0.3071	46.303	14.221	0.964	1.485	48.032	71.341
1977	0.2989	49.151	14.691	0.965	1.564	50.914	79.618
1978	0.2912	52.480	15.284	0.972	1.683	54.007	90.917
1979	0.2933	54.472	15.977	0.973	1.821	55.987	101.964

Table C.15. Petroleum and coal products

Year	Capital input				Capital stock		
	Price	Quantity	Outlay	Quality	Price	Quantity	Value
1948	0.0748	17.126	1.282	0.888	0.434	19.289	8.373
1949	0.0605	18.350	1.110	0.888	0.445	20.669	9.190
1950	0.0668	18.782	1.254	0.889	0.448	21.118	9.464
1951	0.0682	17.805	1.215	0.858	0.515	20.759	10.688
1952	0.0780	19.128	1.492	0.907	0.536	21.078	11.300
1953	0.0784	19.570	1.535	0.920	0.546	21.282	11.626
1954	0.0865	20.345	1.760	0.926	0.539	21.982	11.858
1955	0.0925	20.994	1.941	0.930	0.564	22.580	12.746
1956	0.0877	21.600	1.895	0.927	0.597	23.295	13.903
1957	0.0733	22.639	1.660	0.930	0.626	24.334	15.224
1958	0.0641	23.370	1.499	0.937	0.620	24.943	15.453
1959	0.0833	23.473	1.955	0.936	0.615	25.082	15.432
1960	0.0625	22.875	1.430	0.916	0.612	24.981	15.292
1961	0.0683	22.711	1.551	0.914	0.614	24.849	15.262
1962	0.0671	22.733	1.525	0.912	0.624	24.923	15.561
1963	0.0395	22.844	0.901	0.920	0.643	24.838	15.973
1964	0.0541	22.556	1.219	0.917	0.663	24.610	16.324
1965	0.0622	22.333	1.390	0.916	0.686	24.377	16.735
1966	0.0910	22.446	2.044	0.918	0.712	24.463	17.419
1967	0.0825	22.755	1.877	0.924	0.748	24.637	18.424
1968	0.1015	23.887	2.424	0.941	0.775	25.392	19.682
1969	0.0804	25.122	2.019	0.967	0.829	25.971	21.532
1970	0.0745	25.881	1.928	0.982	0.896	26.363	23.619
1971	0.0753	26.704	2.010	0.993	0.946	26.905	25.460
1972	0.1068	27.535	2.941	1.000	1.000	27.535	27.535
1973	0.0576	28.654	1.652	1.037	1.116	27.624	30.818
1974	0.2207	29.898	6.598	1.087	1.297	27.509	35.665
1975	0.1398	30.747	4.297	1.079	1.490	28.500	42.474
1976	0.1728	31.723	5.481	1.077	1.549	29.443	45.594
1977	0.2754	32.981	9.082	1.082	1.664	30.469	50.688
1978	0.2918	33.669	9.824	1.089	1.846	30.921	57.091
1979	0.4559	33.667	15.350	1.089	1.992	30.907	61.570

Table C.16. Rubber and miscellaneous plastic products

| Year | Capital input | | | | Capital stock | | |
	Price	Quantity	Outlay	Quality	Price	Quantity	Value
1948	0.1122	2.323	0.261	0.856	0.494	2.713	1.340
1949	0.0934	2.559	0.239	0.868	0.505	2.947	1.488
1950	0.0799	2.448	0.196	0.840	0.552	2.916	1.609
1951	0.2932	2.186	0.641	0.778	0.616	2.811	1.733
1952	0.2462	2.627	0.647	0.830	0.620	3.165	1.963
1953	0.1738	3.236	0.563	0.905	0.624	3.575	2.232
1954	0.1074	3.435	0.369	0.910	0.624	3.773	2.354
1955	0.1366	3.625	0.495	0.949	0.648	3.821	2.477
1956	0.1770	3.795	0.672	0.952	0.691	3.985	2.755
1957	0.1521	4.132	0.629	0.973	0.723	4.246	3.069
1958	0.1542	4.274	0.659	0.976	0.727	4.379	3.182
1959	0.1727	4.278	0.739	0.974	0.732	4.391	3.214
1960	0.1503	4.513	0.678	0.976	0.734	4.626	3.397
1961	0.1609	4.774	0.768	0.979	0.739	4.877	3.604
1962	0.1673	4.963	0.830	0.977	0.746	5.077	3.790
1963	0.1510	5.355	0.809	0.986	0.757	5.429	4.110
1964	0.1515	5.591	0.847	0.988	0.761	5.661	4.310
1965	0.1502	5.960	0.895	0.991	0.782	6.016	4.706
1966	0.1690	6.488	1.096	0.996	0.802	6.515	5.224
1967	0.1679	7.154	1.201	1.002	0.839	7.139	5.988
1968	0.1932	7.702	1.488	1.002	0.845	7.688	6.495
1969	0.1882	8.442	1.589	0.998	0.882	8.458	7.459
1970	0.1268	9.166	1.162	1.003	0.936	9.142	8.555
1971	0.1836	9.629	1.768	1.003	0.969	9.603	9.301
1972	0.1933	9.932	1.920	1.000	1.000	9.932	9.932
1973	0.1993	10.642	2.121	1.003	1.050	10.610	11.139
1974	0.1300	11.672	1.517	1.007	1.234	11.593	14.304
1975	0.1784	12.639	2.254	1.007	1.412	12.554	17.730
1976	0.1701	12.727	2.164	1.014	1.474	12.549	18.500
1977	0.2238	13.025	2.915	1.016	1.550	12.813	19.856
1978	0.2077	13.698	2.845	1.017	1.679	13.466	22.605
1979	0.1442	14.350	2.069	1.017	1.826	14.107	25.754

Table C.17. Leather and leather products

Year	Capital input				Capital stock		
	Price	Quantity	Outlay	Quality	Price	Quantity	Value
1948	0.1491	1.603	0.239	0.904	0.521	1.772	0.923
1949	0.0929	1.763	0.164	0.931	0.522	1.894	0.988
1950	0.0467	1.806	0.084	0.935	0.560	1.930	1.080
1951	0.1656	1.797	0.298	0.943	0.647	1.906	1.233
1952	0.1025	2.005	0.206	1.008	0.549	1.990	1.093
1953	0.0937	1.985	0.186	1.014	0.570	1.957	1.116
1954	0.1024	2.014	0.206	1.020	0.537	1.975	1.061
1955	0.0757	2.017	0.153	1.023	0.526	1.971	1.037
1956	0.0982	2.026	0.199	1.031	0.584	1.965	1.147
1957	0.0973	2.056	0.200	1.033	0.603	1.990	1.201
1958	0.0754	1.892	0.143	0.962	0.625	1.967	1.229
1959	0.1143	1.694	0.194	0.886	0.646	1.911	1.235
1960	0.1279	1.613	0.206	0.861	0.643	1.873	1.204
1961	0.0871	1.771	0.154	0.962	0.658	1.841	1.210
1962	0.1245	1.752	0.218	0.962	0.657	1.821	1.196
1963	0.1589	1.763	0.280	0.967	0.650	1.823	1.185
1964	0.1237	1.793	0.222	0.975	0.671	1.838	1.233
1965	0.1414	1.779	0.252	0.976	0.705	1.823	1.284
1966	0.1739	1.803	0.314	0.980	0.705	1.840	1.297
1967	0.1877	1.899	0.357	0.985	0.737	1.928	1.421
1968	0.1740	1.930	0.336	0.987	0.767	1.955	1.499
1969	0.1366	2.009	0.274	0.989	0.802	2.031	1.630
1970	0.1365	2.063	0.282	0.990	0.845	2.084	1.761
1971	0.1454	2.030	0.295	0.991	0.888	2.049	1.819
1972	0.0667	2.034	0.136	1.000	1.000	2.034	2.034
1973	0.1540	1.978	0.305	1.006	1.024	1.967	2.014
1974	0.1217	2.135	0.260	1.028	1.113	2.076	2.311
1975	0.1795	2.143	0.385	1.036	1.288	2.068	2.664
1976	0.2414	2.098	0.506	1.038	1.368	2.020	2.763
1977	0.1493	2.051	0.306	1.016	1.456	2.017	2.938
1978	0.1561	2.030	0.317	1.002	1.648	2.026	3.338
1979	0.1345	2.060	0.277	1.003	1.808	2.054	3.714

Table C.18. Lumber and wood products, except furniture

Year	Capital input				Capital stock		
	Price	Quantity	Outlay	Quality	Price	Quantity	Value
1948	0.1663	5.546	0.922	0.790	0.439	7.024	3.084
1949	0.1145	6.280	0.719	0.813	0.442	7.721	3.410
1950	0.1593	6.370	1.015	0.814	0.462	7.823	3.612
1951	0.1529	6.660	1.018	0.825	0.527	8.076	4.254
1952	0.1150	7.341	0.845	0.850	0.539	8.640	4.655
1953	0.1116	7.283	0.813	0.851	0.542	8.558	4.642
1954	0.1098	7.209	0.791	0.850	0.536	8.478	4.542
1955	0.1471	7.245	1.066	0.854	0.530	8.485	4.498
1956	0.1196	7.670	0.917	0.864	0.594	8.882	5.276
1957	0.0937	8.174	0.766	0.880	0.613	9.294	5.696
1958	0.1137	7.940	0.903	0.878	0.619	9.047	5.603
1959	0.1321	8.089	1.068	0.894	0.631	9.050	5.713
1960	0.1092	8.160	0.891	0.896	0.625	9.106	5.689
1961	0.1033	8.316	0.859	0.903	0.627	9.210	5.773
1962	0.1149	8.167	0.938	0.902	0.640	9.058	5.794
1963	0.1345	8.300	1.117	0.907	0.653	9.151	5.980
1964	0.1459	8.538	1.246	0.910	0.671	9.385	6.301
1965	0.1827	8.767	1.602	0.935	0.690	9.378	6.468
1966	0.1445	9.058	1.309	0.947	0.715	9.562	6.834
1967	0.1555	9.426	1.466	0.957	0.749	9.852	7.375
1968	0.2102	9.475	1.991	0.961	0.800	9.857	7.887
1969	0.2417	9.568	2.312	0.970	0.830	9.865	8.191
1970	0.1734	10.457	1.813	0.991	0.866	10.552	9.143
1971	0.1940	10.742	2.084	0.984	0.945	10.920	10.317
1972	0.2839	11.126	3.158	1.000	1.000	11.126	11.126
1973	0.3711	11.634	4.317	1.009	1.090	11.525	12.560
1974	0.3125	12.216	3.817	1.017	1.183	12.007	14.203
1975	0.2552	13.128	3.350	1.023	1.345	12.834	17.258
1976	0.3523	13.265	4.673	1.025	1.430	12.947	18.518
1977	0.4069	13.586	5.528	1.022	1.568	13.288	20.842
1978	0.4957	14.036	6.958	1.026	1.724	13.681	23.591
1979	0.5619	14.457	8.124	1.028	1.873	14.062	26.337

Table C.19. Furniture and fixtures

Year	Capital input				Capital stock		
	Price	Quantity	Outlay	Quality	Price	Quantity	Value
1948	0.1086	1.699	0.184	0.833	0.485	2.038	0.988
1949	0.1482	1.703	0.252	0.832	0.481	2.047	0.984
1950	0.1423	1.702	0.242	0.829	0.509	2.052	1.044
1951	0.1688	1.856	0.313	0.833	0.579	2.228	1.290
1952	0.1618	1.955	0.316	0.845	0.576	2.313	1.333
1953	0.1262	1.963	0.248	0.845	0.587	2.323	1.363
1954	0.1348	1.939	0.261	0.844	0.580	2.298	1.332
1955	0.1523	2.008	0.306	0.861	0.585	2.332	1.365
1956	0.1591	2.177	0.346	0.894	0.649	2.434	1.580
1957	0.1486	2.281	0.339	0.891	0.674	2.561	1.727
1958	0.1122	2.373	0.266	0.917	0.676	2.588	1.749
1959	0.1315	2.385	0.314	0.916	0.684	2.603	1.781
1960	0.1253	2.430	0.304	0.909	0.684	2.673	1.828
1961	0.1396	2.444	0.341	0.908	0.683	2.692	1.840
1962	0.1604	2.450	0.393	0.906	0.692	2.705	1.872
1963	0.1734	2.583	0.448	0.908	0.704	2.843	2.000
1964	0.1725	2.725	0.470	0.925	0.716	2.946	2.109
1965	0.2190	2.925	0.641	0.980	0.727	2.984	2.171
1966	0.2042	3.103	0.634	0.983	0.747	3.158	2.360
1967	0.1911	3.404	0.651	0.988	0.782	3.446	2.695
1968	0.1869	3.616	0.676	0.988	0.821	3.659	3.002
1969	0.2013	3.725	0.750	0.988	0.854	3.770	3.220
1970	0.1446	4.008	0.580	0.992	0.906	4.041	3.663
1971	0.1487	4.232	0.629	0.999	0.958	4.237	4.061
1972	0.1826	4.336	0.792	1.000	1.000	4.336	4.336
1973	0.1262	4.691	0.592	1.004	1.086	4.672	5.076
1974	0.0992	5.135	0.509	1.015	1.223	5.058	6.187
1975	0.1418	5.374	0.762	1.027	1.385	5.231	7.247
1976	0.1692	5.287	0.894	1.047	1.443	5.051	7.287
1977	0.1813	5.353	0.970	1.042	1.553	5.136	7.975
1978	0.2079	5.562	1.156	1.049	1.694	5.302	8.984
1979	0.2345	5.820	1.365	1.052	1.857	5.531	10.269

Table C.20. Stone, clay, and glass products

Year	Capital input				Capital stock		
	Price	Quantity	Outlay	Quality	Price	Quantity	Value
1948	0.1052	5.726	0.602	0.851	0.438	6.729	2.950
1949	0.1122	6.214	0.697	0.863	0.453	7.200	3.265
1950	0.1558	6.365	0.992	0.867	0.459	7.343	3.368
1951	0.1530	6.797	1.040	0.880	0.524	7.723	4.043
1952	0.1210	7.581	0.917	0.909	0.538	8.343	4.485
1953	0.1410	7.791	1.099	0.922	0.548	8.455	4.632
1954	0.1467	8.080	1.186	0.925	0.551	8.732	4.812
1955	0.1954	8.235	1.609	0.925	0.545	8.898	4.853
1956	0.1693	9.051	1.533	0.933	0.609	9.698	5.909
1957	0.1472	10.186	1.500	0.939	0.644	10.844	6.983
1958	0.1465	10.896	1.596	0.939	0.649	11.604	7.526
1959	0.1703	11.000	1.874	0.949	0.657	11.589	7.611
1960	0.1462	11.331	1.657	0.948	0.662	11.955	7.909
1961	0.1444	11.474	1.657	0.946	0.663	12.134	8.046
1962	0.1443	11.728	1.692	0.952	0.673	12.319	8.288
1963	0.1614	11.869	1.916	0.954	0.685	12.436	8.514
1964	0.1658	12.151	2.014	0.956	0.701	12.713	8.906
1965	0.1616	12.558	2.029	0.971	0.719	12.933	9.293
1966	0.1388	13.051	1.811	0.976	0.745	13.373	9.968
1967	0.1165	13.854	1.614	0.991	0.783	13.986	10.944
1968	0.1333	14.145	1.885	0.995	0.807	14.217	11.470
1969	0.1541	14.146	2.180	0.992	0.852	14.263	12.154
1970	0.1313	14.492	1.903	0.997	0.906	14.530	13.171
1971	0.1645	14.750	2.427	0.998	0.955	14.779	14.110
1972	0.1905	14.902	2.839	1.000	1.000	14.902	14.902
1973	0.1891	15.489	2.928	1.009	1.057	15.349	16.227
1974	0.1417	16.373	2.321	1.023	1.208	16.000	19.323
1975	0.1616	17.173	2.775	1.029	1.379	16.684	23.011
1976	0.2107	17.446	3.676	1.034	1.430	16.880	24.145
1977	0.2020	17.540	3.543	1.032	1.533	17.003	26.065
1978	0.2684	17.955	4.820	1.038	1.675	17.298	28.980
1979	0.2568	18.780	4.823	1.043	1.815	18.005	32.673

Table C.21. Primary metal industries

Year	Capital input				Capital stock		
	Price	Quantity	Outlay	Quality	Price	Quantity	Value
1948	0.0690	31.901	2.202	0.803	0.425	39.721	16.892
1949	0.0644	33.151	2.135	0.815	0.433	40.656	17.596
1950	0.0930	33.270	3.095	0.822	0.443	40.499	17.936
1951	0.1209	33.362	4.033	0.827	0.516	40.341	20.835
1952	0.0825	35.475	2.927	0.847	0.529	41.895	22.173
1953	0.1069	38.146	4.079	0.866	0.538	44.034	23.669
1954	0.0845	39.478	3.334	0.872	0.537	45.261	24.291
1955	0.1237	39.328	4.866	0.881	0.530	44.663	23.668
1956	0.1241	39.637	4.917	0.883	0.608	44.869	27.269
1957	0.1197	41.988	5.028	0.902	0.629	46.547	29.262
1958	0.0822	44.287	3.640	0.916	0.637	48.341	30.798
1959	0.0889	44.787	3.982	0.923	0.642	48.538	31.178
1960	0.0890	44.193	3.934	0.924	0.643	47.815	30.737
1961	0.0781	45.260	3.535	0.932	0.648	48.540	31.442
1962	0.0828	45.480	3.767	0.936	0.654	48.569	31.785
1963	0.0947	45.066	4.269	0.942	0.671	47.843	32.099
1964	0.1097	45.288	4.967	0.946	0.691	47.854	33.086
1965	0.1219	46.466	5.663	0.957	0.713	48.554	34.622
1966	0.1335	48.135	6.425	0.968	0.738	49.718	36.683
1967	0.1063	51.259	5.449	0.983	0.778	52.152	40.585
1968	0.0949	54.451	5.169	1.002	0.799	54.365	43.458
1969	0.0876	55.487	4.858	0.993	0.859	55.900	47.995
1970	0.0834	56.913	4.748	0.999	0.910	56.974	51.848
1971	0.0741	57.827	4.284	1.001	0.958	57.789	55.369
1972	0.0943	57.110	5.384	1.000	1.000	57.110	57.110
1973	0.0982	56.327	5.531	0.990	1.084	56.869	61.619
1974	0.1538	56.271	8.656	1.008	1.256	55.814	70.122
1975	0.1261	57.239	7.218	0.998	1.412	57.357	80.971
1976	0.0935	56.676	5.297	0.961	1.482	58.959	87.370
1977	0.1103	56.923	6.279	0.953	1.587	59.732	94.791
1978	0.1540	57.777	8.898	0.968	1.737	59.684	103.677
1979	0.1840	58.252	10.721	0.978	1.891	59.583	112.675

Table C.22. Fabricated metal industries

Year	Capital input				Capital stock		
	Price	Quantity	Outlay	Quality	Price	Quantity	Value
1948	0.1099	9.911	1.089	0.844	0.431	11.737	5.062
1949	0.0996	10.179	1.014	0.847	0.459	12.018	5.521
1950	0.1387	10.056	1.395	0.854	0.471	11.770	5.541
1951	0.1558	10.813	1.685	0.857	0.529	12.619	6.670
1952	0.1132	12.313	1.394	0.871	0.546	14.136	7.722
1953	0.1095	12.648	1.385	0.885	0.571	14.299	8.165
1954	0.1015	13.445	1.364	0.892	0.577	15.067	8.689
1955	0.1072	13.604	1.459	0.907	0.577	15.007	8.652
1956	0.1032	14.515	1.499	0.902	0.642	16.089	10.330
1957	0.1115	14.907	1.662	0.898	0.670	16.602	11.128
1958	0.1003	15.482	1.553	0.914	0.678	16.932	11.488
1959	0.1059	15.315	1.622	0.919	0.684	16.670	11.396
1960	0.0921	15.577	1.435	0.924	0.687	16.862	11.586
1961	0.1089	15.732	1.712	0.925	0.687	17.008	11.690
1962	0.1224	15.741	1.926	0.924	0.696	17.029	11.860
1963	0.1339	16.059	2.150	0.925	0.706	17.361	12.254
1964	0.1311	16.545	2.169	0.928	0.717	17.834	12.789
1965	0.1627	18.040	2.935	0.963	0.735	18.738	13.777
1966	0.1722	19.585	3.372	0.971	0.757	20.170	15.276
1967	0.1738	20.921	3.637	0.975	0.792	21.466	17.002
1968	0.1726	22.103	3.814	0.979	0.818	22.588	18.471
1969	0.1549	23.263	3.604	0.980	0.858	23.742	20.364
1970	0.1166	24.000	2.799	0.991	0.918	24.209	22.212
1971	0.1315	24.231	3.186	0.999	0.964	24.244	23.364
1972	0.1616	24.334	3.932	1.000	1.000	24.334	24.334
1973	0.1798	24.875	4.472	1.003	1.051	24.807	26.079
1974	0.1429	26.951	3.851	1.021	1.247	26.393	32.912
1975	0.1995	29.900	5.964	1.056	1.407	28.305	39.838
1976	0.2429	29.999	7.288	1.061	1.470	28.261	41.552
1977	0.2804	30.673	8.600	1.062	1.568	28.875	45.285
1978	0.2878	31.801	9.152	1.067	1.710	29.808	50.966
1979	0.3119	33.017	10.298	1.070	1.873	30.848	57.787

Table C.23. Machinery, except electrical

Year	Capital input				Capital stock		
	Price	Quantity	Outlay	Quality	Price	Quantity	Value
1948	0.1346	11.459	1.542	0.890	0.464	12.869	5.966
1949	0.1446	11.954	1.729	0.891	0.487	13.410	6.533
1950	0.1653	11.624	1.922	0.888	0.495	13.096	6.476
1951	0.2251	12.441	2.801	0.899	0.558	13.840	7.726
1952	0.1936	15.445	2.990	0.933	0.577	16.553	9.550
1953	0.1567	16.318	2.556	0.935	0.595	17.452	10.382
1954	0.1434	16.919	2.427	0.937	0.595	18.055	10.739
1955	0.1431	16.588	2.374	0.934	0.590	17.759	10.481
1956	0.1716	17.562	3.014	0.937	0.655	18.733	12.266
1957	0.1527	19.211	2.934	0.947	0.687	20.282	13.940
1958	0.1212	19.867	2.408	0.949	0.693	20.944	14.521
1959	0.1628	19.557	3.184	0.952	0.701	20.547	14.406
1960	0.1411	20.344	2.871	0.954	0.709	21.314	15.113
1961	0.1499	20.393	3.056	0.953	0.711	21.397	15.221
1962	0.1795	20.464	3.673	0.952	0.717	21.497	15.408
1963	0.1743	21.649	3.774	0.959	0.729	22.583	16.458
1964	0.2131	22.247	4.740	0.961	0.733	23.145	16.974
1965	0.2277	24.111	5.490	0.979	0.756	24.617	18.599
1966	0.2356	26.310	6.199	0.988	0.775	26.635	20.640
1967	0.2147	29.219	6.273	0.990	0.813	29.502	23.972
1968	0.2002	31.475	6.301	0.995	0.839	31.645	26.547
1969	0.1914	32.637	6.248	0.995	0.879	32.792	28.840
1970	0.1931	35.009	6.759	0.999	0.930	35.034	32.571
1971	0.1795	36.424	6.539	1.000	0.974	36.435	35.489
1972	0.2138	36.234	7.746	1.000	1.000	36.234	36.234
1973	0.2149	37.510	8.061	1.002	1.050	37.422	39.297
1974	0.1712	40.147	6.875	0.985	1.219	40.740	49.642
1975	0.2066	43.808	9.050	0.968	1.388	45.276	62.825
1976	0.2382	44.147	10.517	0.978	1.444	45.120	65.153
1977	0.2864	44.947	12.874	0.983	1.540	45.712	70.378
1978	0.3115	46.924	14.615	0.987	1.666	47.539	79.183
1979	0.3038	50.227	15.256	0.991	1.829	50.663	92.666

Table C.24. Electrical machinery, equipment, and supplies

Year	Capital input				Capital stock		
	Price	Quantity	Outlay	Quality	Price	Quantity	Value
1948	0.1252	6.297	0.788	0.770	0.501	8.176	4.092
1949	0.1446	6.362	0.920	0.768	0.509	8.279	4.211
1950	0.2160	6.295	1.360	0.761	0.511	8.276	4.231
1951	0.2117	6.918	1.465	0.788	0.590	8.783	5.179
1952	0.2059	8.663	1.783	0.852	0.619	10.162	6.294
1953	0.1814	9.384	1.703	0.865	0.640	10.850	6.939
1954	0.1558	9.903	1.543	0.870	0.636	11.384	7.237
1955	0.1425	9.855	1.404	0.869	0.625	11.337	7.083
1956	0.1555	10.255	1.595	0.870	0.692	11.782	8.157
1957	0.1756	11.584	2.034	0.902	0.725	12.849	9.309
1958	0.1621	11.833	1.918	0.900	0.725	13.147	9.533
1959	0.2043	11.613	2.373	0.895	0.729	12.976	9.465
1960	0.1657	12.252	2.031	0.896	0.732	13.678	10.015
1961	0.1601	13.068	2.093	0.918	0.731	14.235	10.404
1962	0.1682	13.684	2.302	0.922	0.740	14.840	10.976
1963	0.1687	15.235	2.570	0.948	0.756	16.070	12.142
1964	0.1685	15.824	2.666	0.952	0.759	16.614	12.609
1965	0.2401	16.640	3.996	0.959	0.770	17.348	13.356
1966	0.2465	18.529	4.567	0.976	0.795	18.989	15.099
1967	0.2186	21.576	4.716	0.991	0.834	21.767	18.149
1968	0.2051	23.380	4.796	0.994	0.850	23.511	19.977
1969	0.1974	24.477	4.832	0.994	0.889	24.625	21.895
1970	0.1593	26.105	4.159	1.001	0.932	26.067	24.288
1971	0.1952	26.740	5.220	1.002	0.964	26.674	25.716
1972	0.2437	26.527	6.464	1.000	1.000	26.527	26.527
1973	0.2066	27.241	5.628	1.004	1.039	27.139	28.198
1974	0.0997	30.903	3.082	1.034	1.188	29.874	35.476
1975	0.1457	32.665	4.758	1.042	1.337	31.351	41.910
1976	0.1815	31.840	5.778	1.052	1.376	30.272	41.668
1977	0.2738	32.757	8.968	1.051	1.449	31.168	45.170
1978	0.3288	34.463	11.330	1.054	1.564	32.701	51.146
1979	0.3543	36.579	12.961	1.056	1.710	34.638	59.245

Table C.25   Transportation equipment and ordnance, except motor vehicles

Year	Capital input				Capital stock		
	Price	Quantity	Outlay	Quality	Price	Quantity	Value
1948	0.0207	10.644	0.220	0.901	0.447	11.807	5.279
1949	0.0305	10.019	0.305	0.894	0.462	11.209	5.177
1950	0.0433	9.568	0.414	0.885	0.468	10.812	5.063
1951	0.0518	9.320	0.483	0.871	0.528	10.704	5.653
1952	0.0727	11.426	0.831	0.906	0.554	12.614	6.990
1953	0.0898	10.745	0.965	0.783	0.571	13.731	7.836
1954	0.1125	10.625	1.195	0.744	0.584	14.274	8.336
1955	0.0879	10.960	0.963	0.762	0.577	14.375	8.297
1956	0.0766	11.080	0.849	0.781	0.644	14.194	9.142
1957	0.1043	12.308	1.284	0.802	0.667	15.345	10.240
1958	0.0980	12.655	1.240	0.811	0.671	15.598	10.473
1959	0.069	12.499	0.871	0.821	0.674	15.229	10.262
1960	0.0570	12.531	0.715	0.845	0.677	14.822	10.039
1961	0.0898	12.252	1.100	0.862	0.671	14.211	9.539
1962	0.1093	12.176	1.331	0.864	0.681	14.100	9.601
1963	0.1214	12.517	1.519	0.869	0.690	14.407	9.948
1964	0.1201	13.291	1.597	0.883	0.704	15.050	10.592
1965	0.1156	13.529	1.564	0.889	0.727	15.210	11.059
1966	0.1262	14.024	1.769	0.896	0.748	15.646	11.701
1967	0.1225	17.113	2.096	0.916	0.784	18.674	14.647
1968	0.1174	20.454	2.402	0.920	0.821	22.222	18.245
1969	0.0468	21.905	1.026	0.924	0.867	23.703	20.554
1970	0.0551	23.303	1.284	0.933	0.914	24.980	22.828
1971	0.0782	23.174	1.813	1.000	0.957	23.178	22.182
1972	0.0749	22.207	1.663	1.000	1.000	22.207	22.207
1973	0.1201	21.894	2.630	0.998	1.044	21.938	22.898
1974	0.1037	21.929	2.273	1.002	1.224	21.889	26.787
1975	0.1215	21.865	2.658	1.005	1.411	21.756	30.706
1976	0.1223	21.606	2.642	0.995	1.453	21.721	31.568
1977	0.1410	19.796	2.791	0.938	1.554	21.096	32.777
1978	0.1523	19.776	3.012	0.950	1.686	20.827	35.105
1979	0.1320	23.625	3.118	1.065	1.857	22.180	41.189

Table C.26. Motor vehicles and equipment

Year	Capital input				Capital stock		
	Price	Quantity	Outlay	Quality	Price	Quantity	Value
1948	0.1775	7.918	1.405	0.907	0.459	8.729	4.009
1949	0.2718	8.166	2.220	0.908	0.479	8.994	4.309
1950	0.4219	7.598	3.206	0.891	0.483	8.532	4.118
1951	0.2792	8.559	2.390	0.933	0.551	9.175	5.052
1952	0.2470	10.006	2.471	0.973	0.568	10.287	5.848
1953	0.2634	10.635	2.801	0.977	0.580	10.880	6.312
1954	0.2043	11.403	2.329	0.988	0.585	11.545	6.758
1955	0.4239	10.573	4.482	0.941	0.575	11.242	6.469
1956	0.2071	12.345	2.556	0.980	0.646	12.597	8.137
1957	0.2305	13.146	3.031	0.975	0.676	13.489	9.116
1958	0.1000	13.310	1.331	0.985	0.688	13.516	9.298
1959	0.2725	12.636	3.443	0.982	0.689	12.871	8.866
1960	0.2870	13.093	3.758	0.992	0.700	13.196	9.238
1961	0.2647	12.636	3.346	0.983	0.696	12.854	8.946
1962	0.4007	12.512	5.013	0.981	0.704	12.753	8.979
1963	0.4715	12.974	6.117	0.991	0.710	13.096	9.293
1964	0.4456	13.554	6.039	0.997	0.722	13.597	9.823
1965	0.5295	14.881	7.880	1.009	0.743	14.748	10.964
1966	0.4367	16.413	7.168	1.011	0.766	16.233	12.431
1967	0.3544	17.121	6.068	1.009	0.798	16.976	13.547
1968	0.4605	17.312	7.972	1.006	0.822	17.213	14.145
1969	0.4184	17.577	7.354	1.006	0.868	17.475	15.160
1970	0.2258	17.850	4.031	1.005	0.917	17.757	16.280
1971	0.4402	17.601	7.747	1.003	0.954	17.543	16.729
1972	0.4960	17.207	8.535	1.000	1.000	17.207	17.207
1973	0.4434	19.088	8.464	1.007	1.045	18.952	19.801
1974	0.1528	20.574	3.144	1.001	1.193	20.558	24.517
1975	0.2444	22.780	5.568	1.067	1.364	21.356	29.135
1976	0.4645	22.070	10.251	1.070	1.406	20.623	28.992
1977	0.5636	23.371	13.172	1.077	1.493	21.691	32.384
1978	0.5271	25.074	13.217	1.075	1.609	23.320	37.533
1979	0.2688	31.479	8.461	1.276	1.739	24.675	42.899

Table C.27. Professional photographic equipment and watches

Year	Capital input				Capital stock		
	Price	Quantity	Outlay	Quality	Price	Quantity	Value
1948	0.1059	1.168	0.124	0.807	0.519	1.447	0.751
1949	0.1371	1.257	0.172	0.803	0.520	1.566	0.814
1950	0.1546	1.329	0.205	0.804	0.528	1.653	0.873
1951	0.1999	1.670	0.334	0.887	0.600	1.883	1.130
1952	0.1699	2.328	0.395	0.997	0.633	2.336	1.479
1953	0.1690	2.479	0.419	1.001	0.648	2.477	1.605
1954	0.1767	2.691	0.476	1.006	0.654	2.676	1.749
1955	0.1981	2.568	0.509	0.976	0.630	2.633	1.659
1956	0.1901	3.078	0.585	1.004	0.690	3.064	2.113
1957	0.1471	3.534	0.520	1.024	0.720	3.453	2.488
1958	0.1625	3.726	0.605	1.024	0.722	3.639	2.629
1959	0.2045	3.759	0.769	1.018	0.728	3.693	2.690
1960	0.2014	4.007	0.807	1.009	0.730	3.972	2.898
1961	0.1726	4.279	0.739	1.013	0.740	4.224	3.126
1962	0.2304	4.415	1.017	1.001	0.727	4.410	3.207
1963	0.2212	4.367	0.966	0.985	0.742	4.433	3.290
1964	0.2117	4.550	0.963	0.985	0.745	4.617	3.440
1965	0.2799	4.705	1.317	0.990	0.761	4.752	3.615
1966	0.3353	5.148	1.727	1.000	0.786	5.147	4.046
1967	0.2975	5.990	1.782	1.013	0.824	5.915	4.877
1968	0.3053	6.470	1.975	1.007	0.838	6.428	5.387
1969	0.3248	6.857	2.227	0.999	0.878	6.862	6.025
1970	0.2067	7.260	1.501	1.003	0.935	7.241	6.768
1971	0.2182	7.574	1.653	1.000	0.967	7.575	7.322
1972	0.2369	7.817	1.852	1.000	1.000	7.817	7.817
1973	0.2482	8.189	2.033	1.005	1.059	8.145	8.626
1974	0.1867	8.891	1.660	1.006	1.210	8.841	10.701
1975	0.1919	9.775	1.876	1.004	1.363	9.737	13.269
1976	0.2192	9.810	2.150	1.005	1.414	9.758	13.793
1977	0.1970	10.237	2.017	1.006	1.485	10.176	15.113
1978	0.2342	10.645	2.493	1.005	1.612	10.597	17.078
1979	0.1626	11.473	1.866	1.020	1.768	11.252	19.888

Table C.28. Miscellaneous manufacturing industries

| | Capital input | | | | Capital stock | | |
Year	Price	Quantity	Outlay	Quality	Price	Quantity	Value
1948	0.2111	1.710	0.361	0.986	0.568	1.735	0.985
1949	0.2141	1.708	0.366	0.984	0.575	1.735	0.997
1950	0.2373	1.648	0.391	0.971	0.581	1.696	0.986
1951	0.2090	1.797	0.376	0.977	0.649	1.839	1.194
1952	0.2002	1.960	0.392	0.987	0.654	1.986	1.300
1953	0.1747	1.952	0.341	0.982	0.661	1.988	1.314
1954	0.1656	2.016	0.334	0.983	0.661	2.051	1.356
1955	0.2035	2.026	0.412	0.981	0.651	2.065	1.345
1956	0.1953	2.157	0.421	0.972	0.697	2.220	1.548
1957	0.1755	2.321	0.407	0.971	0.717	2.391	1.714
1958	0.1767	2.575	0.455	0.983	0.722	2.620	1.892
1959	0.2241	2.246	0.503	0.958	0.718	2.343	1.683
1960	0.1921	2.392	0.459	0.965	0.721	2.479	1.788
1961	0.2376	2.508	0.596	0.976	0.723	2.569	1.858
1962	0.2197	2.541	0.558	0.976	0.726	2.604	1.890
1963	0.1890	2.771	0.524	0.981	0.743	2.824	2.097
1964	0.1697	2.870	0.487	0.984	0.753	2.917	2.197
1965	0.1912	2.957	0.565	0.986	0.769	2.998	2.306
1966	0.2109	3.147	0.664	0.991	0.779	3.176	2.475
1967	0.2109	3.368	0.710	0.993	0.824	3.393	2.797
1968	0.2245	3.523	0.791	0.993	0.845	3.549	2.999
1969	0.2220	3.733	0.829	0.992	0.883	3.765	3.323
1970	0.1949	3.973	0.775	0.996	0.922	3.990	3.680
1971	0.2428	4.162	1.010	0.996	0.960	4.179	4.010
1972	0.2763	4.381	1.211	1.000	1.000	4.381	4.381
1973	0.2472	4.699	1.161	1.005	1.076	4.677	5.033
1974	0.1613	5.051	0.815	1.014	1.265	4.979	6.296
1975	0.2956	5.504	1.627	1.036	1.415	5.312	7.517
1976	0.3295	5.198	1.713	1.032	1.461	5.035	7.357
1977	0.3498	5.561	1.945	1.032	1.519	5.387	8.180
1978	0.2800	5.960	1.669	1.052	1.681	5.662	9.518
1979	0.1992	6.164	1.228	1.056	1.847	5.837	10.783

Table C.29. Railroads and rail express services

Year	Capital input				Capital stock		
	Price	Quantity	Outlay	Quality	Price	Quantity	Value
1948	0.0441	45.542	2.008	0.791	0.490	57.570	28.204
1949	0.0362	49.142	1.778	0.808	0.495	60.800	30.126
1950	0.0441	51.471	2.271	0.808	0.511	63.730	32.553
1951	0.0440	53.900	2.370	0.822	0.536	65.608	35.163
1952	0.0451	56.483	2.546	0.841	0.555	67.155	37.279
1953	0.0429	58.039	2.489	0.854	0.572	67.988	38.867
1954	0.0332	58.604	1.949	0.858	0.574	68.263	39.201
1955	0.0423	57.870	2.446	0.857	0.598	67.524	40.378
1956	0.0420	57.041	2.395	0.855	0.625	66.742	41.720
1957	0.0398	57.072	2.271	0.859	0.660	66.429	43.823
1958	0.0354	57.244	2.026	0.862	0.682	66.439	45.338
1959	0.0359	56.061	2.011	0.862	0.698	65.065	45.419
1960	0.0328	55.616	1.823	0.862	0.701	64.523	45.258
1961	0.0332	57.087	1.896	0.878	0.713	65.049	46.356
1962	0.0346	56.803	1.965	0.879	0.720	64.640	46.538
1963	0.0382	55.835	2.134	0.879	0.723	63.494	45.929
1964	0.0387	55.794	2.157	0.886	0.725	62.966	45.637
1965	0.0417	57.417	2.395	0.903	0.727	63.563	46.214
1966	0.0455	59.049	2.687	0.921	0.732	64.126	46.926
1967	0.0345	61.903	2.137	0.946	0.746	65.469	48.824
1968	0.0329	63.402	2.085	0.962	0.778	65.902	51.304
1969	0.0356	63.574	2.263	0.969	0.825	65.582	54.092
1970	0.0357	65.261	2.328	0.986	0.884	66.185	58.482
1971	0.0336	65.772	2.212	0.995	0.939	66.085	62.056
1972	0.0378	65.541	2.478	1.000	1.000	65.541	65.541
1973	0.0342	65.605	2.242	1.010	1.057	64.938	68.611
1974	0.0340	66.625	2.268	1.026	1.200	64.962	77.958
1975	0.0343	65.392	2.243	1.006	1.456	65.028	94.681
1976	0.0427	64.657	2.762	1.004	1.549	64.414	99.788
1977	0.0430	64.822	2.789	1.015	1.655	63.835	105.664
1978	0.0488	69.022	3.366	1.073	1.825	64.321	117.415
1979	0.0559	75.795	4.240	1.158	2.035	65.443	133.163

Table C.30. Street railways, bus lines, and taxicabs

Year	Capital input				Capital stock		
	Price	Quantity	Outlay	Quality	Price	Quantity	Value
1948	0.2365	1.488	0.352	0.660	0.560	2.254	1.263
1949	0.2055	1.585	0.326	0.696	0.618	2.276	1.406
1950	0.2270	1.488	0.338	0.706	0.626	2.108	1.320
1951	0.2558	1.488	0.381	0.722	0.651	2.059	1.342
1952	0.2443	1.696	0.415	0.766	0.717	2.215	1.587
1953	0.2281	1.785	0.407	0.798	0.700	2.238	1.566
1954	0.1948	1.893	0.369	0.825	0.726	2.296	1.667
1955	0.2062	2.035	0.420	0.872	0.714	2.332	1.665
1956	0.2158	2.121	0.458	0.907	0.820	2.339	1.917
1957	0.2480	2.027	0.503	0.905	0.847	2.241	1.897
1958	0.2813	1.950	0.548	0.911	0.848	2.140	1.814
1959	0.3386	1.875	0.635	0.918	0.863	2.042	1.762
1960	0.3475	1.858	0.646	0.924	0.849	2.011	1.706
1961	0.3326	1.985	0.660	0.941	0.855	2.109	1.803
1962	0.3493	1.964	0.686	0.945	0.846	2.078	1.757
1963	0.3592	1.934	0.695	0.952	0.848	2.031	1.722
1964	0.3829	1.979	0.758	0.961	0.838	2.061	1.726
1965	0.4181	2.073	0.867	0.971	0.838	2.135	1.789
1966	0.3975	2.141	0.851	0.980	0.838	2.185	1.831
1967	0.3995	2.202	0.880	0.993	0.848	2.218	1.880
1968	0.3969	2.213	0.878	0.994	0.883	2.227	1.967
1969	0.3701	2.201	0.814	0.999	0.908	2.202	2.000
1970	0.3296	2.354	0.776	1.012	0.948	2.327	2.207
1971	0.3263	2.480	0.809	1.011	0.996	2.453	2.444
1972	0.2742	2.529	0.693	1.000	1.000	2.529	2.529
1973	0.1926	2.680	0.516	1.021	0.999	2.626	2.622
1974	0.1560	3.577	0.558	1.145	1.085	3.125	3.392
1975	0.1598	4.201	0.671	1.185	1.154	3.546	4.094
1976	0.1722	4.899	0.844	1.191	1.192	4.115	4.904
1977	0.1795	5.734	1.029	1.211	1.250	4.736	5.920
1978	0.1725	5.925	1.022	1.229	1.372	4.822	6.615
1979	0.1871	6.012	1.125	1.215	1.459	4.948	7.220

Table C.31. Trucking services and warehousing

Year	Capital input				Capital stock		
	Price	Quantity	Outlay	Quality	Price	Quantity	Value
1948	0.2697	3.126	0.843	0.759	0.490	4.118	2.017
1949	0.2453	3.220	0.790	0.779	0.517	4.133	2.138
1950	0.3305	3.111	1.028	0.782	0.518	3.980	2.060
1951	0.2798	3.447	0.965	0.809	0.566	4.263	2.412
1952	0.2976	3.613	1.075	0.827	0.597	4.367	2.607
1953	0.3416	3.477	1.188	0.828	0.599	4.199	2.516
1954	0.3387	3.538	1.198	0.827	0.596	4.280	2.550
1955	0.3845	3.613	1.389	0.847	0.620	4.267	2.644
1956	0.3580	4.072	1.458	0.878	0.677	4.636	3.137
1957	0.3986	4.139	1.650	0.886	0.721	4.670	3.369
1958	0.4035	4.192	1.691	0.896	0.750	4.678	3.509
1959	0.5334	3.953	2.109	0.896	0.770	4.414	3.400
1960	0.4266	4.529	1.932	0.925	0.769	4.896	3.763
1961	0.4646	4.528	2.104	0.933	0.770	4.856	3.737
1962	0.5194	4.504	2.339	0.936	0.770	4.814	3.705
1963	0.4755	4.965	2.361	0.947	0.777	5.242	4.072
1964	0.5001	5.085	2.543	0.955	0.779	5.326	4.148
1965	0.5639	5.387	3.038	0.959	0.791	5.615	4.442
1966	0.5027	6.382	3.208	0.971	0.814	6.570	5.348
1967	0.4511	7.156	3.228	0.981	0.822	7.297	5.998
1968	0.4693	7.238	3.397	0.983	0.855	7.366	6.300
1969	0.4214	8.432	3.553	0.988	0.884	8.537	7.550
1970	0.3927	8.951	3.515	0.992	0.925	9.020	8.344
1971	0.4193	9.396	3.940	0.994	0.988	9.451	9.336
1972	0.4084	10.781	4.403	1.000	1.000	10.781	10.781
1973	0.4923	9.323	4.590	0.997	1.023	9.354	9.565
1974	0.3874	13.694	5.305	1.092	1.132	12.536	14.196
1975	0.3213	16.668	5.355	1.192	1.298	13.984	18.156
1976	0.2798	20.898	5.847	1.207	1.391	17.319	24.090
1977	0.2569	25.698	6.602	1.148	1.490	22.392	33.364
1978	0.2800	27.938	7.822	1.146	1.627	24.380	39.655
1979	0.2651	29.481	7.815	1.151	1.779	25.615	45.559

Table C.32.   Water transportation

Year	Capital input				Capital stock		
	Price	Quantity	Outlay	Quality	Price	Quantity	Value
1948	0.0309	7.207	0.223	0.794	0.467	9.081	4.239
1949	0.0308	7.922	0.244	0.813	0.490	9.749	4.774
1950	0.0308	7.946	0.245	0.827	0.497	9.610	4.774
1951	0.0451	7.859	0.355	0.830	0.529	9.473	5.015
1952	0.0315	8.253	0.260	0.824	0.551	10.015	5.514
1953	0.0283	8.926	0.253	0.837	0.578	10.665	6.164
1954	0.0217	9.337	0.202	0.845	0.593	11.046	6.550
1955	0.0315	9.136	0.287	0.855	0.597	10.681	6.376
1956	0.0373	9.032	0.337	0.856	0.637	10.555	6.724
1957	0.0278	9.230	0.257	0.855	0.687	10.796	7.414
1958	0.0299	9.547	0.286	0.857	0.698	11.135	7.767
1959	0.0366	9.672	0.354	0.865	0.694	11.188	7.763
1960	0.0346	10.859	0.376	0.974	0.718	11.150	8.007
1961	0.0356	10.869	0.387	0.987	0.707	11.010	7.783
1962	0.0390	10.708	0.417	0.992	0.711	10.794	7.675
1963	0.0462	10.516	0.486	0.995	0.726	10.574	7.681
1964	0.0547	10.199	0.558	0.994	0.737	10.256	7.561
1965	0.0575	9.941	0.572	0.996	0.745	9.984	7.434
1966	0.0618	9.816	0.607	0.996	0.757	9.852	7.462
1967	0.0637	9.720	0.619	0.997	0.780	9.752	7.604
1968	0.0751	9.469	0.711	0.996	0.812	9.512	7.727
1969	0.0568	9.359	0.532	0.992	0.853	9.435	8.044
1970	0.0589	9.443	0.556	0.998	0.904	9.464	8.556
1971	0.0565	9.624	0.543	0.996	0.951	9.661	9.184
1972	0.0618	9.735	0.601	1.000	1.000	9.735	9.735
1973	0.0697	10.069	0.702	1.025	1.060	9.820	10.405
1974	0.1065	10.121	1.078	1.025	1.206	9.873	11.903
1975	0.1004	10.503	1.054	1.035	1.365	10.152	13.862
1976	0.1129	10.947	1.236	1.035	1.429	10.576	15.109
1977	0.1053	11.590	1.220	1.039	1.515	11.157	16.900
1978	0.1224	11.771	1.441	1.035	1.648	11.370	18.742
1979	0.1362	11.894	1.620	1.036	1.808	11.485	20.765

Table C.33. Air transportation

Year	Capital input				Capital stock		
	Price	Quantity	Outlay	Quality	Price	Quantity	Value
1948	0.1454	0.612	0.089	0.866	0.452	0.706	0.319
1949	0.2181	0.559	0.122	0.862	0.473	0.649	0.307
1950	0.3157	0.573	0.181	0.866	0.491	0.661	0.324
1951	0.3940	0.564	0.222	0.871	0.548	0.647	0.354
1952	0.3559	0.574	0.204	0.888	0.554	0.647	0.359
1953	0.3593	0.711	0.256	0.909	0.571	0.783	0.447
1954	0.4025	0.776	0.312	0.908	0.575	0.855	0.492
1955	0.3961	0.827	0.328	0.915	0.593	0.903	0.536
1956	0.3822	0.800	0.306	0.921	0.641	0.868	0.557
1957	0.3045	0.921	0.280	0.931	0.684	0.990	0.677
1958	0.3284	1.067	0.350	0.943	0.692	1.131	0.783
1959	0.3856	1.083	0.418	0.946	0.716	1.145	0.820
1960	0.3193	1.481	0.473	0.973	0.723	1.522	1.100
1961	0.3079	1.736	0.535	0.983	0.728	1.767	1.286
1962	0.3783	1.926	0.729	0.987	0.745	1.953	1.455
1963	0.4180	2.041	0.853	0.987	0.777	2.069	1.608
1964	0.5163	1.997	1.031	0.996	0.762	2.005	1.528
1965	0.5879	2.257	1.327	0.991	0.778	2.278	1.771
1966	0.5369	2.742	1.472	0.993	0.787	2.760	2.174
1967	0.4443	3.564	1.583	0.991	0.818	3.597	2.943
1968	0.3052	4.767	1.455	0.993	0.847	4.798	4.066
1969	0.2332	6.511	1.519	1.001	0.881	6.505	5.730
1970	0.1883	7.627	1.436	1.001	0.934	7.616	7.117
1971	0.2023	8.673	1.755	1.004	0.978	8.640	8.447
1972	0.2506	8.331	2.087	1.000	1.000	8.331	8.331
1973	0.2668	8.557	2.283	1.001	1.036	8.545	8.850
1974	0.2664	9.508	2.532	1.013	1.163	9.384	10.911
1975	0.2301	9.062	2.085	1.034	1.268	8.760	11.108
1976	0.3452	8.262	2.852	1.015	1.409	8.143	11.474
1977	0.4508	7.474	3.369	1.017	1.532	7.347	11.255
1978	0.5877	7.104	4.175	1.024	1.649	6.937	11.442
1979	0.5346	6.874	3.675	1.025	1.838	6.705	12.325

Table C.34. Pipelines, except natural gas

Year	Capital input				Capital stock		
	Price	Quantity	Outlay	Quality	Price	Quantity	Value
1948	0.0260	4.045	0.105	0.879	0.539	4.604	2.481
1949	0.0275	4.533	0.125	0.870	0.557	5.207	2.902
1950	0.0400	5.037	0.202	0.873	0.576	5.773	3.324
1951	0.0397	5.501	0.219	0.870	0.599	6.320	3.788
1952	0.0370	5.917	0.219	0.868	0.616	6.815	4.200
1953	0.0340	6.571	0.223	0.871	0.642	7.547	4.849
1954	0.0325	7.107	0.231	0.868	0.643	8.186	5.268
1955	0.0307	7.662	0.235	0.874	0.674	8.768	5.909
1956	0.0318	7.857	0.250	0.870	0.711	9.033	6.422
1957	0.0301	8.094	0.244	0.883	0.761	9.165	6.970
1958	0.0313	8.474	0.265	0.879	0.782	9.639	7.540
1959	0.0342	8.861	0.303	0.903	0.795	9.810	7.794
1960	0.0347	8.782	0.305	0.900	0.787	9.757	7.676
1961	0.0349	9.000	0.314	0.917	0.811	9.820	7.966
1962	0.0337	9.089	0.306	0.928	0.806	9.797	7.899
1963	0.0414	9.807	0.406	0.963	0.794	10.183	8.088
1964	0.0411	10.353	0.425	0.979	0.765	10.578	8.097
1965	0.0415	10.451	0.434	0.987	0.787	10.589	8.330
1966	0.0428	10.499	0.449	0.992	0.800	10.581	8.469
1967	0.0445	10.594	0.471	0.994	0.814	10.655	8.672
1968	0.0437	10.819	0.473	0.996	0.842	10.864	9.147
1969	0.0490	11.163	0.547	0.997	0.876	11.192	9.807
1970	0.0575	11.199	0.644	0.998	0.898	11.222	10.074
1971	0.0591	11.462	0.677	0.998	0.952	11.484	10.933
1972	0.0661	11.938	0.789	1.000	1.000	11.938	11.938
1973	0.0613	11.879	0.728	1.004	1.058	11.837	12.523
1974	0.0497	12.103	0.602	1.009	1.213	11.994	14.551
1975	0.0468	15.385	0.720	1.033	1.505	14.895	22.419
1976	0.0407	21.029	0.856	1.071	1.601	19.635	31.444
1977	0.0258	37.828	0.976	1.477	1.676	25.619	42.935
1978	0.0237	48.629	1.152	1.732	1.885	28.074	52.919
1979	0.0258	54.240	1.398	1.807	2.042	30.009	61.290

Table C.35. Transportation services

Year	Capital input				Capital stock		
	Price	Quantity	Outlay	Quality	Price	Quantity	Value
1948	0.1174	0.827	0.097	0.369	0.505	2.244	1.132
1949	0.0894	1.146	0.102	0.476	0.539	2.409	1.299
1950	0.1388	0.792	0.110	0.317	0.543	2.500	1.358
1951	0.1469	0.736	0.108	0.281	0.589	2.616	1.541
1952	0.1130	1.118	0.126	0.414	0.621	2.699	1.676
1953	0.0814	1.411	0.115	0.519	0.621	2.718	1.689
1954	0.0604	2.160	0.130	0.784	0.615	2.754	1.695
1955	0.0744	2.182	0.162	0.827	0.634	2.639	1.673
1956	0.0872	2.152	0.188	0.846	0.682	2.542	1.733
1957	0.1050	2.077	0.218	0.837	0.723	2.481	1.793
1958	0.0975	1.989	0.194	0.835	0.746	2.382	1.776
1959	0.0965	1.844	0.178	0.812	0.764	2.271	1.735
1960	0.0954	2.127	0.203	0.920	0.755	2.313	1.746
1961	0.1007	2.314	0.233	0.966	0.759	2.394	1.818
1962	0.1058	2.226	0.235	0.956	0.760	2.329	1.771
1963	0.1159	2.164	0.251	0.958	0.761	2.259	1.719
1964	0.1302	2.067	0.269	0.951	0.764	2.175	1.661
1965	0.1460	2.131	0.311	0.970	0.775	2.198	1.703
1966	0.1416	2.396	0.339	1.016	0.798	2.357	1.881
1967	0.1721	2.538	0.437	1.039	0.808	2.441	1.973
1968	0.1173	2.973	0.349	1.083	0.844	2.746	2.318
1969	0.1293	2.755	0.356	1.064	0.877	2.590	2.271
1970	0.1462	2.687	0.393	1.056	0.918	2.544	2.336
1971	0.1488	2.465	0.367	1.037	0.978	2.378	2.325
1972	0.1696	2.201	0.373	1.000	1.000	2.201	2.201
1973	0.1529	2.580	0.395	1.117	1.033	2.311	2.388
1974	0.2448	3.128	0.766	1.224	1.140	2.556	2.913
1975	0.2771	2.999	0.831	1.216	1.280	2.466	3.157
1976	0.3139	3.139	0.985	1.228	1.347	2.556	3.441
1977	0.3285	3.363	1.105	1.234	1.437	2.726	3.918
1978	0.3848	3.415	1.314	1.256	1.573	2.720	4.278
1979	0.4729	3.365	1.591	1.271	1.728	2.648	4.576

Table C.36 Telephone, telegraph, and miscellaneous communication
services

Year	Capital input				Capital stock		
	Price	Quantity	Outlay	Quality	Price	Quantity	Value
1948	0.0669	12.700	0.849	0.534	0.401	23.766	9.525
1949	0.0730	14.292	1.043	0.561	0.415	25.471	10.571
1950	0.0721	15.159	1.093	0.572	0.427	26.488	11.313
1951	0.0948	15.571	1.476	0.575	0.454	27.094	12.306
1952	0.0981	16.265	1.596	0.583	0.466	27.898	13.000
1953	0.1000	18.298	1.829	0.622	0.475	29.414	13.959
1954	0.1001	19.976	1.999	0.616	0.482	32.405	15.616
1955	0.1065	21.921	2.335	0.653	0.515	33.549	17.271
1956	0.0957	24.034	2.300	0.686	0.541	35.025	18.943
1957	0.1016	26.959	2.740	0.697	0.557	38.684	21.548
1958	0.0991	30.821	3.055	0.735	0.577	41.914	24.194
1959	0.1109	33.482	3.714	0.763	0.599	43.902	26.283
1960	0.1188	35.940	4.270	0.782	0.610	45.953	28.036
1961	0.1206	38.851	4.685	0.810	0.635	47.993	30.485
1962	0.1178	41.361	4.872	0.830	0.636	49.862	31.734
1963	0.1381	44.313	6.118	0.842	0.655	52.631	34.479
1964	0.1366	46.119	6.299	0.864	0.668	53.399	35.693
1965	0.1394	48.112	6.706	0.881	0.683	54.641	37.311
1966	0.1510	50.904	7.686	0.908	0.708	56.046	39.687
1967	0.1517	54.347	8.243	0.928	0.737	58.548	43.147
1968	0.1571	57.469	9.031	0.942	0.778	61.024	47.468
1969	0.1609	60.878	9.792	0.956	0.825	63.693	52.531
1970	0.1552	65.151	10.111	0.971	0.877	67.064	58.846
1971	0.1527	70.779	10.808	0.987	0.928	71.710	66.554
1972	0.1493	75.439	11.267	1.000	1.000	75.439	75.439
1973	0.1525	79.444	12.114	1.016	1.062	78.167	82.999
1974	0.1639	83.161	13.633	1.033	1.148	80.500	92.418
1975	0.1974	86.812	17.141	1.041	1.297	83.402	108.153
1976	0.2021	87.328	17.652	1.041	1.375	83.922	115.403
1977	0.2149	88.018	18.914	1.040	1.445	84.609	122.223
1978	0.2281	91.939	20.973	1.053	1.565	87.307	136.624
1979	0.2289	98.578	22.562	1.074	1.696	91.789	155.659

Table C.37. Radio and television broadcasting

	Capital input				Capital stock		
Year	Price	Quantity	Outlay	Quality	Price	Quantity	Value
1948	0.1928	0.322	0.062	0.876	0.552	0.367	0.203
1949	0.1547	0.379	0.059	0.907	0.573	0.418	0.239
1950	0.2183	0.384	0.084	0.918	0.572	0.418	0.239
1951	0.3232	0.375	0.121	0.907	0.601	0.414	0.249
1952	0.3379	0.390	0.132	0.910	0.596	0.428	0.255
1953	0.3903	0.359	0.140	0.910	0.589	0.395	0.233
1954	0.4298	0.379	0.163	0.898	0.584	0.422	0.246
1955	0.5421	0.448	0.243	0.966	0.594	0.463	0.275
1956	0.5040	0.497	0.250	1.006	0.626	0.494	0.310
1957	0.5390	0.496	0.267	0.963	0.650	0.515	0.335
1958	0.5103	0.529	0.270	0.961	0.656	0.551	0.361
1959	0.5936	0.535	0.318	0.956	0.663	0.560	0.371
1960	0.6526	0.569	0.372	0.965	0.659	0.590	0.389
1961	0.5010	0.639	0.320	0.968	0.666	0.660	0.440
1962	0.6615	0.653	0.432	0.992	0.675	0.658	0.444
1963	0.7059	0.651	0.460	0.968	0.685	0.673	0.461
1964	0.5578	0.757	0.422	0.970	0.696	0.781	0.543
1965	0.5889	0.829	0.488	0.972	0.711	0.852	0.606
1966	0.5360	1.004	0.538	0.972	0.727	1.033	0.751
1967	0.4136	1.160	0.480	0.982	0.758	1.181	0.895
1968	0.3909	1.392	0.544	0.984	0.793	1.414	1.122
1969	0.4241	1.496	0.634	0.997	0.844	1.501	1.267
1970	0.3569	1.582	0.565	1.000	0.888	1.582	1.405
1971	0.3913	1.588	0.621	1.001	0.939	1.587	1.490
1972	0.4893	1.705	0.834	1.000	1.000	1.705	1.705
1973	0.4218	1.876	0.791	1.000	1.057	1.875	1.983
1974	0.3422	2.075	0.710	1.008	1.170	2.058	2.407
1975	0.4367	2.307	1.008	1.008	1.315	2.289	3.011
1976	0.5945	2.460	1.463	1.009	1.380	2.437	3.363
1977	0.7921	2.519	1.995	0.977	1.452	2.579	3.746
1978	0.8141	2.622	2.135	0.965	1.566	2.718	4.256
1979	0.7260	2.860	2.077	0.981	1.711	2.917	4.989

Table C.38. Electric utilities

Year	Capital input				Capital stock		
	Price	Quantity	Outlay	Quality	Price	Quantity	Value
1948	0.0603	25.225	1.521	0.764	0.444	33.015	14.671
1949	0.0609	29.069	1.769	0.801	0.466	36.298	16.909
1950	0.0578	33.420	1.933	0.831	0.494	40.209	19.844
1951	0.0609	37.341	2.273	0.855	0.540	43.664	23.581
1952	0.0610	40.798	2.490	0.869	0.543	46.922	25.469
1953	0.0592	45.846	2.715	0.894	0.573	51.277	29.380
1954	0.0598	51.835	3.101	0.920	0.576	56.312	32.453
1955	0.0606	56.708	3.438	0.938	0.609	60.462	36.817
1956	0.0613	60.312	3.694	0.950	0.654	63.481	41.545
1957	0.0610	63.581	3.878	0.953	0.696	66.713	46.450
1958	0.0600	67.154	4.027	0.955	0.705	70.309	49.600
1959	0.0641	70.428	4.511	0.955	0.726	73.717	53.546
1960	0.0690	72.661	5.017	0.956	0.726	75.984	55.172
1961	0.0704	74.793	5.269	0.949	0.720	78.791	56.707
1962	0.0731	76.677	5.607	0.945	0.714	81.118	57.891
1963	0.0749	78.389	5.873	0.943	0.717	83.171	59.610
1964	0.0775	80.609	6.249	0.940	0.724	85.753	62.109
1965	0.0792	83.008	6.571	0.939	0.735	88.365	64.975
1966	0.0802	86.609	6.946	0.937	0.749	92.385	69.158
1967	0.0790	91.664	7.239	0.940	0.776	97.500	75.646
1968	0.0791	98.379	7.779	0.944	0.805	104.180	83.837
1969	0.0786	105.886	8.320	0.946	0.850	111.873	95.095
1970	0.0736	116.066	8.543	0.960	0.901	120.958	108.952
1971	0.0757	129.070	9.768	0.977	0.959	132.132	126.658
1972	0.0730	145.910	10.647	1.000	1.000	145.910	145.910
1973	0.0688	166.036	11.431	1.033	1.057	160.772	170.014
1974	0.0606	186.695	11.313	1.061	1.202	176.023	211.607
1975	0.0759	202.554	15.370	1.080	1.443	187.566	270.750
1976	0.0799	209.266	16.721	1.077	1.551	194.297	301.277
1977	0.0868	218.046	18.933	1.084	1.666	201.170	335.154
1978	0.0894	234.670	20.984	1.101	1.807	213.216	385.271
1979	0.0855	256.930	21.958	1.125	1.970	228.442	450.088

Table C.39.   Gas utilities

Year	Capital input				Capital stock		
	Price	Quantity	Outlay	Quality	Price	Quantity	Value
1948	0.0404	14.586	0.590	0.955	0.436	15.278	6.662
1949	0.0482	15.959	0.770	0.950	0.453	16.801	7.619
1950	0.0448	17.693	0.793	0.960	0.482	18.433	8.875
1951	0.0497	20.460	1.017	0.972	0.525	21.044	11.054
1952	0.0484	23.232	1.124	0.976	0.527	23.795	12.544
1953	0.0498	24.962	1.243	0.982	0.557	25.419	14.160
1954	0.0535	26.756	1.432	0.988	0.557	27.092	15.083
1955	0.0568	27.967	1.589	0.989	0.596	28.274	16.842
1956	0.0597	29.399	1.755	0.987	0.635	29.790	18.925
1957	0.0605	31.302	1.893	0.989	0.671	31.650	21.245
1958	0.0612	33.031	2.021	0.991	0.679	33.345	22.652
1959	0.0662	34.327	2.273	0.995	0.702	34.489	24.207
1960	0.0710	35.647	2.530	0.995	0.701	35.808	25.096
1961	0.0721	37.177	2.681	0.995	0.699	37.380	26.118
1962	0.0730	38.541	2.814	0.993	0.695	38.809	26.972
1963	0.0742	39.709	2.946	0.993	0.700	39.970	27.969
1964	0.0745	40.791	3.038	0.994	0.709	41.020	29.086
1965	0.0746	42.043	3.137	0.995	0.722	42.245	30.492
1966	0.0753	44.009	3.316	0.997	0.737	44.162	32.536
1967	0.0752	46.362	3.487	0.997	0.763	46.491	35.484
1968	0.0779	48.503	3.780	0.999	0.790	48.566	38.378
1969	0.0772	51.193	3.952	0.997	0.840	51.334	43.102
1970	0.0732	53.457	3.912	0.992	0.893	53.882	48.135
1971	0.0810	55.191	4.470	0.994	0.953	55.528	52.939
1972	0.0862	56.535	4.874	1.000	1.000	56.535	56.535
1973	0.0908	57.669	5.239	1.003	1.068	57.485	61.401
1974	0.0888	58.434	5.191	1.002	1.238	58.307	72.167
1975	0.1197	58.654	7.022	1.006	1.485	58.299	86.586
1976	0.1307	58.566	7.652	1.007	1.589	58.148	92.403
1977	0.1485	58.378	8.671	1.011	1.718	57.732	99.204
1978	0.1633	58.936	9.627	1.016	1.877	58.034	108.959
1979	0.1687	59.688	10.067	1.022	2.059	58.385	120.219

Table C.40. Water supply and sanitary services

Year	Capital input				Capital stock		
	Price	Quantity	Outlay	Quality	Price	Quantity	Value
1948	0.0436	3.979	0.173	1.013	0.439	3.927	1.723
1949	0.0559	3.915	0.219	1.006	0.456	3.892	1.774
1950	0.0535	3.864	0.207	1.005	0.483	3.844	1.858
1951	0.0667	3.826	0.255	1.005	0.526	3.806	2.003
1952	0.0746	3.781	0.282	1.005	0.528	3.761	1.985
1953	0.0819	3.778	0.309	1.004	0.557	3.763	2.097
1954	0.0930	3.834	0.357	1.004	0.557	3.819	2.126
1955	0.1061	3.866	0.410	1.004	0.596	3.852	2.296
1956	0.1095	3.936	0.431	1.007	0.636	3.908	2.485
1957	0.1190	4.070	0.484	1.006	0.673	4.043	2.721
1958	0.1242	4.149	0.515	1.005	0.681	4.127	2.809
1959	0.1437	4.147	0.596	1.005	0.703	4.126	2.899
1960	0.1651	4.124	0.681	1.005	0.702	4.104	2.879
1961	0.1761	4.115	0.725	1.003	0.699	4.103	2.867
1962	0.1877	4.098	0.769	1.003	0.695	4.087	2.842
1963	0.2003	4.108	0.823	1.003	0.700	4.098	2.868
1964	0.2175	4.098	0.891	1.002	0.710	4.091	2.902
1965	0.2305	4.109	0.947	1.002	0.722	4.101	2.961
1966	0.2473	4.151	1.026	1.003	0.737	4.140	3.051
1967	0.2589	4.179	1.082	1.002	0.763	4.170	3.183
1968	0.2835	4.222	1.197	1.001	0.791	4.217	3.337
1969	0.3032	4.306	1.306	1.001	0.841	4.301	3.615
1970	0.3113	4.387	1.366	1.001	0.893	4.384	3.914
1971	0.3483	4.482	1.561	1.000	0.953	4.481	4.272
1972	0.3877	4.402	1.707	1.000	1.000	4.402	4.402
1973	0.4163	4.410	1.836	1.000	1.067	4.410	4.706
1974	0.4174	4.342	1.812	1.000	1.233	4.344	5.357
1975	0.5756	4.258	2.451	0.999	1.483	4.262	6.321
1976	0.6401	4.180	2.675	1.000	1.584	4.181	6.623
1977	0.7410	4.090	3.031	1.000	1.712	4.092	7.006
1978	0.8388	4.023	3.374	1.000	1.874	4.022	7.536
1979	0.8910	3.954	3.523	1.000	2.058	3.953	8.135

Table C.41. Wholesale trade

Year	Capital input				Capital stock		
	Price	Quantity	Outlay	Quality	Price	Quantity	Value
1948	0.1923	19.664	3.782	0.790	0.574	24.876	14.290
1949	0.1477	21.145	3.123	0.806	0.566	26.225	14.843
1950	0.1942	21.310	4.138	0.818	0.582	26.066	15.171
1951	0.2160	23.660	5.110	0.837	0.651	28.277	18.403
1952	0.2006	24.310	4.878	0.841	0.652	28.922	18.851
1953	0.1751	24.499	4.291	0.841	0.645	29.143	18.805
1954	0.1578	24.296	3.833	0.836	0.648	29.076	18.850
1955	0.1856	24.925	4.627	0.858	0.664	29.036	19.285
1956	0.1824	27.182	4.957	0.885	0.702	30.705	21.560
1957	0.1858	28.259	5.251	0.900	0.730	31.389	22.919
1958	0.2042	27.899	5.697	0.901	0.731	30.975	22.641
1959	0.2056	27.835	5.723	0.907	0.746	30.692	22.903
1960	0.1842	30.474	5.614	0.917	0.752	33.237	24.990
1961	0.1797	31.742	5.705	0.923	0.760	34.401	26.130
1962	0.1904	32.090	6.111	0.932	0.764	34.425	26.307
1963	0.1964	33.430	6.564	0.938	0.770	35.637	27.431
1964	0.1892	35.479	6.713	0.949	0.780	37.374	29.146
1965	0.2429	37.344	9.073	0.953	0.793	39.203	31.076
1966	0.2012	39.887	8.024	0.964	0.819	41.373	33.891
1967	0.2457	44.503	10.936	0.975	0.826	45.659	37.719
1968	0.2194	47.021	10.316	0.976	0.851	48.201	41.019
1969	0.2234	49.659	11.096	0.991	0.876	50.125	43.926
1970	0.2157	53.745	11.594	0.997	0.913	53.912	49.225
1971	0.2245	57.052	12.806	0.998	0.950	57.169	54.315
1972	0.2806	59.629	16.732	1.000	1.000	59.629	59.629
1973	0.3259	62.433	20.349	1.003	1.088	62.233	67.711
1974	0.3881	66.368	25.760	1.010	1.273	65.687	83.650
1975	0.4213	71.770	30.240	1.013	1.419	70.832	100.516
1976	0.4265	70.708	30.154	1.014	1.502	69.702	104.678
1977	0.4547	74.182	33.732	1.015	1.601	73.111	117.022
1978	0.4380	79.204	34.691	1.016	1.734	77.993	135.266
1979	0.4497	83.774	37.670	1.017	1.948	82.398	160.486

Table C.42. Retail trade

Year	Capital input				Capital stock		
	Price	Quantity	Outlay	Quality	Price	Quantity	Value
1948	0.1153	44.125	5.086	0.810	0.494	54.491	26.896
1949	0.1992	46.671	9.297	0.818	0.483	57.046	27.565
1950	0.1356	46.041	6.243	0.815	0.504	56.478	28.474
1951	0.1294	49.930	6.460	0.834	0.560	59.841	33.535
1952	0.1539	50.380	7.756	0.837	0.563	60.204	33.883
1953	0.1497	49.994	7.482	0.833	0.555	59.986	33.276
1954	0.1259	51.563	6.493	0.841	0.565	61.331	34.669
1955	0.1144	53.674	6.139	0.870	0.601	61.671	37.042
1956	0.1115	62.023	6.916	0.930	0.652	66.699	43.521
1957	0.1193	64.964	7.753	0.946	0.683	68.655	46.873
1958	0.1450	66.554	9.648	0.948	0.681	70.229	47.835
1959	0.1297	66.412	8.613	0.947	0.706	70.099	49.491
1960	0.1332	69.155	9.213	0.954	0.713	72.511	51.693
1961	0.1373	71.239	9.778	0.964	0.721	73.891	53.278
1962	0.1388	71.642	9.941	0.976	0.733	73.398	53.837
1963	0.1525	75.163	11.460	0.977	0.737	76.903	56.649
1964	0.1317	78.800	10.381	0.997	0.765	79.071	60.487
1965	0.1781	82.971	14.777	1.007	0.771	82.413	63.572
1966	0.1728	87.467	15.114	1.008	0.814	86.779	70.628
1967	0.2098	90.861	19.060	1.004	0.809	90.542	73.289
1968	0.1635	91.512	14.958	0.999	0.845	91.633	77.474
1969	0.1673	96.628	16.168	1.002	0.885	96.455	85.355
1970	0.1876	99.891	18.742	1.003	0.913	99.609	90.974
1971	0.1970	100.921	19.877	1.000	0.952	100.886	96.028
1972	0.1900	106.940	20.321	1.000	1.000	106.940	106.940
1973	0.1763	112.935	19.905	1.007	1.060	112.166	118.857
1974	0.1283	119.608	15.344	1.013	1.214	118.091	143.356
1975	0.1818	120.188	21.853	1.020	1.346	117.821	158.596
1976	0.2195	117.908	25.879	1.021	1.431	115.518	165.262
1977	0.2590	121.149	31.376	1.025	1.540	118.201	182.088
1978	0.2700	125.747	33.947	1.024	1.691	122.766	207.640
1979	0.2560	129.982	33.277	1.023	1.902	126.997	241.597

Table C.43. Finance, insurance, and real estate

Year	Capital input				Capital stock		
	Price	Quantity	Outlay	Quality	Price	Quantity	Value
1948	0.0503	200.411	10.084	1.008	0.440	198.886	87.449
1949	0.0522	199.254	10.401	1.005	0.438	198.250	86.793
1950	0.0624	199.776	12.456	1.010	0.453	197.85	89.671
1951	0.0648	200.022	12.952	1.007	0.483	198.577	95.896
1952	0.0720	199.574	14.361	1.006	0.496	198.295	98.312
1953	0.0825	199.031	16.430	1.005	0.496	198.054	98.182
1954	0.0886	201.921	17.890	0.989	0.499	204.177	101.860
1955	0.0908	202.953	18.431	0.986	0.528	205.879	108.624
1956	0.1010	204.913	20.701	0.978	0.545	209.422	114.146
1957	0.0950	206.216	19.581	0.976	0.559	211.193	117.984
1958	0.1054	208.185	21.943	0.973	0.567	214.002	121.394
1959	0.1112	209.557	23.293	0.976	0.584	214.710	125.385
1960	0.0938	211.250	19.824	0.990	0.610	213.394	130.081
1961	0.1147	215.265	24.701	0.990	0.606	217.433	131.802
1962	0.1112	219.660	24.425	0.990	0.623	221.778	138.105
1963	0.1045	225.936	23.608	0.990	0.634	228.189	144.710
1964	0.1059	232.875	24.661	0.994	0.649	234.392	152.064
1965	0.1173	241.235	28.290	0.999	0.672	241.390	162.298
1966	0.1275	246.567	31.433	1.001	0.700	246.205	172.341
1967	0.1335	251.207	33.535	0.997	0.729	251.939	183.563
1968	0.1272	255.094	32.437	0.999	0.770	255.328	196.480
1969	0.1282	258.945	33.205	0.997	0.822	259.662	213.542
1970	0.1341	267.593	35.872	1.001	0.868	267.241	231.891
1971	0.1355	272.816	36.967	0.999	0.925	273.062	252.664
1972	0.1744	280.344	48.902	1.000	1.000	280.344	280.344
1973	0.1575	295.397	46.522	1.014	1.131	291.440	329.757
1974	0.1566	308.448	48.298	1.021	1.360	302.152	411.031
1975	0.1542	308.996	47.643	1.010	1.333	305.808	407.573
1976	0.1728	307.717	53.176	0.999	1.429	308.070	440.085
1977	0.2107	311.200	65.559	1.001	1.590	310.958	494.375
1978	0.2229	317.948	70.857	1.006	1.801	315.990	569.140
1979	0.2347	322.929	75.778	1.002	2.039	322.364	657.178

Table C.44. Services, except private households and institutions

Year	Capital input				Capital stock		
	Price	Quantity	Outlay	Quality	Price	Quantity	Value
1948	0.1757	42.005	7.380	0.726	0.499	57.895	28.894
1949	0.1772	42.953	7.610	0.737	0.497	58.316	28.996
1950	0.1892	42.959	8.128	0.742	0.497	57.889	28.789
1951	0.1919	44.309	8.502	0.756	0.549	58.604	32.198
1952	0.1916	45.888	8.792	0.774	0.573	59.295	33.947
1953	0.2010	46.048	9.254	0.779	0.569	59.093	33.647
1954	0.2037	48.097	9.795	0.786	0.568	61.224	34.755
1955	0.2352	48.428	11.390	0.794	0.588	60.965	35.873
1956	0.2238	52.077	11.657	0.823	0.632	63.301	40.023
1957	0.2317	54.858	12.711	0.833	0.664	65.886	43.730
1958	0.2266	57.719	13.082	0.850	0.666	67.884	45.200
1959	0.2439	59.849	14.599	0.861	0.674	69.511	46.883
1960	0.2453	62.782	15.400	0.870	0.676	72.127	48.759
1961	0.2364	66.307	15.673	0.883	0.691	75.057	51.835
1962	0.2368	71.053	16.822	0.894	0.703	79.476	55.846
1963	0.2313	77.684	17.969	0.906	0.718	85.709	61.530
1964	0.2267	81.981	18.587	0.910	0.728	90.045	65.553
1965	0.2349	86.385	20.288	0.911	0.738	94.800	69.981
1966	0.2316	93.706	21.702	0.923	0.760	101.576	77.171
1967	0.2348	102.870	24.155	0.934	0.785	110.164	86.496
1968	0.2283	110.281	25.177	0.944	0.820	116.835	95.836
1969	0.2181	125.744	27.428	0.974	0.872	129.138	112.583
1970	0.2079	139.145	28.925	0.995	0.918	139.852	128.443
1971	0.2163	145.230	31.418	0.998	0.962	145.462	139.985
1972	0.2232	149.321	33.322	1.000	1.000	149.321	149.321
1973	0.2325	157.478	36.611	1.005	1.045	156.643	163.707
1974	0.2196	168.819	37.080	1.016	1.163	166.177	193.196
1975	0.2438	172.844	42.141	1.017	1.291	169.935	219.349
1976	0.2788	169.504	47.265	1.005	1.335	168.655	225.136
1977	0.3135	168.649	52.872	1.005	1.424	167.872	239.119
1978	0.3327	172.407	57.361	1.010	1.566	170.667	267.247
1979	0.3601	174.916	62.980	1.006	1.734	173.820	301.368

Table C.45. Private households

Year	Capital input				Capital stock		
	Price	Quantity	Outlay	Quality	Price	Quantity	Value
1948	0.0707	387.226	27.383	0.754	0.474	513.488	243.431
1949	0.0690	425.021	29.313	0.778	0.488	546.169	266.753
1950	0.0743	465.009	34.540	0.806	0.515	577.023	297.250
1951	0.0779	518.622	40.412	0.837	0.560	619.911	347.017
1952	0.0845	551.610	46.636	0.848	0.579	650.766	377.023
1953	0.0813	577.383	46.960	0.852	0.589	677.550	399.258
1954	0.0921	610.257	56.202	0.862	0.594	707.698	420.563
1955	0.0892	641.323	57.220	0.869	0.615	738.095	453.790
1956	0.0891	690.657	61.539	0.886	0.646	779.575	503.635
1957	0.0816	726.017	59.274	0.894	0.666	812.081	541.239
1958	0.0916	756.032	69.217	0.900	0.677	840.100	568.879
1959	0.0887	776.685	68.911	0.899	0.694	863.572	599.131
1960	0.0961	810.565	77.887	0.903	0.701	897.836	629.090
1961	0.0965	839.979	81.053	0.905	0.710	927.972	658.406
1962	0.0979	861.610	84.354	0.904	0.721	953.202	687.697
1963	0.0966	894.101	86.405	0.908	0.725	984.814	714.256
1964	0.1019	934.825	95.276	0.914	0.737	1022.451	753.496
1965	0.1099	981.703	107.924	0.923	0.752	1063.502	799.775
1966	0.1128	1038.645	117.119	0.936	0.772	1109.408	856.818
1967	0.1099	1096.663	120.509	0.950	0.797	1153.829	919.808
1968	0.1140	1147.223	130.762	0.960	0.837	1194.641	1000.229
1969	0.1194	1210.728	144.554	0.973	0.875	1244.877	1088.709
1970	0.1241	1272.095	157.884	0.984	0.912	1292.759	1179.581
1971	0.1276	1319.177	168.360	0.991	0.951	1331.714	1266.681
1972	0.1429	1388.307	198.445	1.000	1.000	1388.307	1388.307
1973	0.1555	1480.191	230.199	1.014	1.081	1460.215	1578.240
1974	0.1480	1577.178	233.380	1.028	1.185	1534.058	1817.945
1975	0.1429	1633.787	233.545	1.032	1.290	1583.055	2041.636
1976	0.1601	1682.135	269.320	1.036	1.387	1623.756	2252.364
1977	0.1905	1757.900	334.847	1.044	1.520	1683.989	2559.956
1978	0.2061	1850.518	381.472	1.053	1.689	1758.044	2969.885
1979	0.2142	1945.831	416.707	1.061	1.871	1833.663	3430.885

Table C.46. Institutions

Year	Capital input				Capital stock		
	Price	Quantity	Outlay	Quality	Price	Quantity	Value
1948	0.0166	56.301	0.937	0.958	0.363	58.776	21.320
1949	0.0261	58.449	1.526	0.974	0.368	60.002	22.097
1950	0.0240	60.796	1.459	0.986	0.389	61.642	23.997
1951	0.0155	64.838	1.004	1.009	0.434	64.243	27.909
1952	0.0321	67.861	2.179	1.019	0.451	66.590	30.055
1953	0.0270	70.137	1.892	1.022	0.464	68.595	31.853
1954	0.0372	72.478	2.699	1.025	0.471	70.715	33.324
1955	0.0341	75.282	2.569	1.026	0.493	73.353	36.146
1956	0.0164	78.421	1.289	1.033	0.540	75.935	41.010
1957	0.0222	81.869	1.815	1.039	0.570	78.780	44.941
1958	0.0419	85.534	3.580	1.044	0.581	81.936	47.625
1959	0.0365	89.272	3.257	1.046	0.601	85.355	51.258
1960	0.0468	93.484	4.372	1.050	0.606	89.012	53.939
1961	0.0456	98.081	4.468	1.054	0.614	93.014	57.155
1962	0.0443	103.014	4.564	1.059	0.628	97.251	61.078
1963	0.0384	108.943	4.179	1.067	0.639	102.145	65.282
1964	0.0441	115.074	5.070	1.075	0.655	107.088	70.134
1965	0.0469	122.570	5.755	1.088	0.678	112.673	76.363
1966	0.0479	129.929	6.217	1.095	0.707	118.628	83.915
1967	0.0487	137.444	6.692	1.102	0.738	124.744	92.120
1968	0.0561	143.389	8.045	1.104	0.774	129.869	100.530
1969	0.0671	141.642	9.504	1.077	0.822	131.457	108.105
1970	0.0317	139.424	4.424	1.046	0.880	133.321	117.257
1971	0.0504	137.268	6.919	1.017	0.934	134.994	126.030
1972	0.0719	136.713	9.833	1.000	1.000	136.713	136.713
1973	0.0552	136.623	7.543	0.985	1.129	138.670	156.615
1974	0.0808	136.896	11.060	0.976	1.260	140.229	176.710
1975	0.0777	137.058	10.650	0.972	1.387	140.945	195.528
1976	0.0811	136.414	11.062	0.967	1.523	141.081	214.815
1977	0.1749	136.710	23.906	0.964	1.641	141.799	232.652
1978	0.1483	137.295	20.366	0.964	1.835	142.419	261.314
1979	0.1377	138.145	19.029	0.965	2.065	143.115	295.527

Sectoral Production Accounts: Output, Intermediate Input, and Productivity

Table D.1. Agricultural production

Year	Intermediate input				Output			Tax rate	Rate of productivity growth
	Price	Quantity	Outlay	Quality	Price	Quantity	Revenue		
1948	0.722	29.883	21.573	0.966	0.897	50.277	45.113	0.0002	
1949	0.665	31.928	21.239	0.982	0.774	51.886	40.185	0.0002	0.0061
1950	0.675	32.058	21.654	0.980	0.788	53.113	41.850	0.0002	0.0196
1951	0.765	37.239	28.491	0.968	0.930	55.555	51.659	0.0002	−0.0173
1952	0.757	36.459	27.591	0.973	0.898	55.711	50.005	0.0003	0.0172
1953	0.719	33.963	24.430	0.981	0.811	55.329	44.898	0.0003	0.0357
1954	0.709	35.263	24.998	0.982	0.782	57.407	44.864	0.0003	0.0198
1955	0.698	36.477	25.459	0.986	0.748	59.358	44.428	0.0003	0.0195
1956	0.700	35.522	24.863	0.988	0.734	59.821	43.913	0.0004	0.0346
1957	0.717	36.374	26.064	0.987	0.749	60.502	45.303	0.0005	0.0210
1958	0.741	37.049	27.445	0.986	0.789	62.253	49.106	0.0005	0.0306
1959	0.730	39.347	28.718	0.988	0.761	63.505	48.343	0.0004	−0.0143
1960	0.739	38.494	28.434	0.990	0.762	64.636	49.228	0.0003	0.0292
1961	0.740	38.725	28.648	0.988	0.763	65.671	50.140	0.0002	0.0282
1962	0.752	41.001	30.837	0.992	0.778	67.836	52.769	0.0002	0.0019
1963	0.748	42.157	31.535	0.995	0.762	70.209	53.478	0.0002	0.0331
1964	0.739	41.324	30.555	0.997	0.731	70.717	51.701	0.0002	0.0282
1965	0.773	40.973	31.690	0.997	0.780	71.435	55.713	0.0002	0.0177
1966	0.815	41.809	34.056	0.997	0.832	71.817	59.738	0.0002	0.0141
1967	0.809	43.856	35.490	0.999	0.807	74.670	60.243	0.0002	0.0174
1968	0.834	42.832	35.738	1.000	0.822	74.570	61.305	0.0002	0.0112
1969	0.880	43.326	38.129	1.000	0.868	76.630	66.485	0.0002	0.0304
1970	0.897	43.541	39.039	0.999	0.884	76.992	68.053	0.0002	−0.0037
1971	0.926	46.082	42.684	1.000	0.896	81.516	73.003	0.0003	0.0373
1972	1.000	47.649	47.649	1.000	1.000	82.991	82.991	0.0002	−0.0028
1973	1.189	46.141	54.869	0.995	1.307	81.892	107.010	0.0002	−0.0014
1974	1.304	46.427	60.545	0.995	1.348	80.633	108.726	0.0002	−0.0171
1975	1.350	43.201	58.304	0.993	1.287	83.815	107.843	0.0003	0.0729
1976	1.377	51.503	70.908	0.993	1.295	90.700	117.428	0.0002	−0.0188
1977	1.429	56.811	81.178	0.991	1.310	99.530	130.354	0.0002	0.0400
1978	1.618	57.093	92.362	0.993	1.586	96.427	152.926	0.0002	−0.0407
1979	1.825	59.785	109.129	0.990	1.835	98.271	180.304	0.0002	0.0019

Table D.2. Agricultural services

	Intermediate input				Output				
Year	Price	Quantity	Outlay	Quality	Price	Quantity	Revenue	Tax rate	Rate of productivity growth
1948	0.760	0.893	0.679	1.008	0.445	3.119	1.387	0.0007	
1949	0.684	1.012	0.692	1.018	0.434	3.308	1.435	0.0007	−0.0017
1950	0.698	1.055	0.736	1.012	0.446	3.444	1.535	0.0007	−0.0108
1951	0.804	1.005	0.808	0.998	0.488	3.459	1.688	0.0006	−0.0064
1952	0.784	1.034	0.811	0.998	0.498	3.554	1.771	0.0006	−0.0150
1953	0.733	1.178	0.863	1.001	0.471	3.917	1.846	0.0005	0.0396
1954	0.715	1.137	0.813	0.999	0.455	4.089	1.861	0.0005	0.0520
1955	0.700	1.316	0.921	1.000	0.486	4.102	1.995	0.0005	−0.0568
1956	0.699	1.457	1.018	0.998	0.513	4.146	2.125	0.0005	−0.0381
1957	0.715	1.344	0.961	0.994	0.508	4.093	2.079	0.0005	0.0300
1958	0.747	1.409	1.052	0.983	0.512	4.361	2.233	0.0004	0.0526
1959	0.733	1.810	1.326	0.985	0.577	4.342	2.505	0.0008	−0.1256
1960	0.741	1.856	1.375	0.985	0.563	4.631	2.608	0.0004	0.0842
1961	0.742	1.880	1.395	0.984	0.517	5.196	2.689	0.0007	0.0924
1962	0.727	1.778	1.293	0.992	0.537	5.238	2.812	0.0004	0.0063
1963	0.746	1.967	1.468	1.000	0.546	5.444	2.970	0.0007	−0.0247
1964	0.740	1.902	1.408	1.002	0.606	5.174	3.134	0.0006	−0.0578
1965	0.773	1.850	1.430	1.002	0.645	5.118	3.302	0.0006	−0.0291
1966	0.813	1.815	1.475	1.002	0.696	4.997	3.479	0.0009	−0.0370
1967	0.813	1.943	1.580	0.998	0.685	5.433	3.723	0.0008	0.0279
1968	0.839	1.864	1.565	0.997	0.781	5.076	3.964	0.0010	−0.0777
1969	0.885	1.649	1.459	0.999	0.908	4.584	4.162	0.0043	−0.0728
1970	0.895	1.684	1.507	0.998	0.772	5.653	4.364	0.0030	0.2013
1971	0.924	1.660	1.533	1.000	0.856	5.483	4.695	0.0036	−0.0490
1972	1.000	1.932	1.932	1.000	1.000	5.431	5.431	0.0042	−0.1076
1973	1.187	2.098	2.490	0.995	1.202	5.314	6.388	0.0045	−0.1059
1974	1.308	2.125	2.780	0.996	1.315	5.449	7.167	0.0050	0.0099
1975	1.343	2.602	3.496	0.994	1.412	5.565	7.858	0.0055	−0.0468
1976	1.377	2.543	3.501	0.993	1.410	6.214	8.762	0.0060	0.0669
1977	1.427	2.423	3.459	0.991	1.506	6.385	9.616	0.0062	0.0135
1978	1.610	2.773	4.464	0.994	1.577	7.366	11.619	0.0059	0.0149
1979	1.815	3.012	5.469	0.990	1.756	7.838	13.762	0.0054	0.0002

Table D.3. Metal mining

	Intermediate input				Output				
Year	Price	Quantity	Outlay	Quality	Price	Quantity	Revenue	Tax rate	Rate of productivity growth
1948	0.546	2.467	1.346	0.993	0.567	3.238	1.837	0.0011	
1949	0.557	1.464	0.815	0.995	0.582	2.200	1.281	0.0047	−0.0122
1950	0.574	1.792	1.029	0.996	0.612	2.593	1.587	0.0011	0.0219
1951	0.628	2.260	1.420	0.992	0.700	3.052	2.138	0.0037	−0.0198
1952	0.644	1.938	1.247	0.994	0.724	2.678	1.938	0.0015	−0.0466
1953	0.662	1.983	1.312	0.996	0.742	2.805	2.082	0.0012	0.0182
1954	0.671	1.449	0.972	0.996	0.758	2.223	1.684	0.0018	−0.0167
1955	0.702	2.109	1.481	0.994	0.824	2.814	2.319	0.0013	−0.0209
1956	0.738	2.494	1.841	0.991	0.902	3.187	2.875	0.0015	−0.0012
1957	0.728	2.162	1.574	0.997	0.814	3.089	2.514	0.0016	0.0626
1958	0.725	1.086	0.788	0.999	0.777	2.042	1.587	0.0063	0.0405
1959	0.735	1.208	0.887	0.997	0.805	2.097	1.689	0.0024	−0.0101
1960	0.758	2.129	1.614	0.999	0.833	3.018	2.515	0.0020	−0.0195
1961	0.752	1.921	1.445	1.000	0.806	2.846	2.295	0.0022	0.0164
1962	0.754	1.801	1.357	1.001	0.792	2.817	2.230	0.0027	0.0349
1963	0.756	1.936	1.464	0.999	0.786	3.000	2.357	0.0025	0.0292
1964	0.766	2.228	1.706	0.999	0.802	3.370	2.702	0.0026	0.0150
1965	0.785	2.451	1.924	0.999	0.835	3.637	3.035	0.0030	−0.0237
1966	0.802	2.487	1.994	0.998	0.837	3.876	3.244	0.0028	0.0031
1967	0.827	1.891	1.564	0.995	0.876	3.184	2.790	0.0039	−0.0358
1968	0.855	2.150	1.838	0.997	0.897	3.338	2.993	0.0043	−0.0574
1969	0.893	2.788	2.490	0.998	0.942	4.171	3.929	0.0033	−0.0081
1970	0.947	3.386	3.208	1.000	1.048	4.540	4.758	0.0029	−0.0690
1971	0.971	2.425	2.355	1.001	1.005	3.908	3.926	0.0038	0.0739
1972	1.000	2.429	2.429	1.000	1.000	4.265	4.265	0.0040	0.0758
1973	1.068	2.971	3.172	0.999	1.114	5.438	6.058	0.0033	0.1107
1974	1.274	3.227	4.111	0.993	1.478	5.301	7.838	0.0029	−0.1403
1975	1.372	1.788	2.453	0.995	1.435	3.641	5.225	0.0050	−0.0763
1976	1.455	1.659	2.415	0.993	1.521	4.478	6.811	0.0046	0.2218
1977	1.582	2.236	3.537	0.991	1.705	3.822	6.518	0.0054	−0.2724
1978	1.704	2.109	3.594	0.990	1.855	4.073	7.555	0.0052	0.0646
1979	1.928	3.728	7.189	0.986	2.249	5.031	11.314	0.0038	−0.1324

Table D.4. Coal mining

Year	Intermediate input				Output			Tax rate	Rate of productivity growth
	Price	Quantity	Outlay	Quality	Price	Quantity	Revenue		
1948	0.601	2.682	1.613	0.966	0.654	6.669	4.359	0.0017	
1949	0.603	1.995	1.202	0.969	0.645	4.880	3.146	0.0008	−0.1098
1950	0.612	2.253	1.379	0.972	0.644	5.659	3.641	0.0025	0.0731
1951	0.646	2.235	1.443	0.972	0.660	5.791	3.820	0.0014	0.0186
1952	0.648	1.988	1.289	0.975	0.656	5.123	3.359	0.0027	−0.0125
1953	0.657	1.940	1.275	0.976	0.658	4.875	3.205	0.0028	0.0304
1954	0.637	1.605	1.023	0.977	0.602	4.216	2.537	0.0036	0.0846
1955	0.643	1.866	1.200	0.978	0.593	4.871	2.890	0.0035	0.0599
1956	0.678	1.911	1.295	0.979	0.633	5.255	3.328	0.0042	0.0579
1957	0.708	1.899	1.345	0.980	0.671	5.119	3.434	0.0040	0.0106
1958	0.701	1.498	1.050	0.981	0.642	4.268	2.742	0.0051	0.0234
1959	0.696	1.588	1.106	0.979	0.627	4.278	2.682	0.0060	0.0101
1960	0.700	1.578	1.105	0.979	0.614	4.286	2.630	0.0065	0.0391
1961	0.696	1.485	1.033	0.979	0.600	4.144	2.485	0.0080	0.0444
1962	0.692	1.613	1.116	0.980	0.587	4.322	2.536	0.0083	0.0125
1963	0.694	1.723	1.197	0.977	0.578	4.695	2.712	0.0085	0.0563
1964	0.735	1.610	1.183	0.984	0.662	4.372	2.894	0.0090	−0.0322
1965	0.708	1.805	1.278	0.978	0.583	5.142	2.998	0.0093	0.0741
1966	0.724	1.814	1.313	0.979	0.591	5.336	3.151	0.0102	0.0331
1967	0.737	1.983	1.462	0.996	0.601	5.508	3.313	0.0103	−0.0187
1968	0.759	2.005	1.521	0.998	0.609	5.420	3.301	0.0109	−0.0074
1969	0.796	2.169	1.727	1.001	0.648	5.581	3.619	0.0099	−0.0105
1970	0.878	2.260	1.985	1.001	0.817	5.950	4.861	0.0068	−0.0022
1971	0.946	2.346	2.220	1.000	0.922	5.446	5.023	0.0062	−0.1691
1972	1.000	2.725	2.725	1.000	1.000	5.839	5.839	0.0043	−0.0559
1973	1.109	2.558	2.836	0.998	1.191	5.423	6.457	0.0045	−0.0504
1974	1.494	3.668	5.480	0.985	2.065	5.878	12.139	0.0028	−0.1372
1975	1.727	4.479	7.736	0.972	2.518	6.335	15.952	0.0024	−0.0995
1976	1.798	4.968	8.930	0.977	2.544	6.628	16.863	0.0027	−0.0402
1977	1.891	4.830	9.134	0.981	2.596	6.743	17.502	0.0029	0.0340
1978	2.036	4.405	8.967	0.979	2.787	6.345	17.682	0.0116	−0.0367
1979	2.229	5.245	11.691	0.978	3.012	7.502	22.595	0.0110	0.0370

Table D.5. Crude petroleum and natural gas

Year	Intermediate input				Output			Tax rate	Rate of productivity growth
	Price	Quantity	Outlay	Quality	Price	Quantity	Revenue		
1948	0.491	8.517	4.180	1.002	0.726	11.902	8.646	0.0002	
1949	0.503	5.564	2.801	1.003	0.703	9.656	6.784	0.0004	−0.0238
1950	0.513	6.428	3.300	1.001	0.697	11.048	7.705	0.0004	0.0629
1951	0.548	9.215	5.046	0.996	0.720	14.439	10.391	0.0003	0.0761
1952	0.565	8.657	4.887	0.997	0.724	13.656	9.884	0.0004	−0.0427
1953	0.587	8.452	4.965	0.996	0.765	13.878	10.622	0.0005	0.0104
1954	0.596	9.327	5.557	0.994	0.781	14.579	11.383	0.0004	−0.0112
1955	0.612	9.263	5.672	0.993	0.783	15.468	12.117	0.0004	0.0372
1956	0.633	10.001	6.328	0.990	0.803	16.716	13.422	0.0004	0.0145
1957	0.656	11.634	7.637	0.986	0.861	16.817	14.476	0.0003	−0.0945
1958	0.668	6.778	4.529	0.983	0.850	12.966	11.026	0.0005	−0.0154
1959	0.651	9.624	6.269	0.981	0.838	15.211	12.742	0.0002	−0.0129
1960	0.694	9.958	6.907	0.985	0.844	16.599	14.002	0.0002	0.0616
1961	0.700	10.526	7.368	0.986	0.850	16.875	14.336	0.0003	−0.0233
1962	0.707	10.252	7.245	1.001	0.858	16.528	14.175	0.0003	−0.0209
1963	0.723	10.896	7.878	0.998	0.855	18.312	15.651	0.0002	0.0618
1964	0.731	11.087	8.103	0.999	0.846	18.744	15.851	0.0003	0.0027
1965	0.742	10.380	7.698	0.999	0.848	18.690	15.840	0.0004	0.0168
1966	0.769	11.656	8.963	0.999	0.860	19.620	16.865	0.0004	−0.0239
1967	0.800	12.512	10.008	0.998	0.872	22.254	19.398	0.0004	0.0769
1968	0.830	13.328	11.068	0.998	0.874	23.063	20.161	0.0009	−0.0085
1969	0.871	12.386	10.789	1.000	0.903	22.149	20.011	0.0018	−0.0157
1970	0.909	13.940	12.668	1.000	0.932	24.389	22.733	0.0023	0.0240
1971	0.958	14.423	13.821	1.000	0.992	24.172	23.988	0.0031	−0.0271
1972	1.000	13.195	13.195	1.000	1.000	22.931	22.931	0.0046	−0.0063
1973	1.056	15.510	16.375	0.999	1.164	25.644	29.839	0.0041	0.0125
1974	1.206	26.585	32.054	0.991	1.927	25.434	49.014	0.0030	−0.3533
1975	1.336	23.980	32.030	0.988	2.265	24.360	55.168	0.0030	0.0071
1976	1.410	24.856	35.037	0.984	2.595	24.773	64.293	0.0030	−0.0136
1977	1.534	33.332	51.141	0.972	3.673	21.885	80.380	0.0027	−0.3101
1978	1.649	34.511	56.910	0.971	4.020	22.122	88.941	0.0028	−0.0294
1979	1.829	41.577	76.044	0.964	5.046	22.999	116.057	0.0024	−0.0943

Table D.6.   Nonmetallic mining and quarrying

Year	Intermediate input				Output			Tax rate	Rate of productivity growth
	Price	Quantity	Outlay	Quality	Price	Quantity	Revenue		
1948	0.561	0.513	0.288	0.982	0.663	1.299	0.862	0.0012	
1949	0.573	0.448	0.257	0.986	0.674	1.259	0.849	0.0000	0.0324
1950	0.583	0.558	0.325	0.988	0.692	1.457	1.008	0.0010	0.0645
1951	0.627	0.583	0.365	0.987	0.718	1.600	1.149	0.0009	0.0430
1952	0.637	0.639	0.407	0.991	0.736	1.650	1.214	0.0008	−0.0316
1953	0.653	0.707	0.462	0.994	0.770	1.693	1.303	0.0008	−0.0334
1954	0.664	0.986	0.654	0.995	0.786	1.995	1.568	0.0006	0.0331
1955	0.681	1.013	0.690	0.996	0.807	2.140	1.728	0.0006	0.0286
1956	0.708	1.051	0.745	0.997	0.824	2.276	1.876	0.0005	0.0113
1957	0.733	1.058	0.775	0.998	0.832	2.258	1.878	0.0005	−0.0256
1958	0.741	1.106	0.820	1.000	0.827	2.282	1.887	0.0005	−0.0147
1959	0.748	1.270	0.950	0.999	0.840	2.479	2.083	0.0000	0.0009
1960	0.762	1.173	0.893	1.002	0.839	2.524	2.118	0.0000	0.0582
1961	0.764	1.298	0.992	1.003	0.840	2.605	2.189	0.0005	−0.0095
1962	0.769	1.289	0.991	1.004	0.858	2.663	2.286	0.0004	0.0156
1963	0.776	1.347	1.045	0.998	0.869	2.847	2.473	0.0004	0.0453
1964	0.780	1.426	1.112	1.000	0.873	3.094	2.701	0.0004	0.0210
1965	0.791	1.749	1.383	1.001	0.892	3.301	2.944	0.0003	−0.0512
1966	0.809	1.704	1.379	1.002	0.906	3.419	3.098	0.0003	0.0176
1967	0.828	1.410	1.167	1.000	0.927	3.309	3.068	0.0003	−0.0019
1968	0.851	1.394	1.187	1.000	0.936	3.234	3.029	0.0026	−0.0413
1969	0.882	1.461	1.289	1.001	0.941	3.396	3.194	0.0041	0.0439
1970	0.918	1.489	1.368	1.000	0.947	3.410	3.229	0.0037	−0.0026
1971	0.965	1.386	1.337	1.000	0.986	3.430	3.383	0.0041	0.0046
1972	1.000	1.352	1.352	1.000	1.000	3.570	3.570	0.0048	0.0108
1973	1.063	1.241	1.319	0.999	1.051	3.892	4.090	0.0046	0.0833
1974	1.258	1.334	1.678	0.990	1.297	3.767	4.885	0.0047	−0.1462
1975	1.430	1.703	2.436	0.987	1.578	3.620	5.712	0.0049	−0.1446
1976	1.503	1.730	2.600	0.986	1.444	4.042	5.838	0.0055	0.0811
1977	1.606	1.421	2.282	0.982	1.420	4.182	5.938	0.0062	0.0938
1978	1.720	1.595	2.743	0.982	1.585	4.393	6.963	0.0059	−0.0372
1979	1.928	1.771	3.415	0.975	1.812	4.610	8.356	0.0054	−0.0308

Table D.7.   Contract construction

Year	Intermediate input				Output			Tax rate	Rate of productivity growth
	Price	Quantity	Outlay	Quality	Price	Quantity	Revenue		
1948	0.550	27.981	15.380	0.978	0.510	52.671	26.848	0.0017	
1949	0.555	28.824	15.984	0.981	0.508	54.132	27.484	0.0010	0.0274
1950	0.574	36.162	20.754	0.983	0.519	64.979	33.746	0.0016	0.0225
1951	0.623	33.087	20.624	0.982	0.564	63.705	35.957	0.0011	−0.0026
1952	0.626	33.409	20.929	0.985	0.580	64.644	37.473	0.0018	−0.0042
1953	0.638	35.455	22.635	0.987	0.583	67.983	39.641	0.0017	0.0267
1954	0.646	39.036	25.236	0.989	0.579	73.090	42.349	0.0017	0.0337
1955	0.664	43.410	28.841	0.991	0.591	79.963	47.232	0.0016	0.0119
1956	0.693	42.533	29.475	0.991	0.622	80.283	49.944	0.0018	−0.0025
1957	0.712	42.041	29.920	0.992	0.639	80.126	51.241	0.0018	0.0112
1958	0.719	45.010	32.362	0.993	0.636	83.676	53.232	0.0022	0.0076
1959	0.732	48.962	35.858	0.995	0.643	91.115	58.624	0.0013	0.0153
1960	0.736	48.682	35.851	0.995	0.641	92.009	59.011	0.0015	0.0139
1961	0.737	50.038	36.859	0.996	0.643	94.487	60.791	0.0016	0.0024
1962	0.738	51.285	37.869	0.999	0.650	97.638	63.424	0.0017	−0.0013
1963	0.742	54.324	40.284	1.000	0.655	103.124	67.521	0.0017	0.0070
1964	0.751	54.124	40.625	1.002	0.662	106.266	70.332	0.0018	0.0153
1965	0.762	56.161	42.810	1.003	0.675	111.788	75.474	0.0019	0.0088
1966	0.783	54.678	42.813	1.004	0.701	112.074	78.511	0.0021	−0.0009
1967	0.802	54.115	43.394	0.999	0.729	110.666	80.700	0.0023	−0.0105
1968	0.836	56.589	47.319	1.000	0.767	115.209	88.335	0.0030	0.0016
1969	0.879	56.358	49.531	1.001	0.822	116.195	95.467	0.0040	−0.0110
1970	0.908	54.316	49.306	1.001	0.884	110.617	97.769	0.0049	−0.0174
1971	0.958	60.774	58.248	1.000	0.946	117.546	111.212	0.0056	−0.0080
1972	1.000	66.109	66.109	1.000	1.000	124.670	124.670	0.0064	0.0032
1973	1.075	66.338	71.300	0.998	1.084	126.154	136.734	0.0066	−0.0250
1974	1.236	57.704	71.338	0.995	1.256	111.027	139.479	0.0075	−0.0510
1975	1.367	53.788	73.546	0.993	1.368	104.007	142.301	0.0081	0.0177
1976	1.451	57.954	84.069	0.994	1.431	111.394	159.391	0.0083	0.0213
1977	1.557	62.432	97.185	0.992	1.550	117.653	182.421	0.0082	−0.0095
1978	1.679	69.043	115.930	0.992	1.727	123.972	214.154	0.0079	−0.0449
1979	1.865	68.840	128.391	0.987	1.965	121.924	239.536	0.0080	−0.0392

Table D.8. Food and kindred products

Year	Intermediate input				Output			Tax rate	Rate of productivity growth
	Price	Quantity	Outlay	Quality	Price	Quantity	Revenue		
1948	0.541	55.542	30.050	0.959	0.765	49.839	38.151	0.0555	
1949	0.545	54.472	29.685	0.969	0.705	53.590	37.768	0.0566	0.0865
1950	0.565	54.538	30.803	0.972	0.713	54.835	39.077	0.0599	0.0184
1951	0.619	58.158	36.025	0.971	0.797	56.291	44.843	0.0519	−0.0300
1952	0.623	57.757	36.007	0.977	0.782	58.293	45.594	0.0570	0.0385
1953	0.637	53.553	34.115	0.979	0.739	59.822	44.197	0.0600	0.0855
1954	0.649	53.837	34.925	0.980	0.758	59.642	45.183	0.0561	−0.0045
1955	0.671	51.902	34.829	0.981	0.725	63.448	46.004	0.0569	0.0894
1956	0.715	51.256	36.659	0.981	0.718	66.727	47.902	0.0586	0.0575
1957	0.748	51.093	38.193	0.981	0.741	67.298	49.838	0.0532	0.0136
1958	0.762	53.199	40.541	0.981	0.774	68.311	52.876	0.0513	−0.0125
1959	0.773	52.373	40.506	0.981	0.759	70.791	53.703	0.0525	0.0447
1960	0.780	53.563	41.800	0.982	0.756	73.040	55.248	0.0518	0.0104
1961	0.781	55.380	43.225	0.983	0.768	74.279	57.064	0.0519	−0.0071
1962	0.783	57.140	44.757	0.981	0.775	76.322	59.114	0.0513	−0.0001
1963	0.812	56.025	45.518	0.985	0.770	78.658	60.597	0.0516	0.0444
1964	0.819	57.826	47.375	0.988	0.766	82.305	63.073	0.0556	0.0186
1965	0.830	58.958	48.963	0.992	0.792	82.200	65.143	0.0594	−0.0187
1966	0.848	62.034	52.602	0.996	0.839	83.637	70.168	0.0574	−0.0245
1967	0.827	67.820	56.113	1.000	0.828	89.613	74.182	0.0543	−0.0024
1968	0.852	68.246	58.179	1.000	0.847	91.218	77.243	0.0539	0.0092
1969	0.887	70.445	62.515	1.001	0.889	92.954	82.673	0.0547	−0.0071
1970	0.933	70.254	65.522	1.000	0.927	94.118	87.257	0.0543	0.0152
1971	0.969	71.242	69.046	1.001	0.948	96.986	91.953	0.0546	0.0194
1972	1.000	79.011	79.011	1.000	1.000	102.075	102.075	0.0510	−0.0267
1973	1.047	93.174	97.515	1.000	1.200	101.061	121.306	0.0434	−0.1418
1974	1.211	99.062	119.972	0.997	1.390	105.165	146.171	0.0361	−0.0116
1975	1.349	89.319	120.490	0.996	1.502	102.524	153.971	0.0351	0.0574
1976	1.428	89.772	128.232	0.995	1.468	110.584	162.388	0.0328	0.0677
1977	1.517	89.372	135.613	0.994	1.529	112.767	172.419	0.0316	0.0200
1978	1.625	97.818	158.955	0.993	1.709	115.707	197.715	0.0289	−0.0493
1979	1.797	95.362	171.327	0.990	1.795	119.256	214.098	0.0273	0.0473

Table D.9. Tobacco manufacturers

	Intermediate input				Output				Rate of productivity growth
Year	Price	Quantity	Outlay	Quality	Price	Quantity	Revenue	Tax rate	
1948	0.769	1.034	0.795	1.008	0.453	2.722	1.233	1.0614	
1949	0.693	1.488	1.032	1.014	0.517	2.996	1.550	0.8493	−0.1521
1950	0.705	1.642	1.157	1.009	0.549	2.998	1.647	0.8178	−0.0654
1951	0.805	1.339	1.078	0.997	0.547	3.014	1.649	0.8748	0.1262
1952	0.790	1.112	0.878	0.996	0.486	3.060	1.487	1.1189	0.1235
1953	0.742	1.271	0.943	0.998	0.577	2.899	1.673	0.9644	−0.1323
1954	0.732	1.261	0.923	0.997	0.610	2.694	1.644	0.9376	−0.0749
1955	0.714	1.249	0.891	0.998	0.581	2.801	1.629	0.9781	0.0365
1956	0.712	1.208	0.860	0.997	0.581	2.834	1.646	0.9922	0.0403
1957	0.729	1.218	0.888	0.996	0.605	2.879	1.743	0.9748	0.0142
1958	0.758	1.295	0.982	0.994	0.630	3.029	1.907	0.9518	0.0133
1959	0.747	1.372	1.024	0.994	0.657	3.110	2.043	0.9078	−0.0098
1960	0.749	1.517	1.137	0.995	0.667	3.377	2.252	0.8673	0.0169
1961	0.754	1.582	1.193	0.994	0.675	3.414	2.304	0.8768	−0.0215
1962	0.764	1.490	1.138	0.996	0.682	3.427	2.336	0.8698	0.0133
1963	0.757	1.165	0.882	0.998	0.652	3.425	2.232	0.9488	0.1094
1964	0.747	1.527	1.141	0.998	0.687	3.516	2.414	0.8571	−0.0973
1965	0.781	1.493	1.166	0.998	0.685	3.463	2.372	0.8879	0.0033
1966	0.822	1.557	1.279	0.998	0.733	3.404	2.494	0.8459	−0.0311
1967	0.813	1.493	1.215	0.999	0.762	3.409	2.597	0.8187	0.0329
1968	0.835	1.412	1.178	1.000	0.779	3.354	2.612	0.8211	0.0104
1969	0.878	1.261	1.107	0.999	0.835	3.237	2.703	0.7777	0.0334
1970	0.906	1.166	1.056	1.000	0.900	3.290	2.961	0.7392	0.0500
1971	0.931	1.243	1.158	0.999	0.951	3.323	3.162	0.6851	0.0175
1972	1.000	1.487	1.487	1.000	1.000	3.456	3.456	0.6494	−0.0331
1973	1.189	1.370	1.630	0.996	1.038	3.563	3.700	0.6522	0.0335
1974	1.305	1.754	2.289	0.997	1.248	3.623	4.521	0.5229	−0.1062
1975	1.354	1.990	2.693	0.997	1.466	3.663	5.370	0.4458	−0.0682
1976	1.374	2.167	2.977	0.997	1.603	3.713	5.951	0.4221	−0.0325
1977	1.423	2.146	3.055	0.996	1.816	3.477	6.315	0.3804	−0.0587
1978	1.618	2.200	3.561	0.998	2.055	3.499	7.190	0.3467	−0.0051
1979	1.798	2.062	3.709	0.997	2.298	3.406	7.829	0.3211	0.0030

Table D.10. Textile mill products

	Intermediate input				Output				Rate of productivity growth
Year	Price	Quantity	Outlay	Quality	Price	Quantity	Revenue	Tax rate	
1948	0.701	8.293	5.810	0.953	1.028	10.762	11.058	0.0011	
1949	0.667	9.269	6.181	0.968	0.930	11.167	10.383	0.0007	0.0068
1950	0.688	12.005	8.256	0.968	0.996	12.896	12.842	0.0011	−0.0543
1951	0.757	12.004	9.088	0.958	1.126	12.720	14.327	0.0005	−0.0092
1952	0.742	10.755	7.985	0.967	0.989	12.776	12.640	0.0010	0.0763
1953	0.742	11.365	8.434	0.977	0.956	13.522	12.930	0.0009	0.0249
1954	0.743	10.077	7.487	0.981	0.915	12.456	11.394	0.0010	0.0286
1955	0.730	11.660	8.510	0.982	0.917	14.083	12.907	0.0009	0.0131
1956	0.733	11.627	8.517	0.984	0.914	14.234	13.004	0.0010	0.0190
1957	0.750	11.087	8.316	0.985	0.909	13.857	12.601	0.0010	0.0216
1958	0.771	10.223	7.878	0.986	0.882	13.594	11.988	0.0013	0.0535
1959	0.771	11.691	9.011	0.986	0.899	15.278	13.738	0.0009	0.0111
1960	0.774	11.340	8.773	0.987	0.910	14.866	13.523	0.0010	0.0025
1961	0.777	11.550	8.975	0.988	0.885	15.429	13.661	0.0012	0.0283
1962	0.786	12.530	9.854	0.991	0.898	16.588	14.892	0.0011	0.0066
1963	0.788	12.861	10.137	0.987	0.897	17.080	15.315	0.0012	0.0145
1964	0.785	13.740	10.784	0.988	0.908	18.197	16.516	0.0012	0.0158
1965	0.807	14.106	11.382	0.990	0.914	19.502	17.825	0.0012	0.0364
1966	0.839	14.432	12.116	0.992	0.917	20.841	19.102	0.0014	0.0342
1967	0.840	14.553	12.225	0.994	0.909	21.116	19.185	0.0015	0.0062
1968	0.862	15.740	13.573	0.998	0.948	22.581	21.397	0.0015	0.0008
1969	0.897	15.392	13.813	0.999	0.957	23.086	22.094	0.0018	0.0323
1970	0.925	14.228	13.164	0.999	0.943	22.902	21.595	0.0019	0.0493
1971	0.947	15.019	14.229	0.999	0.944	24.239	22.889	0.0020	0.0213
1972	1.000	17.162	17.162	1.000	1.000	26.719	26.719	0.0021	−0.0046
1973	1.116	17.393	19.414	0.996	1.113	26.651	29.664	0.0021	−0.0175
1974	1.238	16.863	20.874	0.997	1.292	24.542	31.702	0.0023	−0.0390
1975	1.304	14.853	19.369	0.998	1.233	23.829	29.375	0.0028	0.0826
1976	1.371	16.961	23.251	0.997	1.319	26.667	35.165	0.0027	0.0063
1977	1.444	17.579	25.385	0.996	1.339	29.091	38.962	0.0028	0.0649
1978	1.608	17.889	28.765	0.998	1.464	29.919	43.788	0.0028	0.0146
1979	1.782	18.022	32.120	0.997	1.538	31.371	48.256	0.0030	0.0488

Table D.11. Apparel and other fabricated textile products

Year	Intermediate input				Output			Tax rate	Rate of productivity growth
	Price	Quantity	Outlay	Quality	Price	Quantity	Revenue		
1948	0.863	7.938	6.852	0.936	0.836	12.588	10.523	0.0010	
1949	0.802	9.068	7.271	0.949	0.786	13.736	10.792	0.0007	0.0051
1950	0.832	8.683	7.222	0.947	0.789	13.731	10.833	0.0010	0.0176
1951	0.933	8.016	7.478	0.943	0.844	13.615	11.486	0.0006	0.0451
1952	0.875	8.621	7.540	0.958	0.803	14.525	11.663	0.0009	0.0089
1953	0.855	9.270	7.922	0.963	0.792	15.395	12.189	0.0008	0.0074
1954	0.838	9.358	7.839	0.969	0.789	15.098	11.909	0.0009	−0.0072
1955	0.840	10.261	8.616	0.973	0.788	16.415	12.936	0.0009	0.0087
1956	0.845	10.666	9.011	0.978	0.801	17.006	13.619	0.0010	0.0100
1957	0.853	10.891	9.289	0.983	0.799	17.309	13.833	0.0009	0.0122
1958	0.848	10.083	8.548	0.987	0.795	16.477	13.100	0.0012	0.0189
1959	0.856	10.841	9.275	0.986	0.802	17.632	14.148	0.0008	−0.0026
1960	0.866	10.793	9.348	0.985	0.813	17.724	14.404	0.0010	0.0031
1961	0.855	11.065	9.459	0.985	0.815	17.923	14.604	0.0010	0.0060
1962	0.861	11.630	10.011	0.988	0.821	18.975	15.577	0.0010	−0.0016
1963	0.861	12.561	10.820	0.987	0.825	20.111	16.596	0.0011	0.0042
1964	0.866	13.033	11.282	0.987	0.835	20.811	17.376	0.0010	0.0048
1965	0.877	13.382	11.742	0.989	0.842	21.892	18.434	0.0011	0.0175
1966	0.891	13.516	12.047	0.990	0.855	22.660	19.380	0.0013	0.0123
1967	0.893	14.523	12.966	0.995	0.869	23.736	20.631	0.0014	0.0013
1968	0.919	14.922	13.714	0.998	0.898	24.579	22.077	0.0014	0.0131
1969	0.935	15.669	14.647	0.999	0.933	25.163	23.482	0.0017	−0.0098
1970	0.943	14.585	13.746	0.999	0.961	23.580	22.656	0.0018	−0.0110
1971	0.960	15.794	15.156	1.000	0.975	24.858	24.244	0.0019	−0.0011
1972	1.000	16.818	16.818	1.000	1.000	26.920	26.920	0.0020	0.0289
1973	1.082	17.292	18.707	0.999	1.052	27.846	29.288	0.0020	0.0083
1974	1.269	14.898	18.902	0.998	1.155	25.640	29.620	0.0025	0.0295
1975	1.327	14.296	18.965	0.995	1.180	25.500	30.088	0.0027	0.0406
1976	1.403	15.051	21.115	0.995	1.244	27.129	33.753	0.0028	0.0017
1977	1.452	16.831	24.434	0.994	1.318	29.260	38.555	0.0028	0.0078
1978	1.556	15.617	24.298	0.996	1.363	29.106	39.668	0.0031	0.0348
1979	1.684	14.782	24.887	0.993	1.437	28.502	40.968	0.0035	0.0225

Table D.12. Paper and allied products

Year	Intermediate input				Output			Tax rate	Rate of productivity growth
	Price	Quantity	Outlay	Quality	Price	Quantity	Revenue		
1948	0.775	4.933	3.822	0.967	0.653	9.872	6.451	0.0008	
1949	0.727	5.182	3.765	0.980	0.631	9.857	6.218	0.0013	−0.0309
1950	0.767	6.147	4.715	0.977	0.646	12.017	7.762	0.0009	0.0654
1951	0.853	6.765	5.772	0.972	0.766	12.558	9.619	0.0001	−0.0327
1952	0.796	6.833	5.442	0.989	0.752	12.002	9.023	0.0007	−0.0670
1953	0.782	8.058	6.298	0.993	0.744	13.589	10.106	0.0006	0.0031
1954	0.763	8.344	6.370	0.996	0.749	13.734	10.292	0.0006	−0.0159
1955	0.772	9.194	7.099	0.999	0.767	15.013	11.521	0.0006	0.0105
1956	0.781	9.720	7.595	1.002	0.822	15.329	12.596	0.0007	−0.0316
1957	0.781	10.203	7.968	1.002	0.842	15.230	12.818	0.0007	−0.0514
1958	0.778	10.113	7.865	0.994	0.847	14.994	12.693	0.0012	−0.0156
1959	0.797	10.884	8.674	0.996	0.849	16.599	14.086	0.0009	0.0378
1960	0.802	10.962	8.786	0.994	0.860	16.623	14.293	0.0010	−0.0100
1961	0.785	11.104	8.718	0.993	0.836	17.317	14.480	0.0011	0.0249
1962	0.795	11.663	9.276	0.992	0.841	18.274	15.363	0.0010	0.0131
1963	0.800	12.268	9.809	0.991	0.837	19.247	16.106	0.0012	0.0131
1964	0.812	12.533	10.182	0.992	0.839	20.141	16.898	0.0011	0.0264
1965	0.823	13.527	11.132	0.992	0.848	21.582	18.300	0.0012	0.0108
1966	0.839	14.528	12.190	0.994	0.870	23.155	20.146	0.0012	0.0024
1967	0.845	14.864	12.558	0.993	0.888	23.254	20.661	0.0014	−0.0249
1968	0.891	14.662	13.064	0.996	0.892	24.592	21.935	0.0014	0.0483
1969	0.925	15.573	14.404	0.998	0.919	26.222	24.108	0.0017	0.0165
1970	0.909	16.067	14.609	0.997	0.958	25.462	24.402	0.0018	−0.0417
1971	0.939	15.913	14.935	1.000	0.972	25.714	24.990	0.0019	0.0176
1972	1.000	16.400	16.400	1.000	1.000	27.753	27.753	0.0022	0.0533
1973	1.113	17.197	19.143	0.998	1.069	30.159	32.226	0.0020	0.0481
1974	1.265	21.243	26.877	0.998	1.315	31.525	41.460	0.0019	−0.0812
1975	1.271	21.065	26.778	0.997	1.498	27.361	40.975	0.0022	−0.1051
1976	1.365	22.389	30.560	0.997	1.570	30.269	47.533	0.0021	0.0459
1977	1.432	22.401	32.078	0.995	1.625	31.195	50.679	0.0023	0.0181
1978	1.557	22.747	35.409	0.994	1.689	32.915	55.599	0.0024	0.0352
1979	1.670	25.198	42.076	0.992	1.897	34.247	64.950	0.0024	−0.0317

Table D.13. Printing and publishing

| Year | Intermediate input | | | | Output | | | Tax rate | Rate of productivity growth |
	Price	Quantity	Outlay	Quality	Price	Quantity	Revenue		
1948	0.551	5.159	2.843	1.004	0.502	12.629	6.341	0.0025	
1949	0.529	6.568	3.473	1.005	0.518	13.810	7.156	0.0013	−0.0219
1950	0.581	6.244	3.625	1.005	0.524	14.292	7.496	0.0023	0.0610
1951	0.630	6.761	4.260	1.004	0.560	15.010	8.399	0.0011	−0.0158
1952	0.624	6.909	4.309	1.005	0.590	14.767	8.718	0.0018	−0.0381
1953	0.629	7.069	4.449	1.005	0.601	15.362	9.229	0.0018	0.0127
1954	0.625	7.789	4.867	1.005	0.595	16.530	9.833	0.0017	0.0230
1955	0.645	7.977	5.142	1.005	0.611	17.299	10.573	0.0017	0.0235
1956	0.660	8.732	5.763	1.005	0.632	18.291	11.559	0.0016	0.0025
1957	0.645	9.117	5.880	1.005	0.659	18.262	12.034	0.0016	−0.0312
1958	0.640	9.518	6.090	1.003	0.670	18.194	12.195	0.0022	−0.0199
1959	0.673	9.977	6.714	1.004	0.678	19.760	13.388	0.0016	0.0415
1960	0.660	10.759	7.101	1.004	0.696	20.367	14.184	0.0016	−0.0426
1961	0.645	11.348	7.320	1.003	0.705	20.604	14.534	0.0019	−0.0061
1962	0.649	11.667	7.567	1.013	0.716	21.194	15.175	0.0018	0.0087
1963	0.661	11.835	7.828	1.007	0.734	21.445	15.743	0.0019	0.0011
1964	0.674	11.905	8.024	1.007	0.742	22.707	16.859	0.0018	0.0377
1965	0.687	12.800	8.793	1.007	0.755	23.995	18.105	0.0015	0.0049
1966	0.716	13.280	9.513	1.008	0.781	25.263	19.735	0.0016	0.0121
1967	0.719	14.695	10.565	0.997	0.804	26.369	21.190	0.0016	−0.0293
1968	0.794	13.823	10.975	0.998	0.835	26.965	22.517	0.0016	0.0404
1969	0.874	13.742	12.015	0.999	0.876	28.135	24.647	0.0019	0.0321
1970	0.816	14.850	12.123	0.998	0.933	26.738	24.951	0.0019	−0.0893
1971	0.903	13.825	12.484	1.000	0.973	26.800	26.068	0.0020	0.0529
1972	1.000	14.607	14.607	1.000	1.000	29.251	29.251	0.0022	0.0513
1973	1.183	13.288	15.718	0.997	1.041	30.648	31.906	0.0021	0.0811
1974	1.260	14.635	18.436	0.998	1.166	29.916	34.887	0.0024	−0.0708
1975	1.262	14.958	18.880	0.998	1.319	28.070	37.024	0.0025	−0.0691
1976	1.420	15.106	21.451	0.998	1.400	29.663	41.540	0.0026	0.0446
1977	1.604	15.744	25.247	0.997	1.492	32.128	47.927	0.0026	0.0456
1978	1.791	14.342	25.691	0.995	1.549	33.092	51.275	0.0027	0.0582
1979	1.947	15.653	30.478	0.995	1.709	34.400	58.776	0.0028	−0.0195

Table D.14. Chemicals and allied products

Year	Intermediate input				Output			Tax rate	Rate of productivity growth
	Price	Quantity	Outlay	Quality	Price	Quantity	Revenue		
1948	0.612	10.085	6.168	0.991	0.896	11.701	10.490	0.0009	
1949	0.597	10.574	6.313	0.996	0.856	12.628	10.805	0.0013	0.0441
1950	0.624	12.592	7.855	0.994	0.856	15.405	13.186	0.0008	0.0760
1951	0.693	13.750	9.525	0.988	0.964	16.566	15.972	0.0000	−0.0145
1952	0.681	14.187	9.660	0.994	0.931	17.210	16.017	0.0006	−0.0190
1953	0.684	14.917	10.198	0.996	0.933	18.212	16.988	0.0006	−0.0015
1954	0.684	14.791	10.121	0.996	0.940	18.305	17.210	0.0007	0.0028
1955	0.701	16.544	11.602	0.997	0.941	21.185	19.933	0.0006	0.0669
1956	0.728	17.644	12.848	0.996	0.944	22.766	21.480	0.0008	0.0129
1957	0.738	17.792	13.132	0.995	0.958	23.245	22.258	0.0007	−0.0001
1958	0.741	17.537	12.997	0.995	0.962	22.921	22.039	0.0013	−0.0082
1959	0.755	19.486	14.706	0.996	0.957	26.437	25.297	0.0011	0.0664
1960	0.758	19.806	15.017	0.995	0.963	26.458	25.480	0.0013	−0.0230
1961	0.750	19.993	14.994	0.994	0.957	27.138	25.976	0.0014	0.0167
1962	0.755	21.773	16.446	0.995	0.948	29.580	28.053	0.0014	0.0201
1963	0.760	23.668	17.981	0.997	0.948	32.063	30.402	0.0014	0.0206
1964	0.768	25.613	19.676	0.997	0.944	34.762	32.807	0.0014	0.0212
1965	0.779	27.977	21.791	0.997	0.951	37.923	36.079	0.0014	0.0151
1966	0.801	30.238	24.227	0.997	0.963	41.062	39.527	0.0015	0.0014
1967	0.810	31.066	25.175	0.996	0.965	41.977	40.528	0.0018	−0.0186
1968	0.848	30.925	26.233	0.997	0.963	45.479	43.779	0.0018	0.0654
1969	0.892	31.849	28.417	0.999	0.960	48.524	46.575	0.0020	0.0324
1970	0.902	31.965	28.830	0.998	0.975	48.743	47.501	0.0020	−0.0033
1971	0.949	31.435	29.817	1.000	0.992	50.229	49.845	0.0021	0.0407
1972	1.000	32.988	32.988	1.000	1.000	54.861	54.861	0.0022	0.0605
1973	1.092	35.068	38.291	0.998	1.033	60.141	62.100	0.0022	0.0455
1974	1.256	44.917	56.432	0.997	1.308	62.835	82.182	0.0019	−0.1290
1975	1.354	42.413	57.419	0.995	1.552	55.557	86.222	0.0021	−0.0844
1976	1.453	45.797	66.546	0.995	1.613	62.077	100.141	0.0021	0.0465
1977	1.560	48.501	75.673	0.994	1.682	66.572	111.957	0.0021	0.0183
1978	1.682	49.247	82.825	0.993	1.727	70.625	121.977	0.0022	0.0342
1979	1.849	53.580	99.060	0.992	1.934	73.151	141.501	0.0022	−0.0312

Table D.15. Petroleum and coal products

| Year | Intermediate input | | | | Output | | | Tax rate | Rate of productivity growth |
	Price	Quantity	Outlay	Quality	Price	Quantity	Revenue		
1948	0.551	13.558	7.468	0.999	0.706	13.936	9.832	0.0591	
1949	0.552	11.677	6.446	1.002	0.808	10.735	8.677	0.0681	−0.1545
1950	0.563	10.583	5.956	1.000	0.777	10.755	8.359	0.0782	0.0673
1951	0.624	13.605	8.495	0.990	0.881	12.587	11.090	0.0636	−0.0295
1952	0.635	13.527	8.587	0.994	0.869	13.345	11.594	0.0824	0.0502
1953	0.642	14.134	9.075	0.995	0.889	13.749	12.222	0.0806	−0.0104
1954	0.646	13.420	8.664	0.994	0.900	13.446	12.106	0.0830	0.0109
1955	0.662	14.539	9.622	0.994	0.909	14.631	13.299	0.0825	0.0212
1956	0.692	15.552	10.769	0.990	0.941	15.407	14.492	0.0970	−0.0020
1957	0.715	14.765	10.551	0.990	0.988	14.338	14.159	0.1155	−0.0408
1958	0.725	14.960	10.852	0.989	0.939	15.207	14.276	0.1178	0.0502
1959	0.729	14.579	10.622	0.988	0.924	15.734	14.539	0.1293	0.0583
1960	0.748	15.030	11.248	0.990	0.901	16.207	14.609	0.1602	0.0119
1961	0.747	14.250	10.646	0.991	0.902	15.686	14.151	0.1670	0.0147
1962	0.752	14.734	11.086	1.002	0.888	16.372	14.538	0.1686	0.0196
1963	0.762	15.292	11.659	1.008	0.869	16.713	14.516	0.1775	−0.0057
1964	0.770	15.521	11.951	1.008	0.835	18.089	15.108	0.1761	0.0704
1965	0.781	16.863	13.170	1.008	0.864	19.161	16.546	0.1750	−0.0065
1966	0.804	17.500	14.074	1.008	0.905	20.064	18.165	0.1590	0.0151
1967	0.831	18.264	15.171	0.999	0.931	20.593	19.176	0.1491	−0.0100
1968	0.855	18.164	15.523	1.001	0.907	22.323	20.258	0.1575	0.0772
1969	0.889	18.881	16.788	1.001	0.917	23.246	21.324	0.1590	0.0031
1970	0.930	17.499	16.273	1.001	0.915	22.787	20.850	0.1733	0.0334
1971	0.966	18.968	18.329	1.001	0.976	23.711	23.153	0.1609	−0.0258
1972	1.000	19.497	19.497	1.000	1.000	25.431	25.431	0.1556	0.0471
1973	1.053	24.274	25.564	1.000	1.290	23.600	30.445	0.1385	−0.2550
1974	1.213	40.031	48.539	0.997	2.121	27.829	59.023	0.0685	−0.2601
1975	1.356	44.236	60.001	0.995	2.489	27.620	68.743	0.0605	−0.0934
1976	1.436	45.986	66.026	0.995	2.649	28.886	76.530	0.0573	0.0067
1977	1.513	54.445	82.365	0.995	2.964	32.752	97.078	0.0468	−0.0241
1978	1.591	52.919	84.186	0.995	3.088	32.491	100.320	0.0468	0.0112
1979	1.758	66.905	117.627	0.994	4.337	32.281	140.012	0.0327	−0.2050

Table D.16. Rubber and miscellaneous plastic products

	Intermediate input				Output				Rate of productivity growth
Year	Price	Quantity	Outlay	Quality	Price	Quantity	Revenue	Tax rate	
1948	0.695	2.678	1.862	0.944	0.638	5.048	3.223	0.0492	
1949	0.687	2.451	1.683	0.954	0.629	4.704	2.957	0.0487	0.0037
1950	0.695	3.670	2.552	0.959	0.690	5.787	3.992	0.0477	−0.0781
1951	0.762	3.793	2.890	0.957	0.818	6.098	4.991	0.0346	0.0200
1952	0.758	3.474	2.634	0.965	0.787	6.157	4.845	0.0357	0.0277
1953	0.766	3.681	2.820	0.970	0.771	6.634	5.115	0.0349	−0.0023
1954	0.773	3.684	2.849	0.974	0.775	6.268	4.860	0.0330	−0.0367
1955	0.784	4.447	3.487	0.980	0.834	7.100	5.925	0.0316	−0.0314
1956	0.803	4.102	3.292	0.985	0.868	6.924	6.012	0.0381	0.0167
1957	0.821	3.964	3.256	0.989	0.874	6.941	6.067	0.0451	0.0082
1958	0.825	3.965	3.272	0.993	0.886	6.798	6.026	0.0448	0.0046
1959	0.828	4.660	3.860	0.994	0.878	7.976	7.004	0.0438	0.0281
1960	0.838	4.632	3.879	0.995	0.873	8.047	7.025	0.0433	0.0089
1961	0.837	4.522	3.786	0.996	0.852	8.290	7.066	0.0483	0.0404
1962	0.836	4.999	4.181	0.997	0.839	9.382	7.873	0.0518	0.0195
1963	0.838	5.386	4.513	0.995	0.845	9.836	8.316	0.0500	−0.0038
1964	0.838	5.701	4.778	0.996	0.837	10.602	8.870	0.0495	0.0237
1965	0.851	6.210	5.286	0.996	0.842	11.612	9.778	0.0511	0.0107
1966	0.868	6.305	5.476	0.996	0.865	12.254	10.606	0.0471	0.0047
1967	0.881	6.390	5.629	1.001	0.883	12.554	11.088	0.0437	0.0055
1968	0.891	6.899	6.149	1.001	0.901	13.853	12.486	0.0451	0.0225
1969	0.910	7.112	6.473	1.000	0.905	14.897	13.480	0.0474	0.0242
1970	0.937	7.229	6.776	1.000	0.943	14.243	13.437	0.0490	−0.0438
1971	0.974	7.144	6.961	1.000	0.973	14.940	14.537	0.0449	0.0468
1972	1.000	8.881	8.881	1.000	1.000	17.470	17.470	0.0460	0.0107
1973	1.075	9.047	9.727	0.998	1.030	18.884	19.457	0.0456	0.0328
1974	1.337	9.599	12.835	0.987	1.240	18.191	22.553	0.0364	−0.0683
1975	1.539	7.676	11.812	0.984	1.391	15.534	21.609	0.0329	0.0139
1976	1.614	8.336	13.454	0.983	1.478	16.497	24.380	0.0344	−0.0145
1977	1.718	9.731	16.722	0.979	1.570	19.223	30.176	0.0308	0.0301
1978	1.814	10.504	19.056	0.980	1.625	20.877	33.915	0.0293	0.0157
1979	2.069	11.439	23.670	0.968	1.780	22.118	39.370	0.0242	−0.0072

Table D.17. Leather and leather products

Year	Intermediate input				Output			Tax rate	Rate of productivity growth
	Price	Quantity	Outlay	Quality	Price	Quantity	Revenue		
1948	0.649	3.783	2.456	0.979	0.620	6.040	3.743	0.0008	
1949	0.636	3.447	2.191	0.986	0.595	5.630	3.348	0.0007	−0.0013
1950	0.644	3.704	2.384	0.986	0.630	5.618	3.539	0.0009	−0.0620
1951	0.712	3.493	2.486	0.977	0.725	5.328	3.865	0.0007	0.0033
1952	0.708	3.074	2.177	0.983	0.626	5.706	3.572	0.0011	0.1275
1953	0.712	3.277	2.332	0.985	0.627	5.950	3.731	0.0008	0.0063
1954	0.722	2.888	2.084	0.985	0.612	5.672	3.472	0.0012	0.0468
1955	0.730	3.125	2.280	0.987	0.610	6.080	3.710	0.0011	0.0048
1956	0.747	3.207	2.395	0.989	0.643	6.108	3.927	0.0010	−0.0048
1957	0.766	3.073	2.355	0.990	0.646	6.042	3.903	0.0010	0.0212
1958	0.776	3.005	2.333	0.991	0.651	5.827	3.791	0.0013	0.0017
1959	0.781	3.425	2.675	0.991	0.719	5.999	4.314	0.0005	−0.0679
1960	0.792	3.143	2.488	0.991	0.712	5.785	4.117	0.0007	0.0295
1961	0.794	3.133	2.487	0.991	0.715	5.706	4.079	0.0007	−0.0103
1962	0.797	3.096	2.468	0.996	0.727	5.762	4.186	0.0010	0.0103
1963	0.803	2.874	2.306	0.999	0.718	5.704	4.094	0.0007	0.0450
1964	0.809	3.079	2.490	1.001	0.720	5.983	4.309	0.0009	0.0051
1965	0.822	3.194	2.626	1.001	0.739	6.132	4.531	0.0011	−0.0042
1966	0.842	3.369	2.837	1.002	0.797	6.187	4.932	0.0010	−0.0336
1967	0.855	3.343	2.860	0.999	0.798	6.302	5.027	0.0010	0.0319
1968	0.875	3.472	3.039	1.000	0.820	6.548	5.369	0.0011	0.0067
1969	0.901	3.418	3.080	1.000	0.860	6.223	5.350	0.0017	−0.0171
1970	0.935	3.090	2.889	1.000	0.884	5.798	5.127	0.0016	0.0108
1971	0.972	2.904	2.823	1.000	0.906	5.584	5.057	0.0020	0.0129
1972	1.000	3.457	3.457	1.000	1.000	5.644	5.644	0.0019	−0.0930
1973	1.055	3.319	3.500	0.999	1.073	5.502	5.905	0.0020	0.0084
1974	1.238	2.952	3.654	0.996	1.126	5.362	6.037	0.0023	0.0739
1975	1.404	2.645	3.712	0.993	1.166	5.247	6.116	0.0028	0.0825
1976	1.475	2.835	4.180	0.994	1.290	5.450	7.030	0.0027	−0.0342
1977	1.559	2.921	4.554	0.994	1.363	5.351	7.295	0.0030	−0.0222
1978	1.645	3.029	4.982	0.995	1.484	5.360	7.956	0.0030	−0.0260
1979	1.824	3.369	6.146	0.993	1.759	5.225	9.193	0.0029	−0.0754

Table D.18. Lumber and wood products, except furniture

	Intermediate input				Output				Rate of productivity growth
Year	Price	Quantity	Outlay	Quality	Price	Quantity	Revenue	Tax rate	
1948	0.744	3.100	2.307	0.944	0.565	9.480	5.353	0.0009	
1949	0.726	3.115	2.262	0.952	0.526	9.304	4.892	0.0016	0.0161
1950	0.732	4.733	3.463	0.956	0.601	11.239	6.750	0.0008	−0.0487
1951	0.808	4.558	3.684	0.953	0.657	11.224	7.379	0.0014	−0.0072
1952	0.798	4.647	3.706	0.959	0.641	11.237	7.200	0.0008	−0.0058
1953	0.800	4.832	3.868	0.963	0.642	11.374	7.302	0.0008	0.0075
1954	0.809	4.391	3.552	0.965	0.632	10.834	6.849	0.0008	0.0350
1955	0.813	5.172	4.207	0.969	0.653	12.354	8.073	0.0006	0.0251
1956	0.826	5.269	4.354	0.973	0.665	12.469	8.290	0.0007	0.0032
1957	0.847	4.491	3.803	0.977	0.632	11.584	7.326	0.0006	0.0435
1958	0.856	4.234	3.624	0.979	0.619	11.503	7.118	0.0014	0.0458
1959	0.855	4.974	4.252	0.980	0.663	12.659	8.391	0.0008	−0.0181
1960	0.864	4.674	4.037	0.981	0.637	12.436	7.927	0.0010	0.0275
1961	0.864	4.582	3.957	0.982	0.614	12.538	7.695	0.0012	0.0397
1962	0.861	4.820	4.149	0.978	0.622	13.124	8.162	0.0014	0.0103
1963	0.863	5.183	4.472	0.971	0.633	14.068	8.905	0.0012	0.0261
1964	0.864	5.515	4.763	0.971	0.646	14.885	9.619	0.0014	0.0048
1965	0.877	5.294	4.643	0.970	0.657	15.257	10.021	0.0014	0.0309
1966	0.897	5.868	5.262	0.969	0.691	15.442	10.675	0.0015	−0.0495
1967	0.881	6.278	5.531	0.999	0.679	16.316	11.082	0.0016	0.0264
1968	0.894	7.145	6.385	0.999	0.769	16.670	12.820	0.0055	−0.0539
1969	0.914	7.315	6.682	1.000	0.870	16.060	13.972	0.0020	−0.0599
1970	0.942	6.347	5.976	1.000	0.771	16.873	13.001	0.0024	0.1143
1971	0.974	7.112	6.928	1.000	0.875	16.850	14.740	0.0026	−0.0733
1972	1.000	10.179	10.179	1.000	1.000	19.756	19.756	0.0023	−0.0390
1973	1.061	11.979	12.712	0.998	1.247	19.394	24.191	0.0021	−0.1209
1974	1.284	10.200	13.101	0.995	1.288	18.955	24.418	0.0025	0.0789
1975	1.469	8.582	12.603	0.992	1.231	18.635	22.941	0.0030	0.1152
1976	1.531	10.203	15.619	0.992	1.426	20.196	28.794	0.0027	−0.0554
1977	1.617	13.118	21.211	0.989	1.654	22.165	36.670	0.0025	−0.0685
1978	1.711	14.715	25.179	0.990	1.885	23.073	43.488	0.0023	−0.0442
1979	1.913	13.945	26.681	0.986	2.039	23.170	47.253	0.0025	0.0217

Table D.19. Furniture and fixtures

Year	Intermediate input				Output			Tax rate	Rate of productivity growth
	Price	Quantity	Outlay	Quality	Price	Quantity	Revenue		
1948	0.716	1.795	1.286	0.989	0.584	4.269	2.493	0.0011	
1949	0.688	1.952	1.342	0.999	0.585	4.318	2.527	0.0016	0.0028
1950	0.705	2.498	1.762	0.996	0.604	5.272	3.185	0.0008	0.0005
1951	0.783	2.416	1.891	0.989	0.680	5.088	3.461	0.0001	−0.0119
1952	0.755	2.428	1.833	0.998	0.658	5.279	3.471	0.0006	0.0211
1953	0.750	2.870	2.153	1.000	0.664	5.719	3.800	0.0005	−0.0170
1954	0.749	2.802	2.099	1.000	0.666	5.545	3.691	0.0008	0.0177
1955	0.755	3.212	2.424	1.001	0.675	6.329	4.271	0.0009	0.0190
1956	0.769	3.407	2.620	1.003	0.706	6.501	4.590	0.0010	−0.0151
1957	0.783	3.340	2.616	1.004	0.728	6.307	4.592	0.0008	−0.0150
1958	0.795	3.297	2.620	0.996	0.739	6.048	4.468	0.0013	−0.0161
1959	0.808	3.557	2.874	0.997	0.752	6.626	4.985	0.0006	0.0220
1960	0.815	3.374	2.751	0.996	0.759	6.432	4.882	0.0010	0.0044
1961	0.813	3.299	2.682	0.996	0.759	6.321	4.795	0.0013	0.0134
1962	0.819	3.569	2.924	0.997	0.764	6.855	5.240	0.0013	0.0062
1963	0.822	3.899	3.204	0.997	0.770	7.323	5.642	0.0012	0.0097
1964	0.823	4.101	3.376	0.998	0.781	7.730	6.036	0.0013	0.0032
1965	0.837	4.183	3.503	0.998	0.786	8.304	6.527	0.0015	0.0334
1966	0.862	4.368	3.763	0.999	0.810	8.739	7.076	0.0016	−0.0044
1967	0.870	4.619	4.017	0.993	0.832	8.844	7.358	0.0016	−0.0142
1968	0.889	4.935	4.386	0.994	0.867	9.279	8.043	0.0017	−0.0027
1969	0.914	5.398	4.931	0.994	0.913	9.784	8.930	0.0018	−0.0030
1970	0.941	5.221	4.912	0.994	0.941	9.208	8.664	0.0020	−0.0202
1971	0.970	5.560	5.394	0.995	0.970	9.630	9.342	0.0021	0.0003
1972	1.000	6.977	6.977	1.000	1.000	11.616	11.616	0.0020	0.0227
1973	1.074	7.572	8.136	0.999	1.069	12.238	13.080	0.0018	−0.0185
1974	1.262	6.571	8.291	0.997	1.206	11.039	13.314	0.0022	0.0015
1975	1.403	5.382	7.549	0.994	1.293	9.625	12.448	0.0027	0.0367
1976	1.461	6.161	9.002	0.995	1.371	10.722	14.703	0.0026	−0.0037
1977	1.535	7.378	11.324	0.995	1.464	12.138	17.775	0.0025	−0.0076
1978	1.636	8.012	13.108	0.996	1.574	13.057	20.552	0.0025	−0.0002
1979	1.794	8.356	14.995	0.994	1.710	13.584	23.231	0.0025	0.0148

Table D.20. Stone, clay, and glass products

	Intermediate input				Output				
Year	Price	Quantity	Outlay	Quality	Price	Quantity	Revenue	Tax rate	Rate of productivity growth
1948	0.607	2.316	1.407	0.962	0.523	7.272	3.802	0.0009	
1949	0.606	3.409	2.068	0.967	0.551	8.084	4.451	0.0016	−0.0306
1950	0.623	4.285	2.671	0.968	0.567	9.911	5.620	0.0009	0.0603
1951	0.684	4.744	3.249	0.964	0.604	10.941	6.606	0.0003	0.0115
1952	0.672	5.019	3.377	0.969	0.612	10.771	6.593	0.0010	−0.0521
1953	0.681	5.055	3.447	0.972	0.635	11.114	7.058	0.0008	0.0174
1954	0.686	5.089	3.493	0.973	0.655	10.962	7.177	0.0009	−0.0067
1955	0.700	5.830	4.083	0.975	0.676	12.580	8.499	0.0007	0.0440
1956	0.727	6.393	4.651	0.976	0.709	13.015	9.224	0.0009	−0.0351
1957	0.743	6.393	4.755	0.977	0.737	12.733	9.378	0.0008	−0.0328
1958	0.753	6.172	4.650	0.978	0.753	12.344	9.294	0.0015	−0.0082
1959	0.769	7.140	5.494	0.979	0.765	14.186	10.851	0.0007	0.0317
1960	0.777	7.017	5.458	0.980	0.769	13.893	10.683	0.0009	−0.0192
1961	0.775	6.938	5.382	0.981	0.767	13.760	10.559	0.0012	0.0063
1962	0.779	7.179	5.595	0.987	0.767	14.400	11.043	0.0012	0.0174
1963	0.781	7.623	5.954	0.989	0.761	15.500	11.798	0.0012	0.0341
1964	0.786	7.903	6.212	0.989	0.763	16.340	12.475	0.0012	0.0182
1965	0.795	8.635	6.870	0.989	0.764	17.501	13.373	0.0013	0.0098
1966	0.816	9.199	7.507	0.989	0.772	18.293	14.131	0.0016	−0.0058
1967	0.824	8.928	7.363	0.998	0.788	17.587	13.863	0.0014	−0.0240
1968	0.851	9.363	7.972	0.998	0.824	18.399	15.159	0.0016	0.0160
1969	0.884	9.222	8.149	1.000	0.861	18.803	16.180	0.0018	0.0154
1970	0.915	8.928	8.173	1.000	0.905	17.858	16.160	0.0020	−0.0294
1971	0.958	9.306	8.913	1.000	0.966	18.410	17.790	0.0020	0.0106
1972	1.000	10.647	10.647	1.000	1.000	20.697	20.697	0.0022	0.0393
1973	1.058	11.246	11.897	0.999	1.037	22.133	22.960	0.0022	0.0118
1974	1.214	11.898	14.438	0.997	1.172	21.773	25.512	0.0023	−0.0473
1975	1.348	10.812	14.577	0.995	1.338	19.452	26.017	0.0025	−0.0316
1976	1.439	11.179	16.084	0.994	1.437	20.541	29.516	0.0026	0.0242
1977	1.535	12.342	18.941	0.992	1.559	21.446	33.429	0.0026	−0.0232
1978	1.639	12.982	21.278	0.992	1.661	23.287	38.671	0.0025	0.0325
1979	1.818	13.949	25.359	0.992	1.857	23.770	44.133	0.0025	−0.0337

Table D.21. Primary metal industries

	Intermediate input				Output				
Year	Price	Quantity	Outlay	Quality	Price	Quantity	Revenue	Tax rate	Rate of productivity growth
1948	0.562	28.433	15.978	0.992	0.466	48.436	22.565	0.0005	
1949	0.572	25.407	14.542	0.995	0.477	43.079	20.564	0.0014	−0.0101
1950	0.586	22.369	13.106	0.997	0.505	41.607	21.016	0.0007	0.0188
1951	0.628	32.355	20.319	0.996	0.549	55.092	30.230	0.0001	0.0182
1952	0.637	26.851	17.109	0.999	0.560	46.296	25.913	0.0006	−0.0450
1953	0.654	32.047	20.966	1.000	0.585	54.222	31.725	0.0005	0.0162
1954	0.662	22.446	14.870	1.002	0.608	39.739	24.149	0.0005	−0.0521
1955	0.684	31.028	21.215	1.004	0.649	51.344	33.319	0.0005	0.0220
1956	0.713	36.514	26.051	1.004	0.707	55.000	38.859	0.0006	−0.0437
1957	0.730	29.390	21.455	1.006	0.720	48.319	34.795	0.0006	0.0082
1958	0.736	19.329	14.222	1.008	0.720	34.818	25.078	0.0013	−0.0383
1959	0.747	24.690	18.450	1.008	0.742	41.101	30.509	0.0009	−0.0021
1960	0.755	28.155	21.263	1.009	0.748	45.011	33.665	0.0010	0.0086
1961	0.754	25.667	19.342	1.010	0.738	42.026	30.997	0.0012	0.0032
1962	0.757	27.341	20.693	1.008	0.734	45.144	33.152	0.0012	0.0203
1963	0.758	30.840	23.363	1.005	0.732	50.013	36.618	0.0011	0.0217
1964	0.767	35.301	27.086	1.006	0.748	56.152	42.026	0.0011	0.0119
1965	0.779	40.452	31.512	1.006	0.769	62.327	47.934	0.0011	−0.0012
1966	0.795	43.274	34.393	1.006	0.788	66.611	52.504	0.0011	0.0090
1967	0.818	36.706	30.011	0.998	0.805	58.441	47.056	0.0014	−0.0241
1968	0.843	37.229	31.383	0.998	0.828	59.334	49.100	0.0015	−0.0012
1969	0.878	43.120	37.844	0.999	0.876	64.538	56.515	0.0016	−0.0219
1970	0.925	38.426	35.537	0.999	0.946	56.935	53.858	0.0018	−0.0357
1971	0.967	34.665	33.510	1.000	0.968	53.266	51.572	0.0021	0.0168
1972	1.000	41.372	41.372	1.000	1.000	62.191	62.191	0.0021	0.0334
1973	1.058	52.572	55.597	0.999	1.057	75.134	79.448	0.0018	0.0063
1974	1.268	60.948	77.275	0.993	1.372	77.982	106.965	0.0016	−0.0721
1975	1.427	42.568	60.726	0.991	1.522	57.914	88.129	0.0021	−0.0133
1976	1.498	43.864	65.722	0.991	1.611	58.305	93.900	0.0023	−0.0176
1977	1.600	48.359	77.392	0.989	1.734	63.267	109.717	0.0022	0.0052
1978	1.721	54.455	93.728	0.989	1.861	70.764	131.678	0.0021	0.0169
1979	1.934	58.667	113.455	0.986	2.183	72.108	157.428	0.0020	−0.0416

Table D.22. Fabricated metal industries

Year	Intermediate input				Output			Tax rate	Rate of productivity growth
	Price	Quantity	Outlay	Quality	Price	Quantity	Revenue		
1948	0.508	8.405	4.266	0.996	0.519	17.655	9.170	0.0012	
1949	0.517	9.116	4.717	0.997	0.533	17.323	9.236	0.0015	−0.0162
1950	0.539	11.851	6.382	0.998	0.553	21.800	12.046	0.0009	0.0456
1951	0.587	12.987	7.618	0.996	0.616	23.549	14.513	0.0002	−0.0188
1952	0.594	11.508	6.839	0.997	0.608	22.796	13.855	0.0010	0.0007
1953	0.613	13.348	8.182	0.997	0.618	25.857	15.980	0.0009	0.0115
1954	0.628	11.531	7.246	0.998	0.622	23.399	14.554	0.0010	0.0111
1955	0.659	13.272	8.751	0.999	0.648	25.950	16.827	0.0009	0.0030
1956	0.705	13.811	9.734	0.999	0.689	26.667	18.373	0.0009	−0.0045
1957	0.722	13.893	10.031	0.999	0.718	26.751	19.213	0.0009	−0.0057
1958	0.727	13.224	9.608	1.000	0.728	24.792	18.059	0.0016	−0.0076
1959	0.742	14.692	10.906	1.000	0.730	27.702	20.220	0.0010	0.0299
1960	0.750	14.655	10.992	1.000	0.735	27.730	20.373	0.0012	−0.0033
1961	0.745	13.945	10.388	1.000	0.740	26.924	19.932	0.0015	0.0101
1962	0.743	15.249	11.337	1.002	0.742	29.420	21.838	0.0014	0.0154
1963	0.744	16.037	11.930	1.002	0.748	30.739	22.987	0.0015	0.0112
1964	0.757	16.910	12.797	1.003	0.761	32.468	24.696	0.0015	0.0101
1965	0.774	18.311	14.164	1.003	0.770	35.881	27.631	0.0014	0.0282
1966	0.793	20.232	16.043	1.003	0.793	39.561	31.370	0.0014	0.0042
1967	0.812	22.004	17.862	1.000	0.810	42.234	34.215	0.0015	0.0078
1968	0.836	24.270	20.296	1.000	0.831	45.846	38.109	0.0012	0.0152
1969	0.879	23.754	20.871	1.000	0.864	46.104	39.815	0.0028	0.0003
1970	0.936	21.572	20.195	1.001	0.916	41.580	38.082	0.0031	−0.0177
1971	0.967	21.271	20.567	1.001	0.962	40.524	38.964	0.0033	0.0029
1972	1.000	22.913	22.913	1.000	1.000	43.824	43.824	0.0034	0.0172
1973	1.054	24.854	26.198	1.000	1.042	48.157	50.181	0.0033	0.0187
1974	1.301	25.317	32.948	0.997	1.258	46.133	58.049	0.0034	−0.0501
1975	1.451	21.259	30.839	0.996	1.455	39.706	57.777	0.0037	−0.0224
1976	1.534	22.628	34.708	0.996	1.509	43.496	65.622	0.0039	0.0430
1977	1.645	24.168	39.746	0.995	1.603	46.742	74.944	0.0037	0.0212
1978	1.763	27.514	48.518	0.995	1.749	50.200	87.777	0.0036	−0.0232
1979	2.015	27.859	56.129	0.991	1.915	52.167	99.881	0.0037	0.0159

Table D.23. Machinery, except electrical

Year	Intermediate input				Output			Tax rate	Rate of productivity growth
	Price	Quantity	Outlay	Quality	Price	Quantity	Revenue		
1948	0.514	9.731	4.998	0.991	0.481	24.208	11.634	0.0047	
1949	0.527	9.798	5.168	0.993	0.505	22.369	11.301	0.0032	−0.0137
1950	0.547	11.570	6.329	0.994	0.523	25.331	13.235	0.0044	0.0245
1951	0.596	14.670	8.742	0.993	0.572	32.135	18.395	0.0033	0.0311
1952	0.602	15.021	9.039	0.994	0.576	34.124	19.661	0.0044	−0.0046
1953	0.617	15.552	9.595	0.995	0.590	34.421	20.307	0.0045	−0.0195
1954	0.629	12.631	7.949	0.996	0.601	29.616	17.814	0.0051	−0.0079
1955	0.652	15.012	9.795	0.996	0.619	32.476	20.116	0.0051	−0.0024
1956	0.695	16.302	11.323	0.996	0.667	35.344	23.590	0.0052	0.0059
1957	0.723	15.774	11.397	0.996	0.711	33.577	23.864	0.0053	−0.0415
1958	0.732	14.128	10.342	0.996	0.723	29.229	21.141	0.0066	−0.0270
1959	0.746	16.041	11.961	0.995	0.740	33.488	24.794	0.0054	0.0395
1960	0.754	15.528	11.712	0.996	0.749	32.873	24.630	0.0067	−0.0111
1961	0.754	15.103	11.388	0.997	0.754	32.395	24.413	0.0064	0.0109
1962	0.756	16.512	12.489	0.999	0.759	35.935	27.270	0.0055	0.0278
1963	0.760	18.032	13.705	0.999	0.765	38.055	29.094	0.0054	−0.0004
1964	0.770	20.306	15.632	1.000	0.774	43.017	33.277	0.0050	0.0373
1965	0.782	22.259	17.406	1.000	0.786	47.345	37.226	0.0028	0.0111
1966	0.803	26.992	21.672	1.000	0.812	54.935	44.597	0.0015	0.0025
1967	0.823	26.741	22.008	0.999	0.834	54.940	45.824	0.0017	−0.0161
1968	0.850	26.632	22.637	0.999	0.867	54.916	47.594	0.0019	−0.0009
1969	0.887	29.483	26.138	1.000	0.900	59.068	53.165	0.0021	0.0026
1970	0.934	26.822	25.039	1.000	0.941	56.315	52.972	0.0022	0.0116
1971	0.970	26.142	25.354	1.000	0.976	53.559	52.294	0.0025	−0.0067
1972	1.000	31.215	31.215	1.000	1.000	61.979	61.979	0.0025	0.0322
1973	1.045	37.725	39.410	1.000	1.029	72.520	74.612	0.0023	0.0156
1974	1.223	42.330	51.750	0.996	1.158	77.501	89.731	0.0023	−0.0216
1975	1.376	35.209	48.436	0.996	1.340	66.567	89.206	0.0025	−0.0266
1976	1.447	36.911	53.422	0.995	1.401	70.567	98.865	0.0027	0.0268
1977	1.536	40.003	61.435	0.994	1.470	77.550	113.987	0.0026	0.0338
1978	1.648	43.487	71.646	0.993	1.586	83.431	132.293	0.0026	−0.0062
1979	1.828	44.870	82.044	0.989	1.712	88.204	150.989	0.0026	0.0031

Table D.24. Electrical machinery, equipment, and supplies

Year	Intermediate input				Output			Tax rate	Rate of productivity growth
	Price	Quantity	Outlay	Quality	Price	Quantity	Revenue		
1948	0.566	7.803	4.416	0.972	0.678	12.524	8.494	0.0335	
1949	0.575	7.691	4.420	0.976	0.687	12.066	8.288	0.0265	0.0269
1950	0.595	10.676	6.348	0.977	0.708	15.854	11.223	0.0284	0.0357
1951	0.648	11.463	7.427	0.976	0.765	17.396	13.301	0.0294	−0.0021
1952	0.650	12.117	7.873	0.980	0.757	19.468	14.733	0.0269	0.0237
1953	0.664	14.100	9.363	0.982	0.770	22.028	16.962	0.0260	−0.0062
1954	0.676	11.823	7.988	0.984	0.785	19.072	14.964	0.0205	−0.0150
1955	0.695	13.498	9.385	0.986	0.787	21.254	16.737	0.0207	0.0149
1956	0.734	14.046	10.315	0.986	0.832	22.337	18.585	0.0183	0.0004
1957	0.762	12.880	9.812	0.986	0.878	21.610	18.966	0.0182	−0.0032
1958	0.772	11.649	8.993	0.987	0.891	20.126	17.932	0.0192	0.0088
1959	0.784	13.870	10.879	0.987	0.909	23.899	21.713	0.0179	0.0322
1960	0.790	14.810	11.705	0.989	0.903	25.346	22.886	0.0163	−0.0038
1961	0.788	16.232	12.786	0.990	0.894	27.267	24.367	0.0158	0.0220
1962	0.786	18.518	14.561	0.995	0.879	31.116	27.352	0.0152	0.0250
1963	0.787	18.868	14.844	0.998	0.870	32.111	27.953	0.0162	0.0226
1964	0.793	19.255	15.263	0.999	0.862	33.429	28.805	0.0165	0.0290
1965	0.801	21.849	17.503	1.000	0.863	38.660	33.380	0.0074	0.0487
1966	0.819	25.633	20.998	1.000	0.881	44.776	39.431	0.0016	−0.0023
1967	0.840	25.971	21.813	1.000	0.903	45.931	41.480	0.0018	−0.0077
1968	0.862	26.961	23.249	0.999	0.914	48.344	44.205	0.0017	0.0217
1969	0.893	27.020	24.119	1.000	0.925	50.478	46.680	0.0020	0.0316
1970	0.937	25.634	24.021	1.000	0.962	47.949	46.103	0.0020	−0.0052
1971	0.973	23.708	23.060	1.000	0.989	46.530	46.022	0.0021	0.0344
1972	1.000	26.437	26.437	1.000	1.000	52.166	52.166	0.0023	0.0443
1973	1.041	31.033	32.299	1.000	1.017	59.279	60.294	0.0022	0.0050
1974	1.205	31.586	38.058	0.996	1.118	58.306	65.208	0.0024	−0.0377
1975	1.350	25.156	33.969	0.996	1.255	49.622	62.275	0.0028	0.0155
1976	1.419	28.428	40.347	0.995	1.302	55.948	72.819	0.0028	0.0399
1977	1.500	30.630	45.950	0.994	1.346	63.399	85.326	0.0027	0.0636
1978	1.603	33.077	53.036	0.993	1.433	69.427	99.509	0.0027	0.0160
1979	1.772	36.002	63.807	0.990	1.546	75.515	116.771	0.0027	0.0112

Table D.25 Transportation equipment and ordnance, except motor vehicles

Year	Intermediate input				Output			Tax rate	Rate of productivity growth
	Price	Quantity	Outlay	Quality	Price	Quantity	Revenue		
1948	0.546	3.918	2.138	0.965	0.490	8.470	4.154	0.0039	
1949	0.563	4.852	2.730	0.970	0.511	9.350	4.780	0.0013	−0.0006
1950	0.578	5.403	3.125	0.974	0.525	10.172	5.339	0.0036	0.0224
1951	0.629	9.503	5.978	0.975	0.589	16.292	9.599	0.0016	−0.0297
1952	0.639	16.863	10.781	0.980	0.591	27.590	16.304	0.0016	0.0335
1953	0.650	21.371	13.888	0.984	0.602	34.153	20.553	0.0014	0.0222
1954	0.659	17.721	11.684	0.987	0.612	29.792	18.226	0.0016	0.0177
1955	0.683	16.069	10.979	0.989	0.633	27.475	17.405	0.0018	−0.0107
1956	0.723	16.660	12.052	0.991	0.685	27.902	19.118	0.0018	−0.0332
1957	0.751	18.814	14.124	0.993	0.723	30.919	22.355	0.0017	0.0021
1958	0.763	15.599	11.905	0.994	0.737	27.108	19.969	0.0022	0.0116
1959	0.776	16.728	12.987	0.994	0.747	28.218	21.082	0.0019	−0.0035
1960	0.779	15.619	12.160	0.996	0.753	26.412	19.896	0.0020	0.0030
1961	0.777	15.531	12.061	0.997	0.755	26.986	20.375	0.0020	0.0268
1962	0.778	15.825	12.319	0.998	0.757	28.575	21.643	0.0019	0.0179
1963	0.780	16.260	12.679	0.997	0.757	30.098	22.787	0.0023	0.0319
1964	0.789	16.904	13.330	0.996	0.764	31.074	23.733	0.0021	0.0155
1965	0.799	18.568	14.842	0.996	0.776	33.058	25.648	0.0022	−0.0056
1966	0.815	22.606	18.432	0.995	0.790	39.952	31.550	0.0025	0.0093
1967	0.830	24.780	20.560	0.999	0.817	42.973	35.108	0.0022	−0.0157
1968	0.855	25.658	21.950	0.999	0.844	44.637	37.668	0.0012	0.0086
1969	0.886	26.869	23.800	1.000	0.882	43.884	38.709	0.0014	−0.0295
1970	0.930	22.959	21.347	1.000	0.934	37.702	35.221	0.0016	0.0081
1971	0.970	21.548	20.897	1.000	0.970	35.180	34.135	0.0017	0.0131
1972	1.000	21.390	21.390	1.000	1.000	35.474	35.474	0.0020	0.0078
1973	1.038	24.289	25.218	1.000	1.041	39.880	41.496	0.0018	0.0359
1974	1.192	23.893	28.475	0.997	1.182	38.716	45.751	0.0020	−0.0186
1975	1.335	22.715	30.319	0.996	1.315	37.166	48.873	0.0021	−0.0015
1976	1.411	21.592	30.462	0.996	1.410	35.553	50.128	0.0024	−0.0100
1977	1.501	22.231	33.360	0.995	1.509	36.491	55.058	0.0025	0.0037
1978	1.610	26.464	42.614	0.995	1.629	41.509	67.598	0.0023	−0.0057
1979	1.773	31.591	56.016	0.992	1.783	47.958	85.490	0.0022	−0.0070

Table D.26. Motor vehicles and equipment

Year	Intermediate input				Output			Tax rate	Rate of productivity growth
	Price	Quantity	Outlay	Quality	Price	Quantity	Revenue		
1948	0.520	14.345	7.465	1.001	0.553	20.890	11.542	0.0458	
1949	0.533	19.238	10.253	1.003	0.599	25.456	15.249	0.0424	0.0037
1950	0.551	23.552	12.979	1.005	0.596	33.062	19.705	0.0398	0.1129
1951	0.601	19.801	11.909	1.005	0.622	29.314	18.248	0.0434	−0.0282
1952	0.606	18.977	11.502	1.007	0.657	27.438	18.016	0.0550	−0.0517
1953	0.619	25.351	15.701	1.009	0.653	36.005	23.525	0.0552	0.0388
1954	0.630	21.644	13.630	1.010	0.655	31.131	20.381	0.0569	−0.0131
1955	0.652	30.173	19.671	1.012	0.677	43.874	29.703	0.0577	0.0963
1956	0.691	24.066	16.638	1.012	0.712	34.230	24.386	0.0576	−0.0864
1957	0.716	25.278	18.087	1.012	0.739	35.704	26.401	0.0607	0.0088
1958	0.724	19.303	13.974	1.012	0.759	26.137	19.832	0.0615	−0.0750
1959	0.738	23.286	17.179	1.009	0.774	33.248	25.731	0.0629	0.0878
1960	0.743	26.113	19.410	1.007	0.764	37.540	28.678	0.0623	0.0290
1961	0.742	21.978	16.312	1.003	0.760	32.389	24.620	0.0636	−0.0027
1962	0.744	27.588	20.516	1.006	0.766	40.990	31.410	0.0630	0.0594
1963	0.746	29.223	21.806	1.007	0.760	45.340	34.461	0.0637	0.0467
1964	0.756	29.922	22.628	1.008	0.768	46.523	35.723	0.0660	−0.0019
1965	0.769	37.180	28.578	1.008	0.786	56.897	44.694	0.0523	0.0249
1966	0.788	36.853	29.051	1.009	0.800	56.296	45.044	0.0407	−0.0244
1967	0.808	31.619	25.537	1.002	0.808	49.593	40.056	0.0447	−0.0183
1968	0.840	36.697	30.810	1.001	0.833	58.888	49.024	0.0486	0.0550
1969	0.882	36.413	32.104	1.002	0.847	59.417	50.307	0.0513	0.0122
1970	0.915	31.246	28.594	1.000	0.880	48.271	42.475	0.0494	−0.0755
1971	0.959	40.585	38.907	1.000	0.950	61.696	58.625	0.0280	0.0592
1972	1.000	43.681	43.681	1.000	1.000	65.906	65.906	0.0081	0.0021
1973	1.065	49.312	52.529	0.998	1.011	76.391	77.251	0.0098	0.0335
1974	1.232	41.911	51.625	0.997	1.103	64.142	70.767	0.0115	−0.0337
1975	1.356	37.390	50.704	0.996	1.246	57.560	71.702	0.0091	−0.0042
1976	1.445	48.001	69.351	0.997	1.324	74.728	98.969	0.0078	0.0547
1977	1.550	54.069	83.834	0.996	1.416	85.176	120.618	0.0087	0.0233
1978	1.676	57.825	96.892	0.995	1.520	89.828	136.569	0.0098	−0.0105
1979	1.852	55.340	102.476	0.992	1.644	84.594	139.102	0.0109	−0.0401

Table D.27. Professional photographic equipment and watches

	Intermediate input				Output				
Year	Price	Quantity	Outlay	Quality	Price	Quantity	Revenue	Tax rate	Rate of productivity growth
1948	0.578	1.376	0.795	0.985	0.572	3.199	1.831	0.0269	
1949	0.581	1.349	0.783	0.989	0.583	3.138	1.828	0.0224	0.0288
1950	0.597	1.747	1.042	0.987	0.594	3.869	2.299	0.0196	0.0314
1951	0.655	1.806	1.182	0.982	0.652	4.425	2.883	0.0156	0.0049
1952	0.653	1.979	1.293	0.985	0.654	5.019	3.284	0.0094	−0.0002
1953	0.665	1.967	1.307	0.986	0.670	5.296	3.550	0.0100	0.0032
1954	0.673	1.522	1.025	0.986	0.681	4.833	3.290	0.0062	0.0206
1955	0.690	1.793	1.237	0.986	0.694	5.286	3.668	0.0058	0.0262
1956	0.726	1.856	1.347	0.986	0.736	5.569	4.097	0.0064	−0.0231
1957	0.754	1.956	1.474	0.985	0.778	5.596	4.355	0.0066	−0.0465
1958	0.765	1.828	1.399	0.985	0.797	5.458	4.349	0.0071	0.0185
1959	0.776	2.170	1.683	0.985	0.807	6.254	5.046	0.0063	0.0426
1960	0.784	2.233	1.752	0.987	0.817	6.452	5.269	0.0065	−0.0028
1961	0.784	1.965	1.540	0.988	0.818	6.153	5.033	0.0070	−0.0029
1962	0.787	1.468	1.156	0.992	0.831	6.144	5.103	0.0069	0.0454
1963	0.790	1.756	1.387	0.996	0.826	6.535	5.398	0.0072	0.0200
1964	0.797	2.027	1.616	0.997	0.832	6.889	5.731	0.0079	0.0043
1965	0.807	2.462	1.986	0.996	0.843	7.989	6.736	0.0031	0.0509
1966	0.827	2.597	2.149	0.996	0.878	8.956	7.867	0.0019	0.0159
1967	0.849	3.028	2.571	0.999	0.914	9.515	8.693	0.0018	−0.0369
1968	0.873	3.203	2.795	0.999	0.936	10.122	9.475	0.0019	0.0232
1969	0.900	3.201	2.882	1.000	0.942	10.898	10.269	0.0022	0.0493
1970	0.940	3.741	3.516	1.000	0.975	10.523	10.255	0.0023	−0.0695
1971	0.973	3.856	3.751	1.000	0.991	10.735	10.643	0.0025	0.0338
1972	1.000	4.354	4.354	1.000	1.000	12.025	12.025	0.0027	0.0352
1973	1.045	5.126	5.356	1.000	1.023	13.753	14.075	0.0026	0.0282
1974	1.205	6.228	7.505	0.997	1.112	14.969	16.642	0.0025	−0.0282
1975	1.342	5.533	7.424	0.995	1.221	13.856	16.924	0.0028	−0.0019
1976	1.413	6.308	8.911	0.995	1.288	15.346	19.765	0.0028	0.0216
1977	1.488	6.853	10.199	0.994	1.331	16.740	22.278	0.0028	0.0133
1978	1.591	7.539	11.994	0.994	1.448	17.879	25.885	0.0028	−0.0117
1979	1.760	8.444	14.862	0.991	1.597	18.683	29.843	0.0028	−0.0433

Table D.28. Miscellaneous manufacturing industries

	Intermediate input				Output				
Year	Price	Quantity	Outlay	Quality	Price	Quantity	Revenue	Tax rate	Rate of productivity growth
1948	0.601	2.410	1.448	0.969	0.689	4.486	3.090	0.0139	
1949	0.596	2.730	1.628	0.976	0.685	4.588	3.142	0.0116	−0.0001
1950	0.619	3.075	1.903	0.979	0.700	5.196	3.637	0.0120	0.0400
1951	0.680	2.682	1.823	0.978	0.748	4.898	3.664	0.0110	0.0011
1952	0.674	2.597	1.749	0.986	0.731	4.946	3.618	0.0137	0.0179
1953	0.681	3.197	2.176	0.990	0.742	5.608	4.163	0.0123	−0.0062
1954	0.687	2.785	1.913	0.993	0.749	5.137	3.847	0.0123	0.0044
1955	0.705	3.050	2.149	0.996	0.753	5.664	4.266	0.0103	0.0457
1956	0.735	3.216	2.363	0.998	0.778	5.894	4.588	0.0113	0.0036
1957	0.750	3.041	2.282	1.000	0.790	5.725	4.522	0.0112	0.0118
1958	0.757	3.243	2.456	1.001	0.795	5.892	4.682	0.0113	0.0072
1959	0.766	3.460	2.650	0.997	0.797	6.401	5.103	0.0108	0.0443
1960	0.774	3.701	2.866	0.993	0.805	6.574	5.293	0.0111	−0.0207
1961	0.771	3.793	2.924	0.990	0.808	6.775	5.474	0.0110	0.0228
1962	0.775	4.063	3.149	0.993	0.813	7.136	5.800	0.0110	−0.0050
1963	0.779	4.461	3.474	0.996	0.814	7.537	6.133	0.0117	−0.0021
1964	0.786	4.707	3.701	0.996	0.815	7.957	6.487	0.0114	0.0113
1965	0.798	5.234	4.175	0.996	0.826	8.704	7.193	0.0054	0.0085
1966	0.818	5.339	4.367	0.996	0.845	9.086	7.678	0.0025	0.0102
1967	0.834	5.428	4.526	0.999	0.864	9.215	7.966	0.0028	0.0043
1968	0.861	5.607	4.825	0.999	0.888	9.690	8.608	0.0029	0.0259
1969	0.894	5.909	5.281	1.000	0.907	10.273	9.320	0.0029	0.0210
1970	0.927	5.661	5.250	1.000	0.938	9.920	9.301	0.0034	−0.0087
1971	0.963	5.513	5.312	1.000	0.970	10.036	9.736	0.0036	0.0278
1972	1.000	6.729	6.729	1.000	1.000	11.665	11.665	0.0037	0.0230
1973	1.063	6.889	7.321	0.999	1.058	11.860	12.550	0.0035	−0.0123
1974	1.240	6.700	8.306	0.997	1.206	11.232	13.546	0.0040	−0.0437
1975	1.362	5.596	7.625	0.995	1.318	10.335	13.624	0.0043	0.0398
1976	1.441	6.280	9.050	0.996	1.376	11.342	15.603	0.0045	0.0171
1977	1.528	7.033	10.745	0.995	1.450	12.460	18.067	0.0045	0.0144
1978	1.633	7.393	12.073	0.995	1.568	12.656	19.841	0.0049	−0.0303
1979	1.833	9.253	16.964	0.992	1.934	12.880	24.908	0.0040	−0.1318

Table D.29. Railroads and rail express services

	Intermediate input				Output				
Year	Price	Quantity	Outlay	Quality	Price	Quantity	Revenue	Tax rate	Rate of productivity growth
1948	0.515	17.085	8.800	1.007	0.739	22.483	16.626	0.0278	
1949	0.530	14.399	7.638	1.004	0.789	18.762	14.798	0.0240	−0.0438
1950	0.540	15.650	8.444	1.001	0.800	20.382	16.302	0.0258	0.0528
1951	0.581	15.875	9.219	0.994	0.807	22.316	17.999	0.0229	0.0584
1952	0.592	15.662	9.268	0.994	0.856	21.350	18.267	0.0263	−0.0310
1953	0.607	15.621	9.482	0.993	0.879	20.960	18.429	0.0257	−0.0157
1954	0.612	13.666	8.366	0.992	0.856	18.961	16.222	0.0242	0.0083
1955	0.629	14.335	9.013	0.992	0.831	21.108	17.549	0.0231	0.0777
1956	0.657	14.262	9.373	0.990	0.840	21.820	18.335	0.0232	0.0424
1957	0.685	13.631	9.333	0.986	0.877	20.786	18.230	0.0231	−0.0058
1958	0.694	12.360	8.573	0.986	0.898	18.580	16.693	0.0180	−0.0075
1959	0.699	13.063	9.135	0.985	0.908	19.107	17.345	0.0076	0.0091
1960	0.718	12.545	9.007	0.987	0.869	19.496	16.950	0.0080	0.0579
1961	0.725	11.711	8.493	0.987	0.846	19.134	16.185	0.0087	0.0362
1962	0.729	12.073	8.803	0.997	0.834	19.936	16.632	0.0083	0.0272
1963	0.743	12.000	8.920	0.991	0.817	20.697	16.901	0.0055	0.0498
1964	0.749	12.445	9.323	0.992	0.806	21.641	17.450	0.0058	0.0241
1965	0.761	12.711	9.668	0.991	0.796	22.887	18.219	0.0061	0.0497
1966	0.791	12.653	10.011	0.992	0.789	24.043	18.978	0.0071	0.0472
1967	0.814	12.223	9.946	0.997	0.792	23.276	18.441	0.0071	−0.0059
1968	0.839	12.726	10.675	0.998	0.820	23.567	19.331	0.0059	−0.0065
1969	0.877	12.816	11.236	0.999	0.848	23.987	20.335	0.0065	0.0209
1970	0.916	12.749	11.677	1.000	0.894	23.806	21.278	0.0064	0.0043
1971	0.964	13.196	12.726	1.000	0.990	22.896	22.668	0.0061	−0.0437
1972	1.000	13.631	13.631	1.000	1.000	23.994	23.994	0.0062	0.0427
1973	1.072	14.208	15.235	0.998	1.014	26.209	26.582	0.0061	0.0607
1974	1.254	14.409	18.070	0.986	1.159	26.118	30.267	0.0063	−0.0073
1975	1.395	12.846	17.914	0.982	1.286	23.359	30.050	0.0074	−0.0214
1976	1.476	13.134	19.386	0.981	1.357	24.466	33.197	0.0079	0.0389
1977	1.586	12.278	19.475	0.977	1.407	24.407	34.330	0.0087	0.0342
1978	1.697	12.856	21.815	0.977	1.504	25.453	38.283	0.0088	0.0099
1979	1.926	13.030	25.090	0.963	1.662	26.511	44.064	0.0086	0.0169

Table D.30. Street railways, bus lines, and taxicabs

Year	Intermediate input				Output			Tax rate	Rate of productivity growth
	Price	Quantity	Outlay	Quality	Price	Quantity	Revenue		
1948	0.499	6.047	3.015	1.032	0.316	14.952	4.721	0.0167	
1949	0.514	5.608	2.885	1.030	0.351	12.953	4.541	0.0211	−0.0908
1950	0.521	5.597	2.913	1.028	0.379	12.079	4.574	0.0157	−0.0498
1951	0.566	5.220	2.954	1.022	0.404	11.699	4.723	0.0202	0.0127
1952	0.578	5.174	2.989	1.025	0.424	11.401	4.838	0.0167	−0.0307
1953	0.589	5.227	3.077	1.025	0.449	10.953	4.916	0.0158	−0.0455
1954	0.596	4.965	2.958	1.025	0.469	10.108	4.736	0.0114	−0.0375
1955	0.611	4.840	2.960	1.025	0.493	9.688	4.779	0.0114	−0.0173
1956	0.637	4.812	3.064	1.024	0.512	9.599	4.913	0.0109	−0.0030
1957	0.662	4.672	3.094	1.022	0.531	9.484	5.037	0.0112	0.0117
1958	0.665	4.379	2.910	1.025	0.538	8.981	4.829	0.0118	0.0006
1959	0.669	4.462	2.984	1.024	0.568	8.854	5.026	0.0099	−0.0152
1960	0.684	4.525	3.096	1.026	0.584	8.824	5.154	0.0109	−0.0121
1961	0.691	4.258	2.944	1.027	0.599	8.466	5.068	0.0118	−0.0104
1962	0.699	4.399	3.076	1.029	0.620	8.448	5.239	0.0111	−0.0165
1963	0.717	4.391	3.150	1.015	0.636	8.385	5.335	0.0043	−0.0007
1964	0.723	4.410	3.187	1.016	0.660	8.276	5.464	0.0048	−0.0127
1965	0.741	4.437	3.289	1.017	0.687	8.343	5.734	0.0049	−0.0003
1966	0.766	4.431	3.393	1.017	0.707	8.415	5.949	0.0055	0.0057
1967	0.815	4.581	3.735	0.997	0.753	8.519	6.411	0.0050	−0.0182
1968	0.840	4.708	3.954	0.999	0.789	8.562	6.754	0.0049	−0.0081
1969	0.882	4.761	4.197	1.000	0.824	8.502	7.005	0.0064	−0.0086
1970	0.917	4.816	4.416	1.000	0.878	8.336	7.320	0.0075	−0.0424
1971	0.966	4.855	4.689	1.000	0.955	8.137	7.769	0.0091	−0.0299
1972	1.000	5.037	5.037	1.000	1.000	8.019	8.019	0.0111	−0.0308
1973	1.091	5.324	5.810	0.998	1.074	8.007	8.597	0.0114	−0.0240
1974	1.283	5.120	6.569	0.984	1.097	8.748	9.599	0.0119	0.1028
1975	1.423	4.824	6.864	0.979	1.272	8.031	10.219	0.0131	−0.0500
1976	1.509	4.744	7.159	0.978	1.406	7.678	10.795	0.0146	−0.0362
1977	1.626	4.670	7.594	0.975	1.520	7.631	11.596	0.0154	0.0007
1978	1.737	4.760	8.268	0.975	1.686	7.382	12.448	0.0163	−0.0463
1979	1.986	4.500	8.935	0.958	1.773	7.620	13.510	0.0169	0.0482

Table D.31. Trucking services and warehousing

Year	Intermediate input				Output			Tax rate	Rate of productivity growth
	Price	Quantity	Outlay	Quality	Price	Quantity	Revenue		
1948	0.467	8.829	4.122	0.979	0.570	11.993	6.833	0.0163	
1949	0.490	9.166	4.493	0.983	0.556	13.105	7.292	0.0244	0.0631
1950	0.493	12.379	6.108	0.977	0.532	17.785	9.457	0.0162	0.0995
1951	0.537	12.767	6.850	0.976	0.545	19.246	10.498	0.0250	0.0274
1952	0.554	12.878	7.133	0.979	0.562	19.964	11.223	0.0161	0.0174
1953	0.575	13.808	7.939	0.981	0.563	22.224	12.518	0.0163	0.0551
1954	0.582	12.643	7.360	0.983	0.551	21.809	12.021	0.0166	0.0410
1955	0.593	14.811	8.785	0.983	0.611	22.981	14.051	0.0164	−0.0611
1956	0.617	14.689	9.068	0.983	0.581	25.477	14.792	0.0172	0.0849
1957	0.643	14.849	9.546	0.984	0.602	26.004	15.650	0.0175	0.0097
1958	0.657	14.354	9.435	0.985	0.597	26.166	15.626	0.0132	0.0319
1959	0.661	17.032	11.263	0.984	0.644	28.522	18.378	0.0046	−0.0315
1960	0.687	16.296	11.197	0.988	0.636	29.155	18.543	0.0051	0.0314
1961	0.701	16.49	11.565	0.989	0.634	30.253	19.165	0.0059	0.0307
1962	0.706	17.925	12.649	0.995	0.660	31.614	20.878	0.0061	−0.0185
1963	0.730	18.185	13.270	0.988	0.638	34.383	21.947	0.0062	0.0585
1964	0.740	19.298	14.276	0.989	0.646	36.386	23.518	0.0062	0.0083
1965	0.775	19.981	15.490	0.988	0.703	36.743	25.845	0.0060	−0.0338
1966	0.813	20.553	16.714	0.986	0.716	38.943	27.888	0.0064	0.0074
1967	0.861	20.302	17.490	0.993	0.729	39.813	29.042	0.0059	0.0155
1968	0.876	22.732	19.902	0.995	0.807	40.550	32.729	0.0050	−0.0625
1969	0.916	24.000	21.973	0.998	0.867	41.332	35.834	0.0052	−0.0395
1970	0.938	24.570	23.048	0.999	0.890	42.124	37.476	0.0056	0.0046
1971	0.974	27.436	26.730	1.000	0.943	45.520	42.924	0.0052	−0.0010
1972	1.000	29.603	29.603	1.000	1.000	48.071	48.071	0.0052	−0.0137
1973	1.070	30.534	32.679	0.998	1.035	51.668	53.472	0.0053	0.0489
1974	1.209	29.492	35.659	0.988	1.154	50.621	58.405	0.0054	−0.0315
1975	1.368	22.897	31.319	0.985	1.219	44.273	53.982	0.0066	0.0241
1976	1.441	24.813	35.766	0.983	1.280	47.741	61.108	0.0067	−0.0018
1977	1.572	25.346	39.845	0.980	1.401	49.248	68.992	0.0067	−0.0191
1978	1.718	26.794	46.038	0.981	1.479	53.829	79.613	0.0059	0.0276

Table D.32. Water transportation

Year	Intermediate input				Output			Tax rate	Rate of productivity growth
	Price	Quantity	Outlay	Quality	Price	Quantity	Revenue		
1948	0.584	4.619	2.697	0.944	0.465	8.284	3.848	0.0052	
1949	0.593	4.628	2.747	0.952	0.508	7.544	3.835	0.0048	−0.0833
1950	0.589	4.623	2.723	0.956	0.512	7.524	3.851	0.0047	0.0121
1951	0.614	6.127	3.763	0.962	0.536	9.723	5.209	0.0043	0.0296
1952	0.622	5.675	3.532	0.966	0.570	8.698	4.960	0.0052	−0.0561
1953	0.632	5.353	3.383	0.969	0.632	7.763	4.909	0.0053	−0.0695
1954	0.633	4.898	3.100	0.973	0.605	7.391	4.471	0.0049	0.0318
1955	0.638	5.349	3.412	0.977	0.590	8.443	4.978	0.0050	0.0627
1956	0.656	5.776	3.787	0.978	0.596	9.205	5.487	0.0052	0.0256
1957	0.672	5.790	3.890	0.978	0.596	9.522	5.673	0.0057	0.0218
1958	0.692	4.224	2.922	0.977	0.660	6.868	4.533	0.0064	−0.0836
1959	0.696	4.150	2.889	0.977	0.714	6.522	4.656	0.0006	−0.0496
1960	0.728	4.015	2.924	0.977	0.711	6.792	4.826	0.0010	0.0546
1961	0.753	3.365	2.532	0.975	0.736	6.017	4.426	0.0011	−0.0095
1962	0.769	3.502	2.692	0.986	0.721	6.507	4.690	0.0009	0.0561
1963	0.761	3.592	2.733	0.992	0.759	6.394	4.851	0.0008	−0.0258
1964	0.763	3.862	2.945	0.992	0.771	6.787	5.231	0.0010	0.0077
1965	0.762	3.998	3.048	0.991	0.858	6.277	5.383	0.0011	−0.0881
1966	0.793	4.078	3.233	0.993	0.964	6.064	5.848	0.0010	−0.0681
1967	0.799	3.598	2.874	0.998	1.028	5.428	5.582	0.0011	−0.0529
1968	0.799	3.713	2.965	0.998	1.070	5.564	5.951	0.0008	0.0195
1969	0.843	3.274	2.761	0.999	1.024	5.458	5.590	0.0012	0.0735
1970	0.893	3.827	3.419	0.999	0.995	6.410	6.376	0.0008	0.0940
1971	0.960	3.755	3.604	1.000	0.957	6.745	6.454	0.0006	0.0860
1972	1.000	3.766	3.766	1.000	1.000	6.774	6.774	0.0004	0.0098
1973	1.079	5.130	5.537	0.999	0.989	9.011	8.912	0.0004	0.0969
1974	1.185	5.537	6.562	0.994	1.081	9.733	10.522	0.0004	0.0287
1975	1.292	4.613	5.960	0.992	1.211	8.308	10.057	0.0005	−0.0397
1976	1.388	4.617	6.411	0.991	1.224	8.960	10.969	0.0005	0.0721
1977	1.489	5.123	7.628	0.989	1.371	9.099	12.477	0.0006	−0.0517
1978	1.612	5.643	9.094	0.988	1.589	9.294	14.768	0.0005	−0.0693
1979	1.762	6.181	10.891	0.981	1.834	9.389	17.220	0.0004	−0.0638

Table D.33. Air transportation

Year	Intermediate input				Output			Tax rate	Rate of productivity growth
	Price	Quantity	Outlay	Quality	Price	Quantity	Revenue		
1948	0.526	1.149	0.604	0.971	0.854	1.214	1.037	0.0518	
1949	0.551	1.192	0.657	0.973	0.841	1.354	1.138	0.0527	0.1029
1950	0.555	1.196	0.664	0.970	0.785	1.569	1.231	0.0566	0.1420
1951	0.606	1.289	0.782	0.968	0.752	1.948	1.465	0.0613	0.1438
1952	0.619	1.461	0.905	0.972	0.737	2.265	1.668	0.0680	0.0318
1953	0.632	1.780	1.126	0.975	0.733	2.731	2.002	0.0626	0.0298
1954	0.642	1.895	1.217	0.977	0.723	3.025	2.186	0.0486	0.0495
1955	0.653	2.170	1.418	0.979	0.698	3.562	2.486	0.0491	0.0561
1956	0.682	2.318	1.581	0.980	0.695	3.979	2.765	0.0481	0.0339
1957	0.715	2.438	1.742	0.981	0.690	4.420	3.049	0.0472	0.0274
1958	0.717	2.635	1.889	0.985	0.723	4.563	3.298	0.0464	−0.0271
1959	0.718	3.152	2.263	0.984	0.723	5.385	3.892	0.0421	0.0446
1960	0.738	3.352	2.473	0.988	0.776	5.554	4.309	0.0408	−0.0644
1961	0.748	3.423	2.560	0.989	0.829	5.465	4.532	0.0415	−0.0494
1962	0.753	3.755	2.829	0.989	0.876	5.825	5.103	0.0359	−0.0077
1963	0.765	4.115	3.150	0.986	0.822	6.876	5.653	0.0225	0.0992
1964	0.766	4.629	3.548	0.988	0.820	7.823	6.413	0.0204	0.0542
1965	0.784	5.293	4.149	0.988	0.824	9.120	7.518	0.0186	0.0420
1966	0.814	5.985	4.869	0.989	0.831	10.512	8.730	0.0197	0.0083
1967	0.842	7.148	6.016	0.997	0.809	13.020	10.530	0.0162	0.0319
1968	0.850	8.280	7.036	0.998	0.784	15.261	11.965	0.0191	0.0050
1969	0.891	8.906	7.937	0.999	0.829	16.313	13.524	0.0191	−0.0319
1970	0.923	8.848	8.163	1.000	0.885	16.002	14.165	0.0248	−0.0283
1971	0.972	8.749	8.507	1.000	0.951	15.876	15.095	0.0396	−0.0058
1972	1.000	9.230	9.230	1.000	1.000	16.662	16.662	0.0404	0.0226
1973	1.106	9.338	10.332	0.997	1.093	17.014	18.593	0.0406	−0.0074
1974	1.311	9.957	13.053	0.985	1.143	19.305	22.065	0.0377	0.0734
1975	1.469	9.373	13.772	0.973	1.228	18.721	22.992	0.0369	0.0106
1976	1.551	9.853	15.279	0.971	1.353	19.250	26.055	0.0397	0.0054
1977	1.671	10.541	17.612	0.966	1.456	20.647	30.057	0.0391	0.0356
1978	1.792	12.083	21.657	0.965	1.594	22.726	36.233	0.0385	0.0095
1979	2.069	11.596	23.996	0.965	1.688	23.619	39.861	0.0394	0.0326

Table D.34. Pipelines except natural gas

Year	Intermediate input				Output			Tax rate	Rate of productivity growth
	Price	Quantity	Outlay	Quality	Price	Quantity	Revenue		
1948	0.548	0.381	0.209	0.998	1.069	0.417	0.446	0.0471	
1949	0.554	0.350	0.194	0.998	1.119	0.401	0.448	0.0411	−0.0204
1950	0.564	0.347	0.196	1.000	1.160	0.451	0.524	0.0464	0.1053
1951	0.608	0.434	0.264	0.999	1.183	0.529	0.626	0.0406	0.0251
1952	0.625	0.468	0.292	1.000	1.213	0.550	0.667	0.0466	−0.0314
1953	0.635	0.503	0.319	1.001	1.187	0.591	0.701	0.0468	0.0110
1954	0.638	0.524	0.334	1.002	1.163	0.622	0.723	0.0608	0.0130
1955	0.653	0.642	0.419	1.003	1.154	0.704	0.812	0.0381	0.0068
1956	0.684	0.670	0.458	1.004	1.104	0.793	0.875	0.0479	0.0876
1957	0.707	0.639	0.452	1.004	1.132	0.768	0.869	0.0451	−0.0179
1958	0.712	0.615	0.438	1.005	1.201	0.729	0.875	0.0251	−0.0422
1959	0.718	0.651	0.467	1.005	1.213	0.780	0.946	0.0000	0.0319
1960	0.729	0.643	0.469	1.008	1.213	0.780	0.946	0.0000	0.0161
1961	0.734	0.659	0.484	1.010	1.216	0.798	0.971	0.0000	0.0103
1962	0.735	0.724	0.532	1.013	1.225	0.823	1.007	0.0000	−0.0148
1963	0.754	0.625	0.471	0.991	1.196	0.874	1.045	0.0000	0.1110
1964	0.758	0.630	0.478	0.993	1.158	0.923	1.070	0.0000	0.0371
1965	0.771	0.674	0.519	0.995	1.063	1.052	1.118	0.0000	0.0963
1966	0.793	0.690	0.547	0.997	1.017	1.148	1.167	0.0000	0.0805
1967	0.786	0.739	0.581	0.999	0.991	1.239	1.228	0.0000	0.0393
1968	0.814	0.745	0.606	0.998	0.940	1.344	1.264	0.0016	0.0684
1969	0.853	0.726	0.619	0.999	0.963	1.412	1.359	0.0037	0.0477
1970	0.899	0.673	0.605	1.000	0.987	1.474	1.455	0.0055	0.0876
1971	0.954	0.684	0.652	1.000	1.012	1.529	1.548	0.0000	0.0140
1972	1.000	0.607	0.607	1.000	1.000	1.628	1.628	0.0117	0.0921
1973	1.075	0.742	0.798	0.999	1.011	1.741	1.761	0.0119	−0.0049
1974	1.252	0.853	1.069	0.993	1.118	1.726	1.930	0.0124	−0.0861
1975	1.416	0.878	1.243	0.989	1.310	1.741	2.281	0.0127	−0.0876
1976	1.527	0.910	1.389	0.984	1.477	1.761	2.600	0.0127	−0.1180
1977	1.671	0.802	1.340	0.976	1.448	1.868	2.705	0.0140	−0.0784
1978	1.823	0.881	1.605	0.976	1.618	2.003	3.241	0.0133	−0.0856
1979	2.041	0.934	1.905	0.972	2.002	1.924	3.852	0.0122	−0.1061

Table D.35. Transportation services

Year	Intermediate input				Output			Tax rate	Rate of productivity growth
	Price	Quantity	Outlay	Quality	Price	Quantity	Revenue		
1948	0.505	1.311	0.662	0.996	0.239	4.191	1.000	0.0045	
1949	0.509	1.154	0.587	0.995	0.275	3.436	0.945	0.0039	−0.1375
1950	0.520	1.275	0.662	0.993	0.261	3.889	1.017	0.0055	0.1092
1951	0.560	1.445	0.809	0.990	0.305	4.059	1.239	0.0045	−0.0571
1952	0.578	1.545	0.894	0.989	0.323	4.192	1.352	0.0047	−0.0600
1953	0.587	1.628	0.955	0.987	0.347	4.136	1.433	0.0051	−0.0725
1954	0.588	1.840	1.082	0.986	0.368	4.279	1.577	0.0046	−0.0700
1955	0.601	2.251	1.354	0.985	0.383	4.930	1.891	0.0044	−0.0061
1956	0.629	2.270	1.426	0.984	0.419	4.791	2.008	0.0045	−0.0323
1957	0.647	2.483	1.607	0.982	0.477	4.699	2.242	0.0045	−0.0753
1958	0.653	2.513	1.642	0.981	0.483	4.634	2.237	0.0049	−0.0095
1959	0.652	2.673	1.743	0.979	0.494	4.822	2.381	0.0000	−0.0104
1960	0.670	2.959	1.982	0.980	0.544	4.917	2.676	0.0000	−0.0724
1961	0.674	3.835	2.586	0.981	0.593	5.605	3.321	0.0000	−0.0753
1962	0.685	4.206	2.882	0.982	0.596	6.122	3.650	0.0000	0.0138
1963	0.702	4.311	3.027	0.975	0.629	6.100	3.838	0.0003	−0.0259
1964	0.712	3.612	2.570	0.977	0.656	5.239	3.438	0.0000	−0.0224
1965	0.723	4.308	3.116	0.978	0.744	5.473	4.072	0.0002	−0.0962
1966	0.747	4.980	3.722	0.988	0.757	6.345	4.800	0.0002	0.0094
1967	0.765	5.531	4.229	0.998	0.903	6.072	5.485	0.0002	−0.1387
1968	0.800	6.003	4.801	0.998	0.822	7.339	6.035	0.0003	0.1143
1969	0.846	7.274	6.152	0.999	0.963	7.750	7.462	0.0005	−0.1055
1970	0.893	6.071	5.421	1.000	0.978	7.033	6.876	0.0009	0.0478
1971	0.951	7.073	6.726	1.000	1.058	7.756	8.208	0.0011	−0.0240
1972	1.000	7.465	7.465	1.000	1.000	9.089	9.089	0.0014	0.1199
1973	1.064	8.240	8.764	1.000	1.108	9.556	10.590	0.0013	−0.0460
1974	1.199	8.078	9.685	0.997	1.151	10.528	12.113	0.0013	0.0952
1975	1.313	7.902	10.377	0.996	1.470	8.850	13.011	0.0015	−0.1549
1976	1.388	8.495	11.787	0.994	1.612	9.223	14.865	0.0015	−0.0250
1977	1.491	8.869	13.224	0.991	1.848	9.244	17.088	0.0015	−0.0485
1978	1.622	9.715	15.753	0.988	2.096	9.706	20.339	0.0014	−0.0473
1979	1.799	9.948	17.894	0.985	2.418	9.606	23.229	0.0014	−0.0399

Table D.36. Telephone and telegraph and miscellaneous communication services

Year	Intermediate input				Output			Tax rate	Rate of productivity growth
	Price	Quantity	Outlay	Quality	Price	Quantity	Revenue		
1948	0.513	1.925	0.988	0.992	0.638	6.112	3.925	0.1407	
1949	0.521	1.943	1.012	0.992	0.661	6.362	4.233	0.1356	0.0221
1950	0.534	1.968	1.051	0.990	0.692	6.573	4.579	0.1466	0.0248
1951	0.572	2.164	1.239	0.986	0.716	7.222	5.202	0.1381	0.0361
1952	0.588	2.209	1.299	0.987	0.734	7.650	5.652	0.1445	0.0201
1953	0.602	2.435	1.465	0.987	0.757	8.302	6.321	0.1457	0.0006
1954	0.607	2.576	1.563	0.985	0.787	8.505	6.738	0.1034	−0.0169
1955	0.621	2.754	1.710	0.985	0.797	9.273	7.438	0.0863	0.0249
1956	0.647	2.778	1.796	0.983	0.805	9.861	7.989	0.0915	0.0038
1957	0.668	2.735	1.828	0.980	0.819	10.403	8.571	0.0911	0.0159
1958	0.682	2.900	1.977	0.974	0.835	10.855	9.123	0.0936	0.0169
1959	0.686	3.190	2.188	0.973	0.864	11.678	10.150	0.0918	0.0235
1960	0.705	3.358	2.368	0.976	0.870	12.356	10.814	0.0931	0.0014
1961	0.711	3.414	2.428	0.978	0.880	12.923	11.444	0.0941	0.0239
1962	0.716	3.721	2.665	0.986	0.886	13.886	12.384	0.0901	0.0204
1963	0.730	3.949	2.883	0.985	0.903	14.880	13.526	0.0890	0.0254
1964	0.739	4.101	3.030	0.986	0.914	15.860	14.584	0.0874	0.0233
1965	0.750	4.400	3.301	0.985	0.912	17.226	15.817	0.0817	0.0344
1966	0.773	4.680	3.617	0.985	0.918	18.824	17.396	0.0676	0.0295
1967	0.786	4.849	3.813	0.996	0.912	20.227	18.571	0.0878	0.0287
1968	0.820	4.908	4.026	0.996	0.920	21.625	20.023	0.0847	0.0318
1969	0.862	5.509	4.749	0.998	0.925	24.181	22.507	0.0885	0.0305
1970	0.906	5.189	4.699	0.998	0.927	26.066	24.305	0.0925	0.0315
1971	0.960	5.117	4.914	0.998	0.960	27.254	26.339	0.0976	0.0216
1972	1.000	5.494	5.494	1.000	1.000	29.878	29.878	0.0991	0.0464
1973	1.059	5.891	6.242	0.999	1.026	32.603	33.396	0.0938	0.0400
1974	1.178	5.693	6.704	0.996	1.064	34.211	36.235	0.0918	0.0370
1975	1.295	5.656	7.327	0.995	1.101	37.147	40.546	0.0878	0.0798
1976	1.373	5.405	7.422	0.994	1.153	39.785	44.754	0.0850	0.0801
1977	1.466	5.407	7.926	0.991	1.174	42.776	48.575	0.0812	0.0575
1978	1.573	6.087	9.578	0.990	1.197	47.755	55.407	0.0733	0.0520
1979	1.735	5.788	10.042	0.986	1.222	51.551	61.190	0.0664	0.0322

Table D.37. Radio and television broadcasting

| Year | Intermediate input | | | | Output | | | | |
	Price	Quantity	Outlay	Quality	Price	Quantity	Revenue	Tax rate	Rate of productivity growth
1948	0.415	0.606	0.251	1.009	0.437	1.299	0.521	0.0014	
1949	0.426	0.682	0.291	1.007	0.457	1.380	0.579	0.0000	−0.0433
1950	0.438	0.693	0.304	1.003	0.481	1.476	0.652	0.0000	0.0298
1951	0.465	0.713	0.332	1.001	0.471	1.752	0.757	0.0013	0.1267
1952	0.483	0.788	0.381	1.000	0.490	1.897	0.852	0.0004	0.0120
1953	0.500	0.914	0.458	0.999	0.468	2.290	0.982	0.0003	0.0996
1954	0.513	0.851	0.437	0.999	0.490	2.308	1.037	0.0002	0.0019
1955	0.527	0.840	0.442	0.999	0.504	2.509	1.159	0.0001	0.0437
1956	0.548	0.933	0.512	0.998	0.539	2.598	1.285	0.0000	−0.0356
1957	0.567	1.042	0.591	0.997	0.518	2.979	1.415	0.0007	0.0785
1958	0.579	1.186	0.687	0.995	0.530	3.187	1.550	0.0006	−0.0011
1959	0.588	1.022	0.602	0.995	0.580	2.903	1.545	0.0058	−0.0512
1960	0.608	1.097	0.667	0.996	0.579	3.217	1.708	0.0059	0.0443
1961	0.618	1.167	0.722	0.997	0.557	3.411	1.744	0.0069	0.0031
1962	0.630	1.004	0.633	0.990	0.612	3.175	1.784	0.0073	−0.0264
1963	0.673	0.688	0.463	0.982	0.688	2.683	1.695	0.0083	−0.0671
1964	0.693	0.560	0.388	0.981	0.722	2.476	1.641	0.0085	−0.0926
1965	0.713	0.421	0.300	0.981	0.776	2.365	1.684	0.0095	−0.0279
1966	0.736	0.339	0.249	0.981	0.811	2.394	1.780	0.0118	−0.0322
1967	0.759	0.262	0.199	0.998	0.836	2.278	1.747	0.0109	−0.0977
1968	0.797	0.047	0.038	0.999	0.926	2.073	1.762	0.0108	−0.0477
1969	0.834	0.183	0.153	0.999	0.877	2.508	2.017	0.0124	0.0632
1970	0.877	0.031	0.027	1.000	0.932	2.325	1.989	0.0141	−0.0336
1971	0.926	0.030	0.028	1.000	0.915	2.511	2.108	0.0171	0.0603
1972	1.000	0.031	0.031	1.000	1.000	2.484	2.484	0.0177	−0.0554
1973	1.056	0.033	0.035	1.000	1.053	2.389	2.591	0.0181	−0.0917
1974	1.141	0.033	0.038	0.999	1.114	2.223	2.698	0.0208	−0.1202
1975	1.249	0.033	0.041	0.998	1.163	2.366	3.191	0.0207	0.0224
1976	1.330	0.031	0.042	0.997	1.402	1.901	3.934	0.0196	−0.2676
1977	1.419	0.031	0.044	0.995	1.592	1.860	4.810	0.0183	−0.0558
1978	1.513	0.036	0.054	0.993	1.753	1.952	5.388	0.0186	−0.0112
1979	1.654	0.034	0.056	0.990	1.929	1.956	5.785	0.0197	−0.0638

Table D.38. Electric utilities

Year	Intermediate input				Output			Tax rate	Rate of productivity growth
	Price	Quantity	Outlay	Quality	Price	Quantity	Revenue	Tax rate	Rate of productivity growth
1948	0.472	3.881	1.833	0.963	0.786	5.811	4.570	0.0205	
1949	0.489	3.820	1.866	0.967	0.797	6.150	4.899	0.0129	0.0102
1950	0.495	3.992	1.977	0.971	0.792	6.715	5.317	0.0223	0.0175
1951	0.522	4.047	2.111	0.971	0.808	7.297	5.896	0.0136	0.0269
1952	0.540	4.192	2.265	0.975	0.816	7.841	6.397	0.0123	0.0224
1953	0.562	4.457	2.504	0.976	0.821	8.515	6.987	0.0118	0.0076
1954	0.570	4.324	2.467	0.979	0.822	9.046	7.437	0.0119	0.0186
1955	0.590	4.704	2.777	0.983	0.830	9.842	8.168	0.0106	0.0168
1956	0.613	4.971	3.046	0.983	0.837	10.548	8.828	0.0115	0.0199
1957	0.637	5.260	3.351	0.982	0.845	11.144	9.419	0.0117	0.0125
1958	0.655	5.297	3.471	0.987	0.848	11.616	9.848	0.0169	0.0122
1959	0.672	5.544	3.723	0.991	0.850	12.592	10.698	0.0195	0.0453
1960	0.689	5.540	3.818	0.993	0.862	13.232	11.412	0.0202	0.0327
1961	0.701	5.867	4.112	0.996	0.862	14.020	12.083	0.0208	0.0257
1962	0.709	7.127	5.056	0.994	0.865	15.580	13.474	0.0196	0.0243
1963	0.732	7.475	5.471	0.986	0.861	16.596	14.290	0.0193	0.0341
1964	0.739	7.720	5.703	0.989	0.856	17.648	15.114	0.0199	0.0344
1965	0.714	8.554	6.106	0.985	0.852	18.784	15.997	0.0208	0.0037
1966	0.760	8.780	6.672	0.987	0.846	20.264	17.142	0.0228	0.0487
1967	0.773	9.364	7.239	0.990	0.852	21.393	18.228	0.0203	0.0013
1968	0.795	9.924	7.887	0.991	0.856	23.034	19.714	0.0242	0.0196
1969	0.830	10.394	8.625	0.992	0.861	24.805	21.359	0.0289	0.0190
1970	0.889	11.166	9.929	0.992	0.883	26.545	23.434	0.0330	−0.0006
1971	0.962	11.667	11.226	0.992	0.947	27.884	26.405	0.0354	−0.0139
1972	1.000	13.133	13.133	1.000	1.000	29.794	29.794	0.0386	−0.0298
1973	1.080	14.219	15.356	0.998	1.037	32.184	33.384	0.0383	−0.0087
1974	1.368	17.232	23.577	0.976	1.300	32.316	42.012	0.0354	−0.1311
1975	1.560	17.917	27.943	0.965	1.513	33.720	51.006	0.0341	0.0010
1976	1.696	19.580	33.201	0.953	1.622	36.085	58.516	0.0350	0.0101
1977	1.890	21.320	40.300	0.942	1.786	38.518	68.807	0.0338	0.0024
1978	2.038	22.391	45.622	0.938	1.924	40.282	77.493	0.0339	−0.0117
1979	2.276	21.014	47.836	0.932	2.017	40.659	82.024	0.0354	0.0125

Table D.39. Gas utilities

Year	Intermediate input				Output			Tax rate	Rate of productivity growth
	Price	Quantity	Outlay	Quality	Price	Quantity	Revenue		
1948	0.546	2.688	1.468	0.955	0.557	4.537	2.528	0.0143	
1949	0.556	2.601	1.446	0.959	0.564	4.902	2.765	0.0100	0.0697
1950	0.560	3.427	1.918	0.966	0.558	5.889	3.288	0.0148	0.0016
1951	0.582	3.746	2.181	0.968	0.573	6.755	3.874	0.0093	0.0417
1952	0.604	4.320	2.611	0.972	0.604	7.416	4.476	0.0079	−0.0242
1953	0.629	5.106	3.212	0.974	0.637	8.261	5.264	0.0072	−0.0154
1954	0.648	5.340	3.459	0.978	0.665	8.652	5.754	0.0071	−0.0007
1955	0.668	6.084	4.063	0.982	0.692	9.469	6.553	0.0061	−0.0023
1956	0.686	6.676	4.581	0.983	0.707	10.367	7.327	0.0066	0.0170
1957	0.708	7.150	5.065	0.984	0.721	11.131	8.026	0.0067	0.0117
1958	0.730	7.765	5.670	0.987	0.751	11.802	8.868	0.0094	−0.0100
1959	0.744	8.609	6.408	0.990	0.773	12.837	9.922	0.0106	0.0081
1960	0.772	9.541	7.368	0.993	0.815	13.729	11.195	0.0104	−0.0114
1961	0.790	10.004	7.905	0.996	0.841	14.210	11.957	0.0107	−0.0064
1962	0.797	10.915	8.696	0.994	0.846	15.274	12.919	0.0103	0.0056
1963	0.796	11.354	9.035	1.000	0.845	15.930	13.458	0.0103	0.0081
1964	0.788	12.345	9.723	1.000	0.828	17.273	14.296	0.0102	0.0169
1965	0.785	12.940	10.160	1.001	0.824	18.052	14.879	0.0107	−0.0009
1966	0.794	13.552	10.763	1.002	0.817	19.282	15.758	0.0118	0.0252
1967	0.793	14.242	11.299	1.015	0.815	20.353	16.590	0.0107	0.0067
1968	0.801	14.956	11.980	1.016	0.811	21.852	17.726	0.0131	0.0266
1969	0.825	15.875	13.094	1.016	0.822	23.273	19.142	0.0153	0.0071
1970	0.864	17.174	14.834	1.016	0.859	24.452	21.015	0.0168	−0.0158
1971	0.930	17.394	16.180	1.016	0.930	24.863	23.127	0.0185	−0.0012
1972	1.000	17.598	17.598	1.000	1.000	25.224	25.224	0.0209	0.0015
1973	1.083	16.616	17.991	0.999	1.072	24.469	26.243	0.0223	0.0026
1974	1.343	16.728	22.471	0.988	1.296	23.858	30.909	0.0220	−0.0331
1975	1.632	17.223	28.107	0.984	1.674	23.103	38.663	0.0206	−0.0520
1976	1.914	19.032	36.436	0.975	2.075	23.147	48.023	0.0195	−0.0713
1977	2.294	19.332	44.356	0.952	2.540	22.600	57.404	0.0185	−0.0365
1978	2.513	20.143	50.624	0.950	2.799	23.301	65.212	0.0184	−0.0070
1979	2.763	19.337	53.422	0.946	2.936	23.525	69.071	0.0192	0.0351

Table D.40.   Water supply and sanitary services

| Year | Intermediate input | | | | Output | | | Tax rate | Rate of productivity growth |
	Price	Quantity	Outlay	Quality	Price	Quantity	Revenue		
1948	0.565	0.268	0.151	0.923	0.400	1.157	0.463	0.0230	
1949	0.575	0.251	0.144	0.928	0.416	1.248	0.519	0.0151	0.0937
1950	0.579	0.250	0.145	0.934	0.417	1.204	0.502	0.0253	−0.0313
1951	0.602	0.253	0.152	0.936	0.424	1.362	0.577	0.0156	0.1173
1952	0.625	0.267	0.167	0.940	0.433	1.466	0.634	0.0140	0.0609
1953	0.651	0.278	0.181	0.942	0.441	1.567	0.691	0.0136	0.0518
1954	0.670	0.237	0.159	0.946	0.465	1.570	0.729	0.0139	0.0372
1955	0.691	0.269	0.186	0.949	0.504	1.644	0.828	0.0125	0.0115
1956	0.710	0.300	0.213	0.951	0.521	1.703	0.887	0.0134	−0.0037
1957	0.732	0.279	0.204	0.952	0.560	1.717	0.962	0.0143	0.0049
1958	0.755	0.260	0.196	0.955	0.586	1.723	1.010	0.0210	0.0044
1959	0.770	0.314	0.242	0.957	0.608	1.912	1.162	0.0237	0.0673
1960	0.798	0.254	0.203	0.961	0.627	1.965	1.231	0.0253	0.0683
1961	0.817	0.195	0.160	0.964	0.641	1.954	1.253	0.0275	0.0311
1962	0.824	0.271	0.223	0.961	0.658	2.090	1.375	0.0263	0.0162
1963	0.816	0.277	0.226	0.975	0.683	2.137	1.460	0.0264	0.0132
1964	0.807	0.314	0.253	0.976	0.689	2.312	1.593	0.0269	0.0561
1965	0.805	0.252	0.203	0.977	0.706	2.303	1.625	0.0295	0.0189
1966	0.814	0.312	0.254	0.978	0.728	2.470	1.797	0.0320	0.0280
1967	0.816	0.144	0.118	0.987	0.746	2.357	1.758	0.0315	0.0242
1968	0.824	0.190	0.157	0.987	0.776	2.544	1.975	0.0372	0.0391
1969	0.848	0.109	0.092	0.987	0.822	2.545	2.091	0.0463	0.0156
1970	0.889	0.194	0.172	0.987	0.879	2.654	2.333	0.0530	−0.0263
1971	0.957	0.122	0.117	0.988	0.969	2.626	2.545	0.0587	0.0019
1972	1.000	0.150	0.150	1.000	1.000	2.815	2.815	0.0654	0.0683
1973	1.083	0.201	0.218	0.999	1.055	2.941	3.102	0.0660	0.0127
1974	1.343	0.341	0.458	0.988	1.113	3.060	3.407	0.0698	−0.0071
1975	1.632	0.330	0.538	0.984	1.322	3.199	4.227	0.0658	0.0593
1976	1.914	0.257	0.492	0.975	1.462	3.106	4.542	0.0722	0.0095
1977	2.294	0.150	0.344	0.952	1.598	3.069	4.905	0.0758	0.0425
1978	2.513	0.126	0.316	0.950	1.708	3.171	5.415	0.0776	0.0411
1979	2.763	0.091	0.251	0.946	1.787	3.202	5.720	0.0812	0.0404

Table D.41. Wholesale trade

	Intermediate input				Output				
Year	Price	Quantity	Outlay	Quality	Price	Quantity	Revenue	Tax rate	Rate of productivity growth
1948	0.498	7.213	3.590	0.970	0.704	26.877	18.932	0.1545	
1949	0.510	6.588	3.357	0.972	0.677	26.393	17.874	0.1692	0.0007
1950	0.520	7.492	3.898	0.973	0.699	28.824	20.138	0.1737	0.0619
1951	0.558	8.141	4.544	0.969	0.764	30.223	23.100	0.1632	−0.0243
1952	0.574	7.979	4.584	0.973	0.752	30.750	23.136	0.1739	−0.0009
1953	0.592	7.921	4.689	0.975	0.747	31.378	23.445	0.1821	0.0106
1954	0.602	7.782	4.683	0.976	0.749	31.411	23.521	0.1886	0.0109
1955	0.616	8.633	5.319	0.977	0.762	35.126	26.749	0.1828	0.0732
1956	0.639	9.140	5.844	0.978	0.788	36.903	29.075	0.1877	0.0024
1957	0.660	9.126	6.019	0.978	0.812	37.449	30.412	0.1882	0.0056
1958	0.675	8.870	5.986	0.979	0.814	37.714	30.689	0.1954	0.0146
1959	0.680	10.068	6.847	0.978	0.813	41.544	33.768	0.2012	0.0492
1960	0.704	9.996	7.033	0.980	0.812	42.587	34.560	0.2107	−0.0164
1961	0.712	10.298	7.332	0.980	0.806	35.550	35.550	0.2145	0.0252
1962	0.723	10.632	7.682	0.989	0.805	46.699	37.614	0.2197	0.0313
1963	0.737	11.099	8.177	0.997	0.805	48.836	39.325	0.2201	0.0243
1964	0.747	11.614	8.678	0.998	0.819	51.685	42.351	0.2198	0.0203
1965	0.764	12.216	9.337	0.997	0.818	55.565	45.428	0.2270	0.0334
1966	0.791	12.992	10.275	0.996	0.841	59.260	49.837	0.2261	0.0095
1967	0.816	13.163	10.739	0.995	0.850	61.893	52.587	0.2265	0.0137
1968	0.847	14.250	12.073	0.997	0.871	66.878	58.274	0.2323	0.0395
1969	0.882	15.072	13.293	0.998	0.907	70.066	63.583	0.2275	0.0062
1970	0.914	16.148	14.763	0.999	0.932	72.496	67.578	0.2303	−0.0051
1971	0.960	15.759	15.124	1.000	0.947	76.460	72.401	0.2355	0.0382
1972	1.000	17.752	17.752	1.000	1.000	83.306	83.306	0.2174	0.0450
1973	1.063	19.675	20.905	0.999	1.101	87.223	96.022	0.2043	−0.0091
1974	1.192	20.264	24.152	0.994	1.305	85.715	111.829	0.1823	−0.0413
1975	1.318	17.371	22.893	0.991	1.372	85.303	117.037	0.1979	0.0144
1976	1.401	20.065	28.103	0.989	1.447	90.461	130.856	0.1766	0.0137
1977	1.500	17.586	26.372	0.986	1.500	93.106	139.648	0.1786	0.0281
1978	1.608	19.276	31.003	0.985	1.572	98.740	155.232	0.1787	−0.0063
1979	1.773	18.899	33.511	0.980	1.741	100.466	174.940	0.1641	−0.0195

Table D.42. Retail trade

Year	Intermediate input				Output			Tax rate	Rate of productivity growth
	Price	Quantity	Outlay	Quality	Price	Quantity	Revenue		
1948	0.457	40.009	18.290	0.988	0.583	79.625	46.446	0.0429	
1949	0.470	38.510	18.105	0.988	0.575	81.077	46.631	0.0410	0.0212
1950	0.480	38.164	18.324	0.989	0.550	86.789	47.725	0.0463	0.0681
1951	0.512	38.240	19.588	0.986	0.594	86.256	51.245	0.0471	−0.0356
1952	0.532	39.182	20.863	0.987	0.606	89.158	54.045	0.0512	0.0196
1953	0.553	38.117	21.082	0.988	0.601	91.348	54.854	0.0543	0.0378
1954	0.565	38.436	21.698	0.988	0.612	92.227	56.470	0.0497	0.0086
1955	0.582	39.855	23.212	0.988	0.604	99.514	60.078	0.0510	0.0499
1956	0.604	40.147	24.266	0.988	0.618	101.321	62.567	0.0553	−0.0041
1957	0.624	40.428	25.235	0.987	0.635	102.745	65.211	0.0592	0.0083
1958	0.639	40.058	25.610	0.988	0.648	102.031	66.146	0.0604	−0.0002
1959	0.635	43.652	27.713	0.987	0.665	107.778	71.692	0.0594	0.0138
1960	0.672	42.625	28.661	0.989	0.674	108.893	73.412	0.0638	−0.0047
1961	0.682	42.302	28.830	0.989	0.686	108.378	74.309	0.0685	0.0132
1962	0.697	44.391	30.954	0.993	0.691	114.726	79.329	0.0704	0.0288
1963	0.716	45.328	32.462	0.998	0.701	118.166	82.838	0.0725	0.0139
1964	0.727	49.005	35.626	0.999	0.719	126.205	90.694	0.0741	0.0179
1965	0.738	51.534	38.027	0.999	0.729	133.070	97.017	0.0742	0.0176
1966	0.765	52.772	40.352	0.999	0.748	138.409	103.465	0.0746	0.0124
1967	0.790	55.397	43.764	0.999	0.793	140.825	111.629	0.0772	−0.0064
1968	0.824	58.781	48.425	0.999	0.831	147.792	122.754	0.0848	0.0150
1969	0.864	60.820	52.567	1.000	0.889	149.620	132.948	0.0900	−0.0187
1970	0.901	62.934	56.712	1.000	0.935	151.620	141.776	0.0938	−0.0192
1971	0.956	64.091	61.251	1.000	0.986	155.867	153.636	0.0969	0.0146
1972	1.000	66.578	66.578	1.000	1.000	165.809	165.809	0.1016	0.0369
1973	1.057	67.465	71.283	0.999	1.042	172.400	179.617	0.1044	0.0151
1974	1.172	63.207	74.053	0.995	1.137	164.004	186.414	0.1130	−0.0271
1975	1.294	71.307	92.260	0.992	1.282	170.462	218.598	0.1033	−0.0139
1976	1.384	70.467	97.521	0.988	1.345	176.746	237.643	0.1070	0.0292
1977	1.485	74.796	111.064	0.984	1.423	187.309	266.545	0.1080	0.0186
1978	1.585	80.132	127.048	0.983	1.535	194.044	297.851	0.1092	−0.0141
1979	1.741	81.301	141.536	0.979	1.658	197.477	327.323	0.1102	0.0015

Table D.43. Finance, insurance, and real estate

Year	Intermediate input				Output			Tax rate	Rate of productivity growth
	Price	Quantity	Outlay	Quality	Price	Quantity	Revenue		
1948	0.505	26.942	13.614	0.993	0.435	72.565	31.556	0.0079	
1949	0.504	28.690	14.471	1.000	0.448	73.936	33.127	0.0170	−0.0078
1950	0.515	30.859	15.904	0.998	0.463	79.971	36.991	0.0098	0.0403
1951	0.557	34.234	19.063	0.989	0.485	85.610	41.521	0.0170	0.0065
1952	0.573	38.111	21.827	0.990	0.514	89.988	46.252	0.0089	−0.0126
1953	0.582	38.501	22.413	0.993	0.543	90.096	48.931	0.0091	−0.0149
1954	0.585	46.984	27.484	0.993	0.550	101.419	55.809	0.0101	0.0091
1955	0.597	51.006	30.449	0.993	0.570	106.758	60.810	0.0091	0.0029
1956	0.617	53.294	32.859	0.993	0.588	110.475	64.968	0.0091	0.0035
1957	0.636	56.085	35.653	0.991	0.607	115.120	69.891	0.0088	0.0093
1958	0.648	59.733	38.682	0.990	0.614	122.195	74.982	0.0189	0.0208
1959	0.636	61.286	38.948	0.989	0.572	136.333	77.932	0.0201	0.0880
1960	0.668	71.576	47.846	0.992	0.643	137.905	88.636	0.0186	−0.0857
1961	0.674	82.283	55.479	0.993	0.648	151.256	97.981	0.0187	0.0098
1962	0.690	84.103	58.015	0.993	0.673	153.307	103.188	0.0185	−0.0108
1963	0.705	93.509	65.931	0.992	0.698	162.546	113.406	0.0183	−0.0133
1964	0.714	92.932	66.327	0.994	0.707	165.196	116.862	0.0202	0.0056
1965	0.727	100.977	73.460	0.995	0.718	178.737	128.389	0.0187	0.0165
1966	0.757	106.594	80.698	0.996	0.753	186.617	140.540	0.0173	−0.0007
1967	0.781	109.481	85.475	0.998	0.783	191.502	149.933	0.0179	0.0007
1968	0.816	119.488	97.507	0.998	0.819	205.169	168.054	0.0185	0.0046
1969	0.861	129.439	111.390	0.999	0.866	216.016	186.974	0.0178	−0.0072
1970	0.900	138.987	125.050	1.000	0.899	228.355	205.330	0.0168	0.0015
1971	0.952	153.581	146.224	1.000	0.948	247.663	234.753	0.0175	0.0090
1972	1.000	165.871	165.871	1.000	1.000	262.313	262.313	0.0166	0.0013
1973	1.067	170.307	181.660	0.999	1.042	273.484	284.967	0.0171	0.0041
1974	1.178	164.378	193.589	0.996	1.115	272.846	304.296	0.0178	0.0089
1975	1.281	171.960	220.289	0.995	1.209	278.298	336.386	0.0175	−0.0139
1976	1.347	176.638	237.864	0.994	1.256	292.081	366.852	0.0178	0.0265
1977	1.435	181.411	260.256	0.993	1.335	307.859	410.930	0.0182	0.0240
1978	1.547	188.981	292.379	0.992	1.423	324.053	461.083	0.0192	0.0064
1979	1.710	193.496	330.803	0.988	1.550	334.545	518.693	0.0200	0.0034

Table D.44. Services, excluding private households, institutions

Year	Intermediate input				Output			Tax rate	Rate of productivity growth
	Price	Quantity	Outlay	Quality	Price	Quantity	Revenue		
1948	0.511	52.278	26.723	0.966	0.381	115.582	43.587	0.0137	
1949	0.522	54.173	28.268	0.971	0.393	118.647	45.584	0.0131	0.0016
1950	0.533	56.465	30.083	0.973	0.405	122.588	48.410	0.0117	0.0018
1951	0.568	57.164	32.481	0.971	0.433	124.008	52.261	0.0112	−0.0053
1952	0.586	59.428	34.840	0.976	0.453	127.190	55.933	0.0106	−0.0113
1953	0.597	62.219	37.168	0.978	0.473	130.052	59.659	0.0101	−0.0115
1954	0.604	64.066	38.681	0.980	0.493	130.165	62.379	0.0074	−0.0266
1955	0.619	67.423	41.722	0.982	0.511	135.519	68.040	0.0066	0.0031
1956	0.643	72.147	46.384	0.984	0.536	143.848	75.190	0.0061	−0.0030
1957	0.663	76.202	50.511	0.983	0.557	150.702	81.720	0.0056	−0.0024
1958	0.676	78.465	53.049	0.984	0.569	154.784	85.818	0.0060	−0.0019
1959	0.684	85.301	58.307	0.985	0.589	164.293	94.427	0.0067	−0.0040
1960	0.704	86.155	60.647	0.986	0.603	166.808	98.771	0.0069	−0.0123
1961	0.709	91.547	64.874	0.986	0.619	173.936	105.593	0.0069	−0.0050
1962	0.723	95.541	69.037	0.988	0.636	180.121	112.814	0.0069	−0.0113
1963	0.743	100.015	74.279	0.987	0.652	189.014	121.385	0.0071	−0.0005
1964	0.755	109.298	82.471	0.987	0.676	202.381	134.098	0.0070	−0.0039
1965	0.769	115.887	89.116	0.987	0.701	210.922	145.371	0.0072	−0.0105
1966	0.794	123.325	97.867	0.988	0.728	223.292	160.477	0.0059	−0.0032
1967	0.811	131.061	106.247	0.999	0.761	231.891	175.298	0.0057	−0.0198
1968	0.844	136.659	115.382	0.999	0.803	238.767	191.065	0.0061	−0.0127
1969	0.876	148.620	130.231	1.000	0.852	253.678	214.923	0.0064	−0.0195
1970	0.918	157.075	144.144	1.000	0.904	264.658	236.858	0.0065	−0.0101
1971	0.961	160.623	154.303	1.000	0.963	265.979	254.599	0.0068	−0.0160
1972	1.000	168.975	168.975	1.000	1.000	280.435	280.435	0.0068	0.0073
1973	1.052	183.472	192.953	0.999	1.065	300.543	318.397	0.0069	−0.0008
1974	1.172	181.585	212.849	0.997	1.147	307.950	350.384	0.0072	0.0163
1975	1.297	183.104	237.469	0.995	1.261	312.562	391.073	0.0071	0.0035
1976	1.385	190.463	263.834	0.994	1.349	324.513	436.186	0.0073	0.0050
1977	1.479	201.502	298.037	0.992	1.449	341.359	492.688	0.0071	0.0024
1978	1.576	216.805	341.607	0.992	1.554	364.849	561.528	0.0069	0.0059
1979	1.731	222.895	385.932	0.989	1.723	371.715	638.084	0.0067	−0.0158

Table D.45. Private households

Year	Intermediate input				Output			Tax rate	Rate of productivity growth
	Price	Quantity	Outlay	Quality	Price	Quantity	Revenue		
1948	0.000	0.000	0.000	0.000	0.484	61.461	29.747	0.0000	
1949	0.000	0.000	0.000	0.000	0.473	66.887	31.670	0.0000	0.0000
1950	0.000	0.000	0.000	0.000	0.508	73.108	37.113	0.0000	0.0000
1951	0.000	0.000	0.000	0.000	0.533	80.748	43.074	0.0000	0.0000
1952	0.000	0.000	0.000	0.000	0.579	85.067	49.251	0.0000	0.0000
1953	0.000	0.000	0.000	0.000	0.560	88.619	49.651	0.0000	0.0000
1954	0.000	0.000	0.000	0.000	0.632	92.926	58.773	0.0000	0.0000
1955	0.000	0.000	0.000	0.000	0.615	97.998	60.273	0.0000	0.0000
1956	0.000	0.000	0.000	0.000	0.615	105.318	64.807	0.0000	0.0000
1957	0.000	0.000	0.000	0.000	0.568	110.291	62.597	0.0000	0.0000
1958	0.000	0.000	0.000	0.000	0.634	114.670	72.720	0.0000	0.0000
1959	0.000	0.000	0.000	0.000	0.617	117.423	72.464	0.0000	0.0000
1960	0.000	0.000	0.000	0.000	0.667	122.467	81.684	0.0000	0.0000
1961	0.000	0.000	0.000	0.000	0.671	126.348	84.787	0.0000	0.0000
1962	0.000	0.000	0.000	0.000	0.681	129.433	88.161	0.0000	0.0000
1963	0.000	0.000	0.000	0.000	0.673	134.030	90.236	0.0000	0.0000
1964	0.000	0.000	0.000	0.000	0.710	139.775	99.192	0.0000	0.0000
1965	0.000	0.000	0.000	0.000	0.765	146.315	111.892	0.0000	0.0000
1966	0.000	0.000	0.000	0.000	0.785	154.306	121.141	0.0000	0.0000
1967	0.000	0.000	0.000	0.000	0.767	162.530	124.691	0.0000	0.0000
1968	0.000	0.000	0.000	0.000	0.797	169.524	135.139	0.0000	0.0000
1969	0.000	0.000	0.000	0.000	0.836	178.288	148.993	0.0000	0.0000
1970	0.000	0.000	0.000	0.000	0.869	186.953	162.383	0.0000	0.0000
1971	0.000	0.000	0.000	0.000	0.895	193.300	172.910	0.0000	0.0000
1972	0.000	0.000	0.000	0.000	1.000	203.068	203.068	0.0000	0.0000
1973	0.000	0.000	0.000	0.000	1.088	216.059	234.998	0.0000	0.0000
1974	0.000	0.000	0.000	0.000	1.038	229.280	237.936	0.0000	0.0000
1975	0.000	0.000	0.000	0.000	1.005	237.036	238.120	0.0000	0.0000
1976	0.000	0.000	0.000	0.000	1.125	244.103	274.674	0.0000	0.0000
1977	0.000	0.000	0.000	0.000	1.336	255.017	340.711	0.0000	0.0000
1978	0.000	0.000	0.000	0.000	1.446	268.151	387.638	0.0000	0.0000
1979	0.000	0.000	0.000	0.000	1.502	281.633	423.066	0.0000	0.0000

Table D.46. Institutions

Year	Intermediate input				Output			Tax rate	Rate of productivity growth
	Price	Quantity	Outlay	Quality	Price	Quantity	Revenue		
1948	0.458	1.520	0.697	0.990	0.261	12.058	3.147	0.0000	
1949	0.472	1.457	0.687	0.989	0.314	12.539	3.938	0.0000	0.0064
1950	0.483	1.465	0.708	0.988	0.316	12.739	4.029	0.0000	−0.0228
1951	0.513	1.690	0.867	0.985	0.289	13.584	3.925	0.0000	−0.0037
1952	0.535	1.698	0.908	0.985	0.377	14.012	5.285	0.0000	−0.0038
1953	0.556	1.899	1.056	0.985	0.370	14.545	5.380	0.0000	−0.0144
1954	0.567	1.736	0.984	0.985	0.427	14.782	6.310	0.0000	0.0039
1955	0.584	1.979	1.156	0.985	0.425	15.444	6.563	0.0000	−0.0156
1956	0.606	2.273	1.378	0.984	0.356	16.068	5.726	0.0000	−0.0218
1957	0.627	1.997	1.251	0.983	0.385	16.591	6.392	0.0000	0.0269
1958	0.640	2.308	1.477	0.982	0.508	17.073	8.673	0.0000	−0.0357
1959	0.635	3.552	2.256	0.980	0.528	18.145	9.579	0.0000	−0.0860
1960	0.671	2.173	1.458	0.981	0.561	18.443	10.347	0.0000	0.0429
1961	0.681	2.594	1.767	0.981	0.585	19.045	11.141	0.0000	−0.0390
1962	0.690	3.175	2.192	0.997	0.613	19.751	12.107	0.0000	−0.0504
1963	0.712	4.249	3.023	0.999	0.620	20.712	12.841	0.0000	−0.0420
1964	0.722	3.908	2.822	0.999	0.654	21.173	13.847	0.0000	0.0065
1965	0.734	3.973	2.918	0.999	0.676	22.268	15.053	0.0000	0.0093
1966	0.758	4.850	3.678	0.999	0.726	23.365	16.963	0.0000	−0.0374
1967	0.784	5.619	4.408	1.001	0.755	24.967	18.850	0.0000	−0.0053
1968	0.817	4.942	4.036	1.000	0.806	25.358	20.439	0.0000	0.0093
1969	0.855	4.945	4.231	1.001	0.869	26.714	23.215	0.0000	0.0282
1970	0.895	11.394	10.202	1.001	0.893	27.506	24.566	0.0000	−0.1990
1971	0.952	9.572	9.116	1.001	0.969	27.720	26.860	0.0000	0.0662
1972	1.000	7.793	7.793	1.000	1.000	29.338	29.338	0.0000	0.1167
1973	1.059	11.402	12.079	1.000	1.027	31.584	32.437	0.0000	−0.0517
1974	1.178	9.075	10.694	0.996	1.094	32.603	35.671	0.0000	0.1017
1975	1.319	11.471	15.135	0.992	1.242	33.272	41.308	0.0000	−0.0846
1976	1.434	12.523	17.960	0.985	1.343	34.081	45.774	0.0000	−0.0098
1977	1.559	5.813	9.063	0.977	1.423	36.034	51.262	0.0000	0.2711
1978	1.672	9.764	16.321	0.975	1.521	37.558	57.136	0.0000	−0.1001
1979	1.829	11.456	20.958	0.974	1.635	38.336	62.679	0.0000	−0.0491

Table D.47. Federal public administration

	Intermediate input				Output				
Year	Price	Quantity	Outlay	Quality	Price	Quantity	Revenue	Tax rate	Rate of productivity growth
1948	0.000	0.000	0.000	0.000	0.270	17.367	4.681	0.0000	
1949	0.000	0.000	0.000	0.000	0.288	17.619	5.078	0.0000	0.0000
1950	0.000	0.000	0.000	0.000	0.301	17.968	5.401	0.0000	0.0000
1951	0.000	0.000	0.000	0.000	0.318	22.518	7.161	0.0000	0.0000
1952	0.000	0.000	0.000	0.000	0.336	23.950	8.036	0.0000	0.0000
1953	0.000	0.000	0.000	0.000	0.348	22.737	7.905	0.0000	0.0000
1954	0.000	0.000	0.000	0.000	0.348	21.398	7.452	0.0000	0.0000
1955	0.000	0.000	0.000	0.000	0.374	21.625	8.080	0.0000	0.0000
1956	0.000	0.000	0.000	0.000	0.397	22.056	8.766	0.0000	0.0000
1957	0.000	0.000	0.000	0.000	0.415	22.198	9.206	0.0000	0.0000
1958	0.000	0.000	0.000	0.000	0.460	21.865	10.053	0.0000	0.0000
1959	0.000	0.000	0.000	0.000	0.465	22.190	10.314	0.0000	0.0000
1960	0.000	0.000	0.000	0.000	0.490	22.567	11.052	0.0000	0.0000
1961	0.000	0.000	0.000	0.000	0.508	23.226	11.807	0.0000	0.0000
1962	0.000	0.000	0.000	0.000	0.515	24.423	12.588	0.0000	0.0000
1963	0.000	0.000	0.000	0.000	0.542	24.750	13.408	0.0000	0.0000
1964	0.000	0.000	0.000	0.000	0.578	24.753	14.313	0.0000	0.0000
1965	0.000	0.000	0.000	0.000	0.600	25.114	15.076	0.0000	0.0000
1966	0.000	0.000	0.000	0.000	0.621	26.701	16.574	0.0000	0.0000
1967	0.000	0.000	0.000	0.000	0.626	28.737	17.975	0.0000	0.0000
1968	0.000	0.000	0.000	0.000	0.680	29.103	19.783	0.0000	0.0000
1969	0.000	0.000	0.000	0.000	0.732	28.897	21.139	0.0000	0.0000
1970	0.000	0.000	0.000	0.000	0.853	27.394	23.377	0.0000	0.0000
1971	0.000	0.000	0.000	0.000	0.915	27.724	25.366	0.0000	0.0000
1972	0.000	0.000	0.000	0.000	1.000	27.411	27.411	0.0000	0.0000
1973	0.000	0.000	0.000	0.000	1.075	27.006	29.025	0.0000	0.0000
1974	0.000	0.000	0.000	0.000	1.124	28.071	31.544	0.0000	0.0000
1975	0.000	0.000	0.000	0.000	1.234	28.357	34.992	0.0000	0.0000
1976	0.000	0.000	0.000	0.000	1.312	28.944	37.969	0.0000	0.0000
1977	0.000	0.000	0.000	0.000	1.411	29.090	41.036	0.0000	0.0000
1978	0.000	0.000	0.000	0.000	1.520	29.573	44.960	0.0000	0.0000
1979	0.000	0.000	0.000	0.000	1.601	29.712	47.570	0.0000	0.0000

Table D.48. Federal government enterprises

	Intermediate input				Output				
Year	Price	Quantity	Outlay	Quality	Price	Quantity	Revenue	Tax rate	Rate of productivity growth
1948	0.000	0.000	0.000	0.000	0.271	6.186	1.676	0.0000	
1949	0.000	0.000	0.000	0.000	0.283	6.568	1.857	0.0000	0.0000
1950	0.000	0.000	0.000	0.000	0.302	6.407	1.935	0.0000	0.0000
1951	0.000	0.000	0.000	0.000	0.319	6.715	2.140	0.0000	0.0000
1952	0.000	0.000	0.000	0.000	0.335	7.270	2.433	0.0000	0.0000
1953	0.000	0.000	0.000	0.000	0.338	7.124	2.407	0.0083	0.0000
1954	0.000	0.000	0.000	0.000	0.337	7.152	2.410	0.0170	0.0000
1955	0.000	0.000	0.000	0.000	0.363	7.121	2.588	0.0151	0.0000
1956	0.000	0.000	0.000	0.000	0.383	7.165	2.744	0.0138	0.0000
1957	0.000	0.000	0.000	0.000	0.394	7.389	2.914	0.0148	0.0000
1958	0.000	0.000	0.000	0.000	0.430	7.549	3.247	0.0139	0.0000
1959	0.000	0.000	0.000	0.000	0.428	7.809	3.343	0.0132	0.0000
1960	0.000	0.000	0.000	0.000	0.450	8.054	3.627	0.0160	0.0000
1961	0.000	0.000	0.000	0.000	0.473	8.170	3.866	0.0194	0.0000
1962	0.000	0.000	0.000	0.000	0.487	8.319	4.051	0.0249	0.0000
1963	0.000	0.000	0.000	0.000	0.530	8.309	4.401	0.0245	0.0000
1964	0.000	0.000	0.000	0.000	0.559	8.362	4.677	0.0195	0.0000
1965	0.000	0.000	0.000	0.000	0.588	8.517	5.005	0.0170	0.0000
1966	0.000	0.000	0.000	0.000	0.595	9.226	5.490	0.0140	0.0000
1967	0.000	0.000	0.000	0.000	0.609	9.654	5.881	0.0114	0.0000
1968	0.000	0.000	0.000	0.000	0.670	9.780	6.553	0.0090	0.0000
1969	0.000	0.000	0.000	0.000	0.718	9.997	7.177	0.0093	0.0000
1970	0.000	0.000	0.000	0.000	0.824	10.245	8.442	0.0076	0.0000
1971	0.000	0.000	0.000	0.000	0.885	10.061	8.899	0.0079	0.0000
1972	0.000	0.000	0.000	0.000	1.000	9.670	9.670	0.0081	0.0000
1973	0.000	0.000	0.000	0.000	1.086	9.654	10.484	0.0070	0.0000
1974	0.000	0.000	0.000	0.000	1.204	9.808	11.805	0.0058	0.0000
1975	0.000	0.000	0.000	0.000	1.345	9.586	12.895	0.0055	0.0000
1976	0.000	0.000	0.000	0.000	1.473	9.466	13.944	0.0053	0.0000
1977	0.000	0.000	0.000	0.000	1.606	9.225	14.814	0.0056	0.0000
1978	0.000	0.000	0.000	0.000	1.694	9.474	16.052	0.0062	0.0000
1979	0.000	0.000	0.000	0.000	1.842	9.566	17.621	0.0064	0.0000

Table D.49. State and local educational services

	Intermediate input				Output				
Year	Price	Quantity	Outlay	Quality	Price	Quantity	Revenue	Tax rate	Rate of productivity growth
1948	0.000	0.000	0.000	0.000	0.271	13.883	3.766	0.0000	
1949	0.000	0.000	0.000	0.000	0.286	14.621	4.176	0.0000	0.0000
1950	0.000	0.000	0.000	0.000	0.294	15.392	4.527	0.0000	0.0000
1951	0.000	0.000	0.000	0.000	0.316	15.921	5.036	0.0000	0.0000
1952	0.000	0.000	0.000	0.000	0.326	17.115	5.574	0.0000	0.0000
1953	0.000	0.000	0.000	0.000	0.336	18.143	6.096	0.0000	0.0000
1954	0.000	0.000	0.000	0.000	0.354	19.211	6.797	0.0000	0.0000
1955	0.000	0.000	0.000	0.000	0.363	20.366	7.402	0.0000	0.0000
1956	0.000	0.000	0.000	0.000	0.388	21.467	8.320	0.0000	0.0000
1957	0.000	0.000	0.000	0.000	0.409	22.938	9.373	0.0000	0.0000
1958	0.000	0.000	0.000	0.000	0.430	24.355	10.470	0.0000	0.0000
1959	0.000	0.000	0.000	0.000	0.448	25.728	11.514	0.0000	0.0000
1960	0.000	0.000	0.000	0.000	0.469	27.703	12.979	0.0000	0.0000
1961	0.000	0.000	0.000	0.000	0.498	28.746	14.321	0.0000	0.0000
1962	0.000	0.000	0.000	0.000	0.527	29.945	15.784	0.0000	0.0000
1963	0.000	0.000	0.000	0.000	0.552	31.653	17.463	0.0000	0.0000
1964	0.000	0.000	0.000	0.000	0.573	33.788	19.345	0.0000	0.0000
1965	0.000	0.000	0.000	0.000	0.592	35.936	21.285	0.0000	0.0000
1966	0.000	0.000	0.000	0.000	0.635	38.189	24.255	0.0000	0.0000
1967	0.000	0.000	0.000	0.000	0.688	39.776	27.377	0.0000	0.0000
1968	0.000	0.000	0.000	0.000	0.745	41.772	31.126	0.0000	0.0000
1969	0.000	0.000	0.000	0.000	0.807	43.472	35.086	0.0000	0.0000
1970	0.000	0.000	0.000	0.000	0.882	45.206	39.856	0.0000	0.0000
1971	0.000	0.000	0.000	0.000	0.941	46.883	44.138	0.0000	0.0000
1972	0.000	0.000	0.000	0.000	1.000	48.570	48.570	0.0000	0.0000
1973	0.000	0.000	0.000	0.000	1.063	50.485	53.665	0.0000	0.0000
1974	0.000	0.000	0.000	0.000	1.124	51.998	58.426	0.0000	0.0000
1975	0.000	0.000	0.000	0.000	1.237	53.146	65.735	0.0000	0.0000
1976	0.000	0.000	0.000	0.000	1.341	53.945	72.352	0.0000	0.0000
1977	0.000	0.000	0.000	0.000	1.437	54.652	78.556	0.0000	0.0000
1978	0.000	0.000	0.000	0.000	1.512	56.304	85.124	0.0000	0.0000
1979	0.000	0.000	0.000	0.000	1.628	57.243	93.193	0.0000	0.0000

Table D.50. State and local public administration

Year	Intermediate input				Output			Tax rate	Rate of productivity growth
	Price	Quantity	Outlay	Quality	Price	Quantity	Revenue		
1948	0.000	0.000	0.000	0.000	0.308	15.462	4.755	0.0000	
1949	0.000	0.000	0.000	0.000	0.313	16.828	5.266	0.0000	0.0000
1950	0.000	0.000	0.000	0.000	0.321	17.513	5.618	0.0000	0.0000
1951	0.000	0.000	0.000	0.000	0.341	17.959	6.124	0.0000	0.0000
1952	0.000	0.000	0.000	0.000	0.363	18.405	6.678	0.0000	0.0000
1953	0.000	0.000	0.000	0.000	0.377	19.211	7.238	0.0000	0.0000
1954	0.000	0.000	0.000	0.000	0.392	20.131	7.901	0.0000	0.0000
1955	0.000	0.000	0.000	0.000	0.407	20.746	8.435	0.0000	0.0000
1956	0.000	0.000	0.000	0.000	0.427	21.779	9.301	0.0000	0.0000
1957	0.000	0.000	0.000	0.000	0.446	22.813	10.185	0.0000	0.0000
1958	0.000	0.000	0.000	0.000	0.460	24.124	11.108	0.0000	0.0000
1959	0.000	0.000	0.000	0.000	0.476	24.386	11.619	0.0000	0.0000
1960	0.000	0.000	0.000	0.000	0.505	24.738	12.491	0.0000	0.0000
1961	0.000	0.000	0.000	0.000	0.513	26.539	13.613	0.0000	0.0000
1962	0.000	0.000	0.000	0.000	0.529	27.342	14.459	0.0000	0.0000
1963	0.000	0.000	0.000	0.000	0.552	27.882	15.394	0.0000	0.0000
1964	0.000	0.000	0.000	0.000	0.569	29.064	16.528	0.0000	0.0000
1965	0.000	0.000	0.000	0.000	0.597	30.156	18.009	0.0000	0.0000
1966	0.000	0.000	0.000	0.000	0.634	31.338	19.860	0.0000	0.0000
1967	0.000	0.000	0.000	0.000	0.684	32.379	22.153	0.0000	0.0000
1968	0.000	0.000	0.000	0.000	0.730	33.951	24.772	0.0000	0.0000
1969	0.000	0.000	0.000	0.000	0.794	34.643	27.515	0.0000	0.0000
1970	0.000	0.000	0.000	0.000	0.875	35.663	31.211	0.0000	0.0000
1971	0.000	0.000	0.000	0.000	0.935	37.557	35.117	0.0000	0.0000
1972	0.000	0.000	0.000	0.000	1.000	39.162	39.162	0.0000	0.0000
1973	0.000	0.000	0.000	0.000	1.079	40.802	44.032	0.0000	0.0000
1974	0.000	0.000	0.000	0.000	1.168	41.833	48.864	0.0000	0.0000
1975	0.000	0.000	0.000	0.000	1.259	43.613	54.889	0.0000	0.0000
1976	0.000	0.000	0.000	0.000	1.352	44.310	59.898	0.0000	0.0000
1977	0.000	0.000	0.000	0.000	1.461	44.829	65.486	0.0000	0.0000
1978	0.000	0.000	0.000	0.000	1.554	46.564	72.358	0.0000	0.0000
1979	0.000	0.000	0.000	0.000	1.666	47.492	79.136	0.0000	0.0000

Table D.51. State and local government enterprises

Year	Intermediate input				Output			Tax rate	Rate of productivity growth
	Price	Quantity	Outlay	Quality	Price	Quantity	Revenue		
1948	0.000	0.000	0.000	0.000	0.267	2.394	0.640	0.0000	
1949	0.000	0.000	0.000	0.000	0.283	2.495	0.707	0.0000	0.0000
1950	0.000	0.000	0.000	0.000	0.290	2.621	0.760	0.0000	0.0000
1951	0.000	0.000	0.000	0.000	0.309	2.784	0.859	0.0000	0.0000
1952	0.000	0.000	0.000	0.000	0.327	3.233	1.056	0.0000	0.0000
1953	0.000	0.000	0.000	0.000	0.344	3.308	1.138	0.0000	0.0000
1954	0.000	0.000	0.000	0.000	0.360	3.296	1.187	0.0000	0.0000
1955	0.000	0.000	0.000	0.000	0.382	3.337	1.274	0.0000	0.0000
1956	0.000	0.000	0.000	0.000	0.395	3.320	1.310	0.0000	0.0000
1957	0.000	0.000	0.000	0.000	0.410	3.338	1.368	0.0000	0.0000
1958	0.000	0.000	0.000	0.000	0.430	3.472	1.494	0.0000	0.0000
1959	0.000	0.000	0.000	0.000	0.453	3.863	1.750	0.0000	0.0000
1960	0.000	0.000	0.000	0.000	0.477	4.054	1.934	0.0000	0.0000
1961	0.000	0.000	0.000	0.000	0.496	3.959	1.962	0.0000	0.0000
1962	0.000	0.000	0.000	0.000	0.518	4.231	2.192	0.0000	0.0000
1963	0.000	0.000	0.000	0.000	0.539	4.312	2.325	0.0000	0.0000
1964	0.000	0.000	0.000	0.000	0.567	4.543	2.574	0.0000	0.0000
1965	0.000	0.000	0.000	0.000	0.601	4.618	2.777	0.0000	0.0000
1966	0.000	0.000	0.000	0.000	0.655	4.582	3.000	0.0000	0.0000
1967	0.000	0.000	0.000	0.000	0.697	4.631	3.227	0.0000	0.0000
1968	0.000	0.000	0.000	0.000	0.735	4.977	3.658	0.0000	0.0000
1969	0.000	0.000	0.000	0.000	0.791	5.179	4.094	0.0000	0.0000
1970	0.000	0.000	0.000	0.000	0.844	5.447	4.597	0.0000	0.0000
1971	0.000	0.000	0.000	0.000	0.928	5.537	5.140	0.0000	0.0000
1972	0.000	0.000	0.000	0.000	1.000	5.606	5.606	0.0000	0.0000
1973	0.000	0.000	0.000	0.000	1.093	5.872	6.419	0.0000	0.0000
1974	0.000	0.000	0.000	0.000	1.163	6.303	7.330	0.0000	0.0000
1975	0.000	0.000	0.000	0.000	1.243	6.816	8.470	0.0000	0.0000
1976	0.000	0.000	0.000	0.000	1.338	6.837	9.149	0.0000	0.0000
1977	0.000	0.000	0.000	0.000	1.438	6.786	9.756	0.0000	0.0000
1978	0.000	0.000	0.000	0.000	1.526	7.122	10.869	0.0000	0.0000
1979	0.000	0.000	0.000	0.000	1.634	7.371	12.043	0.0000	0.0000

Notes

1. Overview

1. The study by Leontief (1953) excludes capital input, while the studies by Kendrick (1961a; 1973; 1983) and Kendrick and Grossman (1980) exclude intermediate input.

2. The studies by Kendrick (1961a; 1973; 1983) and Kendrick and Grossman (1980) are based on the existence of a value-added aggregate. References to models of production and productivity growth based on value-added are given in Chapter 2.

3. The analysis of changes in the structure of intermediate input by sector of origin was originated by Leontief (1953). Changes in the structure of intermediate input for the United States have been analyzed by Bezdek (1978), Bezdek and Dunham (1976; 1978), Bezdek and Wendling (1976), Carter (1953; 1957; 1960; 1963; 1967; 1970a; 1970b), Vaccara (1972), Vaccara and Simon (1968), and Wolff (1986). References to changes for other countries can be found in Carter (1970a) and in the conference volumes edited by Barna (1963), Carter and Brody (1970), Brody and Carter (1972), and J. Polenske and Skolka (1976).

4. The breakdown of capital input by class of asset and legal form of organization was originated by Christensen and Jorgenson (1969; 1970; 1973a; 1973b). Changes in the structure of capital input for the United States were discussed by Jorgenson and Griliches (1972a; 1972b) and Jorgenson (1980). Gollop and Jorgenson (1980) and Fraumeni and Jorgenson (1980, 1986) presented the first results based on this approach at the sectoral level; Fraumeni and Jorgenson (1986) updates their earlier study.

5. The breakdown of labor input by demographic characteristics was originated by Denison (1962; 1967; 1974; 1979; 1985). Changes in the structure of labor input for the United States were discussed by Jorgenson and Griliches (1972a; 1972b). Gollop and Jorgenson (1980, 1983) presented the first results based on this approach at the sectoral level. Gollop and Jorgenson (1983) updated their earlier study.

6. This approach to interindustry analysis was originated by Hudson and Jorgenson (1974, 1976, 1978a, 1978b, 1978c) and is discussed by Jorgenson (1982).

7. Interindustry analysis based on fixed coefficients was originated by Leontief (1941, 1953). Additional references are given in the conference volumes edited by Netherlands Economic Institute (1953), Barna (1956; 1963), Carter and Brody (1970), Brody and Carter (1972), and Polenske and Skolka (1976). Interindustry analysis based on fixed coefficients for intermediate inputs and substitution between capital and labor inputs within a value-added aggregate for each sector was originated by Johansen (1959). Additional references are given by Bergman (1985), Johansen (1976), and Taylor (1975).

8. Duality between prices and quantities in production was introduced by Hotelling (1932) and later revived and extended by Samuelson (1953; 1960), and Shephard (1953; 1970). Hotelling (1932) and Samuelson (1953) develop the dual formulation of production theory on the basis of the Legendre transformation. This approach is employed by Jorgenson and Lau (1974a; 1974b) and Lau (1976; 1978a). Shephard (1953) utilizes distance functions to characterize the duality between prices and quantities. This approach is employed by Diewert (1974), Hanoch (1978), McFadden (1978), and Uzawa (1964). Surveys of duality in the theory of production are presented by Diewert (1982) and Samuelson (1983).

9. References to Divisia index numbers are presented in Chapter 2, footnote 8.

10. The translog production function was introduced by Christensen, Jorgenson, and Lau (1971; 1973).

11. The translog index of productivity growth was introduced by Christensen and Jorgenson (1970). It was first derived from the translog production function by Jorgenson and Nishimizu (1978).

12. The translog index numbers were introduced by Fisher (1922) and have been discussed by Tornquist (1936), Theil (1965), and Kloek (1966). They were first derived from the translog production function by Diewert (1976).

13. The translog production function was first applied at the sectoral level by Berndt and Christensen (1973b, 1974), using a value-added aggregate. The translog production function incorporating intermediate input was applied at the sectoral level by Berndt and Jorgenson (1973) and Berndt and Wood (1975). References to sectoral production studies incorporating intermediate input are given by Jorgenson (1986).

14. Alternative approaches to generating data and analyzing the sources of U.S. economic growth at the aggregate level are discussed by the Bureau of Labor Statistics (1983), Christensen and Jorgenson (1969; 1970; 1973a; 1973b), Christensen, Cummings, and Jorgenson (1980; 1981), Denison (1962; 1967; 1969; 1974; 1979; 1985), Jorgenson and Griliches (1972a; 1972b), Jorgenson (1984), Kendrick (1961; 1973; 1983), Kendrick and Grossman (1980), and Solow (1957; 1960; 1963).

15. An aggregate production function was introduced by Cobb and Douglas (1928). References to aggregate production studies based on this approach are given in a survey paper by Douglas (1948) and by Douglas (1967; 1976). Early studies of producer behavior, including those based on the Cobb–Douglas production function, have been surveyed by Heady and Dillon (1961) and Walters (1963). Samuelson (1979) discusses the impact of Douglas's research. Econometric studies based on the

CES production function are surveyed by Griliches (1967), Jorgenson (1974), Kennedy and Thirlwall (1972), Nadiri (1970), and Nerlove (1967). More recent studies are surveyed by Jorgenson (1986).

16. The relationship of sectoral and aggregate indices of technical change was first discussed by Leontief (1953) and Debreu (1954). Additional references are given in Chapter 2.

17. The method of iterative proportional fitting is a generalization of the RAS method for the biproportional matrix model, discussed by Bacharach (1965). The method of iterative proportional fitting is presented by Bishop, Fienberg, and Holland (1975).

18. The duality between prices and quantities of capital services is discussed by Christensen and Jorgenson (1973a), pp. 265–83, and by Jorgenson (1973; 1980).

19. References to data on interindustry transactions in the U.S. are given in Chapter 5.

20. Reclassifications, redefinitions, and transfers employed in constructing the U.S. interindustry transaction accounts are discussed by Walderhaug (1973).

21. References to the decomposition of quality change are given in Chapter 8.

22. References to share elasticities are given in Chapter 7.

23. References to biases of technical change are given in Chapter 7.

24. References to models of production based on value-added and references to Hicks neutrality of technical change are given in Chapter 2.

25. The characterization of the translog production function in terms of constant share elasticities is discussed by Jorgenson (1986).

26. References to Harrod neutrality and Solow neutrality of technical change are given in Chapter 9.

2. Methodology

1. The concept of separability is due to Leontief (1947a; 1947b) and Sono (1961).

2. The concept of homothetic separability was introduced by Shephard (1953, 1970).

3. A proof of this proposition is given by Lau (1969, 1978a).

4. The definition of productivity growth that is neutral, in the sense that the ratio of marginal products of capital and labor for any ratio of capital and labor inputs is independent of time, is due to Hicks (1932). This definition was generalized to more than two inputs by Burmeister and Dobell (1969).

5. The price function was introduced by Samuelson (1953).

6. A proof of this proposition is given by Lau (1978a).

7. The translog production function was introduced by Christensen, Jorgenson, and Lau (1971, 1973). The treatment of productivity growth outlined below is due to Jorgenson and Nishimizu (1978).

8. The quantity indices were introduced by Fisher (1922) and have been discussed by Tornquist (1936), Theil (1965), and Kloek (1966). These indices were first derived from the translog production function by Diewert (1976). The corresponding index of productivity growth was introduced by Christensen and Jorgenson (1970). The

translog index of productivity was first derived from the translog production function by Jorgenson and Nishimizu (1978). Earlier, Diewert (1976) had interpreted the ratio of translog indices of output and input as an index of productivity under the assumption of Hicks neutrality.

9. This characterization of price and quantity indices was originated by Shephard (1953; 1970). This corrects an error in Christensen and Jorgenson (1973a), p. 261.

10. The durable goods model of production was originated by Walras (1954). Capital as a factor of production has been discussed by Diewert (1980) and by Jorgenson (1973; 1980).

11. The dual to the durable goods model of production was originated by Hotelling (1925) and Haavelmo (1960). The dual to this model has been further developed by Arrow (1964) and Hall (1968).

12. Price and quantity indices associated with the durable goods model of production are special cases of the indices proposed by Hicks (1946). A presentation of Hicks's approach to aggregation and references to the literature are given by Diewert (1980), pp. 434–438.

13. The system of vintage accounts described below was originated by Christensen and Jorgenson (1973). This system is discussed by Jorgenson (1980).

14. The simplified system of vintage accounts was originated by Christensen and Jorgenson (1969, 1970, 1973) and has been employed by Fraumeni and Jorgenson (1980).

15. The model of production based on value-added has been discussed by Arrow (1974), Bruno (1977), Diewert (1980), Sato (1976), and Sims (1969; 1976). Sato provides references to the literature. Index numbers for value-added were introduced by Geary (1944) and have been discussed by Armstrong (1975), Diewert (1980), Domar (1961), Hill (1971), Karmel (1954), Kendrick (1961a; 1973; 1983), Kendrick and Grossman (1980), Massell (1961), Statistical Office of The United Nations (1968, 66–70), and in the conference volume edited by Kendrick (1968).

16. Duality of the model of production based on value-added has been discussed by Arrow (1974), Bruno (1977), Diewert (1980), and Sato (1976).

17. An alternative approach to the construction of a translog index of sectoral value-added has been proposed by Diewert (1980).

18. The derivation of a production possibility frontier from the multisectoral model of production was introduced by Debreu (1951, 285), and has been discussed by Bergson (1961; 1975), Diewert (1980), Fisher (1982), Fisher and Shell (1972), Moorsteen (1961), and Weitzman (1983).

19. This definition of aggregate productivity growth is due to Debreu (1954, 52–54), and has been discussed by Diewert (1976; 1980), Hulten (1973a), Jorgenson and Griliches (1967), and Richter (1966).

20. This condition for the existence of an aggregate production function is due to Denny (1972) and Hall (1973). For further discussion see Denny and Pinto (1978) and Lau (1978a).

21. The price possibility frontier was introduced by Lau (1972) and has been discussed by Jorgenson and Lau (1974a, 1974b).

22. The existence of a value-added aggregate equal to the sum of the quantities of value-added in all sectors is an implication of Hicks (1946) aggregation. For further discussion see Bruno (1978) and Diewert (1978).

23. The relationship between aggregate and sectoral indices of productivity growth was first discussed by Leontief (1953) and Debreu (1954) under the assumption that prices paid for primary-factors of production are the same for all sector.

24. The relationship between aggregate and sectoral indices of productivity growth under the assumption that prices of primary-factors of production differ among sectors was first discussed by Kendrick (1961a) and Massell (1961).

25. This expression generalizes a formula originally proposed by Domar (1961), correcting the procedure introduced by Leontief (1953). Domar's approach, like Leontief's, is based on the assumption that prices paid for primary-factors of production are the same for all sectors. Domar's approach has been discussed by Baumol and Wolff (1985), Diewert (1980), Gollop (1979; 1983), Hulten (1978), and Jorgenson (1980) and has been employed by Fraumeni and Jorgenson (1980; 1986), Nishimizu (1974), Nishimizu and Hulten (1978), and Wolff (1985). Leontief's approach has been discussed in Statistical Office of the United Nations, (1968) "Gross Output and All Inputs, The Gross System of Productivity Measurement" pp. 69–70, and has been employed by Ezaki (1978), Star (1974), and Watanabe (1971).

26. A closely related approach, using a sectoral model of production based on value-added rather than the sectoral model based on output that we employ, was introduced by Bergson (1961), Domar (1961), Kendrick (1961), Massell (1961), and Moorsteen (1961) and has been discussed by Bergson (1975), Fisher (1982), Fisher and Shell (1972), Statistical Office of the United Nations, (1968) "Value Added and Primary Inputs: The Net System of Productivity Measurement," p. 69, and Weitzman (1983). This approach has been employed by Armstrong (1975), Kendrick (1961a, 1973, 1983), Kendrick and Grossman (1980), and Massell (1961).

3. Sectoral Labor Input

1. The initial design of our approach to the measurement of labor input, the collection of data, and much of the required estimation was carried out in collaboration with Peter Chinloy. The results of his measurement and analysis of labor input for the U.S. economy at the aggregate level are reported in Chinloy (1974; 1980; 1981).

2. The 81,600 cell total is the product of the number of characteristic divisions within each industrial, occupational, and demographic dimension (51.2.2.8.5.10). A substantial number of these cells have zero entries; an example is the number of 14–15 year-old laborers with four or more years of college in each of the 2040 cells cross-classified by industry, occupation, sex, and employment class. In implementing the multiproportional matrix model discussed below, we need not identify the empty cells prior to estimation; these cells are treated symmetrically with those for which entries are not zero.

3. Kendrick purposely avoids disaggregating the employed population by demographic or occupational characteristics. In Kendrick's view, any difference in the productivity of an hour worked by laborers of differing personal characteristics should be

captured not in a measure of factor input, but in an index of productivity change. By contrast, Denison posits that disaggregation by personal characteristics is essential for measuring labor input. In his view, however, shifting composition of industrial and occupational characteristics does not reflect changes in the level of labor input, but should be included in the measure of productivity change.

4. A detailed discussion of the method of iterative proportional fitting is presented by Bishop, Fienberg, and Holland (1975) especially pp. 83–102 and 188–191.

5. Most of the definitional changes introduced by the Census Bureau in January 1967 affect the distinction between the unemployed and those who are not in the labor force. See Stein (1967). These changes do not influence this study, but changes in the interviewers' questioning policy and the Bureau's classificatory criteria do have an impact. Beginning in January 1967, (1) those persons previously classified as unemployed, who were absent from their jobs during the entire survey week because of vacations, strikes, etc. but were looking for other jobs, were classified as employed; (2) former proprietors who later incorporated their businesses were assigned to the wage and salary class rather than the self-employed category; and (3) 14–15 year-old laborers were no longer considered part of the labor force.

6. Results based on the *Current Population Survey* were used to initialize the multiproportional matrix model for 1966 and earlier years.

7. Unfortunately, there are no available data, covering the postwar period which classify hours worked by education.

8. Barger (1971) has applied Gjeddebaek's method to the estimation of mean earnings from data available in frequency form.

9. Detailed discussions of quality indices and applications to disaggregated labor data can be found in doctoral dissertations by Barger (1971) and Chinloy (1974). Chinloy (1980; 1981) presents an application to U.S. aggregate data and Jorgenson (1984) gives an application to data for individual industrial sectors.

10. Kendrick (1961; 1973) relies occasionally on Bureau of Labor Statistics (1973b) data on hours paid (see Kendrick, 1973, 156). For a detailed discussion of the hours paid series used at the sectoral level, see Kendrick (1961, 382, mining; 496, contract construction; 503, wholesale and retail trade; 515, transportation; 559, communications and public utilities). In a more recent study Kendrick and Grossman (1980, 25) rely on BLS hours-paid data for all laborers except proprietors and unpaid family workers (Kendrick 1983, 56) employs the same data sources as Kendrick and Grossman.

11. Kenison (1979, 155) provides a detailed description of the extrapolation procedure through 1976, Denison (1985, 64) gives a description of the procedure through 1982.

12. Bureau of the Census (1972), Table 5. The Census occupational category for ''managers'' best identifies the group of nonsupervisory workers underlying BLS estimates. The occupations of nonsupervisory workers are defined in the technical note to Bureau of Labor Statistics (1976), p. 774.

13. The Bureau of Labor Statistics does not provide estimates of hours paid for the self-employed or unpaid family workers. For these groups Denison and, for the most part, Kendrick use household survey data on hours worked.

14. Admittedly, Kendrick does distinguish between the hours worked by proprietors and unpaid family workers and those worked by wage and salary employees whenever the former group is a "significant fraction" of the particular industry's labor force. By not weighting the two employment class labor intensities differentially, Kendrick eliminates any potential effect of changing labor composition. Kendrick (1961, 26) and Kendrick (1973, 12). Kendrick and Grossman (1981, 26) adopt an even stricter definition of labor input.

15. See, for example, Denison (1985, 157–158).

4. Sectoral Capital Input

1. As previously noted, the investment data from the Faucett–BLS study do not include tenant-occupied housekeeping residential structures.

2. We use the methodology described in the earlier study by Fraumeni and Jorgenson (1980), based upon depreciation methods and asset lives, as employed by Gollop and Jorgenson (1980). See Fraumeni and Jorgenson (1980, 96–97).

3. We use data from the Jack Faucett Associates report (1973c) to disaggregate mining and the public utilities portion of communications and public utilities. We use Table 6.2 from the *Survey of Current Business* to disaggregate agriculture, transportation, and the communications portion of communications and public utilities. The remaining five aggregates—construction, wholesale trade, retail trade, finance, insurance and real estate, and services—each correspond to one of our forty-six industries.

4. The data in Table 1.1 are presented in millions, while the data in Table 1.2 are presented in billions, so that the implicit inventory deflator in the base year, 1972, will not equal 1.000. This problem did not arise for plant and equipment, as implicit price deflators normalized to 1.000 in the base year are available from Table 7.19 and Table 7.20 of the *Survey of Current Business*.

5. The detailed asset categories are the twenty-two producers' durable equipment and ten private nonresidential structures categories employed by Hulten and Wykoff (1981c).

6. The RAS procedure is based on Bacharach (1965).

7. The Hulten–Wykoff (1981c) classification of consumers durables includes: motor vehicles and parts, furniture, kitchen and household appliances, radio and television receivers, recorders, musical instruments, wheel goods, durable toys, sports equipment, and other.

8. We distinguish between investment and asset deflators when the valuation of investment differs significantly from the valuation of capital stocks, as in the case of inventories.

9. We begin with asset deflators from the Bureau of Economic Analysis. We produce investment and asset deflators, employing separate scaling procedures.

10. The "hedonic technique" for price measurement originated by Court (1939) and employed, for example, by Griliches (1961) is based on a number of varieties that are perfect substitutes. The hedonic technique is analyzed by Muellbauer (1975) and surveys of the literature have been given by Griliches (1971) and by Triplett (1975).

11. Hulten and Wykoff have estimated vintage price functions for structures from a sample of 8066 observations on market transactions in used structures. These data were collected by the Office of Industrial Economics of the U.S. Department of the Treasury in 1972 and were published in *Business Building Statistics* (1975). They have estimated vintage price functions for equipment from prices of machine tools collected by Beidleman (1976) and prices of other types of equipment collected from used equipment dealers and from auction reports of the U.S. General Services Administration.

12. The 1971 distribution is used for all subsequent years.

13. This practice is consistent with the convention adopted by the Bureau of Economic Analysis (1974) in allocating value added among employee compensation, property-type income, and indirect business taxes in the construction of the 1967 input-output matrix. Property-type income is defined to include noncorporate profits, which is the sum of the return to capital and the labor of self-employed persons, and the statistical discrepancy. We allocate the statistical discrepancy in proportion to noncorporate profits.

14. The portion of rental income of persons resulting from the imputed value of owner-occupied housing is allocated to the household industry.

15. The information on capital consumption allowances comes from the Bureau of Economic Analysis study of gross product originating. The noncorporate-corporate ratio we describe here is used throughout that study.

16. Nonprofit institutions not serving persons include such groups as fraternal organizations and clubs.

17. For industries with very small noncorporate sectors, the imputed value of the income of self-employed persons allocated to labor compensation is occasionally negative, due to the limits imposed by the accuracy of the data. In these cases we assume that self-employed labor compensation moves in proportion to wage and salary labor compensation. As a result, we define a noncorporate rate of return differs from the corporate rate of return for the affected years.

18. One rate is used for all industries for plant; similarly one rate is used for all industries for equipment. See Jorgenson and Sullivan (1981, Table 10, 194).

19. See, for example, Denison (1969, 6).

5. Sectoral Output and Intermediate Input

1. See Walderhaug (1973) for a full discussion of the redefinition and reclassification adjustments necessary to bridge national accounts and input-output definitions.

2. The six interindustry accounts sectors (and the corresponding BEA sector numbers) are nonferrous metal ores mining (6), transportation and warehousing (65), electric, gas, water, and sanitary services (68), finance and insurance (70), business services (73), and medical, educational services, and nonprofit organizations (77).

3. We employed BEA interindustry transactions data for 1947 and 1958. Data for 1958 are published in the *Survey of Current Business* (1965). Data for 1947 obtained from unpublished studies by BEA (1968).

4. Data for the more detailed 1963 table from the *Survey of Current Business* (1969) is required for industries obtained from Faucett's BLS industry classification. We assume that 367-order industries are a constant proportion of 80-order industries for all years. The less detailed tables, 1947 and 1958, are required for industries from Faucett's interindustry classification. The more detailed tables are available on a consistent basis only for 1963 and 1967, so the 1963 table was used.

5. This assumption was also made by Faucett (1975), so that our adjustments are consistent with those made by Faucett.

6. The eleven benchmark years are 1947, 1958, 1961, 1963, and 1966–1972. 80-order data for 1958, 1963 and 1967 are published in the *Survey of Current Business* (1965; 1967; 1974c). Data for 1947, 1961, 1966, and 1968–1972 were obtained from studies by BEA (1968; 1970; 1972; 1975 for 1968–1970; 1977; 1979).

6. Growth in Sectoral Output

1. This index of productivity growth was introduced by Christensen and Jorgenson (1970). It was first derived from the translog production function by Jorgenson and Nishimizu (1978).

7. Sectoral Substitution and Technical Change

1. Share elasticity was introduced by Christensen, Jorgenson, and Lau (1971; 1973) and Samuelson (1973).

2. The bias of productivity growth was introduced by Hicks (1932). An alternative definition of the bias of productivity growth was introduced by Binswanger (1974a; 1974b). Alternative definitions of biases of productivity growth are compared by Binswanger (1978b).

3. The following discussion of share elasticities and concavity follows that of Jorgenson (1986). Representation of conditions for concavity in terms of the Cholesky factorization is due to Lau (1978; 1979).

4. The translog production function was introduced by Christensen, Jorgenson, and Lau (1971; 1973).

5. Share elasticities were first employed as constant parameters of an econometric model of producer behavior by Christensen, Jorgenson, and Lau (1971; 1973). Constant share elasticities and biases of productivity growth are employed by Jorgenson and Fraumeni (1981) and Jorgenson (1983; 1984). Binswanger (1974a; 1974b; 1978c) uses a different definition of biases of productivity growth.

6. The following discussion of concavity for the translog production function is based on that of Jorgenson (1986).

7. Productivity growth is assumed to be Hicks neutral by Christensen, Jorgenson, and Lau (1971; 1973) and by Berndt and Christensen (1973b; 1974) in studies based on translog production and cost functions.

8. The methodology for testing separability was originated by Jorgenson and Lau (1975). This methodology has been discussed by Blackorby, Primont, and Russell (1977) and by Denny and Fuss (1977). An alternative approach has been developed by Woodland (1978).

9. The following formulation of an econometric model of production is based on that of Jorgenson and Fraumeni (1981) and Jorgenson (1984b).

10. A review of the literature on induced productivity growth is given by Binswanger (1978).

8. Aggregate Labor and Capital Inputs

1. Detailed discussions of quality indices and applications to disaggregated labor data can be found in the doctoral dissertations by Barger (1971) and Chinloy (1974). Chinloy (1980, 1981) presents an application to U.S. aggregate data and Jorgenson (1984b) gives an application to data for individual industrial sectors. Extremely valuable assistance in programming the computations was provided by Peter Derksen.

2. When two factors are positively correlated, both first-order contributions capture the factors' joint effect. When two factors are negatively correlated, the opposing effects are measured in both first-order contributions. In each case, the second-order contribution guarantees that the joint effect is counted only once.

9. Growth in Aggregate Output

1. Our econometric model is discussed in more detail by Jorgenson (1985a).

2. Neutrality of productivity growth in the sense of Harrod (1947), Hicks (1932), and Solow (1960) is discussed by Burmeister and Dobell (1969).

3. The role of an aggregate production account in a complete accounting system for the U.S. economy is discussed by Christensen and Jorgenson (1969, 1970, 1973a, 1973b) and Jorgenson (1980).

4. The following discussion of share elasticities and concavity follows that of Jorgenson (1986). Representation of conditions for concavity in terms of the Cholesky factorization is due to Lau (1978, 1979).

5. The following discussion of concavity for the translog production function follows that of Jorgenson (1986).

6. The following formulation of an econometric model of production is based on that of Jorgenson (1986).

7. Application of the Bonferroni inequality to simultaneous tests of hypotheses is discussed by Savin (1984).

References

Ackerman, Susan R. 1973. Used cars as a depreciating asset. *Western Economic Journal* 11: 463–474.

Armstrong, Alan. 1974. *Structural change in the British economy 1948–1968 (A Programme for Growth 12)*. London: Chapman and Hall.

Arrow, Kenneth J. 1964. Optimal capital policy, the cost of capital, and myopic decision rules. *Annals of the Institute of Statistical Mathematics* 16: 16–30.

——— 1974. The measurement of real value added. In *Nations and households in economic growth*, ed. Paul A. David and Melvin W. Reder. New York: Academic.

Bacharach, Michael. 1965. Estimating non-negative matrices from marginal data. *International Economic Review* 6: 294–310.

——— 1970. *Biproportional matrices and input-output change*. Cambridge: Cambridge University Press.

Bancroft, Gertrude, and Stuart Garfinkle. 1963. Job mobility in 1961. *Special Labor Force Report* 35.

Barger, William J. 1971. The measurement of labor input: U.S. manufacturing industries, 1948–1966. Dissertation, Harvard University.

Barna, Tibor, ed. 1956. *The structural interdependence of the economy*. New York: Wiley.

——— ed., 1963. *Structural interdependence and economic development*. London: Macmillan.

Baumol, William J., and Edward N. Wolff. 1984. On interindustry differences in absolute productivity. *Journal of Political Economy* 92: 1017–1034.

Beidleman, Carl R. 1976. Economic depreciation in a capital goods industry. *National Tax Journal* 29: 379–390.

Bergman, Lars. 1985. Extensions and applications of the MSG-Model: A brief survey. In *Production, multi-sectoral growth and planning*, ed. Finn R. Forsund, Michael Hoel, and Svein Longva. Amsterdam: North-Holland.

Bergson, Abram. 1961. *The real national income of the Soviet Union since 1928*. Cambridge, Mass.: Harvard University Press.

541

————— 1975. Index numbers and the computation of factor productivity. *Review of Income and Wealth* 21: 259–278.

Berndt, Ernst R., and Laurits R. Christensen. 1973a. The internal structure of functional relationships: Separability, substitution, and aggregation. *Review of Economic Studies* 40: 403–410.

————— 1973b. The translog function and the substitution of equipment, structures, and labor in U.S. manufacturing 1929–68. *Journal of Econometrics* 1: 81–113.

————— 1974. Testing for the existence of a consistent aggregate index of labor input. *American Economic Review* 64: 391–404.

Berndt, Ernst R., and Dale W. Jorgenson. 1973. Production structure. In *U.S. energy resources and economic growth,* ed. Dale W. Jorgenson and Hendrik S. Houthakker. Washington: Energy Policy Project.

Berndt, Ernst R., and David O. Wood. 1975. Technology, prices, and the derived demand for energy. *Review of Economics and Statistics* 56: 259–268.

————— 1979. Engineering and econometric interpretations of energy-capital complementarity. *American Economic Review* 69: 342–354.

Bezdek, Roger H. 1978. Postwar structural and technological changes in the American economy. *Omega* 6: 211–225.

Bezdek, Roger H., and Constance K. Dunham. 1976. On the relationship between change in input-output coefficients and changes in product mix. *Review of Economics and Statistics* 58: 375–379.

————— 1978. Structural change in the American economy, by functional industry group. *Review of Income and Wealth* 24: 93–104.

Bezdek, Roger H., and Robert M. Wendling. 1976. Disaggregation of structural change in the American economy, 1947–1966. *Review of Income and Wealth* 22: 167–186.

Binswanger, Hans P. 1974a. The measurement of technical change biases with many factors of production. *American Economic Review* 64: 964–976.

————— 1974b. A microeconomic approach to induced innovation. *Economic Journal* 84: 940–958.

————— 1978. Issues in modeling induced technical change. In *Induced innovation,* ed. Hans P. Binswanger and Vernon W. Ruttan. Baltimore: Johns Hopkins University Press.

Bishop, Yvonne M.M., Steven E. Fienberg, and Paul W. Holland. 1975. *Discrete multivariate analysis.* Cambridge, Mass.: M.I.T. Press.

Blackorby, Charles, Daniel Primont, and R. Robert Russell. 1978. *Duality, separability, and functional structure: Theory and economic applications.* New York: North-Holland.

Board of Governors of the Federal Reserve System. 1981. *Balance sheets for the U.S. economy 1945–80: Flow of funds.* Washington: Federal Reserve System.

Brody, Andras, and Anne P. Carter, eds. 1972. *Input-output techniques.* Amsterdam: North-Holland.

Bruno, Michael. 1978. Duality, intermediate inputs, and value added. In *Production economics: A dual approach to theory and applications,* ed. Melvyn Fuss and Daniel McFadden. Vol. 2. Amsterdam: North-Holland.

Bureau of the Census. 1958. *Enterprise statistics: 1948, Part 3: Link of Census establishment and IRS corporation data.* Series ES3, No. 3. Washington: U.S.
Department of Commerce.

———— 1963. *U.S. census of population: 1960, Industrial characteristics.* Final
Report PC(2)-7F. Washington: U.S. Department of Commerce.

———— 1972. *Census of Population: 1970, Occupation by industry.* Final Report
PC(2)-7C. Washington: U.S. Department of Commerce.

———— 1973a. *Census of population: 1970, Earnings by occupation and education.* Final Report PC(2)-8B. Washington: U.S. Department of Commerce.

———— 1973b. *Census of population: 1970, Industrial characteristics.* Final
Report PC(2)-7B. Washington: U.S. Department of Commerce.

———— 1973c. *Census of population: 1970, Occupational characteristics.* Final
Report PC(2)-7A. Washington: U.S. Department of Commerce.

———— 1978. *Annual survey of manufactures, 1976.* Washington: U.S. Government Printing Office.

———— 1980. *Annual Survey of manufactures, 1978.* Washington: U.S. Government Printing Office.

———— 1981. *1977 census of manufactures, Volume I, Subject statistics.* Washington: U.S. Government Printing Office.

Bureau of Economic Analysis. 1965. Transaction table of 1958 input-output study and
revised direct and total requirement data. *Survey of Current Business* 45:
33–55.

———— 1968. *Input-output transactions: 1961.* Staff Paper in Economics and
Statistics No. 16. Washington: U.S. Department of Commerce.

———— 1969. Input-output structure of the U.S. economy: 1963. *Survey of Current
Business* 49: 16–47.

———— 1970. *The input-output structure of the United States economy: 1947.*
Washington: U.S. Department of Commerce.

———— 1972. *Input-output transactions: 1966.* Staff Paper in Economics and
Statistics No. 19. Washington: U.S. Department of Commerce.

———— 1974a. Gross national product by industry, Work File 1205–01–01. Washington: U.S. Department of Commerce.

———— 1974b. Gross national product by industry, Work File 1205–04–06, Washington: U.S. Department of Commerce.

———— 1974c. The input-output structure of the U.S. economy: 1967. *Survey of
Current Business* 54: 24–56.

———— 1974d. *The input-output structure of the U.S. economy: 1967. Supplement
to the Survey of Current Business.* Washington: U.S. Department of Commerce.

———— 1975a. *Interindustry transactions in new structures and equipment, 1963
and 1967. Supplement to the Survey of Current Business.* Washington: U.S.
Department of Commerce.

———— 1975b. *Summary input-output tables of the U.S. economy: 1968, 1969,
1970.* BEA Staff Paper No. 27. Washington: U.S. Department of Commerce.

———— 1976a. *Fixed nonresidential business and residential capital in the United States, 1925–1975.* Washington: U.S. Department of Commerce.

———— 1976b. U.S. national income and product accounts, 1973 to second quarter 1976. *Survey of Current Business* 56: 22–68.

———— 1977a. *Input-output table of the U.S. economy.* BEA Staff Paper No. 28. Washington: U.S. Department of Commerce.

———— 1977b. *The national income and product accounts of the United States, 1929–1974: Statistical tables.* Washington: U.S. Department of Commerce.

———— 1979. Dollar-value tables for the 1972 input-output study. *Survey of Current Business* 59: 51–72.

———— 1981a. Fourteen current dollar components of gross product originating by industry. Work File 1205–01–03. Washington: U.S. Department of Commerce.

———— 1981b. *The national income and product accounts of the United States, 1929–1976: Statistical tables.* Washington: U.S. Department of Commerce.

———— *Survey of Current Business.* Various monthly issues.

Bureau of Labor Statistics. 1960. *Trends in output per man-hour in the private economy, 1909, 1958.* Bulletin 1249. Washington: U.S. Department of Labor.

———— 1963. *Manufacturing industries 1962: Employer expenditures for selected supplementary compensation practices for production and related workers.* Bulletin 1428. Washington: U.S. Department of Labor.

———— 1968. Household data. *Employment and Earnings and Monthly Report on the Labor Force* 14: 25–47.

———— 1971. *BLS handbook of methods for surveys and studies.* Bulletin 1711. Washington: U.S. Department of Labor.

———— 1973a. *Employment and earnings statistics of the United States.* Bulletin No. 1312. Washington: U.S. Department of Labor.

———— 1973b. Historical productivity measures. Unpublished working paper prepared by the Productivity and Technology Division of the Bureau of Labor Statistics. Washington: U.S. Department of Labor.

———— 1976. *Employment and earnings, United States, 1909–75.* Bulletin 1312–10. Washington: U.S. Department of Labor.

———— 1979a. *Capital stock estimates for input-output industries: Methods and data.* Bulletin 2034. Washington: U.S. Department of Labor.

———— 1979b. *Time series data for input-output industries.* Bulletin 2018. Washington: U.S. Department of Labor.

———— 1983. *Trends in multifactor productivity, 1948–81.* Bulletin 2178. Washington: U.S. Department of Labor.

Burmeister, Edwin, and Rodney Dobell. 1969. Disembodied technological change with several factors. *Journal of Economic Theory* 1: 1–8.

Cagan, Philip. 1965. Measuring quality changes and the purchasing power of money: An exploratory study of automobiles. *National Banking Review* 3: 217–236.

Carter, Anne P. (Grosse). 1953. The technological structure of the cotton textile industry. In *Studies in the structure of the American economy,* ed. Wassily Leontief. New York: Oxford University Press.

———— 1957. Capital coefficients as economic parameters: The problem of instability. In *Conference on research in income and wealth: Problems of capital formation.* Princeton: Princeton University Press.

———— 1960. Investment, capacity utilization, and change in input structures in the tin can industry. *Review of Economics and Statistics* 42: 282–291.

———— 1963. Incremental flow coefficients for a dynamic input-output model with changing technology. In *Structural interdependence and economic development,* ed. Tibor Barna. London: Macmillan.

———— 1967. Changes in the structure of the American economy, 1957 to 1958 and 1962. *Review of Economics and Statistics* 49: 209–224.

———— 1970a. A linear programming system analyzing embodied technological change. In *Contributions to input-output analysis,* ed. Anne P. Carter and Andras Brody. Amsterdam: North-Holland.

———— 1970b. *Structural change in the American economy.* Cambridge, Mass.: Harvard University Press.

Carter, Anne P., and Andras Brody. 1970a. *Applications of input-output analysis.* Amsterdam: North-Holland.

———— 1970b. *Contributions to input-output analysis.* Amsterdam: North-Holland.

Chinloy, Peter T. 1974. Issues in the measurement of labor input. Dissertation, Harvard University.

———— 1977. Hedonic price and depreciation indexes for residential housing: A longitudinal approach. *Journal of Urban Economics* 4: 469–482.

———— 1980. Sources of quality change in labor input. *American Economic Review* 70: 108–119.

———— 1981. *Labor productivity.* Cambridge, Mass.: Abt.

Chow, Gregory C. 1957. *The demand for automobiles in the United States.* Amsterdam: North-Holland.

———— 1960. Statistical demand functions for automobiles and their use for forecasting. In *The demand for durable goods,* ed. Arnold C. Harberger. Chicago: University of Chicago Press.

Christensen, Laurits R., Dianne Cummings, and Dale W. Jorgenson. 1978. Productivity growth, 1947–1973: An international comparison. In *The impact of international trade and investment on employment,* ed. William Dewald. Washington: U.S. Government Printing Office.

———— 1980. Economic growth, 1947–1973: An international comparison. In *New development in productivity measurement,* ed. John W. Kendrick and Beatrice Vaccara. Chicago: University of Chicago Press.

———— 1981. Relative productivity levels, 1947–1973. *European Economic Review* 16: 61–94.

Christensen, Laurits R., and Dale W. Jorgenson. 1969. The measurement of U.S. real capital input, 1929–1967. *Review of Income and Wealth* 15: 293–320.

———— 1970. U.S. real product and real factor input, 1929–1967. *Review of Income and Wealth* 16: 19–50.

———— 1973a. Measuring the performance of the private sector of the U.S. economy, 1929–1969. In *Measuring economic and social performance,* ed. Milton Moss. New York: Columbia University Press.

———— 1973b. U.S. income, saving, and wealth, 1929–1969. *Review of Income and Wealth,* 19: 329–362.

Christensen, Laurits R., Dale W. Jorgenson, and Lawrence J. Lau. 1971. Conjugate duality and the transcendental logarithmic production function. *Econometrica* 39: 255–256.

———— 1973. Transcendental logarithmic production frontiers. *Review of Economics and Statistics* 55: 28–45.

Cobb, Charles W., and Paul H. Douglas. 1928. A theory of production. *American Economic Review* 18: 139–165.

Coen, Robert, 1975. Investment behavior, the measurement of depreciation, and tax policy. *American Economic Review* 65: 59–74.

———— 1980. Depreciation, profits, and rates of return in manufacturing industries. In *The measurement of capital,* ed. Dan Usher. Chicago: University of Chicago Press.

Conrad, Klaus. 1985. *Produktivitatslucken nach Wirtschaftszweigen in internationalen vergleich.* Berlin: Springer.

Conrad, Klaus, and Dale W. Jorgenson. 1985. Sectoral productivity gaps between the United States, Japan, and Germany, 1960–1979. In Vereins für Socialpolitik, *Probleme und Perspektiven der weltwirtschaftlichen Entwicklung.* Berlin: Duncker and Humblot.

Creamer, Daniel. 1972. Measuring capital input for total factor productivity analysis: Comments by a sometime estimator. *Review of Income and Wealth* 18: 55–78.

Debreu, Gerard. 1951. The coefficient of resource utilization. *Econometrica* 19: 273–292.

———— 1954. Numerical representations of technological change. *Metroeconomica* 6: 45–54.

Denison, Edward F. 1957. Theoretical aspects of quality change, capital consumption, and net capital formation. In *Conference on research in income and wealth: Problems of capital formation.* Princeton: Princeton University Press.

———— 1961. Measurement of labor input: Some questions of definition and the adequacy of data. In *Conference on research in income and wealth: Output, input, and productivity measurement.* Princeton: Princeton University Press.

———— 1962. *Sources of economic growth in the United States and the alternatives before us.* New York: Committee for Economic Development.

———— 1966. Discussion. *American Economic Review* 66: 76–78.

———— 1967. *Why growth rates differ.* Washington: Brookings Institution.

———— 1969. Some major issues in productivity analysis: An examination of estimates by Jorgenson and Griliches. *Survey of Current Business* 49: 1–27.

———— 1972. Final comments. *Survey of Current Business* 52: 95–110.

———— 1974. *Accounting for United States economic growth, 1929 to 1969.* Washington: Brookings Institution.

———— 1979. *Accounting for slower economic growth.* Washington: Brookings Institution.

———— 1985. *Trends in American economic growth, 1929–1982.* Washington: Brookings Institution.

Denison, Edward F., and William K. Chung. 1976. *How Japan's economy grew so fast.* Washington: Brookings Institution.

Denny, Michael. 1972. Trade and the production sector: An exploration of models with multi-product technologies. Dissertation, University of California, Berkeley.

Denny, Michael, and Melvyn Fuss. 1977. The use of approximation analysis to test for separability and the existence of consistent aggregates. *American Economic Review* 67: 404–418.

Denny, Michael, and Cheryl Pinto. 1978. An aggregate model with multi-product technologies. In *Production economics: A dual approach to theory and applications,* ed. Melvyn Fuss and Daniel McFadden. Vol. 2. Amsterdam: North-Holland.

Diewert, W. Erwin. 1974. Applications of duality theory. In *Frontiers of quantitative economics,* ed. Michael Intriligator and David A. Kendrick. Vol. 2. Amsterdam: North-Holland.

———— 1976. Exact and superlative index numbers. *Journal of Econometrics* 4: 115–146.

———— 1978. Hicks' aggregation theorem and the existence of a real value-added function. In *Production economics: A dual approach to theory and applications,* ed. Melvyn Fuss and Daniel McFadden. Vol. 2. Amsterdam: North-Holland.

———— 1980. Aggregation problems in the measurement of capital. In *The measurement of capital,* ed. Dan Usher. Chicago: University of Chicago Press.

———— 1982. Duality approaches to microeconomic theory. In *Handbook of mathematical economics,* ed. Kenneth J. Arrow and Michael D. Intriligator. Vol. 2. Amsterdam: North-Holland.

Divisia, François. 1925. L'indice monétaire et la théorie de la monnaie. *Revue d'Economie Politique* 39: 842–61; 980–1008; 1121–1151.

———— 1928. *Economique rationnelle:* Paris: Gaston Doin.

———— 1952. *Exposés d'économique.* Vol l. Paris: Dunod.

Domar, Evsey. 1961. On the measurement of technological change. *Economic Journal* 71: 709–729.

Douglas, Paul H. 1948. Are there laws of production? *American Economic Review* 38: 1–41.

———— 1967. Comments on the Cobb-Douglas production function. In *The theory and empirical analysis of production,* ed. Murray Brown. New York: Columbia University Press.

———— 1976. The Cobb-Douglas production function once again: Its history, its testing, and some empirical values. *Journal of Political Economy,* 84: 903–916.

Eisner, Robert. 1972. Components of capital expenditures: Replacement and modernization. *Review of Economics and Statistics* 54: 297–305.

Executive Office of the President. 1967. *Standard industrial classification manual.* Washington: Bureau of the Budget.

———— 1972. *Standard industrial classification manual.* Washington: Bureau of the Budget.

Ezaki, Mitsuo, 1978. Growth accounting of postwar Japan: The input side. *Economic Studies Quarterly* 29: 193–215.

Fabricant, Solomon S. 1940. *The output of manufacturing industries, 1899–1937.* New York: National Bureau of Economic Research.

———— 1983. The productivity-growth slowdown: A review of the "facts." In *Energy, productivity, and growth,* ed. Sam H. Schurr, Sidney Sonenblum, and David O. Wood. Cambridge, Mass.: Oelgeschlager, Gunn, and Hain.

Feldstein, Martin S., and David K. Foot. 1974. The other half of gross investment: Replacement and modernization expenditures. *Review of Economics and Statistics* 56: 49–58.

Feller, William. 1968. *An introduction to probability theory and its applications.* 3rd ed. New York: Wiley.

Fisher, Franklin M. 1972. On perfect aggregation in the national output deflator and generalized Rybczynski theorems. *International Economic Review* 23: 43–60.

Fisher, Franklin M., and Karl Shell. 1972. The pure theory of the national output deflator. In *The economic theory of price indexes,* ed. Franklin M. Fisher and Karl Shell. New York: Academic Press.

Fisher, Irving. 1922. *The making of index numbers.* Boston: Houghton Mifflin.

Fraumeni, Barbara M. 1980. The role of capital in U.S. economic growth. Dissertation, Boston College.

Fraumeni, Barbara M., and Dale W. Jorgenson. 1980. The role of capital in U.S. economic growth, 1948–1976. In *Capital efficiency and growth,* ed. George von Furstenberg. Cambridge, Mass.: Ballinger.

———— 1986. The role of capital in U.S. economic growth, 1948–1979. In *Measurement issues and behavior of productivity variables,* ed. Ali Dogramaci. Boston: Martinus Nijhoff.

Frohn, Joachim, Rolf Krengel, Peter Kuhbier, Karl H. Oppenlander, and Luitpold Uhlmann. 1973. *Der technische Fortschritt in der Industrie.* Berlin: Duncker and Humblot.

Gallant, A. Ronald, and Dale W. Jorgenson. 1980. Statistical inference for a system of simultaneous, nonlinear, implicit equations in the context of instrumental variables estimation. *Journal of Econometrics* 11: 275–302.

Geary, R.C. 1944a. The concept of net volume of output with special reference to Irish data. *Journal of the Royal Statistical Society* 107: 251–92.

———— 1944b. Some thoughts on the making of Irish index numbers. *Journal of the Statistical and Social Inquiry Society of Ireland* 17: 345–70.

Gjeddebaek, Nils F. 1949. Contribution to the study of grouped observations: Application of the method of maximum likelihood in case of normally distributed observations. *Skandinavisk Aktuarietidskrift* 32: 135.

Goldsmith, Raymond W. 1962. *The national wealth of the United States in the postwar period.* New York: National Bureau of Economic Research.

Gollop, Frank M. 1974. Modeling technical change and market imperfections: An econometric analysis of U.S. manufacturing, 1947–1971. Dissertation, Harvard University.

———— 1979. Accounting for intermediate input: The link between sectoral and aggregate measures of productivity growth. In National Research Council, *The measurement and interpretation of productivity growth.* Washington: National Academy of Sciences.

———— 1982. Growth accounting in an open economy. In *Developments in econometric analysis of productivity,* ed. Ali Dogramaci. Boston, Kluwer-Nijhoff.

———— 1985. Analysis of the productivity slowdown: Evidence for a sector-biased or sector-neutral industrial strategy. In *Productivity growth and U.S. competitiveness,* ed. William J. Baumol and Kenneth McLennan. Oxford: Oxford University Press.

Gollop, Frank M., and Dale W. Jorgenson. 1980. U.S. productivity growth by industry, 1947–1973. In *New developments in productivity measurement,* ed. John W. Kendrick and Beatrice Vaccara. Chicago: University of Chicago Press.

———— 1983. Sectoral measures of labor cost for the United States, 1948–1978. In *The measurement of labor cost,* ed. Jack E. Triplett. Chicago: University of Chicago Press.

Griliches, Zvi. 1960a. The demand for a durable input: U.S. farm tractors, 1921–57. In *The demand for durable goods,* ed. Arnold C. Harberger. Chicago: University of Chicago Press.

———— 1960b. Measuring inputs in agriculture: A critical survey. *Journal of Farm Economics* 42: 1411–1427.

———— 1961. Hedonic indexes for automobiles: An econometric analysis of quality change. In *The price statistics of the federal government.* New York: National Bureau of Economic Research.

———— 1967. Production functions in manufacturing: Some empirical results. In *The theory and empirical analysis of production,* ed. Murray Brown. New York: Columbia University Press.

———— 1971a. Hedonic price indexes revisited. In *Price indexes and quality change,* ed. Zvi Griliches. Cambridge, Mass.: Harvard University Press.

———— ed. 1971b. *Price indexes and quality change.* Cambridge, Mass.: Harvard University Press.

Griliches, Zvi, and Dale W. Jorgenson. 1966. Sources of measured productivity change: Capital input. *American Economic Review* 56: 50–61.

Groes, Nils, and Peter Bjerregaard. 1978. *Real product, real factor input and productivity in Denmark, 1950–1972.* Copenhagen: University of Copenhagen, Institute of Economics.

Haavelmo, Trygve. 1960. *A study in the theory of investment.* Chicago: University of Chicago Press.

Hall, Robert E. 1973. The specification of technology with several kinds of output. *Journal of Political Economy* 81: 878–892.

———— 1968. Technical change and capital from the point of view of the dual. *Review of Economic Studies* 35: 35–46.

———— 1971. The measurement of quality changes from vintage price data. In *Price indexes and quality change,* ed. Zvi Griliches. Cambridge, Mass.: Harvard University Press.

———— 1973. The specification of technology with several kinds of output. *Journal of Political Economy* 81: 878–892.

Hall, Robert E., and Dale W. Jorgenson. 1967. Tax policy and investment behavior. *American Economic Review* 57: 391–414.

———— 1971. Application of the theory of optimum capital accumulation. In *Tax incentives and capital spending,* ed. Gary Fromm. Amsterdam: North-Holland.

Hanoch, Giora. 1978. Symmetric duality and polar production functions. In *Production economics: A dual approach to theory and applications,* ed. Melvyn Fuss and Daniel McFadden. Vol. 1. Amsterdam: North-Holland.

Harrod, Roy. 1948. *Towards a dynamic economics.* London: Macmillan.

Heady, Earl O., and John L. Dillon. 1961. *Agricultural production functions.* Ames: Iowa State University Press.

Hicks, John R. 1946. *Value and capital.* Oxford: Oxford University Press.

———— 1963. *The theory of wages.* London: Macmillan.

Hill, T.P. 1971. *The measurement of real product.* Paris: O.E.C.D.

———— 1979. *Profits and rates of return.* Paris: O.E.C.D.

Hotelling, Harold. 1925. A general mathematical theory of depreciation. *Journal of the American Statistical Association* 20: 340–353.

———— 1932. Edgeworth's taxation paradox and the nature of demand and supply functions. *Journal of Political Economy* 40: 577–616.

Hudson, Edward A., and Dale W. Jorgenson. 1974. U.S. energy policy and economic growth, 1975–2000. *Bell Journal of Economics and Management Science* 5: 461–514.

———— 1976. U.S. tax policy and energy conservation. In *Econometric studies of U.S. energy policy,* ed. Dale W. Jorgenson. Amsterdam: North-Holland.

———— 1978a. Policies to reduce U.S. energy growth. *Resources and Energy* 1: 205–230.

———— 1978b. Energy policy and U.S. economic growth. *American Economic Review* 68: 118–123.

———— 1978c. Energy prices and the U.S. economy, 1972–1976. *Natural Resources Journal* 18: 877–897.

Hulten, Charles R. 1973a. Divisia index numbers. *Econometrica* 41: 1017–1026.

———— 1973b. The measurement of total factor productivity in U.S. manufacturing, 1948–1966. Dissertation, University of California, Berkeley.

———— 1978. Growth accounting with intermediate inputs. *Review of Economic Studies* 45: 511–518.

Hulten, Charles, and Frank C. Wykoff. 1981a. Economic depreciation and the taxation of structures in United States manufacturing industries: An empirical analysis. In *The measurement of capital*, ed. Dan Usher. Chicago: University of Chicago Press.

———— 1981b. The estimation of economic depreciation using vintage asset prices: An application of the Box-Cox power transformation. *Journal of Econometrics* 15: 367–396.

———— 1981c. The measurement of economic depreciation. In *Depreciation, inflation and the taxation of income from capital*, ed. Charles R. Hulten. Washington: Urban Institute Press.

Internal Revenue Service. 1974. *Source book, statistics of income: Active corporation income tax returns*. Washington: U.S. Government Printing Office.

Jack Faucett Associates. 1973a. *Data development for the I-O energy model: Final report*. Washington: Energy Policy Project.

———— 1973b. *Development of capital stock series by industry sector*. Washington: Office of Emergency Preparedness.

———— 1973c. *Measures of working capital*. Washington: U.S. Department of the Treasury.

———— 1975. *Output and employment for input-output sectors*. Washington: U.S. Bureau of Labor Statistics.

Johansen, Leif. 1976. *A multi-sectoral study of economic growth*. Amsterdam: North-Holland.

Jorgenson, Dale W., and Zvi Griliches. 1967. The explanation of productivity change. *Review of Economic Studies* 34: 249–283.

———— 1971. Divisia index numbers and productivity measurement. *Review of Income and Wealth* 17: 53–55.

———— 1972a. Issues in growth accounting: A reply to Edward F. Denison. *Survey of Current Business* 52: 65–94.

———— 1972b. Issues in growth accounting: Final reply. *Survey of Current Business* 52: 111.

Jorgenson, Dale W. 1968. Industry changes in non-labor costs: Comment. In *The industrial composition of income and product*, ed. John W. Kendrick. New York: Columbia University Press.

———— 1973. The economic theory of replacement and depreciation. In *Econometrics and economic theory*, ed. Willy Sellekaerts. New York, Macmillan.

———— 1980. Accounting for capital. In *Capital, efficiency and growth*, ed. George von Furstenberg. Cambridge, Mass.: Ballinger.

———— 1982. Econometric and process analysis models for the analysis of energy policy. In *Perspectives on resource policy modeling: Energy and minerals*, ed. Rafi Amit and Mordecai Avriel. Cambridge, Mass.: Ballinger.

———— 1984a. The contribution of education to U.S. economic growth. In *Education and economic productivity*, ed. Edwin Dean. Cambridge, Mass.: Ballinger.

———— 1984b. The role of energy in productivity growth. In *International comparisons of productivity and causes of the slowdown*, ed. John W. Kendrick. Cambridge, Mass.: Ballinger.

———— 1986. Econometric methods for modeling producer behavior. In *Handbook of econometrics,* ed. Zvi Griliches and Michael D. Intriligator. Vol. 3. Amsterdam: North-Holland.

Jorgenson, Dale W., and Jean-Jacques Laffont. 1974. Efficient estimation of nonlinear simultaneous equations with additive disturbances. *Annals of Social and Economic Measurement* 3: 615–640.

Jorgenson, Dale W., Masahiro Kuroda, and Mieko Nishimizu. 1986. Japan-U.S. industry-level productivity comparisons, 1960–1979. In *Productivity in the U.S. and Japan,* ed. Charles R. Hulten and J. Randolph Norsworthy. Chicago: University of Chicago Press.

Jorgenson, Dale W., and Lawrence J. Lau. 1974a. Duality and differentiability in production. *Journal of Economic Theory* 9: 23–42.

———— 1974b. The duality of technology and economic behavior. *Review of Economic Studies* 41: 181–200.

———— 1975. The structure of consumer preferences. *Annals of Social and Economic Measurement* 4: 49–101.

Jorgenson, Dale W., and Mieko Nishimizu. 1978. U.S. and Japanese economic growth, 1952–1974: An international comparison. *Economic Journal* 88: 707–726.

Jorgenson, Dale W., and Martin A. Sullivan. 1981. Inflation and corporate capital recovery. In *Depreciation, inflation and the taxation of income from capital,* ed. Charles R. Hulten. Washington: Urban Institute Press.

Karmel, Peter H. 1954. The relations between chained indexes of input, gross output, and net output. *Journal of the Royal Statistical Society* 117: 441–458.

Kendrick, John W. 1961a. *Productivity trends in the United States.* Princeton: Princeton University Press.

———— 1961b. Some theoretical aspects of capital measurement. *American Economic Review* 51: 102–111.

———— ed., 1968a. *The industrial composition of income and product.* New York: Columbia University Press.

———— 1968b. Industry changes in non-labor costs. In *The industrial composition of income and product,* ed. John W. Kendrick. New York: Columbia University Press.

———— 1973. *Postwar productivity trends in the United States, 1948–1969.* New York: National Bureau of Economic Research.

———— 1976. *The national wealth of the United States.* New York: Conference Board.

———— 1983. *Interindustry differences in productivity growth.* Washington: American Enterprise Institute.

———— 1984. International comparisons of recent productivity trends. In Japan Productivity Center, *Measuring productivity.* New York: Unipub.

Kendrick, John W., and Elliot S. Grossman. 1980. *Productivity in the United States: Trends and cycles.* Baltimore: Johns Hopkins University Press.

Kennedy, Charles. 1964. Induced bias in innovation and the theory of distribution. *Economic Journal* 74: 541–547.

Kennedy, Charles, and A.P. Thirlwall. 1972. Technical progress: A survey. *Economic Journal* 82: 11–72.

Kloek, Tuun. 1966. *Indexcijfers: Enige methodologisch aspecten*. The Hague: Pasmans.

Kunze, Kent. 1979. Evaluation of work-force composition adjustment. In National Research Council, *Measurement and interpretation of productivity*. Washington: National Academy of Sciences.

Lau, Lawrence J. 1969. Duality and the structure of utility functions. *Journal of Economic Theory* 1: 374–396.

———— 1972. Profit functions of technologies with multiple inputs and outputs. *Review of Economics and Statistics* 54: 281–289.

———— 1974. Comments on applications of duality theory. In *Frontiers of quantitative economics*, ed. Michael D. Intriligator and David A. Kendrick. Vol. 2. Amsterdam: North-Holland.

———— 1976. A characterization of the normalized restricted profit function. *Journal of Economic Theory* 12: 131–163.

———— 1978a. Applications of profit functions. In *Production economics: A dual approach to theory and applications*, ed. Melvyn Fuss and Daniel McFadden. Vol. 1. Amsterdam: North-Holland.

———— 1978b. Testing and imposing monotonicity, convexity, and quasi-convexity constraints. In *Production economics: A dual approach to theory and applications*, ed. Melvyn Fuss and Daniel McFadden. Vol. 1. Amsterdam: North-Holland.

Lee, Bun Song. 1978. Measurement of capital depreciation within the Japanese fishing fleet. *Review of Economics and Statistics* 60: 225–237.

Leontief, Wassily. 1947a. Introduction to a theory of the internal structure of functional relationships. *Econometrica* 15: 361–373.

———— 1947b. A note on the interrelation of subsets of independent variables of a continuous function with continuous first derivatives. *Bulletin of the American Mathematical Society* 53: 343–350.

———— 1953. Structural change. In *Studies in the structure of the American economy*, ed. Wassily Leontief. New York: Oxford University Press.

Loftus, Shirley F. 1972. Stocks of business inventories in the United States, 1928–1971. *Survey of Current Business* 52: 29–32.

Malpezzi, S., L. Ozanne, and T. Thibodeau. 1980. Characteristic prices of housing in fifty-nine metropolitan areas. Working Paper 1367–1. Washington: Urban Institute.

Manvel, A.D. 1968. Trends in the value of real estate and land, 1956–1966. In National Commission on Urban Problems, *Three land research studies*. Washington: U.S. Government Printing Office.

Massell, Benton F. 1961. A disaggregated view of technical change. *Journal of Political Economy* 69: 547–557.

McFadden, Daniel. 1978. Cost, revenue, and profit functions. In *Production economics: A dual approach to theory and applications*, ed. Melvyn Fuss and Daniel McFadden. Vol. 1. Amsterdam: North-Holland.

Merrilees, William J. 1971. The case against Divisia index numbers as a basis in a social accounting system. *Review of Income and Wealth* 17: 81–86.

Milgrim, Grace. 1973. Appendix II, Estimates of the value of land in the U.S. held by various sectors of the economy, annually, 1952–1968. In *Institutional investors and corporate stock: A background study,* ed. Raymond W. Goldsmith. New York: Columbia University Press.

Moorsteen, Richard H. 1961. On measuring productive potential and relative efficiency. *Quarterly Journal of Economics* 75: 451–467.

Muellbauer, John. 1975. The cost of living and taste and quality change. *Journal of Economic Theory* 10: 269–283.

Musgrave, John. 1976. Fixed nonresidential business and residential capital in the United States, 1925–1975. *Survey of Current Business* 56: 46–52.

Nadiri, Mohammed I. 1970. Some approaches to the theory and measurement of total factor productivity: A survey. *Journal of Economic Literature* 8: 1137–1178.

Nelson, Richard R. 1973. Recent exercises in growth accounting: New understanding or dead end. *American Economic Review* 63: 462–468.

Nerlove, Marc L. 1967. Recent empirical studies of the CES and related production functions. In *The theory and empirical analysis of production,* ed. Murray Brown. New York: Columbia University Press.

Netherlands Economic Institute. 1953. *Input-output relations.* Leiden: H.E. Stenfert Krose.

Nishimizu, Mieko. 1974. Total factor productivity analysis: A disaggregated study of the postwar Japanese economy with explicit consideration of intermediate inputs. Dissertation, Johns Hopkins University.

Nishimizu, Mieko, and Charles R. Hulten. 1978. The sources of Japanese economic growth: 1955–1971. *Review of Economics and Statistics* 60: 351–361.

Norsworthy, J. Randolph. 1984a. Capital input measurement: Options and inaccuracies. In Japan Productivity Center, *Measuring productivity.* New York: Unipub.

————— 1984b. Growth accounting and productivity measurements. *Review of Income and Wealth* 30: 309–329.

Norsworthy, J. Randolph, Michael J. Harper, and Kent Kunze. 1979. The slowdown in productivity growth: Analysis of some contributing factors. *Brookings Papers on Economic Activity* 2: 387–421.

Norsworthy, J. Randolph, and Michael J. Harper. 1981. The rate of capital formation in the recent slowdown in productivity growth. In *Aggregate and industry-level productivity analysis,* ed. Ali Dogramaci and P.U. Adams. Boston: Kluwer-Nijhoff.

Norsworthy, J. Randolph, and David H. Malmquist. 1983. Input measurement and productivity growth in Japanese and U.S. manufacturing. *American Economic Review* 73: 947–967.

Office of Tax Analysis. 1973. Unpublished tables: Investment and asset life by industry and type of equipment; use of depreciation methods by industry and equipment type; investment by industry and equipment type; and investment by industry. Washington: U.S. Department of the Treasury.

Ohta, Makota, and Zvi Griliches. 1975. Automobile prices revisited: Extensions of the hedonic price hypothesis. In *Household production and consumption,* ed. Nestor Terleckj. New York: Columbia University Press.

Pechman, Joseph A. 1983. *Federal tax policy.* Washington: Brookings Institution.

Perrella, Vera C. 1970. Multiple job holders in May, 1969. Special Labor Force Report No. 123. Washington: U.S. Department of Labor.

Polenske, Karen R., and Kiri V. Skolka. 1976. *Advances in input-output analysis.* Cambridge, Mass.: Ballinger.

Ramm, Wolfhard. 1970. Measuring the services of household durables: The case of automobiles. *Proceedings of the business and economics section.* Washington: American Statistical Association.

Richter, M.K. 1966. Invariance axioms and economic indexes. *Econometrica* 34: 239–255.

Samuelson, Paul A. 1953. Prices of factors and goods in general equilibrium. *Review of Economic Studies* 21: 1–20.

———— 1960. Structure of a minimum equilibrium system. In *Essays in economics and econometrics,* ed. Ralph W. Pfouts. Chapel Hill: University of North Carolina Press.

———— 1965. A theory of induced innovation along Kennedy-Weizsacker lines. *Review of Economics and Statistics* 47: 343–356.

———— 1973. Relative shares and elasticities simplified: Comment. *American Economic Review* 63: 770–771.

———— 1979. Paul Douglas's measurement of production functions and marginal productivities. *Journal of Political Economy* 87: 923–939.

———— 1983. *Foundations of economic analysis.* Cambridge, Mass.: Harvard University Press.

Sato, Kazuo. 1976. The meaning and measurement of the real value added index. *Review of Economic Statistics* 58: 434–442.

Savin, N. Eugene. 1984. Multiple hypothesis testing. In *Handbook of econometrics,* ed. Zvi Griliches and Michael D. Intriligator. Vol. 2. Amsterdam: North-Holland.

Shephard, Ronald W. 1953. *Cost and production functions.* Princeton: Princeton University Press.

———— 1970. *Theory of cost and production functions.* Princeton: Princeton University Press.

Sims, Christopher. 1969. Theoretical basis for a double-deflated index of real value added. *Review of Economic Statistics* 51: 470–471.

———— 1977. Remarks on real value added. *Annals of Social and Economic Measurement* 6: 127–132.

Social Security Administration. 1980. *Social Security Bulletin, Annual Statistical Supplement, 1977–1979.* Washington: U.S. Government Printing Office.

Solow, Robert M. 1957. Technical change and the aggregate production function. *Review of Economics and Statistics* 39: 312–320.

———— 1960. Investment and technical progress. In *Mathemati-*

cal methods in the social sciences, 1959, ed. Kenneth J. Arrow, Samuel Karlin, and Patrick Suppes. Stanford: Stanford University Press.

————— 1963. *Capital theory and the rate of return.* Amsterdam: North-Holland.

Sono M. 1961. The effect of price changes on the demand and supply of separable goods. *International Economic Review* 2: 239–271.

Star, Spencer. 1974. Accounting for the growth of output. *American Economic Review* 64: 123–135.

Star, Spencer, and Robert E. Hall. 1976. An approximate Divisia index of total factor productivity. *Econometrica* 44: 257–264.

Statistical Office of the United Nations. 1968. *A system of national accounts.* Studies in Methods, Series F, No. 2, Rev. 3. New York: Department of Economic and Social Affairs, United Nations.

Stein, Robert L. 1967. New definitions for employment and unemployment. *Employment and Earnings and Monthly Report on the Labor Force* 13: 3–27.

Stone, Richard, and J.A.C. Brown. 1962. *A computable model of economic growth (A programme for growth 1).* London: Chapman and Hall.

Takayama, Akira. 1974. On biased technological progress. *American Economic Review* 64: 631–639.

Taubman, Paul, and Robert Rasche. 1969. Economic and tax depreciation of office buildings. *National Tax Journal* 22: 334–346.

Taylor, Lance. 1975. Theoretical foundations and technical implications. In *Economy-wide models and development planning,* ed. Charles K. Blitzer, Peter B. Clark, and Lance Taylor. Oxford: Oxford University Press.

Terborgh, George. 1954. *Realistic depreciation policy.* Washington: Machinery and Allied Products Institute.

Theil, Henri. 1965. The information approach to demand analysis. *Econometrica* 33: 67–87.

Thor, Carl G., George E. Sadler, and Elliot S. Grossman. Comparison of total factor productivity in Japan and the United States. In Japan Productivity Center, *Measuring productivity.* New York: Unipub.

Tornquist, Leo. 1936. The Bank of Finland's consumption price index. *Bank of Finland Monthly Bulletin* 10: 1–8.

Triplett, Jack E. 1975. The measurement of inflation: A survey of research on the accuracy of price indexes. In *Analysis of inflation,* ed. Paul H. Earl. Lexington: Heath.

————— 1983. Introduction: An essay on labor cost. In *The measurement of labor cost,* ed. Jack E. Triplett. Chicago: University of Chicago Press.

U.S. Congress, House of Representatives, Ways and Means Committee. 1969. *Unemployment compensation.* Hearings, Ninety-first Congress, First Session, October 1-7.

Usher, Dan. 1974. The suitability of the Divisia index for the measurement of economic aggregates. *Review of Income and Wealth* 20: 273–288.

Uzawa, Hirofumi. 1964. Duality principles in the theory of cost and production. *International Economic Review* 5: 216–220.

Vaccara, Beatrice N. 1972. Changes over time in input-output coefficients for the

United States. In *Applications of input-output analysis,* ed. Anne P. Carter and Andras Brody. Amsterdam: North-Holland.

Vaccara, Beatrice N., and Nancy W. Simon. 1968. Factors affecting the postwar industrial composition of real product. In *The industrial composition of output,* ed. John W. Kendrick. New York: Columbia University Press.

Vasquez, Thomas. 1974. ADR paper. Washington: U.S. Department of the Treasury, Office of Tax Analysis.

von Weizsacker, C. Christian. 1962. A new technical progress function. Cambridge, Mass.: M.I.T., Department of Economics.

Walderhaug, Albert J. 1973. The composition of value added in the 1963 input-output study. *Survey of Current Business* 53: 34–44.

Waldorf, William. 1973. Quality of labor in manufacturing. *Review of Economic Statistics* 55: 284–291.

Walras, Leon. 1954. *Elements of pure economics.* Trans. William Jaffe. Homewood: Irwin.

Walters, Alan A. 1963. Production and cost functions: An econometric survey. *Econometrica* 31: 1–66.

Walters, Dorothy. 1968. *Canadian income levels and growth: An international perspective.* Ottawa: Economic Council of Canada.

———— 1970. *Canadian growth revisited, 1950–1967.* Ottawa: Economic Council of Canada.

Watanabe, Tsunehiko. 1971. A note on measuring sectoral input productivity. *Review of Income and Wealth* 17: 335–340.

Ward, Michael. 1976. *The measurement of capital.* Paris: O.E.C.D.

Weitzman, Martin L. 1983. On the meaning of comparative factor productivity. In *Marxism, central planning, and the Soviet economy,* ed. Padma Desai. Cambridge, Mass.: M.I.T. Press.

Wolff, Edward N. 1985. Industrial composition, interindustry effects, and the U.S. productivity slowdown. *Review of Economics and Statistics* 67: 268–277.

Wykoff, Frank C. 1970. Capital depreciation in the postwar period: Automobiles. *Review of Economics and Statistics* 52: 168–176.

Wykoff, Frank C., and Charles R. Hulten. 1979. *Economic depreciation of the U.S. capital stock: A first step.* Washington: U.S. Department of the Treasury, Office of Tax Analysis.

Young, Allan. 1969. Alternative estimates of corporate depreciation and profits: Part I. *Survey of Current Business* 48: 17–28.

Young, Allan, and John C. Musgrave. 1980. Estimation of capital stock in the United States. In *The measurement of capital,* ed. Dan Usher. Chicago: University of Chicago Press.

Index